Ethical, Legal, and Pedagogical Perspectives on AI in Education

Kristen Carlson
https://orcid.org/0000-0002-4559-8531
Minnesota State University, Moorhead, USA

IGI Global
Scientific Publishing
Publishing Tomorrow's Research Today

Vice President of Editorial	Melissa Wagner
Director of Acquisitions	Mikaela Felty
Director of Book Development	Jocelynn Hessler
Production Manager	Mike Brehm
Cover Design	Jose Rosado

Published in the United States of America by
IGI Global Scientific Publishing
701 East Chocolate Avenue
Hershey, PA, 17033, USA
Tel: 717-533-8845 | Fax: 717-533-7115
Website: https://www.igi-global.com E-mail: cust@igi-global.com

Library of Congress Cataloging-in-Publication Data

Names: Carlson, Kristen, 1986- editor.
Title: Ethical, legal, and pedagogical perspectives on AI in education / [edited by] Kristen Carlson.
Description: Hershey, PA : IGI Global Scientific Publishing, [2026] | Includes bibliographical references and index. | Summary: "This book aims to serve as a foundational resource for understanding AI's impact on education from ethical, legal, and pedagogical perspectives"-- Provided by publisher.
Identifiers: LCCN 2025015984 (print) | LCCN 2025015985 (ebook) | ISBN 9798337330006 (hardcover) | ISBN 9798337330013 (paperback) | ISBN 9798337330020 (ebook)
Subjects: LCSH: Artificial intelligence--Educational applications. | Education--Effect of technological innovations on.
Classification: LCC LB1028.43 .E84 2026 (print) | LCC LB1028.43 (ebook) | DDC 370.78/563--dc23/eng/20250513
LC record available at https://lccn.loc.gov/2025015984
LC ebook record available at https://lccn.loc.gov/2025015985

British Cataloguing in Publication Data
A Cataloguing in Publication record for this book is available from the British Library.

Table of Contents

Editorial Advisory Board

Detailed Table of Contents

to cybersecurity threats and AI-driven surveillance risks. The study highlights the absence of sector-specific guidelines in India's Digital Personal Data Protection (DPDP) Act 2023 and the lack of AI ethics frameworks for higher education.

Bias in AI-driven educational tools can manifest in several forms, including data bias, where training data reflects societal inequities; algorithmic bias, where AI design discriminates against groups; and interaction bias, where systems fail to accommodate diverse backgrounds. These biases can reinforce inequalities and hinder equitable education. Fairness can be framed through group fairness, individual fairness, counterfactual fairness, procedural fairness, and causal fairness. Mitigating bias involves pre-processing techniques like reweighting, in-processing methods with fairness constraints, and post-processing adjustments for equitable outcomes. Tools like AI Fairness 360, Fairlearn, TensorFlow Fairness Indicators, and the What-If Tool help detect and mitigate bias, fostering fairness and inclusivity in AI-driven education. Ensuring fairness in AI enhances accessibility, promotes trust, and supports diverse learning needs in digital education.

This chapter examines the growing role of generative AI tools, such as large language models, in higher education and argues that instructors must intentionally develop students' AI literacies, awareness, evaluation, ethical use, and creative collaboration, to promote responsible and effective learning. After reviewing established literacy frameworks, this chapter presents practical classroom strategies for prompt design, output assessment (e.g., adapted CRAAP test), and ethical reflection. The chapter also illustrates how AI can function as a collaborator and outlines methods for assessing AI competencies and embedding AI guidelines in syllabi. The chapter concludes by discussing challenges and future directions, finally recommending that instructors and institutions continuously evolve their pedagogies and practices as the AI landscape continues to develop.

The emergence and adoption of Generative Artificial Intelligence (AI) in education, especially ChatGPT, has garnered significant attention from educators and researchers alike. The most notable and attractive feature of this chatbot is its ability to offer personalised assistance to its users. In order to explore how ChatGPT creates a personalised learning environment for students and facilitates their learning processes, a systematic review of empirical studies was conducted. This review adhered strictly to PRISMA guidelines and included 10 empirical studies for meta-synthesis. The results revealed that the chatbot is highly valued for its ability to provide a social presence in students' learning journeys. This social presence is crucial as it creates a more engaging and interactive learning experience, which is often missing in traditional educational settings. One of the key findings from the review is that ChatGPT's personalised support enhances students' self-paced learning. By providing immediate feedback, answering questions, and offering explanations tailored to the student's level of understanding, the chatbot helps students learn at their own pace. The review highlights important implications for policy, practice, and research, emphasising the integration of ChatGPT into educational frameworks to support personalised learning and enhance teaching practices. It also calls for further research to examine the long-term effects of AI chatbots on student learning outcomes.

This chapter highlights the transformative role of artificial intelligence (AI) in education, focusing on its impact on teaching methodologies, assessment strategies, and student engagement. AI-driven adaptive learning platforms personalize education by analyzing student performance and tailoring content to individual needs. Additionally, AI assists educators by automating administrative tasks, enabling data-driven instruction, and identifying learning gaps. However, ethical concerns such as bias in AI algorithms, student data privacy, and transparency in AI decision-making must be addressed. The chapter also explores compliance with legal frameworks, including the General Data Protection Regulation (GDPR), the Family Educational Rights and Privacy Act (FERPA), and intellectual property laws, which are crucial for ensuring responsible AI use in education. The legal complexities surrounding AI-generated content ownership and liability in AI malfunctions further necessitate the establishment of clear policies and risk management strategies. Moreover, AI's integration requires pedagogical adaptations, ensuring that AI complements human instruction rather than replacing it. Blended learning models, AI-augmented teacher

This chapter examines the pedagogical considerations and implications of integrating artificial intelligence (AI) with Islamic Religious Education (IRE). As generative AI reshapes modern education, its role in Islamic-based learning settings warrants significant consideration. The contextualisation of AI in education, with a justification for focusing on IRE, is discussed first. Foundational concepts are defined, which include AI in education (AIEd), and major pedagogical principles common to all Islamic traditions are also discussed, along with their practical applications. Opportunities and challenges are presented. The chapter introduced Islamic pedagogical views and addressed teacher AI readiness, concluding with suggested pedagogical strategies that align with the use of AI and Islamic values. The chapter concludes by calling for collaborative-based initiatives and outlines the next steps in research for curriculum development, professional development, and AI ethics in IRE.

The integration of Artificial Intelligence (AI) applications into education is possible in all disciplines, and teaching abstract concepts becomes significantly easier by providing an individualized learning environment. In Turkey, considering the developing technology, the 21st century and the goals of the Ministry of National Education (MoNE), the use of technology in education and especially the use of AI applications, which have recently come to the fore, has become a necessity. With STEM, individuals are expected to have 21st century skills by combining mathematics, engineering, science and technology disciplines. Individuals of our

In the world of digitalization, Artificial Intelligence (AI) is bringing a deep revolution in higher education. This study examines the emergence of New Age Pedagogy, a learner-centered AI enhanced model that prepares different pupils' cognitive, emotional, social and metacognitive needs. AI-based tools, from intelligent tutoring systems to personalized and instant analytical feedback, increase learner participation, performance, and self-regulation, helping cultivate different learning methods and contributing to effective educational impact. The issue of using the AI calls pressing ethical questions such as data privacy misconception, algorithmic bias, academic dishonesty, and transparency and trust erosion. Such risks emphasize the necessity of strong ethics of governance, reflective curriculum design and humanity-AI partnership. The chapter argues for incorporating ethics in educational frameworks and advocates for participatory and interdisciplinary approaches to policy making focused on the ecological interrelations of AI, systems within an educational space.

This chapter examines the potential of Artificial Intelligence (AI) to transform higher education, with a focus on personalized learning. The ability of AI to tailor educational experiences significantly improves student engagement, motivation, and academic achievement. The integration of AI introduces ethical challenges, such as data privacy concerns, algorithmic bias, and the need for human oversight in educational practices. Furthermore, although AI can automate specific educational processes, the role of lecturers is crucial in delivering pedagogical interpretation and emotional support. The implementation of balanced strategies integrates AI with conventional teaching methods, recognizing the significance of human insight in fostering critical thinking and maintaining academic integrity. Higher education institutions can responsibly leverage AI's capabilities to develop inclusive, personalized, and equitable learning environments by fostering collaboration among lecturers, policymakers, and technology providers.

This chapter explores the transformative potential of Artificial Intelligence (AI) in Indian higher education by analyzing current trends, benefits, challenges, and future prospects. It highlights how AI is reshaping pedagogy, enhancing personalized learning, streamlining administrative processes, and preparing students for future job markets. Drawing on secondary data and literature, the study identifies key barriers such as infrastructural gaps, faculty readiness, cost, ethical concerns, and linguistic limitations. The chapter concludes with forward-looking policy recommendations to promote inclusive, scalable, and ethical AI adoption across diverse educational contexts in India.

Artificial intelligence (AI) has become increasingly integrated into language research by providing opportunities, while researchers' perceptions of ethical issues AI usage in research seem untouched in the research context. This study aims to explore language researchers' perceptions of the ethical implications of AI in research practices. In this qualitative research, data were collected through written responses from 20 language researchers and analyzed thematically. The study concluded that while AI offers efficiency and innovation, researchers are concerned with ethical risks, institutional policies, and clearer guidelines to ensure responsible AI use in language research. To maintain the integrity and sustainability of AI in language research, some practical recommendations for language researchers are also noted regarding language researchers, university administrators, policymakers, and academic publishers.

Preface

Artificial Intelligence (AI) has rapidly transitioned from an emerging technological concept to a transformative force shaping educational systems worldwide. Across K–12, higher education, teacher preparation, and educational research, AI technologies are redefining how learning is personalized, how teaching is supported, how data are collected and analyzed, and how institutions govern academic practices. Alongside these opportunities, however, arise complex ethical dilemmas, legal responsibilities, and pedagogical challenges that demand careful, critical, and context-sensitive consideration. *Ethical, Legal, and Pedagogical Perspectives on AI in Education* is conceived as a comprehensive reference work that addresses these pressing concerns through interdisciplinary and global scholarship.

This edited volume brings together contributions from researchers and practitioners across diverse geographic regions, educational systems, and disciplinary traditions. The chapters collectively examine how AI intersects with issues of regulation, data privacy, bias, fairness, accessibility, inclusion, language, culture, religion, and pedagogy. Rather than presenting AI as a neutral or purely technical tool, the book foregrounds the human, social, and institutional dimensions of AI adoption, emphasizing that educational technologies are shaped by values, policies, and pedagogical choices.

A strong legal and policy foundation anchors the volume. Several chapters explore regulatory frameworks governing AI use in education, including data protection laws, institutional accountability, and emerging national and international policies. Particular attention is given to evolving regulatory contexts in countries such as India and the United States, highlighting challenges related to student privacy, surveillance, and compliance gaps. These discussions underscore the importance of proactive governance and ethical oversight as AI becomes embedded in educational infrastructures.

Equally central to this volume are ethical considerations surrounding bias, fairness, accessibility, and equity. Contributors critically analyze how AI-driven educational tools can reproduce social inequities through biased data, algorithmic design, and exclusionary practices. At the same time, the book showcases pathways for responsible AI development, including fairness frameworks, inclusive design principles, and assistive technologies that support learners with disabilities and diverse needs. These chapters collectively argue that ethical AI in education requires intentional design, transparency, and sustained institutional commitment.

Pedagogical innovation forms another core pillar of the book. Multiple chapters examine how AI reshapes teaching and learning across disciplines, including science education, language education, religious education, and higher education more broadly. Topics such as AI literacies, critical thinking, personalized learning, student engagement, and self-paced learning are explored through both theoretical and practical lenses. The volume emphasizes that while AI can enhance learning experiences, educators remain central to fostering critical inquiry, ethical reflection, and meaningful human connection.

Teacher education and professional development receive sustained attention throughout the book. Several chapters focus on preparing current and future educators to work effectively and ethically in AI-enhanced classrooms. Collaborative models, curriculum redesign, mentorship, and institutional readiness are presented as key strategies for empowering educators to lead AI integration rather than merely adapt to it. These contributions highlight the importance of human-centered, inclusive, and sustainable approaches to teacher training in an AI-driven era.

As a reference book, *Ethical, Legal, and Pedagogical Perspectives on AI in Education* is intended for a broad audience, including scholars, educators, teacher educators, policymakers, institutional leaders, and graduate students. The volume offers conceptual frameworks, empirical insights, policy analyses, and practical strategies that can inform research, teaching, curriculum development, and governance. By bringing ethical, legal, and pedagogical perspectives into dialogue, this book seeks to support informed decision-making and responsible innovation.

Ultimately, this volume advances the position that the future of AI in education must be guided not only by technological capability, but by shared commitments to equity, accountability, cultural sensitivity, and educational purpose. It is our hope that this book will serve as a critical resource for those seeking to understand, shape, and ethically steward the role of artificial intelligence in education worldwide.

CHAPTER 1: AI REGULATION IN K–12 AND HIGHER EDUCATION INSTITUTIONS

This chapter explores the complex regulatory environment governing the use of artificial intelligence across K–12 and higher education systems. It examines critical legal and ethical concerns related to data privacy, security, and institutional responsibility, highlighting key regulatory frameworks such as GDPR, FERPA, COPPA, SOPIPA, HIPAA, relevant CFR provisions, and NIST guidelines. The chapter also discusses the rapidly evolving regulatory context in India, emphasizing institutional obligations when handling personal and cross-border data. By mapping overlapping legal requirements, the chapter underscores the importance of compliance-driven governance models for responsible AI adoption in education.

CHAPTER 2: AI, BIG DATA, AND STUDENT PRIVACY: A POLICY PERSPECTIVE IN INDIAN HIGHER EDUCATION

This chapter analyzes the growing use of AI and Big Data in Indian higher education and the resulting policy, legal, and ethical challenges. It reveals significant gaps in institutional data governance, with many universities lacking standardized policies to protect student data from misuse, surveillance, and cybersecurity threats. Through an examination of existing laws and policies, including the Digital Personal Data Protection (DPDP) Act 2023, the chapter highlights the absence of sector-specific AI guidelines and ethics frameworks. The chapter calls for robust policy reforms to ensure privacy protection, accountability, and ethical AI implementation in Indian universities.

CHAPTER 3: DISSECTING BIAS AND FAIRNESS IN AI-DRIVEN EDUCATIONAL TOOLS

This chapter investigates how bias manifests in AI-driven educational technologies through data, algorithmic, and interactional dimensions, often reinforcing existing social and educational inequalities. It presents key theoretical frameworks for understanding fairness, including group, individual, counterfactual, procedural, and causal fairness. The chapter outlines technical strategies for bias mitigation across pre-processing, in-processing, and post-processing stages and introduces practical tools such as AI Fairness 360, Fairlearn, and TensorFlow Fairness Indicators. Emphasizing equity-centered design, the chapter demonstrates how fairness in AI enhances trust, accessibility, and inclusive learning outcomes.

CHAPTER 4: FUTURE-FACING PEDAGOGY: EMPOWERING STUDENTS THROUGH AI LITERACIES

This chapter argues for the intentional development of AI literacies as generative AI tools become integral to higher education. It situates AI literacy within existing information and digital literacy frameworks and offers practical instructional strategies for prompt design, critical evaluation of AI outputs, and ethical reflection. The chapter reframes AI as a collaborative learning partner and outlines methods for assessing AI competencies and embedding AI-use guidelines into course syllabi. It concludes by emphasizing the need for continuously evolving pedagogical practices that respond to rapid developments in AI technologies.

CHAPTER 5: SYSTEMATIC REVIEW ON AI CHATBOTS AS A PROVISION FOR SELF-PACED LEARNING

This chapter presents a systematic review of empirical studies examining the role of AI chatbots, particularly ChatGPT, in supporting self-paced learning. The findings highlight the value of AI chatbots in enhancing student engagement through social presence, personalized feedback, and immediate instructional support. The review demonstrates how chatbots assist learners who struggle with traditional instructional models while raising important considerations for policy and classroom practice. The chapter concludes by calling for further longitudinal research into learning outcomes and the responsible integration of AI chatbots into educational frameworks.

CHAPTER 6: CHALLENGES AND OPPORTUNITIES IN AI–HUMAN COLLABORATIVE TEACHING

This chapter examines the evolving relationship between artificial intelligence and human educators, focusing on collaborative teaching models that enhance learning rather than replace instructional roles. It explores AI-driven adaptive learning, automated assessment, and data-informed instruction while addressing ethical concerns related to bias, data privacy, transparency, and content ownership. Legal considerations, including GDPR and FERPA compliance, are discussed alongside pedagogical strategies such as blended learning, gamification, and AI-augmented instruction. The chapter emphasizes institutional responsibility for ethical governance, educator training, and balanced regulatory approaches.

CHAPTER 7: ENHANCING STUDENT ENGAGEMENT WITH AI: PERSONALIZED LEARNING AND ADAPTIVE MOTIVATION STRATEGIES

This chapter explores how AI-driven personalization and adaptive motivational strategies can significantly enhance student engagement in digital learning environments. Drawing on pedagogical theory and global case studies, it highlights AI's capacity to tailor instruction, provide real-time feedback, and sustain motivation through gamification and emotionally responsive systems. Ethical, legal, and equity considerations are integrated throughout the discussion, reinforcing the need for responsible implementation. The chapter concludes with policy recommendations and educational innovations aimed at fostering inclusive, transparent, and learner-centered AI-enhanced education.

CHAPTER 8: HARNESSING AI FOR ACCESSIBILITY AND INCLUSIVE LEARNING SPACES

This chapter examines the potential of AI to advance accessibility and inclusive education through frameworks grounded in Critical Disability Theory and Universal Design for Learning. It demonstrates how ethically designed AI tools can proactively reduce systemic barriers and support diverse learners, particularly students with disabilities. Through legal, theoretical, and practical perspectives, the chapter also addresses risks such as algorithmic bias, surveillance, and digital divides. It calls for a shift toward inclusive-by-design approaches that position accessibility as a foundational principle in AI-enhanced learning environments.

CHAPTER 9: PEDAGOGICAL PERSPECTIVES ON ARTIFICIAL INTELLIGENCE IN ISLAMIC RELIGIOUS EDUCATION

This chapter provides a comprehensive review of AI integration within Islamic Religious Education (IRE), contextualizing AI technologies within Islamic pedagogical traditions and values. It defines key concepts related to AI in education and examines opportunities and challenges associated with generative AI in religious learning contexts. The chapter addresses teacher readiness, ethical considerations, and pedagogical alignment with Islamic principles. It concludes by proposing collaborative initiatives and future research directions to guide curriculum development, professional training, and ethical AI use in IRE.

CHAPTER 10: DESIGNING AN AI-SUPPORTED TEACHING MODULE WITH A STEM APPROACH FOR SCIENCE EDUCATION

This chapter focuses on the design and implementation of an AI-supported STEM teaching module for science education within the Turkish educational context. Emphasizing individualized learning and 21st-century skill development, the chapter describes how AI-enhanced instructional design supports students' understanding of abstract scientific concepts. Aligned with national educational goals, the AI-supported EBA module demonstrates how technology integration can address individual differences and enhance learning effectiveness. The chapter highlights the role of AI in fostering active, productive, and technologically literate learners.

CHAPTER 11: FOSTERING CRITICAL THINKING IN AI-ASSISTED ENGLISH LANGUAGE LEARNING ENVIRONMENTS

This chapter examines the role of AI in enhancing critical thinking within English Language Teaching (ELT). It emphasizes the importance of critical thinking for meaningful language use and illustrates how AI-driven tools provide personalized feedback, interactive learning experiences, and tailored challenges. The chapter highlights the continued centrality of teachers in designing reflective and inquiry-based learning tasks. Ethical considerations are addressed to ensure AI implementation supports learning while preserving students' rights and educators' professional responsibilities.

CHAPTER 12: GENERATIVE AI'S IMPACT ON ENGLISH LANGUAGE EDUCATION

This chapter critically examines the implications of generative AI for English as an Additional Language (EAL) education, particularly in relation to linguistic imperialism and the privileging of Standard English. While generative AI tools can increase access to dominant language norms, the chapter argues that they may also reinforce cultural and linguistic biases. Grounded in critical pedagogy, the chapter proposes instructional strategies that promote critical language awareness and honor linguistic diversity. It positions AI as both a pedagogical opportunity and an ethical challenge within post-secondary language education.

CHAPTER 13: THE NEW AGE PEDAGOGY: LEARNING DIMENSIONS AND ETHICAL CHALLENGES OF AI IN HIGHER EDUCATION

This chapter introduces a learner-centered "New Age Pedagogy" that integrates AI to address cognitive, emotional, social, and metacognitive dimensions of learning. It highlights the benefits of AI-based tools for engagement, feedback, and self-regulation while critically examining ethical risks such as data misuse, algorithmic bias, academic dishonesty, and erosion of trust. The chapter advocates for ethics-driven governance, reflective curriculum design, and interdisciplinary policymaking. It emphasizes the importance of human–AI partnerships in sustaining meaningful educational ecosystems.

CHAPTER 14: TRANSFORMING HIGHER EDUCATION THROUGH AI-DRIVEN PERSONALIZED LEARNING

This chapter explores the transformative role of AI in personalized learning within higher education. It examines how AI-enabled customization enhances student engagement, motivation, and academic achievement while raising ethical concerns related to privacy, bias, and human oversight. The chapter underscores the continued importance of lecturers in providing pedagogical interpretation, mentorship, and emotional support. By advocating for balanced integration of AI with traditional teaching methods, the chapter highlights collaborative approaches to creating equitable and inclusive learning environments.

CHAPTER 15: THE FUTURE OF AI IN INDIAN HIGHER EDUCATION

This chapter analyzes current trends and future prospects for AI adoption in Indian higher education. It highlights AI's potential to enhance pedagogy, administrative efficiency, and workforce readiness while identifying challenges such as infrastructure limitations, faculty preparedness, financial constraints, ethical risks, and linguistic diversity. Drawing on existing literature, the chapter offers policy recommendations aimed at fostering inclusive, scalable, and ethically grounded AI integration. It envisions a future in which AI supports equitable educational development across India's diverse institutions.

CHAPTER 16: THE ETHICS OF USING ARTIFICIAL INTELLIGENCE IN LANGUAGE RESEARCH

This chapter investigates language researchers' perceptions of ethical issues surrounding AI use in research practices. Based on qualitative data, it reveals concerns related to ethical risks, institutional oversight, and the absence of clear guidelines, despite AI's potential to enhance research efficiency and innovation. The chapter highlights the need for stronger ethical frameworks and policy clarity to ensure responsible AI adoption. Practical recommendations are provided for researchers, administrators, policymakers, and publishers to support ethical and sustainable research practices.

CHAPTER 17: INTEGRATING AI IN TEACHER TRAINING: PREPARING FUTURE EDUCATORS

This chapter examines the need to reimagine teacher education programs to prepare educators for AI-enhanced classrooms. It emphasizes curriculum redesign, pedagogical innovation, ethical reflection, and systemic support as key components of effective teacher training. The chapter highlights the importance of AI literacy, digital fluency, equitable access, and adaptive assessment. Drawing on global policy trends and best practices, it proposes a human-centered framework for building inclusive and sustainable teacher education ecosystems.

CHAPTER 18: TRANSFORMATIVE ALLIANCES: A COLLABORATIVE MODEL FOR AI INTEGRATION IN TEACHER TRAINING

This chapter presents a multidisciplinary, collaborative model for integrating generative AI into teacher preparation programs. Developed through a faculty alliance, the model emphasizes ethical transparency, co-creation, professional learning, and inclusive pedagogy. By revising curricula, modeling responsible AI practices, and developing flexible classroom policies, the alliance supports preservice teachers in critically engaging with AI. The chapter offers a replicable framework for educator preparation programs navigating the evolving role of AI in education.

Chapter 1
AI Regulation in K-12 and Higher Education Institutions

Tushar
https://orcid.org/0000-0001-7190-7687
United College of Engineering and Research, Prayagraj, India

Pooja Jaiswal
https://orcid.org/0009-0007-2507-1525
University of Allahabad, Prayagraj, India

Nandita Pradhan
https://orcid.org/0009-0006-8819-1009
United College of Engineering and Research, Prayagraj, India

Shivani Mishra
https://orcid.org/0009-0006-0110-7039
United College of Engineering and Research, Prayagraj, India

Prabhat Chandra Shrivastava
https://orcid.org/0000-0003-0766-6422
Faculty of Science, University of Allahabad, Prayagraj, India

Ajit Kumar Yadav
United College of Engineering and Research, Prayagraj, India

ABSTRACT

The growing application of artificial intelligence (AI) in education, from early childhood to higher education, raises exciting possibilities and difficult legal issues. Data privacy, security, and ethics are common concerns. This landscape is governed by a complex web of regulations, including GDPR, FERPA, COPPA, SOPIPA, and HIPAA. NIST recommendations and CFR parts also matter. Due to these advancements, India's regulatory environment is changing swiftly. Every educational institution that handles personal data, especially of EU nationals, must comply with GDPR. The major US student education record law is FERPA.

DOI: 10.4018/979-8-3373-3000-6.ch001

1. INTRODUCTION

The adoption of Artificial Intelligence (AI) in education is reshaping students' knowledge understanding, teachers' teaching modes and entire institution management. From algorithms suggesting optimum personalized learning approaches, to adaptive assessments and administrative automations to predictive analytics and beyond, AI-based tech is redesigning classrooms and campuses across the globe. In the context of K–12, AI promotes an early identification of students needing academic help, and a personalisation of support to student learning. In higher education the context expands significantly, impacting on admissions decisions, academic advisement, assisting to detect plagiarism and powering advanced research projects. But this increasing dependence on AI also comes with a host of thorny issues, above all in the areas of privacy, data protection and ethics. Today, schools and universities maintain large amounts of personal data about students in sensitive categories such as academic records, history of behavior incidents, medical information and unique personal identifying information. A reevaluation of the laws and regulations that now guide data and technology use in education is needed to answer these questions. There are already a number of laws (GDPR in the EU, FERPA, COPPA, SOPIPA, HIPAA in the U.S.) that govern our use of data; however these frameworks were mostly written long before anyone could train an image recognition system on billions of photos and may not adequately protect against the risks or afford opportunities for capabilities specific to modern machine learning systems. For instance, while FERPA governs parental access and consent to student records, it does not detail how AI-based profiling should be disclosed. The right to explanation and the principle of data minimization are also introduced in the GDPR, however, how these apply for algorithmic recommendations at educational institutions is recondite. Data protection frameworks, such as the GDPR, which mandate stringent guidelines on data storage, processing, and transfer, have been extensively examined in previous studies. The literature also highlights the challenges posed by jurisdictional conflicts, where contradictory laws on data handling and privacy are imposed by different countries. In addition, the National Institute of Standards and Technology (NIST) have published an AI Risk Management Framework for ensuring responsible AI development, although its voluntary status largely negated any enforcement within education. So, the patchwork of regulation we have now, although undoubtedly useful is still not comprehensive and certainly not fit for purpose in a digital age.

This chapter will explain how these privacy protection laws and existing frameworks can be used as a guide to reevaluate, repurpose and harmonize them so that ethical AI is applied in the classroom. It makes the case for a 'doing more' culture which is centred on understanding and not just being seen to do what is required urging education providers not to tick boxes but promote high ethical standards. In this way, schools and universities create systems of trust, transparency and accountability that respect students' rights while realizing the benefits of AI. Then, if this set of regulatory instruments is tuned up to be more coherent and closer to educational realities, enabling institutions to promote responsible, equitable, human-centered practice in AI for teaching and learning as well as administration.

1.1. Global Influence: The GDPR and Its Educational Impact

The GDPR of the European Union began in 2018 and is one of the world's most sweeping international privacy laws. It gives users the means to control their own data, and lays down strict rules on the collection, processing or storage of personal data. While this will be most applicable within the EU, its extra-territorial impact is that any educational establishment globally processing data belonging to people in the EU must ensure compliance with GDPR. For example, a U.S. university serving European students in an online degree program will need to follow the GDPR's consent rules about explicit opt-in as well as data portability and the right to be forgotten. With the increased emphasis on transparency, consent and data minimization introduced by GDPR, it is now a very different landscape when working with students' data in an educational context. AI-based EdTech developers will have to include "privacy by design and by default", with data protection built into the development of the technology as a guiding principle from its very start. By placing the responsibility in the hands of education institutions, this shift also compels these to be more considered when evaluating AI vendors and bringing on technology that prioritises student privacy. One obstacle, however, is reconciling GDPR principles with other regional laws such as FERPA in the United States, which may differ in its interpretation of students' data rights. It would be to the advantage of multinationals if there was a natural steppingstone from one standard to another, removing the need for overlapping or entirely different approaches and reducing complexity and administrative burden.

1.2. FERPA: Protecting Student Education Records

FERPA is a key privacy law protecting student data in the United States. Enforced by the Family Policy Compliance Office (FPCO), FERPA provides parents and eligible students with certain rights, including the right to inspect, correct, and control privacy of education records. If AI systems are used to examine or hold onto student performance records, those systems must comply with FERPA so they don't share that information without permission. For example, if a school relies on an AI platform to predict student success or issue insights about behavior, the platform must have controls in place so that access to data is available only to people who are authorized to see it and can share it. FERPA also mandates that schools receive parental or student consent before they release personally identifiable information (PII) to third party vendors like those that provide AI software.

1.3. COPPA and SOPIPA: Safeguarding Children's Online Data

That means COPPA and SOPIPA for K–12. COPPA is meant to protect children under age 13 by requiring parents' permission before collecting personal information online. As applicable for education tech, for example learning apps and online game or AI tutoring systems designed for early learners. Meanwhile SOPIPA, which was legislated in California, offers K–12 students some protection by prohibiting ed-tech companies from selling or to target their advertising with student data. It insists that the information it gathers may only be used for education. This statute has served as a model and foundation for other states' attempts to regulate and laid down the crucial founding case against commercial exploitation of student data. But schools often struggle to reconcile those laws with the AI technology they purchase from a multitude of vendors. So, for example, a school district deploying an AI-powered homework platform might have to validate that the product is indeed COPPA-compliant in its entirety while also adhering to SOPIPA's prohibitions on data commercialization.

1.4. HIPAA: When Health Data and Education Overlap

HIPAA covers medical and health information, while FERPA applies to educational records. This line can be hard to draw in school settings, where AI systems may track students' health or emotional well-being. Most K–12 schools fall under FERPA, not HIPAA, when it comes to student health records the schools maintain. But HIPAA can come into play if schools share data with non-school-based health care providers. As more schools use AI to predict attendance, monitor emotions and even deliver special education services, it becomes increasingly important to know where these lines are. "If FERPA and HIPAA dovetailed better, schools and health entities could pair with more ease. This would enable AI to be utilised in a manner that enhances student wellness, while safe guarding against data misuse and privacy intrusion.

1.5. The NIST AI RMF: Building Trustworthy AI

AI RMF is published by the National Institute of Standards and Technology to allow organizations to create and use ethical AI systems. It is voluntary and more broadly accepted than FERPA or GDPR. Essentially, NIST's framework is a means to systematically recognize, control, and reduce the risk of AI systems including but not restricted to concepts of transparency, responsibility, robustness, and equity.

The Need for Seamless Transitions between Frameworks

Even though there's some good in each regulation, too many overlapping regimes can lead to mass confusion and waste and lots of different applications. "We do need a more standardized and interoperable solution. Flows across systems would even promote greater uniformity in the application of privacy principles, allow for cross-border cooperation and facilitate compliance training for educators and administrators. Common guidelines could allow, for example, a multinational university to manage GDPR compliance when working with students from European nations without ignoring FERPA requirements governing its U.S. students. A simple checklist for compliance, one that links both COPPA (the federal Children's Online Privacy Protection Act) and SOPIPA requirements, might also help edtech companies construct products that fulfill state and federal expectations.

They would also incentivize privacy-by-design systems of AI technologies that are designed at the outset to be ethically global, helping minimize risks of student profiling, data misuse and algorithmic discrimination. These types of activities can ensure when we are using AI for education purposes it is not only legally defensible, but ethically justifiable.

The Role of Case Studies in Enhancing Understanding

The construction of legal structures and texts on which any law-based themes are based is well organized and strictly systematic. Some strong content structure and worked examples support vastly improved reader engagement and understanding. For instance:

- **Case Study 1:** A US school district attempted AI-enabled attendance and behavior monitoring; hit a huge backlash for breaking FERPA due to sharing data with unauthorized third parties. This is just one example of how overseeing vendors can go awry and result in non-compliance and a lack of trust from students.
- **Case Study 2:** A European university that had used AI to watch students take exams remotely was hit with G.D.P.R. complaints after students claimed it had over surveilled them. This is a clear case of being damned if you do and damned if you don't when it comes to academic honesty v/s privacy.
- **Case Study 3:** SOPIPA is a bill passed in California where the policing of it led software companies to reimagine their business model from ad-driven

revenue base to subscription-based educational solutions an instance of law leading ethical innovation.

Not only do these specific examples clarify the potential reach of each regulation, but they also highlight best practices upon which schools can rely. They breathe life into abstract legal principles, showing that responsible AI can enrich rather than erode education in a manner that honors the dignity and autonomy of students.

A Comprehensive Literature Review That Places These Laws in the Context of Ongoing Discussions, and Knowledge Gaps

AI integration decisions are frequently made without a solid empirical basis in terms of long-term effects, safety, or efficacy. Because of this evidence gap, institutional policies and regulatory efforts are usually predicated on conjecture or anecdotal evidence rather than thorough research, which increase the risk of the widespread use of harmful or ineffective AI tools, potentially wasting money, and having a detrimental effect on students' development. This disparity is a crucial call for scholarly study to guide practice and policy.

The paucity of research on the long-term effects on learning outcomes and student development is closely related. Although there have been early worries about decreased brain activity and lower critical-thinking scores linked to an excessive reliance on AI, there are surprisingly few thorough longitudinal studies looking at the long-term cognitive, social, and emotional effects of AI on students.

Additionally, there are significant gaps as shown in Table 1 comprehensive regulatory frameworks that are specifically tailored to the unique challenges of AI, especially in the United States. Clearer rules regarding data ownership, strong algorithmic transparency, and efficient accountability frameworks are desperately needed for AI systems, particularly those that use automated decision-making and student profiling.

Standardized auditing and evaluation procedures for AI bias and fairness are also required. Standardized, independent auditing and evaluation procedures to systematically identify, quantify, and reduce bias in educational AI systems are mainly lacking, despite the fact that algorithmic bias in these systems is widely acknowledged and has been documented. Considering the increasingly global nature of EdTech companies and the cross-border flow of student data, it is imperative to investigate how global standards can be developed to ensure consistent protection and ethical use of AI across different jurisdictions.

Table 1. Identified knowledge gap for research imperative and its reasons

Identified Knowledge Gap	Research Imperative/Direction	Why this Matters
Absence of impartial proof regarding AI's efficacy or safety	Perform thorough, empirical research on the effectiveness and equity of AI in a range of educational contexts and student populations.	To prevent the broad use of harmful or ineffectual AI tools and to guide evidence-based policy and practice.
Too few studies on the long-term effects on student development	To evaluate AI's long-term effects on students' critical thinking, agency, and social and emotional development, longitudinal studies should be started.	To safeguard the growth of students and guarantee that AI enhances rather than reduces fundamental human abilities.
Regulatory framework gaps specific to AI	Investigation of novel ethical and legal frameworks that is especially suited to AI in education, going beyond modifications of current legislation.	To address the particular difficulties of AI data processing and algorithmic impact, as well as to guarantee complete legal protection.
Lack of standardized tools for bias auditing/ mitigation	Create independent, standardized auditing and evaluation procedures to identify, quantify, and lessen algorithmic bias in AI systems used in education.	To prevent systematic discrimination against vulnerable student populations and advance equitable AI.
Research on international harmonization for EdTech AI is scarce.	Analyze policies in comparison and investigate models for global collaboration and harmonization of AI laws in education.	To promote ethical AI development worldwide and guarantee uniform cross-border student protection.

2. DIFFERENT TYPES OF AI REGULATIONS AND ACTS

Fast-growing AI might change K–12 education. Various machine learning applications have shown the promise of AI-driven and data-driven methods in various computing fields. Several initiatives are bringing machine learning to K–12 and higher school computer courses. Understanding intuition and agency in machine learning systems is crucial as it enters K–12 computer education. Computing education study finds it harder to understand the issues of teaching machine learning in K–12 since schools and teachers are already striving to integrate computational thinking and AI into curriculum. AI regulations and acts is shown in Figure 1. Education AI operates under patchwork laws:

(i) K-12: Regulated by FERPA, COPPA, and state-level laws (e.g., California Student Privacy Act).
(ii) In higher education, ethical AI research requires GDPR (EU), HIPAA (health data), and institutional IRBs.

Gaps: Education lacks federal AI framework, producing unequal supervision.

Figure 1. Various AI Regulation and Acts

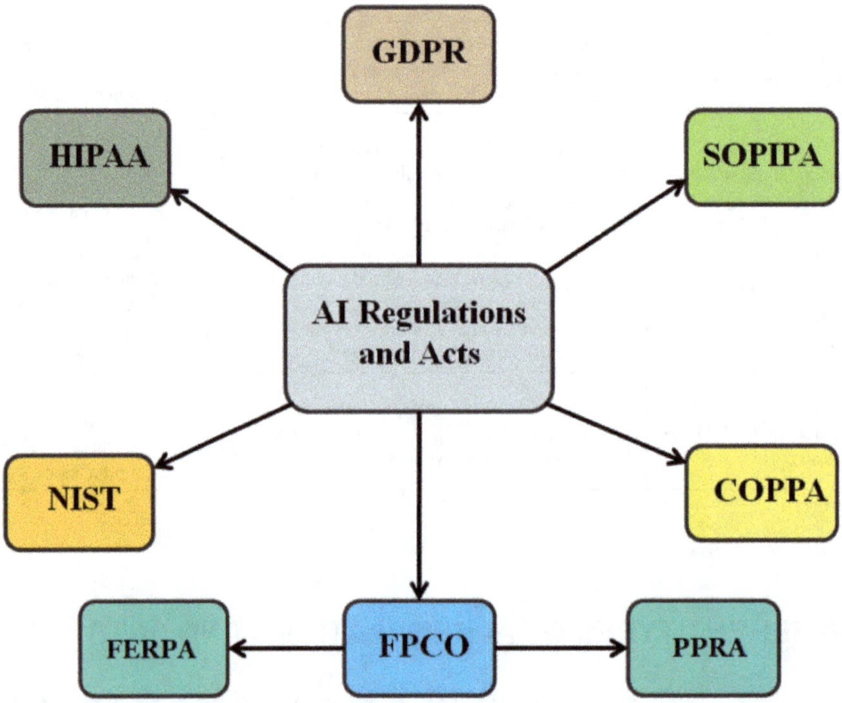

2.1 GDPR in Educational Institutions (K-12 and Higher Education)

Companies must follow severe GDPR data protection standards while collecting, processing, and storing personal data. The tool, created through 36 classroom interventions with 213 children and usability evaluations, is a low-entry point for teaching categorization ideas, supports creative and collaborative learning, and is GDPR-compliant for safe classroom usage (Kahila et al., 2024). The method emphasised four AI/ML education subject areas using concepts from literature. First, the design follows K-12 AI instruction and tool design knowledge (Gresse von Wangenheim et al., 2021). Second, inquiry-based and design-oriented teaching encouraged children to construct and create knowledge. Third, the tool promoted children's rights by using personal data while complying with GDPR (Pothong and Livingstone, 2023). Fourth, the UX design followed workflows and had few instructional scaffolding to meet accessibility and usability criteria (Schaper et al., 2023). Strict requirements for the protection of user data are imposed on organizations by regulations such as GDPR and the California Consumer Privacy Act (Tushar et al., 2026).

In K-12 Institutions

Among the key tenets Create a culture of compliance in K–12 schools and districts, according to GDPR, are that data was collected lawfully, fairly and transparently. When student personal data especially from AI systems is collected and used, policymakers should ensure clear communication with parents and students. Loading governance bodies will be required to implement the principle of data minimization, purpose limitation and storage-reduction so that only limited to what's needed data is retained. Scholars need to emphasize accuracy and develop strong security systems to avoid unauthorized intrusion. Institutions also need to be able to prove compliance through documented policies and practices as they integrate AI use in classrooms with GDPR's ethical and legal obligations meant to safeguard student privacy.

In Higher Education Institutions

In the higher learning sector, GDPR explains personal data must be processed particularly via AI in a lawful, fair and transparent manner. There is a requirement that students be notified of the collection purposes and consent is obtained as necessary. Policymakers must require that principles such as data minimization, accuracy, purpose limitation and storage limitation be enforced: Only the data necessary to fulfill tasks should be taken and kept in a safe manner. No AI tools can use data not originally intended for education. Only with ethical standards, such as anonymisation, impact assessments and adherence to security systems in place can research pay the proper respect due students' rights and ensure its work is fully GDPR compliant.

2.2 FPCO in Educational Institutions (K-12 and Higher Education)

The Family Policy Compliance Office (FPCO) enforces two federal education statutes that safeguard student and family rights:

(i) The Family Educational Rights and Privacy Act (FERPA) is the main statute FPCO oversees. As said, FERPA safeguards student education records.

(ii) The Protection of Pupil Rights Amendment (PPRA) requires parental approval for surveys, analyses, or evaluations financed by the U.S. Department of Education that gather sensitive student information.

FPCO's Role and AI in K-12 and Higher Education

The FPCO's enforcement of FERPA and PPRA directly impacts how educational institutions can use AI tools, particularly concerning student data.

In K-12 Institutions

The Family Policy Compliance Office (FPCO) offers significant guidance on FERPA and PPRA to safeguard student data in K–12 schools, including AI. AI vendors that receive access to education records must be deemed "school officials" and provide a service that schools would have used, be acting under the authority of the school, and use data exclusively for authorized educational purposes. You cannot commercialize use, create a profile using or train on student data. Schools should let parents know about the collection, use and access rights to their children's data. FERPA guarantees parents the right to control information about their children and FPCO withholds publications of decisions from AI so long as those decisions can be explained by a human through review following standards of fairness and that conform to requirements.

In Higher Education Institutions:

In the postsecondary setting, FERPA (administered by the Family Policy Compliance Office [FPCO]) protects student education records and confers certain rights to students when they are 18 or attending college. According to FERPA, students need to be notified and well-aware of and how AI technologies are using their personal data. AI is already used by universities for academic personalization, admissions screenings, advising or research. The FPCO mandates consent or a valid FERPA exception for any AI system that processes student data. For purposes of research, the institution must adhere to ethical standards, receive FPCO permission, and utilize de-identification or anonymization procedures to prevent student identity. Similar to K–12, higher education institutions should ensure that third-party AI vendors are "school officials" under FERPA.

2.1.1 FERPA in Educational Institutions (K-12 and Higher Education)

Student education data are protected by the Family Educational Rights and Privacy Act (FERPA). Parents have some rights over their children's school records, which students take up at 18 or when they begin college. All educational agencies and institutions that accept U.S. Department of Education subsidies must comply with FERPA. Representing students and protecting student privacy is shown in Figure 2. For instance, AI might help teachers customize educational resources. However, AI-enabled systems need more student data to do so. This information need not be demographic. It might also be student choices, other hobbies, relationships, or experiences. This data's fate, deletion, and access worry educators (Zacamy and Roschelle, 2022; Baker et al. 2022). Teachers must assess whether federal or state privacy rules, such as FERPA, apply to student data shared with or retained in AI-enabled systems to address educational disparities. Educators must also evaluate whether chatbots or automated tutors that provide conversational or textual instruction to pupils produce legal records.

Figure 2. Representing students and protecting student privacy

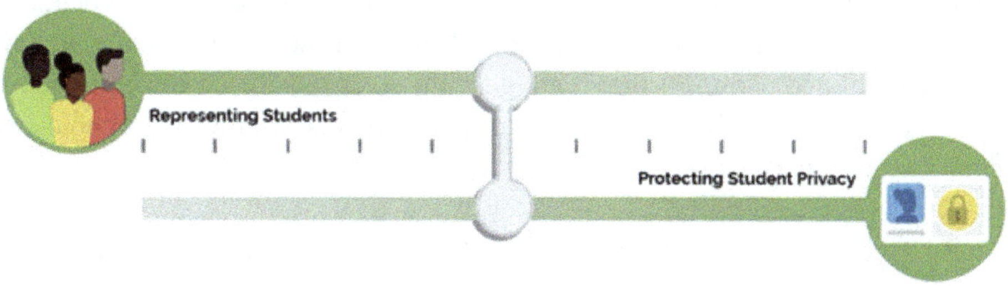

The integration of Artificial Intelligence (AI) in K-12 and higher education institutions presents a complex interplay with FERPA, introducing both opportunities and significant challenges for student data privacy.

AI and FERPA in K-12 Education

K–12 schools are under scrutiny, given the vulnerability and age of their students. COPPA mandates that, when using AI-driven technologies, one must receive parental consent especially in children under 13. Most AI tools are produced by third-party vendors, and under FERPA's "school official" exception, schools can share student data protected by the law with those vendors but only under tight restrictions. These would include providing a service the school normally offered internally, requiring that the school retain control of data use and maintenance, using that data only for contracted educational purposes, and having strong data security practices. Importantly, vendors may not use student data to train commercial AI models or for any purposes other than educational without separate explicit consent. These guidances make clear the need to safeguard students' privacy and use AI in K–12 responsibly, transparently, and within federal privacy laws.

AI and FERPA in Higher Education

Colleges and universities face problems that are identical to those of K–12, particularly when they have adult students who enjoy full FERPA rights. Most approved students (age 18 or in post-secondary) will have to give consent for their education records to be disclosed. AI systems that process pupil data must have valid consent especially if the data is used for non-educational purposes such as targeted advertising or data-driven careers advice. If AI factors into decisions, be it admissions or financial aid or academic status or discipline, there is a requirement of transparency and appeals processes echoing GDPR's "right to explanation." De-identifying Student Data AI's role in research makes it necessary to anonymize (or de-identify) your student data, even if the information found its way to you under broad educational consent. Contracts with third-party artificial intelligence vendors should explicitly label them as "school officials" and forbid the use of student data in training commercial models. Security of Data: It must be encrypted, and have access control and audit. Furthermore, generative AI tools need to be curated to guard against student PII contamination of public model training and uphold academic integrity and FERPA.

2.1.2 PPRA in Educational Institutions (K-12 and Higher Education)

The Protection of Pupil Rights Amendment (PPRA) governs U.S. Department of Education activities. It grants parents control over surveys, marketing data collecting, and physical tests or screenings.

PPRA for AI in Education

To comply with PPRA, schools must seek written parental agreement before requiring minor pupils to engage in ED-funded surveys, analyses, or evaluations that contain sensitive information.

In order to meet the requirements of the Protection of Pupil Rights Amendment (PPRA), schools must obtain written consent when students are required to take part in related surveys, evaluations, or analysis that are funded by the U.S. Department of Education and include personally identifiable information. This protects student privacy and complies with federal guidelines. Such consent shall be obtained from the parent when procurement of such information would encompass inquiry into matters such as political beliefs of the student or the student's parent; or any mental or psychological problem of the student or a member of his family; or any sexual behavior or attitudes; illegal, anti-social, self-incriminating and demeaning behavior; critical appraisals of other individuals with whom respondents have close family relationships; privileged and analogous relationships (such as those afforded by law to doctors, mediators etc. In addition, consent is needed if information includes significant others' critical appraisals or discussions of legally protected relationships (e.g., those between attorneys, physicians, clergy and clients). PPRA is intended to protect student privacy and ensure that parents retain control over their children's attendance at certain survey-based activities in school.

2.3 COPPA in Educational Institutions (K-12 and Higher Education)

US federal law COPPA compels commercial websites, online services, and mobile apps to protect children under 13's privacy (Coates et al. 2016). K-12 schools increasingly employ third-party online teaching tools and services, whereas COPPA targets commercial firms.

AI and COPPA in K-12 Education

Because schools commonly function as parent's "agent" in consenting pupils to utilize educational internet services, COPPA has a major influence on K-12 institutions. Schools can agree to the collecting of children's information on behalf of parents, as per instructions from the Federal Trade Commission (FTC), which enforces COPPA.

In order to comply with the Children's Online Privacy Protection Act (COPPA), K–12 schools need to ensure that AI-based educational technology systems adhere to stringent privacy guidelines, especially when gathering data from students under 13. They need to be predominantly educational and not rely on student data for commercial activities like advertising, profiling or developing general AI models. AI offerings often need a lot of student data academic performance, behavior patterns, usage and even personal biometric like facial recognition so privacy questions surface. Schools, therefore, must verify that ed-tech vendors are completely COPPA-compliant.

Schools should notify parents about AI tools, data collection, and protection, allowing them to understand their rights and voice concerns. AI can benefit from massive datasets, but schools and suppliers must still prioritize data reduction. Only data necessary for AI education should be gathered and stored.

Complex AI models can make it difficult to disclose how they make judgments regarding a kid (e.g., learning group placement, content recommendation). This does not violate COPPA, but it raises ethical questions about algorithmic bias and fairness, which can be connected to "use" of personal information.

COPPA and Higher Education Institutions

COPPA does not apply to higher education adult students (13 and over). Specifically, the legislation protects minors under 13. There are indirect factors:

When a university collects data online from children under 13, both the researchers and the institution (if operating the online service) are subject to COPPA regulations. This is important if AI is employed in research. Universities training future K-12 teachers should inform students about COPPA and its implications for AI use in classrooms. COPPA applies to university programs that gather personal information from children under 13 who participate in online activities. The ethical principles of COPPA (data privacy, transparency, informed consent) are generally considered good practice for all student data, regardless of age, especially when using AI systems to profile or make significant decisions about students.

Legal Frameworks for AI in Education: Navigating Overlaps and Tensions between FERPA, COPPA, and Ethical Governance

Student data privacy, legal compliance, and ethical use of AI have become growingly complicated and vital concerns at the intersection between student data privacy and artificial intelligence (AI) in schools and administration. There are legally enshrined protections for student data like (FERPA) and the Children's Online Privacy Protection Act (COPPA). But they sit on top of a foundation that leans toward tensions and interpretation, particularly in weighing innovation with privacy, parental rights and institutional obligations in AI-rich environments.

Particularly contentious are tensions among AI being data-intensive and the goal of minimum data safeguards in both FERPA and COPPA. The AI tools within many K–12 schools such as adaptive assessments and behavior analytics rely on collecting enormous amounts of personal data, from academic performance to biometric inputs (think: facial recognition) to interaction histories. FERPA requires schools to control the releases of education records and make parental rights to access and amend such records available. In the meantime, COPPA limits what online services can do with personal data gathered from children under 13 without explicit consent. But when schools operate as the intermediaries signing off for parents that introduce a gray area where AI systems might be allowed to work legally but still raise ethical concerns particularly with opaque algorithmic decision-making.

Third-party vendor management is a common issue under both FERPA and COPPA. For the "school official" exception to apply under FERPA, AI vendors must operate under the direct control of an institution and process data only for authorized educational purposes. COPPA further bolsters those protections by requiring ed-tech vendors to specify how data is used and prevent commercial use of student records. Yet the emergence of cross-user learning AI models (e.g., training on pooled student data) contradicts these limits. The tension is that it must not allow vendors to use data on users to create non-education-oriented commercial AI development even as many powerful AI tools develop through generalized exposure of their code to broad data usage.

Transparency and explainability is a second, overlapping issue. FERPA brings parents' and eligible students' rights to know what is being done with educational records up front, while COPPA requires that parents are clearly informed of data collection. With AI systems making important decisions on placement in classes, disciplining students, and content recommendations, that explainability is becoming increasingly crucial. While these systems might be legal under existing privacy regulations, the reliance on convoluted explanations to justify AI decisions is potential violations of the spirit of informed consent and accountability.

In higher education, COPPA loses some bite, because it applies only to children under 13. But FERPA is still key here, controlling students' rights in their data once people are considered eligible students. Colleges using AI for admissions, advising or research would need to obtain students' explicit consent or rely on FERPA's narrow exceptions. And here, FERPA-compliant de-identification standards become crucial to research, especially when AI is used to traverse and understand large-scale trends or behaviors. Colleges of education that work in teacher training also should teach COPPA concepts into curriculum, so future educators understand what ethical AI looks like in youth education.

Ultimately, while FERPA and COPPA provide a floor of protections in this space the jurisdictional holes, overlapping obligations, and procedural rigidity demonstrate that there is room for a more cohesive, dynamic regulatory framework better suited to technology. Closing these gaps is critical to ensuring that AI adoption is not only legal, but transparent, ethical, and respectful of student rights.

2.4 SOPIPA in Educational Institutions (K-12 and Higher Education)

Because California is a major market for educational technology (ed tech) businesses, the Student Online Personal Information Protection Act (SOPIPA) is prominent. Many national ed-tech suppliers tailor their services to conform to the strongest state legislation, like SOPIPA, to avoid having to produce various versions for different states (Colonna, 2022). SOPIPA applies to K-12 student websites, apps, and online services as of 2016. SOPIPA's main goal is K-12 student data privacy. Online educational service providers have certain restrictions.

(i) Online service providers cannot sell student data.
(ii) Students cannot be targeted by advertisers using student data. This includes "retargeting ads" depending on student internet activity.
(iii) Operators cannot create student profiles for non-educational purposes. AI excels at profiling and classifying users, thus this is important.

SOPIPA and AI in K-12 Education

California: SOPIPA-driven implementation of AI tools. The role out of AI-based tools in K–12 education is strongly influenced by California's Student Online Personal Information Protection Act (SOPIPA) which sets stringent data privacy requirements. SOPIPA basically imposes purpose limitation and data minimization, by insisting that AI tools only collect student data necessary to accomplish the educational mission. It makes it explicit you can't use such data for training commercial AI models like predictive purchase or career-movement models." Any ed-tech provider that uses student data for product development or resale would run afoul of SOPIPA. Vendor agreements would have to explicitly, and finally, limit this. While SOPIPA doesn't include an explicit requirement for explainability, its focus on consent and ethical data use suggests that transparency is important schools should inform parents in some way how AI received data and what insights it drew from them. Finally, SOPIPA demands that AI systems have strong security to prevent them from being hacked and/or misused. These regulatory requirements require robust vendor agreements to maintain compliance, promoting ethical and legal integration of AI in classrooms.

SOPIPA and Higher Education Institutions

While SOPIPA only covers K–12 students, its principles can be relevant to higher education. Although not bound by the SOPIPA, many universities share those ethical standards, particularly as AI makes its way into academic and administrative systems. Data protection, commercial profiling and targeted advertising are not only issues of compliance but form part of wider institutional obligation. What's more, colleges and universities often rely on AI tools from vendors who provide services to the K–12 market. These vendors might bring SOPIPA-compliant data usage practices to their apps used in higher education, thereby influencing how student data is processed. Moreover, students entering college today especially from California may have grown up with SOPIPA safeguards in place during their K–12 lives. Consequently, they probably expect to see the same data privacy and clarity of purpose at university.

2.5 HIPAA in Educational Institutions (K-12 and Higher Education)

A federal legislation in the United States called the Health Insurance Portability and Accountability Act (HIPAA) sets national requirements to safeguard the confidentiality and integrity of personally identifiable health information, or Protected Health Information (PHI). For all personally identifiable health information, the HIPAA Rules are well known for offering a nationwide baseline of data privacy, security, and breach notification safeguards. To demonstrate why this isn't always the case when it comes to health data that is gathered, produced, utilized, or revealed in the context of predictive or generative AI, a little background knowledge is required (Covered entity concerns exam, 2003).

HIPAA in K-12 Education Institutions

Indeed, HIPAA rarely covers K–12 schools because most do not fall within the definition of "covered entities" under HIPAA. Even when schools have nurses or psychologists, they generally don't conduct electronic transactions such as insurance billing to spur HIPAA compliance. Instead, students' health records kept by schools are subject to FERPA, which is the controlling authority. FERPA classifies such information as part of a student's "education record," and HIPAA specifically excepts these records. However, exceptions exist. For example, a healthcare provider that is not part of the school e.g., an immunization clinic at which the child is receiving vaccinations and that does not specifically operate on behalf of the school under HIPAA must obtain parental consent prior to disclosing this information. At such point as information received from third-party providers becomes part of a student's educational record (1) through receipt from them or (2) by recording it in some way, FERPA protections cover that information. Finally, it should be noted that even private schools not receiving federal money would be subject to the reach of HIPAA since FERPA would not cover them. If they are "covered entities" under HIPAA e.g., because they submit claims for health care services electronically, they must abide by HIPAA's PHI safeguarding requirements.

HIPAA in Higher Education Institutions

HIPAA works differently in higher education than it does in K–12 because of wider healthcare roles. The vast majority of student's health records think counseling center or student clinic records are "education" (or treatment) records, which are exempt from HIPAA under FERPA. But if a university is a "hybrid entity" then HIPAA might apply. This extends to institutions that operate self-funded student health plans or who have medical clinics performing electronic billing for service (including for non-students). In those cases, any of your student health records that are not FERPA-protected is HIPAA-protected. And if the university receives or creates Protected Health Information (PHI) through its health research, HIPAA's Privacy and Security Rules apply.

Strong administrative, technological, and physical protections for Electronic Protected Health Information (ePHI) are required under HIPAA's Security Rule. These strict security requirements (such as encryption, access restrictions, audit logs, and integrity controls) must be followed by any AI system handling ePHI in a HIPAA-covered setting. The Privacy Rule of HIPAA regulates the use and disclosure of PHI. Any use of an AI system that handles PHI must adhere to the Privacy Rule's authorizations (e.g., for treatment, payment, healthcare operations, or with specific patient authorization).

2.6 NIST in Educational Institutions (K-12 and Higher Education)

By developing measurement science, standards, and technology, the National Institute of Standards and Technology (NIST), a non-regulatory organization within the U.S. Department of Commerce, contributes significantly to the advancement of American innovation and economic competitiveness. NIST doesn't make legally enforceable rules, but its recommendations and frameworks especially the NIST AI Risk Management Framework (AI RMF) are generally accepted as best practices and frequently have an impact on industry standards, laws, and policies throughout the world. The US National Institute of Standards and Technology (NIST) initiative, which involves workshops and discussions with the public and private sectors regarding the development of federal standards for dependable artificial intelligence systems, is one example of how efforts to research and develop standards have been sparked in the US by worries about the potential misuse or unexpected consequences of AI (NCSL, 2022).

The NIST AI Risk Management Framework (AI RMF):

The NIST AI RMF is a voluntary framework that was released in January 2023 with the goal of assisting organizations of all kinds, including educational institutions, in managing the risks associated with AI systems while encouraging the development and responsible application of AI in a trustworthy manner. It highlights a methodical approach to four main tasks:

(i) **Govern:** Creating explicit procedures, records, and guidelines inside companies to promote a culture of risk management, establish frameworks for recognizing and foreseeing hazards, and determine how to mitigate their effects.
(ii) **Map:** Putting AI systems in perspective, seeing possible ethical, legal, and security risks, comprehending how AI advances larger objectives, and foreseeing effects beyond its intended purpose.
(iii) **Measure:** Applying quantitative or qualitative methods to evaluate the risks associated with AI, including monitoring metrics for reliable attributes (e.g., validity, reliability, safety, security, resilience, accountability, transparency, explainability, privacy-enhancement, fairness, bias management).
(iv) **Manage**: Creating backup plans, assigning funds, handling problems as they arise, and using lessons learned to enhance risk management.

NIST AI RMF in K-12 Institutions

The NIST AI Risk Management Framework (AI RMF) cannot necessarily be specifically adapted to K–12 but provides vital advice at the same time in regards to adopting AI by educational institutions. It prioritizes principles of fairness, accountability, transparency, privacy and security essential for trustworthiness in the use of AI at schools. The framework also assists institutions in recognizing and mitigating risks from issues such as algorithmic bias, student privacy breaches and cybersecurity threats. For example, bias in AI-facilitated grading or behavior monitoring can disproportionately impact marginalized types of students, while systems that are data-intensive lines up with FERPA and COPPA. It is the RMF's "Map," "Measure," "Manage" and "Govern" functions that help schools navigate these risks. It also champions transparency, by pushing for explainable AI that ensures parents and teachers know why a decision was made about their children. Furthermore, due diligence in the selection of AI vendors is also recommended where AI vendors should be required to meet ethical and legal standards. Finally, AI literacy is promoted among students and staff to create an informed and ethical use. In sum, the AI RMF provides a proactive systematic method for incorporating AI in education that is both secure and equitable.

NIST AI RMF in Higher Education Institutions

One such framework, NIST AI Risk Management Framework (AI RMF) may be especially pertinent for higher education institutions whose activities are centred on teaching, research and complex administration. In research, it contributes to ethical AI development by mitigating issues around data privacy, bias and transparency particularly when working with human subjects or sensitive data. When it comes to teaching, universities can leverage the RMF to review risks related to AI-powered advising, grading and learning tools and guide responsible policies. But for administrative uses admissions, financial aid the framework guarantees fairness and reduces algorithmic error. It acts as a good base for developing courses in AI ethics & governance, which would help students becoming responsible practitioners of AI. The RMF promotes governance through institutionalization by distributing the AI risk stakeholder responsibilities including IT, legal, and academic affairs. While it is not legally enforceable, compliance serves as an indication of the commitment to ethical AI and could increase institutional credibility, ensure future lawfulness (like the EU's proposed AI Act or India's DPDP Act), and secure research funding.

3. CONCEPTUAL FRAMEWORK: TECHNO-LEGAL GOVERNANCE FOR ETHICAL AI IN EDUCATION

A techno-legal governance framework an interdisciplinary platform that uses technological insight and legal and ethical overview is used in this chapter for responding to the challenges presented by AI in education. This framework acknowledges that although AI holds transformative potential for personalized learning, predictive analytics, and administrative efficiency, it also entails substantial risks related to privacy, accountability, bias, and student agency. An exclusively technology driven or legal solution is not enough; what we need is 'hybrid governance.

At the centre of this framework is the idea of student-centred data ethics which prioritises transparency, fairness and explainability in decision-making fueled by AI. It demands that schools make sure these AI tools work responsibly and in the spirit of trust and inclusion. This includes building the transparency of algorithms, so that students and their families can know how decisions (like placing them in a course or predicting behavioral risk) have been made. The framework is anchored within the law and will audit existing regulatory tool (the GDPR, FERPA, COPPA, SOPIPA and HIPAA) as foundational footings rather than comprehensive actions. It also explores new models such as the NIST AI Risk Management Framework towards evolving dynamic, proactive compliance approaches. These instruments should serve as a mechanism for ensuring data protection as well as guiding ethically beneficial AI design and usage. Operationally, the techno-legal governance model is biased toward institutional capacity-building schools and universities are incentivized to hire data stewards, conduct ethical impact assessments, and place human oversight over automation. As an example, by promoting common understanding among principals, technologists and policy makers, this model enables a more responsible use of AI within schools. In the end, techno-legal governance provides a pragmatic road map to reconcile AI innovation with legal responsibility and ethical fortitude such that education progress is not achieved at the expense of student rights or social justice.

K-12 AI Implementation Framework

1. Structures of Institutional Governance

Evaluation committees at the district level use multi-phase audits to carry out methodical screening procedures for educational AI systems. Organizations like the Ed-Tech Triage Team of the Los Angeles Unified School District operationalize this strategy. Standardized assessment tools are used by these cross-functional organizations to evaluate:

Curriculum conformity with educational goals
Adherence to regulations (COPPA/FERPA data privacy restrictions)
Protections for algorithmic equity before deployment permission.

2. Integration of Developmental Pedagogy

Constructivist methods are used in age-differentiated curriculum frameworks to gradually enhance computational cognition. This approach is best demonstrated by the MIT Design and AI Literacy (DAILy) program, which contains modules on ethical reasoning and experiential prototyping exercises for students in the concrete operational level (grades 6–8) that are closely related to the CSTA K–12 Computer Science Standards.

Higher Education AI Governance Framework

1. Oversight of Research Ethics

Institutional Review Boards will use rigorous assessment procedures to assess artificial intelligence research involving human participants. According to 45 CFR §46.111 regulatory requirements, studies that use learner data or algorithmic interventions must undergo a thorough examination. This includes:

Algorithmic impact assessments outlining potential discriminatory effects
Risk reduction techniques for unforeseen behavioral consequences;
Validated informed consent frameworks addressing data processing activities

2. Architecture of Academic Integrity

For the creation of computational material, postsecondary institutions use tiered mitigation systems:

Policy Recalibration: Updated honor codes that specifically forbid undisclosed synthetic authorship (e.g., Stanford University Administrative Guide Policy 4.2.1)

Authentication Infrastructure: deployment of probabilistic authorship validation systems (e.g., Turnitin's proprietary detection engine) exhibiting 97% empirical accuracy

Pedagogical Intervention: Instruction in ethical prompt building tailored to a particular discipline.

4. DISCUSSION

Implications for Educators, Policymakers, and Researchers

The inclusive regulatory environment of considering ethical use of Artificial Intelligence (AI) in education is a major concern for multiple stakeholders – teachers, policy makers and researchers. As AI is redefining both teaching, learning and institutions' management, steering that complex ecosystem of legal, ethical and technical responsibility will be a shared challenge and need to become a priority.

For Educators

Teachers are the ones on the ground using AI in educational contexts, from schools as to colleges and universities. As AI tools come with transformative benefits like personalized learning, adaptive testing and actional behavioral insights for educators —— they also require that those same educators are informed, discerning and transparent. Teachers need to know the limits of data collection, as with AI tools that collect sensitive student information. FERPA and COPPA, for instance, establish strict boundaries around what it will gather and how it must be handled. Educators therefore need instruction in data literacy and digital ethics that will enable them to scrutinize ed-tech tools to ascertain whether they are behaving in accordance with the law (federal or school-based). Critical is to have educators act as champions of student rights, seeing that AI deployment will not take away agency, inclusion or fairness in the classroom.

For Policymakers

Key Points: Policymakers in federal, state, and institutional systems will need to grapple with regulatory fragmentation that currently guides AI in education. There is no single law that regulates this complex role of AI, which also leads to implementation deficits and accountability problems. FERPA, COPPA, SOPIPA and HIPAA are applicable but under certain requirements, as is GDPR, while it adds steps for institutions abroad or worldwide platforms. As a result, policymakers should aim to align these frameworks or create clearer guidance which actually speaks to AI-specific risks in educational environments. Best efforts should also be placed on clear language in vendor contracts, standard parental notifications and oversight mechanism that permit continuous monitoring of AI systems implemented within schools. In addition, we should consider making the voluntary NIST AI Risk Management Framework (AI RMF) more institutionalized across sectors such that consideration is given to frameworks in place that enable organizations to implement proactive governance circumstances beyond compliance and build public trust.

For Researchers

Education technology researchers (and particularly those who focus on education technology, data science or public policy) also have a role to play in defining the future of AIEd. But they have ethical and legal considerations to weigh when designing studies that use student data or creating AI tools based on them. In academia, the research use of identifiable education records is governed by FERPA as well and may necessitate de-identification or explicit consent. COPPA goes even further for minors (in particularly in the online world). And scientists have to conduct responsible impact assessments to prevent AI models from reinforcing bias or inequality. Additionally, researchers are in an ideal position to assess the actual impact of AI interventions in practice that feed evidence-based recommendations to educators and policy makers. There is also a growing necessity for interdisciplinary research that connects novel technical capabilities to social science perspectives, so that AI tools not only perform well, but do so in a fair and transparent way.

5. CHALLENGES IN EDUCATIONAL AI IMPLEMENTATION

Systemic challenges with the Use of AI in Education

1. Inadequate Enforcement

Resource Limitations: For thorough AI vendor audits, educational institutions are severely lacking in technical know-how, funding, and staffing. This leads to non-compliance with ethical norms (Grozdanovski and De Cooman, 2025) and legal frameworks (GDPR, FERPA) by impeding the verification of algorithmic fairness, data protection measures, and pedagogical efficacy claims.
Technical Opacity: Complex machine learning systems' intrinsic lack of transparency makes evaluation difficult. Even stakeholders with technical expertise are unable to detect inherent biases in proprietary systems or evaluate internal decision-making procedures. Standardization Vacuum: Institutions lack verified assessment parameters when domain-specific audit procedures are absent, which makes it more difficult to evaluate educational AI systems systematically.

2. Misalignment of Technology and Policy

Regulatory Latency: As generative AI (such as transformer-based LLMs) advances faster than policy creation cycles, governance gaps are created during crucial adoption stages. As a result, educational institutions function without clear legal or moral guidelines.
Dynamic System Complexity: Ongoing algorithmic upgrades call for ongoing compliance monitoring, which calls for institutional resources above and beyond standard technology management procedures.
Unquantified Longitudinal Impacts: The continuous incorporation of AI in learning environments has unreported cognitive, developmental, and social repercussions that regulatory mechanisms are unable to adequately address.

3. Inequities in Structure

Infrastructural Disparities: Adoption obstacles faced by underfunded schools include:
Inadequate internet connectivity and device availability • Exorbitant acquisition and maintenance expenses
A poor technical support system that favors wealthy districts through digital segregation.

Algorithmic discrimination produces discriminating results in automated assessment scoring, personalized learning paths, and training data that incorporates past biases.

Students from underprivileged groups are disproportionately affected by behavioral intervention programs.
Gaps in Professional Development: The lack of ethical AI integration training among educators in economically disadvantaged areas exacerbates implementation disparities.
Market Exclusion: Fair access to pedagogically sound AI solutions is hampered by vendors giving preference to universities with substantial financial resources.

6. FUTURE CHALLENGES

Existing legal frameworks such as GDPR, FERPA, FPCO, COPPA, SOPIPA, HIPAA, NIST, and the larger CFR face a dynamic and complicated set of future issues due to the quick development and integration of AI in K–12 and higher education. The fundamental characteristics of AI technology, its quick development, and the particular circumstances of educational settings are the main causes of these difficulties. These are the main obstacles of the future:

a. Explainability and the "Black Box" Issue

Challenge: A lot of sophisticated AI models, including deep learning, function as "black boxes," making it hard to comprehend how they make certain judgments or forecasts.
Impact on Regulations:

(i) **The Right to Explanation under the GDPR:** This law expressly gives people the right to understandable information on the reasoning behind automated decision-making. One of the biggest challenges will be making complicated AI judgments clear to parents, students, and even professors.
(ii) **FERPA/FPCO & openness:** Without clear explainability, it will be difficult to provide sufficient openness on how AI affects student education records and choices (such as individualized learning paths, disciplinary actions).
(iii) **Bias Detection:** If the decision-making process is opaque, it becomes practically hard to detect and mitigate algorithmic bias, a major problem across all legislation.

b. Pervasive Data Collection and Re-identification Risks

Challenge: Because AI thrives on large datasets, a variety of student data (academic, behavioral, biometric, and emotional) is continuously and frequently passively collected. Additionally, people can be re-identified from data that appears to have been anonymized or de-identified using sophisticated AI algorithms.

Impact on Regulations:

(i) **GDPR's Data Minimization:** The notion of data minimization is at odds with the need for large datasets. Achieving the advantages of AI while genuinely reducing data will be a problem of the future.

(ii) **FERPA/COPPA/SOPIPA:** The meanings of "education record" and "personally identifiable information" shall be continuously examined. Given that AI can readily re-identify people, how much data is actually "de-identified"? The distinction between profiling for educational and non educational reasons will become increasingly hazy.

(iii) **HIPAA:** Advanced AI re-identification techniques may eventually threaten HIPAA's privacy protections, even for de-identified PHI.

c. Algorithmic Bias and Discrimination

Challenge: AI programs that have been trained on skewed historical data have the potential to reinforce or magnify current social injustices, producing unfair results in areas such as disciplinary actions, student support, grading, and admissions.

Impact on Regulations:

(i) **CFR (such as Title VI of the Civil Rights Act, ADA):** The CFR's current nondiscrimination provisions will be put to the test. It will be difficult to prove and address AI-driven prejudice; new auditing procedures and court rulings will be needed.

(ii) NIST AI RMF: Although NIST offers a framework for dealing with bias, it will be extremely difficult to put into practice, monitor continuously, and hold people accountable for prejudice in quickly developing AI systems.

d. Evolving AI Capabilities and Unforeseen Uses (Generative AI)

Challenge: Large language models, for example, are examples of generative AI that may produce new material, raise concerns about academic integrity (cheating, plagiarism), and perhaps produce inaccurate or dangerous content.

Impact on Regulations:

(i) **Academic Integrity regulations:** Establishing new definitions of authorship and ethical usage will be necessary as institutions find it difficult to modify current regulations to accommodate AI-generated work.

(ii) **FERPA/COPPA/SOPIPA:** Students may violate "no commercial use" restrictions or general privacy standards if they provide personally identifiable information (PII) to public generative AI models (for example, to assist with homework).

(iii) **Content Moderation:** Controlling AI-generated content (such as deepfakes in educational courses) and guaranteeing its safety and correctness will become more difficult.

e. Speed of Technological Change vs. Regulatory Lag

Challenge: Because AI technology is developing at an exponential rate, it is challenging for regulatory organizations and legislative bodies to keep up with thorough and pertinent rules.

Impact on All Regulations: The laws in place were not created with contemporary AI in mind. Among the difficulties of the future are:

(i) **Interpretation and Application:** In light of new AI applications, regulators such as FPCO will constantly have difficulties understanding current rules (FERPA, COPPA).

(ii) **Enforcement:** Without clear jurisdiction or technological know-how within regulatory authorities, it will be more difficult to enforce laws against sophisticated, internationally functioning AI organizations.

(iii) **Need for New Law:** There will be constant demand to pass AI-specific laws that classify risks and need certain controls, such as the EU AI Act. These laws must then be integrated with already-existing sector-specific regulations.

f. Resource and Expertise Gaps in Educational Institutions

Challenge: The technological know-how, funding, and committed personnel needed to properly comprehend, deploy, and oversee AI systems for regulatory compliance are frequently lacking in K–12 and higher education institutions.

Impact on All Regulations:

(i) **Compliance Burden:** It will become more difficult to guarantee adherence to several overlapping laws (GDPR, FERPA, COPPA, SOPIPA, HIPAA, NIST principles, CFR) for AI technologies.

(ii) **Vendor Dependence:** Institutions that rely on outside AI suppliers have a heavy burden in carrying out careful due diligence and efficiently managing contracts. Standardizing vendor responsibility and compliance will be a future concern.

(iii) **Teacher/Educator Training:** It will continue to be difficult to provide educators the skills they need to utilize AI sensibly and recognize possible ethical or privacy concerns.

g. Global Harmonization and Data Flow

Challenge: AI laws are being developed by several nations and areas (e.g., EU AI Act, India's DPDP Act). As a result, online learning platforms and international higher education institutions face a fragmented environment.

Impact on GDPR & Beyond: It will become more difficult for universities with foreign students or research partnerships to make sure their AI systems adhere to several, sometimes incompatible, international data protection and AI ethical standards.

CONCLUSION

The use of Artificial Intelligence (AI) in K–12 and higher education offer enormous potential to improve student learning, administrative functionality, and institutional decision-making. But to realize these benefits in a way that is morally and justly conscientious, we must pay special attention to messily complex regulatory terrain. At the moment there is no single holistic legal regime for AI systems in educational environments. Instead, establishments must look at what is possible in a web of related federal regulations, including those that have been patched like FERPA, COPPA, PPRA and HIPAA (and new state-level laws like California's

SOPIPA), international standards such as the GDPR and NIST AI Risk Management Framework and guidance documents.

For teachers, the shape of this landscape demands more than checking off a technical to-do list. Teachers and school leaders must be knowledgeable about their responsibilities related to data privacy, student privacy and fairness of algorithms. Their task is to make sure AI tools are transparent, equitable and used to augment not replace human-centered learning.

Policymakers have an important role in resolving regulatory ambiguities and establishing AI-specific educational standards. A unified legal perspective on AI would close the disconnect between the pace of tech progress and student data privacy, so institutions could use AI in a way that honors basic rights with certainty. Scientists themselves also have to build into their work consideration of ethics and regulation. This requires the building of AI systems that are not only accurate, but fair; ones that can give explanations for their predictions and at the same time are aware of the broader social impact on education.

Finally, the ethical use of AI in education requires collaborative action between educators, policy makers and researchers. Student safety, equity and public trust need to be the foundation of all AI schemes. Working across disciplines, and coalescing around common principles of ethical innovation, AI can be harnessed as a force for good that can change the postsecondary educational landscape.

AI in education must always be used as follows:

(i) Purpose limited: Information is only gathered and utilized for valid educational objectives.
(ii) Transparent: Parents and students in grades K–12 are aware of how AI technologies utilize their data.
(iii) Secure: Student information is shielded from abuse or illegal access.
(iv) Under control: Organizations keep an eye on student data and make sure suppliers don't exploit it for profit or to train their general artificial intelligence models without explicit, separate agreement.
    (iv) Respectful of rights: Even when AI is used in the development or upkeep of educational records, parents and students still have the right to access, examine, and seek changes to them.

REFERENCES

Baker, R. S., Esbenshade, L., Vitale, J., & Karumbaiah, S. (2022). Using demographic data as predictor variables: A questionable choice. https://doi.org/DOI: 10.35542/osf.io/y4wvj

Coates, H., Kelly, P., & Mahat, M. (2016). The regulation of standards in higher education. *Education*. Advance online publication. DOI: 10.1093/obo/9780199756810-0158

Colonna, L. (2022). The AI regulation and higher education: Preliminary observations and critical perspectives. SSRN *Electronic Journal.*

Covered entity issues exam. (2003). *The Practical Guide to HIPAA Privacy and Security Compliance.*

Gresse von Wangenheim, C., Hauck, J. C., Pacheco, F. S., & Bertonceli Bueno, M. F. (2021). Visual tools for teaching machine learning in K-12: A ten-year systematic mapping. *Education and Information Technologies*, *26*(5), 5733–5778. PMID: 33967587

Grozdanovski, L., & De Cooman, J. (2025). Individual safeguards in the era of AI: Fair algorithms, fair regulation, fair procedures. *Cambridge Forum on AI: Law and Governance*, *1*(e18), 1–9.

Kahila, J., Vartiainen, H., Tedre, M., Arkko, E., Lin, A., Pope, N., Jormanainen, I., & Valtonen, T. (2024). Pedagogical framework for cultivating children's data agency and creative abilities in the age of AI. *Informatics in Education*, 323-360.

NCSL, 2022. *Legislation Related to Artificial Intelligence.* Levantino, F. P., & Paolucci, F. (2025).

Pothong, K., & Livingstone, S. (2023). Child rights by design: Unboxing children from the child-only digital corner. *AoIR Selected Papers of Internet Research.*

Schaper, M., Tamashiro, M. A., Smith, R. C., Van Mechelen, M., & Iversen, O. S. (2023). Five design recommendations for teaching teenagers' about artificial intelligence and machine learning. *Proceedings of the 22nd Annual ACM Interaction Design and Children Conference*, 298-309.

Tushar, P. N., Shrivastava, P. C., Jaiswal, P., Singh, S., & Mishra, V. (2026). Legal challenges in cloud computing. In I. Oncioiu (Ed.), Law and regulation of AI, blockchain, and digital rights (pp. 63–102). IGI Global Scientific Publishing. DOI: 10.4018/979-8-3373-3186-7.ch003

Zacamy, J., & Roschelle, J. (2022). Navigating the tensions: How could equity-relevant research also be agile, open, and scalable? Digital Promise. http://hdl.handle.net/20.500.12265/159

APPENDIX

Abbreviations

AI - Artificial Intelligence
GDPR - General Data Protection Regulation
FERPA - Family Educational Rights and Privacy Act
FPCO - Family Policy Compliance Office
COPPA - Children's Online Privacy Protection Act
SOPIPA - Student Online Personal Information Protection Act
HIPAA - Health Insurance Portability and Accountability Act
NIST - National Institute of Standards and Technology
CFR - Code of Federal Regulations
PHI - Protected Health Information
AI RMF - Artificial Intelligence Risk Management Framework
DPDP - Digital Personal Data Protection
PPRA - Protection of Pupil Rights Amendment
FTC - Federal Trade Commission
Ed-tech - Educational Technology
AICTE - All India Council for Technical Education
PII - Personally Identifiable Information
IDEA - Individuals with Disabilities Education Act
EAR - Export Administration Regulations
BIS - Bureau of Industry and Security
DAILy - Design and AI Literacy
CSTA - Computer Science Teachers Association's
LLM's - Large Language Models
EU - European Union

Chapter 2
AI, Big Data, and Student Privacy:
A Policy Perspective in Indian Higher Education

Kusum Lata
https://orcid.org/0009-0005-2938-4129
D.G.C. Gurugram, Gurugram University, Gurugram, India

ABSTRACT

The integration of Artificial Intelligence (AI) and Big Data in Indian higher education has led to significant transformations in student learning, administrative decision-making, and institutional governance. However, data privacy, algorithmic bias, and regulatory gaps remain major concerns, with most universities lacking standardized policies for AI-driven student data management. This study investigates the current policy landscape, legal gaps, privacy risks, and ethical concerns in AI-enabled higher education in India. Using secondary data sources, including government reports, academic studies, and institutional policies, this study finds that most Indian universities do not comply with robust data protection measures, exposing students to cybersecurity threats and AI-driven surveillance risks. The study highlights the absence of sector-specific guidelines in India's Digital Personal Data Protection (DPDP) Act 2023 and the lack of AI ethics frameworks for higher education.

1. INTRODUCTION

Artificial Intelligence (AI) and Big Data are revolutionizing higher education across the globe, including in India, where universities are increasingly adopting AI-driven learning analytics, automated decision-making, and predictive student performance

DOI: 10.4018/979-8-3373-3000-6.ch002

modeling. AI applications in education have expanded beyond traditional classroom settings, impacting student assessment, faculty recruitment, and institutional administration. AI-powered tools such as plagiarism detection software, adaptive learning platforms, and chatbot-based student counseling are now integral to Indian universities. With the rise of Digital India initiatives and National Education Policy (NEP) 2020, the adoption of AI and Big Data has accelerated, aiming to create an inclusive, technology-driven, and data-informed education system (MHRD, 2021).

However, while AI and Big Data enhance the efficiency and accessibility of education, they also raise serious concerns about student privacy, data security, algorithmic bias, and ethical decision-making. Indian educational institutions handle vast amounts of sensitive student data, including demographic details, academic performance, online learning behavior, biometric data for attendance, and even psychometric assessments. Unlike Europe's General Data Protection Regulation (GDPR), India has only recently introduced the Digital Personal Data Protection (DPDP) Act 2023, which lacks specific guidelines for the education sector.

The problem is further exacerbated by data breaches and cybersecurity threats targeting Indian universities. In recent years, several Indian higher education institutions, including IITs, IIMs, and private universities, have suffered cyberattacks, leading to the leakage of thousands of student records. In 2021, the AIIMS Delhi student database was breached, exposing sensitive student medical data (CyberPeace Foundation, 2021).

Moreover, the lack of student awareness regarding data collection and usage is alarming. A study by Negi, (2024) found that 82% of Indian students were unaware of how universities collect and utilize their personal data. This lack of transparency results in unethical data collection, potential surveillance, and commercialization of student information without informed consent. AI-driven assessments and facial recognition-based attendance tracking, while efficient, raise ethical questions regarding student autonomy, privacy rights, and the potential misuse of biometric data (Akhtar, T. (2025).

Thus, this chapter aims to examine the policy landscape governing AI and Big Data in Indian higher education, identify challenges in student data protection, and propose policy interventions to ensure ethical AI deployment in universities. The study will rely on secondary data sources, including government reports, academic studies, and institutional policies, to provide a comprehensive analysis of the student privacy debate in India's AI-driven education sector.

2. REVIEW OF RELATED LITERATURE

2.1 AI and Big Data in Higher Education: Global and Indian Perspectives

Globally, the application of Artificial Intelligence (AI) in education has been extensively studied, focusing on learning analytics, personalized education, and automated assessments. In the United States and Europe, AI-driven models predict student dropouts, optimize learning strategies, and provide personalized learning experiences based on cognitive ability and engagement levels (Baker, R.S., 2021). However, these advancements also introduce challenges related to data ownership, algorithmic bias, and ethical AI governance (Selwyn, 2022).

In the Indian context, AI adoption in universities is still in its early stages, yet the government has been actively promoting AI-driven EdTech solutions. The National Education Policy (NEP) 2020 advocates for AI-based student assessments, personalized learning, and online proctoring tools, but it does not comprehensively address privacy risks, data protection measures, or ethical AI concerns (MHRD, 2021). The "AI for All" initiative launched by the Indian government aims to train students in AI skills but lacks guidelines on responsible AI usage in educational settings (Mehta, 2023).

2.2 Privacy Risks and Data Protection in AI-Based Education

Studies on data privacy in higher education indicate that students often lack control over their personal data, and institutions fail to establish proper safeguards (Sharma et al, 2024). Research has shown that AI-driven educational tools, such as facial recognition attendance systems and learning analytics platforms, often operate without explicit student consent or adequate anonymization of data (Chinnasamy et al., 2024).

In the Indian higher education sector, universities collect vast amounts of student data, but institutional policies on data security remain inconsistent and underdeveloped. A survey by the Internet Freedom Foundation (2022) found that only 12% of Indian universities had published a student data protection policy. Unlike in Europe, where the General Data Protection Regulation (GDPR) mandates strict data protection rules, Indian students lack a legal framework to challenge data misuse (Mehta, 2023).

2.3 Algorithmic Bias and Ethical AI Governance in Education

AI-driven grading and assessment tools in Indian universities have shown bias against students from rural, non-English-speaking backgrounds. A study by Deepshikha. (2025), found that AI-based evaluations favored urban students due to training datasets being skewed toward privileged demographics. Such biases perpetuate educational inequalities and call for stronger algorithmic accountability measures.

Despite the increasing adoption of AI and Big Data in Indian higher education, there is a significant lack of research focusing on student privacy, data security, and ethical AI governance in universities. Most studies have emphasized the technological benefits of AI in education but have not addressed the policy implications and legal voids concerning student data protection. Furthermore, there is no comprehensive policy framework in India that regulates AI-based student surveillance, algorithmic decision-making, or institutional data security practices. This study seeks to fill this gap by providing a policy-oriented perspective on student privacy in Indian higher education, focusing on AI ethics, legal frameworks, and institutional best practices.

Recent interdisciplinary research spanning education, law, data science, and ethics has deepened understanding of how AI and Big Data are transforming higher education while simultaneously creating new privacy and accountability challenges. Scholars such as Williamson and Piattoeva, (2022) and Knox (2022) describe the phenomenon of *datafied education*, where universities function as data ecosystems capturing and monetizing every aspect of student behavior. This datafication enables predictive learning analytics and “student success profiling,” yet also transforms learners into subjects of continuous monitoring. Williamson and Piattoeva, (2022) characterizes this as *platform governance*, where commercial EdTech companies influence institutional practices through data-driven infrastructures. The theoretical parallels with Zuboff’s (2019) concept of *surveillance capitalism* are striking both suggest that human behavior is commodified for predictive and commercial gain. In India, this pattern manifests through the rapid integration of EdTech platforms, predictive analytics, and AI-based monitoring systems that often operate without robust privacy oversight.

Educational theorists such as Selwyn (2022) and Holmes et al. (2022) have also emphasized the shift from traditional human evaluation to automated decision-making. Holmes et al. argue that AI systems used for grading and performance prediction are often *black boxes*students and teachers are rarely informed about how these systems function or influence outcomes. Algorithmic opacity undermines trust and accountability, particularly in contexts like India where digital literacy and institutional transparency are uneven. Selwyn (2022) cautions that education’s digital transformation must be examined through the lens of *power relations*AI in classrooms is not merely a pedagogical tool but a governance mechanism that redistributes authority between institutions, corporations, and students.

Indian literature, though more limited, mirrors these concerns. The *National Strategy for Artificial Intelligence* (NITI Aayog, 2018) positioned education as a core sector for AI innovation but neglected ethical and privacy safeguards. Akhtar, T. (2025) observed that while universities widely deploy AI-powered plagiarism detectors and proctoring software, few have defined protocols for consent, data retention, or algorithmic accountability. Pandey and Jha (2022) similarly note that outsourcing AI-based services to private EdTech firms creates opaque accountability chains, as universities delegate responsibility for data governance to external vendors.

At the global level, UNESCO (2021) and the OECD (2023) warn that the expansion of AI in education may exacerbate digital inequality if ethical safeguards are not embedded. OECD data shows that fewer than 25% of national education systems worldwide have adopted AI ethics guidelines, and most lack mechanisms for student consent or data-access rights. In the Indian context, studies by Sharma et al, (2024) and David et al (2025) have empirically documented algorithmic bias in AI-driven admission and grading systems. These findings reinforce international observations that AI systems replicate and amplify social inequalities present in training data particularly disadvantaging students from rural, regional-language, or low-income backgrounds.

Cybersecurity and institutional readiness represent another crucial area of concern. Mehta (2023) and the CyberPeace Foundation (2021) report that Indian universities often lack dedicated cybersecurity frameworks or encryption protocols, making them prime targets for cyberattacks. Globally, universities have become one of the most targeted sectors for ransomware and data theft (IBM Security Report, 2022). In India, breaches such as the 2021 AIIMS Delhi hack. The lack of mandatory data-protection officers or institutional audits means that privacy violations often go undetected or unpunished.

The question of *student awareness and consent* has been studied by Negi A. (2024) and Dhar, R., & Nath, S. (2024), who demonstrate that most Indian students remain unaware of how their data are collected, stored, or shared. This *information asymmetry* between institutions and students perpetuates passive consent students comply with digital data collection as part of academic participation. Dhar, R., & Nath, S. (2024) emphasizes that this undermines informed consent, transforming privacy from a right into a procedural formality. UNESCO (2021) has urged educational institutions to make transparency and participation foundational principles of ethical AI adoption. Yet, in practice, Indian universities rarely disclose data policies or provide opt-out mechanisms for students.

Ethical scholarship has increasingly proposed frameworks such as *data justice* (Heeks, 2022) and the *FAT principles*Fairness, Accountability, and Transparency

(Floridi et al., 2021) as essential for responsible AI deployment. These frameworks argue that ethical AI governance must encompass representation (who is included in data), distribution (who benefits), and procedural justice (who participates in decisions). Empirical evidence from European universities operating under the GDPR suggests that implementing FAT principles increases trust and reduces the likelihood of algorithmic bias (Heeks, 2022). These frameworks provide the ethical and philosophical grounding for the current study's analysis of AI governance and student privacy in India.

Comparative research also reveals sharp differences between Western and Indian higher education in *policy maturity and institutional preparedness*. Levy (2021) notes that universities in Europe and North America benefit from clear data governance regimes, while Asian institutions operate in more fragmented regulatory environments. Mishra, Chatterjee, and Sengupta (2023) observe that Indian universities often use disparate AI systems across departments without centralized oversight, increasing the risk of inconsistencies and data exposure. The absence of unified data-management infrastructure complicates compliance with emerging privacy laws such as the Digital Personal Data Protection (DPDP) Act 2023.Further, Selwyn and Jandrić (2020) argue that AI-driven assessment challenges the *moral economy* of education undermining creativity, empathy, and critical thought. These pedagogical critiques echo ethical concerns about the depersonalization of learning environments and the erosion of student agency under AI surveillance.

Finally, the literature emphasizes policy reform as the ultimate safeguard against ethical risks. International bodies such as UNESCO (2021), OECD (2023), and the European Commission (2023) advocate for national AI ethics frameworks aligned with human rights and democratic accountability. In India, the University Grants Commission (UGC, 2023) has initiated discussions on digital education and AI governance, yet implementation remains minimal. Mehta (2023) argue that India's DPDP Act 2023, though a milestone, lacks sector-specific provisions for higher education and fails to ensure student data rights such as access, correction, and erasure. Scholars converge on the need for multi-stakeholder frameworks combining technological standards, institutional ethics committees, and legal enforcement to ensure privacy and fairness in AI-enabled education.

The existing literature demonstrates that while AI and Big Data promise transformative potential for higher education, they also generate profound ethical, legal, and social implications. Across global and Indian studies, three consistent themes emerge:

1. The rise of data-driven educational governance that privileges efficiency over privacy;

2. The persistence of algorithmic bias and inequality in AI-driven academic systems; and
3. The inadequacy of legal and institutional mechanisms to safeguard student rights.

This study builds upon these insights by analyzing policy gaps, governance mechanisms, and ethical imperatives necessary for ensuring that AI in Indian higher education evolves responsibly, transparently, and in alignment with democratic and human-rights principles.This study seeks to fill this gap by providing a policy-oriented perspective on student privacy in Indian higher education, focusing on AI ethics, legal frameworks, and institutional best practices.

3. RESEARCH QUESTIONS

1. How do Indian universities handle student data in AI-driven education systems, and what are the associated privacy risks?
2. What policy measures should be implemented to ensure ethical AI deployment in Indian higher education institutions?

4. HYPOTHESES

H1: The absence of a standardized data protection policy in Indian universities leads to increased student privacy risks.
H2: AI-driven educational technologies in India operate with minimal transparency, leading to ethical concerns regarding student data usage.

5. RESEARCH METHODOLOGY

This study adopt a secondary research methodology, utilizing existing literature, government reports, academic studies, and institutional policies to analyze the intersection of AI, Big Data, and student privacy in Indian higher education. Data collected from official reports such as AISHE (All India Survey on Higher Education), National Digital University reports, and policy documents from UGC (University Grants Commission). Additionally, academic research from peer-reviewed journals, legal analyses of the DPDP Act 2023, and case studies of Indian universities implementing AI-driven education technologies also examined. This qualitative approach allow for a comprehensive analysis of privacy risks, legal gaps, and best practices in AI-based student data management.

5.1.Theoretical and Conceptual Framework

The relationship between Artificial Intelligence, Big Data, and student privacy in higher education can be best understood through a multidisciplinary theoretical lens that integrates socio-technical, ethical, and policy-oriented perspectives. At its core, this study draws from *Surveillance Capitalism Theory (Zuboff, 2019)*, the *Socio-Technical Systems (STS) framework*, and principles of *AI Ethics and Data Justice*, while also situating the discussion within the *Digital Governance and Human-Rights-Based Approach (HRBA)*. Together, these perspectives explain how the integration of AI technologies in education simultaneously enhances institutional efficiency and jeopardizes fundamental student rights to privacy, autonomy, and equity.

From the standpoint of *Surveillance Capitalism Theory*, the increasing deployment of AI-driven systems in universities represents a shift from education as a public good to a data-driven enterprise, where student behavior, engagement patterns, and learning analytics are commodified as data assets. Zuboff (2019) argues that modern institutions whether corporate or educational extract behavioral data to predict and shape future actions, often without users' explicit consent. In the Indian higher-education context, where AI-powered learning platforms, remote proctoring tools, and facial-recognition systems have become common, universities inadvertently reproduce this logic of surveillance capitalism. Student interactions with digital platforms generate vast datasets academic records, biometric identifiers, psychological profiles that can be monetized or misused by third-party vendors. This theoretical lens helps explain why privacy risks are not incidental but structural outcomes of data-driven education systems that prioritize efficiency and predictive control over student autonomy.

Complementing this is the *Socio-Technical Systems (STS) framework*, which emphasizes that technology and society co-evolve. AI and Big Data in higher education are not neutral tools; their impacts depend on institutional norms, regulatory frameworks, and cultural attitudes toward privacy. According to STS theory, the design and deployment of AI in universities reflect existing power structures and policy gaps. For instance, when AI-based grading systems in India exhibit bias against regional-language essays or when surveillance tools disproportionately affect marginalized students, these outcomes arise from the sociotechnical design of algorithms trained on skewed data and implemented without ethical oversight. The STS framework thus provides a holistic understanding of how social context, institutional capability, and technological architecture together determine the consequences of AI adoption in universities. It aligns closely with your study's finding that the lack of standardized policies and weak data-governance capacity in Indian institutions amplifies the ethical risks of AI.

The *AI Ethics and Data Justice* perspective further grounds this analysis in moral and normative principles. Drawing from UNESCO's *Recommendation on the Ethics of Artificial Intelligence* (2021) and Heeks' (2022) notion of "data justice," this study interprets fairness, accountability, and transparency as central pillars of ethical AI governance. Data justice extends beyond data protection to encompass representation (who is included or excluded in datasets), distribution (who benefits from data use), and procedural justice (who has voice in decision-making). In India's higher-education sector, where algorithmic opacity and digital inequality are prevalent, data-justice theory underscores the importance of democratizing AI governance. It helps explain why marginalized students those from rural, low-income, or non-English-speaking backgrounds face disproportionate harm from biased algorithms. Ethical AI frameworks advocate for "explainable AI" and human-in-the-loop decision systems, ensuring that automated outcomes can be reviewed and contested principles directly echoed in your paper's policy recommendations.

At the regulatory level, the *Digital Governance and Human-Rights-Based Approach (HRBA)* offers another crucial layer. This framework, rooted in international human-rights law, interprets privacy as a fundamental right linked to dignity, autonomy, and equality. The HRBA shifts the focus from technological capability to institutional responsibility, emphasizing accountability of the state and universities in safeguarding student rights. It aligns with Article 21 of the Indian Constitution (Right to Privacy) and international standards like the GDPR and UNESCO guidelines. Applying HRBA to AI governance means that universities must ensure consent, transparency, and proportionality in data collection and use. It transforms AI deployment from a discretionary institutional choice into a rights-based obligation. Within this framework, your study's emphasis on policy gaps and lack of regulatory oversight gains theoretical grounding: the absence of explicit student data-protection mechanisms violates the normative expectations of human-rights-based governance.

The *conceptual framework* that emerges from integrating these theories positions student privacy as the central dependent variable shaped by four interrelated independent constructs: (1) technological infrastructure and AI adoption; (2) institutional governance and data-management capacity; (3) regulatory and policy environment; and (4) ethical-awareness and digital literacy among stakeholders. AI and Big Data function as enabling technologies that influence data-collection intensity and algorithmic decision-making. Institutional governance—including the presence of data-protection officers, ethics committees, and cybersecurity protocols—determines how responsibly these technologies are deployed. The regulatory environment, including national laws like the DPDP Act 2023 and UGC/AICTE guidelines, provides external accountability mechanisms that can either strengthen or weaken student privacy protections. Finally, the ethical and digital-literacy dimension reflects how informed students and faculty are about their data rights and responsibilities. Collectively, these four variables interact to produce outcomes ranging from enhanced learning efficiency to potential privacy violations. A weakness in any one dimension say, low regulatory oversight or limited ethical literacy can lead to systemic vulnerabilities, as evidenced by the repeated data breaches and algorithmic biases identified in your findings.

This conceptual synthesis can be visualized as a multi-layered model: at the core lies *student privacy and trust*; surrounding it are concentric layers of *technological design*, *institutional governance*, *legal frameworks*, and *ethical culture*. The innermost layer (technology) determines how data are collected and processed; the second layer (institutional governance) controls access, storage, and consent; the third layer (policy and regulation) enforces compliance; and the outermost layer (ethical and digital culture) sustains awareness and accountability. The model illustrates that safeguarding student privacy in AI-enabled education requires alignment across all layers no single mechanism suffices. For instance, strong technology without ethical literacy still enables misuse, while robust laws without enforcement yield little practical protection. Hence, the conceptual framework advocates an integrated, systems-level approach to privacy governance in education.

These theoretical and conceptual perspectives also help interpret the empirical patterns discussed later in your paper. The widespread lack of transparency and student consent aligns with the predictions of surveillance capitalism and weak digital governance. Algorithmic bias observed in AI-based grading and admissions exemplifies structural inequities explained by STS and data-justice theories. Similarly, cybersecurity vulnerabilities and policy gaps correspond to deficiencies in institutional governance as defined in the conceptual model. By embedding the analysis within these theoretical constructs, the study gains explanatory depth moving beyond descriptive documentation of privacy violations to a systemic understanding of why such risks persist.

In essence, this framework situates your study at the intersection of *technology, ethics, and governance*. It underscores that the challenges of AI and Big Data in Indian higher education are not purely technological but fundamentally socio-political and ethical. Addressing them demands multi-level reforms technical (secure data architecture), institutional (AI ethics committees), regulatory (sector-specific privacy laws), and cultural (digital-rights literacy). The theoretical integration of surveillance capitalism, socio-technical systems, data justice, and human-rights-based governance thus provides a comprehensive scaffold for analyzing student privacy in the age of intelligent education systems. It not only supports your hypotheses linking weak institutional frameworks to heightened privacy risks but also strengthens the rationale for the policy interventions proposed in the later sections. Within this conceptual architecture, AI can be re-imagined not merely as a technological innovation but as a test of educational ethics and democratic accountability in 21st-century India.

Figure 1. Conceptual Model of Student Privacy in AI-Enabled Higher Education

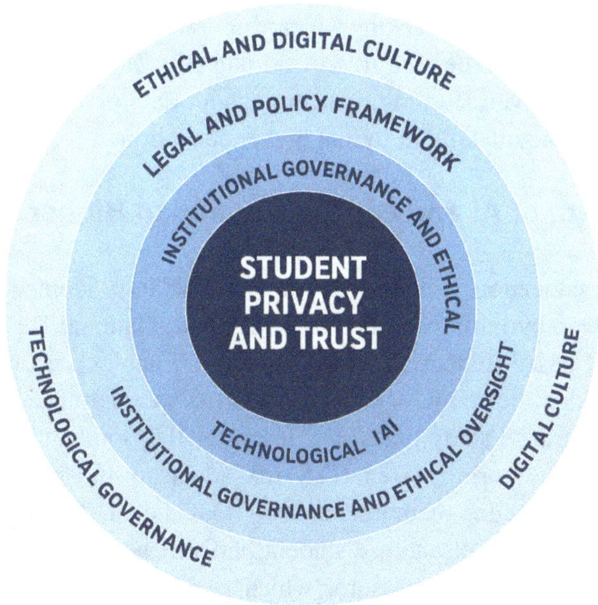

6. AI AND BIG DATA IN INDIAN HIGHER EDUCATION: AN OVERVIEW

The integration of Artificial Intelligence (AI) and Big Data in Indian higher education is transforming how universities manage student learning, administrative processes, and institutional decision-making. AI-driven tools are being increasingly used for personalized learning, student performance analytics, faculty recruitment, plagiarism detection, and even emotional intelligence assessment. Big Data analytics, on the other hand, allows institutions to process vast amounts of student-related data, offering predictive insights into dropout rates, learning difficulties, and course performance trends. However, while these technological innovations enhance efficiency, they also introduce privacy concerns, algorithmic biases, and ethical challenges in handling student data.

India's higher education sector is the second-largest in the world, with over 40 million students enrolled in approximately 1,100 universities and 43,000 colleges

(AISHE, 2021). The push for Digital India initiatives and the implementation of the National Education Policy (NEP) 2020 have fueled the adoption of AI in Indian universities, encouraging adaptive learning models, facial recognition attendance systems, online proctoring, and AI-assisted academic decision-making (MHRD, 2021). Despite these advancements, student privacy and data security remain largely unregulated, with institutions lacking a clear framework for data protection and AI ethics. This section examines the role of AI and Big Data in Indian universities, the benefits of AI-driven learning, concerns about data privacy, and the broader implications for policymaking in Indian higher education.

6.1 The Growth of AI and Big Data in Indian Higher Education

AI-powered education technologies are now widely adopted across Indian universities, driven by initiatives such as SWAYAM, National Digital University, and AICTE's AI-based student monitoring tools. AI enables personalized learning by analyzing student behavior, academic performance, and engagement levels to recommend customized study plans. For instance, IIT Bombay has developed an AI-driven intelligent tutoring system (ITS) that adapts to student progress and provides personalized learning recommendations (David et al, 2025)).

Machine learning modelsanalyze student performance data to predict dropout risks and recommend remedial measures, which have been successfully implemented at institutions like IIM Bangalore and Delhi University. Likewise, AI chatbots and virtual assistants are being deployed to enhance student support services. Universities such as IIT Madras and Amity University have implemented AI-based chatbots that provide academic counseling, career guidance, and administrative assistance.

6.2 Role of Big Data in University Decision-Making

Big Data analytics has emerged as a crucial tool for higher education institutions in India, allowing universities to analyze vast amounts of student-related data to improve academic and administrative decision-making. Institutions collect and process data from multiple sources, including student enrollment records, course participation logs, exam performance metrics, and digital footprints from online learning platforms (Dhar, R., & Nath, S., 2024). For example, learning analytics platforms are now widely adopted to track student progress in online courses, particularly in Massive Open Online Courses (MOOCs) like NPTEL and SWAYAM. These platforms collect student interaction data, including quiz performance, video engagement, and forum participation, to identify at-risk students and tailor intervention strategies (Mishra et al., 2023).

Additionally, faculty recruitment and research assessment in Indian universities are increasingly being driven by AI and Big Data. Universities such as IISc Bangalore and JNU utilize AI-powered bibliometric analysis tools to evaluate research impact based on publication citations, h-index, and research collaboration networks ((Sharma et al, 2024)). This data-driven approach ensures transparency in faculty hiring and funding allocation but also raises concerns regarding over-reliance on quantitative metrics rather than qualitative assessments.

6.3 AI in Student Assessment and Automated Grading

One of the most significant applications of AI in Indian higher education is automated grading and student assessment. AI-driven Natural Language Processing (NLP) models are being used to assess essay-based exams, plagiarism detection, and even emotional tone in student responses. Tools like Turnitin, Grammarly, and iThenticate are widely used for plagiarism detection, ensuring academic integrity in student submissions (Chinnasamy et.al, 2024). Additionally, automated essay grading systems are being piloted in various universities, reducing faculty workload and ensuring objective assessment. Delhi University and Christ University Bangalore have experimented with AI-assisted grading systems for evaluating descriptive answers in undergraduate exams (Akhtar, T. (2025). While these systems enhance efficiency, they also pose ethical concerns regarding algorithmic bias, as AI models may fail to understand nuanced arguments, cultural contexts, or creative writing styles.

6.4 AI in Surveillance and Student Monitoring

Another controversial application of AI in Indian higher education is student surveillance and proctoring systems. The rise of online learning and remote examinations during the COVID-19 pandemic has led to widespread adoption of AI-based remote proctoring tools that monitor student behavior during exams through facial recognition, eye-tracking, and keystroke pattern analysis.

Platforms such as ProctorU, Mettl, and ExamSoft have been widely used in Indian universities for online exam invigilation, but they have raised serious privacy concerns (Internet Freedom Foundation, 2022). Students have protested against the intrusive nature of AI-based proctoring systems, arguing that constant surveillance creates psychological stress and disproportionately affects students with disabilities or those from marginalized backgrounds (The Hindu, 2022). Additionally, facial recognition attendance systems are increasingly replacing traditional roll-call methods in universities like VIT Vellore, BITS Pilani, and Hyderabad University. While these systems enhance efficiency and prevent proxy attendance, they also raise concerns about biometric data security and the lack of explicit student consent (Mehta, 2023).

6.5 AI and Algorithmic Bias in Higher Education

Algorithmic bias in AI-driven education technologies remains a significant concern in India. AI models used for student evaluation, admissions, and recruitment may inadvertently favor privileged demographics while disadvantaging students from rural backgrounds, lower-income families, and non-English-speaking communities. A study by David et al (2025) found that AI-based grading systems used in Indian universities tended to assign lower scores to essays written in regional languages compared to English-medium submissions.

Similarly, AI-based admission screening tools used by private universities may unintentionally favor applicants from elite schools with better digital footprints, disadvantaging students from government schools or economically weaker sections (Sharma et al, 2024). These biases necessitate greater transparency and accountability in AI-driven decision-making in Indian universities.

6.6 Data Privacy and Cybersecurity Risks in AI-Based Education

The rapid adoption of AI in Indian higher education has outpaced the development of robust data privacy policies and cybersecurity measures. Indian universities frequently collect student data without clear policies on data storage, retention, or third-party access (Chinnasamy et.al, 2024). The Digital Personal Data Protection (DPDP) Act 2023, India's first comprehensive data privacy law, provides a broad legal framework but lacks specific provisions for the education sector (Mehta, 2023). Cybersecurity threats targeting Indian universities have increased in recent years. In 2021, AIIMS Delhi's student database was hacked, exposing sensitive student health records (CyberPeace Foundation, 2021).

The integration of AI and Big Data in Indian higher education offers numerous advantages, including personalized learning, predictive analytics, automated assessments, and administrative efficiency. However, these technologies also pose significant privacy risks, algorithmic biases, and ethical dilemmas that Indian universities are yet to fully address. The absence of strong data protection policies and AI governance frameworks necessitates urgent policy interventions to ensure ethical AI deployment while safeguarding student rights in Indian higher education.

7. PRIVACY CONCERNS IN AI-ENABLED HIGHER EDUCATION

The rapid adoption of Artificial Intelligence (AI) and Big Data in Indian higher education has transformed the way universities collect, store, and analyze student data. AI-driven tools are now extensively used for student assessment, faculty evaluation, predictive analytics, and administrative decision-making. However, this widespread integration raises significant privacy concerns, as most Indian universities lack clear guidelines on student data protection, informed consent, and cybersecurity protocols. Unlike the General Data Protection Regulation (GDPR) in the European Union, India's Digital Personal Data Protection (DPDP) Act 2023 is still in its nascent stage, and its application in the education sector remains ambiguous (Mehta, 2023).

The major privacy concerns in AI-enabled education in India include lack of transparency in data collection, cybersecurity threats, algorithmic biases, ethical concerns surrounding student surveillance, and absence of regulatory oversight. This section explores these challenges in detail, supported by statistical data, case studies, and expert analyses.

7.1 Lack of Transparency in Data Collection

One of the primary privacy issues in AI-based higher education is the lack of transparency in student data collection and processing. Many Indian universities do not provide clear policies on how student data is collected, stored, or shared. For example, Delhi University's online proctoring system records video feeds, keystroke patterns, and browsing history during exams, but students are rarely informed about how long their data is stored or who has access to it (Chinnasamy et.al, 2024). A similar issue was observed at IITs and IIMs, where AI-driven adaptive learning platforms collect data on student interaction patterns, quiz performance, and engagement levels, but students are not given the option to opt out of data tracking.

7.2 Risks of Data Breaches and Cybersecurity Threats

The growing reliance on AI-driven student databases has made Indian universities prime targets for cyberattacks and data breaches. In recent years, several major security incidents have exposed sensitive student information, raising concerns about weak cybersecurity measures in the education sector.

Table 1. Major Data Breaches in Indian Higher Education Institutions

Year	Institution	Nature of Breach	Data Exposed	Source
2021	AIIMS Delhi	Cyberattack on student health records	Medical and personal records of 100,000+ students compromised	CyberPeace Foundation (2021)
2023	Private University (Unnamed)	Ransomware attack on student database	Financial details, enrollment data	Internet Freedom Foundation (2023)
2023	Indian Institute of Science (IISc)	Unauthorized access to research data	Student login credentials, research papers	Cybersecurity Report (2023)

These breaches highlight *the vulnerability of student databases*, particularly *when universities do not implement strong encryption, multi-factor authentication, or periodic cybersecurity audits* (Negi A. 2024). A study by the *Internet Freedom Foundation (2023)* found that *only 18% of Indian universities have cybersecurity teams dedicated to protecting student data*, and *nearly 70% of institutions store student records on unsecured servers*. This *lack of robust cybersecurity infrastructure* increases the risk of *data theft, unauthorized access, and potential misuse of student information.*

7.3 Algorithmic Bias and Discrimination in AI-Based Assessments

Another major concern in AI-enabled education is the risk of algorithmic bias, where AI-based grading systems, admission screening tools, and student performance analytics unintentionally favor certain demographics over others. For example, AI-based admission screening systems used by private universities tend to favor students from elite schools with extensive digital footprints, putting students from government schools and rural backgrounds at a disadvantage (David et al, 2025)). Automated grading tools have also been found to assign lower scores to essays written in regional languages, as most AI models are trained primarily on English-language datasets (Akhtar, T. (2025). This bias not only affects admissions and assessments but also impacts student scholarships and funding opportunities, as AI-based decision-making tools are increasingly used to determine eligibility for financial aid and merit-based scholarships (Chinnasamy et.al, 2024).

7.4 Surveillance and Ethical Concerns in AI-Based Education

AI-powered facial recognition, remote proctoring, and behavior-tracking systems have raised serious ethical concerns among students and faculty members.

During the COVID-19 pandemic, AI-based remote proctoring tools such as ProctorU and Mettl were widely used for online examinations. These tools monitor eye movements, facial expressions, and keystroke patterns to detect potential cheating. However, students have protested against these surveillance measures, arguing that they violate privacy, cause anxiety, and disproportionately affect students with disabilities (The Hindu, 2022). In 2022, students at Hyderabad University staged protests against the mandatory use of facial recognition attendance systems, citing concerns over biometric data privacy and unauthorized data storage (Internet Freedom Foundation, 2022). Additionally, universities such as BITS Pilani and VIT Vellore have implemented AI-powered emotion recognition software to analyze student engagement during lectures. While these technologies claim to improve learning outcomes, they raise ethical questions about autonomy, consent, and psychological impact (Mehta, 2023).

7.5 Absence of Strong Regulatory Oversight

Unlike the European Union's GDPR, which provides strong legal protections for student data, India's DPDP Act 2023 lacks sector-specific guidelines for higher education. Most universities do not have clear data governance policies, and there is no regulatory body to monitor AI ethics in education ((Negi A. 2024).). A study by Dhar, R., & Nath, S. (2024). found that only 14% of Indian universities have a dedicated data protection officer, and less than 30% of institutions inform students about their data rights. This lack of legal safeguards leaves student data vulnerable to misuse by third-party EdTech companies and AI software vendors. Without a clear regulatory framework, Indian universities continue to collect, analyze, and share student data without accountability, raising serious privacy and ethical concerns.

The unregulated use of AI and Big Data in Indian higher education has significantly increased student privacy risks. Universities collect vast amounts of student data, but lack transparency in data policies, fail to implement strong cybersecurity measures, and rely on AI models that reinforce existing biases. Additionally, AI-based surveillance tools infringe upon student autonomy and mental well-being, further exacerbating privacy concerns.

Given these challenges, India urgently needs a regulatory framework that mandates transparency, consent, cybersecurity standards, and AI ethics in higher education. Without such measures, student privacy will remain at risk, and the benefits of AI in education may be overshadowed by ethical concerns and potential misuse of data.

7.6. MAJOR FINDINGS

The rapid adoption of *AI and Big Data in Indian higher education* has *transformed student learning experiences, administrative processes, and decision-making in universities*. However, this shift has also introduced *critical privacy concerns, legal ambiguities, and ethical dilemmas*. The following are the major findings of this study, organized around the core objectives:

1. Widespread AI Adoption Without Standardized Data Protection Policies

The study finds that *Indian universities have rapidly integrated AI-powered educational tools*, including *learning analytics platforms*, *plagiarism detection software*, *chatbot-based student assistance, and automated grading systems.* AI is also being used for *predictive analytics*, helping institutions identify students at risk of *dropout or academic failure*. However, despite these advancements, *there is no standardized national framework guiding AI ethics, transparency, or accountability in educational institutions* (Mehta, 2023).

A *2023 report by the Internet Freedom Foundation (IFF)* noted that *only 14% of Indian universities have a dedicated data protection officer*, leaving student records vulnerable to *data breaches and unauthorized access.*

2. Rising Cybersecurity Threats in Indian Universities

With *large-scale AI deployment*, universities are *collecting, storing, and processing vast amounts of student data*, making them prime targets for *cyberattacks and hacking attempts*. The study identifies *multiple cybersecurity breaches in Indian higher education institutions*, highlighting *poor data encryption standards and weak cybersecurity infrastructure.*

3. Algorithmic Bias in AI-Based Student Evaluations and Admissions

AI models used for *grading, admissions, and student performance tracking* often exhibit *algorithmic biases that favor certain demographics over others*. The study finds that *students from rural backgrounds, lower-income families, and non-English-speaking communities are disproportionately affected* by AI-based assessments.

A study by David et al (2025) found that AI-powered grading systems in Indian universities *scored essays written in English 15% higher than those written in regional languages*, reflecting *bias in training datasets.*

4. AI-Based Surveillance and Ethical Concerns in Student Monitoring

The study identifies *serious ethical concerns* regarding the use of *AI-driven surveillance tools, such as facial recognition attendance systems and remote proctoring software*. While these tools help *prevent cheating and proxy attendance*, they also *violate student privacy and contribute to psychological stress.*

During the COVID-19 pandemic, *remote proctoring software like ProctorU and Mettl* were widely used in Indian universities, but students protested against their *intrusive nature and unfair targeting of marginalized students* .Additionally, in 2022, *Hyderabad University students protested against mandatory facial recognition attendance systems*, citing *concerns over biometric data misuse and unauthorized surveillance* (Internet Freedom Foundation, 2022).

5. Legal and Policy Gaps in Student Data Protection

Despite the introduction of *India's Digital Personal Data Protection (DPDP) Act 2023, there are no sector-specific guidelines for AI governance in education.* Unlike the *EU's GDPR, which provides explicit student data rights*, the *DPDP Act does not grant students the right to access, modify, or delete their AI-processed academic records* (Mehta, 2023). Furthermore, the *National Education Policy (NEP) 2020* promotes *AI integration in education* but *fails to address the risks associated with AI-driven surveillance, cybersecurity, and algorithmic discrimination* (MHRD, 2021).

6. Lack of Institutional Oversight and AI Governance Mechanisms

The *University Grants Commission (UGC) and AICTE* have not yet developed *standardized AI governance policies*, leading to *inconsistent implementation of AI ethics across universities.* While *elite institutions like IITs and private universities have introduced internal AI ethics policies*, the vast majority of Indian universities *lack structured AI deployment guidelines* (Akhtar, T. (2025).

8. POLICY LANDSCAPE AND LEGAL GAPS IN INDIA

The rapid adoption of *Artificial Intelligence (AI) and Big Data* in Indian higher education has significantly outpaced the development of robust legal and regulatory frameworks governing student data privacy. While AI-driven learning analytics, automated assessments, and biometric surveillance tools offer efficiency and personalization, they also raise critical ethical and legal concerns. *India lacks a comprehensive legal framework that explicitly governs student data protection in educational institutions*, making student records vulnerable to unauthorized access, misuse, and exploitation. Although *the Digital Personal Data Protection (DPDP) Act 2023* provides a general legal foundation for data protection, its applicability to higher education remains ambiguous, leaving universities and students without clear safeguards (Mehta, 2023).

8.1 The Digital Personal Data Protection (DPDP) Act 2023 and Its Limitations

The *DPDP Act 2023* is India's first comprehensive data protection law aimed at regulating the collection, processing, and storage of personal data. However, the Act *does not contain specific provisions for student data protection* in higher education institutions. Unlike the *General Data Protection Regulation (GDPR) in Europe*, which mandates *clear consent mechanisms, right to data access, and stringent data retention policies*, the *DPDP Act lacks explicit regulations for how student data should be handled by universities and EdTech platforms* ((Negi A. 2024)).

One of the *primary limitations* of the DPDP Act is that it *does not grant students the explicit right to access or delete their academic records collected through AI-driven platforms*. Many universities *store student records indefinitely*, often sharing them with *third-party AI vendors, online learning platforms, and private research agencies* without students' informed consent. Additionally, there are *no legal repercussions for universities that fail to implement strong data security measures,* further increasing the risk of data breaches.

8.2 The National Education Policy (NEP) 2020 and Its Gaps

The *National Education Policy (NEP) 2020* promotes the *integration of AI, Big Data, and EdTech platforms* in Indian higher education but *does not outline clear data protection measures*. The policy encourages *the use of AI-powered personalized learning models, facial recognition for attendance, and online assessment systems,* yet it *fails to address the ethical and privacy implications of such technologies* (MHRD, 2021).

The lack of *institutional guidelines on AI ethics and student data management* has led to a situation where universities *adopt AI technologies without ensuring transparency or accountability*. For instance, while institutions such as *IIT Bombay and IISc Bangalore* have begun implementing AI-based student monitoring systems, *there is no standardized framework on how student data should be anonymized, stored, and protected from cyber threats* (Chinnasamy et.al, 2024).

8.3 Institutional Data Protection Policies: The Absence of Standardization

Only a few *elite institutions, such as IITs and private universities like Ashoka and OP Jindal*, have developed *data protection policies outlining the handling of student data*. However, these policies *vary widely between institutions and are not legally binding*, leading to inconsistencies in implementation (David et al, 2025).

A study by Dhar, R., & Nath, S. (2024). found that:

- *Only 14% of Indian universities* have a dedicated data protection officer.
- *Less than 30% of institutions inform students* about how their data is collected and used.
- *Over 60% of universities* lack an explicit policy on *how long student data is retained* and who has access to it.

The absence of standardized regulations *allows universities to collect and store student data indefinitely*, often outsourcing data processing to *third-party AI vendors without oversight*(Akhtar, T. (2025). This raises concerns about *data security, unauthorized profiling, and potential misuse by private entities.*

8.4 The Role of the University Grants Commission (UGC) and AICTE

The University Grants Commission (UGC) and the All India Council for Technical Education (AICTE) have yet to establish comprehensive guidelines on AI governance and student data privacy. While the AICTE has promoted AI-driven learning platforms and digital tools, it has not issued regulations to ensure transparency, student consent, or cybersecurity compliance in AI-based education (Internet Freedom Foundation, 2023). The lack of centralized oversight has created a fragmented and inconsistent approach to AI adoption, where universities implement surveillance-based learning technologies without accountability (Mehta, 2023). To address these challenges, India must develop clear legal frameworks and institutional policies that prioritize student data protection while enabling responsible AI innovation.

9. RECOMMENDATIONS AND POLICY INTERVENTIONS

The use of Artificial Intelligence (AI) and Big Data in higher education has reshaped academic environments in India, enabling universities to implement smart learning platforms, predictive analytics, and student monitoring systems. However, this transformation has also introduced a wide range of challenges—most notably, privacy violations, algorithmic bias, cybersecurity vulnerabilities, and an overall lack of regulatory oversight. As Indian higher education moves further into the digital age, it becomes crucial to design, implement, and enforce coherent policy frameworks that balance innovation with privacy, transparency, and accountability. This section proposes a series of comprehensive, evidence-based policy interventions aimed at addressing these gaps in the AI and Big Data ecosystem of Indian academia.

9.1 Develop a National AI and Data Ethics Framework for Higher Education

At present, India lacks a centralized framework guiding the ethical use of AI in higher education. The European Union has already adopted a risk-based approach through its AI Act, which classifies AI systems according to the risk they pose to fundamental rights. Similarly, UNESCO has released global guidelines on the ethics of AI in education. India must develop a national AI ethics framework specifically tailored for the education sector. This framework should be led by the Ministry of Education in collaboration with NITI Aayog, the University Grants Commission (UGC), the All India Council for Technical Education (AICTE), and domain experts in AI ethics, law, education technology, and cybersecurity.

The framework should mandate that universities conduct *Ethical Impact Assessments (EIAs)* before deploying AI systems in classrooms or administrative processes. These assessments should evaluate whether the system respects student rights, maintains transparency in decision-making, and avoids reinforcing historical inequalities. Each educational AI tool must also be registered in a national registry, including details of the algorithm used, data sources, vendors, privacy risks, and expected outcomes.Moreover, institutions should be required to publicly declare their use of AI technologies, provide explanations for AI-based decisions (e.g., automated grading or admissions), and offer human review mechanisms. This would enhance both transparency and trust among students, parents, and faculty.

9.2 Enforce Mandatory Data Protection Policies in All Higher Education Institutions

While the Digital Personal Data Protection (DPDP) Act 2023 provides a broad legal framework, it falls short of providing clear directives for data governance in educational settings. Universities should be required to adopt *customized, enforceable data protection policies* aligned with the principles of the DPDP Act but extending further to address the unique requirements of academic data.

Each university must establish a *Student Data Governance Policy* covering data collection, storage, access, sharing, retention, and deletion protocols. The policy should clarify the types of data collected (e.g., biometric, academic, behavioral), the legal basis for processing, third-party access conditions, and students' rights to opt-out or access their information.

Data minimization should be a guiding principle. Universities should only collect what is strictly necessary for academic purposes. Additionally, all student data must be stored in *encrypted formats*, hosted on secure servers within India, and retained only for specified durations. Institutions should be required to undergo *annual data protection audits* and publish audit summaries for public review.

9.3 Institutionalize Informed Consent and Data Transparency Mechanisms

A cornerstone of ethical AI deployment is informed consent. In Indian universities, AI-powered tools are often implemented without consulting students or informing them about how their data will be used. The practice of blanket consent embedded in admission forms or online learning platforms is inadequate and misleading.

Universities must adopt *granular and contextual consent frameworks*. Students should be given clear, readable privacy notices before each instance of data collection, particularly for invasive tools such as facial recognition systems or predictive behavioral analytics. These notices must outline what data is being collected, why it's needed, how it will be used, how long it will be stored, and with whom it may be shared.Further, institutions should provide students with *data dashboards* where they can view, correct, download, or delete their personal data. These dashboards should be modeled after successful examples from GDPR-compliant platforms in the EU, offering *real-time transparency and user agency*. No AI-based assessment or surveillance mechanism should be mandatory; students must always have the right to opt out without academic penalty.

9.4 Establish Independent AI Ethics Committees in Universities

To oversee the ethical deployment of AI and resolve grievances related to algorithmic bias or data misuse, each university should set up an *AI Ethics Committee (AIEC)*. These committees should include representatives from the faculty, legal experts, technologists, students, and civil society members. Their responsibilities would include:

- Reviewing new AI implementations and providing ethical clearance
- Investigating student complaints related to AI systems (e.g., discriminatory grading or surveillance practices)
- Conducting regular bias audits of algorithms used in assessments or administrative decision-making
- Ensuring compliance with national AI ethics guidelines

In addition, universities should be mandated to submit *annual AI Ethics Reports* detailing the types of AI systems in use, their outcomes, reported incidents, and corrective actions taken. This would ensure internal accountability and contribute to a national repository of AI best practices.

9.5 Integrate AI Ethics and Digital Literacy in Curriculum

Digital and data literacy are critical in a world increasingly governed by algorithms. Indian universities should introduce *mandatory AI ethics modules in undergraduate and postgraduate curricula* across disciplines. These modules should cover topics such as data protection laws, algorithmic fairness, surveillance ethics, consent, and digital rights.For students in technology programs, there should be an added emphasis on responsible AI development, ensuring they understand not only how to build AI systems but also how to evaluate their social impact. Similarly, education and humanities students should be trained in how to critically assess algorithmic tools in pedagogical settings.Educating future professionals on ethical AI usage will not only protect student rights in the present but will help cultivate a generation of responsible technologists, educators, and policymakers.

9.6 Strengthen Cybersecurity Infrastructure Across Universities

Cyberattacks on academic institutions have become more frequent and more damaging, with major breaches at AIIMS Delhi, private universities, and EdTech firms exposing hundreds of thousands of student records. Strengthening cybersecurity in higher education must become a national priority.

All universities should be required to:

- Appoint *Chief Information Security Officers (CISOs)* or *Data Protection Officers (DPOs)*
- Conduct *quarterly vulnerability assessments and penetration tests*
- Maintain updated *incident response protocols and data breach notification procedures*

- Use *multi-factor authentication (MFA)* and *end-to-end encryption* on all academic data systems

The Ministry of Education, in collaboration with CERT-In (Computer Emergency Response Team – India), should create a *National Academic Cybersecurity Framework (NACF)* with clear standards and certification processes. Institutions found to be in violation should face penalties, including withdrawal of funding or AI tool deactivation.

9.7 Audit AI Systems for Fairness, Accountability, and Transparency (FAT Principles)

AI systems used for grading, admissions, student profiling, or research evaluation must be regularly audited using the *FAT principles—Fairness, Accountability, and Transparency*. AI audits should be conducted by independent third-party organizations that assess:

- Dataset representativeness (to detect demographic or linguistic biases)
- Decision logic explainability (so students and faculty can understand AI outcomes)
- Disparate impacts on different student groups (e.g., women, Dalits, students with disabilities)

Auditors must be empowered to recommend algorithmic modifications, suspension of biased systems, or full disclosure of system logic to affected students. Any AI tool that fails to meet basic fairness thresholds should be prohibited for academic use.

9.8 Regulate and Monitor Third-Party AI Vendors and EdTech Platforms

Many universities in India use third-party platforms for AI-powered assessments, learning analytics, and proctoring. These vendors often operate without adequate oversight, posing serious risks to data security and privacy.Government agencies must create *licensing and certification protocols for EdTech vendors*, requiring them to comply with national standards on:

- Data minimization and user consent
- Transparency in algorithmic decision-making
- Non-commercial use of student data
- Storage of data within Indian jurisdiction

Further, universities must disclose all vendor relationships publicly and conduct *due diligence audits* before engaging with new AI-based services. Contracts must include clauses preventing data resale or repurposing, and breach of contract should lead to disqualification from providing services in any educational institution.

9.9 Create a National Repository for AI Use in Higher Education

Transparency across institutions can be fostered by maintaining a *National Repository of AI Tools and Practices* in Indian higher education. This repository, hosted by the Ministry of Education or UGC, would include:

- Detailed descriptions of AI tools deployed by universities
- Performance metrics, biases encountered, and student feedback
- Incident reports related to AI misuse or malfunctions
- Research on ethical AI development in Indian education

Such a repository would encourage knowledge sharing, help smaller institutions adopt safe technologies, and allow regulators to monitor trends and anticipate emerging risks.

9.10 Include Civil Society in Policymaking and Oversight

Finally, to ensure the development of inclusive and equitable policies, the government must actively engage civil society organizations, student unions, privacy advocacy groups, and academic researchers in drafting and reviewing AI regulations. Public consultations should be institutionalized before passing any major legislation related to AI in education. The involvement of independent watchdogs will ensure that student voices are heard, and commercial interests of EdTech firms are balanced with public accountability and ethical integrity.

The future of AI in Indian higher education must be rooted in ethical design, privacy-by-default infrastructure, regulatory enforcement, and participatory governance. With the exponential growth of AI in academia, India stands at a pivotal juncture. These policy interventions spanning legal reforms, institutional governance, consent protocols, cybersecurity mandates, AI audits, and curriculum changes will help build an education system that not only leverages the power of technology but protects the dignity, rights, and future of every student. The choice is not between innovation and privacy, but about embedding human-centered values into the innovation process itself.

CONCLUSION

The integration of Artificial Intelligence (AI) and Big Data in Indian higher education is undoubtedly revolutionizing the academic landscape—improving personalization, efficiency, and predictive decision-making across institutions. However, this digital transformation comes at a significant cost if not managed ethically and responsibly. This chapter has revealed that despite the extensive use of AI-driven tools and analytics in universities, India lacks a comprehensive, sector-specific policy framework to regulate student data, address privacy risks, and ensure ethical AI deployment. The findings underscore the urgency of a regulatory overhaul. Most Indian universities operate without clear data protection policies, offer minimal transparency to students, and frequently adopt AI tools without informed consent. Furthermore, algorithmic biases embedded in AI-driven assessments and admission tools threaten to exacerbate existing educational inequities. Cybersecurity infrastructure in higher education is also significantly underdeveloped, leaving institutions highly vulnerable to data breaches and unauthorized exploitation of sensitive student information.

To mitigate these risks and build trust, India must adopt a multifaceted approach. This includes establishing a National AI Ethics Framework for education, enforcing standardized student data protection laws, introducing institutional AI Ethics Committees, mandating algorithmic audits, and enhancing cybersecurity readiness across universities. Equally important is the empowerment of students through digital literacy and transparency in how their data is collected and used. In short, for AI to truly serve as a transformative force in Indian higher education, it must be aligned with the principles of fairness, accountability, transparency, and inclusivity. This chapter advocates for urgent, coordinated policy actions that uphold student rights and institutional integrity in the age of intelligent education systems. Only by embedding ethics at the core of AI deployment can India responsibly harness technology for equitable and sustainable educational futures.

REFERENCES

NITI Aayog. (2018). National strategy for artificial intelligence: #AIForAll. Government of India. National Strategy for Artificial Intelligence

Akhtar, T. (2025). Ethical AI governance in higher education: A framework for fair automation. *International Research Journal of Modernization in Engineering Technology and Science*, *4*(2). https://www.irjmets.com/upload_newfiles/irjmets7

Baker, R. S. (2021). Artificial Intelligence in Education: Bringing It All Together. In *OECD Digital Education Outlook 2021: Pushing the frontiers with AI, blockchain, and robotics* (pp. 43–56). OECD Publishing. Retrieved from oecd-baker.pdf.

Chinnasamy, P., Pushpalatha, M., Nirmala, V., Vidhya, V., Ayyasamy, R. K., & Priya, D. (2024). AI-driven assessment and evaluation: Enhancing sustainability in educational practices. In Proceedings of the 2024 3rd International Conference on Automation, Computing and Renewable Systems (ICACRS) (pp. 1–6). IEEE. https://doi.org/DOI: 10.1109/ICACRS62842.2024.10841634

CyberPeace Foundation. (2021). Report on cyberattacks on Indian universities. CyberPeace Research Report.

David, D., Rajeshwari, B., & Timhna, S. (2025). Algorithmic bias and discrimination in India: A looming crisis. Journal of Education and Social Change. Advance online publication. https://doi.org/DOI: 10.1177/24551333251343358

Deepshikha. (2025). A comprehensive review of AI-powered grading and tailored feedback in universities. Discover Artificial Intelligence, 5, Article 251. https://link.springer.com/article/10.1007/s44163-025-00517-0

Dhar, R., & Nath, S. (2024). Digital surveillance and civil rights: Assessing the impact on privacy. Chanakya Law Review, 5(1), 66–86. Retrieved from https://cnlu.ac.in/wp-content/uploads/2025/05/Digital-Surveillance-And-Civil-Rights-Assessing-The-Impact-On-Privacy-by-Dr.-Rumi-Dhar-Ms.-Sonia-Nath.pdf

Floridi, L., Cowls, J., Beltrametti, M., Chatila, R., Chazerand, P., Dignum, V., Luetge, C., Madelin, R., Pagallo, U., Rossi, F., Schafer, B., Valcke, P., & Vayena, E. (2021). An ethical framework for a good AI society: Opportunities, risks, principles, and recommendations. Minds and Machines, 31(2), 137–163. https://doi.org/ retrieved from AI4People-An Ethical Framework for a Good AI Society: Opportunities, Risks, Principles, and Recommendations - PubMedDOI: 10.1007/s11023-020-09527-8

Heeks, R. (2022). *Data justice and digital development: Pathways for a fair information society*. Routledge.

Holmes, W., Porayska-Pomsta, K., Holstein, K., Sutherland, E., Baker, T., Shum, S. B., & Koedinger, K. R. (2022). Ethics of AI in Education: Towards a Community-Wide Framework. *International Journal of Artificial Intelligence in Education, 32*(3), 504–526. DOI: 10.1007/s40593-021-00239-1

Internet Freedom Foundation. (2022). The state of student data protection in Indian higher education. Internet Freedom Foundation Report. India: Freedom on the Net 2022 Country Report | Freedom House

Knox, J. (2022). *Artificial intelligence and education futures: Critical perspectives and key debates*. Routledge.

Levy, K. (2021). *Student privacy in the digital age: Balancing AI innovation and data protection*. Harvard University Press.

Mehta, A. (2023). Cybersecurity in Indian universities: Challenges and policy solutions. In Mehta, A. (Ed.), *Legal gaps in AI regulation in Indian higher education* (pp. 77–96). Springer.

MHRD. (2021). National [Ministry of Human Resource Development, Government of India. NEP_Final_English.pdf]. *Educational Policy*, •••, 2020.

Mishra, P., Chatterjee, A., & Sengupta, S. (2023). Predictive analytics in higher education: An Indian perspective. *Journal of Learning Analytics and Policy*, *9*(1), 23–38.

Negi, A. (2024). Privacy of students in the digital age. *Indian Journal of Legal Review*, *4*(2), 1399–1404. https://ijlr.iledu.in/wp-content/uploads/2024/08/V4I2153.pdf

OECD. (2023). *Is Education Losing the Race with Technology?: AI's Progress in Maths and Reading, Educational Research and Innovation*. OECD Publishing., DOI: 10.1787/73105f99-

Pandey, R., &Jha, M. (2022). The state of EdTech regulation in India: Evaluating accountability and transparency. Policy Insights journal.7(3), 42–57.

Postdigital Living in the Age of Covid-19: Unsettling What We See as Possible - PMC

Security, I. B. M. (2022). Cost of a data breach report 2022. IBM Corporation. https://www.ibm.com/reports/data-breach

Selwyn, N. (2022). *Education and technology: Key issues and debates* (3rd ed.). Bloomsbury Academic.

Selwyn, N., & Jandrić, P. (2020). Postdigital Living in the Age of Covid-19: Unsettling What We See as Possible. Postdigital science and education, 2(3), 989–1005. https://doi.org/DOI: 10.1007/s42438-020-00166-9

Sharma, S., Singh, G., & Sharma, C. S. (2024). Artificial intelligence in Indian higher education institutions: A quantitative study on adoption and perceptions. *International Journal of System Assurance Engineering and Management*. Advance online publication. DOI: 10.1007/s13198-023-02193-8

UNESCO. (2021). Recommendation on the ethics of artificial intelligence. UNESCO. https://unesdoc.unesco.org/ark:/48223/pf0000381137

University Grants Commission. (2023). National Programme on Artificial Intelligence (NPAI) Skilling Framework. Committee on Creating Skilling Framework for AI. https://www.ugc.gov.in/pdfnews/5732498_Report-on-NPAI-Skilling-Framework .pdf

Williamson, B., & Piattoeva, N. (2022). Education Governance and Datafication. Education and Information Technologies, 27, 3515-3531. Williamson, B. and Piattoeva, N. (2022) Education Governance and Datafication. [- References - Scientific Research Publishing]. *Education and Information Technologies*, *27*, 3515–3531.

Zuboff, S. (2019). *The age of surveillance capitalism: The fight for a human future at the new frontier of power*. PublicAffairs.

Chapter 3
Dissecting Bias and Fairness in AI-Driven Educational Tools:
Addressing Bias in EdTech Tools Using Equity AI

Wasswa Shafik
https://orcid.org/0000-0002-9320-3186
Dig Connectivity Research Laboratory (DCRLab), Uganda

ABSTRACT

Bias in AI-driven educational tools can manifest in several forms, including data bias, where training data reflects societal inequities; algorithmic bias, where AI design discriminates against groups; and interaction bias, where systems fail to accommodate diverse backgrounds. These biases can reinforce inequalities and hinder equitable education. Fairness can be framed through group fairness, individual fairness, counterfactual fairness, procedural fairness, and causal fairness. Mitigating bias involves pre-processing techniques like reweighting, in-processing methods with fairness constraints, and post-processing adjustments for equitable outcomes. Tools like AI Fairness 360, Fairlearn, TensorFlow Fairness Indicators, and the What-If Tool help detect and mitigate bias, fostering fairness and inclusivity in AI-driven education. Ensuring fairness in AI enhances accessibility, promotes trust, and supports diverse learning needs in digital education.

DOI: 10.4018/979-8-3373-3000-6.ch003

1. INTRODUCTION

We begin our work with a general discussion of AI-driven educational tools, as those are the focus of our study. We consider AI models in use across the educational pipeline, including models that help with admissions, teacher training, instruction, and assessments in educational settings. We argue that serving many different roles across many different student populations introduces a broad and diverse set of stakeholder perspectives and concerns about the practice of AI (Archambault et al., 2024). AI in education is one of the fastest-growing areas in the ed-tech market, with expectations of explosive growth over the next decade. We argue that, as these models grow in reach and influence, democratic and constitutional considerations become more urgent. Our work takes inspiration from legal and policy thinking that calls for audits, evaluations, and impact analyses, particularly as it applies to actions taken by governments or to which the government contributes, such as through contractual arrangements with companies (Gade, Geyik, Kenthapadi, Mithal, & Taly, 2020).

The idea of developing audit and accountability mechanisms to check the results achieved by educational products—one of the key mechanisms highlighted by our policy panel—is not in itself new. Management scholars dating back to the 1940s and 1950s have recognized a variety of different marginalized constituencies or stakeholders of action, and social scientists have developed specific frameworks for accountability over the use of AI (Kuck, 2023). The availability of data combined with rapid advances in AI technology enables the design of applications with the potential for real educational and societal benefits, and society is naturally interested in understanding whether educational tools are living up to human expectations. If AI is being used to submit marks in a proprietary product, concerns over the privacy of the AI techniques used to develop those models are valid and important (Usman Hadi et al., 2024).

Defining fairness and bias may seem simple, but these concepts have proven to be challenging in the context of AI-driven applications. Generally, unfairness refers to treating different groups of people inconsistently; these concepts can have many dimensions and implications in educational technology. Bias can arise from both human and algorithmic choices. Educational technology tools have the potential to perpetuate and reduce stereotypes, but currently, there is limited regulation and guidance to reduce the negative impact that unfairness and bias could have on individuals and society (Hort et al., 2023). In this chapter, we discuss major issues related to bias and unfairness in AI-driven educational tools and suggest research lines for the future. Bias and unfairness can arise in various phases during the creation of AI-driven tools that are used in education – from data gathering to decision-making. AI-driven educational tools refer to tools that use a combination of algorithms and training data to deliver educational content or experiences. They operate in a myriad of settings that include formal educational instruction, workforce retraining, and informal lifelong learning. AI-driven educational tools can, for example, be used to recognize words in oral language assessments, provide adaptive feedback in science instruction, and auto-grade mathematics assignments (Hurtgen & Moller, 2020). Such tools have the potential to drastically reduce the cost and effort of tutoring and testing when compared to hiring human labor, but they do pose the challenge of ensuring equitable performance across diverse student populations. In AI, an expert system is a computer system emulating the decision-making ability of a human expert. Expert systems are designed to solve complex problems by reasoning through bodies of knowledge, represented mainly as if–then rules rather than through conventional procedural programming code, as sampled in Figure 1.

Figure 1. Categories of expert systems

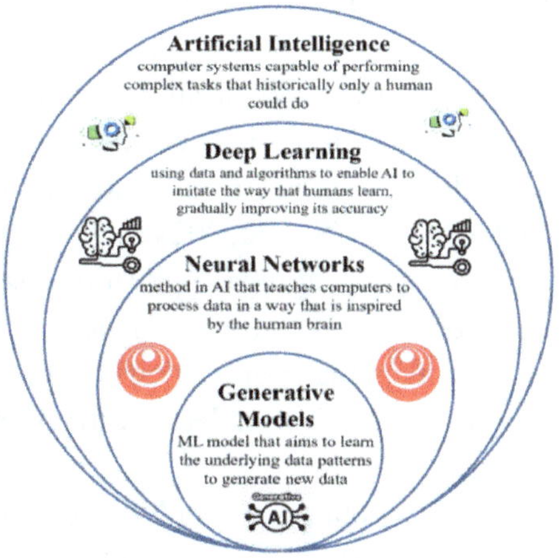

The education system in the U.S. has deep disparities, ranging from the funding of public schools, the distribution of experienced teachers, and access to advanced coursework to college acceptance. These racial and socio-economic disparities lead to long-lasting inequalities that often produce a deep sense of unfairness in educational outcomes. It is particularly poignant and unfair to examine the fact that these education systems produce different life outcomes based on a child's race and identity (Shafik, 2024i). Therefore, when thinking about the fairness of using machine learning in education, it is essential to understand the larger context within which these tools operate and to ensure that they do not further disadvantage the children who use them by violating the principles of fairness. However, the age of COVID-19 laid bare a chronically underfunded system that heavily relies on classroom instruction. The inability of the system to provide effective alternatives by transitioning portions of in-class instruction to mostly virtual instruction for all students, with the necessary digital divide for some, underscores the need for many innovative educational tools that work remotely (Abubakari et al., 2024a). Given the serious challenges faced by the educational sector due to the pandemic, the development and evaluation of AI-driven educational tools have the potential to provide effective help to both teachers and students. The tools that we develop can leverage natural language processing and machine learning techniques to interact with students by providing personalized instruction and aiding teachers (Shafik, 2024e). We hypothesize that AI-facilitated education can offer pedagogical and resource support that has been previously difficult to provide and evaluate.

2. UNDERSTANDING BIAS IN AI SYSTEMS

AI-based systems are trained on large datasets in order to learn the relationships between input features and outputs. As a result, AI-driven educational tools are not immune to human biases and historical societal and cultural inequalities; rather, they amplify those biases. Bias is the difference between the predicted value and the true value of the prediction, while fairness is a measure of the independence between specific input features and outcomes (Shafik, 2024c). Bias can be particularly problematic in high-stakes AI-driven educational applications, such as admissions and assessment. These potential biases have the consequence of embedding discrimination. The issue goes beyond educational applications to other fields, such as health care and judicial systems, leading to a broader call for AI ethical considerations (Dorsey & Michaels, 2022).

Understanding bias and fairness in AI is a multidisciplinary endeavor, bridging social science, cognitive science, computer science, philosophy, and law. A number of terms may be used to refer to different types of bias in AI systems. Observe that when discovering unfairness in AI systems, it may be useful for instructors and institutions adopting or using AI tools to be familiar with implicit bias and stereotype threats. When making difficult prediction tasks, it is not realistic to expect AI to be completely fair (Mehta et al., 2023). However, it is possible to mitigate many kinds of bias discovered in AI. Given the automation of bias and discrimination with the widespread adoption of AI tools, addressing these issues requires not only the introduction of technical approaches but also practical work in bridging different fields: educative work aimed at enabling interaction among affected parties, as well as ethical guidelines and the establishment of future international policies (ALORDIAH, 2023).

2.1. Types of Bias

AI-driven digital technologies, such as those using machine learning and data mining, are increasingly finding their way into the education domain. These algorithms access, refine, and analyze huge pedagogical databases containing data on individuals, learning activities, learning environments, and learning achievements in real-time or close to real-time and then present or facilitate decisions and actions. When exposed to biased data, digital implantation technologies absorb and then reuse these biases to facilitate, ingrain, and/or perpetuate biased decision-making (Farrelly & Baker, 2023). They do this either through the configuration and development of biased algorithms, which erode the scientific integrity and legitimacy of such algorithms, and/or via the unjust inference they deliver, which in turn results in decisions and actions that disadvantage individuals or groups in society unfairly. The presence of unjustified bias within educational data-driven implantation technologies is a critically important issue that remains largely unexplored in the educational technology sector (Du et al., 2024). In the implementation of any AI-driven educational tool, it is important to use only data that is free from bias and to sanitize the data proactively, or even neutralize the biased component within the data at the point of the data's entry, and thus remove bias before subsequent systems ingest it.

2.2. Causes of Bias

For example, "stereotype threat," that is, diminished test-taking performance due to the heightened anxiety levels that result from the activation of negative stereotypes about the test-taker group. Other related concerns include the negative impacts of engagement with adaptive tools when used in connection with high-stakes testing (Muhic, 2024). For example, suppose students were to become aware that their test or quiz questions are subtly biased against them in certain ways. In that case, they might lose motivation to take test modules or disengage from the test, effectively disenfranchising themselves from the learning opportunities that testing provides. With this paper, we take the position that it is desirable to design adaptive tools to limit the introduction of biases of this kind, and we stress that with contemporary AI technologies, it is increasingly possible to improve tools in this way through ethical analysis and intervention (Ryan, 2023).

3. FAIRNESS IN AI SYSTEMS

The World Economic Forum identified bias and discrimination as the most concerning issues associated with the use of artificial intelligence in 2016. In 2017, a global initiative started to standardize measures of fairness, accountability, and transparency in machine learning. Around the same time, a policy was established to not "encode marginalization." Last year, an organization added an article on principles that identify diversity in their code of ethics (Mashhadi et al., 2022). Despite the increased concern about fairness, AI developers still face the challenge of defining fairness in a specific context, choosing among the many mathematical and algorithmic definitions, and implementing the selected definition to ensure that harmful biases are identified and corrected. Many software programs and algorithms can embed communication biases such as racial, cultural, and gender biases, for instance. It was reported that a word embedding tool established racial and gender stereotypes. In the same story, an example was provided of how it helped complete the sentence "man is to computer programmer as woman is to x." Unfortunately, the x word was "homemaker." A study described the search success of a young white woman as more than double that of a young white man, examples of AI-driven tools are presented in Figure 2 (Griep et al., 2023).

Figure 2. Sampled academic AI-driven tools

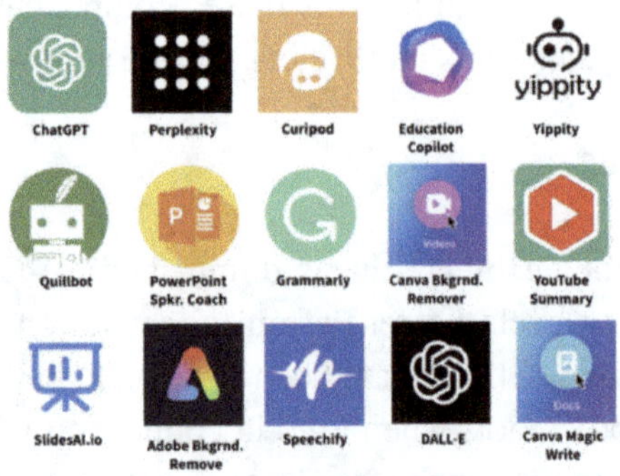

3.1. Definition and Principles

Bias can be manifested in different aspects and stages of the machine learning process, from the creation of the training dataset to the deployment of the results. To help expose and address these potential biases, different authorities have delivered different sets of principles, tools, and resources. These attempts understand that the impact of automatic decisions on human rights means that institutions using these systems must work to identify and address potential sources of algorithmic bias (Al Ka'bi, 2023). In this section, I will present and discuss our review of nine sets of rules related to the responsible use of AI and algorithms for decision-making. One way to understand ethics in artificial intelligence and machine learning systems is to think about it as common guidelines that the research community has established to help decision-makers implement AI in a way that represents ethical and social justice principles. Guidelines help address issues that arise in the development or deployment of AI. Each set of principles has been created with specific needs in mind and can be used to answer different problems or perspectives (Kuck, 2023; Shafik, 2025b). Understanding how institutions can apply these principles in specific settings is also valuable, as Table 1 presents the identified challenges of these educational tools.

Table 1. Key Challenges in AI-driven Educational Tools

Challenge	Description	Impact on Students	Potential Bias Type	Possible Solutions	Reference
Data bias	Biases in training data affecting outcomes	Unequal educational opportunities	Historical, Sampling	Diversify training datasets	(Shafik, 2024f)
Algorithmic bias	Inherent biases in the AI model's design	Disproportionate impact on marginalized groups	Gender, Racial, Socioeconomic	Audit and test models for bias regularly	(Zakaria et al., 2024)
Lack of representation	Underrepresentation of certain groups in training data	Exclusion of diverse perspectives	Demographic, Cultural	Include diverse voices in the development	(Abubakari & Rahman, 2024)
Overfitting	AI models tailoring solutions to specific data sets	Limited ability to generalize to diverse students	Sampling, Data	Regularly update and expand datasets	(Abubakari et al., 2023)
Stereotyping	AI reinforces negative stereotypes through recommendations or content	Harmful reinforcement of societal stereotypes	Racial, Gender	Use bias detection tools to correct outputs	(Abubakari & Kalinaki, 2024)
Teacher-student interaction	AI replacing human interaction in personalized learning	Loss of nuanced support for individual needs	Emotional, Social	Combine AI with human oversight	(Archambault et al., 2024)
Performance variance	AI-driven tools may favor certain student learning styles over others	Some students may not engage effectively	Learning Style	Adapt models to accommodate multiple styles	(Gade, Geyik, Kenthapadi, Mithal, & Taly, 2020)

continued on following page

Table 1. Continued

Challenge	Description	Impact on Students	Potential Bias Type	Possible Solutions	Reference
Content curation	AI curating content based on historical trends, excluding novel approaches	Restricts access to diverse or innovative content	Cultural, Ideological	Enable more dynamic content sourcing	(Usman Hadi et al., 2024)
Feedback loops	AI systems reinforce biases by using their own previous decisions as data	Continuous disadvantage for affected students	Confirmation, Data	Implement transparent feedback correction	(Usman Hadi et al., 2023)
Access to technology	Disparity in access to technology influencing educational outcomes	The digital divide between students	Socioeconomic, Geographic	Ensure equitable access to devices	(Shree & Patidar, 2020)
Transparency	Lack of clarity about AI decision-making processes	Inability to challenge or correct AI decisions	Procedural	Improve transparency in AI algorithms	(Shafik, 2024d)
Ethical concerns	Ethical implications of using AI to monitor and assess students	Invasion of privacy, bias in assessments	Privacy, Discrimination	Develop ethical guidelines for AI usage	(Shafik, 2025b)
Model explainability	Difficulty in understanding how AI makes decisions	Uncertainty in student outcomes	Decision-making	Create interpretable models and reports	(Shafik, 2023)

3.2. Challenges in Ensuring Fairness

There are multiple challenges to ensuring fairness and equal opportunity progress in today's educational systems, and AI and data-driven technologies are often combined with these complex issues. We focus in this section on the primary stakeholders and potential points of bias entering an AI-driven educational system, and we outline the current state of available tools and insights for addressing these biases. Existing educational systems and content have historically been created with the goal of providing a quality education to all students (Ryan, 2023). The assumption of providing equal services and opportunities to all students motivates the establishment of a public education system, which is an essential foundation of modern country-wide governance. In practice, though, many obstacles exist in educational systems that may inadvertently create bias or unequal access to opportunities. These obstacles may manifest at a higher level, at the level of school, curriculum, or teacher, or even towards individual students. In this chapter, we examine the potential contributions of networked technologies and aggregated data to these challenges. Specifically, we review the use of AI-driven personalized learning systems and search for evidence of impacts on student learning, time on task, and the quality of motivation towards learning (Intelligence et al., 2019). We also explore current work and open questions for embedding considerations of fairness and bias within these AI systems.

4. ETHICAL CONSIDERATIONS IN AI-DRIVEN EDUCATION

The thought that a machine might automatically classify or be involved in the classification of human traits is worrisome to many. Because a learning machine extends beyond what we have programmed it to do, it can learn to recognize patterns and draw defensible inferences that we have not explicitly authorized; that is, inferences that are not based upon our formal knowledge, thinking, or human-refined logic and algorithms. These processes can happen without our explicit knowledge, our permission, or our agreement (Dorsey & Michaels, 2022). Given that an AI-driven educational system can repeatedly make decisions concerning students—often using only a small proportion of information about each student and always operating with incomplete information—this situation creates the potential for hidden systemic ethical biases and unfairness for inadvertent inferences compatible with large costs for students. Consequently, there is increasing concern about the ethical use of AI and AI-driven learning systems in education. These concerns cover a great variety of subjects and range according to the specific motivations of different scholars (Archambault et al., 2024). Despite the diversity of both causes and types of mishandling of the use of machine learning for educational purposes, most topics traditionally treated within the field of professional ethics have overlapping interests related to one primary concern: bias.

4.1. Privacy and Data Protection

It is possible to take the perspective of the individuals about whom the algorithm is making decisions as well. A central right of individuals about whom information is used in such systems is informational self-determination. A person or a group of people ought to have access to and control over the data that is generated as part of actions taken by or on their behalf. Without control of the data, it becomes difficult for them to take steps to remedy situations where the tool has negatively influenced their life. A more specific right as part of informational self-determination is privacy (Gade, Geyik, Kenthapadi, Mithal, & Taly, 2020). Everyone has the right to respect their private and family life, home, and correspondence. Additionally, a range of organizations around the world have developed guidelines, laws, and regulations that respect this right. From a privacy perspective, people ought to be able to participate in public debates and discussions without experiencing an unfair level of discrimination based on characteristics such as race, gender, religion, political belief, sexual orientation, disability, etc (Kuck, 2023).

There needs to be a sound reason with proper justification for opening up these public spaces to additional tranquility. Additionally, it is important to note that requiring a sound justification for increasing the tranquility of particular subgroups that are disproportionately subjects of biased AI predictions may be less pernicious than many cases of algorithmic unfairness (Usman Hadi et al., 2023). However, it still limits the rights of minorities to engage in public discussions, and so still implies moral costs. Moreover, privacy and confidentiality are required to protect individuals from receiving different treatments based on their predictive risk of engaging in particular behavior. Given an AI-driven tool that aims to predict whether an individual is at risk of engaging in a particular behavior, it becomes possible for a third party to discriminate against that individual based on the estimated predicted risk (Hurtgen & Moller, 2020).

4.2. Transparency and Accountability

As a consequence of teachers' concerns about the accuracy and validity of AI-driven educational tools, as well as the need to understand decision-making and results, there is a call for transparency and accountability. In the Trust in the AI system model, a system is perceived as transparent if it is understandable, its processes are traceable, and it enables users to review, explain, and reject results. These enable users to build trust in and use a system (Gade, Geyik, Kenthapadi, Mithal, Taly, et al., 2020). In essence, it aims to communicate the mission, purpose, values, priorities, trade-offs, and decision-making processes of an AI system to stakeholders. This communication should be done in a clear, consistent, and understandable manner with educational stakeholders, including students and their parents, and other important decision-makers, including the Ministry of Education, the Learning Management System provider, teachers, and society at large. The model makes clear the need for well-defined guidelines and centralized management principles that guide and reinforce the ethical and moral dimensions of AI, data processing, applications, and use, as well as an understanding from policymakers of the potential implications of AI use in schools (Al Ka'bi, 2023). When possible, transparent AI-driven educational tools should provide methodologies, ease of explanation, and possible confidence in the generated materials for enhancing the understanding of the underlying algorithms used for decision-making, results, and outcomes. Based on the understanding of these concepts above, educational stakeholders are expected to engage with AI-driven educational tools, leading to adequate accountability (Archambault et al., 2024).

5. IMPACT OF BIAS AND UNFAIRNESS IN EDUCATION

"In many cases, what we have determined to be education and educational institutions did not consider me, people like me, or my views, and instead intentionally discriminated against me. We were specifically excluded. This isn't a history lesson. This is ongoing. It's right now."

Bias in technology applications, such as AI-driven educational tools, often propagate biases in society, weakening the opportunities to address inequality in the schools that education was designed to do (Hurtgen & Moller, 2020; Shafik, 2025a). In this section, we will consider how this can happen and what to do about it, and consider how K-12 online learning may benefit from adopting a theory of social justice.

Perfect fairness in schools is an aspirational goal. Public schools attempt to provide learning opportunities that give all students the skills, knowledge, and systems to allow them to build useful and fulfilling lives. Yet, we already know that this is an overly idealized vision. We still live in a country with active residential segregation, although some school districts have attempted to disrupt this by encouraging voluntary school integration. Unfortunately, even in these districts, schools tend to mirror existing race and income disparities, with public schools typically more integrated than the residential communities they serve (Shafik, 2024b). For example, Black and Latinx students are likely to attend schools with higher levels of poverty than schools attended by White students and often receive less funding overall. While schooling contributes to economic mobility, opportunities to participate in a well-funded school are only theoretical 'choices' for many families and, therefore, lead to disparities in educators, curricula, and learning environments. This leads to inequity in educational opportunities for students. By embedding biases against marginalized communities, AI-driven educational tools can magnify these existing inequities further, potentially reducing student protections, closing doors for students, and having a negative effect on society overall (Al Ka'bi, 2023; Shafik et al., 2024).

5.1. Student Outcomes

Student Outcomes

As AI-driven educational tools are deployed in real classrooms, we have the opportunity to see how they affect outcomes for a wide variety of students—not just in terms of measures such as learning gains or test scores but also in terms of motivation, peer interactions, and other important dimensions of educational success. It is especially interesting to consider differential effects, examining whether the benefits of educational technology flow equally to all students or whether certain subgroups are better or worse advantaged (Usman Hadi et al., 2024). Here, a number of research questions suggest themselves, each with both practical and theoretical significance. Do various subgroups of students learn better or worse when using educational technology? Do subgroups with different amounts of prior knowledge of the subject matter take away similar amounts of new knowledge? Are there any differences across gender or race? Are students in inclusive classrooms helped or hindered by technology (Muhic, 2024)?

Are low-performing students more likely to disengage when technology is made part of the curriculum? Does the use of online platforms encumber high-performing students? If there are measured differences in experiences and outcomes that advantaged groups have over others, the question of whether these differences are actually advantages comes quickly into play. While some differences in student experiences may be trivial from a developmental standpoint, others may be quite meaningful, signaling that some students are encountering barriers to learning that others are not (Farnadi et al., 2018). Teachers and Ed-Tech developers would be wise to understand the sources of such differences better and think about how they can be remediated or at least better understood. Answering these questions provides not only evidence on the practical impact of certain tools but also helps with the larger question of how technology is likely to reshape higher education landscapes (Al Ka'bi, 2023).

5.2. Inequality and Discrimination

There are two basic concepts of fairness: equality in opportunity or procedure and equality in outcome. In the education context, the more agreed-upon definition of the fairness of educational opportunities concept in terms of race and its link with education is the negative use of discrimination, defined as the act of treating one group differently on the basis of a classification that is not relevant to the group's action or interests. It is considered the simplest and least controversial conception of equality in procedural fairness violations (Griep et al., 2023). Differential treatment occurs when one group is intentionally granted or denied a benefit that, on the basis of relevant characteristics, it seems to be entitled to or disqualified from. However, usually in the education field, the result of treatment is the best way to discover discrimination. With respect to inequality, it should be noted that although closely linked, both are not synonyms. One is a difference or lack of difference in the status of subjects across social categories, while the other is morally unjust and, as such, should be avoided. Being different is not necessarily wrong or unfair. With respect to educational assessment, any of these positive differentiated indicators are acceptable in principle (Ryan, 2023). They reflect the status of student performance on a set of skills and competencies that the test is able to privilege.

On the other hand, the construction of these test features is rather subjective, particularly in high-stakes decision tests, and is usually governed by the socio-economic and cultural status of students who will participate in them. Educational assessment establishes a positive differentiation that reflects a current reality and does not help to improve it; rather, it freezes the current pattern of performances in the test features. Educational assessment is a powerful and privileged tool in monitoring societies and initiating or combating inequality and discrimination practices (Shafik, 2024a). The educational system promotes unequal treatment, at the student level and educational opportunity level, if it considers a personal characteristic irrelevant and assigns them a different result, elementary or procedural, than expected, based on their intrinsic personal characteristics. Educational assessment results are paramount for the promotion of the values of equality and non-discrimination in educational systems, ranking them, supporting their growth, and the individuals that should direct their performances (Abubakari et al., 2024b).

6. MITIGATING BIAS AND ENSURING FAIRNESS IN AI-DRIVEN EDUCATIONAL TOOLS

Several mitigations can be considered when developing AI-driven education tools to reduce the effects of AI biases and ensure fairness. First, simply acknowledging their existence can help prevent unfair consequences or misuses by promoting increased understanding. Second, including the affected communities as active participants is highly important. Data-driven decisions must often be made, and input from domain experts and end users is crucial to understanding the social, political, and cultural implications of the tool as well as its consequences for the users (Shafik, 2024i). Including the community from the early stages, ensuring transparency, traceability, and accountability, and making the decision-making process clear seem to be best practices in learning systems. A governance structure or an ethical framework can support the team in making ethically sound decisions, which are of high importance in ensuring fairness and reducing bias. The framework should stress the ethical aspects of development, especially when basic human rights are involved. Using interdisciplinary knowledge and skills and focusing on benefits for users are key components of good inclusive development. In data practices, it is crucial to ensure a representative and bias-free dataset, understand the historical context of a bias in the data, and use thorough testing to mitigate bias-contained technology (Shafik, 2025c). Thus, using the right metrics in the subject can measure fairness in learning systems and ensure unbiased insertion into student practice.

6.1. Algorithmic Fairness Techniques

The field of fairness and bias mitigation is rich, with many methods and tools already in place. Our analysis considers a subset of this large and diverse body of work. The discussed mitigation strategies are widely used in practice, presenting a diverse range in the number of assumptions they make about both fairness-relevant features and the connection between these features and decisions, and are all implemented within a unified and widely accessible platform. The project implements bias detection functionalities by taking the predictions of a model as input alongside ground truth information about protected attributes from any classification task (ALORDIAH, 2023; Shafik, 2024h). To proceed with fairness analyses, practitioners must first choose a 'harm' concept to model and be able to extract fairness-relevant features from the original data.

When protected attributes are directly available and causally connected to discrimination, their use in assessing and ensuring fairness is straightforward. They dictate not only estimation targets when selecting the harm to measure but also appropriate mitigation strategies. Critics might prefer that the design and deployment of the tool be amended to encourage better outcomes from the perspective of equity rather than simply allowing the status quo; an AI-driven personalized student intervention tool should reasonably be expected to take action to reduce discrimination, for instance. In the case that there are multiple proxy attributions for a given protected classification attribute, all potentially overloading attributions must be properly allocated accordingly in the analysis (Dorsey & Michaels, 2022; Shafik et al., 2024). The proxy and real attributions are not assumed to match in any special way; if they do, perfectly accurate auditing becomes easier.

6.2. Data Collection and Processing Best Practices

Accurate and inclusive AI-driven tools require comprehensive, unbiased, and diverse data on their users. Inclusion also involves understanding how to provide context and adapt user interfaces and interactions to the needs of such a diverse population. Using well-labeled, diverse data sets helps ensure that the machine-learned model used in these tools is representative of the user base. Unfortunately, issues of biased data generated from student submissions and data privacy may make handling this challenge especially difficult in education (Abubakari et al., 2024b). A wide range of behaviors needs to be both supported and predicted when learners are interacting with the tool, including how they might be physically interacting with the user interface. When engineers provide a variety of options for this physical interaction, it makes the tool accessible to a greater and more diverse audience. Because of the unique challenges faced by students with disabilities in K-12 education, exploring ways to address these challenges is particularly important (Shafik, 2024g). Overall, addressing concerns of bias and fairness in an educational context requires understanding users' unique needs and being respectful of and accommodating to those needs, as presented in Table 2.

Table 2. Methods for Ensuring Fairness in AI-driven Educational Tools

Method	Description	Goal	Challenges	Example	Reference
Bias detection algorithms	Tools that identify and mitigate bias within datasets and AI models	To minimize unfair discrimination	False positives, Model Complexity	Fairness-aware machine learning algorithms	(Archambault et al., 2024)
Regular audits	Systematic reviews of AI models and outputs for bias and fairness	Ensure ongoing fairness and accountability	Resource-intensive	External audit of an AI-based grading system	(Gade, Geyik, Kenthapadi, Mithal, & Taly, 2020)
Data diversification	Including diverse data sources to better represent all student groups	To ensure AI models are inclusive	Data collection challenges	Collect data from underrepresented regions	(Usman Hadi et al., 2024)
Human oversight	Involving human educators in monitoring AI-driven tools	Reduce reliance on AI and correct potential biases	High cost, Limited availability	Teachers review AI-generated learning paths	(Hort et al., 2023)
Adaptive learning systems	AI systems that adjust learning strategies based on student performance	Personalize education for all learners	Overfitting, Lack of flexibility	AI-driven tutoring systems	(Hurtgen & Moller, 2020)
Transparency frameworks	Providing clear explanations of AI decision-making processes	Increase trust and allow intervention	Complexity, Accountability issues	Open-source AI educational tools	(Intelligence et al., 2019)
Ethics boards	Establishing groups of experts to guide the ethical development of AI	Ensure responsible development of educational AI	Slow decision-making	Advisory boards in AI-based education projects	(Muhic, 2024)

continued on following page

Table 2. Continued

Method	Description	Goal	Challenges	Example	Reference
Model explainability	Building AI models that are interpretable by non-experts	Enhance understanding and trust	Complexity, Trade-offs	Explainable AI for grading predictions	(Shree & Patidar, 2020)
Participatory design	Involving diverse stakeholders (e.g., students, teachers) in tool design	Develop inclusive AI tools	Stakeholder alignment	Co-designing adaptive learning tools	(Gade, Geyik, Kenthapadi, Mithal, Taly, et al., 2020)
Bias-mitigating algorithms	Implementing algorithms to address identified biases directly	Minimize bias in educational outcomes	Reduced accuracy, Trade-offs	Fairness-driven recommendation systems	(Rossi, 2020)
Real-time feedback	AI systems that provide instant feedback to students	Empower students to improve while minimizing bias	High computational cost	Adaptive assessment tools	(Farnadi et al., 2018)
Peer review systems	Allowing peers to assess AI educational tools for fairness and accuracy	Increase external accountability	Conflicting views	Student and teacher evaluations of AI tools	(Cachel & Rundensteiner, 2022)
Continuous learning	AI models that evolve based on new data and feedback	Maintain fairness as conditions change	Data privacy, Overfitting	Dynamic content curation for diverse students	(Manyika et al., 2019)

7. REGULATORY FRAMEWORKS AND GUIDELINES

Federal and state laws internalize children's rights protection and privacy in their educational systems. They assign custodial responsibilities to educational institutions such as schools and guide them with data protection standards. Children are vulnerable and cannot protect themselves from potential data abuse like informed adults; therefore, more protective privacy frameworks proceed under the assumption that stakeholders around children are actively equipped with legal norms and correct incentives to safeguard children's interests and comply with relevant privacy and data protection standards (Dorsey & Michaels, 2022). For example, privacy laws protect the privacy of educational data and ensure access rights for students using this data, prohibiting unauthorized release of student educational records. Data protection regulations confer data rights on parents and legal guardians regarding educational journey data and outline their responsibilities to protect children's data and procure parental consent (ALORDIAH, 2023).

Since educational data are the sum of their parts, when it is not offered directly by educational institutions themselves, the performance of diverse educational complement service providers and vendors is higher because the educational, private data used in these advanced supporting services inherently respect higher qualifications characterized by relevant privacy and data protection rules. These external service providers use different rigorous assessments and offer detailed sub-services to fully benefit from children's education data, promoting school policy-level uniform standards, better customization, and efficient resource allocation (Ryan, 2023). While the quality of raw source data must be optimal to provide students with knowledge of global and localized education, the involvement of third-party vendors in advanced services like standardized education and mastering the data spectrum is only beneficial as the private sector moves towards educational services that help improve educational data. The participation of technology-advanced commercial solution providers has intensified the long-standing lack of expertise (Du et al., 2024). In recent years, those in supporting areas have created a new realm of free simulator degree programs to help establish new sales leads and collaborations that target the increasing portion of the costs expended by big and small school officials. The use of technology in learning and exams, and automated test preparation all call for optimization, scalability, and technical capabilities. With regard to these legal constraints, regulations have also gradually evolved. The agreement of stakeholders on a more just trajectory may provide a conducive climate for regulators in their actions, centering on public-sector rights, duties of care, and multiple benefits that have been highlighted (Griep et al., 2023).

7.1. Existing Regulations

The commercial use of AI-driven automated decision-making systems in educational settings is subject to regulatory constraints. However, laws and regulations vary from one jurisdiction to another. Introduced in 1974, the Family Educational Rights and Privacy Act aims to protect student information collected, stored, and processed by schools and shared with other agencies and organizations. Schools must have signed consent from a parent or an eligible student to disclose education records to third parties, including automated decision-making systems (Mehta et al.,

2023). However, consent is not required for school officials or other entities when processing student data to improve instruction or the general operation of schools.

It is important to differentiate between the use of commercial tools developed and deployed by third parties and tools used by organizations for their internal purposes. Educational institutions, such as school districts, state or local education agencies, and community colleges, where these types of tools are used, are subject to the Family Educational Rights and Privacy Act (Farrelly & Baker, 2023). However, this act does not extend to the use of commercial educational tools by individuals to solve their foreign language learning, SAT preparation, or personal development data problems. In such cases, companies are essentially business associates, which are not subject to the act. The Health Insurance Portability and Accountability Act, which concerns communication between doctors and insurance agencies, does not extend to related industries. The use of educational sites similar to that of their parent companies is subject to the privacy policy of the platform, e.g., the data usage rules of the organization providing the service (Mashhadi et al., 2022).

7.2. Proposed Guidelines

In this position paper, we try to address carefully the question of "fairness" in AI-driven educational tools. The position we aim to take is that by understanding that "fairness" is not a single notion and is affected both by the particularities of the educational context and the particularities of the stakeholders within the educational context, we are more likely to be able to consider diverse accounts of fairness when designing AI-driven educational tools in the first place. Educational tools, especially those that are built to make use of AI, need to be designed more humanely and with a multi-stakeholder viewpoint in mind (Cachel & Rundensteiner, 2022). While generic guidelines on fairness have addressed many pressing issues, human biases, and dataset shortcomings can only be addressed intelligently with input from a variety of stakeholder viewpoints.

We therefore propose a set of guidelines for both the ML community as well as AI-driven educational tool builders. For ML researchers: 1) The main purpose of educational content is to improve students' knowledge. Therefore, when designing ML algorithms, consider users' values in the development process. Researchers should be mindful of public perceptions and moral intuition in order to make the algorithms more trustworthy. 2) This is an opportunity to work on smart education that can address educational content from multiple viewpoints. Researchers are encouraged to work on platforms that support diverse educational content and values. 3) We conclude by urging algorithm designers to be vigilant about the emotional and valuable impacts of the systems they design and support inspection and introspection of those algorithms in real-time within educational tools (Shree & Patidar, 2020). They take responsibility when public accommodation of those hazards breaks.

8. CASE STUDIES AND EXAMPLES

In this section, we offer a more in-depth look at a few innovative and well-regarded AI-driven educational tools, as well as examples intended to illustrate common themes and potential pitfalls throughout the case studies and the report more broadly. In particular, we discuss a mental health chatbot designed for deployment on smartphones, a quantified affect detector from the domain of learning at scale, a few example visualization tools, and an OCR tool (Archambault et al., 2024). These examples are discussed in more depth in this section, which is then followed by a synthesis of lessons learned related to governance, making the case for why these case studies matter.

The first AI-driven educational tool is a mental health chatbot designed for deployment on smartphones. This tool uses AI to deliver scalable psychological intervention, driven by principles of cognitive behavioral therapy, to address specific issues such as worrying, social anxiety, depression, and stress. We use this chatbot as an example of a conversational AI tool that can create potential privacy and security issues. Second, we consider the quantified affect detector, a tool developed for learning at scale. Like the chatbot, this tool is designed to detect emotion. It processes students' implicit emotional states and cognitive responses through modern information processing pipelines and collectively extracts learning signals from those to understand the learning process better (Hort et al., 2023). We use this tool as an example of an AI-driven educational tool that could create pernicious bias, specifically, in this case, within the field of learning at scale. Third, we convey a brief example of work within sensorimotor systems through cognitive augmented reality. Finally, we consider examples of tools that make heavy use of computer vision, including an OCR tool and preliminary work algorithmically detecting eye gaze through computer vision in virtual and augmented reality (Shree & Patidar, 2020).

This approach was applied in a popular language learning product that serves diverse populations of students with various language backgrounds. Existing academic research on learner engagement, learning outcomes, and system bias was leveraged to define the socially desirable classification. This work demonstrates the feasibility of this direction of debiasing methods in addressing biases in large-scale, multimodal task-learning systems in the context of real-world educational products (Gade, Geyik, Kenthapadi, Mithal, Taly, et al., 2020). Bias mitigation at the stages of the development and testing of educational technologies will lead to more equitable opportunities for all learners and enhance opportunities for reaching systematic educational goals. It is a notification presented for the Educational Data Mining community for validating AI-developed educational technology through pedagogical success metrics to ensure the fair, empirically justified usage of these tools in real-world educational settings. The promise of recent breakthroughs in AI has made it an attractive area for educational technology development. However, much of the work has focused on creating and deploying systems using mostly technical benchmarks, not on solving pedagogical problems that meet the needs of students and teachers. More importantly, it is increasingly important not only to suggest that a tool works but to validate that claim through pedagogical success metrics such as task engagement and learning outcomes (Cachel & Rundensteiner, 2022). Furthermore, AI-developed educational technologies must also not exacerbate, and ideally help mitigate, disparities in motivation and performance across diverse groups of learners. Bias and fairness challenges in AI-driven educational tools manifest differently across contexts. Table 1 synthesizes fourteen global cases, revealing how data imbalance, socio-cultural assumptions, and algorithmic design choices perpetuate inequities among learners. While biases vary, ranging from language misrepresentation in Finland to gendered algorithms in Uganda and Australia, common patterns emerge: insufficient contextual data, lack of participatory model design, and minimal transparency mechanisms. Applying Equity AI frameworks demonstrates how integrating fairness-aware modeling, localized data pipelines, and inclusive evaluation metrics can mitigate such disparities. Embedding these lessons reinforces that bias is not solely a technical problem but a socio-technical phenomenon requiring ethical, contextual, and participatory interventions

Table 1. Global Case Studies on Bias and Fairness in AI-Driven Educational Tools

Region / Country	AI-Driven Tool / Platform	Type of Bias Observed	Empirical Evidence or Data Insight	User Perspective (Students / Teachers)	Mitigation through Equity AI Approaches
United States	Adaptive Learning Platform for K–12 Mathematics (e.g., DreamBox Learning)	Algorithmic bias – performance models underestimated minority students' abilities.	U.S. Dept. of Education (2023): 7–12% lower prediction accuracy for underrepresented groups.	Teachers doubted fairness of recommendations; minority students felt stereotyped.	Introduced fairness-aware training and demographic balancing of datasets.
India	AI-based Online Exam Proctoring System	Cultural/technical bias – false flagging due to attire and environmental noise.	Audit (2022): 18% false positives for students with religious attire.	Students perceived surveillance as discriminatory.	Hybrid human–AI verification model with contextual calibration.
Kenya	Mobile Learning App for Rural Schools	Data bias – urban-centered training data misaligned with rural learning contexts.	EdTech Hub (2024): Rural content relevance 43% vs. 82% urban.	Teachers reported misaligned lessons; rural learners disengaged.	Localization through participatory dataset design and teacher co-creation.
Brazil	Blended Learning Recommender System	Measurement bias – bandwidth-dependent engagement metrics.	National pilot (2023): Engagement inflation of 21% for high-connectivity students.	Teachers noted unfair grading for low-access learners.	Equitable weighting of engagement metrics including offline activity logs.
Finland	Adaptive Language-Learning AI Tool	Representation bias – limited accent and linguistic diversity.	Ministry review (2024): 15% higher misclassification for non-native accents.	Immigrant students frustrated; teachers intervened manually.	Added multilingual corpora and user-centric retraining.
South Africa	Automated Essay Scoring System	Cultural-linguistic bias – penalized local idioms and phrasing.	Local university study (2023): 10–14% lower average scores for African English variants.	Students felt alienated; teachers questioned validity.	Retrained NLP model with culturally diverse essays and linguistic fairness metrics.
China	Intelligent Tutoring System for STEM	Socioeconomic bias – students from rural schools received lower personalized feedback scores.	Provincial study (2022): 20% fewer high-quality hints for rural users.	Teachers in rural areas felt excluded from optimization cycles.	Integrated federated learning to balance representation from rural schools.

continued on following page

Table 1. Continued

Region / Country	AI-Driven Tool / Platform	Type of Bias Observed	Empirical Evidence or Data Insight	User Perspective (Students / Teachers)	Mitigation through Equity AI Approaches
United Kingdom	AI-Powered Admissions Recommendation Tool	Data bias – overrepresentation of elite schools in training datasets.	Audit (2023): 9% higher acceptance suggestions for private-school applicants.	Students from public schools saw reduced algorithmic favorability.	Introduced socio-demographic fairness constraints and transparency dashboard.
Uganda	Digital Literacy Assessment AI	Gender bias – female students systematically scored lower due to skewed behavioral data.	Makerere study (2024): 12% lower scores despite equivalent task accuracy.	Female learners expressed decreased motivation.	Bias reweighting using gender-balanced behavioral benchmarks.
Canada	AI Feedback Tool for Academic Writing	Algorithmic bias – flagged non-native English structures unfairly.	University of Toronto (2023): False error rate 17% higher for ESL students.	Students reported demotivation; instructors offered manual overrides.	Introduced adaptive linguistic profiling and inclusive error models.
Bangladesh	Mobile AI Tutor for Secondary Science	Infrastructure bias – models failed under low-connectivity conditions.	UNESCO (2024): 28% reduced functionality in low-bandwidth zones.	Rural teachers found system unreliable.	Developed offline-first AI models and local content caching.
Germany	AI-Enhanced Grading System	Measurement bias – emphasized speed over comprehension.	Pilot (2023): Fast typists scored 10% higher regardless of content quality.	Students criticized unfair weighting; teachers adjusted rubric manually.	Adjusted scoring model to decouple speed and accuracy.
Nigeria	Adaptive STEM Learning Platform	Socioeconomic bias – ignored multilingual contexts and local curricula.	Field evaluation (2024): Only 40% content aligned with local syllabus.	Teachers in public schools reported exclusion of local knowledge.	Integrated localized content ontology and teacher-driven data labeling.
Australia	Early Learning AI Recommender	Gender and cultural bias – recommended gender-stereotyped activities.	National audit (2023): 65% of STEM suggestions targeted male students.	Parents and teachers raised gender-equity concerns.	Implemented Equity AI fairness filters and diversity-aware recommendation modules.

9. FUTURE DIRECTIONS AND RESEARCH OPPORTUNITIES

Future directions for increasing fairness in educational AI-driven tools include research that investigates the extent to which personalization in education tools can exacerbate bias-related harms. Research should identify and measure how at-risk school demographics, including children from low-income backgrounds, underrepresented groups, and international students, can be harmed by inequitable treatment (Archambault et al., 2024). By identifying the current state and risk points, the strongest potential for meaningful and accurate AI analysis across the AI-supported educational ecosystem will be possible. By understanding the various factors presented, AI vendors, policymakers, educational institutions, and others will find opportunities to incorporate fairness in their technologies more broadly (Rossi, 2020). By defining and validating computational measures of fairness under different interventions and in several learning contexts, AI researchers are in a strong position to provide guidance driven by ethical principles and, ultimately, policy. AI is designed for learning systems that create value following standardized rules, results, and standards. Willingly submitting to human-driven exams, AI vendors working to improve the fairness of their systems are at a competitive disadvantage. Providing additional insights and guidelines through non-test-based methods of fairness may help to address such issues (Dorsey & Michaels, 2022; Du et al., 2024). Therefore, the best measures and solutions to behavioral fairness concerns remain open questions for which policy guidance could provide a driving force.

9.1. Emerging Technologies

Digital technologies afford many benefits that can facilitate learning, including access to high-quality learning experiences no matter where students live, flexible learning for diverse sets of students, and the opportunity to conduct data-driven research on learning at scales not otherwise possible. However, it is important to acknowledge that these same technologies must be critically examined and developed to meet the needs of all students and educators and to ensure they are used in ethical and fairways. Many emergent digital technologies could change or augment teaching and learning. We provide this list as a mirror to the trends we explore, focusing less on areas that are well-researched and focusing more on areas that are evolving in many disciplines (Al Ka'bi, 2023). They include novel learning paradigms, blended and hybrid learning environments, intelligent user interfaces, and new devices. Each of these technologies presents unique opportunities, challenges, and potential discrimination or fairness concerns. For instance, contributions to both science and society include agents for intelligent tutoring, virtual companions and mentors, expressive and mindfully engaging interfaces, speech interfaces, and educational experiences for students who face accessibility issues. Additionally, the trends described illustrate that there are certain challenges in computer science, such as privacy and data management. For every technology described, thought needs to be applied to avoid negative externalities and potential harm. Computing education, ethics, fairness, law, and public policy can all play roles in investigating and defining possible societal problems or helping avoid them (Mehta et al., 2023). There is a clear opportunity for additional research and education to support fairness, accountability, transparency, and inclusion as digital technologies continue to evolve.

9.2. Interdisciplinary Collaboration

Individuals in computer science, education research, and related fields must encourage more interdisciplinary collaborations to ensure a more comprehensive understanding, creation, and construction of AI-driven educational technologies. Collaborations will enable researchers to explore the potential implementation of ethical AI principles in educational software and platforms. Collaboration should not be optional but a given at every stage of the research process. The field has the potential to expand knowledge on context-specific variables affecting learning and is designed to celebrate diverse populations (Dorsey & Michaels, 2022). The development of ethical AI-driven educational tools and conducting research with diverse populations are second nature to education researchers. It is now time to encourage and invite other researchers from diverse backgrounds to join these efforts.

Educational technology and edtech have an impact on diverse learners and have the potential to provide unique and innovative learning experiences. Innovative AI-driven apps may inspire, guide, and capture students' imagination as they explore infrequently addressed areas of science, like biotechnology, pharmacogenetics, and cyber-pharmacology. For collaboration between researchers from a broad range of disciplines to be effective and productive, strong working relationships should be deliberately developed. Successfully developing a strong and collaborative cross-disciplinary team requires a shift in both culture and mindset (Farrelly & Baker, 2023). The research environment needs to be one in which international and interdisciplinary working is the norm, and those at the senior management level should establish that culture. Domain expertise is essential for well-performing AI systems and the development of AI tools, and researchers with domain expertise often identify ethical concerns specific to the application. One example of such a critical ethical feature would involve the prediction of standardized admissions scores based on facial recognition models (Farnadi et al., 2018). The potential for ethical issues should encourage research towards the analysis of these algorithms and promote the fair use of machine learning technologies.

10. CONCLUSION

AI-driven educational tools hold immense potential to transform the academic landscape through personalized learning experiences and efficient assessment methods, but their integration also brings significant concerns regarding bias and fairness. Data bias, algorithmic bias, and performance variance can disproportionately affect marginalized and underrepresented student groups, leading to discriminatory outcomes and limiting the diversity of learning opportunities. To mitigate these challenges, it is crucial to implement bias detection algorithms, conduct regular audits of AI systems, and diversify training data. Ensuring transparency and explainability in AI decision-making processes can build trust within academic communities and facilitate effective interventions. Human oversight remains indispensable, as educators can provide nuanced judgment and correct biases that AI models might overlook. Participatory design, involving diverse stakeholders such as students, educators, and technologists, is essential for shaping AI tools that align with equity and inclusivity values. By adopting these strategies, academic institutions can better manage the risks associated with AI-driven tools while leveraging their potential to create more equitable, personalized, and effective learning environments. Ultimately, ensuring fairness in AI applications within education is not just a technical challenge but an ethical imperative for fostering academic success for all students.

REFERENCES

Abubakari, M. S., & Kalinaki, K. (2024). Digital Competence in Islamic Education for Lifelong Learning: Preliminary Analysis Using DigComp 2.1 Framework. In *Embracing Technological Advancements for Lifelong Learning* (pp. 1–31). IGI Global.

Abubakari, M. S., & Rahman, A. F. (2024). Modelling Online Learning Satisfaction of Secondary School Students in Indonesia: The Role of Family and School Support. *Journal of Computing Research and Innovation*, *9*(1), 107–120.

Abubakari, M. S., Shafik, W., & Hidayatullah, A. F. (2024a). Evaluating the Potential of Artificial Intelligence in Islamic Religious Education: A SWOT Analysis Overview. In *AI-Enhanced Teaching Methods* (pp. 216–239). IGI Global.

Abubakari, M. S., Shafik, W., & Hidayatullah, A. F. (2024b). Evaluating the Potential of Artificial Intelligence in Islamic Religious Education: A SWOT Analysis Overview. In *AI-Enhanced Teaching Methods* (pp. 216–239). IGI Global.

Abubakari, M. S., Zakaria, G. A. N., Musa, J., & Kalinaki, K. (2023). Validating the Digital Competence (Dig-Comp 2.1) Framework in Higher Education Using Confirmatory Factor Analysis: Non-Western Perspective. *Canadian Journal of Educational and Social Studies*, *3*(6), 15–26.

Al Ka'bi, A. (2023). Proposed artificial intelligence algorithm and deep learning techniques for development of higher education. *International Journal of Intelligent Networks*, *4*. Advance online publication. DOI: 10.1016/j.ijin.2023.03.002

ALORDIAH, C. O. (2023). APPRECIATING THE AI REVOLUTION: EMPOWERING EDUCATIONAL RESEARCHERS THROUGH AI TOOLS FOR WRITING RESEARCH ARTICLES. *Zamfara International Journal of Humanities*, *2*(01). Advance online publication. DOI: 10.36349/zamijoh.2023.v02i01.013

Archambault, S. G., Ramachandran, S., Acosta, E., & Fu, S. (2024). Ethical dimensions of algorithmic literacy for college students: Case studies and cross-disciplinary connections. *Journal of Academic Librarianship*, *50*(3). Advance online publication. DOI: 10.1016/j.acalib.2024.102865

Cachel, K., & Rundensteiner, E. (2022). FINS auditing framework: Group fairness for subset selections. *AIES 2022 - Proceedings of the 2022 AAAI/ACM Conference on AI, Ethics, and Society*. https://doi.org/DOI: 10.1145/3514094.3534160

Dorsey, D. W., & Michaels, H. R. (2022). Validity Arguments Meet Artificial Intelligence in Innovative Educational Assessment. In *Journal of Educational Measurement* (Vol. 59, Issue 3). https://doi.org/DOI: 10.1111/jedm.12331

Du, K., Geiger, J., Killen, T., Porta, A. E., & O'Brien, T. (2024). The Paradigm Shift in Education in Big Data Era: Exploring the Intersection of Historical Assessment Frameworks and AI-Powered Assessment Methods in Education. *Journal of Education and Training Studies, 12*(2). Advance online publication. DOI: 10.11114/jets.v12i2.6582

Farnadi, G., Babaki, B., & Getoor, L. (2018). Fairness in Relational Domains. *AIES 2018 - Proceedings of the 2018 AAAI/ACM Conference on AI, Ethics, and Society*. https://doi.org/DOI: 10.1145/3278721.3278733

Farrelly, T., & Baker, N. (2023). Generative Artificial Intelligence: Implications and Considerations for Higher Education Practice. In *Education Sciences* (Vol. 13, Issue 11). https://doi.org/DOI: 10.3390/educsci13111109

Gade, K., Geyik, S., Kenthapadi, K., Mithal, V., & Taly, A. (2020). Explainable AI in Industry: Practical Challenges and Lessons Learned. *The Web Conference 2020 - Companion of the World Wide Web Conference, WWW 2020*. https://doi.org/DOI: 10.1145/3366424.3383110

Gade, K., Geyik, S. C., Kenthapadi, K., Mithal, V., Taly, A., & Machinery, A. C. (2020). Implications Tutorial: Explainable AI in Industry: Practical Challenges and Lessons Learned. In *FAT* '20: PROCEEDINGS OF THE 2020 CONFERENCE ON FAIRNESS, ACCOUNTABILITY, AND TRANSPARENCY* (Issue ACM Conference on Fairness, Accountability, and Transparency (FAT)).

Griep, K., Stone, L., Edwards, S., Hill, M., Cui, J., Liu, C., Jia, Q., & Song, Y. (2023). Ensuring Ethical, Transparent, and Auditable Use of Education Data and Algorithms on AutoML. *ACM International Conference Proceeding Series*. https://doi.org/DOI: 10.1145/3639479.3639492

Hort, M., Moussa, R., & Sarro, F. (2023). Multi-objective search for gender-fair and semantically correct word embeddings. *Applied Soft Computing, 133*. Advance online publication. DOI: 10.1016/j.asoc.2022.109916

Hurtgen, H., & Moller, M. (2020). *Rethinking AI talent strategy as AutoML comes of age*. McKinsey Quantum Black.

Intelligence, A., Rajpurkar, P., Irvin, J., Bagul, A., Ding, D., Duan, T., Mehta, H., Yang, B., Zhu, K., Laird, D., Ball, R. L., Langlotz, C., Shpanskaya, K., Lungren, M. P., Ng, A. Y., Egziabher, T. B. G., Edwards, S., , . ., , . ., … Iansiti, M. (2019). Maximising the AI opportunity How to harness the potential of AI effectively and ethically. *Lawfare, 9*(3).

Kuck, K. (2023). Generative Artificial Intelligence: A Double-Edged Sword. *2023 IEEE IFEES World Engineering Education Forum and Global Engineering Deans Council: Convergence for a Better World: A Call to Action, WEEF-GEDC 2023 - Proceedings*. https://doi.org/DOI: 10.1109/WEEF-GEDC59520.2023.10343638

Manyika, J., Silberg, J., & Presten, B. (2019). What do we do about the biases in AI? In *Harvard Business Review*.

Mashhadi, A., Zolyomi, A., & Quedado, J. (2022). A Case Study of Integrating Fairness Visualization Tools in Machine Learning Education. *Conference on Human Factors in Computing Systems - Proceedings*. https://doi.org/DOI: 10.1145/3491101.3503568

Mehta, P., Chillarge, G. R., Sapkal, S. D., Shinde, G. R., & Kshirsagar, P. S. (2023). Inclusion of children with special needs in the educational system, artificial intelligence (AI). In *AI-Assisted Special Education for Students With Exceptional Needs*. https://doi.org/DOI: 10.4018/979-8-3693-0378-8.ch007

Muhic, M. (2024). THE TRANSFORMATIVE POTENTIAL OF GENERATIVE AI IN EDUCATION. *INTED2024 Proceedings, 1*. https://doi.org/DOI: 10.21125/inted.2024.0201

Rossi, F. (2020). *How IBM Is Working Toward a Fairer AI.*

Ryan, P. (2023). Ethical Considerations in the Transformative Role of AI Chatbots in Education. SSRN *Electronic Journal*. https://doi.org/DOI: 10.2139/ssrn.4623611

Shafik, W. (2023). Introduction to ChatGPT. In *Advanced Applications of Generative AI and Natural Language Processing Models*. https://doi.org/DOI: 10.4018/9798369305027.ch001

Shafik, W. (2024a). An Overview of Artificial Intelligence-Enhanced Teaching Methods. *AI-Enhanced Teaching Methods*, 132–159.

Shafik, W. (2024b). Deep Learning Impacts in the Field of Artificial Intelligence. In *Deep Learning Concepts in Operations Research* (pp. 9–26). Auerbach Publications., DOI: 10.1201/9781003433309-2

Shafik, W. (2024c). Enhancing AI-Enabled Education Through Mobile Learning and Bring Your Own Device (BYOD) Integration. In *Exploring Youth Studies in the Age of AI* (pp. 140–173). IGI Global.

Shafik, W. (2024d). Generative AI for Social Good and Sustainable Development. In *Generative AI: Current Trends and Applications* (pp. 185–217). Springer.

Shafik, W. (2024e). Mobile Learning and Bring Your Own Device (BYOD): Enhancing Education in the Digital Age. In *Integrating Cutting-Edge Technology Into the Classroom* (pp. 240–267). IGI Global.

Shafik, W. (2024f). Social Media Insights Into Consumer Behavior. In *Intersection of AI and Business Intelligence in Data-Driven Decision-Making* (pp. 283–308). IGI Global., DOI: 10.4018/979-8-3693-5288-5.ch010

Shafik, W. (2024g). Sustainable Development. In Viana Hassan, A. S. S. B. (Ed.), *Building Community Resiliency and Sustainability With Tourism Development* (1st ed., Vol. 1, pp. 1–30). IGI Global., DOI: 10.4018/979-8-3693-5405-6.ch001

Shafik, W. (2024h). Toward a More Ethical Future of Artificial Intelligence and Data Science. In *The Ethical Frontier of AI and Data Analysis* (pp. 362–388). IGI Global.

Shafik, W. (2024i). Towards Trustworthy and Explainable AI Educational Systems. In *Explainable AI for Education: Recent Trends and Challenges* (pp. 17–41). Springer.

Shafik, W. (2025a). Digital twins tools and technologies. In *Digital Twins for Smart Cities and Villages* (pp. 55–80). Elsevier., https://doi.org/https://doi.org/10.1016/B978-0-443-28884-5.00003-8

Shafik, W. (2025b). Human-Computer Interaction (HCI) Technologies in Socially-Enabled Artificial Intelligence. In *Future of Digital Technology and AI in Social Sectors* (pp. 121–150). IGI Global.

Shafik, W. (2025c). Machine Learning Techniques for Multicriteria Decision-Making. In *Multi-Criteria Decision-Making and Optimum Design with Machine Learning* (pp. 165–194). CRC Press.

Shafik, W., Kalinaki, K., Fahim, K. E., & Adam, M. (2024). Safeguarding Data Privacy and Security in Federated Learning Systems. In *Federated Deep Learning for Healthcare* (pp. 170–190). CRC Press., DOI: 10.1201/9781032694870-13

Shree, C., & Patidar, D. (2020). AI for Social Good: Addressing Global Challenges and Empowering Communities. [TURCOMAT]. *Turkish Journal of Computer and Mathematics Education, 11*(1). Advance online publication. DOI: 10.61841/turcomat.v11i1.14407

Usman Hadi, M. al tashi, qasem, Qureshi, R., Shah, A., muneer, amgad, Irfan, M., Zafar, A., Bilal Shaikh, M., Akhtar, N., Wu, J., Mirjalili, S., Al-Tashi, Q., & Muneer, A. (2023). A Survey on Large Language Models: Applications, Challenges, Limitations, and Practical Usage. Authorea Preprints.

Usman Hadi, M., Al Tashi, Q., Qureshi, R., Shah, A., Muneer, A., Irfan, M., Zafar, A., Bilal Shaikh, M., Akhtar, N., Zohaib Hassan, S., Shoman, M., Wu, J., Mirjalili, S., Shah, M., Al-Tashi, Q., & Ali Al-Garadi, M. (2024). Large Language Models: A Comprehensive Survey of its Applications, Challenges, Limitations, and Future Prospects. *Authorea Preprints*.

Zakaria, G. A. N., Yusmaliana, D., Abdullah, Z. H., Abubakari, M. S., Narongrak-shakhet, I., & Amonov, B. (2024). Gender-Neutral Pathways to Positive Behavior: Investigating the Role of Self-Actualisation and Academic Achievement in Secondary Education. [IJOLAE]. *Indonesian Journal on Learning and Advanced Education*, *7*(1), 1–17.

Chapter 4
Future-Facing Pedagogy: Empowering Students Through AI Literacies

J. J. Wallace
https://orcid.org/0000-0002-9690-4148
Transylvania University, USA

Julie Perino
https://orcid.org/0000-0002-7530-0679
Transylvania University, USA

Iva Katzarska-Miller
https://orcid.org/0000-0001-7200-1924
Transylvania University, USA

ABSTRACT

This chapter examines the growing role of generative AI tools, such as large language models, in higher education and argues that instructors must intentionally develop students' AI literacies, awareness, evaluation, ethical use, and creative collaboration, to promote responsible and effective learning. After reviewing established literacy frameworks, this chapter presents practical classroom strategies for prompt design, output assessment (e.g., adapted CRAAP test), and ethical reflection. The chapter also illustrates how AI can function as a collaborator and outlines methods for assessing AI competencies and embedding AI guidelines in syllabi. The chapter concludes by discussing challenges and future directions, finally recommending that instructors and institutions continuously evolve their pedagogies and practices as the AI landscape continues to develop.

DOI: 10.4018/979-8-3373-3000-6.ch004

INTRODUCTION

The increased popularity of Artificial Intelligence (AI) tools and their integration into nearly every aspect of society, business, and technology necessitates a cultural and pedagogical shift in higher education. While AI has been slowly increasing in capabilities since the mid-20th century (Mucci, 2024) it has only been with the introduction of generative AI (Caballar, 2024) and large language models (LLM) (Amazon Web Services [AWS], 2025) that the ability to utilize this technology productively in nearly all aspects of education and learning has emerged. AI and LLMs enable real-time content creation and collaboration with AI tools, presenting a unique and exciting opportunity for transformative pedagogical development.

With the release of ChatGPT (OpenAI) in November 2022, educators have been grappling with the rapid changes that make pedagogical development with AI daunting and in constant flux. A recent survey of AI policy at U.S. institutions of higher education found that 63% of institutions encourage the use of AI, but only 41% provide detailed guidance, 56% offer sample syllabi, and 50% provide examples of classroom integration (McDonald et al., 2025). Additionally, a 2024 international survey of faculty found that 61% of faculty have used AI in their teaching practices; however, 88% also report using AI only moderately to minimally for tasks such as creating teaching materials, administrative tasks, demonstrating AI to students, and boosting student engagement (Digital Education Council [DEC], 2025). Clearly, we have room to grow in terms of developing our and our students' AI literacies.

While the use of AI is increasing, educators in higher education settings must be reminded that AI has limitations, is constantly changing in scope of use, and poses ethical dilemmas related to the generation of content. Concerns include problems with bias and representation (Selwyn, 2024), development of student literacies, such as critical thinking and judgment (Darwin et al., 2024; Goyal, 2025), and environmental impact, such as emissions and resource consumption (United Nations Environmental Programme [UNEP], 2024; Kerr, 2024). Despite these concerns, research shows that AI use in the classroom can increase student engagement (Nguyen et al., 2024), improve self- and peer feedback (Darvishi et al., 2024), and improve efficiency (Pearson, 2024). Striking a balance between the ethical use of AI and fostering student growth and critical skills is paramount. Research and practice into AI demonstrate that individuals with training and expertise receive higher-quality outcomes than those who simply try to use it as a replacement for a search engine or to generate a quick response. For students to successfully work with AI, they need to recognize the value of the knowledge they bring with them as their prompts and iterations on those prompts help them receive more valuable outputs (Caddy, 2025; Inkpen, et al. 2023); moreover, students need to know that AI responses do not have value without human contribution.

In this chapter, we explore foundational principles of AI literacies, practical classroom strategies, and ethical considerations in higher education. The organization of the chapter moves from theoretical understanding to classroom applications that reflect both how instructors develop AI competence and how they can effectively teach these skills to students. We begin by establishing the conceptual framework of the AI literacies that instructors need before they can guide students successfully to use AI. Next, we discuss practical interaction skills, critical evaluations of AI outputs, and academic integrity through how to cite AI. The chapter concludes with recommendations for integrating AI literacies into curricula and assessing student learning outcomes. As already mentioned, we acknowledge that there are multiple ethical concerns regarding AI usage. While we consider ethics in teaching students to evaluate AI outputs, the chapter will not address in detail the academic or broader societal ethical implications of AI usage. Furthermore, we understand that the implementation of the practical applications presented in the chapter pose unique challenges to higher education instructors depending on the size of the institution and its AI policies; course level variation such as number of students, level and content area will also impact implementation. While these contextual factors are beyond the scope of this chapter, we encourage educators to adapt the strategies presented in the chapter, drawing on their professional experience to navigate challenges as they present themselves.

AI LITERACIES

Defining AI Literacies

To understand AI literacies, it helps to consider the broader evolution of what we mean by "literacy." In 1996, the New London Group–a coalition of educational researchers–argued that literacies should encompass the "competent control of representational forms" (p. 61) across media, technologies, and contexts. They emphasized that without instruction in multiple, contextual literacies that extended beyond knowledge of standard written language, learners from varied backgrounds would be unable to navigate the world around them successfully. In particular, they argued that learners from minoritized groups would not have access to the same knowledges and opportunities as non-minoritized learners (The New London Group, 1996).

Since then, educators have expanded literacy to literacies, including domains like visual (Kress, 2007), computer (Eyman & Reilly, 2006; Haas, 1996), digital (Glister, 1997; Jones & Hafner, 2021), critical, media, and information literacies (Yancey, 2004). These multiliteracies equip students to read and write and also to analyze, create, and act across diverse contexts. Teaching AI literacies builds on this multiliteracies framework. AI literacies require students to engage their digital, data, and computational literacies (Long & Magerko, 2020; Wang et al., 2023). The research consensus is clear: effective AI use requires foundational knowledge of computer systems and data analysis.

Moreover, there is a consensus that users gain greater AI competence when they have the data and computational literacies discussed above. For those in computational and data studies, a key literacy that students as AI users can develop is coding. While this literacy is discipline-specific, it underlines a main point throughout the discussion on AI. Learning AI literacies is not the same as using AI to generate a response. Individuals who progress in their AI literacies can use them to brainstorm, create, and build. As we reference in other sections of this chapter, co-creation involves active effort and thinking on the user's part. Materials that are co-created with AI are perceived as the product of the human co-creator, rather than AI's, because the user's prompting drives the AI to refine the ideas and content it generates, which it cannot do independently. Students who develop AI literacies will find that working with AI to generate a good, insightful response to a prompt takes as much or more time as creating a product of similar value on their own.

While there are multiple working definitions of AI literacies (Almatrafi et al., 2024, DEC, 2025; Long & Magerko, 2020; Wang et. al, 2022; Weber et al., 2023; Yee et al., 2023), the principles that have most utility for those of us in the higher education classroom include:

- Having an awareness of AI and its role in modern technologies.
- Evaluating and analyzing the information provided by AI.
- Navigating AI use ethically.
- Recognizing that AI is a tool that doesn't create new information but that can foster human creativity.

While these literacies are straightforward, students cannot develop them without teachers direct instruction and examples to help them move beyond the novice level.

AI Literacies Considerations

Part of students' problems in applying the first aspect of AI literacies – having an awareness of it - is that ubiquitous elements of AI have been built into our computer, tablet, and phone technologies with increasing embeddedness. In addition to autotext, spellcheck, and grammar check, machine learning-based AI have become common across multiple domains of society, from everyday shopping and banking apps to social media, healthcare, and education programs (Almatrafi et al., 2024). What this means is that students' recognition and analysis of AI can start with obvious

LLM-based AI like ChatGPT and Claude, but classroom conversations should also incorporate ideas about the ways other algorithm-based apps employ AI. In their systematic review of discussions of AI literacies, Almatrafi et al. (2024) found that fostering this awareness in students "enable[s] [them] to make informed interactions with this technology and avoid blind reliance [upon them]" (Core Constructs section, Know & understand).

As will be discussed in more depth in the Evaluating AI Output section, understanding of AI's biases and evaluating its outputs are critical components of engaging with AI, which is why they comprise the second element of AI literacies. The DEC AI Literacy Framework (2025) suggests providing students with sample AI text to analyze and asking students to use lateral reading (the practice of opening new tabs or sources to verify a website's reliability by cross-checking with other information sources; McGrew, 2024) to learn more about the topic in order to verify the AI provided information. Wineberg et al. (2022) found that explicit instruction in this process increased students' abilities to evaluate digital information.

Beyond teaching strategies that enhance students' abilities to assess information, instructors need to guide students in analyzing the word choices and biases that AI may incorporate into its output on a particular topic. Sano-Franchini (2025) demonstrated the ways that AI incorporated an anti-education bias into summaries from a paragraph from one of her articles. She shared a side-by-side view of a summary she had written herself versus a summary written by ChatGPT and conducted a linguistic analysis to demonstrate how ChatGPT altered the tone and meaning of her work. Incorporating demonstrations and analysis activities can also help students develop a greater awareness of AI's role in technologies and how AI is shaped by and reinforces cultural biases present in its training data.

Navigating the ethical use of AI involves multiple factors, all of which students need instructors to discuss directly, and which have multiple areas for students to develop and deepen their understanding of AI. The DEC (2025) recommends teaching students about AI's role in surveillance and biased hiring systems and suggests using case studies to help students recognize the ways AI has contributed to these problems. As was referenced in the introduction, students also need to learn about AI's role in environmental pollution (UNEP, 2024). Teaching students about AI's environmental impact can involve research projects or in-class debates and role-playing. Such activities should emphasize teaching students to respect and understand the technologies they use on a daily basis, as no technology is resource-neutral.

As we discuss in other sections of this chapter, teaching students to use AI ethically also involves teaching them to cite and reflect on their AI use. The benefits of this instruction into ethical AI literacies include the ways that students' reflections on their AI use helps them grow more competent in understanding potential benefits of AI use, which may help them learn to value AI more as a resource and less as a plagiarism machine. In terms of using AI to bolster creativity via brainstorming and idea generation, these literacies will be discussed further in the pedagogy section, but they involve the ways that AI tools can be used as co-researchers, co-creators of content, and study buddies.

Cultivating AI literacies by teaching students to recognize, ethically use, analyze and evaluate, and creatively leverage AI is crucial. Teaching students these literacies empowers them to become informed and responsible digital citizens. For more example assignments that will help students develop these AI literacies, consult Yee et al. (2023).

TALKING TO AI

Teaching students AI literacies involves helping them understand the communication skills for generating relevant AI responses. These skills differ from traditional literature/resource searches because, when using AI, users can no longer rely on Boolean Operators, special characters, and using simple search terms to generate good results. Instead, users must prompt the AI, which means to provide a description of what we want the AI to do (Henrickson & Merono-Penuela, 2025). AI is designed to respond as chatbots and communicating with AI is like a conversation, requiring writing in full sentences, asking questions, and providing context to ensure appropriate results. Each prompt should be followed by an iterative process to refine and adjust the AI response until it meets the desired quality and caliber (Jha et al., 2023). Warzel (2023) notes that iterative prompting is quickly becoming one of the "most important job skills of this century."

Popular AI models, such as Anthrop\c's Claude, Google's Gemini, and OpenAI's ChatGPT, all provide prompting guidelines that help users interact and communicate effectively (Anthrop\c, 2025; Google, 2025; OpenAI, 2025). These guidelines can be reduced to: Prompt Specificity, Response Guidelines, and Response Refinement.

- **Prompt Specificity** involves writing clear, concise prompts that may include defined roles (e.g., "Act as a science teacher"), relevant examples, and steps broken down into smaller tasks—a process sometimes called chaining (Gadesha & Kavlakogly, 2024).
- **Response Guidelines** help shape the AI's reply by specifying desired formats (e.g., lists, paragraphs), tone (e.g., persuasive, explanatory), or length (e.g., word count or page limit).
- **Response Refinement** focuses on iterative follow-ups to improve the response. This includes asking for clarifications, exploring alternative perspectives, or adjusting tone and content to better suit the task.

When used together, these three guidelines help students and educators create precise prompts that elicit high-quality responses. Refer to the QR code (Figure 1) for examples of "good" and "better" prompts.

Figure 1. Talking to AI Supplemental Materials (URL: https://tinyurl.com/3wtpjx2z)

Other techniques such as zero- and few-shot prompting are also useful to share with students (Sanwal & Arora, 2023; Shah, 2024). Teachers can instruct students to use zero-shot prompting when the task is simple and the need for speed over precision is warranted. In that kind of scenario, no context or concrete examples are included in the prompt. Or, instructors can teach students to use few-shot prompting when the task is more complex, and precision, accuracy, and relevancy need to be prioritized. With few-shot prompting, one or more examples are included in the prompt to prime the model and create a pseudo-training session that helps the AI understand the context of the prompt.

When teaching students to use AI, it is also important to help students understand that they can learn from the AI's responses. Using an AI to learn or asking it to expand on its "reasoning" is called chain of thought (CoT) prompting (Choi & Chang, 2025; Lee et al., 2024), which involves asking the AI to outline its thought processes. CoT prompting helps users better understand how the AI would approach creating a response for the user's prompt. This technique allows the user to evaluate response creation for nuances, biases, and areas for improvement, which creates the opportunity to refine the CoT process, effectively guiding the AI to a reasoning model that best fits the user's context and situation, before the AI generates its response. This technique can be especially useful in the classroom because it can help students reason through a complex task before they begin their work.

Using these strategies, educators can frame AI interaction as a form of academic dialogue that requires practice and critical engagement. Sasson Lazovsky et al. (2024) explored the differences and similarities between asking questions and prompting

AI. They surmised that effectively communicating with AI creates a "symbiotic relationship" that encourages creativity, clarity, and precision of language, adaptability, critical thinking, empathy, goal orientation, and cognitive flexibility (Sasson Lazovsky et al., 2024). These skills, while crucial for developing strong AI literacies, are also critical and necessary skills for students to develop in higher education. Mapping the skills required for effective prompting to Bloom's Taxonomy illustrates that higher education already teaches the key competencies for communicating well with AI. For example, the ability to read, understand, evaluate, and apply knowledge from a book/resource is the same as for AI-generated content (Blakeslee, 2004).

With greater fluency in prompt construction and refinement, students will improve upon their AI interactions, leveraging it not just as a search engine, but as a thinking partner. Once students have developed the necessary skills to prompt AI, the next step is to help students critically evaluate the responses AI generates.

EVALUATING AI OUTPUT

Verifying AI outputs begins with an understanding of the limitations inherent in these systems. As we discussed in the AI literacies section, LLMs have remarkable capabilities but are prone to specific weaknesses that students must learn to identify (Bommasani et al., 2021). These include "hallucinations" (fabricated information presented as fact; Bowman, 2024), perpetuating biases and stereotyping (Ranjan et al., 2024), and knowledge limitations tied to the models' training cutoffs (Mousavi et al., 2025).

To address these weaknesses, students should be taught a systematic process for evaluating AI-generated content as part of developing their AI literacies. Despite being digital natives, students often struggle to accurately assess the credibility and accuracy of digital information without targeted educational interventions (Wineburg & McGrew, 2019). These educational approaches should emphasize a process that begins with the verification of cited sources for accuracy and credibility, followed by cross-checking whether the content is current and factually correct, then assessing potential biases, oversimplifications, and logical structure, and finally considering the broader societal and ethical implications of the generated information.

First, if the output includes citations, students should be taught to check whether these references exist, and if they do exist, whether they are credible sources. Next, students should assess whether the output accurately represents the content of the source (Maynez et al., 2020). In other words, does the content cited in the output match the information provided in the source? Second, students should verify the factual correctness of the information, which involves cross-checking facts, statistics, figures, and claims by using other reliable sources. Students should be encouraged to use multiple credible sources to verify information, especially for controversial and more complex topics where AI might present an oversimplified or one-sided perspective. Third, students should evaluate the logical structure and consistency of the content, as LLM systems currently struggle with complex reasoning chains (Mitchell, 2025). This includes identifying logical fallacies, examining the quality of the arguments, and evaluating whether the conclusions drawn are reasonable based on the assumptions provided. Students should question whether the AI output addresses all relevant aspects of the topic, or provides an oversimplified explanation, which has been identified as a common limitation in current LLMs (Gibney, 2024). Students should ask themselves: Does the AI output present multiple perspectives on a contested issue? Are there omissions that might impact understanding of the topic? Finally, students should assess the contextual relevance of the output by asking questions like: Does the information align with the intended audience, purpose, and scope of the work?

Teaching students to recognize biases in AI outputs by considering both what is present in the text and what is missing, is essential for developing critical AI literacies. As was referenced in the AI Literacies section, biases in AI systems can manifest in various forms, ranging from dataset and statistical to cultural and linguistic ones (Ranjan, 2024; Schwartz et al., 2022). Bender et al. (2021) emphasize the importance of recognizing that AI output often reflects the biases present in its training data. Bias identification should start with evaluating the diversity of viewpoints presented in the content. Students should consider whether the output reflects a balanced perspective, or it privileges a specific view point. Students should also question whose voices are being included and excluded, and whether the framing of information perpetuates existing assumptions and stereotypes of social groups. Students should pay attention to the language choices in AI outputs, evaluating whether the terminology used, examples provided, and cultural references represent a specific world view, or demonstrate a variety of perspectives.

In learning to analyze AI responses for biased content, students must recognize that their use and evaluation of AI-generated content has ethical and societal implications that extend beyond their personal academic performance. When AI outputs that contain biased or inaccurate information are shared, they can contribute to spreading of misinformation, which can have implications for public discourse and decision making (Kreps et al., 2022). Furthermore, uncritical acceptance of biased AI content can impact social justice efforts by perpetuating systematic inequalities and beliefs about social groups. Students should understand that having strong AI-output evaluation skills can have implications for their future professional practices, where biased or inaccurate information can impact their clients or communities (Jobin et al., 2019). Additionally, by developing AI literacies students prepare themselves to be responsible citizens that can use AI technology in ways that offset potential AI harms to society (Gonzalez-Mohino et al., 2023).

One way to help students develop this ethical approach to evaluating AI information is to teach them practical models like the CRAAP test (Blakeslee, 2004). Although the CRAAP (Currency, Relevance, Authority, Accuracy, Purpose) test was originally developed to evaluate traditional information sources rather than AI-generated content, it can be effectively adapted to allow students to assess AI output (Todd, 2023).

- For *Currency*, students should ask whether the AI information includes current information on the topic, recognizing that AI systems may not have been trained on most recent data.
- When evaluating *Relevance,* students should determine whether the AI information taps into their specific topic.
- Determining *Authority* can be particularly challenging, but students should consider who are the tool creators and what is their intent (i.e., company mission), which can help with understanding their perspectives and identify underlying biases.
- For *Accuracy*, students should verify the claims, statistics, and any other information by cross-referencing it with other reliable sources.
- Finally, for *Purpose* students should consider how any underlying biases in the training data could have impacted the output.

Two additional evaluation frameworks that complement the CRAAP test are the SIFT method (Stop, Investigate the source, Find better coverage, Trace claims to original context; Caulfield, 2019) and RADAR framework (Rationale, Authority, Date, Accuracy, Relevance; Mandalios, 2013). Teaching students these frameworks develops their AI literacies. After students have developed the skills to critically evaluate AI output, they also must learn to properly document and cite their use of AI tools in academic work.

CITING AI WORK

When and how to cite AI contributions to academic or creative works has become an increasingly debated topic (Meehan, 2023). The United States Copyright Office (2025) (U.S. Copyright Office, 2025), the European Union (European Union [EU], 2024), journals and publishers (American Psychological Association [APA], 2023; Elsevier, 2025,), AI companies (OpenAI, 2022), and educators continue to grapple with the implications of using AI in creative works. The consensus as of writing this chapter is that only humans can qualify as authors, and AI cannot claim authorship or copyright ownership (U.S. Copyright Office, 2025, part 2 copyrightability). Istrate (2023) states that AI, as a tool, should be recognized or cited for its contribution to the final product. Despite these guidelines, lawsuits on the topic of intellectual property are currently being debated (ChatGPT is Eating the World, 2025; Madigan, 2025). While the role of AI contribution in research writing could change in the future, students can only navigate AI ethically if they are reminded of the rules and regulations for proper citation. Below we review strategies for ensuring students navigate AI citation ethically.

The first step in ethical AI citation is knowing when to cite. AI developers and other organizations have shared stances toward AI authorship. The APA dictates that AI cannot be an author, but its use must be detailed in the methods section (APA, 2023), with examples available on their website (McAdoo, 2024). Journal of American Medical Association (JAMA) similarly prohibits AI authorship, mandating disclosure of AI tools in acknowledgments or methods (Flanagin, et al., 2023). Best practice for educational institutions often involves acknowledging AI use visibly (Istrate, 2023), ensuring transparency of how AI was used (Feng, 2024), and attributing responsibility to human authors (Leung et al., 2023). Instructing students in these strategies will differ between courses, professors, disciplines, and institutions but, in general, students should cite AI tools whenever the tool generates text, ideas, summaries, or media that contribute to their work. This includes paraphrased or reworded content, not just verbatim output. Having a clear citation policy in the course syllabus and a list of ways AI can be used to complete every assignment is the best way to ensure students are following classroom guidelines and properly citing AI contributions to their creative processes and final products.

Once when to recognize AI contributions is established, the second step is defining how AI should be cited. In general, the AI program being used should be cited in text (where appropriate) and on the works cited page (see Table 1 for examples). Additionally, some citation style guides have suggested that writers cite the AI program and include a description of how AI was used to increase transparency. Reflecting on and disclosing how AI was used can be completed through the use of metacognitive reflection (Zakrajsek, 2025) and/or requiring AI use statements at the end of the student's work (Iannantuono, 2024). These tools foster transparency and encourage students to think critically about their writing process.

Once higher education instructors have taught students to interact, evaluate, and cite AI effectively, they must also establish clear classroom policies and frameworks that guide ethical integration of AI throughout the course. This includes developing AI syllabus policy, assignment guidelines, and assessment strategies that promote responsible AI use.

Table 1. Popular Citation Style Examples

Style	QR Code	Example Works Cited Entry
APA		OpenAI. (2023). *ChatGPT* (Mar 14 version) [Large language model]. https://chat.openai.com/chat
MLA		"Describe the symbolism of the green light in the book *The Great Gatsby* by F. Scott Fitzgerald" prompt. *ChatGPT*, 13 Feb. version, OpenAI, 8 Mar. 2023, chat.openai.com/chat.
Chicago		ChatGPT, response to "Explain how to make pizza dough from common household ingredients," OpenAI, March 7, 2023. Edited for style and content.
AMA		*ChatGPT*. Version 4.5. OpenAI; 2025. Accessed February 28, 2025. https://openai.com/

PEDAGOGICAL APPROACHES

AI Syllabus and Assignment Policies

We strongly recommend that every course have an AI policy syllabus-statement. Regardless of whether AI use is allowed or not, an AI policy syllabus-statement sets clear expectations for AI use, prevents misuse and plagiarism, encourages open communication between instructors and students, and encourages critical thinking about the role of AI in student learning. A well-developed AI policy syllabus-statement should provide

- A description of the tools that the teacher considers AI (e.g., is it just generative AI, or also editing tools like Grammarly?),
- An explanation of permitted and forbidden uses of AI embedded in a conversation about academic integrity and plagiarism,
- Instructions for citing AI output properly,
- A clear statement of the impact of unethical use on students' grades (Katzarska-Miller & Wallace, 2025).

When AI is completely prohibited, an explanation of why students will not be using it should be provided. For limited AI use, faculty should define the scope, program used, and the when and how AI will be used. For unlimited AI use, faculty should outline citation policy and describe the reflective metacognition required from students on their AI use.

In addition to including a holistic course AI policy, faculty should consider including AI statements on each assignment. Students can be required, encouraged, or prohibited from using AI for specific course components and assignments even in a class where AI is permitted. Two practical applications for communicating these policies with students include the Traffic Light System (Mormando, 2023) and AI Menus (Liu, 2024). The traffic light system uses red, yellow, or green lights to designate allowance for AI usage.

- Red light indicates that AI usage is not permitted for the activity or assignment.
- Yellow light designates that permission for the instructor is required before using AI.
- Green light signifies that the instructor encourages students to use AI tools.

These options can be used selectively depending on the learning objectives and goals of the specific assignments. For example, red light can be used for traditional quizzes and exams, yellow light for research projects, and green light for creative tasks (Mormando, 2023). AI Menus clearly state an instructor's stance toward AI by providing students with a list of acceptable AI programs and uses, which can be applied to the course (course menu) or for a specific assignment (assignment menu). The role of instructors, based on their knowledge of their students and teaching context, is to guide students to use the tools that best suit specific tasks and desired skills for students to develop in the course (Liu, 2024).

AI Learning Outcomes

Beyond establishing comprehensive AI policies, faculty should consider how to embed the AI literacies described above into their course design and learning objectives. Effective curriculum integration requires instructors to incorporate AI awareness into existing curriculum, while maintaining academic rigor and supporting student learning outcomes. A modified version of Bloom's taxonomy (Rivers & Holland, 2023; Scheuer-Larsen & Lauridsen, 2023) offers students opportunities to develop cognitive skills in relation to AI tools and applications. The modified version maintains the six cognitive levels Remember, Understand, Apply, Analyze, Evaluate, and Create, but reframes them to consider the role of AI at each stage. For example, at the Analyze stage, AI can compare and contrast information or derive trends, while students can be taught to break down the output and determine its quality and relevance (Scheuer-Larsen & Lauridsen, 2023). Although AI can be used at each cognitive level, it can efficiently handle more foundational cognitive tasks such as information retrieval (Remember) and explanation of concepts (Understand), allowing students to focus more attention on evaluation skills (Evaluate) and novel ideas (Create; Katzarska-Miller & Wallace, 2025). Regardless of the level of cognitive skill, students still need to critically evaluate the AI output.

Katzarska-Miller and Wallace (2025) provide three examples of how AI can be incorporated into existing curricula to help achieve student learning outcomes.

- AI as a co-researcher: where AI can help search for and summarize information, analyze data, text, image, or video, and find additional resources and avenues to explore.
- AI as a study buddy: helping students identify themes, solving problems (math, coding, etc.), taking notes, and creating study guides, along with practice tests and problems, serving as a tutor and course teaching assistant.
- AI as a collaborator (co-creator of content): generating text, presentations, images, and serving as a writing partner in editing and proofreading students' work.

AI as Collaborator

Of these examples, AI as a collaborator can be the most challenging and potentially fruitful practice to develop because it is the aspect where students engage most with AI and learn the most about humans' roles in generating quality AI outputs. As a writing partner, AI can help students generate ideas, develop their drafts, and provide them with formative feedback and editing assistance (Bushnell, 2025; Foster, 2022; Gasaymeh et al., 2024; Kim et al., 2025; Yee et al., 2023). Framing AI as a "writing partner" positions it not as a passive tool or a human substitute, but as a potential co-authoring agent that can help scaffold learners' development as writers (Open AI, 2025).

Not only can students be taught to use AI as a collaborator for their writing projects, they can also be taught how to use AI at different stages of their research processes. According to Klebeck (2024), librarians recommend using AI to help students develop their research questions. This is because AI, through its training data and internet access in newer models, has access to scholarship that includes discipline-specific terms and ideas. Often, students find scholarly language to be a barrier when trying to find and understand relevant research. Students can query AI for synonyms for their search terms, ask the bot to respond as an expert in the field being researched, and receive links to further information on the topic. This generative capacity extends beyond research questions to encompass brainstorming paper topics and soliciting opinions on a topic, which students can use to help them create rebuttals to popular stances toward the topic (Yee et al., 2023). In this way, AI can be used as an idea generation tool, rather than replacing students' thinking.

Other ways AI can be used to co-create information include multimedia creation, which instructors and students can utilize to assist in designing images, video, and audio content. Image-generating AI can create images in various styles, include a wide range of content, and be revised completely or based on a base-image style (Miller, 2023). Morrison and Caswell (2025) recommend ChatGPT as the best overall image generator because the "simplest text prompts can yield accurate depictions without further explanations" (para. 13). The other models they recommend, such as Midjourney and Leonardo, can create similar-quality images but have more challenging user interfaces and require more effort on the user's part. AI-generated images, videos, and audio can help students without technical expertise to create, edit, and refine multimedia components of projects. They can also be used to represent course information in multimedia forms, making it more accessible to students by providing them with multiple ways to engage with and learn from the material (Hey, 2025; Kharbach, 2024). This aligns with research on multimodal learning, which suggests that combining visual and auditory elements can enhance cognitive processing and retention (CAST, 2024; Mayer, 2021).

While students and teachers can gain much from using AI to create media, as with all other AI use, doing so creates ethical concerns primarily regarding the AI's training data, much of which may have been created from internet images without artists' consent (Jiang et al., 2023). Because of this issue and an instructor's need to balance their class time between teaching AI and other content, AI image-generators should be evaluated on their ease of use/instruction and the ethics of the company that runs the AI model. In terms of image-generating AI, Adobe Firefly rates as a model that is easy to use and whose training data (the Adobe Stock Image Library) is ethically sourced (Morrison & Caswell, 2025). Training data from other generators may violate the copyright of human artists, as AI creators often scrape the internet for images without adhering to copyright laws (Morrison & Caswell, 2025). Beyond the training data quandary, to be ethical, AI use needs to support human work and not replace it, in the same way that we teach students to use other AI tools. Part of this means helping students be transparent in acknowledging how and when they use AI to generate media, citing the tools they use, and carefully evaluating the output of the AI to ensure that it doesn't present potentially harmful or biased content.

AI and Assessment

Once an instructor has taught students when, how, and why to use AI, a new question arises: How can instructors assess students' AI literacies? We find that traditional assessment methods are still valuable in doing this kind of work. For example, instructors can provide students with self-assessment questionnaires that they can use to measure their perceived competencies in AI literacies (e.g., Scale for the Assessment of non-Experts' AI Literacy [SNAIL]; Laupichler et al., 2023). This self-assessment is important as it allows students to share their perspective toward their literacies' development, but other kinds of assessment can also help faculty assess students' competencies in these literacies

- Objective AI literacy tests can measure competencies in a variety of areas, such as understanding of AI, usage of AI, etc. (Litner, 2024; Long & Magerko, 2020).
- Quizzes and concept mapping can be used to assess students' knowledge-base and measure students' understanding of foundational AI concepts and vocabulary.
- Performance-based assessment can be used to have students apply their AI knowledge in real-world or simulated situations, emphasizing practical and creative competencies.
- Reflective assessments, such as learning journals and self-assessment checklists, can help students develop their metacognitive awareness about what they know about AI and how they can use it.
- Rubric-based assessment, where a rubric is aligned with AI competencies, can assess student work across multiple dimensions.

These traditional methods can help instructors and students track progress through the different AI literacies.

While traditional assessments are valuable for assessing students' AI literacies, the use of AI as an assessment tool that assists instructors in grading and providing feedback on student work has gained traction (Owan et al., 2023). Instructors have reported using AI for grading to save time, providing students with timely feedback, and reducing subjectivity in grading (Cutler, 2024; Kumar, 2023; Schwartz, 2025). However, some instructors find using AI more time-consuming when trying to provide meaningful feedback on complex assignments than doing it manually (Taylor, 2024). Student reactions have been mixed. Some of the positives relate to students appreciating receiving timely feedback (Schwartz, 2025) and perceiving AI as fairer evaluators than teachers (Chai et al., 2024). However, recently there has been more negative reactions such as ethical objections, where many students feel it is unethical for instructors to use AI to assess their work, especially when students are prohibited from using AI themselves (Schwartz, 2025). Other issues include potential bias against certain writing styles and non-native English speakers (Wargo & Anderson, 2024), AI lack of understanding students' work (Juliani, 2024), and privacy concerns (Soares, 2024).

If instructors decide to use AI to assess students' work they need to take into consideration students' privacy, as well as legal, and ethical concerns (Kumar, 2023). Before using any AI tool to assess student work, instructors must check their school's AI usage policy and ensure that AI grading aligns with institutional guidelines. Furthermore, instructors should ensure that AI-generated feedback aligns with the intended learning outcomes of the course. Instructors should also reduce potential biases the AI model may have toward different writing styles or non-standard English forms; they can do so by tailoring the model they work with to be less reactive toward non-standard forms and by carefully evaluating the AI's output. Additionally, instructors should verify that the AI tools comply with data protection regulations by paying special consideration to FERPA. Students should be made aware that their work is going to be assessed with AI tools and be given the option to opt out of receiving this form of feedback. Finally, instructors should clarify what aspects of grading or feedback are AI-assisted and which are human-reviewed.

CHALLENGES AND FUTURE DIRECTIONS

Artificial-intelligence tools have the potential to bring significant change and positive impacts on student learning outcomes. However, their benefits could be outweighed by issues such as equity, bias, and the rapidly changing landscape of technology. The efficacy of AI in education hinges on addressing several challenges, some of which can be addressed at the institutional and classroom level, while others are beyond educators' control. These challenges include closing infrastructure gaps, mitigating ethical risks, countering bias, and designing AI literacies to facilitate continuous evolution.

Infrastructure gaps that can impact the ability of students to utilize AI include robust hardware, high-speed internet connectivity, and equitable access, all of which are prerequisites for meaningful engagement. The U.S. Department of Education estimates that local bandwidth gaps, dated student devices, and lack of universal access to paid tools constrain digital initiatives in rural and minority-serving institutions, creating AI-driven inequity (Cardona et al., 2023). Meeting these challenges will require coordinated investments by institutions, including considerations such as campus Wi-Fi upgrades, device loan or access programs, and cloud-budget planning. Addressing infrastructure gaps will allow equitable and reliable access to the technology needed so that AI does not become an accelerator of existing inequalities.

In addition to ensuring equitable access, institutions of higher education must prioritize mitigating ethical risks related to information integrity and data privacy. Many universities are also updating academic integrity policies with AI-specific clauses regarding use, disclosure, and sanctions, although these policies must adapt to evolving federal regulations. Ethical concerns also extend to the environmental impact of AI's computational demands, as noted by MIT researchers highlighting AI's significant carbon emissions (Zewe, 2025), as well as intellectual property law, long-term societal impacts related to employment and social structures, and the potential for misinformation.

Bias, both algorithmic and human, presents another unresolved challenge to AI use. For example, detectors designed to flag AI-generated writing have produced false positives that disadvantage English second-language learners and neurodivergent writers. A widely circulated case involved a Purdue University professor whose succinct email responses were labeled "AI-written" by colleagues and online commenters; the instructor, who is diagnosed with autism, noted that brevity was a communication preference rather than evidence of non-human authorship (Pindell, 2025). Cases like this illustrate how cultural expectations and bias about "warmth" or style can unfairly disadvantage certain groups, underscoring the need for awareness of not only how AI produces responses but also how humans interpret those outputs. The purposeful addition of digital and multiple literacies, including media, data, and AI into student learning outcomes may help mitigate the inclusion or use of biased AI information in academic and creative works.

Given the rapid pace of AI development, educators must also recognize the need for agility. The 2024 *Stanford AI Index* reveals that language model performance has doubled in months, with new capabilities emerging frequently (Human-Centered Artificial Intelligence, 2024). Since specific AI competencies can quickly become outdated, AI literacies should prioritize transferable skills, including clear prompt formulation, output evaluation, source verification, bias auditing, and transparent citation. Pedagogy should be iterative, supported by transparent institutional policies and adaptable syllabi that acknowledge potential policy changes within a given academic year or semester. This nimbleness will foster the development of effective and informed AI users.

While AI tools have the potential to enhance learning outcomes, realizing this potential hinges on addressing critical issues of equity, ethics, and adaptability. By focusing on closing infrastructure gaps, mitigating ethical risks, countering bias, and fostering a dynamic approach to AI literacies, instructors can ensure that AI serves to augment, rather than hinder, student success. The journey toward responsible and effective AI integration will be ongoing, requiring continuous evaluation and adaptation to the ever-evolving technological landscape.

AI USE STATEMENT

Throughout the development of this chapter, several AI tools were used for various purposes, including idea generation, brainstorming, outlining, organizing, editing, language refinement, and generating examples. Wherever AI-generated text has not been paraphrased or adapted, direct quotations and in-text citations acknowledge its contribution. This practice reflects our commitment to transparency and academic integrity in AI-assisted scholarship.

AI Tools Utilized

- ChatGPT 4o, o1, o3 (OpenAI, April-May 2025 versions)
- Claude 3.7 Sonnet (Anthropic, April 2025 version)
- Gemini for Workspace (Google, April-May 2025 versions)
- Grammarly (April 2025 version)
- Say What You See (Google AI, April 2025 version)

REFERENCES

Almatrafi, O., Johri, A., & Lee, H. (2024). A systematic review of AI literacy conceptualization, constructs, and implementation and assessment efforts (2019-2023). *Computers and Education Open*, *6*, 100173. Advance online publication. DOI: 10.1016/j.caeo.2024.100173

Amazon Web Services. (2025). *What is LLM (Large language model)?* https://aws.amazon.com/what-is/large-language-model/

American Psychological Association. (2023). *APA journals policy on generative AI: Additional guidance.* American Psychological Association. https://www.apa.org/pubs/journals/resources/publishing-tips/policy-generative-ai

Anthropic. (2025). *Prompt engineering overview.* Anthropic. https://docs.anthropic.com/en/docs/build-with-claude/prompt-engineering/overview

Bender, E. M., Gebru, T., McMillan-Major, A., & Shmitchell, S. (2021). On the dangers of stochastic parrots: Can language models be too big? *Proceedings of the 2021 ACM Conference on Fairness, Accountability, and Transparency*, 610-623. DOI: 10.1145/3442188.3445922

Blakeslee, S. (2004). The CRAAP Test. *LOEX Quarterly*, *31*, 6–7.

Bommasani, R., Hudson, D. A., Adeli, E., Altman, R., Arora, S., von Arx, S., . . . Liang, P. (2021). *On the opportunities and risks of foundation models*. arXiv. *L* arXiv.2108.07258DOI: 10.48550

Bowman, S. R. (2024). Eight things to know about large language models. *Critical AI*, *2*(2). Advance online publication. DOI: 10.1215/2834703X-11556011

Bushnell, J. T., & Harrison, W. (2025). A new muse: how guided AI use impacts creativity in online creative writing courses.

Caballar, R. D. (2024, August 9). *Generative AI vs. predictive AI: What's the difference?* IBM. https://www.ibm.com/think/topics/generative-ai-vs-predictive-ai-whats-the-difference

Caddy, B. (2025, February 20). *I've become a ChatGPT expert by levelling up my AI prompts – here are my 8 top tips for success.* TechRadar: The Technology Experts. https://www.techradar.com/computing/artificial-intelligence/ive-become-a-chatgpt-expert-by-levelling-up-my-ai-prompts-here-are-my-8-top-tips-for-success

Cardona, M. A., Rodríguez, R. J., & Ishmael, K. (2023). *Artificial intelligence and the future of teaching and learning: Insights and recommendations.* Office of Educational Technology. https://files.eric.ed.gov/fulltext/ED631097.pdf?utm_source=chatgpt.com

CAST. (2024). *Universal Design for Learning Guidelines version 3.0.* https://udlguidelines.cast.org

Caulfield, M. (2019, June 19). *SIFT (The four moves).* https://hapgood.us/2019/06/19/sift-the-four-moves/

Chai, F., Ma, J., Wang, Y., Zhu, J., & Han, T. (2024). Grading by AI makes me feel fairer? How different evaluators affect college students' perception of fairness. *Frontiers in Psychology, 15*, 1221177. Advance online publication. DOI: 10.3389/fpsyg.2024.1221177 PMID: 38371704

ChatGPT Is Eating the World. (2025). *Master list of AI copyright lawsuits.* ChatGPT Is Eating the World. https://chatgptiseatingtheworld.com/updated-the-master-list-of-ai-copyright-lawsuits-current-total-38/

Choi, W. C., & Chang, C. I. (2025). A survey of techniques, key components, strategies, challenges, and student perspectives on prompt engineering for large language models (LLMs) in education. *Preprints*. DOI: 10.20944/preprints202503.1808.v1

Cutler, D. (2024, May 8). *How AI can enhance the grading process.* Edutopia. https://www.edutopia.org/article/using-ai-grading-tools-enhance-proces

Darvishi, A., Khosravi, H., Sadiq, S., Gašević, D., & Siemens, G. (2024). Impact of AI assistance on student agency. *Computers & Education, 210*, 104967. Advance online publication. DOI: 10.1016/j.compedu.2023.104967

Darwin, Rusdin, D., Mukminatien, N., Suryati, N., Laksmi, E. D., & Marzuki. (2024). Critical thinking in the AI era: An exploration of EFL students' perceptions, benefits, and limitations. *Cogent Education, 11*(1), 2290342. Advance online publication. DOI: 10.1080/2331186X.2023.2290342

Digital Education Council. (2025). *Digital education council global AI faculty survey 2025 AI meets academia: What faculty think.* Digital Education Council. https://www.digitaleducationcouncil.com/post/digital-education-council-global-ai-faculty-survey

Elsevier. (2025). *The use of generative AI and AI-assisted technologies in writing for Elsevier.* Elsevier. https://www.elsevier.com/about/policies-and-standards/the-use-of-generative-ai-and-ai-assisted-technologies-in-writing-for-elsevier

European Union. (2024). *The Act Texts.* EU Artificial Intelligence Act. https://artificialintelligenceact.eu/the-act/

Eyman, D., & Reilly, C. (2006). Revising with word processing/technology/document design. In Horning, A., & Becker, A. (Eds.), *Revision: History, theory and practice* (pp. 102–115). Parlor Press.

Feng, G. C. (2024). Best practices for responsibly using AI tools in social sciences research. *Cogent Social Sciences, 10*(1), 2420484. Advance online publication. DOI: 10.1080/23311886.2024.2420484

Flanagin, A., Bibbins-Domingo, K., Berkwits, M., & Christiansen, S. L. (2023). Nonhuman "authors" and implications for the integrity of scientific publication and medical knowledge. *Journal of the American Medical Association, 329*(8), 637–639. DOI: 10.1001/jama.2023.1344 PMID: 36719674

Foster, D. (2022). *Generative deep learning: Teaching machines to paint, write, compose, and play* (2nd ed.). O'Reilly Media, Inc.

Gadesha, V., & Kavlakogly, E. (2024, April 23). *What is prompt chaining?* IBM. https://www.ibm.com/think/topics/prompt-chaining

Gibney, E. (2024, July 24). *AI models fed AI-generated data quickly spew nonsense.* Nature. https://www.nature.com/articles/d41586-024-02420-7

Gonzalez-Mohino, M., Rodriguez-Domenech, M. Á., Callejas-Albiñana, A. I., & Castillo-Canalejo, A. (2023). Empowering critical thinking: The role of digital tools in citizen participation. *Journal of New Approaches in Educational Research, 12*(2), 258–275. DOI: 10.7821/naer.2023.7.1385

Google. (2025.). *Learn about Gemini for Google Workspace.* Google. https://support.google.com/a/users/answer/14200040

Goyal, A. (2025). AI as a cognitive partner: A systematic review of the influence of AI on metacognition and self-reflection in critical thinking. *International Journal of Innovative Science and Research Technology, 10*(3), 1231–1238. DOI: 10.38124/ijisrt/25mar1427

Haas, C. (1996). *Writing technology: Studies on the materiality of literacy*. Routledge.

Henrickson, L., & Mereño-Peñuela, A. (2025). Prompting meaning: A hermeneutic approach to optimising prompt engineering with ChatGPT. *AI & Society, 40*, 903–918. DOI: 10.1007/s00146-023-01752-8

Hey, A. (2025, January 27). *10 best AI educational video makers.* Coursebox. https://www.coursebox.ai/blog/best-ai-educational-video-makers

Human-Centered Artificial Intelligence. (2024). *Artificial intelligence index report 2024. Chapter 6: Education.* Stanford University. https://hai.stanford.edu/ai-index/2024-ai-index-report/education?utm_source=chatgpt.com

Inkpen, K., Chappidi, S., Mallari, K., Nushi, B., Ramesh, D., Michelucci, P., & Quinn, G. (2023). Advancing human-AI complementarity: The impact of user expertise and algorithmic tuning on joint decision making. *ACM Transactions on Computer-Human Interaction, 30*(5), 1–29.

Istrate, O. (2023). How to cite ChatGPT and AI products. *Revista de Pedagogie Digitala, 2*(1), 3–8. DOI: 10.61071/RPD.2347

Jha, S., Jha, S. K., Lincoln, P., Bastian, N. D., Velasquez, A., & Neema, S. (2023). Dehallucinating large language models using formal methods guided iterative prompting. *Proceedings of 2023 IEEE International Conference on Assured Autonomy*, 149-152. DOI: 10.1109/ICAA58325.2023.00029

Jiang, H. H., Brown, L., Cheng, J., Khan, M., Gupta, A., Workman, D., & Gebru, T. (2023, August). AI Art and its Impact on Artists. In *Proceedings of the 2023 AAAI/ACM Conference on AI, Ethics, and Society* (pp. 363-374)

Jobin, A., Ienca, M., & Vayena, E. (2019). The global landscape of AI ethics guidelines. *Nature Machine Intelligence, 1*(9), 389–399. DOI: 10.1038/s42256-019-0088-2

Jones, R. H., & Hafner, C. A. (2021). *Understanding digital literacies: A practical introduction* (2nd ed.). Routledge., DOI: 10.4324/9781003177647

Juliani, A. J. (2024, September 19). The BIG Problem with using A.I. for assessment. *A. J. Juliani.* https://www.ajjuliani.com/blog/the-big-problem-with-using-ai-for-assessment

Katzarska-Miller, I., & Wallace, J. (2025). Beyond policies: Developing AI literacy through structured syllabus statements and pedagogical integration. *Journal of Faculty Development, 39*(2), 73–75. https://www.ingentaconnect.com/content/magna/jfd/2025/00000039/00000002/art00012#expand/collapse

Kerr, D. (2024, July 12). *AI brings soaring emissions for Google and Microsoft, a major contributor to climate change.* NPR. https://www.npr.org/2024/07/12/g-s1-9545/ai-brings-soaring-emissions-for-google-and-microsoft-a-major-contributor-to-climate-change

Kharbach, M. (2024). *6 best AI video generators.* Educators Technology. https://www.educatorstechnology.com/2023/02/6-best-ai-video-generators-for-teachers-2.html

Kim, J., Yu, S., Detrick, R., & Li, N. (2025). Exploring students' perspectives on generative AI-assisted academic writing. *Education and Information Technologies*, *30*(1), 1265–1300. DOI: 10.1007/s10639-024-12878-7

Klebeck, L. (2024, February 5). *Research librarians describe many ways to use artificial intelligence*. Gonzaga University. https://www.gonzaga.edu/news-events/stories/2024/2/5/research-librarians-describe-many-ways-to-use-ai

Kreps, S., McCain, R. M., & Brundage, M. (2022). All the news that's fit to fabricate: AI-generated text as a tool of media misinformation. *Journal of Experimental Political Science*, *9*(1), 104–117. DOI: 10.1017/XPS.2020.37

Kress, G. R. (2007). *Literacy in the new media age* (Reprinted). Routledge.

Kumar, R. (2023). Faculty members' use of artificial intelligence to grade student papers: A case of implications. *International Journal for Educational Integrity*, *19*, 9. Advance online publication. DOI: 10.1007/s40979-023-00130-7

Laupichler, M. C., Aster, A., Haverkamp, N., & Raupach, T. (2023). Development of the "Scale for the assessment of non-experts' AI literacy"–An exploratory factor analysis. *Computers in Human Behavior Reports*, *12*, 100338. Advance online publication. DOI: 10.1016/j.chbr.2023.100338

Lee, A. V. Y., Teo, C. L., & Tan, S. C. (2024). Prompt engineering for knowledge creation: Using chain-of-thought to support students' improvable ideas. *AI*, *5*(3), 1446–1461. DOI: 10.3390/ai5030069

Leung, T. I., de Azevedo Cardoso, T., Mavragani, A., & Eysenbach, G. (2023). Best practices for using AI Tools as an author, peer reviewer, or editor. *Journal of Medical Internet Research*, *25*, 51584. Advance online publication. DOI: 10.2196/51584 PMID: 37651164

Liu, D. (2024, April 18). *Menus, not traffic lights: A different way to think about AI and assessments*. The University of Sydney. https://educational-innovation.sydney.edu.au/teaching@sydney/menus-not-traffic-lights-a-different-way-to-think-about-ai-and-assessments/

Long, D., & Magerko, B. (2020). What is AI literacy? Competencies and design considerations. *Proceedings of the 2020 CHI Conference on Human Factors in Computing Systems,* 1-16. DOI: 10.1145/3313831.3376727

Madigan, D. (2025, January 9). *AI lawsuit developments in 2024: A year in review*. Copyright Alliance. https://copyrightalliance.org/ai-lawsuit-developments-2024-review/

Mandalios, J. (2013). RADAR: An approach for helping students evaluate Internet sources. *Journal of Information Science, 39*(4), 470–478. DOI: 10.1177/0165551513478889

Mayer, R. E. (2021). *Multimedia learning* (3rd ed.). Cambridge University Press.

Maynez, J., Narayan, S., Bohnet, B., & McDonald, R. (2020). *On faithfulness and factuality in abstractive summarization*. arXiv /arXiv.2005.00661DOI: 10.48550

McAdoo, T. (2024). *How to cite ChatGPT.* American Psychological Association. https://apastyle.apa.org/blog/how-to-cite-chatgpt

McDonald, N., Johri, A., Ali, A., & Collier, A. H. (2025). Generative artificial intelligence in higher education: Evidence from an analysis of institutional policies and guidelines. *Computers in Human Behavior: Artificial Humans, 3*, 100121. Advance online publication. DOI: 10.1016/j.chbah.2025.100121

McGrew, S. (2024). Teaching lateral reading: Interventions to help people read like fact checkers. *Current Opinion in Psychology, 55*, 101737. Advance online publication. DOI: 10.1016/j.copsyc.2023.101737 PMID: 38039950

Meehan, S. R. (2023, January 30). *When AI is writing, who is the author?* Inside Higher Ed. https://www.insidehighered.com/views/2023/01/31/teaching-ai-writing-terms-co-authorship-opinion

Miller, M. (2023, September 12). *10 Free AI image generators for classroom uses.* Ditch that textbook. https://ditchthattextbook.com/ai-image-generators/

Mitchell, M. (2025). Artificial intelligence learns to reason. *Science, 387*(6740), eadw5211. Advance online publication. DOI: 10.1126/science.adw5211 PMID: 40112073

Mormando, S. (2023, November 9). *Creating AI usage guidelines for students.* Edutopia. https://www.edutopia.org/article/creating-ai-usage-guidelines-students/

Morrison, R., & Caswell, A. (2025). *I've created thousands of AI images and these are the best AI image generators of 2025.* Tom's Guide. https://www.tomsguide.com/best-picks/best-ai-image-generators

Mousavi, S. M., Alghisi, S., & Riccardi, G. (2025). *LLMs as repositories of factual knowledge: Limitations and solutions*. arXiv. /arXiv.2501.12774DOI: 10.48550

Mucci, T. (2024, October 21). *The history of artificial intelligence*. IBM. https://www.ibm.com/think/topics/history-of-artificial-intelligence

Nguyen, A., Kremantzis, M., Essien, A., Petrounias, I., & Hosseini, S. (2024). Enhancing student engagement through artificial intelligence (AI): Understanding the basics, opportunities, and challenges. *Journal of University Teaching & Learning Practice, 21*(6). https://open-publishing.org/journals/index.php/jutlp/article/view/818/772

Open, A. I. (2025). *Text generation guide.* OpenAI. https://platform.openai.com/docs/guides/text

Owan, V. J., Abang, K. B., Idika, D. O., Etta, E. O., & Bassey, B. A. (2023). Exploring the potential of artificial intelligence tools in educational measurement and assessment. *Eurasia Journal of Mathematics, Science and Technology Education, 19*(8), em2307. Advance online publication. DOI: 10.29333/ejmste/13428

Pearson. (2024, June 24). *End of semester AI report: More college students say AI is helping them get better grades.* Pearson. https://plc.pearson.com/en-GB/news-and-insights/news/end-semester-ai-report-more-college-students-say-ai-helping-them-get-better

Pindell, R. (2025). *The challenge of AI checkers.* Center for Transformative Teaching, University of Nebraska-Lincoln. https://teaching.unl.edu/ai-exchange/challenge-ai-checkers/?utm_source=chatgpt.com

Ranjan, R., Gupta, S., & Singh, S. N. (2024). *A comprehensive survey of bias in LLMs: Current landscape and future directions.* arXiv. /arXiv.2409.16430DOI: 10.48550

Rivers, C., & Holland, A. (2023, August 30). *How can generative AI intersect with Bloom's taxonomy?* Times Higher Education. https://www.timeshighereducation.com/campus/how-can-generative-ai-intersect-blooms-taxonomy

Sano-Franchini, J. (2025, April 10-13). *Timely, (un)disciplinary, and solutions-oriented: Remembering and enacting abundance in these times when we just have to keep going* [Chair's address]. *2025 Conference on College Composition and Communication*, Baltimore, MD, United States.

Sanwal, U., & Arora, K. (2023, July 19). *Zero shot vs. few shot prompt engineering: Which one is the best for your business?* SearchUnify. https://www.searchunify.com/su/sudo-technical-blogs/zero-shot-vs-few-shot-prompt-engineering-which-one-is-the-best-for-your-business/

Sasson Lazovsky, G., Raz, T., & Kenett, Y. N. (2025). The art of creative inquiry—From question asking to prompt engineering. *The Journal of Creative Behavior, 59*(1), e671. Advance online publication. DOI: 10.1002/jocb.671

Scheuer-Larsen, C., & Lauridsen, P. (2023, December 14.). *Bloom's taxonomy and AI.* Viden AI. https://viden.ai/en/blooms-taxonomy-and-ai/

Schwartz, R., Schwartz, R., Vassilev, A., Greene, K., Perine, L., Burt, A., & Hall, P. (2022). *Towards a standard for identifying and managing bias in artificial intelligence.* National Institute of Standards and Technology., DOI: 10.6028/NIST.SP.1270

Schwartz (2025, February 14). *Is it Ethical to use AI to grade?* Education Week. https://www.edweek.org/technology/is-it-ethical-to-use-ai-to-grade/2025/02

Selwyn, N. (2024). On the limits of artificial intelligence (AI) in education. *Nordisk Tidsskrift for Pedagogikk og Kritikk, 10*(1), 3–14. DOI: 10.23865/ntpk.v10.6062

Shah, D. (2024, October 27). *Zero-shot vs few-shot prompting.* Portkey. https://portkey.ai/blog/zero-shot-vs-few-shot-prompting

Soares, W. (2024, December 13). *AI tools and student data: Teachers can endanger kids' privacy without robust training.* Chalkbeat._https://www.chalkbeat.org/2024/12/13/ai-tools-used-by-teachers-can-pu--student-privacy-and-data-at-risk/

Taylor, P. (2024, September 6). *The imperfect tutor: Grading, feedback and AI.* Inside Higher Ed. https://www.insidehighered.com/opinion/career-advice/teaching/2024/09/06/challenges-using-ai-give-feedback-and-grade-students

The New London Group. (1996). A pedagogy of multiliteracies: Designing social futures. *Harvard Educational Review, 66*(1), 60–93. DOI: 10.17763/haer.66.1.17370n67v22j160u

Todd, V. (2023, March 1). *Referencing Generative AI and why students should take the CRAAP test: Advice from the library.* Teche. https://teche.mq.edu.au/2023/03/suggested-strategies-for-referencing-generative-ai-and-why-your-students-should-take-the-craap-test-advice-from-the-library/

United Nations Environment Programme. (2024, September 21). *AI has an environmental problem. Here's what the world can do about that.* UN Environment Programme. https://www.unep.org/news-and-stories/story/ai-has-environmental-problem-heres-what-world-can-do-about

U.S. Copyright Office. (2025). *Copyright and artificial intelligence.* U.S. Copyright Office. https://copyright.gov/ai/

Wang, B., Rau, P.-L. P., & Yuan, T. (2023). Measuring user competence in using artificial intelligence: Validity and reliability of artificial intelligence literacy scale. *Behaviour & Information Technology, 42*(9), 1324–1337. DOI: 10.1080/0144929X.2022.2072768

Wargo, K., & Anderson, B. (2024, December 5). *Striking a balance: Navigating the ethical dilemmas of AI in higher education.* Educause. https://er.educause.edu/articles/2024/12/striking-a-balance-navigating-the-ethical-dilemmas-of-ai-in-higher-education

Warzel, C. (2023) *The most important job skill of this century.* The Atlantic. https://www.theatlantic.com/technology/archive/2023/02/openai-text-models-google-search-engine-bard-chatbot-chatgpt-prompt-writing/672991

Weber, P., Pinski, M., & Baum, L. (2023). Toward an objective measurement of AI literacy" (2023). *Proceedings of Pacific Asia Conference on Information Systems,* 60. https://aisel.aisnet.org/pacis2023/60

Wineburg, S., Breakstone, J., McGrew, S., Smith, M. D., & Ortega, T. (2022). Lateral reading on the open Internet: A district-wide field study in high school government classes. *Journal of Educational Psychology*, *114*(5), 893–909. DOI: 10.1037/edu0000740

Wineburg, S., & McGrew, S. (2019). Lateral reading and the nature of expertise: Reading less and learning more when evaluating digital information. *Teachers College Record*, *121*(11), 1–40. DOI: 10.1177/016146811912101102

Yancey, K. B. (2004). Made not only in words: Composition in a new key. *College Composition and Communication*, *56*(2), 297–328. DOI: 10.58680/ccc20044045

Yee, K., Whittington, K., Doggette, E., & Uttich, L. (2023). *ChatGPT assignments to use in your classroom today*. UCF Created OER Works. 8. https://stars.library.ucf.edu/oer/8

Zakrajsek, T. (2025, May 8). *Teaching students AI strategies to enhance metacognitive processing.* The Scholarly Teacher. https://www.scholarlyteacher.com/post/teaching-students-ai-strategies-to-enhance-metacognitive-processing

Zewe, A. (2025, January 17). *Explained: Generative AI's environmental impact.* MIT News. https://news.mit.edu/2025/explained-generative-ai-environmental-impact-0117?utm_source=chatgpt.com

KEY TERMS AND DEFINITIONS

AI Literacies: The skills and knowledges that users develop to understand, evaluate, and use AI tools.

Co-creation: Process by which users and AI systems generate or refine content together.

CRAAP Framework: A set of criteria (Currency, Relevance, Authority, Accuracy, Purpose) for evaluating information quality.

Generative AI: AI: systems (e.g., large language models) that produce content (e.g., text, images, code) based on learned patterns and user input.

Metacognition: Awareness of one's thinking processes and learning when and after interacting with AI.

Pedagogy: Strategies for developing students AI literacies and adapting AI for useful classroom practices.

Prompting: The skill of writing clear and specific instructions to elicit a desired response from AI.

Chapter 5
Systematic Review on AI Chatbots as a Provision for Self-Paced Learning

Aisha Naz Ansari
https://orcid.org/0000-0003-0938-8980
Institute for Educational Development, Aga Khan University, Karachi, Pakistan

ABSTRACT

The emergence and adoption of Generative Artificial Intelligence (AI) in education, especially ChatGPT, has garnered significant attention from educators and researchers alike. The most notable and attractive feature of this chatbot is its ability to offer personalised assistance to its users. In order to explore how ChatGPT creates a personalised learning environment for students and facilitates their learning processes, a systematic review of empirical studies was conducted. This review adhered strictly to PRISMA guidelines and included 10 empirical studies for meta-synthesis. The results revealed that the chatbot is highly valued for its ability to provide a social presence in students' learning journeys. This social presence is crucial as it creates a more engaging and interactive learning experience, which is often missing in traditional educational settings. One of the key findings from the review is that ChatGPT's personalised support enhances students' self-paced learning. By providing immediate feedback, answering questions, and offering explanations tailored to the student's level of understanding, the chatbot helps students learn at their own pace. The review highlights important implications for policy, practice, and research, emphasising the integration of ChatGPT into educational frameworks to support personalised learning and enhance teaching practices. It also calls for further research to examine the long-term effects of AI chatbots on student learning outcomes.

DOI: 10.4018/979-8-3373-3000-6.ch005

INTRODUCTION

Generative Artificial Intelligence (AI) is becoming increasingly vital across various domains, including education. Within the educational landscape, generative AI - particularly chatbots - has emerged as a prominent tool in teaching and learning. The rapid evolution of AI technology, expanding at an annual rate of 21%, has led to the development of chatbots capable of simulating human-like intelligence (Albayrak et al., 2018; Guarda & Augusto, 2021; Niranjanamurthy et al., 2023; Singh & Thakur, 2020; Weizenbaum, 1966). These chatbots engage in natural language conversations using advanced algorithms and natural language processing techniques, evolving into sophisticated knowledge-based systems (Goar et al., 2023).

Generative AI, including ChatGPT, offers personalised guidance and feedback, adapts curricular content to address individual knowledge gaps, and automates grading processes by providing instant responses. These features not only reduce the burden on educators by streamlining qualitative assessments but also enhance the overall efficiency of instructional delivery (Ansari et al., 2024; Rawat et al., 2023). In the context of professional education, such tools have demonstrated promise in supporting personalised learning, improving reasoning, and facilitating the understanding of complex concepts. Furthermore, they contribute to skill development across a range of disciplines, including health and social science disciplines (Ansari et al., 2024; Sallam et al., 2023).

ChatGPT has attracted significant attention for its ability to support complex educational activities, including personalised and interactive learning, formative assessments, and continuous feedback for instructional improvement (AlAli & Wardat, 2024). It has the potential to transform traditional models of higher education into more personalised, quality-driven, and student-centered experiences that foster critical thinking, self-regulated learning, and creativity (Xu et al., 2023). By analysing student data, generating study materials, and adapting to individual needs, the chatbot contributes to the cultivation of essential 21st century skills (Tabib & Alrabeei, 2024). In higher education, AI chatbots personalise learning by adapting to each student's unique needs and learning styles. ChatGPT offers individualised responses and tailored support, enhancing the educational experience through the use of natural language processing and sophisticated algorithms. This capability enables students to receive real-time assistance, personalised feedback, and curated learning resources, fostering an adaptive and engaging learning environment.

The integration of generative AI such as ChatGPT into education presents opportunities to transform the goals, content, processes, and approaches of teaching to meet the demands of future societies (Ahmad et al., 2024; Bhutta et al., 2025; Karakose & Tülübas, 2023). It has the potential to empower students in their learning journeys, enhance cognitive and metacognitive skills, and nurture critical and foundational competencies. Nonetheless, concerns remain regarding the risks of generating inaccurate or biased content, perpetuating existing prejudices embedded in training data, and compromising data privacy (AlAli & Wardat, 2024; Ansari et al., 2025; Sallam et al., 2023). There are also apprehensions that overreliance on such tools in education could impede the development of students' critical thinking and communication abilities.

Rationale of the Review

The increasing integration of generative AI tools in higher education has prompted considerable interest in their potential to enhance student learning experiences. Among these tools, AI chatbots such as ChatGPT have emerged as prominent agents capable of delivering personalised instruction, facilitating real-time feedback, and supporting diverse learning needs (Ansari et al., 2024). However, there remains a need to systematically synthesise the existing evidence on how these tools influence key dimensions of the student learning experience, including engagement, attitude, and learning outcomes.

The aim of this systematic review is to explore how ChatGPT contributes to personalised learning in higher education by analysing its impact on these core dimensions. Specifically, this study seeks to address the review question: *How does ChatGPT provide a personalised learning experience to students in higher education?*

By addressing this question, the review offers a comprehensive understanding of the mechanisms through which ChatGPT supports personalised learning and the extent to which it enhances educational experiences in higher education settings.

RESEARCH CONTEXT

The rapid proliferation of generative AI technologies, particularly in higher education, has transformed the pedagogical landscape by enabling personalised, data-driven, and interactive learning experiences. ChatGPT, a widely adopted AI chatbot, exemplifies this shift by offering real-time feedback, adaptive support, and engagement opportunities tailored to individual learners. As institutions increasingly experiment with such tools, questions have emerged around their pedagogical value, effectiveness, and the challenges they present in diverse educational contexts.

Despite the growing body of research on AI in education, much of the literature remains fragmented across disciplines and focuses on disparate outcomes such as engagement, academic performance, and user perceptions. A comprehensive understanding of how ChatGPT specifically contributes to personalised learning in higher education is lacking. In this context, a systematic review of literature provides a rigorous and structured approach to synthesising existing evidence, identifying patterns, and revealing knowledge gaps. This method is particularly well-suited to the present study, as it enables the integration of insights across multiple empirical studies while maintaining transparency, reproducibility, and methodological clarity.

The choice of a systematic review is thus grounded in the need to consolidate and critically synthesise a rapidly evolving research field. It offers a means to generate evidence-based insights that inform educational practice, guide institutional decision-making, and shape future research on the pedagogical implications of AI chatbots like ChatGPT in higher education settings.

METHODOLOGY

The current systematic review analysed how ChatGPT promotes self-paced learning among students in higher education settings. Following PRISMA guidelines, this review consolidated published evidence to inform policymakers, practitioners, and researchers. The inclusion and exclusion criteria and a search query were established to gather relevant literature, which underwent screening at two levels to ensure transparency and minimise bias in reporting results (Newman & Gough, 2020).

Inclusion and Exclusion Criteria

In alignment with systematic review guidelines (Sanfilippo et al., 2020), specific inclusion and exclusion criteria were developed to ensure the relevance and rigour of the review. The primary aim was to examine how ChatGPT, as a generative AI tool, supports personalised learning in higher education.

Table 1. Inclusion/Exclusion Criteria

Criteria	Inclusion	Exclusion
AI Tool	Studies specifically involving ChatGPT	Studies not involving ChatGPT
Educational Setting	Higher education (e.g., universities, institutions)	Primary, secondary, or non-educational contexts
Focus of Study	Examines personalised learning experiences (e.g., self-paced learning, individualised support)	Studies not addressing personalised learning
Disciplinary Scope	Any academic discipline within higher education	Non-academic or general-purpose applications
Publication Type	Peer-reviewed journal articles	Blogs, opinion pieces, editorials, or reviews

continued on following page

Table 1. Continued

Criteria	Inclusion	Exclusion
Language	English	Non-English studies
Publication Period	Published between 2022 and 2024	Published before 2022 or after 2024

Search Strategy

In line with systematic review protocols, efforts were made to ensure a comprehensive and representative selection of literature. An open search strategy was developed to gather the maximum available literature on how AI chatbot provides personalised learning experiences. Search terms included 'ChatGPT,' 'personalised learning,' 'self-paced learning,' and 'higher education.' The search query ('ChatGPT' AND ('personalised learning' OR 'self-paced learning') AND 'higher education') was applied to seven selected databases: Scopus, Taylor and Francis, JSTOR, IEEE Xplore, PubMed, Wiley Library, and Emerald, on April 20, 2024. The Scopus database was primarily used for this review due to its broad interdisciplinary coverage and its indexing of high-quality, peer-reviewed literature. Although Web of Science and ERIC are widely recommended in education-related systematic reviews, these databases were not accessible in Pakistan. To mitigate this constraint, alternative strategies were adopted to enhance the breadth and reliability of the search. These included using comprehensive index, manual searches of key journals, and cross-referencing from relevant articles. This approach ensured that studies meeting the inclusion criteria, particularly those related to ChatGPT and personalised learning in higher education, were adequately captured. In total, the search yielded 608 references (Scopus: 15; Taylor and Francis: 32; JSTOR: 1; IEEE Xplore: 87; PubMed: 2; Wiley Library: 15; Emerald: 456), which were imported into Covidence. Out of these, 49 duplicate references were automatically excluded, leaving 559 references for further review, as presented in figure 1.

Figure 1. Flow of literature screening

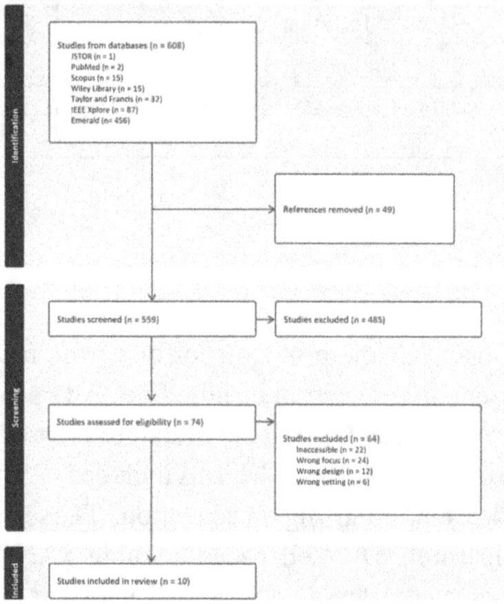

Literature Screening

The imported results underwent screening at two stages by two independent reviewers using the pre-established inclusion criteria. In the first stage, all 559 references were screened at the title and abstract level, excluding 485 studies that did not meet the criteria. This left 74 studies for the second stage of full-text screening, which led to the exclusion of 64 studies due to inaccessibility, a focus on AI chatbots without addressing their impact, other research designs such as opinion, discussion, and review papers and a focus on school settings. Consequently, 10 studies qualified for inclusion in the analysis and reporting. During both stages of screening, the reviewers discussed and resolved conflicts in case of differing opinions on the articles.

Data Extraction

A total of 10 studies were included in the data extraction process. An extraction sheet was developed to capture key components of the studies, such as objectives, educational level, discipline, context, methods, and findings. Two reviewers reviewed and extracted each study, with a consensus reached before finalising the extracted data. The extracted data were then cleaned and analysed for reporting. A summary table of the included studies is presented (table 2).

Table 2. Summary of included studies

Author & Year	Sample	Setting	Methodology	Findings
Ayman et al., (2023)	Across university	Multidisciplinary higher education (Egypt)	Quantitative	75% faculty supported ChatGPT integration despite concerns.
Chan et al., (2023)	12 engineering faculty	Engineering education (Guatemala)	Qualitative	ChatGPT improved student engagement. Faculty noted challenges in bias and technical adaptation.
Dos Santo & Cury, (2023)	80 computer science students	University programming course (Brazil)	Quasi experimental	ChatGPT group outperformed traditional instruction in coding tasks. Higher engagement but challenges with abstract problems.
Gao et al., (2024)	516 university students	Multi-disciplinary higher education (USA)	Quantitative	ChatGPT provides human-like traits (empathy, personality) enhance student engagement. Credibility boosts learning outcomes.
Khan et al., (2023)	201 students + 5 faculty	Computer science and engineering (Bangladesh)	Mixed methods	76% students used ChatGPT for assignments; 44% reported reduced critical thinking. Faculty emphasised need for ethical guidelines.
Li et al., (2024)	23 pre-service STEM teachers	University teacher training course (China)	Quasi experimental	ChatGPT reduced cognitive load and improved task efficiency. In-service teachers yielded better final project outcomes.
Silva et al., (2024)	40 computer science students	Introductory programming course (Brazil)	Quantitative	75% of students found ChatGPT helpful for debugging. Concerns about over-reliance and plagiarism.
Sudirman & Rahmatillah, (2023)	213 entrepreneurship students	Technopreneurship course (Indonesia)	Quantitative	95% found ChatGPT informative and enjoyable. Enhanced creativity and feasibility of ideas.

continued on following page

Table 2. Continued

Author & Year	Sample	Setting	Methodology	Findings
Tossell et al., (2024)	24 engineering students	Human Factors Engineering (USA)	Mixed methods	Students valued AI feedback but preferred human grading. Increased ethical trust in AI post-use.
Zhang et al., (2023)	292 university students	Language learning (China)	Quantitative	AI chatbots improved language outcomes. Technological proficiency moderated effectiveness.

Data Analysis

The data from the included studies (n=10) were cleaned and analysed using thematic analysis. This process involved categorising and combining the findings from the extracted studies into themes about the impact of AI chatbots in higher education (Thomas & Harden, 2008). The procedure included multiple readings of the findings to gain familiarity with the data, coding the extracted data, combining the codes into categories, and combining those categories into emergent themes. This systematic review provides comprehensive insights into how the AI chatbot facilitates personalised, self-paced learning in higher education, emphasising its potential to enhance the educational experience through real-time assistance, personalised feedback, and tailored learning resources.

RESULTS

This section presents a meta-synthesis of the ten included studies to unpack the use of ChatGPT in providing personalised learning experience for students. It begins by describing the actual implementation of ChatGPT in instructional settings, followed by an analysis of its impact on student learning experiences, with a specific focus on its personalised nature.

Implementation of ChatGPT in Instructional Settings

The analysis of included studies reveals that ChatGPT has been implemented across diverse instructional settings in higher education, serving as a personalised learning companion, a curriculum enhancement tool, and a facilitator of student engagement. Its integration has been guided by pedagogical objectives aimed at improving feedback loops, promoting self-paced learning, and cultivating critical thinking. This section further synthesises the modes of implementation, instructional strategies employed, challenges encountered, and effective practices adopted by educators.

Modes of Integration: ChatGPT was commonly used in three instructional roles. First, as a virtual teaching assistant or peer, it provided real-time feedback on student work, responded to queries beyond class hours, and served as a collaborative partner in activities such as programming and brainstorming (Chan et al., 2023; Li et al., 2024; Dos Santo & Cury, 2023). Second, it acted as a curriculum enhancement tool, generating customised learning materials and engaging students across disciplines including coding, language acquisition, and entrepreneurship (Silva et al., 2024; Sudirman & Rahmatillah, 2023; Zhang et al., 2023). Third, ChatGPT supported scaffolded learning by being embedded in multi-phase tasks (e.g., exploration → application → evaluation), enabling structured engagement and iterative refinement of student work (Silva et al., 2024; Tossell et al., 2024).

Instructional Strategies: Successful implementations were characterised by active and collaborative learning designs. Students used ChatGPT to ideate, draft, and refine project-based assignments while educators moderated its output to ensure academic rigour (Chan et al., 2023; Dos Santo & Cury, 2023). Critical engagement was also emphasised where students were tasked with evaluating the accuracy, reliability, and ethical implications of AI-generated responses (Khan et al., 2023; Tossell et al., 2024). Moreover, hybrid models that blended AI support with human instruction emerged as a dominant strategy to balance innovation with oversight (Li et al., 2024).

Challenges and Mitigation Strategies: Despite its potential, the implementation of ChatGPT was not without challenges. Concerns about accuracy, student overreliance, ethical risks (e.g., plagiarism), and technical literacy were recurrent. Mitigation strategies included educator-led moderation, training on prompt engineering, revised assessment formats (e.g., oral presentations, in-person evaluations), and clear institutional guidelines on ethical AI use (Ayman et al., 2023; Silva et al., 2024; Zhang et al., 2023).

Effective Practices: The reviewed studies highlight five effective practices for meaningful integration of ChatGPT in instructional settings: i) defining specific use cases (e.g., feedback vs. brainstorming); ii) scaffolding student-AI interaction across phases of learning; iii) fostering critical evaluation of AI output; iv) maintaining active human oversight to align with learning goals; and v) adapting assessments to prevent misuse.

Overall, the implementation of ChatGPT in instructional contexts has proven to be promising when carefully designed and supervised. It supports a shift towards personalised, student-centered learning, yet its effectiveness depends on intentional instructional design, ethical framing, and integration within broader pedagogical frameworks.

Personalised Learning With ChatGPT Impacting Student Learning Experiences

The ten studies included in this review provide empirical insights into the impact of the chatbot on students' personalised learning experiences in higher education. While none of these studies exclusively focused on student learning experiences, they collectively investigated various aspects such as performance, engagement, and attitudes. These studies highlight the transformative potential of AI chatbots, especially ChatGPT, in higher education. The findings reveal patterns that support AI chatbot's ability to enhance engagement levels, cultivate positive attitudes toward learning, and potentially improve learning outcomes. This underscores ChatGPT's significant role in creating a more engaging and effective learning environment.

The available evidence, including studies by Ayman et al. (2023) and Chan et al. (2023), underscores the transformative potential of the targeted chatbot for personalised learning in educational settings. These studies highlight both the opportunities and challenges of integrating the chatbot into teaching and learning processes, particularly in higher education. Notably, three-quarters of teaching staff acknowledged the integration of ChatGPT, yet uncertainties remained about its impact on teaching and learning outcomes. Arguably, the impact of AI chatbot's personalised features on student learning experiences is compelling. Positive effects include enhanced student engagement and improved attitudes toward learning. Gao et al. (2024) found that students using AI chatbots experienced human-like interactions that increased their engagement and fostered a positive attitude toward AI tools in education. This suggests that ChatGPT can create interactive and engaging learning environments, encouraging active participation and a favourable attitude toward innovative technologies (Ahmad et al., 2024; Bhutta et al., 2025).

Empirical studies (e.g., Dos Santos & Curry, 2023; Li et al., 2024; Silva et al., 2024; Sudirman & Rahimatillah, 2023; Zhang et al., 2023) have documented the significant impact of AI chatbots on student learning experiences through personalised learning support. For instance, in programming courses, ChatGPT as a virtual peer instructor enabled students to outperform traditionally instructed groups by demonstrating better programming skills and conceptual understanding (Dos Santos & Curry, 2023). This success was attributed to the personalised learning support available to students through AI chatbots. In a Technopreneurship course, chatbots facilitated informative and entertaining learning experiences, aiding in idea generation for mobile apps (Sudirman & Rahimatillah, 2023).

Additionally, Silva et al. (2024) noted improved student perceptions of educational support and individual learning experiences through ChatGPT's assistance with programming challenges. Meanwhile, Li et al. (2024) also found that AI chatbots enhanced critical thinking, task completion efficiency, and reduced cognitive load in an iSTEM course, as students used it for self-paced learning. Zhang et al. (2023) discovered a significant correlation between students' understanding of ChatGPT and their language learning achievements, with technological proficiency moderating this relationship. However, concerns about the increasing reliance on AI chatbots, such as potential plagiarism and a decline in critical thinking and creativity, must be addressed (Khan et al., 2023). These risks emphasise the need for caution in AI integration to maintain academic integrity and encourage independent thinking. Tossell et al. (2024) suggest that balancing the benefits and drawbacks of AI in education requires human oversight and clear guidelines to enhance learning experiences while preserving student autonomy.

In summary, the studies reflect the diverse impact of AI chatbot's personalised assistance on student learning experiences, including improvements in language acquisition, critical thinking, and collaborative learning outcomes. Teachers' perspectives on ChatGPT vary, indicating both optimism and apprehension about its broader impact. This underscores the need for ongoing research and a balanced approach to effectively leverage chatbots in education, considering implementation strategies, ethical considerations, and continuous assessment to ensure positive outcomes.

META-SYNTHESIS

AI chatbots have become transformative tools that provide personalised learning assistance, significantly impacting student learning experiences across various dimensions such as performance, engagement, and attitudes. Studies emphasise its potential to enhance learning outcomes and foster positive attitudes toward learning, highlighting the importance of responsible implementation and teacher guidance (Ayman et al., 2023; Chan et al., 2023). Practical involvement and personalised learning experiences facilitated by chatbots contribute to enriched and effective learning (Sudirman & Rahimatillah, 2023; Zhang et al., 2023). The transformative influence of ChatGPT's personalised assistance on performance, engagement, and attitudes through perceived human-like traits and credibility reshapes overall learning experiences positively (Dos Santos & Curry, 2023; Gao et al., 2024). While acknowledging its positive impact, studies provide contrasting perspectives, including ethical considerations and the complementary nature of human expertise (Li et al., 2024; Silva et al., 2024). Convenience and support are highlighted alongside potential drawbacks related to academic integrity and student reliance (Khan et al., 2023; Tossell et al., 2024).

The impact of ChatGPT's personalised assistance on student learning outcomes is multifaceted and significant. It enhances student engagement, motivation, and the speed of quality learning by stimulating interest (Duong et al., 2023). Students find it useful for improving listening skills, writing proficiency, grammar, and vocabulary acquisition (Karataş et al., 2024). It also positively influences academic performance, notably in engineering and programming, where the chatbot users showed improved scores compared to control groups (Alneyadi & Wardat, 2023; Dos Santos & Curry, 2023). This improvement is attributed to the chatbot's ability to aid in grasping complex concepts through interactive learning (Al Shloul et al., 2024).

Despite varied perspectives on its impact, some studies highlight improvements in critical thinking and problem-solving (Qawqzeh, 2024), while others indicate minimal influence on performance and grading outcomes (Kosar et al., 2024). This suggests AI chatbot's potential to revolutionise education by promoting enhanced engagement and personalised learning experiences (Valova et al., 2024). Its transformative impact is evident in changing students' attitudes toward learning, significantly boosting motivation and engagement, particularly in cultivating interest (Valova et al., 2024). Additionally, undergraduate students have a prevalent positive attitude toward using the chatbot as a learning tool (Ajlouni et al., 2023). However, concerns about the accuracy of ChatGPT-generated data and some discomfort in using the platform have been raised (Ajlouni et al., 2023).

A study among teaching staff found that 75% support integrating AI chatbots into teaching practices, although uncertainties about its overall impact on teaching and learning processes remain (Shoufan, 2023). Students appreciate ChatGPT's capabilities, finding it fascinating, motivating, and beneficial for study and work, yet they also recognise its limitations and express the need for further enhancements (Shoufan, 2023). Overall, AI chatbots' impact on student learning outcomes and attitudes is substantial, emphasising its potential to enhance engagement, motivation, and personalised learning experiences while also highlighting the need to address concerns and optimise its use in educational settings (Ansari et al., 2024; Ansari et al., 2026).

The integration of ChatGPT in education brings both significant benefits and challenges (Ansari et al., 2025). It enhances student engagement and motivation yet also raises concerns about ethical issues like cheating and diminished critical thinking skills (Xie & Ding, 2023). To maximise its benefits while upholding educational ethics, responsible implementation, ongoing faculty training, and continuous assessment are essential (Ayman et al., 2023; Khan et al., 2023). Although some experiments show significant positive effects on student performance in specific contexts (Dos Santos & Curry, 2023; Li et al., 2024; Sudirman & Rahimatillah,

2023), others report contrasting trends, such as in a first-year undergraduate programming course (Kosar et al., 2024).

Ethical considerations are crucial, focusing on maintaining critical thinking skills and ethical conduct. Potential decreases in creativity and patience and ethical misconduct due to over-reliance on AI chatbots must be addressed (Awal, 2024; Ayman et al., 2023). Fully leveraging ChatGPT's benefits requires responsible implementation and continuous assessment, considering factors like contextual relevance, instructor expertise, and the educational environment (Ayman et al., 2023). To sum it up, ChatGPT significantly and multifacetedly impacts student learning experiences, offering valuable support, enhancing engagement, and shaping positive learning attitudes. However, careful implementation, ethical considerations, and balancing AI support with human guidance are crucial to maximising its benefits in education.

DISCUSSION

The synthesis reveals that ChatGPT's personalised assistance has both positive and negative aspects. On the positive side, ChatGPT enhances student learning experiences by mimicking human-like traits to encourage engagement, creating interactive environments, promoting outperformance, offering virtual peer assistance, providing informative and entertaining content, supporting activities like idea generation, reducing cognitive load, improving the perception of educational support, enhancing critical thinking and task completion efficacy through collaboration, aiding in language acquisition, accelerating learning and motivation, and offering personalised recommendations with prompt responses to boost curiosity and motivation (Aydin & Zeinolabedini, 2024; Ayman et al., 2023; Chan et al., 2023; Li et al., 2024; Dos Santos & Curry, 2023; Silva et al., 2024; Sudirman & Rahimatillah, 2023; Zhang et al., 2023). However, a notable negative impact is the over-reliance on ChatGPT, which can potentially diminish critical and creative thinking skills and raise ethical concerns such as plagiarism (Awal, 2024; Ayman et al., 2023; Khan et al., 2023; Tossell et al., 2024). Empirical evidence suggests that integrating ChatGPT alone may not yield better outcomes, but human oversight and supervision can facilitate enhanced student learning experiences (Tossell et al., 2024).

Interestingly, the positive impacts on students' learning experiences can be understood within the framework of their social-emotional needs. ChatGPT's ability to provide human-like support, such as empathy and relevant responses, significantly increases students' curiosity and motivation, sustains their interest, and provides an enjoyable yet informative learning experience (Abdillah et al., 2023). Students have become comfortable with chatbots, often preferring AI over human assistance because they feel accepted, listened to, empathised with, non-threatened, and non-judged by ChatGPT (Crawford et al., 2024). While it is beneficial to have personalised and customised support at their fingertips, it is concerning that students are increasingly choosing AI over human interaction.

These findings can be interpreted through the theoretical framework of social presence theory to understand how ChatGPT promotes self-paced learning opportunities. Initially conceptualised by Short et al. (1976), social presence theory emphasises the importance of interpersonal relationships in mediated interactions. Gunawardena (1995) refined this concept, defining social presence as the extent to which a person is perceived as a 'real person' in technology-mediated communication. Empirical evidence has shown that social presence significantly influences audience satisfaction in computer-mediated communication, explaining around 60% of the variance (Gunawardena & Zittle, 1997). Similarly, perceived social presence has been found to predict overall learning outcomes in online courses (Richardson & Swan, 2003). This theory is relevant in understanding the connection between ChatGPT and social presence, particularly for students whose learning experiences are enhanced by the integration of ChatGPT.

Figure 2. Mechanism of ChatGPT impacting student learning experiences

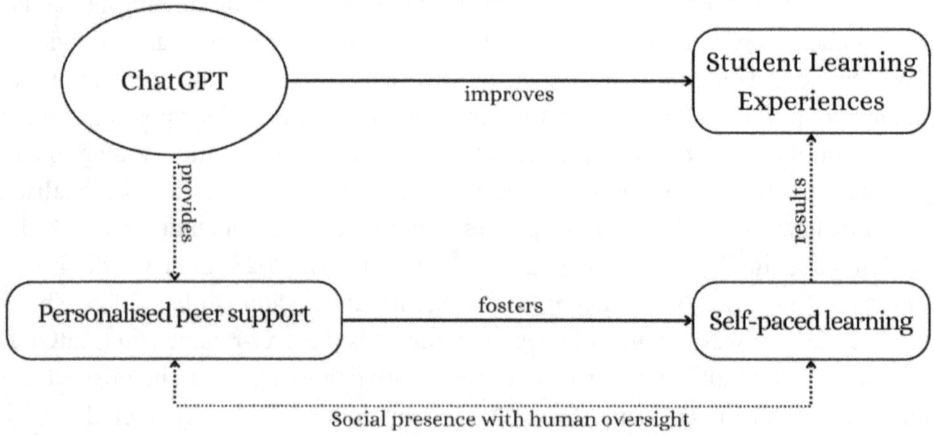

As illustrated in Figure 2, the role of ChatGPT in social presence can be understood through two key elements. Firstly, as an AI language model, ChatGPT engages users through text-based interactions, creating a simulated conversational experience despite lacking physical presence. Secondly, users tend to perceive ChatGPT as a conversational partner, attributing social qualities to it, thereby enhancing the concept of social presence. According to Gunawardena (1995), users' perception of the communication medium as "social" significantly impacts social presence. Students view ChatGPT as a social medium due to its conversational nature, responsiveness, and ability to sustain dialogue, providing personalised peer support with human-like traits such as tone, responsiveness, and conversational flow. When ChatGPT displays attributes like empathy and understanding, users experience heightened social presence, creating an interactive and informative environment. Additionally, students evaluate the quality of interactions with ChatGPT, and meaningful, relevant, and engaging responses contribute to a higher perceived social presence. The anonymity and non-judgmental nature of ChatGPT foster a sense of comfort, reduce social anxiety, and enhance perceived social presence. Its consistent behaviour establishes reliability, akin to interactions with a familiar conversational partner, strengthening social presence. This leads to improved motivation, accelerated learning, and sustained student interest, resulting in enhanced engagement, learning performance, and attitude toward learning.

However, while ChatGPT contributes to social presence, it requires human oversight to ensure a positive impact on student learning experiences. This suggests that while ChatGPT cannot replace human interaction, it can complement it, necessitating a collaborative effort to maximise output quality (Ansari et al., 2025). Educators should acknowledge the reality of AI and integrate it into academic purposes without discouraging its use. Teachers should use ChatGPT as a co-facilitator and supervise its use by students (Ahmad et al., 2024; Bhutta et al., 2025). AI chatbots cannot entirely replace human oversight, especially for students prone to becoming overly reliant on them. Therefore, the responsibility of teachers has not decreased but increased (Ahmad et al., 2024; Ansari et al., 2024). This review confirms previous findings by emphasising that ChatGPT is a convenient tool that promotes a comfortable environment for students but requires human oversight to ensure credibility and maximise output quality.

CONCLUSION

This systematic review examined how ChatGPT, as a generative AI tool, contributes to personalised learning experiences in higher education by synthesising recent empirical literature. The findings demonstrate that ChatGPT positively influences student engagement, learning attitudes, and outcomes through human-like interaction, instant feedback, and tailored support. These contributions align with contemporary pedagogical goals focused on self-paced, adaptive, and student-centred learning. Furthermore, the review illustrates how the concept of social presence plays a vital role in understanding ChatGPT's impact, as students perceive the chatbot as a supportive and empathetic learning partner. This perception enhances motivation, curiosity, and comfort, fostering a conducive environment for personalised learning.

However, the review also reveals several limitations. For instance, restricted access to databases such as Web of Science and ERIC, possibly excluding relevant literature. The review focused only on peer-reviewed studies published in English between 2022 and 2024 and specifically on ChatGPT, which limits the generalisability of findings across broader AI tools, languages, and contexts. Additionally, the absence of a meta-analytical approach due to the qualitative nature of most included studies restricts the ability to derive statistical generalisations. Disciplinary variations in the use and effectiveness of ChatGPT were also not deeply explored, indicating a need for more in-depth investigations.

Despite these limitations, this review contributes to a growing body of knowledge on AI in education and provides practical insights. Educators are encouraged to integrate ChatGPT as a pedagogical co-facilitator, ensuring students are guided to use it ethically and critically. Institutions should develop support structures, policies, and professional development to promote the responsible use of AI. Future research should explore longitudinal and cross-disciplinary effects of AI chatbots, particularly in underrepresented educational contexts, and examine how they can be equitably integrated into diverse learning environments. With thoughtful integration and human oversight, ChatGPT holds significant potential to enrich higher education by fostering more responsive, personalised, and engaging learning experiences.

FUNDING

This systematic review received no specific grant from any funding agency in the public, commercial, or not-for-profit sectors.

REFERENCES

Abdillah, H. Z., Partino, P., & Madjid, A. (2023). Enhancing student well-being through AI ChatGPT in the smart education university learning environment: A preliminary review of research literature. In *E3S Web of Conferences* (Vol. 440, p. 05005). EDP Sciences.

Ahmad, S., Ahmed, A., Bhutta, S. M., & Ansari, A. N. (2024). Transforming teaching learning with chatbots in higher education: Quest, opportunities and challenges for quality enhancement. In *The evolution of artificial intelligence in higher education* (pp. 111–127). IGI Global Scientific Publishing.

Ajlouni, A. O., Wahba, F. A. A., & Almahaireh, A. S. (2023). Students' attitudes towards using ChatGPT as a learning tool: The case of the University of Jordan. *International Journal of Interactive Mobile Technologies*, *17*(18), 18.

Al Shloul, T., Mazhar, T., Iqbal, M., Yaseen Ghadi, Y., Malik, F., & Hamam, H. (2024). Role of activity-based learning and ChatGPT on students' performance in education. *Computers and Education: Artificial Intelligence*, *5*, 100219.

AlAli, R., & Wardat, Y. (2024). How ChatGPT will shape the teaching learning landscape in future. *Journal of Educational and Social Research*, *14*(2), 336–345.

Albayrak, N., Özdemir, A., & Zeydan, E. (2018, May). An overview of artificial intelligence based chatbots and an example chatbot application. In 2018 26th Signal Processing and Communications Applications Conference (SIU) (pp. 1–4). IEEE.

Alneyadi, S., & Wardat, Y. (2023). ChatGPT: Revolutionizing student achievement in the electronic magnetism unit for eleventh-grade students in Emirates schools. *Contemporary Educational Technology*, *15*(4), ep448.

Ansari, A. N., Ahmad, S., & Bhutta, S. M. (2024). Mapping the global evidence around the use of ChatGPT in higher education: A systematic scoping review. *Education and Information Technologies*, *29*(9), 11281–11321.

Ansari, A. N., Ahmad, S., & Bhutta, S. M. (2026). Use of ChatGPT in Higher Education: Development and Validation of Questionnaire. In *The Intersection of AI and Student Development in Learning* (pp. 377–402). IGI Global Scientific Publishing.

Ansari, A. N., Panjwani, F., Ahmad, S., & Bhutta, S. M. (2025). Malaise of Artificial Intelligence in Education: A reflective stance. In *Examining AI Disruption in Educational Settings: Challenges and Opportunities* (pp. 359-380). IGI Global Scientific Publishing.

Awal, M. R. (2024). *Curse or blessing? Students' experience from ChatGPT with an application of Colaizzi's phenomenological descriptive method of enquiry and content analysis*. Higher Education, Skills and Work-Based Learning., DOI: 10.1108/HESWBL-12-2023-0120

Aydin, S., & Zeinolabedini, M. (2024). *Integrating artificial intelligence into foreign language learning: Learners' perspectives*. Online Submission.

Ayman, S. E., El-Seoud, S. A., Nagaty, K., & Karam, O. H. (2023). The influence of ChatGPT on student learning and academic performance. In *2023 International Conference on Computer and Applications (ICCA)* (pp. 1–5). IEEE.

Bhutta, S. M., Ahmad, S., Ansari, A. N., Ahmed, A., & Ali, K. Q. (2025). Exploring knowledge, will, skills, technological support, and use of ChatGPT in higher education: A cross-sectional survey. In *AI adoption and diffusion in education* (pp. 359–382). IGI Global Scientific Publishing.

Chan, M. M., Amado-Salvatierra, H. R., Hernandez-Rizzardini, R., & De La Roca, M. (2023). The potential role of AI-based chatbots in engineering education: Experiences from a teaching perspective. In 2023 IEEE Frontiers in Education Conference (FIE) (pp. 1–5). IEEE.

Crawford, J., Allen, K. A., Pani, B., & Cowling, M. (2024). When artificial intelligence substitutes humans in higher education: The cost of loneliness, student success, and retention. *Studies in Higher Education*, •••, 1–15.

Dos Santos, O. L., & Cury, D. (2023, October). Challenging the confirmation bias: Using ChatGPT as a virtual peer for peer instruction in computer programming education. In 2023 IEEE Frontiers in Education Conference (FIE) (pp. 1–7). IEEE.

Duong, C. D., Vu, T. N., & Ngo, T. V. N. (2023). Applying a modified technology acceptance model to explain higher education students' usage of ChatGPT: A serial multiple mediation model with knowledge sharing as a moderator. *International Journal of Management Education*, *21*(3), 100883.

Gao, L., López-Pérez, M. E., Melero-Polo, I., & Trifu, A. (2024). Ask ChatGPT first! Transforming learning experiences in the age of artificial intelligence. *Studies in Higher Education*, •••, 1–25.

Goar, V., Yadav, N. S., & Yadav, P. S. (2023). Conversational AI for natural language processing: A review of ChatGPT. *International Journal on Recent and Innovation Trends in Computing and Communication*, *11*, 109–117.

Guarda, T., & Augusto, M. F. (2021). Chatbots and business strategy. In *International Conference on Innovations in Bio-Inspired Computing and Applications* (pp. 557–566). Springer International Publishing.

Gunawardena, C. N. (1995). Social presence theory and implications for interaction and collaborative learning in computer conferences. *International Journal of Educational Telecommunications*, *1*(2), 147–166.

Gunawardena, C. N., & Zittle, F. J. (1997). Social presence as a predictor of satisfaction within a computer-mediated conferencing environment. *American Journal of Distance Education*, *11*(3), 8–26.

Karakose, T., & Tülübas, T. (2023). How can ChatGPT facilitate teaching and learning: Implications for contemporary education. *Educational Process: International Journal*, *12*(4), 7–16.

Karataş, F., Abedi, F. Y., Ozek Gunyel, F., Karadeniz, D., & Kuzgun, Y. (2024). Incorporating AI in foreign language education: An investigation into ChatGPT's effect on foreign language learners. *Education and Information Technologies*, •••, 1–24.

Khan, M. M. R. R., Habib, S. B., Tasnim, S. T., & Islam, M. A. (2023). Educational AI and ethical growth: Exploring the effects of ChatGPT on student learning strategies, critical thinking, and academic ethics from a Bangladeshi academic perspective. In 2023 26th International Conference on Computer and Information Technology (ICCIT) (pp. 1–6). IEEE.

Kosar, T., Ostojić, D., Liu, Y. D., & Mernik, M. (2024). Computer science education in ChatGPT era: Experiences from an experiment in a programming course for novice programmers. *Mathematics*, *12*(5), 629.

Li, T., Ji, Y., & Zhan, Z. (2024). Expert or machine? Comparing the effect of pairing student teacher with in-service teacher and ChatGPT on their critical thinking, learning performance, and cognitive load in an integrated-STEM course. *Asia Pacific Journal of Education*, •••, 1–16.

Newman, M., & Gough, D. (2020). *Systematic reviews in educational research: Methodology, perspectives and application*. Springer.

Niranjanamurthy, M., Kantharaju, V., Satish, S., Umashankar, N., & Raviram, V. (2023). Chat generative pretrained transformer (ChatGPT) for data analysis. In 2023 3rd International Conference on Mobile Networks and Wireless Communications (ICMNWC) (pp. 1–6). IEEE.

Qawqzeh, Y. (2024). Exploring the influence of student interaction with ChatGPT on critical thinking, problem solving, and creativity. *International Journal of Information and Education Technology (IJIET)*, *14*(4), 317–324.

Rawat, S., Mittal, S., Nehra, D., Sharma, C., & Kamboj, D. (2023). Exploring the potential of ChatGPT to improve experiential learning in education. In *Proceedings of the 5th International Conference on Information Management & Machine Intelligence* (pp. 1–8).

Richardson, J. C., & Swan, K. (2003). Examining social presence in online courses in relation to students' perceived learning and satisfaction. *Journal of Asynchronous Learning*, *7*(1), 68–88.

Sallam, M., Salim, N. A., Barakat, M., & Ala'a, B. (2023). ChatGPT applications in medical, dental, pharmacy, and public health education: A descriptive study highlighting the advantages and limitations. *Narra J*, *3*(1). PMID: 38450035

Sanfilippo, F., Tigano, S., Palumbo, G. J., Astuto, M., & Murabito, P. (2020). Importance of inclusion criteria in systematic reviews. *British Journal of Anaesthesia*, *125*(5), e398–e399. PMID: 32739043

Short, J., Williams, E., & Christie, B. (1976). *The social psychology of telecommunications*. John Wiley & Sons.

Shoufan, A. (2023). Exploring students' perceptions of ChatGPT: Thematic analysis and follow-up survey. *IEEE Access : Practical Innovations, Open Solutions*.

Silva, C. A. G. D., Ramos, F. N., de Moraes, R. V., & Santos, E. L. D. (2024). ChatGPT: Challenges and benefits in software programming for higher education. *Sustainability*, *16*(3), 1245.

Singh, S., & Thakur, H. K. (2020, June). Survey of various AI chatbots based on technology used. In 2020 8th International Conference on Reliability, Infocom Technologies and Optimization (Trends and Future Directions) (ICRITO) (pp. 1074–1079). IEEE.

Sudirman, I. D., & Rahmatillah, I. (2023, June). Artificial intelligence-assisted discovery learning: An educational experience for entrepreneurship students using ChatGPT. In 2023 IEEE World AI IoT Congress (AIIoT) (pp. 786–791). IEEE.

Tabib, F. M., & Alrabeei, M. M. (2024). Can guided ChatGPT use enhance students' cognitive and metacognitive skills? In *Artificial intelligence in education: The power and dangers of ChatGPT in the classroom* (pp. 143–154). Springer Nature Switzerland.

Thomas, J., & Harden, A. (2008). Methods for the thematic synthesis of qualitative research in systematic reviews. *BMC Medical Research Methodology*, *8*, 45. PMID: 18616818

Tossell, C. C., Tenhundfeld, N. L., Momen, A., Cooley, K., & de Visser, E. J. (2024). Student perceptions of ChatGPT use in a college essay assignment: Implications for learning, grading, and trust in artificial intelligence. *IEEE Transactions on Learning Technologies*.

Valova, I., Mladenova, T., & Kanev, G. (2024). Students' perception of ChatGPT usage in education. *International Journal of Advanced Computer Science and Applications*, *15*(1), 1–10.

Weizenbaum, J. (1966). ELIZA—A computer program for the study of natural language communication between man and machine. *Communications of the ACM*, *9*(1), 36–45.

Xie, X., & Ding, S. (2023, September). Opportunities, challenges, strategies, and reforms for ChatGPT in higher education. In *2023 International Conference on Educational Knowledge and Informatization (EKI)* (pp. 14–18). IEEE Computer Society.

Xu, X., Wang, X., Zhang, Y., & Ma, W. (2023). *Can ChatGPT facilitate the implementation of personal learning environments in tertiary education: Benefits and risks*. International Society for Technology, Education, and Science.

Zhang, Y., Viriyavejakul, C., & Sumettikoon, P. (2023). Integrating chatbots in educational administration for improved language learning outcomes. *Eurasian Journal of Educational Research*, *104*(104), 142–159.

Chapter 6
Challenges and Opportunities in AI-Human Collaborative Teaching

Pankaj Bhanudas Vaishnav
https://orcid.org/0009-0005-3542-2427
Al Seeb Vocational College, Muscat, Oman

ABSTRACT

This chapter highlights the transformative role of artificial intelligence (AI) in education, focusing on its impact on teaching methodologies, assessment strategies, and student engagement. AI-driven adaptive learning platforms personalize education by analyzing student performance and tailoring content to individual needs. Additionally, AI assists educators by automating administrative tasks, enabling data-driven instruction, and identifying learning gaps. However, ethical concerns such as bias in AI algorithms, student data privacy, and transparency in AI decision-making must be addressed. The chapter also explores compliance with legal frameworks, including the General Data Protection Regulation (GDPR), the Family Educational Rights and Privacy Act (FERPA), and intellectual property laws, which are crucial for ensuring responsible AI use in education. The legal complexities surrounding AI-generated content ownership and liability in AI malfunctions further necessitate the establishment of clear policies and risk management strategies. Moreover, AI's integration requires pedagogical adaptations, ensuring that AI complements human instruction rather than replacing it. Blended learning models, AI-augmented teacher roles, and gamified learning environments are examined as strategies to promote student-centered education while preserving the essential human connection in

DOI: 10.4018/979-8-3373-3000-6.ch006

teaching. To fully harness AI's potential; institutions must adopt ethical guidelines, provide professional development for educators, and establish regulatory measures that balance innovation with accountability.

1. INTRODUCTION

Artificial Intelligence (AI) is transforming education, reshaping traditional teaching methodologies, and enhancing student engagement in unprecedented ways. The integration of AI in classrooms is not merely a technological upgrade but a paradigm shift that redefines the roles of educators and learners. AI is taking over a great deal of what has previously been viewed as the human domain (Luckin, 2018: 137). It is particularly seen in areas such as grading and assessment, routine administrative communication, and even aspects of mentoring and personalized feedback. These shifts illustrate how AI is emerging not just a supportive tool but an active agent influencing both instructional practices and the teacher–student relationship.

In this context, AI-human collaborative teaching refers to a pedagogical model in which artificial intelligence systems and human educators work together in a complementary manner, rather than one replacing the other. Porayska-Pomsta et al. (2024) observe that in this model, artificial intelligence functions as an augmentative partner rather than a substitute for human educators. It enables a division of labor where routine and data-driven tasks are automated while teachers focus on creativity, critical thinking, and personalized support. AI-driven collaboration positions the technology as a supportive assistant to teachers while keeping some space for emotional engagement and creativity. For instance, an adaptive platform such as Carnegie Learning's MATHia provides students with tailored practice problems and real-time feedback, while the teacher uses the analytics generated by the system to identify struggling learners and design targeted interventions. This division of labor exemplifies collaboration—AI amplifies efficiency, and the human teacher sustains relational and cognitive depth. This chapter explores the challenges and opportunities associated with this evolving collaboration, considering ethical, legal, and pedagogical dimensions.

AI's role in education spans multiple domains, including personalized learning, automated assessment, and intelligent tutoring systems. Numerous applications of AI in education (AIED) have emerged, delivering support and intelligent feedback across various subjects (Wang et al., 2024). Adaptive learning technologies powered by AI analyze student performance and tailor instruction to individual needs and fosters a more inclusive learning environment. AI-driven analytics assist educators in identifying students' strengths and weaknesses, enabling timely interventions.

Furthermore, AI-powered chatbots and virtual assistants provide students with real-time support, bridging the gap between traditional instruction and digital learning.

Despite these advancements, the integration of AI in education raises critical ethical considerations. The use of AI in classrooms necessitates careful scrutiny of data privacy and security, ensuring that student information remains protected. AI systems may inadvertently reinforce biases present in training data, leading to unfair assessments or discriminatory outcomes. The ethical deployment of AI in teaching, therefore, requires transparency, accountability, and continuous monitoring to mitigate potential biases and uphold educational equity.

Legal implications also play a significant role in the adoption of AI-driven educational technologies. Governments and institutions must establish regulatory frameworks that govern AI's use in classrooms, ensuring compliance with data protection laws and ethical guidelines. Issues such as intellectual property rights, liability in AI-assisted decision-making, and the legal responsibilities of AI developers and educators must be addressed to create a legally sound educational ecosystem. It requires a systematic approach that takes into account societal structural conditions (Walter, 2024). From a pedagogical perspective, AI-human collaborative teaching demands a reevaluation of instructional strategies. Educators must adapt to an AI-enhanced learning environment, leveraging AI tools while maintaining the human touch essential for cognitive and socio-emotional development. Effective AI integration requires educators to develop new skill sets, including digital literacy and data interpretation, to maximize AI's potential without compromising the human elements of teaching.

Looking ahead, AI's role in education is poised for further innovation, presenting both opportunities and challenges. Luckin (2025) describes it as the early stages of the fourth industrial revolution which is happening all around us. AI-human collaboration can potentially lead to sustainable and scalable educational models that enhance learning experiences globally. However, ensuring the responsible development and deployment of AI technologies in education will be crucial in shaping a future where AI serves as an ally rather than a disruptor. This chapter aims to provide a comprehensive analysis of these dimensions, offering insights into the evolving landscape of AI-human collaborative teaching and its implications for the future of education.

1.2 Objectives of the Chapter

The primary aim of this chapter is to investigate the implications of AI-human collaboration in teaching and learning. The discussion will highlight the following objectives:

1. **Understanding AI's Role in Education**: Analyzing AI's functions in enhancing instruction, assessment, and student engagement.
2. **Ethical Considerations**: Addressing privacy, bias, and ethical concerns related to AI in classrooms.
3. **Legal Implications**: Exploring legal frameworks governing AI deployment in educational institutions.
4. **Pedagogical Adaptations**: Examining new instructional strategies for AI-human collaborative teaching.

Considering these objectives, it is essential to begin by mapping AI's current functions in education. A clear understanding of its role in instruction, assessment, and engagement establishes the groundwork for addressing the ethical, legal, and pedagogical dimensions that follow. Section 2 therefore introduces AI's role as the foundation for the chapter's broader analysis.

2. UNDERSTANDING AI'S ROLE IN EDUCATION

AI has been progressively integrated into the education sector, offering various benefits across instructional design, assessment methodologies, and student engagement. This section explores how AI enhances instruction through intelligent tutoring systems, machine learning-driven personalization, and content generation tools.

2. 1. Instructional Enhancement

One of the most significant contributions of AI to education is instructional enhancement. AI-driven platforms provide personalized and adaptive learning experiences tailored to individual student needs. These technologies help bridge learning gaps, cater to diverse learning styles, and improve overall educational outcomes. However, overreliance on adaptive systems may also create challenges, such as reducing students' ability to develop independent learning strategies or fostering dependency on algorithmic guidance. Addressing these concerns requires careful integration of AI tools in ways that complement, rather than replace, human-led instruction.

2.1.1 Intelligent Tutoring Systems (ITS)

AI-driven Intelligent Tutoring Systems (ITS) serve as virtual tutors that adapt to students' learning paces. Clugston (2024) states that these systems use real-time data analytics to assess student performance and provide customized feedback.

For instance, Carnegie Learning's MATHia is an AI-powered ITS that helps students grasp complex mathematical concepts by offering real-time assistance and personalized learning paths. Similarly, platforms like Squirrel AI in China analyze students' strengths and weaknesses, modifying lesson plans dynamically to ensure optimal comprehension.

2.1.2 Personalized Learning through Machine Learning

Machine learning algorithms enable personalized learning by analyzing students' behavioral data, including response times, accuracy, and engagement levels. AI-driven platforms like DreamBox Learning adapt in real-time, ensuring that each student receives content appropriate to their skill level. For example, if a student struggles with algebraic expressions, the system can provide additional practice exercises or alternative explanations tailored to their specific needs. Fitria (2021: 140) observes that AI technology has a significant impact in improving the quality and learning patterns to be more practical and effective. This type of adaptive learning fosters individualized instruction, reducing the one-size-fits-all approach that traditional education often employs.

2.1.3 AI-Powered Content Generation

AI has revolutionized content creation in education by assisting educators in developing dynamic and adaptive curricula. Tools such as Knewton's Alta and Coursera's AI-powered course design help instructors generate customized course materials based on student performance data. These platforms analyze educational content and provide recommendations for instructional adjustments. AI-generated content can range from quizzes and interactive simulations to comprehensive lesson plans, ensuring that educators can focus on teaching rather than spending excessive time on content development.

2.1.4 Real-World Applications and Success Stories

Artificial Intelligence (AI) has significantly transformed instructional methodologies by providing innovative solutions to learning experiences. Several real-world applications demonstrate AI's effectiveness in personalizing education, streamlining teaching efforts, and improving student engagement.

Duolingo: AI-Driven Personalized Language Learning Duolingo, a widely used language-learning application, integrates AI to tailor lessons according to users' proficiency levels. The platform employs machine learning algorithms to analyze user responses, predict potential errors, and provide personalized feedback. Through adaptive learning technology, Duolingo ensures that each learner progresses at an optimal pace, reinforcing concepts they struggle with and introducing new material as they advance. Research by Jiang et al.(2024) indicates that AI-driven personalization in language learning platforms like Duolingo enhances retention rates and overall engagement.

Quillionz: AI-Assisted Assessment Creation Quillionz, an AI-based question generator, supports educators by automating the process of quiz and assessment creation. By leveraging Natural Language Processing (NLP), the platform scans inputted content and generates multiple-choice questions, short-answer prompts, and discussion topics. This tool not only saves educators' valuable time but also ensures that assessments align with key learning objectives. According to Nguyen et al.(2024), AI-powered question generation tools like Quillionz improve the efficiency and consistency of formative assessments, allowing teachers to focus more on instructional delivery.

Google's Socratic: AI-Enhanced Academic Assistance Google's Socratic app leverages AI to assist students in understanding academic subjects through visual and text-based explanations. By using image recognition and NLP, the app scans homework questions and provides step-by-step solutions along with relevant learning resources. Socratic's AI model identifies key concepts and retrieves curated content, making learning more interactive and accessible. A study by Yanuarto et al.(2021) highlights how AI-powered tutoring applications like Socratic contribute to improved comprehension and independent learning among students.

Taken together, these examples reveal both the diversity and commonality of AI applications in education. While Duolingo emphasizes personalized pacing, Quillionz streamlines assessment design, and Socratic enhances academic support, they all share a commitment to improving accessibility, efficiency, and learner autonomy. The similarities highlight AI's role in reducing repetitive tasks for educators and offering adaptive, learner-centered pathways. At the same time, their differences point toward a future where AI tools may increasingly specialize—some focusing on language acquisition, others on instructional support, and others on real-time academic assistance. These trends suggest that the future of AI in education lies not in a single dominant platform but in a collaborative ecosystem of tools that collectively redefine the teaching–learning process. The continued evolution of AI presents boundless opportunities, but it also necessitates careful consideration of ethical, legal, and pedagogical challenges, which will be explored further in this chapter.

Table 1. Comparative Analysis of AI Tools in Education

Tool	Primary Function	Strengths	Limitations	Future Implications
Duolingo	Personalized language learning	Adaptive pacing, gamification, improved retention	May encourage surface-level learning if not supplemented by deeper practice	AI will expand adaptive strategies across subjects, not just language learning
Quillionz	Automated quiz and assessment creation	Saves time, aligns with learning objectives, ensures consistency	Limited creativity in question generation	Future tools may blend automation with teacher creativity for richer assessments
Socratic	Academic assistance and homework help	Step-by-step explanations, resource curation, supports independent learning	Risk of overreliance, reduced critical thinking	Future AI tutors may become real-time study companions, guiding but not replacing human reasoning

Thus, AI in education cannot be understood solely as a set of technical solutions; it must be critically assessed for how it reshapes learning dynamics, redistributes authority between teacher, student, and algorithm, and influences long-term educational equity.

2.2 Assessment Innovations

Assessment is a crucial component of the educational process, and AI has introduced several innovations that improve efficiency, accuracy, and fairness in student evaluations.

2.2.1 Automated Grading Systems

AI-driven automated grading systems have significantly reduced the administrative burden on educators. Tools like Gradescope and Turnitin employ machine learning algorithms to assess student responses, providing immediate feedback on assignments and exams. Automated grading is particularly effective for multiple-choice tests, but advancements in natural language processing (NLP) allow AI to evaluate essays and open-ended responses. For example, the EdX platform's AI-based grading system can assess student essays with remarkable accuracy, offering insights into writing quality, grammar, and coherence. Research by Gnanaprakasam & Lourdusamy (2024) suggests that AI-based grading enhances consistency and reduces grading bias, ensuring fair evaluation across diverse student submissions. Furthermore, AI-enhanced grading systems provide real-time feedback, allowing students to identify areas for improvement promptly. Studies indicate that students who receive AI-generated feedback on writing assignments demonstrate improved performance over time, as they can refine their work based on objective, data-driven suggestions. This approach supports formative assessment practices, fostering continuous learning and skill development. As AI continues to evolve, automated grading solutions are expected to further enhance their accuracy and adaptability, contributing to a more efficient and equitable assessment process.

Despite these advantages, concerns remain regarding the accuracy and reliability of AI-driven grading. Several studies highlight that while AI performs well on structured tasks, it may struggle with nuanced or creative responses, sometimes penalizing unconventional but valid arguments (Liu & Kunnan, 2016; Wetzler et al., 2025). Critics also point out the "black box" nature of algorithmic grading, where teachers and students may not fully understand how scores are generated, raising questions of transparency and trust. Moreover, overreliance on automated grading risks marginalizing the role of human judgment in evaluating critical thinking, originality, and cultural context in student work. As AI continues to evolve, automated grading solutions are expected to improve in accuracy and adaptability, but their effective use will depend on combining algorithmic efficiency with human oversight. This hybrid approach can ensure that assessments remain both equitable and pedagogically meaningful.

2.2.2 Predictive Analytics for Student Performance

AI-driven predictive analytics play a pivotal role in assessing student performance trends and identifying those at risk of falling behind. Platforms like IBM Watson Education analyze past academic performance, attendance records, and engagement levels to forecast potential challenges students may face. These insights enable educators to implement early intervention strategies, such as personalized tutoring or targeted support, to improve learning outcomes. Research by Bird (2023) highlights that predictive analytics systems have helped institutions reduce dropout rates and enhance student retention by providing timely academic assistance.

As AI continues to evolve, automated grading and predictive analytics solutions are expected to further enhance their accuracy and adaptability, contributing to a more efficient and equitable assessment process.

2.2.3 AI-Based Proctoring Systems

With the rise of online learning, maintaining assessment integrity has become a significant concern. AI-based proctoring systems, such as Proctorio and Examity, use facial recognition, eye-tracking, and behavioral analysis to monitor students during online exams. These systems detect suspicious activities, such as looking away from the screen or unauthorized materials, and flag potential violations for human review. Research by Gudiño Paredes et al. (2021) suggests that AI proctoring solutions significantly reduce instances of academic dishonesty while streamlining remote assessment security. However, perspectives from students and faculty reveal a more complex picture. Many students report feeling that constant monitoring is intrusive and anxiety-inducing, leading to heightened stress during exams (Woldeab & Brothen, 2021). Faculty members, too, have expressed concern that proctoring software may erode trust in the teacher–student relationship and shift the focus from learning to surveillance (Johri & Hingle, 2023). Moreover, privacy concerns remain significant, with critics pointing out the risks of storing sensitive biometric data and the potential for bias in facial recognition algorithms to unfairly disadvantage students from diverse backgrounds.

While AI-proctored exams offer enhanced security, concerns about privacy and potential biases in facial recognition algorithms necessitate careful implementation and oversight. Ethical considerations, such as data security and algorithmic fairness, remain key areas of discussion in AI-driven proctoring. Lim et al. (2023) advocate for a balanced approach that incorporates human oversight alongside AI monitoring that can ensure both integrity and fairness in remote assessments. As AI continues to evolve, automated grading, predictive analytics, and AI-based proctoring solutions are expected to further enhance their accuracy and adaptability, contributing to a more efficient and equitable assessment process.

2.2.4 Real-World Applications and Success Stories

Artificial intelligence (AI) has been increasingly integrated into educational assessment tools, leading to enhanced personalized learning experiences and improved educational outcomes. Several institutions and ed-tech companies have successfully implemented AI-driven assessment solutions:

Pearson's AI-Driven Assessment Tools

Pearson has developed AI-powered study tools that provide personalized support to students. These tools leverage generative AI alongside Pearson's vetted content to offer individualized practice and feedback, helping students master key course concepts. During beta tests in the fall of 2023, tens of thousands of students engaged with these tools, reporting strong levels of engagement and positive feedback (Pearson, 2024). Additionally, Pearson introduced an AI tool for instructors to efficiently create personalized assignments. Integrated into Pearson's MyLab and Mastering platforms, this tool assists educators in designing courses, assigning homework, and monitoring student progress in real-time, thereby enhancing teaching effectiveness.

Likewise, Carnegie Learning has implemented an adaptive learning program that utilizes AI algorithms to assess students' knowledge gaps in mathematics (Techflow, 2022). By providing targeted instruction based on individual needs, this program has demonstrated significant improvements in students' math proficiency and problem-solving skills.

Project LISTEN's Reading Tutor

Project LISTEN, a research initiative at Carnegie Mellon University, developed the Reading Tutor - a computer-based system that listens to children read aloud. The tutor corrects errors, offers assistance with difficult words, provides hints, assesses progress, and presents more advanced text as the child improves. Field tests in schools across the United States, Canada, Ghana, and India have shown that the Reading Tutor effectively supports the development of reading skills in children.

2.2.5 AI Integration in Business Education

The University of Toronto's Rotman School of Management implemented an AI assistant called All Day TA, designed by professors Joshua Gans and Kevin Bryan (Murray, 2025). This AI tool successfully handled 12,000 student queries over a semester, demonstrating AI's potential to enhance educational experiences by providing instant support and feedback. The tool has since been adopted by approximately 100 universities world.

AI-Powered Chatbots in Catholic Education

Brisbane Catholic Education (BCE) launched the Catholic CoPilot chatbot across 146 schools. Designed to filter lessons through a religious lens, this AI-driven tool assists in preparing lesson plans, marking assignments, and writing report cards, potentially saving teachers nearly 10 hours per week. The chatbot draws from BCE's curriculum and approved Catholic resources, providing tailored answers that align with the institution's educational values. These examples illustrate the diverse applications of AI-driven assessment tools in education, highlighting their potential to personalize learning, provide immediate feedback, and support educators in delivering effective instruction.

China's national education system has increasingly integrated artificial intelligence (AI) to enhance educational processes, including the grading of student assignments. This integration aims to alleviate teacher workloads and improve grading consistency across the country. As of 2018, approximately 60,000 schools in China—accounting for one in every four schools—have been testing AI-driven systems capable of automatically grading student essays and assignments. These systems utilize machine learning algorithms to assess the general logic and meaning of students' work, offering suggestions for improvement where necessary. The AI's evaluations have shown a high degree of agreement with human graders, aligning 92% of the time in a test involving 120 million participants (Wiggers, 2018).

2.2.6 Benefits of AI Integration

The adoption of AI in grading has led to several notable advantages:

- **Efficiency**: Automated grading systems significantly reduce the time required to evaluate large volumes of student work. It also allows teachers to focus more on instructional activities.
- **Consistency**: AI algorithms apply uniform criteria when assessing assignments and minimize the subjectivity and potential biases associated with human grading.
- **Personalized Feedback**: Advanced AI systems can provide tailored feedback to students, identifying specific areas for improvement and facilitating targeted learning interventions.

2.2.7 Case Study: Squirrel AI Learning

Squirrel AI Learning, an educational technology company in China, has developed an Intelligent Adaptive Learning System (IALS) that employs AI to customize lessons, practice sessions, and evaluations for individual students. By breaking down subjects into thousands of "knowledge points," the system identifies and addresses specific learning gaps. As of 2019, Squirrel AI Learning had opened 2,000 learning centers across 200 cities, serving over a million students in Asia (Elliott, 2024). The integration of AI-powered grading tools within China's education system exemplifies a significant shift towards leveraging technology to enhance educational outcomes. By automating routine tasks such as grading, educators can allocate more time to personalized instruction, ultimately benefiting student learning experiences. For a visual overview of how AI is transforming education in China, you might find the following video informative:

By leveraging AI for assessment innovations, educators can streamline grading processes, identify struggling students early, and maintain academic integrity in online learning environments. However, these advancements must be implemented with ethical considerations to ensure fairness, privacy, and inclusivity in education.

2.3 Student Engagement

Artificial Intelligence (AI) has become instrumental in enhancing student engagement by offering interactive and adaptive learning experiences. One notable application is the use of AI-driven chatbots, which provide instant support and personalized learning opportunities to students.

2.3.1 AI-Driven Chatbots for Instant Support

AI-powered chatbots, such as IBM's Watson Assistant and Duolingo's AI tutor, offer students immediate feedback and assistance. These chatbots can answer queries, clarify doubts, and guide learners through educational modules, ensuring continuous engagement. For instance, Arizona State University implemented an AI chatbot named "Sunny" to assist students with course-related questions, significantly improving response times and student satisfaction. Research has demonstrated the positive impact of AI chatbots on student engagement and learning outcomes. A systematic literature review by Labadze et al.(2023) identified that students benefit from AI-powered chatbots in three key areas: homework and study assistance, personalized learning experiences, and skill development. Similarly, a meta-analysis by Wu & Yu (2024) found that AI chatbots have a substantial effect on students' learning outcomes, with more pronounced effects observed in higher education settings.

Furthermore, a study by Bimpong (2025) explored the impact of generative AI educational chatbots on the academic support experiences of international students in U.S. research universities. The findings suggest that these chatbots enhance academic performance and engagement among international students. AI-driven chatbots play a crucial role in enhancing student engagement by providing instant support, personalized learning experiences, and fostering skill development, thereby contributing positively to educational outcomes.

At the same time, questions of accessibility and inclusivity remain central. While many chatbots can provide multilingual support, studies show that less commonly spoken languages are often underserved, limiting inclusivity in diverse classrooms (Okonkwo & Ade-Ibijola, 2021). Furthermore, accessibility for differently-abled learners is inconsistent: some chatbots integrate with screen readers and voice assistants, while others pose barriers for visually impaired or neurodiverse students (Lin et al., 2024). This reflects a broader concern that without universal design principles, AI chatbots risk reinforcing educational inequalities rather than reducing them.

Therefore, while AI-driven chatbots represent a powerful tool for personalized, on-demand student support, their deployment should be accompanied by intentional strategies to enhance linguistic diversity, accessibility, and inclusivity. Doing so ensures that such technologies do not merely scale efficiency but also uphold equity in learning environments.

2.3.2 Gamification with AI

Artificial Intelligence (AI) significantly enhances gamification techniques in education, making learning more interactive and motivating. Platforms like Kahoot!, Quizizz, and Prodigy utilize AI to adapt educational content to students' progress, ensuring a balanced level of challenge and reward. By adjusting difficulty levels in real-time and personalizing feedback, AI-driven gamification sustains learner motivation while preventing disengagement from overly repetitive or overly complex tasks.

Beyond entertainment, gamification serves broader educational objectives. Research indicates that AI-supported gamified environments stimulate intrinsic motivation by fostering a sense of achievement, competition, and progress (Alabbasi, 2017). They also align closely with formative assessment practices, as game-based systems provide immediate feedback and allow teachers to monitor performance trends at both individual and group levels. In this way, gamification becomes not only a tool for engagement but also a pedagogical strategy to reinforce learning outcomes, support mastery learning, and encourage self-regulated study behaviors.

AI Integration in Gamified Learning Platforms

- **Kahoot!:** This platform allows educators to create interactive quizzes and games. Recent developments include AI-powered quiz builders that enable teachers to generate quizzes instantly from a topic or website, streamlining the content creation process.
- **Quizizz:** Quizizz offers gamified quizzes where AI algorithms analyze student responses to adjust the difficulty of subsequent questions, providing a personalized learning experience. This adaptability helps maintain student engagement by offering appropriate challenges.
- **Prodigy:** Prodigy is an educational platform that incorporates AI to personalize learning experiences. It analyzes student responses and adjusts difficulty levels to keep learners engaged without causing frustration. Research indicates that students who used Prodigy regularly saw significantly greater improvements in math scores compared to those who did not use the platform.

2.3.3 Impact on Student Motivation and Engagement

Studies have shown that the use of gamified learning platforms positively impacts student motivation and engagement. España-Delgado (2023) carried out a mixed-method study to investigate students' perceptions regarding the implementation of game-based learning platforms like Kahoot!, Quizizz, and Quizalize during virtual English as a Foreign Language (EFL) classes. The study found that these platforms enhanced students' motivation toward language learning.

The integration of AI in gamification platforms such as Kahoot!, Quizizz, and Prodigy has transformed educational experiences by making learning more interactive and tailored to individual student needs. This personalization not only sustains student engagement but also contributes to improved learning outcomes.

AI enhances gamification techniques in education, making learning more interactive and motivating. Platforms like Kahoot! and Quizizz use AI to adapt quizzes to students' progress, ensuring a balanced level of challenge and reward. Similarly, AI-driven educational games, such as those on the Prodigy platform, analyze student responses and adjust difficulty levels to keep learners engaged without causing frustration.

2.4 Adaptive Learning Tools for Personalized Engagement

Adaptive learning platforms, such as Smart Sparrow and Kidaptive, play a pivotal role in personalizing educational experiences by tailoring lesson difficulty to individual learning paces (Contrino et al., 2024). This approach ensures that students are appropriately challenged without feeling overwhelmed, thereby enhancing motivation and retention rates.

2.4.1 Smart Sparrow

Smart Sparrow's Adaptive eLearning Platform enables educators to create interactive and adaptive online resources that provide instant, personalized feedback to students. Barclay et al. (2020), performed a study involving the implementation of "Smart Quizzes" using Smart Sparrow's platform which demonstrated that 81% of students achieved mastery across all modules by successfully answering all assessment questions. These quizzes adapted in real-time to student interactions, offering tailored feedback that guided learners through complex concepts.

2.4.2 Kidaptive

Kidaptive's Adaptive Learning Platform (ALP) combines data from various learning contexts, such as educational games and parent observations, to dynamically adjust educational content as learners engage with the material. This system creates a personalized learning environment, generating individualized insights and activity suggestions for each learner. A case study on Kidaptive highlighted its use of advanced algorithms to analyze learning patterns, response times, error patterns, engagement levels, and subject mastery, thereby offering a unique learning experience for every student.

2.4.3 Impact on Engagement and Performance

The effectiveness of adaptive learning platforms extends beyond individual case studies. A meta-analysis examining adaptive e-learning environments found that these systems are particularly effective in improving skills among health professionals and students. The adaptivity process within these environments may be more beneficial for skill acquisition rather than merely imparting factual knowledge, as it generates less cognitive load. Adaptive learning tools like Smart Sparrow and Kidaptive enhance personalized engagement by adjusting educational content to match individual learning paces. This personalization not only maintains appropriate challenge levels but also significantly improves motivation, engagement, and learning outcomes.

While AI's expanding role highlights its potential to enrich instruction and learning, these benefits cannot be separated from the ethical challenges they generate. Issues of data privacy, algorithmic bias, and transparency demand equal attention to ensure that technological innovation supports equity and trust in education. Section 3 therefore examines the ethical considerations that underpin responsible AI integration.

3. ETHICAL CONSIDERATIONS

While Artificial Intelligence (AI) offers numerous benefits in educational settings, it also raises significant ethical concerns, particularly regarding data privacy and security. AI systems often require extensive student data to function effectively, which can lead to potential security breaches if not properly managed. To mitigate these risks, educational institutions must implement robust data protection strategies, including data encryption, secure access controls, and adherence to relevant regulations such as the General Data Protection Regulation (GDPR) and the Family Educational Rights and Privacy Act (FERPA).

3.1 Data Privacy and Security in AI-Driven Education

The integration of AI in educational environments necessitates the collection and analysis of vast amounts of student data, encompassing academic records, behavioral patterns, and personal information. This extensive data collection heightens the risk of unauthorized access and potential misuse. Balaban (2024) explains that AI systems can be susceptible to data manipulation, where malicious actors introduce false or manipulated data into AI training datasets, leading to biased or compromised AI model outcomes.

3.1.1 Regulatory Compliance: GDPR and FERPA

Compliance with data protection regulations is crucial for educational institutions utilizing AI technologies. The GDPR, implemented by the European Union, mandates strict guidelines on data processing and grants individuals significant control over their personal information. Similarly, in the United States, FERPA protects the privacy of student education records, requiring schools to obtain consent before sharing such data. Poth (2024) states that schools must ensure that any AI tools used in the classroom comply with FERPA regulations, particularly when sharing student data with third-party providers. These frameworks establish essential guardrails, but they also present ongoing challenges for institutions struggling to balance innovation with compliance.

3.1.2 Best Practices for Data Protection

To safeguard student information, educational institutions should adopt the following best practices:

- **Data Encryption:** Implement encryption protocols to protect data both in transit and at rest, ensuring that unauthorized parties cannot access sensitive information.
- **Secure Access Controls:** Establish strict access controls to limit data access to authorized personnel only, reducing the risk of internal breaches.
- **Third-Party Compliance:** Ensure that third-party AI providers adhere to strict privacy guidelines to prevent unauthorized access and misuse of data. This includes incorporating privacy-compliant practices in product development and staying informed on legal obligations.
- **Transparency:** Maintain transparency in data collection practices to build trust among institutions, students, and parents. Clearly communicate what data is being collected, how it will be used, and who will have access to it.

While these recommendations are essential, their practical implementation often encounters barriers. Financial constraints can hinder smaller institutions from investing in advanced encryption technologies or regular compliance audits. Similarly, a lack of adequately trained personnel may delay the adoption of sophisticated data governance practices. Even when policies are in place, ensuring consistent enforcement across departments can be challenging, particularly when collaborating with multiple third-party vendors (Kelso et al., 2024). These hurdles highlight the importance of not only setting standards but also providing institutions with the resources, training, and policy support necessary to implement them effectively.

3.1.3 Emerging Privacy-Preserving Techniques

To further enhance data privacy, emerging techniques such as federated learning are being explored. Federated learning enables AI models to be trained across multiple decentralized devices that hold local data samples, without requiring the transfer of raw data to a central server. This approach has shown promise in balancing predictive performance and privacy in educational contexts.

For example, a study by Zhang et al. (2023) piloted federated learning in a university learning analytics project that aimed to predict student dropout risks. Instead of pooling sensitive student data into a centralized database, the federated approach allowed each participating institution to train models locally and share only the model parameters. Results showed that this approach maintained strong predictive accuracy while preserving student privacy, making it a viable solution for multi-institution collaborations. Similarly, federated learning has been applied in adaptive tutoring systems, where models learn from student interactions across schools without exposing individual learners' personal data. Hence, AI has the potential to revolutionize education, addressing ethical considerations—particularly data privacy and security—remains essential. Incorporating privacy-preserving innovations such as federated learning ensures responsible implementation while maintaining the trust of all stakeholders involved.

3.2 Algorithmic Bias

Artificial Intelligence (AI) systems have the potential to inadvertently perpetuate existing biases present in their training data, leading to unfair educational outcomes. Such biases can arise from unrepresentative data samples that reflect societal inequalities. Addressing these challenges requires a multifaceted approach involving diverse AI development teams, comprehensive testing across varied demographic groups, and regular audits of AI decision-making processes. Educational institutions must collaborate with AI developers to implement bias detection mechanisms, ensuring that AI-driven recommendations and assessments are equitable for all students.

3.2.1 Manifestations of Algorithmic Bias in Education

Algorithmic bias in educational settings can manifest in various ways, affecting different demographic groups (Obed Boateng & Bright Boateng, 2025). It is important to distinguish algorithmic bias from data bias: while data bias stems from historical inequalities, incomplete datasets, or skewed sampling that feed into machine learning systems, algorithmic bias refers to distortions introduced by the design of the algorithm itself—such as the way models weigh features or classify outcomes. In practice, the two often intersect, amplifying inequities when biased data are processed through biased algorithms (Mehrabi et al., 2019).

Racial Bias: A study titled "Inside the Black Box: Detecting and Mitigating Algorithmic Bias across Racialized Groups in College Student-Success Prediction" found that predictive algorithms used to forecast college student success produced false negatives for 19% of Black students and 21% of Latinx students, incorrectly predicting that these students would not succeed in college.
Gender Bias: Research has shown that AI algorithms can reproduce existing gender biases, potentially influencing admissions processes, assessment outcomes, and even recommendations for STEM pathways, thereby reinforcing systemic underrepresentation of women in certain academic fields.
Disability Bias: AI-driven educational tools may not adequately accommodate students with disabilities, leading to unequal learning experiences and accessibility challenges (Idowu et al., 2024). For example, speech-recognition systems trained primarily on neurotypical or non-accented speech may struggle with diverse communication patterns, limiting inclusivity in digital classrooms.

These manifestations underscore the importance of designing AI in education with fairness-by-design principles, continuous auditing, and participatory input from diverse student groups.

3.2.2 Strategies to Mitigate Algorithmic Bias

To promote fairness and equity in AI-driven educational systems, the following strategies are recommended:

1. **Diversify AI Development Teams:** Ensuring diversity among AI developers can help identify and address potential biases during the design and implementation phases.
2. **Comprehensive Testing:** Evaluating AI models on diverse demographic groups can uncover biases that may not be apparent in homogeneous samples.
3. **Regular Audits:** Implementing routine audits of AI decision-making processes can detect and correct biased outcomes.
4. **Bias Detection Mechanisms:** Collaborating with AI developers to integrate bias detection tools within educational platforms can proactively identify and mitigate unfair practices.
5. **Transparency and Accountability:** Maintaining clear documentation of AI algorithms and their decision-making criteria allows for greater scrutiny and trust among stakeholders.

While the theoretical strategies listed—and in particular, the need for regular audits—are well established, evidence shows they are infrequently implemented in real-world educational settings. For instance: A survey by Farheen et al. (2025) reveals that while educators are increasingly aware of algorithmic bias, formal bias audits remain uncommon in classrooms, especially in K–12 environments. Familiarity with AI tools does lead to more nuanced critical awareness, but school systems often lack structured auditing procedures. Similarly, research by Mökander et al. (2024) indicates that many schools depend on vendor guarantees instead of conducting their own equity or fairness assessments—often due to financial constraints and limited technical staff capacity. These findings highlight a critical gap between best practice guidelines and on-the-ground implementation. Addressing algorithmic bias in education thus calls not just for policy articulation but also for practical support—such as dedicated funding, staff training, and external audit mechanisms to ensure regular, independent evaluation of fairness.

Hence, addressing algorithmic bias in educational AI systems is crucial to prevent the reinforcement of existing inequalities. By implementing diverse development practices, rigorous testing, and continuous monitoring, educational institutions can work towards equitable AI-driven outcomes for all students.

3.3 Teacher-Student Relationship

The integration of Artificial Intelligence (AI) in education offers numerous benefits, such as personalized learning experiences and efficient administrative processes. However, an over-reliance on AI may inadvertently diminish meaningful teacher-student interactions, which are essential for effective learning and student development. However, an over-reliance on AI may inadvertently diminish meaningful teacher–student interactions, which research shows are foundational to learning outcomes. Socio-emotional learning (SEL) frameworks emphasize that supportive teacher–student relationships foster skills such as self-awareness, empathy, collaboration, and resilience—competencies that are difficult for AI systems to replicate (OECD, 2021). When these relational aspects are weakened, students may experience reduced motivation, engagement, and sense of belonging in the classroom.

While AI can provide valuable instructional support, it lacks the emotional intelligence and mentorship that human educators offer. Therefore, ethical guidelines must be developed to balance AI and human instructional roles, ensuring that AI serves as a complementary tool rather than a substitute for teachers. Educators should use AI to enhance, rather than replace, personalized guidance, fostering a learning environment where human connections remain at the core of education.

3.3.1 Impact of AI on Teacher-Student Relationships

The increasing integration of AI in educational settings has raised concerns about its potential to erode the quality of teacher-student relationships. A study by Luo Jess (2024) observed that the rise of Generative AI (GenAI) is causing an "erosion of trust" between students and teachers in higher education . This erosion stems from uncertainties regarding AI's role in learning and assessment, potentially leading to reduced interpersonal interactions and a diminished sense of community within educational environments.

Furthermore, University of Illinios (2024) research indicates that an over-reliance on AI may reduce teacher-student interactions and take away from the social-emotional aspects of learning. If these interactions diminish, students' social skills and interpersonal development could suffer.

3.3.2 Ethical Guidelines for AI Integration

To address these challenges, several organizations have proposed ethical guidelines for AI use in education:

- **European Commission's Ethical Guidelines:** These guidelines provide practical advice to educators on integrating AI and data usage into school education, emphasizing the importance of maintaining human oversight and prioritizing student well-being. In practice, many European school systems are developing institutional protocols—such as mandatory human review of AI-generated grading or placement recommendations—to ensure that final decisions remain under educator control (Porayska-Pomsta et al., 2024).
- **UNESCO's Recommendations:** UNESCO advocates for a human-rights-centered approach to AI ethics, emphasizing principles such as proportionality, safety, and security to prevent harm and ensure that AI use in education aligns with legitimate educational aims (UNESCO, 2025) .

3.3.3 Balancing AI and Human Instructional Roles

To ensure that AI serves as a complementary tool rather than a substitute for teachers, the following strategies are recommended:

1. **Maintain Human Oversight:** Teachers should oversee AI-driven instructional processes to ensure that the technology supports educational goals without compromising the teacher-student relationship.

2. **Promote AI Literacy:** Educators and students should be educated about the capabilities and limitations of AI, fostering a critical understanding of when and how to use AI tools effectively (Yongpradit, 2024).
3. **Encourage Collaborative Learning:** AI should be used to facilitate collaborative learning environments where teachers and students engage in meaningful interactions, supported by AI-driven insights.
4. **Regular Ethical Audits:** Educational institutions should conduct regular assessments of AI tools to ensure they align with ethical standards and do not inadvertently harm teacher-student dynamics.

While AI has the potential to enhance educational experiences, it is crucial to implement it thoughtfully to preserve the integrity of teacher-student relationships. By establishing ethical guidelines and maintaining a balanced approach, educators can leverage AI's benefits while ensuring that human connections remain at the heart of education. These ethical challenges discussed in this section do not only raise pedagogical concerns but also intersect with formal regulatory frameworks. To address these issues systematically, education systems must engage with legal instruments that govern AI use. Section 4 therefore explores the legal implications of AI in education, focusing on data protection, compliance, and institutional responsibilities.

4 LEGAL IMPLICATIONS OF AI IN EDUCATION

The integration of artificial intelligence (AI) in education introduces a spectrum of legal considerations that institutions, policymakers, and educators must address to ensure ethical and lawful use. Key areas of concern include regulatory compliance, intellectual property rights, liability, and accountability.

4.1 Regulatory Compliance

Educational institutions deploying AI must navigate a complex landscape of local, national, and international regulations to ensure that AI applications align with legal standards and institutional policies. In practice, discrepancies between frameworks such as the EU's GDPR and the U.S. FERPA create compliance challenges for cross-border educational collaborations, since the former emphasizes individual data subject rights while the latter prioritizes parental access and institutional discretion (Slade et al., 2023). For example, U.S. universities offering online courses to EU students have faced difficulties reconciling GDPR's "right to be forgotten" with FERPA's requirement that institutions maintain certain educational records. This tension illustrates how international collaborations and cross-border data flows can complicate compliance for AI-enabled learning platforms.

4.1.1 Data Protection Laws

AI systems in education often process extensive student data, raising significant privacy and security concerns. Compliance with data protection laws is crucial:

- **General Data Protection Regulation (GDPR):** Enforced by the European Union, the GDPR sets stringent guidelines on data collection, processing, storage, and sharing. Educational institutions must ensure that AI tools handle student data transparently and securely to comply with these regulations.
- **Family Educational Rights and Privacy Act (FERPA):** In the United States, FERPA protects the privacy of student education records. Schools must ensure that any AI tools used in the classroom comply with FERPA regulations, particularly when sharing student data with third-party providers (Poth, 2024).
- **Children's Online Privacy Protection Act (COPPA):** This U.S. federal law restricts data collection from children under 13 without parental consent. AI applications targeting young students must adhere to COPPA guidelines to avoid legal repercussions.

Non-compliance with these regulations can lead to legal penalties, reputational harm, and erosion of public trust.

4.1.2 Intellectual Property Rights

The use of AI in education raises intricate questions about intellectual property (IP), particularly concerning the creation, use, and ownership of AI-generated content.

AI-Generated Content and Copyright

Gaffar & Albarashdi (2024) explore how AI-generated originality's impact on copyright regulations is the need of the hour. Determining authorship and ownership of AI-generated works is legally complex which can be discussed in the following way:

Authorship Ambiguities: Since most legal jurisdictions only grant copyright to original works of authorship by human authors, the definition of "originality" is central to the copyright status of AI-generated works. For instance, the U.S. Copyright Office recently rejected copyright protection for a fully AI-generated artwork, ruling in *Thaler v. Perlmutter* that only works with human authorship are eligible for copyright (Grossman & Barger, 2023). Similarly, some universities, such as the University of Sydney (2025), have issued policies clarifying that AI-generated outputs cannot be claimed as original student work for copyright or academic integrity purposes. These examples highlight how both courts and institutions are beginning to navigate the authorship ambiguities of AI-generated content. In the European Union, (2025) EU Parliament's 2023 discussions on the AI Act have highlighted that AI-generated outputs cannot enjoy copyright unless there is a demonstrable element of human creative contribution. In Asia, the Government of India's 2023 advisory on AI in education similarly stressed that AI outputs should be treated as tools rather than independent creators, with copyright resting on the human user who directs and edits the work. These emerging policies show how different jurisdictions are converging on the principle of requiring human authorship for IP rights in education and beyond.

Institutional Policies: Educational institutions must establish clear guidelines on the use and ownership of AI-generated content to prevent potential disputes and ensure compliance with copyright laws.

Use of Copyrighted Material in AI Training

AI models often require vast datasets for training, which may include copyrighted materials. However, AI developers frequently use such content without seeking permission from rights holders (Buick, 2024). It leads to legal dispute in the following way.

Fair Use Considerations: In the United States, the use of copyrighted work for AI training has been argued to fall under fair use due to its transformative nature. However, this interpretation is subject to legal scrutiny and ongoing litigation. For instance, lawsuits filed by authors and artists in both the U.S. and UK against AI companies such as OpenAI and Stability AI highlight the uncertainty—if courts rule against AI firms, educational institutions may face stricter licensing requirements and higher costs when adopting AI tools trained on copyrighted datasets (Authors Guild et al. v. OpenAI, 2023; Getty Images (US), Inc. v. Stability AI, 2023).

Licensing Requirements: Educational institutions must be cautious when using AI tools trained on copyrighted materials without proper licensing, as this could lead to infringement claims.

4.1.3 Liability and Accountability

As AI systems become more autonomous, determining liability for their actions becomes increasingly complex:

- **AI Decision-Making:** When AI systems make decisions that negatively impact students, such as biased grading or disciplinary actions, institutions may be held accountable for these outcomes.
- **Transparency and Ability to Explain:** Ensuring that AI decision-making processes are transparent and explainable is crucial for accountability. Institutions must implement mechanisms to audit and justify AI-driven decisions to stakeholders.
- **Legal Frameworks:** Existing laws may not fully address the nuances of AI-related liabilities, necessitating updates to regulations and the development of new legal standards (Bondari, 2025).

Bias and Discrimination

AI systems trained on biased data can perpetuate existing prejudices:

- **Equity Concerns:** Biased AI algorithms can lead to discriminatory practices in educational settings, affecting admissions, grading, and disciplinary measures.
- **Legal Implications:** Institutions deploying biased AI systems may face legal challenges under anti-discrimination laws. It is imperative to implement measures that identify and mitigate biases in AI applications.

4.1.4 Ethical Considerations

Beyond legal compliance, ethical considerations play a vital role in the deployment of AI in education:

- **Student Autonomy:** Overreliance on AI tools may undermine student autonomy and critical thinking skills. Educators must balance AI assistance with opportunities for independent learning.
- **Informed Consent:** Students and parents should be informed about how AI tools are used in educational settings, including data collection practices and the potential impact on learning outcomes.

While AI offers transformative potential in education; it is accompanied by significant legal and ethical challenges. Educational institutions must proactively address regulatory compliance, intellectual property rights, liability, accountability, and ethical considerations to harness AI's benefits responsibly.

Alignment with Institutional Policies and National Educational Standards

AI deployment must also align with national educational standards and institutional policies. For instance, institutions must establish ethical guidelines governing AI's role in grading, admissions, and student support. Likewise, AI should be designed to support, not replace, human educators, ensuring compliance with labor laws and teachers' rights. At the same time, AI-driven educational content should adhere to curriculum guidelines to maintain academic integrity and standardization.

4.2. Intellectual Property Rights

The advent of artificial intelligence (AI) in educational content creation introduces complex legal challenges concerning copyright and ownership. As AI tools become adept at generating educational materials, assessments, and even research papers, it is imperative to establish clear policies defining intellectual property (IP) rights.

4.2.1 Copyright and Ownership of AI-Generated Content

The advent of artificial intelligence (AI) in educational content creation introduces complex legal challenges concerning copyright and ownership. As AI tools become increasingly capable of generating educational materials, assessments, and research papers, establishing clear policies to define intellectual property (IP) rights is essential. Kelly (2024) opines that legal frameworks worldwide vary in recognizing AI-generated content as intellectual property, raising key questions about ownership. The determination of ownership involves multiple stakeholders, including institutions, instructors, and AI developers. If an educational institution commissions the development of AI tools for content creation, it may claim ownership of the generated materials. Similarly, educators who utilize AI tools to develop course content might assert ownership, particularly if they contribute significant input or customization. On the other hand, companies or individuals responsible for creating AI tools could claim rights over the outputs, especially if specified in end-user agreements. In the United States, the U.S. Copyright Office maintains that works lacking human authorship do not qualify for copyright protection, a stance reinforced by a recent court ruling that upheld the denial of copyright registration for AI-generated art created without human intervention.

4.2.2 Derivative Works

AI-generated content may incorporate elements from pre-existing copyrighted materials, raising concerns about derivative works. If AI-generated educational content includes substantial portions of existing works without permission, it may constitute copyright infringement. To mitigate this risk, institutions must implement compliance measures to ensure that AI-assisted teaching materials do not violate copyright laws. This includes verifying the originality of AI-generated outputs and obtaining necessary licenses for any incorporated materials.

Fair Use and Licensing

Educators must discern whether AI-generated content falls under fair use provisions or necessitates specific licensing:

- **Fair Use Doctrine:** In some jurisdictions, the use of copyrighted material for purposes such as criticism, comment, teaching, or research may qualify as fair use. However, the application of fair use to AI-generated content remains a contentious legal area.
- **Licensing Agreements:** Securing licenses for AI-generated content, especially when derived from copyrighted sources, is prudent to mitigate legal risks. This ensures that the use of such content complies with intellectual property laws and respects the rights of original creators.

AI continues to permeate educational content creation; stakeholders must proactively address the legal implications concerning copyright and ownership. Establishing clear policies and adhering to legal frameworks are essential steps to navigate the complexities of AI-generated content in education.

4.2.3 Clear Policies on AI-Assisted Materials

To ensure the ethical and legal use of AI in education, institutions should develop clear policies governing AI-assisted materials. Equally important, institutions should include training modules for both faculty and students on intellectual property (IP) rights and responsibilities in the context of AI-generated materials, so that ethical and legal awareness becomes part of the learning process. These policies should define the permissible use of AI-generated content in educational settings, specifying whether such materials can be used for teaching, assessments, or research. Additionally, institutions must establish attribution requirements, ensuring that AI-generated works are properly credited to maintain academic integrity and transparency. Licensing agreements between AI vendors and educational institutions should also be clearly outlined, addressing ownership rights, data privacy, and compliance with copyright laws. Furthermore, guidelines on students' use of AI tools for academic work are essential to prevent issues related to plagiarism and academic dishonesty. Institutions should provide clear directives on how AI-generated content should be cited, differentiate between acceptable and unacceptable uses of AI in coursework, and implement measures to detect and address potential misuse. By establishing comprehensive policies, educational institutions can promote responsible AI integration while upholding academic and legal standards.

4.3 Liability and Accountability

AI's role in education extends to student assessment, admissions, and personalized learning recommendations. Determining accountability when AI-driven decisions impact student outcomes is a pressing legal concern.

4.3.1 Who Is Responsible for AI-Driven Decisions?

Legal frameworks should define responsibility distribution among stakeholders, including:

- **Educational Institutions:** Schools and universities deploying AI tools must ensure their accuracy, fairness, and reliability. They may be held liable if AI-driven decisions result in discrimination or unfair treatment.
- **AI Developers and Vendors:** AI providers must ensure their systems are free from biases and errors. Institutions should negotiate contracts that specify vendor liability in case of AI failures.
- **Educators and Administrators:** Faculty members using AI must understand its limitations and retain oversight over AI-generated recommendations, ensuring that human judgment remains integral to decision-making.

4.3.2 Bias and Discrimination Concerns

Bias and discrimination concerns are critical when integrating AI into education, as AI algorithms can inadvertently reinforce biases in grading, admissions, and disciplinary actions. If left unchecked, these biases can lead to unfair treatment of students, disproportionately affecting marginalized groups. To address this, institutions must conduct regular audits of AI systems to identify and mitigate potential biases in decision-making processes. Ensuring that AI-driven decisions comply with anti-discrimination laws is equally important, as failure to do so could result in legal consequences and ethical violations. Additionally, students should be provided with a clear and accessible avenue to appeal AI-generated assessments and decisions, allowing for human oversight and correction in cases where AI outputs may be inaccurate or biased. By implementing these measures, educational institutions can foster a fair and inclusive learning environment while maintaining accountability in AI-driven processes.

4.3.3 Legal Consequences of AI Malfunction

The legal consequences of AI malfunctions in education can be significant, affecting students, educators, and institutions alike. Errors in AI systems can lead to incorrect student placements, which may impact academic success by assigning students to courses or programs that do not align with their abilities or needs. Similarly, unfair grading caused by algorithmic miscalculations or biases can result in disputes, appeals, and even legal actions from students or parents challenging the fairness of AI-driven assessments. Additionally, AI systems that handle sensitive student data pose a risk of data breaches, which can lead to lawsuits, regulatory penalties, and reputational damage for institutions. To mitigate these risks, educational institutions should implement robust risk management strategies, including liability insurance to cover potential legal claims and contingency plans to address AI failures effectively. By proactively preparing for AI-related errors, institutions can uphold educational integrity, maintain compliance with legal standards, and protect students' rights.

The integration of AI in education offers numerous benefits, but it also necessitates careful legal considerations. Ensuring compliance with data protection laws, defining intellectual property rights, and establishing clear accountability measures are crucial steps in mitigating legal risks. Institutions must work collaboratively with legal experts, educators, and AI developers to create policies that promote ethical AI use while protecting students' rights. By proactively addressing these legal implications, the education sector can harness AI's potential while maintaining fairness, transparency, and legal integrity. Legal frameworks mentioned above, establish boundaries for the responsible use of AI, they do not address how teaching itself must evolve in response to these technologies. The real challenge for educators lies in adapting pedagogy so that AI complements rather than constrains learning. Section 5 therefore examines pedagogical strategies that foster meaningful AI–human collaboration in classrooms.

5. PEDAGOGICAL ADAPTATIONS IN AI-DRIVEN EDUCATION

The integration of artificial intelligence (AI) into education requires pedagogical adaptations to optimize learning while retaining the essential human aspects of teaching. AI has the potential to transform traditional educational methodologies, making learning more personalized, engaging, and efficient. However, its implementation must be balanced with human interaction to ensure a holistic learning experience. This necessitates a shift towards blended learning approaches, AI-augmented teacher roles, and student-centered learning environments.

5.1 Blended Learning Approaches

Blended learning, which combines artificial intelligence (AI)-driven tools with traditional teaching methods, has emerged as a transformative approach in modern education. This pedagogical strategy leverages the strengths of both AI technologies and human instruction to create a more personalized and flexible learning environment. Park & Doo (2024) highlights that AI serves as both direct mediator and enhances student autonomy. It acts as a supplementary assistant, facilitating effective interactions within blended learning contexts.

The integration of AI into traditional teaching encompasses several key components that enrich the educational experience. Automated assessments enable AI tools to grade assignments and quizzes instantly, providing immediate feedback that supports timely interventions and promotes continuous learning. Adaptive content delivery systems utilize AI to analyze student performance data, tailoring instructional materials to meet individual learning needs and pacing. Additionally, AI-powered virtual tutors, such as chatbots and virtual assistants, offer on-demand support by answering student queries and reinforcing concepts, thereby extending learning opportunities beyond the classroom. Ounejjar et al. (2024) explain the development of platforms like SmartBlendEd which demonstrates how AI-optimized scheduling can enhance blended learning environments by personalizing learning pathways for students. Nevertheless, the adoption of blended learning faces challenges such as the digital divide, where unequal access to reliable technology and internet can exclude certain learners, as well as issues like student and teacher resistance to technology or tech fatigue that may limit long-term engagement (Vaishnav, 2025).

The effectiveness of AI applications in blended learning is further supported by empirical research. Ji et al.(2024) examined AI performance assessment systems and found that they positively influence students' continuous learning motivation indirectly through factors such as expectation confirmation, perceived usefulness, and learning satisfaction. These findings suggest that AI-driven assessments, when designed to provide personalized feedback, can enhance the overall learning experience and encourage sustained engagement.

The thoughtful integration of AI into blended learning environments holds significant potential to enrich educational practices. By combining AI's capabilities in real-time data analysis and personalized support with the nuanced understanding and adaptability of human instructors, educational institutions can create more responsive and effective learning experiences. Continued research and development in this area are essential to fully realize the benefits of AI-enhanced blended learning and to address any emerging challenges associated with its implementation.

5.1.2 Flipped Classrooms and AI Analytics

The integration of artificial intelligence (AI) analytics into flipped classroom models has significantly enhanced the effectiveness of this pedagogical approach. In flipped classrooms, students engage with learning materials prior to attending in-person sessions, allowing classroom time to be dedicated to interactive discussions and problem-solving activities. AI analytics play a pivotal role in this model by tracking student engagement with pre-class materials, identifying areas where students may struggle, and providing personalized learning paths to ensure each student progresses at an appropriate pace.

One notable application of AI in flipped classrooms is the use of AI-based chatbots to facilitate student interaction with pre-class content. A mini-review by Lo & Hew,(023) examined the integration of AI-based chatbots into flipped learning environments, highlighting benefits such as increased student interaction with learning content and improved class preparation. The study also noted that AI chatbots could provide data-driven teaching and learning, allowing educators to tailor in-class discussions based on real-time analytics.

Furthermore, AI-driven adaptive learning systems have been integrated into flipped classrooms to enhance programming education. Katona & Gyonyoru (2025) explored the integration of an AI-powered adaptive learning system within the flipped classroom model. The findings suggested that such integration could improve student engagement and learning outcomes by providing personalized learning experiences tailored to individual student needs.

In addition to enhancing student engagement, AI analytics have been utilized to monitor and support self-regulated learning (SRL) in flipped classrooms. A study by Cabı & Türkoğlu (2025) investigated the impact of a learning analytics-based feedback system on students' academic achievement and SRL in a flipped learning environment. The results indicated that the feedback system positively influenced students' academic performance and their ability to self-regulate their learning processes.

By leveraging AI analytics, educators can design more effective lesson plans that focus on critical thinking and problem-solving during class time. The insights gained from AI analytics enable teachers to identify common areas of difficulty among students, allowing for targeted in-class interventions. This data-driven approach ensures that classroom activities are aligned with student needs, thereby enhancing the overall learning experience.

5.2 AI-Augmented Teacher Roles

The integration of artificial intelligence (AI) in education is transforming traditional teaching roles, positioning educators to focus more on mentorship and the cultivation of critical thinking skills. By automating administrative tasks such as grading, scheduling, and performance tracking, AI allows teachers to dedicate more time to personalized student support and the development of higher-order cognitive abilities. This shift not only enhances instructional quality but also enriches the overall learning experience.

AI-driven tools have been instrumental in alleviating the administrative burdens that often consume a significant portion of educators' time. For instance, platforms like GoGuardian, in partnership with Google Cloud, have introduced features that identify student learning gaps and assign differentiated tasks to address these gaps, thereby streamlining the assessment process and reducing manual workload. Similarly, Slagg (2023) observes that AI applications can automate routine tasks such as grading assignments and generating progress reports, enabling teachers to focus on more impactful educational activities.

With administrative tasks managed by AI, educators can assume roles that emphasize mentorship and the fostering of critical thinking. This transition allows teachers to engage more deeply with students, guiding them through complex problem-solving processes and encouraging analytical reasoning. AI's ability to personalize learning experiences further supports this dynamic, as educators can tailor their instructional strategies to meet individual student needs, thereby promoting a more effective and engaging learning environment.

However, a recent study by Puja et al. (2025) found that while some teachers viewed AI tools as supportive enhancements, many others—especially in rigid, AI-driven frameworks—felt their professional autonomy and pedagogical control were undermined. Educators expressed concern that increasing reliance on AI could narrow their instructional role to supervision or content oversight, potentially eroding their agency and erasing the nuanced judgment central to effective teaching. Striking a balance between automation and the preservation of core teaching responsibilities is therefore essential. By reducing the time spent on administrative duties, teachers can focus on developing students' critical thinking and creativity, skills essential for success in the 21st century. This synergy between AI technology and human instruction fosters a more interactive and personalized educational experience, preparing students to navigate an increasingly complex world.

5.2.1 Training Educators to Work with AI

Integrating artificial intelligence (AI) into education necessitates comprehensive professional development programs to prepare educators for effective collaboration with these technologies. Such programs should focus on equipping teachers with the skills to interpret AI-generated insights, integrating AI tools into lesson planning, and ensuring ethical AI use to prevent bias and maintain data privacy compliance. However, it is important to recognize equity challenges: while well-resourced universities may offer large-scale AI-focused training, underfunded institutions—particularly in developing regions—often lack the financial, technical, or infrastructural capacity to deliver such PD initiatives (Diliberti et al., 2025). This disparity risks widening the digital divide among educators unless policy-level interventions and collaborative capacity-building efforts are implemented.

5.2.2 Equipping Educators with Skills to Interpret AI-Generated Insights

To harness the full potential of AI in education, teachers must develop the ability to understand and apply AI-generated data. Professional development initiatives should include training on data literacy, enabling educators to analyze student performance metrics and tailor instruction accordingly. For example, the International Society for Technology in Education (ISTE) offers courses that help educators identify various types of AI and build tools to make AI accessible for both teachers and students.

5.2.3 Integrating AI Tools into Lesson Planning

Effective integration of AI tools into lesson planning can enhance instructional strategies and student engagement. Educators should be trained to incorporate AI applications that support personalized learning, automate routine tasks, and provide real-time feedback. Organizations like EdTechTeacher offer professional learning events and custom training opportunities focused on AI integration in education, guiding teachers on best practices for embedding AI tools into their curricula.

5.2.4 Ensuring Ethical AI Use

As AI becomes more prevalent in classrooms, addressing ethical considerations is paramount. Professional development programs must emphasize the importance of using AI responsibly, focusing on preventing biases and ensuring compliance with data privacy regulations. Resources such as Carnegie Learning's guidelines on teaching ethical AI practices to K-12 students provide valuable insights into promoting critical thinking, analyzing AI biases, and understanding the implications of AI in education.

By embracing AI as a supportive tool and engaging in targeted professional development, teachers can enhance their pedagogical impact while maintaining the essential human connection in education. This approach ensures that educators are well-prepared to navigate the evolving educational landscape and leverage AI to enrich the learning experience.

5.3 Student-Centered Learning

Artificial intelligence (AI) has revolutionized education by enabling student-centered learning through the creation of adaptive learning environments tailored to individual needs, preferences, and learning styles. These AI-driven platforms analyze student performance to detect strengths and weaknesses, adjusting content delivery accordingly. For instance, a study by Maity & Deroy (2024) highlights the integration of generative AI into personalized intelligent tutoring systems, facilitating dynamic content generation and real-time feedback to enhance learning experiences. Adaptive learning environments also adjust the difficulty levels of lessons and assessments based on student progress. A meta-analysis by X. Wang et al. (2024) found that AI-enabled adaptive learning systems have a medium to large positive effect on students' cognitive learning outcomes compared to non-adaptive interventions, underscoring the efficacy of personalized learning pathways.

Moreover, AI-powered platforms offer diverse learning formats, such as videos, interactive exercises, or text-based explanations, catering to individual learning styles. A study by Sajja et al. (2023) introduced an AI-enabled intelligent assistant designed to provide personalized learning support, including generating quizzes and offering tailored learning pathways, thereby enhancing student engagement and satisfaction. By leveraging AI to create adaptive learning environments, educators can provide personalized educational experiences that maximize student potential. These environments not only enhance engagement and motivation but also promote self-directed learning, as students receive the appropriate level of challenge and support tailored to their unique needs.

5.3.1 Gamification and Interactive Learning

Artificial intelligence (AI) is transforming gamification and interactive learning by embedding rewards, simulations, and real-time feedback into adaptive platforms. Gamified features such as points, badges, and leaderboards have been shown to increase student participation, though research highlights that sustaining motivation requires carefully designed long-term engagement strategies (Smiderle et al., 2020).

Interactive AI-enabled simulations, including virtual labs, allow students to practice in risk-free environments, while frameworks such as the GAFCC model (Yang et al., 2023) demonstrate how goal-setting, feedback, and collaboration can enhance effectiveness. Recent studies on adaptive gamification emphasize AI's ability to personalize challenges and feedback (Suresh Babu & Dhakshina Moorthy, 2024), thereby creating tailored, immersive experiences. These innovations underscore AI's capacity to support student-centered learning while requiring educators to design sustainable engagement practices.

These pedagogical adaptations demonstrate how AI can be meaningfully integrated into teaching, yet they also highlight unresolved tensions around ethics, law, and educational equity. Bringing these strands together, the conclusion reflects on the broader challenges and opportunities of AI–human collaborative teaching, offering directions for future practice and research.

6. CONCLUSION

The integration of artificial intelligence (AI) in education marks a transformative shift in how instruction, assessment, and student engagement are approached. AI has the potential to revolutionize learning experiences by offering personalized education, automating administrative tasks, and enhancing student support systems. Through adaptive learning platforms, AI tailors content to individual student needs, fostering a more inclusive and effective learning environment. Furthermore, AI-driven analytics assist educators in identifying learning gaps, enabling data-informed instructional strategies that enhance academic outcomes. However, while AI offers significant benefits, its deployment in educational settings must be carefully managed to maintain the integrity and quality of education.

Ethical considerations play a crucial role in ensuring AI's responsible use in education. The reliance on AI for decision-making in grading, admissions, and disciplinary actions raises concerns about bias and fairness. AI algorithms, if not carefully designed and regularly audited, may reinforce existing societal inequalities. Additionally, student data privacy remains a major concern, necessitating stringent data protection measures. Compliance with regulations such as the General Data Protection Regulation (GDPR), the Family Educational Rights and Privacy Act (FERPA), and the Children's Online Privacy Protection Act (COPPA) is essential to safeguard sensitive student information. Ethical AI usage mandates transparency, accountability, and mechanisms that allow students and educators to challenge AI-generated outcomes when necessary.

The legal landscape surrounding AI in education is complex and evolving. Institutions must navigate intellectual property rights concerning AI-generated content, determine liability in cases of AI malfunctions, and ensure compliance with national and international regulations. The ownership of AI-generated materials remains a legal gray area, necessitating clear policies on attribution, licensing, and fair use. Furthermore, institutions must adopt risk management strategies to mitigate potential legal challenges arising from AI-related errors, such as incorrect student placements or data breaches. Establishing comprehensive legal frameworks will provide clarity and protect the interests of all stakeholders involved.

Pedagogical adaptations are essential for integrating AI into classrooms effectively. AI should complement, rather than replace, traditional teaching methods, fostering a balanced approach through blended learning models. Teachers must embrace new roles as facilitators, mentors, and critical thinkers while leveraging AI's capabilities to enhance instructional delivery. Professional development programs should equip educators with the necessary skills to interpret AI-generated insights, integrate AI tools into lesson planning, and ensure ethical AI use. Additionally, gamified AI-driven platforms and adaptive learning environments can significantly enhance student motivation and engagement, making learning more interactive and personalized.

In conclusion, AI's role in education presents both immense opportunities and significant challenges. While AI has the potential to revolutionize learning, its successful integration requires addressing ethical concerns, complying with legal standards, and implementing pedagogical adaptations that preserve the human essence of teaching. Looking forward, the future of AI in education will depend on proactive policy development, international cooperation, and a commitment to global equity to ensure that benefits are accessible across diverse educational contexts. To move in this direction, institutions should prioritize four key recommendations for practice: (i) establish clear and transparent AI governance policies, (ii) guarantee equitable access to AI tools and infrastructure, (iii) embed ethical safeguards, including privacy protection and bias auditing, and (iv) invest in continuous professional development for educators. By aligning innovation with responsibility, educational systems can create sustainable, inclusive, and human-centered pathways for AI integration.

REFERENCES

Alabbasi, D. (2017). Exploring Graduate Students' Perspectives towards Using Gamification Techniques in Online Learning. *Turkish Online Journal of Distance Education*, 180–180. DOI: 10.17718/tojde.328951

Authors Guild et al. v. OpenAI*: Hearing on Inc., No. 1:23-cv-08292* (2023). https://www.courtlistener.com/docket/67810584/authors-guild-v-openai-inc/

Balaban, D. (2024, March 29). Privacy And Security Issues Of Using AI For Academic Purposes Forbes]. *Cybersecurity*. https://www.forbes.com/sites/davidbalaban/2024/03/29/privacy-and-security-issues-of-using-ai-for-academic-purposes/

Barclay, N., Westine, C. D., Claris, A., & Martin, F. (2020). Development and Implementation of Adaptive Learning to Engage Learners in Engineering Technology. *Journal of Formative Design in Learning*, *4*(2), 107–118. DOI: 10.1007/s41686-020-00050-6

Bimpong, B. W. (2025, February 13). The Impact of Generative AI Educational Chatbots on the Academic Support Experiences of Students in U.S. Research Universities [NASPA]. *Students Affaira Administration in Higher Education*. https://naspa.org/blog/the-impact-of-generative-ai-educational-chatbots-on-the-academic-support-experiences-of-students-in-u-s-research-universities?utm

Bird, K. (2023, Fall). Predictive Analytics in Higher Education: The Promises and Challenges of Using Machine Learning to Improve Student Success. *Air Professional File*. Advance online publication. DOI: 10.34315/apf1612023

Boateng, O., & Boateng, B. (2025). Algorithmic bias in educational systems: Examining the impact of AI-driven decision making in modern education. *World Journal of Advanced Research and Reviews*, *25*(1), 2012–2017. DOI: 10.30574/wjarr.2025.25.1.0253

Bondari, N. (2025, February 4). *AI, Copyright, and the Law: The Ongoing Battle Over Intellectual Property Rights*. Gould School of Law, USC University of Southern California. https://sites.usc.edu/iptls/2025/02/04/ai-copyright-and-the-law-the-ongoing-battle-over-intellectual-property-rights/

Buick, A. (2024). Copyright and AI training data—Transparency to the rescue? *Journal Of Intellectual Property Law and Practice*, jpae102. https://doi.org/DOI: 10.1093/jiplp/jpae102

Cabı, E., & Türkoğlu, H. (2025). The Impact of a Learning Analytics Based Feedback System on Students' Academic Achievement and Self-Regulated Learning in a Flipped Classroom. *International Review of Research in Open and Distance Learning, 26*(1), 175–196. DOI: 10.19173/irrodl.v26i1.7924

Clugston, B. (2024, July 19). Advantages and disadvantages of AI in education [Educational]. *Education Career Tips.* https://www.ucanwest.ca/blog/education-careers-tips/advantages-and-disadvantages-of-ai-in-education

Contrino, M. F., Reyes-Millán, M., Vázquez-Villegas, P., & Membrillo-Hernández, J. (2024). Using an adaptive learning tool to improve student performance and satisfaction in online and face-to-face education for a more personalized approach. *Smart Learning Environments, 11*(1), 6. DOI: 10.1186/s40561-024-00292-y

Diliberti, M. K., Lake, R. J., & Weiner, S. R. (2025, April 8). More Districts Are Training Teachers on Artificial Intelligence [RAND Research & Commentary Research Reports]. *Findings from the American School District Panel.* https://www.rand.org/pubs/research_reports/RRA956-31.html

Elliott, D. (2024, July 29). This AI tutor could make humans 10 times smarter, its creator says [World Economic Forum]. *Education and Skills.* https://www.weforum.org/stories/2024/07/ai-tutor-china-teaching-gaps/?utm

España-Delgado, J. A. (2023). Kahoot, Quizizz, and Quizalize in the English Class and their Impact on Motivation. *HOW, 30*(1), 65–84. DOI: 10.19183/how.30.1.641

European Parliament. (2025). *Generative AI and Copyright.* JURI Committee European Parliament's Committee on Legal Affairs. https://www.europarl.europa.eu/RegData/etudes/STUD/2025/774095/IUST_STU%282025%29774095_EN.pdf

Farheen, S., Cheema, A. A., Ullah, R. S., & Bandeali, M. M. (2025). Equity and bias in AI educational tools: A critical examination of algorithmic decision-making in classrooms. *The Critical Review of Social Sciences Studies, 3*(3), 67–85.

Fitria, T. N. (2021, December). Artificial Intelligence (AI) In Education: Using AI Tools for Teaching and Learning Process. *Prosiding Seminar Nasional & Call for Paper STIE AAS.* https://www.researchgate.net/publication/357447234_Artificial_Intelligence_AI_In_Education_Using_AI_Tools_for_Teaching_and_Learning_Process

Gaffar, H., & Albarashdi, S. (2024). Copyright Protection for AI-Generated Works: Exploring Originality and Ownership in a Digital Landscape. *Asian Journal of International Law*, 1–24. https://doi.org/DOI: 10.1017/S2044251323000735

Getty Images (US), Inc. v. Stability AI: *Hearing on Inc., No. 1:23-cv-00135* (2023). https://www.courtlistener.com/docket/66788385/getty-images-us-inc-v-stability-ai-inc

Gnanaprakasam, J., & Lourdusamy, R. (2024). The Role of AI in Automating Grading: Enhancing Feedback and Efficiency. In Kadry, S. (Ed.), *Artificial Intelligence* (Vol. 28). IntechOpen., DOI: 10.5772/intechopen.1005025

Grossman, D., & Barger, K. (2023). *Thaler v. Perlmutter District of Columbia District Court* [IP/Entertainment Case Law Updates]. https://www.loeb.com/en/insights/publications/2023/08/thaler-v-perlmutter

Gudiño Paredes, S., Jasso Peña, F. D. J., & De La Fuente Alcazar, J. M. (2021). Remote proctored exams: Integrity assurance in online education? *Distance Education*, *42*(2), 200–218. DOI: 10.1080/01587919.2021.1910495

Idowu, J. A., Koshiyama, A. S., & Treleaven, P. (2024). Investigating algorithmic bias in student progress monitoring. *Computers and Education: Artificial Intelligence*, *7*, 100267. DOI: 10.1016/j.caeai.2024.100267

Ji, H., Suo, L., & Chen, H. (2024). AI performance assessment in blended learning: Mechanisms and effects on students' continuous learning motivation. *Frontiers in Psychology*, *15*, 1447680. DOI: 10.3389/fpsyg.2024.1447680 PMID: 39737232

Jiang, X., Peters, R., Plonsky, L., & Pajak, B. (2024). The Effectiveness of Duolingo English Courses in Developing Reading and Listening Proficiency. *CALICO Journal*, *41*(3), 249–272. DOI: 10.1558/cj.26704

Johri, A., & Hingle, A. (2023). Students' technological ambivalence toward online proctoring and the need for responsible use of educational technologies. *Journal of Engineering Education*, *112*(1), 221–242. DOI: 10.1002/jee.20504

Katona, J., & Gyonyoru, K. I. K. (2025). Integrating AI-based adaptive learning into the flipped classroom model to enhance engagement and learning outcomes. *Computers and Education: Artificial Intelligence*, *8*, 100392. DOI: 10.1016/j.caeai.2025.100392

Kelly, J. (2024, March 11). An introduction to copyright law and practice in education, and the concerns arising in the context of GenerativeAI [Advice and Guidance]. *AI in Universities and Colleges*. https://nationalcentreforai.jiscinvolve.org/wp/2024/03/11/copyright-and-concerns-arising-around-generative-ai/

Kelso, E., Soneji, A., Rahaman, S., Soshitaishvili, Y., & Hasan, R. (2024). *Trust, Because You Can't Verify:Privacy and Security Hurdles in Education Technology Acquisition Practices* (Version 2). arXiv. https://doi.org/DOI: 10.48550/ARXIV.2405.11712

Labadze, L., Grigolia, M., & Machaidze, L. (2023). Role of AI chatbots in education: Systematic literature review. *International Journal of Educational Technology in Higher Education*, *20*(1), 56. DOI: 10.1186/s41239-023-00426-1

Lim, T., Gottipati, S., & Cheong, M. L. F. (2023). Ethical Considerations for Artificial Intelligence in Educational Assessments. In Keengwe, J. (Ed.), (pp. 32–79). Advances in Educational Technologies and Instructional Design. IGI Global., DOI: 10.4018/979-8-3693-0205-7.ch003

Lin, M. P.-C., Liu, A. L., Poitras, E., Chang, M., & Chang, D. H. (2024). An Exploratory Study on the Efficacy and Inclusivity of AI Technologies in Diverse Learning Environments. *Sustainability*, *16*(20), 8992. DOI: 10.3390/su16208992

Liu, S., & Kunnan, A. J. (2016). Investigating the Application of Automated Writing Evaluation to Chinese Undergraduate English Majors: A Case Study of WriteToLearn. *CALICO Journal*, *33*(1), 71–91. DOI: 10.1558/cj.v33i1.26380

Lo, C. K., & Hew, K. F. (2023). A review of integrating AI-based chatbots into flipped learning: New possibilities and challenges. *Frontiers in Education*, *8*, 1175715. DOI: 10.3389/feduc.2023.1175715

Luckin, R. (2018). *Machine Learning and Human Intelligence The future of education for the 21st century*. UCL Institute of Education Press, University College London. https://search.worldcat.org/title/Machine-Learning-and-Human-Intelligence-:-the-future-of-education-for-the-21st-century./oclc/1100936842

Luckin, R. (2025). *Is education ready for artificial intelligence?* [Cambridge Assessment Netwok and Research]. How Educators Can Help Future Learners Outwit the Robots. https://www.cambridgeassessment.org.uk/insights/is-education-ready-ai-rose-luckin/

Luo (Jess), J. (2024). How does GenAI affect trust in teacher-student relationships? Insights from students' assessment experiences. *Teaching in Higher Education*, •••, 1–16. DOI: 10.1080/13562517.2024.2341005

Maity, S., & Deroy, A. (2024). *Generative AI and Its Impact on Personalized Intelligent Tutoring Systems* (Version 1). arXiv. https://doi.org/DOI: 10.48550/ARXIV.2410.10650

Mehrabi, N., Morstatter, F., Saxena, N., Lerman, K., & Galstyan, A. (2019). *A Survey on Bias and Fairness in Machine Learning* (Version 3). arXiv. https://doi.org/DOI: 10.48550/ARXIV.1908.09635

Mökander, J., Schuett, J., Kirk, H. R., & Floridi, L. (2024). Auditing large language models: A three-layered approach. *AI and Ethics*, *4*(4), 1085–1115. DOI: 10.1007/s43681-023-00289-2

Murray, S. (2025, March 16). Business schools ease their resistance to AI [Financial Times]. *Schools Are Using AI-Powered Teaching Assistants, Automated Feedback Systems and AI-Driven Grading Tools*. https://www.ft.com/content/daa0f68d-774a-4e5e-902c-5d6e8bf687dc?utm

Nguyen, T. L., Nguyen, H. L., & Le, D. H. (2024). Teachers' Perspectives on AI-Driven Quillionz for Generating EFL Reading Comprehension Quizzes. *Proceedings of the AsiaCALL International Conference, 6*, 20–34. https://doi.org/DOI: 10.54855/paic.2462

OECD. (2021). *Beyond Academic Learning: First Results from the Survey of Social and Emotional Skills 2019*. OECD., DOI: 10.1787/92a11084-

Okonkwo, C. W., & Ade-Ibijola, A. (2021). Chatbots applications in education: A systematic review. *Computers and Education: Artificial Intelligence*, *2*, 100033. DOI: 10.1016/j.caeai.2021.100033

Ounejjar, L. A., Lachgar, M., Ouhayou, O., Laanaoui, M. D., Refki, E., Makaoui, R., & Saoud, A. (2024). SmartBlendEd: Enhancing blended learning through AI-optimized scheduling and user-centric design. *SoftwareX*, *27*, 101891. DOI: 10.1016/j.softx.2024.101891

Park, Y., & Doo, M. Y. (2024). Role of AI in Blended Learning: A Systematic Literature Review. *International Review of Research in Open and Distance Learning*, *25*(1), 164–196. DOI: 10.19173/irrodl.v25i1.7566

Pearson. (2024, July 18). Pearson Unveils AI Tool to Help Educators Save Time and Prioritize Student Learning [Educational]. *PR Newswire*. https://www.prnewswire.com/news-releases/pearson-unveils-ai-tool-to-help-educators-save-time-and-prioritize-student-learning-302199879.html?utm_source=chatgpt.com

Porayska-Pomsta, K., Holmes, W., & Nemorin, S. (2024). *The Ethics of AI in Education*. https://doi.org/DOI: 10.48550/ARXIV.2406.11842

Poth, R. D. (2024, October 29). AI and the Law: What Educators Need to Know [Edutopia]. *ChatGPT & Generative AI*. https://www.edutopia.org/article/laws-ai-education

Puja, T., Digar, S. F., Anjana, B., & Rakhi, T. (2025). AI in classrooms: Impact on teacher identity and autonomy. *I-Manager's Journal on School Educational Technology*, *20*(4), 39. DOI: 10.26634/jsch.20.4.21964

Sajja, R., Sermet, Y., Cikmaz, M., Cwiertny, D., & Demir, I. (2023). *Artificial Intelligence-Enabled Intelligent Assistant for Personalized and Adaptive Learning in Higher Education* (Version 1). arXiv. https://doi.org/DOI: 10.48550/ARXIV.2309.10892

Slagg, A. (2023, November 14). *AI for Teachers: Defeating Burnout and Boosting Productivity AI can unlock instructors' powers while reducing their workload.* [EdTech]. https://edtechmagazine.com/k12/article/2023/11/ai-for-teachers-defeating-burnout-boosting-productivity-perfcon

Smiderle, R., Rigo, S. J., Marques, L. B., Peçanha De Miranda Coelho, J. A., & Jaques, P. A. (2020). The impact of gamification on students' learning, engagement and behavior based on their personality traits. *Smart Learning Environments*, *7*(1), 3. DOI: 10.1186/s40561-019-0098-x

Suresh Babu, S., & Dhakshina Moorthy, A. (2024). Application of artificial intelligence in adaptation of gamification in education: A literature review. *Computer Applications in Engineering Education*, *32*(1), e22683. DOI: 10.1002/cae.22683

Techflow. (2022, November 1). AI in Education: Global Success Stories Unveiled [Educational]. *TechFLow*. https://teachflow.ai/ai-in-education-global-success-stories-unveiled

UNESCO. (2025). *Ethics of Artificial Intelligence The Recommendation* [The Recommendation]. Global AI Ethics and Governance Observatory. https://www.unesco.org/en/artificial-intelligence/recommendation-ethics

University of Illinios. (2024, October 24). *AI in Schools: Pros and Cons* [College of Education]. https://education.illinois.edu/about/news-events/news/article/2024/10/24/ai-in-schools--pros-and-cons

University of Sydney. (2025). *Academic integrity- Artificial intelligence* (What is generative artificial intelligence?) [Dataset]. https://www.sydney.edu.au/students/academic-integrity/artificial-intelligence.html

Vaishnav, P. (2025). The Paradox of Technology in English Language Education: Connected Or Excluded? *Asian Journal of Education and Social Studies*, *51*(8), 938–950. DOI: 10.9734/ajess/2025/v51i82291

Walter, Y. (2024). Embracing the future of Artificial Intelligence in the classroom: The relevance of AI literacy, prompt engineering, and critical thinking in modern education. *International Journal of Educational Technology in Higher Education, 21*(1), 15. DOI: 10.1186/s41239-024-00448-3

Wang, S., Wang, F., Zhu, Z., Wang, J., Tran, T., & Du, Z. (2024). Artificial intelligence in education: A systematic literature review. *Expert Systems with Applications, 252*, 124167. DOI: 10.1016/j.eswa.2024.124167

Wang, X., & Huang, R. "Tammy," Sommer, M., Pei, B., Shidfar, P., Rehman, M. S., Ritzhaupt, A. D., & Martin, F. (2024). The Efficacy of Artificial Intelligence-Enabled Adaptive Learning Systems From 2010 to 2022 on Learner Outcomes: A Meta-Analysis. *Journal of Educational Computing Research, 62*(6), 1568–1603. DOI: 10.1177/07356331241240459

Wetzler, E. L., Cassidy, K. S., Jones, M. J., Frazier, C. R., Korbut, N. A., Sims, C. M., Bowen, S. S., & Wood, M. (2025). Grading the Graders: Comparing Generative AI and Human Assessment in Essay Evaluation. *Teaching of Psychology, 52*(3), 298–304. DOI: 10.1177/00986283241282696

Wiggers, K. (2018, May 28). *Chinese schools are testing AI that grades papers almost as well as teachers* [VentureBeat]. https://venturebeat.com/ai/chinese-schools-are-testing-ai-that-grades-papers-almost-as-well-as-teachers/?utm

Woldeab, D., & Brothen, T. (2021). Video Surveillance of Online Exam Proctoring: Exam Anxiety and Student Performance. *International Journal of E-Learning & Distance Education Revue Internationale Du E-Learning Et La Formation à Distance, 36*(1). https://www.ijede.ca/index.php/jde/article/view/1204

Wu, R., & Yu, Z. (2024). Do chatbots improve students learning outcomes? Evidence from a meta-analysis. *British Journal of Educational Technology, 55*(1), 10–33. DOI: 10.1111/bjet.13334

Yang, Q.-F., Lian, L.-W., & Zhao, J.-H. (2023). Developing a gamified artificial intelligence educational robot to promote learning effectiveness and behavior in laboratory safety courses for undergraduate students. *International Journal of Educational Technology in Higher Education, 20*(1), 18. DOI: 10.1186/s41239-023-00391-9

Yanuarto, W. N., Jaelani, A., Purwanto, J., & Zakaria, M. I. (2021). Socratic as Mathematics Learning Application for Differential Equations Concept. *Hipotenusa : Journal of Mathematical Society, 3*(1), 97–110. DOI: 10.18326/hipotenusa.v3i1.5309

Yongpradit, P. (2024, January 18). *AI and education: Kids need AI guidance in school. But who guides the schools?* [Education and Skills]. World Ecconomic Forum. https://www.weforum.org/stories/2024/01/ai-guidance-school-responsible-use-in-education/

Zhang, T., Liu, H., Tao, J., Wang, Y., Yu, M., Chen, H., & Yu, G. (2023). Enhancing Dropout Prediction in Distributed Educational Data Using Learning Pattern Awareness: A Federated Learning Approach. *Mathematics*, *11*(24), 4977. DOI: 10.3390/math11244977

Chapter 7
Enhancing Student Engagement With AI:
Personalized Learning and Adaptive Motivation Strategies

Andi Asrifan
https://orcid.org/0000-0002-9934-6129
Universitas Negeri Makassar, Indonesia

Rismawati Rismawati
https://orcid.org/0000-0001-8046-6764
Universitas Muhammadiyah Palopo, Indonesia

Iskandar Sulaiman
Universitas Negeri Makassar, Indonesia

Abdullah Abdullah
Universitas Negeri Makassar, Indonesia

Nurdin Noni
Universitas Negeri Makassar, Indonesia

ABSTRACT

This chapter examines the potential of Artificial Intelligence (AI) to improve student engagement via individualized learning and adaptive motivational techniques. It offers a comprehensive investigation of student participation in the digital age, supported by theoretical and pedagogical frameworks. The discourse emphasizes AI's ability to customize training, facilitate immediate feedback, and enhance motivation via gamification, adaptive responses, and emotional intelligence. Global case studies illustrate practical uses, while ethical, legal, and equity aspects highlight

DOI: 10.4018/979-8-3373-3000-6.ch007

the necessity of responsible implementation. The chapter finishes with governmental proposals and educational innovations designed to maintain AI-enhanced learning environments that are inclusive, transparent, and centered on the learner. This approach ultimately envisions a world where AI enhances participation and fosters comprehensive and transformative educational experiences.

FOUNDATIONS OF STUDENT ENGAGEMENT AND AI INTEGRATION IN EDUCATION

1.1 Understanding Student Engagement in the Digital Era

Student involvement has become a crucial concept in modern educational research, especially in technology-enhanced learning settings. Engagement is acknowledged as a complex phenomenon that includes behavioral, emotional, and cognitive aspects, each differently influencing learners' perseverance, accomplishment, and academic satisfaction (Philippe et al., 2020; Yousafzai et al., 2020; Bond et al., 2020). In the realm of digital education, these aspects must be redefined and reorganized to accommodate progressively hybrid and asynchronous learning paradigms.

The digital age has revolutionized conventional methods of student engagement and altered the interactions among learners, content, peers, and instructors. Previously, physical presence acted as a surrogate for involvement; however, contemporary indicators include login frequency, participation in discussion boards, time spent on tasks, and reaction to digital feedback mechanisms (Demartini et al., 2024; Hussain & Khan, 2021). Nonetheless, these behavioral markers inadequately reflect the extent of cognitive engagement or emotional connection—two essential elements that support significant learning experiences (Jeganathan et al., 2024).

The quality of instructional design, clarity of learning objectives, and relevance of content to students' own goals significantly impact cognitive engagement in digital platforms. In the absence of systematic scaffolding and continuous feedback, pupils may exhibit superficial conformity rather than authentic intellectual engagement (Reeve, 2012). Likewise, emotional engagement—defined as a student's sense of belonging, interest, or enjoyment—may be diminished in digital contexts due to isolation, insufficient real-time connection, or the perceived impersonality of AI-mediated communication (Nandini et al., 2024; Olanipekun, 2025).

As educational institutions progressively incorporate Artificial Intelligence (AI) to enhance personalization and automation, inquiries emerge regarding its effects on student engagement. AI systems can improve behavioral engagement via gamified interfaces and adaptive task sequencing; nevertheless, their impact on deeper motivation and agency is still inadequately examined (Holmes et al., 2019).

Furthermore, the ethical aspect of engagement warrants examination: are students genuinely engaged, or are they being influenced by algorithmic prompts that mimic engagement behaviors? Comprehending engagement in the digital age necessitates a sophisticated, multifaceted paradigm that considers the interaction of learner agency, technology capabilities, and pedagogical purpose. Only via the analysis of these interdependencies can we create AI-enhanced learning environments that foster genuine involvement instead of compliance-based participation.

1.2 The Role of Artificial Intelligence in 21st Century Pedagogy

The emergence of Artificial Intelligence (AI) in education has transformed the parameters of pedagogy in the 21st century. Transcending conventional instructional methods, AI introduces enhanced engagement, adaptability, and accuracy in addressing varied student requirements. In this revolutionary environment, AI has transitioned from a futuristic notion to a current force that actively influences the delivery, personalization, and experience of knowledge (Nandini et al., 2024; Yousafzai et al., 2020).

Fundamentally, AI in education serves to enhance teaching and learning by facilitating systems that can analyze data, forecast results, and tailor to specific learner profiles. Intelligent tutoring systems, natural language processing engines, virtual agents, and predictive analytics platforms have initiated responsive learning environments that customize instructional materials in real-time to align with students' ability, pace, and preferences. These technologies enable educators to transition from a uniform approach to one that promotes differentiated education on an unprecedented scale (Binhammad et al., 2024; Inthanon & Wised, 2024).

The incorporation of AI necessitates a transformation of the educator's role, shifting from mere content provider to learning architect and facilitator of intricate cognitive interaction. Educators are now required to design learning experiences augmented by AI, prioritizing critical thinking, creativity, and collaboration (Olanipekun, 2025). In this redefined paradigm, education is enhanced by automation, enabling educators to concentrate more intently on mentorship, empathy, and facilitating inquiry-based learning.

Furthermore, AI improves engagement by providing real-time feedback, detecting knowledge deficiencies, and allowing for ongoing and adaptive formative assessments. These dynamic capabilities empower students to take an active role in their educational journey by providing timely feedback on their progress and areas for enhancement (Jeganathan et al., 2024; Kumar, 2023). The interactivity inherent in AI tools fosters student autonomy and self-directed learning, essential qualities for lifelong learning growth.

Notwithstanding its potential, the incorporation of AI in education requires careful consideration. Ethical issues regarding data protection, algorithmic bias, and openness in decision-making are fundamental to ethical implementation (Olanipekun, 2025; Rivas et al., 2024). Technological innovation alone does not ensure pedagogical efficacy; it requires deliberate instructional design and human-centered methodologies. AI possesses significant potential to transform education, not by supplanting human instruction, but by enhancing its accessibility and adaptability. When connected with effective pedagogical ideas, AI serves as a formidable ally in enhancing profound and meaningful student engagement within the changing educational context.

1.3 Ethical and Pedagogical Considerations in AI-Enhanced Engagement

As Artificial Intelligence (AI) becomes more integrated into educational settings, its ramifications extend beyond mere utility and efficiency to encompass ethical and pedagogical considerations. AI offers significant potential to improve student engagement via personalization and automation; however, it also introduces essential concerns that need to be addressed for responsible and equitable implementation (Nandini et al., 2024; Striking a Balance: Navigating the Ethical Dilemmas of AI in Higher Education, 2024).

A primary ethical concern in AI-mediated interaction is data privacy. AI systems frequently depend on the ongoing collection and analysis of learner data to modify content, produce insights, or initiate interventions. Although these methods may improve learning results, they also pose concerns related to monitoring, illegal access, and the abuse of sensitive information (Al-Zahrani, 2024; Paolucci et al., 2024). Students may lack full awareness of the utilization and goals of their data, prompting issues regarding informed consent, agency, and autonomy.

Moreover, algorithmic bias poses a substantial risk to fairness in educational participation. AI systems developed using unrepresentative or biased data can unintentionally perpetuate existing inequities, marginalizing pupils based on race, gender, socioeconomic background, or learning preferences. If not meticulously constructed and supervised, AI systems may favor specific groups while marginalizing others in learning analytics and prediction models (Chen, 2023; Luttges et al., 2023; Somorin & Ademola, 2024). Guaranteeing equity necessitates ongoing evaluation, inclusive design methodologies, and transparency in algorithmic determinations.

From an educational perspective, the incorporation of AI should not diminish education to a transactional, efficiency-oriented endeavor. Engagement should not be conflated with mere obedience or gamified reactions. Although AI can facilitate feedback and customize content delivery, the core of significant learning is in interpersonal interactions, critical inquiry, and the development of empathy and reflection (Olanipekun, 2025; Yaseen et al., 2025). Pedagogical frameworks must consequently direct AI implementation to enhance—not supplant—human interaction in education.

Educators encounter the difficulty of preserving professional autonomy in AI-enhanced classrooms. As intelligent systems provide recommendations, evaluate assignments, or track interaction patterns, educators must retain the authority to question, override, or reinterpret AI-generated proposals. Education should consistently emphasize context, intuition, and student expression, aspects that no algorithm can entirely emulate. Ethical and pedagogical factors must be central to any AI-driven engagement strategy. By emphasizing trust, diversity, and educational integrity, stakeholders can guarantee that AI not only improves student involvement but also reinforces the core ideals of democratic and transformative education.

PERSONALIZED LEARNING THROUGH ARTIFICIAL INTELLIGENCE

2.1 Conceptualizing Personalized Learning: Principles and Frameworks

Personalized learning is a revolutionary educational methodology that customizes learning experiences to address the distinct needs, interests, and objectives of individual students. In contrast to conventional instructional paradigms that frequently depend on standardized curriculum and consistent pace, customized learning prioritizes differentiation, learner autonomy, and contextual relevance (Inthanon & Wised, 2024; Jeganathan et al., 2024). In the era of Artificial Intelligence (AI), this methodology acquires enhanced scalability and precision, facilitating more dynamic and responsive learning environments.

Personalized learning fundamentally relies on several essential ideas. It acknowledges that learners advance at different rates and possess varied backgrounds, prior knowledge, and interests in the classroom. Secondly, it fosters learner agency by enabling students to make significant decisions on the content, methodology, and timing of their learning (Do et al., 2023; Ernst & Stelley, 2024; Singh et al., 2024). Third, it utilizes ongoing feedback and formative evaluation to drive instructional choices and direct students along adaptive pathways. These ideas are based on recognized educational theories, such as constructivism, mastery learning, and self-regulated learning.

Frameworks for executing personalized learning typically incorporate essential elements such as learner profiles, individualized learning trajectories, and competency-based advancement. Learner profiles encompass students' cognitive inclinations, emotional conditions, and behavioral tendencies, offering a data-driven basis for tailored interventions. Learning pathways are designed to correspond with students' objectives, strengths, and requirements, frequently facilitating asynchronous advancement and interdisciplinary connections (Jeganathan et al., 2024; Kanchon et al., 2024; Plooy et al., 2024). Competency-based progression allows students to move upon exhibiting proficiency, rather than conforming to inflexible schedules or seat-time mandates.

AI technologies improve the practicality and efficacy of personalized learning by analyzing extensive learner data in real-time. Algorithms can discern performance trends, forecast learning trajectories, and suggest resources or activities customized to individual profiles. Intelligent systems can enhance education by modifying task complexity, providing specific feedback, and promoting reflection via analytics dashboards (Graaf et al., 2023; Lim et al., 2022).

Nonetheless, envisioning individualized learning within AI-augmented environments necessitates a reevaluation of pedagogical functions and system architecture. Educators must reconcile automation with human discernment, ensuring that personalization does not foster excessive dependence on technology or compromise the social aspects of learning. Furthermore, frameworks must be comprehensive, principled, and flexible to various educational environments. The use of AI into personalized learning beyond optimization; it involves re-envisioning the educational experience as a dynamic, student-centric journey enhanced by technical intelligence and human compassion.

2.2 AI Technologies for Delivering Personalized Education

The incorporation of Artificial Intelligence (AI) in education has expedited the transformation of personalized learning from a theoretical concept to a practical implementation. Through the utilization of sophisticated algorithms, adaptable interfaces, and data-centric systems, AI technologies have empowered educators to provide learning experiences that are customized in real-time to meet the specific needs of individual students. These technologies extend beyond material delivery; they analyze, react to, and predict learner behaviors to promote enhanced engagement and academic development (Binhammad et al., 2024; Nandini et al., 2024; Sonni, 2025).

The Intelligent Tutoring System (ITS) is a leading instrument in this field. These systems emulate human-like instruction by evaluating student responses, recognizing misconceptions, and delivering immediate, context-relevant feedback. ITS platforms can facilitate learning by modulating difficulty levels, recommending additional resources, or guiding students back to fundamental concepts as necessary. Borchers et al. (2023), Kumar (2023), Shih et al. (2023) Their interactivity and responsiveness render them particularly useful in facilitating mastery learning.

Natural Language Processing (NLP) is a transformational technology that facilitates tailored dialogue-based learning. AI systems utilize NLP to understand, interpret, and produce human language, enabling tailored interactions with students (Binhammad et al., 2024; Yang et al., 2025). Chatbots can offer round-the-clock academic assistance, address content-related inquiries, or assist learners with tasks while adjusting tone and difficulty according to the user's competence level.

Simultaneously, learning analytics and predictive modeling are essential for forecasting learner trajectories. Through the aggregation of data regarding engagement patterns, assessment outcomes, and interaction histories, AI systems can forecast which kids are susceptible to underachievement and propose specific remedies. These insights enable educators to take preemptive action, customizing assistance solutions prior to the escalation of problems (AlTwijri & Alghizzi, 2024; Shi et al., 2024).

Recommendation systems, akin to those utilized in e-commerce and streaming services, are progressively being implemented in educational environments. These systems recommend educational resources, modules, or activities according to students' preferences, learning styles, and past performance. This personalization boosts relevance and promotes self-directed learning and motivation (Binhammad et al., 2024; Duan et al., 2025).

Additionally, emotion AI—an emerging subdiscipline—examines facial expressions, vocal intonation, and behavioral indicators to identify emotional states such as displeasure, boredom, or confusion. By identifying these emotional signals, AI systems can dynamically alter the learning environment, providing encouragement or modifying task requirements to sustain emotional and cognitive equilibrium. These AI technologies are collectively revolutionizing personalized education. Their deliberate implementation converts static instructional models into dynamic ecosystems that acknowledge, appreciate, and intelligently assist each learner's path.

From a theoretical standpoint, these AI systems should be assessed not just for technological efficiency but also through motivational and engagement paradigms. Intelligent tutoring systems and recommendation engines may enhance competence and success expectancy; nevertheless, their long-term effects on intrinsic motivation remain ambiguous if they do not foster autonomy and relatedness. This contradiction is further explored in the discourse on adaptive motivation mechanisms.

Although emerging AI systems provide robust means for customisation, other significant problems arise. What pedagogical conditions enable adaptive systems to foster authentic involvement instead of mere compliance? How can educators analyze and address AI-generated recommendations while maintaining professional autonomy? How do these systems address equality, bias, and learner diversity? The succeeding parts address these problems through discussions on motivational theory, ethical considerations, and implementation challenges.

2.3 Implementation Challenges and Equity Concerns

The potential of Artificial Intelligence (AI) in customized learning is revolutionary; nonetheless, its execution presents considerable hurdles and risks. The trajectory of AI-enhanced education is influenced by intricate technological, pedagogical, and ethical considerations that might either exacerbate or mitigate current educational disparities (Al-Zahrani, 2024; Nandini et al., 2024; Pahi et al., 2024). It is crucial to address these challenges to guarantee that AI-driven personalization significantly enhances inclusive and fair learning environments.

A significant difficulty pertains to the availability and quality of data. AI systems necessitate substantial quantities of precise, varied, and representative data to generate meaningful predictions and recommendations. Numerous educational institutions, especially in under-resourced environments, exhibit insufficient, inconsistent, or fragmented data infrastructure (Adhikari et al., 2024; Rana et al., 2024). This data deficiency may result in biased models that overlook the diversity of student experiences, thereby marginalizing learners from the advantages of personalization.

The issue of algorithmic bias is closely connected. If training datasets embody historical inequalities or cultural uniformity, AI systems may maintain or exacerbate those disadvantages (Bozkurt et al., 2023; Nandini et al., 2024). Adaptive learning platforms may be ineffective for students whose learning behaviors diverge from the normative patterns integrated into the system. In the absence of transparent and inclusive design practices, personalization may serve as a tool of exclusion instead of empowerment.

Moreover, differences in infrastructure and internet access persist as a significant equity issue. Personalized learning solutions frequently assume reliable access to devices, stable internet connectivity, and digital literacy—assumptions that are not generally applicable. Students in rural locales, economically disadvantaged households, or conflict-impacted regions may have systemic obstacles to accessing AI-enhanced education (Mustafa et al., 2024; Olanipekun, 2025). These technical disparities threaten to solidify educational inequity, notwithstanding AI's assertions of democratizing learning.

Ethical problems around student privacy and consent present an additional element of complexity. AI-driven personalization entails ongoing surveillance, data harvest, and behavioral profiling, which—if executed without informed consent—may violate students' rights and autonomy. Insufficient regulation and a deficiency of openness can undermine trust among students, educators, and institutions. Educator training and institutional readiness are pivotal for the successful incorporation of AI.

Educators may be inadequately trained to recognize AI-generated insights, modify curriculum accordingly, or critically evaluate algorithmic conclusions. In the absence of comprehensive professional development and pedagogical coherence, AI tools are likely to be misapplied or inadequately exploited. To attain fair outcomes, the application of AI must be directed by ethical foresight, inclusive design, and a dedication to assisting all learners, particularly those most vulnerable to marginalization.

ADAPTIVE MOTIVATION STRATEGIES IN AI-POWERED LEARNING

3.1 Theoretical Perspectives on Motivation in Educational Technology

This section explores how motivational theories offer a critical perspective for assessing whether AI-enabled customisation truly enhances engagement or simply improves short-term performance. Motivation is a fundamental factor influencing student involvement, persistence, and accomplishment. In technology-mediated learning environments, comprehending motivational processes is more essential, as digital platforms transform student interactions with content, instructors, and peers. Adaptive AI-driven systems present novel opportunities to enhance and maintain learner motivation; nonetheless, their design must be grounded in solid theoretical frameworks to guarantee significant effectiveness (Olanipekun, 2025; Pahi et al., 2024).

Self-Determination Theory (SDT) is a pivotal concept that asserts intrinsic motivation thrives when three psychological needs—autonomy, competence, and relatedness—are satisfied. AI technologies can enhance autonomy by enabling students to select their learning trajectories, foster competence through structured feedback, and promote relatedness via socially intelligent agents that replicate peer or teacher interactions (Egunjobi & Adeyeye, 2024; Olanipekun, 2025). Nonetheless, when AI systems enforce inflexible learning frameworks or excessive monitoring, they jeopardize these motivational factors.

The Expectancy-Value Theory is another significant model that elucidates motivation as a function of learners' anticipated success and the value they attribute to the job. In AI-enhanced systems, adaptive feedback and personalized goal-setting can shape these perceptions (Ajani et al., 2024). When students believe that the system recognizes their capabilities and modifies tasks accordingly, their expectations for success rise. Concurrently, relevance-driven content recommendations can enhance task value by aligning with learners' interests and ambitions.

Flow Theory, conceived by Mihaly Csikszentmihalyi, introduces a dynamic aspect to motivation. It characterizes ideal learning experiences as instances in which individuals are completely engaged, harmonizing challenge and skill. Artificial intelligence can enhance flow by tracking learner performance and dynamically modifying task complexity to sustain engagement (Das et al., 2023; Rivas et al., 2024). When the difficulty level is excessively low, learners experience boredom; when it is excessively high, they encounter anxiety. Adaptive systems strive to maintain learners within the flow channel.

Moreover, Goal Orientation Theory differentiates between mastery and performance objectives. AI systems can promote mastery orientation by prioritizing progress, effort, and personal development over competition or external comparison. Motivational messaging, dashboard feedback, and gamification components can be synchronized with these goal frameworks (Ajani et al., 2024; Winkens & Hamstra, 2023). By anchoring AI-driven learning environments in these theoretical frameworks, designers and educators may transcend superficial engagement and cultivate profound, enduring motivation. A robust theoretical framework guarantees that technology facilitates not only performance but also the cultivation of lifelong learning habits and autonomous academic resilience.

3.2 AI-Supported Motivational Interventions

Artificial Intelligence (AI) provides a robust array of tools for the design and execution of motivating interventions tailored to the distinct requirements, preferences, and emotional conditions of learners. Utilizing real-time data and predictive algorithms, AI systems may generate dynamic, tailored settings that not only provide information but also maintain and augment student motivation during the learning process.

A prevalent method in AI-driven settings is gamification, which incorporates game-like components such as points, badges, levels, and leaderboards into the educational experience. These features are frequently modified in response to learner performance and engagement metrics. When executed proficiently, gamification can enhance intrinsic motivation by including challenge, feedback, and a sense of accomplishment (Huang & Chuang, 2025; Ng et al., 2024; Ortiz-Rojas et al., 2025). Artificial intelligence augments this methodology by tailoring difficulty levels, suggesting certain tasks to sustain engagement, and ensuring that incentives correspond with learners' objectives and preferences.

Another significant intervention entails adaptive feedback systems. In contrast to conventional static feedback, AI-driven feedback is instantaneous, contextually aware, and customized to the learner's present level of comprehension. These systems examine trends in student responses to detect misconceptions, provide alternate learning tactics, and enhance mastery (Kumar, 2023; Nandini et al., 2024; Topping et al., 2025). Adaptive feedback fosters self-efficacy and resilience through focused encouragement and constructive advice, which are essential for motivational development.

Emotional AI, a burgeoning domain in educational technology, presents a new dimension of motivational assistance. Through the utilization of sensors, facial recognition, and behavioral analytics, AI is capable of identifying emotional states such as frustration, boredom, or perplexity. The system can modify content delivery, recommend breaks, or activate motivating messages aimed at re-engaging learners. This emotional adaptation cultivates a more empathic and responsive learning environment, enabling students to feel comprehended and supported (Jeganathan et al., 2024; Plooy et al., 2024).

Furthermore, AI systems can provide tailored goal-setting interventions. Through the examination of student learning histories and preferences, intelligent systems can propose both short-term and long-term objectives that are suitably demanding and significant. The objectives are monitored via dashboards and visual progress indicators, enhancing a sense of direction and achievement (Egunjobi & Adeyeye, 2024; Huang & Chuang, 2025).

Motivational interventions enhanced by AI are most effective when they are structured to conform to fundamental psychological principles. Instead than controlling behavior, these systems should focus on fostering genuine involvement, self-regulation, and a growth mentality. When integrated judiciously, AI serves as a motivating ally—promoting learners to not just succeed but to flourish.

3.3 Assessing the Impact of AI on Learner Motivation

Evaluating the influence of Artificial Intelligence (AI) on student motivation is crucial for comprehending the efficacy and ethical considerations of intelligent educational systems. Although AI technologies provide innovative avenues for enhancing engagement and tailored experiences, their role in maintaining motivation requires empirical validation through multidimensional and context-sensitive evaluation frameworks.

Motivation is intrinsically multifaceted, encompassing emotional, cognitive, and behavioral aspects. Consequently, evaluation methods must transcend superficial indicators—such as login frequency or job completion rates—to encompass more profound motivational changes. A way entails integrating learning analytics with self-report tools, including motivational scales derived from Self-Determination Theory or Expectancy-Value Theory (Ortiz-Rojas et al., 2025; Wibowo, 2025). These instruments assess perceived autonomy, competence, relevance, and effort regulation, providing a comprehensive perspective on learners' motivational orientations in AI-mediated environments.

Real-time behavioral data gathered by AI systems can provide nuanced markers of motivational dynamics. Metrics including time-on-task, response latency, help-seeking behavior, and interaction patterns with adaptive material can be examined to deduce engagement levels and motivational trends. A reduction in exploratory activity or heightened disengagement with feedback may indicate diminishing intrinsic motivation (Wibowo, 2025; Yaseen et al., 2025). The ability of AI to monitor these changes over time enables detailed understanding of motivational trajectories.

Affective computing technologies enhance assessment by detecting emotional indicators via facial expressions, vocal tone, and physiological signs. These data points can assist in identifying emotional states such as annoyance, boredom, or curiosity, which are intricately linked to motivation (Demartini et al., 2024; Hamzah & Abdalla, 2024; Xu et al., 2024). When implemented judiciously, emotion identification facilitates timely interventions that enhance motivation in real time.

Furthermore, qualitative assessments, such as student comments, focus groups, and teacher observations, provide essential contextual insights into learners' experiences with AI systems. Such narratives frequently reveal motivating variables that quantitative data may neglect, such trust in the system, perceived equity, or sentiments of empowerment vs manipulation (Shi et al., 2024; Walter, 2024).

Assessment must also evaluate long-term motivational results, including persistence in learning, the cultivation of self-regulated learning mechanisms, and the transfer of motivation beyond the AI-enhanced setting. These results ascertain whether AI promotes lasting learner autonomy or simply transient conformity (Bognár et al., 2024; Nandini et al., 2024; Wang & Li, 2024). To guarantee that AI augments rather than undermines motivation, evaluative processes must be rooted in ethical, pedagogical, and psychological principles. A balanced strategy—integrating technology accuracy with human understanding—is essential for harnessing the complete motivational potential of AI-driven learning environments.

CASE STUDIES AND BEST PRACTICES IN AI-DRIVEN ENGAGEMENT

4.1 Global Case Studies of AI-Enhanced Student Engagement

Artificial Intelligence (AI) has been progressively integrated into many global educational systems to improve student engagement via personalized, adaptive, and data-driven learning experiences. Global case studies provide significant insights into the opportunities and problems associated with AI integration across many social and infrastructural contexts (Egunjobi & Adeyeye, 2024; Nandini et al., 2024; Roshanaei et al., 2023). These instances illustrate technological innovation and emphasize the intricate relationship among education, policy, and digital equity.

The Ministry of Education in Singapore has used AI-driven platforms in public schools to facilitate differentiated instruction and provide real-time analytics. The Learning Feedback Assistant offers students prompt, individualized feedback on writing assignments, concurrently supplying teachers with insights to modify course pacing and assist underperforming learners. Engagement measures indicate enhanced time-on-task, elevated student confidence, and diminished anxiety via prompt and constructive feedback mechanisms (Graaf et al., 2023; Meyer et al., 2023; Topping et al., 2025).

In Finland, a nation recognized for its learner-centered educational approach, AI tools are included to enhance inquiry-based learning. A prominent instance is the MathCraft system, which employs gamified AI algorithms to modify issue difficulty according to student advancement. The system preserves motivation via adaptive challenges and fosters profound mathematical reasoning. Educators serve as facilitators, analyzing AI data to promote collaborative discourse and critical analysis (Bayaga, 2024).

In India, the non-profit organization Mindspark provides AI-driven education to underfunded urban and rural schools. The platform mitigates deficiencies in fundamental reading and numeracy by tailoring training in local languages and according to national curricula. Assessments indicate substantial educational advancements among underprivileged students, particularly when the platform is integrated with instructor-led facilitation (Hoop et al., 2023; Jeganathan et al., 2024). This scenario highlights AI's ability to address learning disparities when implemented with contextual awareness.

In the United States, numerous school districts have implemented AI-driven dashboards and recommendation systems in blended learning frameworks. Platforms such as DreamBox and Knewton facilitate student interaction with content tailored to their skill levels and learning preferences. These tools enable educators to analyze engagement patterns, anticipate learning deficiencies, and deliver focused assistance. Nonetheless, apprehensions over data privacy and excessive dependence on automation persist as subjects of policy discourse (Olanipekun, 2025; Paolucci et al., 2024). These global instances highlight the complex nature of AI-enhanced engagement. Success is not exclusively dictated by technological sophistication, but by its integration within pedagogical objectives, local requirements, and inclusive educational aspirations. From the perspective of Self-Determination Theory, these instances indicate that AI-enhanced engagement is most efficacious when systems facilitate learner autonomy and substantive teacher mediation, rather than depending exclusively on automated adaptation.

4.2 Educator Experiences and Institutional Reflections

The effective incorporation of Artificial Intelligence (AI) in educational environments relies not just on technology infrastructure but is also fundamentally dependent on the attitudes, skills, and insights of educators and institutions. Educators, as primary enablers of learning, possess essential insights into the practical realities of AI integration. Their experiences highlight both the advantages and limitations of employing AI to improve student engagement.

Educators frequently indicate that AI tools have improved their capacity to tailor lessons and track student development more efficiently. Real-time analytics dashboards and adaptive learning platforms provide teachers with detailed information into individual student performance, engagement patterns, and behavioral trends. These conclusions endorse varied pedagogical approaches, prompt interventions, and focused scaffolding—particularly in heterogeneous settings where student requirements differ significantly. Numerous instructors characterize this data-driven support as empowering, facilitating more effective planning and adaptive instruction (Goyibova et al., 2025; Smets et al., 2020).

Nonetheless, the use of AI presents considerable pedagogical and emotional obstacles. Educators often articulate apprehensions regarding diminished instructional autonomy when AI systems provide automated recommendations or interventions. Some individuals have discomfort when evaluating feedback generated by algorithms, especially when it conflicts with their professional judgment or contextual understanding of students. This tension highlights the necessity for human supervision and critical analysis in the application of AI-generated insights.

Professional development surfaces as a consistent element in educators' reflections. The successful deployment frequently depends on continuous training in both the technical and pedagogical aspects of AI. Educators require assistance not just in utilizing new tools but also in effectively incorporating them into curriculum, matching them with learning objectives, and addressing ethical issues such as data privacy and student autonomy (Lee & Kwon, 2024; Olanipekun, 2025).

From an institutional standpoint, reflections indicate that the implementation of AI necessitates a cultural transformation. Institutions that foster collaborative learning environments, prioritize innovation, and emphasize student-centered methodologies are more adept at implementing AI. Administrative leadership, interdepartmental cooperation, and explicit data ethics norms facilitate more seamless integration processes. In contrast, institutions that implement AI as a top-down endeavor without engaging stakeholders frequently face resistance and diminished utilization. Educator experiences and institutional reflections provide a substantive perspective on AI-enhanced engagement. They indicate that technology by itself does not alter learning; rather, it is the deliberate, reflective, and empowered application of AI—steered by professional discernment and ethical purpose—that engenders significant transformation in educational practices.

4.3 Scalability, Sustainability, and Long-Term Impact

As Artificial Intelligence (AI) rapidly permeates educational systems, inquiries regarding scalability, sustainability, and long-term effects become progressively essential. The overarching problem extends beyond pilot initiatives and localized triumphs; it involves converting AI-enhanced interaction into a comprehensive, sustainable educational breakthrough that equitably benefits all learners.

Scalability denotes the capacity of AI projects to extend across many educational settings without sacrificing efficacy or integrity. Although initial implementations frequently succeed in affluent, metropolitan, or experimental contexts, expanding AI tools to rural, under-resourced, or multilingual settings presents infrastructural, cultural, and pedagogical obstacles. Success relies not just on technological reproduction but also on contextual flexibility. Scalable solutions must be adaptable, compatible with existing systems, and attuned to local curricular objectives and pedagogical practices (El-Hamamsy et al., 2023; Palada et al., 2024).

Sustainability requires long-term sustainability concerning finance, infrastructure, training, and policy alignment. Numerous AI initiatives face the peril of stagnating once initial funding or pilot-phase impetus wanes. Effective integration necessitates strong institutional dedication, continuous professional development for educators, and strategic collaborations among educational institutions, technology developers, and policymakers (Southworth et al., 2023). Furthermore, ethical sustainability must be emphasized—ensuring that systems maintain transparency, equity, and the safeguarding of student data throughout time.

Institutional sustainability entails establishing governance structures for the monitoring, evaluation, and iteration of AI systems. Ongoing professional development, ethical auditing processes, and feedback systems from educators and learners are essential to enhance AI technologies and maintain trust. In the absence of institutional learning integrated into the process, AI risks becoming into a static or outdated instrument rather than a dynamic teaching partner.

Assessing the enduring effects of AI on student engagement necessitates a transition from immediate metrics—such as examination scores or completion rates—toward more holistic measures of educational development. This encompasses the cultivation of learner autonomy, critical thinking, emotional resilience, and dispositions for lifelong learning. Institutions must monitor not only academic success but also the impact of AI systems on pedagogical relationships, equity outcomes, and learner well-being across time. The objective is to guarantee that AI augments—not supplants—the intrinsic human quality of education. To ensure that AI-enhanced engagement is scalable, sustainable, and impactful, it must be founded on inclusive design, ethical foresight, and ongoing interaction between technology and pedagogy.

FUTURE DIRECTIONS, ETHICAL REFLECTIONS, AND POLICY IMPLICATIONS

5.1 Future Trends in AI and Student Engagement

The future of student participation in education will be significantly influenced by the integration of Artificial Intelligence (AI) with new educational frameworks. As AI technologies advance, they offer enhanced customisation and more human-centric engagement that surpass conventional educational models. Future trends indicate the emergence of intelligent systems that are not only reactive but also proactive, compassionate, and co-creative in promoting lifelong learning.

A significant trend is the progression of context-aware AI, which transcends static adaptation to dynamically react to learners' settings, emotional conditions, and social interactions. AI systems will utilize multimodal data inputs—such as voice, facial expressions, physiological signals, and location data—to customize learning experiences in real-time with enhanced emotional sensitivity and relevance. These systems might adjust not only content complexity but also tone, pace, and interaction style to align with the learner's changing requirements (Kanchon et al., 2024; Olanipekun, 2025).

A nascent frontier is the integration of AI with immersive technologies, including Augmented Reality (AR), Virtual Reality (VR), and Mixed Reality (MR). These interfaces are anticipated to convert engagement from passive screen interaction to immersive, experience learning. AI-powered virtual instructors and intelligent avatars will assist students in simulations, collaborative exploratory tasks, and gamified settings, enhancing engagement through presence, interaction, and flow (Egunjobi & Adeyeye, 2024; Wang et al., 2025).

The future anticipates collaborative AI, wherein intelligent agents engage not only with learners but also in conjunction with educators, peers, and parents to facilitate comprehensive learning experiences. These AI systems will operate as co-learners and co-facilitators, cooperatively adjusting instructional tactics depending on input from several stakeholders (Tong & Hu, 2024). This collaborative agency between humans and robots will transform roles, duties, and relational dynamics within the classroom.

Ethical and inclusive design will be crucial to these advancements. Future AI systems must exhibit transparency, accountability, and be devoid of cultural, racial, and socioeconomic prejudices. This entails the creation of algorithms that accommodate various learning styles, languages, and accessibility requirements, guaranteeing that forthcoming interaction models are both pioneering and fair (Gaskins, 2022; Roshanaei et al., 2023). As AI becomes more embedded in education, student involvement will transform into a multifaceted, individualized, and morally conscious experience. Institutions, educators, and technologists must cooperatively construct this future—rooted not only in innovation but also in principles that preserve the dignity, autonomy, and humanity of every learner.

5.2 Ethical and Legal Considerations in Personalized AI Learning

As personalized Artificial Intelligence (AI) becomes more embedded in education, ethical and legal considerations must be prioritized in system design, implementation, and governance. Although AI has the capacity to democratize education and improve engagement, it also presents intricate challenges related to privacy, consent, equity, accountability, and the safeguarding of learner autonomy (Al-Zahrani, 2024).

A fundamental ethical challenge in AI-driven personalization is data privacy and surveillance. Personalized learning systems depend on ongoing data collecting, encompassing academic performance, behavioral habits, and emotional indicators. In the absence of explicit consent procedures, students may lack awareness regarding the collection, analysis, and dissemination of personal data. This lack of transparency undermines informed decision-making and may foster conditions of passive surveillance, diminishing trust and student autonomy.

The topic of algorithmic bias and prejudice is closely interconnected. AI systems developed with biased or incomplete datasets can reinforce existing societal disparities. Students from minority backgrounds may be inaccurately classified, inadequately supported, or disproportionately identified for intervention due to biased algorithmic assumptions. Ensuring equity necessitates thorough audits of AI models, diversified training datasets, and inclusive design methodologies that consider a broad spectrum of learner profiles and cultural contexts (Dieterle et al., 2022; Gaskins, 2022; Gurevich et al., 2022; Olanipekun, 2025).

From a legal perspective, adherence to data protection regulations—such as the General Data Protection Regulation (GDPR) in the European Union and the Children's Online Privacy Protection Act (COPPA) in the United States—is crucial. Educational institutions must guarantee that AI systems comply with legal requirements of data minimization, parental approval for minors, secure data storage, and the right to erasure. Noncompliance not only subjects schools to legal liability but also jeopardizes their reputational integrity and student safety (D'Souza et al., 2024).

An increasing necessity exists to implement accountability frameworks in AI-assisted decision-making. When AI systems impact learning trajectories, assessments, or student evaluations, educators and institutions must retain accountability for ultimate decisions. Excessive delegation of authority to algorithms jeopardizes the personalization of education and compromises pedagogical discernment. Ethical instruction regarding AI should be included into curriculum to equip learners for informed digital citizenship. Students must comprehend the influence of AI on their educational settings and be encouraged to interrogate, contest, and engage in the development of ethical learning technology. In establishing the future of AI in education, ethical and legal vigilance is essential; it is fundamental to safeguarding the rights, dignity, and equity of all learners.

5.3 Policy Recommendations and Pedagogical Innovations

To fully harness the promise of Artificial Intelligence (AI) in improving student engagement, educational systems must implement comprehensive policies and innovative pedagogical practices. These frameworks must facilitate the incorporation of AI technologies while ensuring equity, transparency, and human-centered values are preserved. Sustainable effect necessitates the concurrent evolution of policy and pedagogy to establish environments where technology enhances, rather than supplants, meaningful, customized learning. Policy proposals should commence with the formation of ethical AI governance frameworks.

Educational ministries and school authorities ought to establish explicit protocols for data gathering, algorithmic openness, and learner permission. These policies must enforce regular audits of AI systems for bias, accessibility, and performance, and necessitate that all stakeholders—teachers, students, parents, and administrators—are informed participants in the implementation process. Regulatory clarity is essential for establishing institutional confidence and reducing harm (Corrêa et al., 2023; Nandini et al., 2024; Shen et al., 2024).

Furthermore, policy must prioritize inclusion and equitable access. AI-enhanced participation should not be an exclusive privilege of affluent institutions. Public investments must prioritize digital infrastructure, specialized language assistance, and device accessibility for underrepresented or geographically marginalized communities. National and regional policy frameworks should promote collaboration between technology developers and educators to jointly design culturally sensitive AI solutions that address varied student needs (Roshanaei et al., 2023).

Innovative educational models must be devised to correspond with AI's adaptive capabilities in education. These models ought to foster blended learning settings that integrate algorithmic personalization with collaborative, inquiry-driven, and experiential learning methodologies. Educators ought to be motivated to incorporate AI tools not as substitutes for teaching, but as enhancers of student autonomy, inquisitiveness, and self-management (Moundridou et al., 2024; Shi et al., 2024).

Teacher professional development is essential. Policymakers must finance and institutionalize AI literacy initiatives that enable educators to comprehend, assess, and tailor AI systems to their educational objectives. Training must encompass ethical literacy, data interpretation competencies, and critical engagement with AI feedback to preserve educator autonomy (Hazari, 2024; Olanipekun, 2025; Williams et al., 2022).

The student voice and digital citizenship must be integrated into both policy and instruction. Students ought to be afforded opportunity to critically engage with AI, comprehend its impact on their educational experiences, and contribute to the formation of ethical learning environments (Ng et al., 2023). Deliberate policy formulation and educational innovation are the twin catalysts for a future in which AI facilitates transformative, inclusive, and profoundly engaging education for everyone.

CONCLUSION

The incorporation of Artificial Intelligence (AI) in education is transforming student interactions with curriculum, peers, and educators. This chapter has explored the transformative capacity of AI to improve engagement via personalization, real-time feedback, and adaptive motivational tactics. AI-driven systems may customize educational experiences to meet individual requirements, monitor emotional and behavioral metrics, and deliver interventions that enhance cognitive, emotional, and behavioral aspects of participation.

Nonetheless, technical progress by itself does not ensure substantial engagement. The genuine worth of AI is in its capacity to augment, rather than supplant, the human aspects of education and learning. Educators continue to serve as important facilitators, interpreters, and ethical guardians of AI applications. Effective AI implementation necessitates deliberate instructional design, ongoing professional development, and the collaborative establishment of ethical learning environments that empower educators and learners alike.

The enduring effectiveness of AI in education relies on inclusive and sustainable policies. Concerns including algorithmic bias, data privacy, and discrepancies in digital access must be resolved to prevent the worsening of current educational inequalities. Legal frameworks must guarantee transparency, accountability, and learner autonomy, while institutional initiatives must promote equal access to AI tools across many contexts.

The future of AI-enhanced education should be shaped by collaborative collaborations involving educators, learners, policymakers, and technologists. By integrating innovation with pedagogical integrity and ethical foresight, AI can cultivate dynamic, individualized, and socially equitable learning experiences.

Ultimately, the aim of AI should be to enhance—not undermine—the relational, introspective, and transformative attributes that characterize effective education. Across the discussion, engagement and motivation theories provide a critical lens for distinguishing between AI systems that support learner agency and those that risk reducing learning to algorithmic optimization.

REFERENCES:

Adhikari, P., Hamal, P., & Baidoo, F. (2024). Artificial Intelligence in fraud detection: Revolutionizing financial security. *International Journal of Science and Research Archive*, *13*(1), 1457. DOI: 10.30574/ijsra.2024.13.1.1860

Ajani, O. A., Gamede, B. T., & Matiyenga, T. C. (2024). Leveraging artificial intelligence to enhance teaching and learning in higher education: Promoting quality education and critical engagement. Journal of Pedagogical Sociology and Psychology. https://doi.org/DOI: 10.33902/jpsp.202528400

Al-Zahrani, A. M. (2024). Unveiling the shadows: Beyond the hype of AI in education. *Heliyon*, *10*(9). Advance online publication. DOI: 10.1016/j.heliyon.2024.e30696 PMID: 38737255

AlTwijri, L., & Alghizzi, T. M. (2024). Investigating the integration of artificial intelligence in English as foreign language classes for enhancing learners' affective factors: A systematic review [Review of Investigating the integration of artificial intelligence in English as foreign language classes for enhancing learners' affective factors: A systematic review]. Heliyon, 10(10). Elsevier BV. https://doi.org/DOI: 10.1016/j.heliyon.2024.e31053

Bayaga, A. (2024). Enhancing M Enhancing mathematics problem-solving skills in AI-driven environment: Integrated SEM-neural network approach. *Computers in Human Behavior Reports*, *16*, 100491. DOI: 10.1016/j.chbr.2024.100491

Binhammad, M. H. Y., Othman, A., Abuljadayel, L., Mheiri, H. A., Alkaabi, M., & Almarri, M. (2024a). Investigating Advanced Generative Dialogue Systems for Educational Chatbots. *Creative Education*, *15*(8), 1593. DOI: 10.4236/ce.2024.158096

Bognár, L., Ágoston, G., Bacsa-Bán, A., Fauszt, T., Gubán, G., Joós, A., Juhász, L., Kocsó, E., Kovács, E., Maczó, E. C., Kollár, A. I. M., & Strauber, G. (2024). Re-Evaluating Components of Classical Educational Theories in AI-Enhanced Learning: An Empirical Study on Student Engagement. *Education Sciences*, *14*(9), 974. DOI: 10.3390/educsci14090974

Borchers, C., Carvalho, P. F., Xia, M., Liu, P., Koedinger, K. R., & Aleven, V. (2023). What Makes Problem-Solving Practice Effective? Comparing Paper and AI Tutoring. In Lecture notes in computer science (p. 44). Springer Science+Business Media. https://doi.org/DOI: 10.1007/978-3-031-42682-7_4

Bozkurt, A., Xiao, J., Lambert, S., Pazurek, A., Crompton, H., Koseoglu, S., Farrow, R., Bond, M., Nerantzi, C., Honeychurch, S., Bali, M., Dron, J., Mir, K., Stewart, B., Costello, E., Mason, J., Stracke, C. M., Romero-Hall, E., Koutropoulos, A., . . . Jandrić, P. (2023). Speculative futures on ChatGPT and generative artificial intelligence (AI): A collective reflection from the educational landscape. Zenodo (CERN European Organization for Nuclear Research). https://doi.org/DOI: 10.5281/zenodo.7636568

Chen, Z. (2023). Ethics and discrimination in artificial intelligence-enabled recruitment practices. *Humanities & Social Sciences Communications*, *10*(1). Advance online publication. DOI: 10.1057/s41599-023-02079-x

Corrêa, N. K., Galvão, C., Santos, J. W., Pino, C. D., Pinto, E. P., Barbosa, C., Massmann, D., Mambrini, R., Galvão, L., Terem, E., & Oliveira, N. de. (2023). Worldwide AI ethics: A review of 200 guidelines and recommendations for AI governance [Review of Worldwide AI ethics: A review of 200 guidelines and recommendations for AI governance]. Patterns, 4(10), 100857. Elsevier BV. https://doi.org/DOI: 10.1016/j.patter.2023.100857

D'Souza, R., Mathew, M., Mishra, V., & Surapaneni, K. M. (2024). Twelve tips for addressing ethical concerns in the implementation of artificial intelligence in medical education. *Medical Education Online*, *29*(1). Advance online publication. DOI: 10.1080/10872981.2024.2330250 PMID: 38566608

Das, A. K., Malaviya, S., & Singh, M. K. (2023). The Impact of AI-Driven Personalization on Learners Performance. *International Journal on Computer Science and Engineering*, *11*(8), 15. DOI: 10.26438/ijcse/v11i8.1522

de Hoop, T., Ring, H., Siwach, G., Dias, P. R. G., Tembo, G., Rothbard, V., & Toungui, A. (2023). Impact of Technology-Aided Activity-Based Learning Approaches on Learning Outcomes: Experimental Evidence from Community Schools in Rural Zambia. *Journal of Research on Educational Effectiveness*, *17*(4), 836. DOI: 10.1080/19345747.2023.2268072

Demartini, C. G., Sciascia, L., Bosso, A., & Manuri, F. (2024). Artificial Intelligence Bringing Improvements to Adaptive Learning in Education: A Case Study. *Sustainability*, *16*(3), 1347. DOI: 10.3390/su16031347

Dieterle, E., Dede, C., & Walker, M. E. (2022). The cyclical ethical effects of using artificial intelligence in education. *AI & Society*, *39*(2), 633. DOI: 10.1007/s00146-022-01497-w PMID: 36185064

Do, H., Bich, N., & Nguyen, M. H. (2023). 3How do constructivism learning environments generate better motivation and learning strategies? The Design Science Approach. *Heliyon, 9*(12). Advance online publication. DOI: 10.1016/j.heliyon.2023.e22862 PMID: 38125439

Duan, C., Yang, J., Cui, Q., Zhang, W., Wan, X., & Zhang, M. (2025). Enhancing the Recommendation of Learning Resources for Learners via an Advanced Knowledge Graph. *Applied Sciences (Basel, Switzerland), 15*(8), 4204. DOI: 10.3390/app15084204

Egunjobi, D., & Adeyeye, O. (2024). Revolutionizing Learning: The Impact of Augmented Reality (AR) And Artificial Intelligence (AI on Education. *International Journal of Research Publication and Reviews, 5*(10), 1157. DOI: 10.55248/gengpi.5.1024.2734

El-Hamamsy, L., Monnier, E.-C., Avry, S., Chessel-Lazzarotto, F., Liégeois, G., Bruno, B., Zufferey, J. D., & Mondada, F. (2023). An adapted cascade model to scale primary school digital education curricular reforms and teacher professional development programs. *Education and Information Technologies, 29*(9), 10391. DOI: 10.1007/s10639-023-12043-6

Ernst, J., & Stelley, H. (2024). Supporting Young Children's Self-Regulation Through Nature-Based Practices in Preschool. *Behavioral Sciences (Basel, Switzerland), 14*(11), 1013. DOI: 10.3390/bs14111013 PMID: 39594313

Gaskins, N. R. (2022). Interrogating Algorithmic Bias: From Speculative Fiction to Liberatory Design. *TechTrends, 67*(3), 417. DOI: 10.1007/s11528-022-00783-0 PMID: 36160677

Goyibova, N., Muslimov, N., Sabirova, G., Kadirova, N., & Samatova, B. (2025). Differentiation Approach in Education: Tailoring Instruction for Diverse Learner Needs [Review of Differentiation Approach in Education: Tailoring Instruction for Diverse Learner Needs]. MethodsX, 14, 103163. Elsevier BV. https://doi.org/DOI: 10.1016/j.mex.2025.103163

Gurevich, E., Hassan, B. E., & Morr, C. E. (2022). Equity within AI systems: What can health leaders expect? *Healthcare Management Forum, 36*(2), 119. DOI: 10.1177/08404704221125368 PMID: 36226507

Hamzah, H. A., & Abdalla, K. K. (2024). EEG-based emotion recognition systems; comprehensive study. *Heliyon, 10*(10). Advance online publication. DOI: 10.1016/j.heliyon.2024.e31485 PMID: 38818173

Hazari, S. (2024). Justification and Roadmap for Artificial Intelligence (AI) Literacy Courses in Higher Education. *Journal of Educational Research and Practice*, *14*(1). Advance online publication. DOI: 10.5590/jerap.2024.14.1.07

Huang, H. C., & Chuang, H. W. (2025). A Pilot Study on AI-Powered Gamified Chatbot with OMO Strategy for Enhancing Parental Nutrition Knowledge. *Digital*, *5*(2), 13. DOI: 10.3390/digital5020013

Hussain, S., & Khan, M. Q. (2021). Student-Performulator: Predicting Students' Academic Performance at Secondary and Intermediate Level Using Machine Learning. *Annals of Data Science*, *10*(3), 637. DOI: 10.1007/s40745-021-00341-0 PMID: 38624826

Inthanon, W., & Wised, S. (2024). Tailoring Education: A Comprehensive Review of Personalized Learning Approaches Based on Individual Strengths, Needs, Skills, and Interests [Review of Tailoring Education: A Comprehensive Review of Personalized Learning Approaches Based on Individual Strengths, Needs, Skills, and Interests]. *Journal of Education and Learning Reviews*, *1*(5), 35. DOI: 10.60027/jelr.2024.779

Jeganathan, S., Raj, L. A., Parthasarathy, S., Khan, A. A. A., & Sathick, K. J. (2024). OptCatB: Optuna Hyperparameter Optimization Model to Forecast the Educational Proficiency of Immigrant Students based on CatBoost Regression. *Journal of Internet Services and Information Security*, *14*(3), 111. DOI: 10.58346/jisis.2024.i2.008

Kanchon, Md. K. H., Sadman, M., Nabila, K. F., Tarannum, R., & Khan, R. (2024). Enhancing personalized learning: AI-driven identification of learning styles and content modification strategies. *International Journal of Cognitive Computing in Engineering*, *5*, 269. DOI: 10.1016/j.ijcce.2024.06.002

Kumar, P. S. (2023). Transformative Role of ICT in 21st Century Learning: Enhancing Educational Effectiveness and Equitability. *International Journal for Research in Applied Science and Engineering Technology*, *11*(12), 91. DOI: 10.22214/ijraset.2023.57028

Lee, S. J., & Kwon, K. (2024). A systematic review of AI education in K-12 classrooms from 2018 to 2023: Topics, strategies, and learning outcomes [Review of A systematic review of AI education in K-12 classrooms from 2018 to 2023: Topics, strategies, and learning outcomes]. Computers and Education Artificial Intelligence, 6, 100211. Elsevier BV. https://doi.org/DOI: 10.1016/j.caeai.2024.100211

Lim, L., Bannert, M., van der Graaf, J., Singh, S., Fan, Y., Surendrannair, S., Raković, M., Molenaar, I., Moore, J. D., & Gašević, D. (2022). Effects of real-time analytics-based personalized scaffolds on students' self-regulated learning. *Computers in Human Behavior*, *139*, 107547. DOI: 10.1016/j.chb.2022.107547

Luttges, B. L., Gardner, M., Quirk, A., Stone, C., Rao, A., Ungar, L., Hutt, S., Hickman, L., D'Mello, S. K., & Duckworth, A. (2023). Using artificial intelligence to assess personal qualities in college admissions. *Science Advances*, *9*(41). Advance online publication. DOI: 10.1126/sciadv.adg9405 PMID: 37824610

Meyer, J., Jansen, T., Schiller, R., Liebenow, L. W., Steinbach, M., Horbach, A., & Fleckenstein, J. (2023). Using LLMs to bring evidence-based feedback into the classroom: AI-generated feedback increases secondary students' text revision, motivation, and positive emotions. *Computers and Education Artificial Intelligence*, *6*, 100199. DOI: 10.1016/j.caeai.2023.100199

Moundridou, M., Matzakos, N., & Doukakis, S. (2024). Generative AI tools as educators' assistants: Designing and implementing inquiry-based lesson plans. *Computers and Education Artificial Intelligence*, *7*, 100277. DOI: 10.1016/j.caeai.2024.100277

Mustafa, F., Nguyen, H. T. M., & Gao, X. (2024). The challenges and solutions of technology integration in rural schools: A systematic literature review. *International Journal of Educational Research*, *126*, 102380. DOI: 10.1016/j.ijer.2024.102380

Nandini, N., Indora, P., & Singh, R. (2024). Artificial Intelligence in Journalism: An Overview of its Applications and Uses. *Journal of Communication Management (London)*, *3*(3), 237. DOI: 10.58966/jcm2024337

Ng, D. T. K., Leung, J. K. L., Su, J., Ng, C. W., & Chu, S. K. W. (2023). Teachers' AI digital competencies and twenty-first century skills in the post-pandemic world. *Educational Technology Research and Development*, *71*(1), 137. DOI: 10.1007/s11423-023-10203-6 PMID: 36844361

Ng, D. T. K., Xinyu, C., Leung, J. K. L., & Chu, S. K. W. (2024). Fostering students' AI literacy development through educational games: AI knowledge, affective and cognitive engagement. *Journal of Computer Assisted Learning*, *40*(5), 2049. DOI: 10.1111/jcal.13009

Olanipekun, S. O. (2025). Ethical frameworks for AI in journalism: Balancing technological innovation and journalistic integrity. *World Journal of Advanced Research and Reviews*, *25*(1), 1342. DOI: 10.30574/wjarr.2025.25.1.0187

Ortiz-Rojas, M., Chiluiza, K., Valcke, M., & Bolaños-Mendoza, C. (2025). How gamification boosts learning in STEM higher education: A mixed methods study. *International Journal of STEM Education*, *12*(1). Advance online publication. DOI: 10.1186/s40594-024-00521-3

Pahi, K., Hawlader, S., Hicks, E., Zaman, A., & Phan, V. (2024). Enhancing active learning through collaboration between human teachers and generative AI. *Computers and Education Open*, *6*, 100183. DOI: 10.1016/j.caeo.2024.100183

Palada, B., Chandan, V. S., & Gowda, C. P., & Nikitha, Prof. (2024). The Role of Augmented Reality (AR) in Education. *International Journal for Research in Applied Science and Engineering Technology*, *12*(3), 1400. DOI: 10.22214/ijraset.2024.59079

Paolucci, C., Vancini, S., Bex, R. T., Cavanaugh, T., Salama, C., & Araujo, Z. de. (2024). A review of learning analytics opportunities and challenges for K-12 education [Review of A review of learning analytics opportunities and challenges for K-12 education]. Heliyon, 10(4). Elsevier BV. https://doi.org/DOI: 10.1016/j.heliyon.2024.e25767

Philippe, S., Souchet, A. D., Lameras, P., Petridis, P., Caporal, J., Coldeboeuf, G., & Duzan, H. (2020). Multimodal teaching, learning and training in virtual reality: a review and case study. In Virtual Reality & Intelligent Hardware (Vol. 2, Issue 5, p. 421). Elsevier BV. https://doi.org/DOI: 10.1016/j.vrih.2020.07.008

Plooy, E. du, Casteleijn, D., & Franzsen, D. (2024). Personalized adaptive learning in higher education: a scoping review of key characteristics and impact on academic performance and engagement [Review of Personalized adaptive learning in higher education: a scoping review of key characteristics and impact on academic performance and engagement]. Heliyon, 10(21). Elsevier BV. https://doi.org/DOI: 10.1016/j.heliyon.2024.e39630

Rana, Md. M., Siddiqee, M. S., Sakib, Md. N., & Ahamed, Md. R. (2024). Assessing AI Adoption in Developing Country Academia: A Trust and Privacy-Augmented UTAUT Framework. *Heliyon*. Advance online publication. DOI: 10.1016/j.heliyon.2024.e37569 PMID: 39315142

Rivas, I. M. A., Fernández, S. P., & Fernández, M. (2024). Artificial Intelligence in Slow Journalism: Journalists' Uses, Perceptions, and Attitudes. *Journalism and Media*, *5*(4), 1836. DOI: 10.3390/journalmedia5040111

Roshanaei, M., Olivares, H., & Lopez, R. R. (2023). Harnessing AI to Foster Equity in Education: Opportunities, Challenges, and Emerging Strategies. *Journal of Intelligent Learning Systems and Applications*, *15*(4), 123. DOI: 10.4236/jilsa.2023.154009

Shen, X., Brown, H., Tao, J., Strobel, M., Tong, Y., Narayan, A., Soh, H., & Doshi-Velez, F. (2024). Directions of Technical Innovation for Regulatable AI Systems. *Communications of the ACM*. Advance online publication. DOI: 10.1145/3653670

Shi, L., Ding, A.-C. E., & Choi, I. (2024). Investigating Teachers' Use of an AI-Enabled System and Their Perceptions of AI Integration in Science Classrooms: A Case Study. *Education Sciences, 14*(11), 1187. DOI: 10.3390/educsci14111187

Shih, S.-C., Chang, C.-C., Kuo, B., & Huang, Y. (2023). Mathematics intelligent tutoring system for learning multiplication and division of fractions based on diagnostic teaching. *Education and Information Technologies*, *28*(7), 9189. DOI: 10.1007/s10639-022-11553-z PMID: 36643382

Singh, N., Misra, R., Quan, W., Radić, A., Lee, S.-M., & Han, H. (2024). An analysis of consumer's trusting beliefs towards the use of e-commerce platforms. *Humanities & Social Sciences Communications, 11*(1). Advance online publication. DOI: 10.1057/s41599-024-03395-6

Smets, W., Neve, D. D., & Struyven, K. (2020). Responding to students' learning needs: How secondary education teachers learn to implement differentiated instruction. *Educational Action Research*, *30*(2), 243. DOI: 10.1080/09650792.2020.1848604

Somorin, K., & Ademola, O. E. (2024). Ethical Imperatives in the Era of AI Journalism: Navigating the Intersection of Technology and Responsibility. *Advances in Multidisciplinary & Scientific Research Journal Publication*, *12*(2), 31. DOI: 10.22624/aims/humanities/v12n2p4

Sonni, A. F. (2025). Digital transformation in journalism: Mini review on the impact of AI on journalistic practices. *Frontiers in Communication, 10*. Advance online publication. DOI: 10.3389/fcomm.2025.1535156

Southworth, J., Migliaccio, K. W., Glover, J., Glover, J., Reed, D. M., McCarty, C., Brendemuhl, J. H., & Thomas, A. (2023). Developing a model for AI Across the curriculum: Transforming the higher education landscape via innovation in AI literacy. *Computers and Education Artificial Intelligence*, *4*, 100127. DOI: 10.1016/j.caeai.2023.100127

Striking a Balance: Navigating the Ethical Dilemmas of AI in Higher Education. (2024). https://er.educause.edu/articles/2024/12/striking-a-balance-navigating-the-ethical-dilemmas-of-ai-in-higher-education

Tong, R. J., & Hu, X. (2024). Future of Education with Neuro-Symbolic AI Agents in Self-Improving Adaptive Instructional Systems. *Frontiers of Digital Education.*, *1*(2), 198. DOI: 10.1007/s44366-024-0008-9

Topping, K. J., Gehringer, E. F., Khosravi, H., Gudipati, S., Jadhav, K., & Susarla, S. (2025). Enhancing peer assessment with artificial intelligence. *International Journal of Educational Technology in Higher Education*, *22*(1). Advance online publication. DOI: 10.1186/s41239-024-00501-1

van der Graaf, J., Raković, M., Fan, Y., Lim, L., Singh, S., Bannert, M., Gašević, D., & Molenaar, I. (2023). How to design and evaluate personalized scaffolds for self-regulated learning. *Metacognition and Learning*, *18*(3), 783. DOI: 10.1007/s11409-023-09361-y

Walter, Y. (2024). Embracing the future of Artificial Intelligence in the classroom: The relevance of AI literacy, prompt engineering, and critical thinking in modern education. *International Journal of Educational Technology in Higher Education*, *21*(1). Advance online publication. DOI: 10.1186/s41239-024-00448-3

Wang, L., & Li, W. (2024). The Impact of AI Usage on University Students' Willingness for Autonomous Learning. *Behavioral Sciences (Basel, Switzerland)*, *14*(10), 956. DOI: 10.3390/bs14100956 PMID: 39457827

Wang, T., Wu, T., Liu, H., Brown, C., & Chen, Y. (2025). Generative Co-Learners: Enhancing Cognitive and Social Presence of Students in Asynchronous Learning with Generative AI. *Proceedings of the ACM on Human-Computer Interaction*, *9*(1), 1. DOI: 10.1145/3701198

Wibowo, H. A. (2025). AN EXPLICATION OF HOW WEBSITE DESIGN ACTUALLY SHAPES ONLINE CUSTOMER LOYALTY: INCORPORATING SEM AND PERSON-ITEMS MAP ANALYSIS. *International Journal of Social Service and Research*, *5*(1), 123. DOI: 10.46799/ijssr.v5i1.1190

Williams, R., Ali, S., Devasia, N., DiPaola, D., Hong, J., Kaputsos, S. P., Jordan, B. T., & Breazeal, C. (2022). AI + Ethics Curricula for Middle School Youth: Lessons Learned from Three Project-Based Curricula. *International Journal of Artificial Intelligence in Education*, *33*(2), 325. DOI: 10.1007/s40593-022-00298-y PMID: 35935456

Winkens, J., & Hamstra, M. R. W. (2023). Does encouraging mastery goals benefit performance in a scoring exercise? It may depend on chronic self-adopted achievement goals. *Scandinavian Journal of Psychology*, *65*(2), 339. DOI: 10.1111/sjop.12979 PMID: 37951843

Xu, Y., Lin, Y., Zhou, X., & Shan, X. (2024). Utilizing emotion recognition technology to enhance user experience in real-time. *Computers and Artificial Intelligence*, *2*(1), 1388. DOI: 10.59400/cai.v2i1.1388

Yang, Y., Ma, Y., Hao, F., Cheng, Y., & Han, Z. (2025). Minimizing Hallucinations and Communication Costs: Adversarial Debate and Voting Mechanisms in LLM-Based Multi-Agents. *Applied Sciences (Basel, Switzerland), 15*(7), 3676. DOI: 10.3390/app15073676

Yaseen, H., Mohammad, A. S., Ashal, N., Abusaimeh, H., Ali, A. A. A., & Sharabati, A. A. (2025). The Impact of Adaptive Learning Technologies, Personalized Feedback, and Interactive AI Tools on Student Engagement: The Moderating Role of Digital Literacy. *Sustainability, 17*(3), 1133. DOI: 10.3390/su17031133

Yousafzai, B. K., Hayat, M., & Afzal, S. (2020). Application of machine learning and data mining in predicting the performance of intermediate and secondary education level student. *Education and Information Technologies*, *25*(6), 4677. DOI: 10.1007/s10639-020-10189-1

ADDITIONAL READING

Bond, M., Bedenlier, S., Marín, V. I., & Händel, M. (2021). Emergency remote teaching in higher education: Mapping the first global online semester. *International Journal of Educational Technology in Higher Education*, *18*(1), 50. DOI: 10.1186/s41239-021-00282-x PMID: 34778537

Demartini, C. G., Sciascia, L., Bosso, A., & Manuri, F. (2024). Artificial intelligence bringing improvements to adaptive learning in education: A case study. *Sustainability*, *16*(3), 1347. DOI: 10.3390/su16031347

du Plooy, E., Casteleijn, D., & Franzsen, D. (2024). Personalized adaptive learning in higher education: A scoping review of key characteristics and impact on academic performance and engagement. *Heliyon*, *10*(21), e39630. DOI: 10.1016/j.heliyon.2024.e39630 PMID: 39524879

Graesser, A. C., Sabourin, J. L., & Hu, X. (2022). Dialog-based intelligent tutoring systems. *Computers & Education*, *173*, 104271. DOI: 10.1016/j.compedu.2021.104271

Huang, A. Y. Q., Lu, O. H. T., & Yang, S. J. H. (2022). Effects of artificial intelligence–enabled personalized recommendations on learners' learning engagement, motivation, and outcomes in a flipped classroom. *Computers & Education*, *194*, 104684. DOI: 10.1016/j.compedu.2022.104684

Lee, S. J., & Kwon, K. (2024). A systematic review of AI education in K–12 classrooms: Topics, strategies, and learning outcomes. *Computers and Education: Artificial Intelligence*, *6*, 100211. DOI: 10.1016/j.caeai.2024.100211

Southworth, J., Migliaccio, K. W., Glover, J., Reed, D. M., & McCarty, C. (2023). Developing a model for AI across the curriculum: Transforming higher education through AI literacy. *Computers and Education: Artificial Intelligence*, *4*, 100127. DOI: 10.1016/j.caeai.2023.100127

KEY TERMS AND DEFINITIONS

Adaptive Learning Systems: AI-powered educational systems that adapt content, tempo, and feedback according on learners' performance, behavior, and educational requirements.

Artificial Intelligence In Education: The utilization of machine learning, data analytics, and sophisticated algorithms to enhance teaching, learning, assessment, and educational decision-making.

Ethical AI Implementation: The accountable implementation of AI technologies in education that emphasizes transparency, equity, data confidentiality, and learner independence.

Learner Engagement: A multifaceted concept that includes behavioral engagement, emotional commitment, and cognitive involvement in educational activities.

Learning Analytics: The quantification, aggregation, and examination of learner data to comprehend and enhance educational processes and results.

Motivational Adaptation: The implementation of adaptive tactics and technologies to maintain or augment learner motivation by addressing fluctuations in interest, effort, and emotional condition.

Personalized Learning: A pedagogical method that customizes educational experiences according to each learner's abilities, interests, objectives, and learning pathways.

Self-Determination Theory: A psychological model elucidating motivation via the satisfaction of autonomy, competence, and relatedness.

Technology-Enhanced Pedagogy: Instructional methodologies that incorporate digital and AI-driven tools to enhance educational experiences while preserving pedagogical objectives.

Chapter 8
Harnessing AI for Accessibility and Inclusive Learning Spaces

Kristin Burgess
https://orcid.org/0009-0009-4598-7578
Metro State University, USA

ABSTRACT

This chapter explores how artificial intelligence can be leveraged to enhance accessibility and foster inclusive learning environments. Grounded in Critical Disability Theory and Social Dominance Theory, it examines the intersections of AI, UDL, ableism, and educational equity. Through legal, theoretical, and practical lenses, the chapter highlights how AI tools, when ethically and intentionally applied, can dismantle systemic barriers, support diverse learners, and personalize education. Real-world scenarios illustrate AI's potential to empower students with disabilities, while also addressing risks such as bias, surveillance, and digital divides. Ultimately, the chapter calls for a shift from reactive accommodations to proactive, inclusive design, positioning accessibility as a foundational commitment that can include AI.

INTRODUCTION

Warning: The following chapter will use provocative language. The content is intended for adult readers who are prepared to engage in active critical thinking.

Education is crucial for understanding the world and our distinct ecosystems. As education systems at every level become more diverse, keeping up with the constant state of flux (yes, that four-letter word) — rather than the dreaded six-letter 'change' that often feels like a four-letter curse — can make adopting new pedagogy, tech-

DOI: 10.4018/979-8-3373-3000-6.ch008

nology, and practices feel overwhelmingly challenging. According to the National Center for Education Statistics, in 2022, 27.6 million elementary and secondary public-school students identified as having a racial or ethnic composition other than White. This number is 5.5 million more than that of white students (NCES, 2022). While postsecondary education remains predominantly white at 52%, compared to approximately 47% of students of color (NCES, 2024), the population of students with disabilities in postsecondary schools is increasing. In the 2019-2020 academic year, NCES reported that 32% of postsecondary students indicated having a disability (NCES, 2023). Speaking of disability (that ten-letter word that still somehow gets treated like a four-letter curse), Welding (2023) observes that up to 63% of college students with disabilities choose not to disclose them. This means that a statistically significant number of individuals may be navigating traditional learning environments without equitable access.

Educators, administrators, policymakers, and others continue to seek the elusive solution that creates inclusive learning spaces that will work for all students. Along the way, we have seen a multitude of approaches used. Some have been more successful than others and stuck around, while others have disappeared over time. This chapter will focus on one segment of technology, Artificial Intelligence (AI) – a two-letter abbreviation currently viewed by many as a curse - and explore how it can be harnessed to create greater accessibility and more inclusive learning environments.

Accessibility in Education

If you are new to education, or even if you are a seasoned veteran, you may not have a solid understanding of why accessibility is essential. In the United States, as well as other countries across the globe, ableism is deeply rooted in our cultures. Researchers such as Cherney (2019) and Dolmage (2017) have examined the rhetorical basis for ableism and its connection to the prioritization of accessibility in education. Other researchers, such as Jun (2009), have noted the similarities between ableism and other 'isms' that allow the dominant group to maintain power over non-dominant groups.

Individuals with disabilities form the largest minority group. The World Health Organization (2023) reports that globally, one in six people has a significant disability. In the United States, that figure increases to one in four, according to the Centers for Disease Control (2024). According to Welding (2023), only 49.5% of college and university students with disabilities graduate, compared to 68% of their peers without disabilities. In a recent study by Burgess (2025), students with disabilities indicated that many barriers hinder their completion of post-secondary education, including ableism. Those same students reported that accommodations and the use of Universal Design for Learning help create more inclusive learning environments, thereby enhancing their success.

Universal Design for Learning (UDL) is an emerging practice in post-secondary education. However, it has been more widely adopted in primary and secondary learning environments. This may be due in part to the Higher Education Opportunity Act (HEOA) of 2008, which emphasized that pre-service teacher training programs should incorporate instructional principles that align with UDL. This has provided teachers within the P-12 arena with more exposure to UDL as compared to their counterparts in higher education. "Universal Design for learning is rooted in neuroscience and seeks to find ways of teaching that minimize barriers and maximize learning opportunities. Universal Design for Learning seeks to make learning inclusive to all learners" (Burgess, 2025). Later in this chapter, we will look at how UDL connects with the use of artificial intelligence and disability accommodations.

Understanding the cultural and pedagogical imperatives for accessibility is essential, but recognizing that accessibility is not only a best practice but also a legal obligation is equally crucial. In the United States and many other countries, a robust legal framework exists to protect the rights of individuals with disabilities and ensure equitable access to education. The following section examines the legal foundations that support accessibility in educational settings in the United States, providing context for how laws such as the Americans with Disabilities Act (ADA) and Section 504 of the Rehabilitation Act influence institutional responsibilities and student rights.

Legal Foundations

As previously noted, people with disabilities make up the largest minority group globally, yet they have long faced systemic oppression by dominant societal groups. The number of people with disabilities reported by groups such as the World Health Organization or the Centers for Disease Control likely underrepresents the actual number, in part because disclosing disability status is voluntary. Persistent stigma surrounding disability continues to discourage many individuals from disclosing their status.

Historically, numerous laws have codified the exclusion of people with disabilities. In the United States, for example, 'ugly laws' enacted in the late 19th century criminalized the presence of individuals with visible disabilities in public spaces (Schweik, 2009). Other discriminatory policies included forced sterilization of people labeled as developmentally disabled, sub-minimum wage allowances, and involuntary institutionalization. These legal structures often reflected the interests of dominant groups, reinforcing social hierarchies.

It was not until the 1960s that disability rights advocates in the United States began to dismantle many of these oppressive laws. Landmark U.S. legislation such as the Rehabilitation Act of 1973, the Individuals with Disabilities Education Act (IDEA) of 1975, and the Americans with Disabilities Act (ADA) of 1990 (amended in 2008) marked significant progress by prohibiting discrimination based on disability. In December 2006, the United Nations adopted the Convention on the Rights of Persons with Disabilities. However, despite these advances, implementation has been inconsistent, and many of the original goals remain unrealized even decades later (Burgess, 2025). For example, the United States is one of only seven countries in the United Nations that have not ratified the Convention on the Rights of Persons with Disabilities.

In the United States, two laws have had the most profound impact on higher education: Section 504 of the Rehabilitation Act and the Americans with Disabilities Act (ADA). Because most colleges and universities receive federal funding, they are required to comply with Section 504. The ADA extends protections to both public and private institutions under Titles II and III. Enrollment data shows that the percentage of students with disabilities in postsecondary education has grown from 2–3% in the 1970s to over 11% by 2016 (Miller, 2019). While this increase may suggest progress, it also reflects the ongoing need for accommodations and the persistence of barriers in higher education (Weis & Bittner, 2022).

Both Section 504 and the ADA advocate for accommodations to ensure equitable access to students' learning environments. These laws require students to disclose their disabilities to the institution and engage in an interactive process with the school to identify appropriate and reasonable accommodations. In some instances, schools may request documentation of the student's disability to confirm that they are a qualified individual. There are limitations to these accommodations, including the fact that the institution is not obligated to apply them retroactively, and accommodations cannot fundamentally alter a course or program. The responsibility for implementing accommodations might be shared among the student, faculty, or other staff members at the institution. For example, a student with accommodations for extended testing time and a distraction-reduced testing environment may need to schedule their exams with the Access or disability office. At the same time, it is generally the institution's responsibility to provide course materials in alternative formats for those students who require them. Accommodations modify existing processes or policies to create equitable access.

While legislative milestones like the ADA and Section 504 have laid the groundwork for greater inclusion, they cannot solely dismantle the deeply rooted social structures that perpetuate inequality. To fully grasp the persistence of ableism and the barriers faced by individuals with disabilities, particularly in higher education, it is crucial to examine the underlying power dynamics and ideologies that shape these experiences. The following section introduces the theoretical framework guiding this chapter, drawing on Social Dominance Theory and Critical Disability Theory to analyze how systemic oppression is upheld and how it might be disrupted.

THEORETICAL FRAMEWORK

Grounded in Critical Disability Theory (Hosking, 2008) and Social Dominance Theory (Sidanius & Pratto, 2004), this chapter explores the role of artificial intelligence (AI) in shaping inclusive learning environments. These frameworks reveal how relativism and subjectivism—often disguised as neutrality in technological systems—are, in fact, socially constructed through power and identity dynamics. When applied to AI, this perspective exposes how algorithmic tools can both reinforce and challenge structures of privilege and oppression.

Critical Disability Theory (CDT) challenges the medical model of disability by emphasizing that disability is a socially constructed identity shaped by systemic barriers and cultural narratives. Social Dominance Theory (SDT) complements this by explaining how dominant groups maintain social hierarchies through institutional mechanisms. In the context of AI, these theories help reveal how technologies may encode ableist assumptions or replicate existing inequities. For example, AI-driven learning analytics may favor neurotypical patterns of engagement, marginalizing students whose learning styles differ from normative expectations.

Furthermore, the perception of AI as objective or neutral is critically examined. CDT and SDT remind us that all technologies are designed within cultural contexts that reflect dominant ideologies. This is particularly relevant in educational AI systems, where design choices—such as which data are collected, how success is measured, and whose voices are included—can either perpetuate or challenge systemic exclusion. For instance, voice recognition tools that fail to accommodate diverse speech patterns or adaptive platforms lacking multilingual support illustrate how AI can inadvertently reinforce exclusion.

Nevertheless, these same tools possess transformative potential. When developed through participatory design and aligned with Universal Design for Learning (UDL) principles, AI can support autonomy, access, and agency. A multilingual medical student using AI to simplify dense medical texts exemplifies how learners can creatively adapt technology to meet their needs. However, SDT warns that access to such tools is not evenly distributed. Digital divides, policy gaps, and institutional resistance may restrict the advantages of AI for marginalized students.

Models of Disability

Students with disabilities represent the largest and most diverse minority group in education, and their numbers continue to grow, particularly in post-secondary education. These students often encounter persistent barriers to accessing their learning environments. These barriers are not only physical but are also deeply rooted in historical and cultural narratives created by the dominant group to marginalize individuals with disabilities.

From the earliest civilizations, disability has often been viewed through a lens of moral or spiritual deficiency. Societies believed that differences in body or mind reflected flaws in the soul, justifying exclusionary practices such as infanticide and slavery. Over time, various models have emerged to understand the concept of disability. These models may be used individually or in combination.

- The moral model frames disability as a personal or familial failing, often seen as a punishment or test of character.
- The charity model views individuals with disabilities as needing pity and aid from others.
- The medical model views disability as a defect within the individual that needs to be cured or corrected.
- The social model emphasizes that disability exists when society creates environments and/or policies that create barriers for those with impairments.
- The human rights model recognizes that impairments are a natural part of human diversity and that all individuals are entitled to equal rights and opportunities.

Each of these models, as well as others, continues to influence how students with disabilities experience their learning environments. Historically, post-secondary education has been designed primarily for wealthy, able-bodied men, and it has been slow to adapt to changes in demographics (Burgess, 2025). As Simi Linton (1998) observed, academic narratives often lag behind evolving civic understandings of disability, failing to reflect or support more progressive, inclusive approaches.

UNDERSTANDING ARTIFICIAL INTELLIGENCE (AI)

Can artificial intelligence play the role of a superhero and save the day? Perhaps not entirely, however, AI technologies, when developed and used ethically, have the potential to dismantle long-standing barriers by personalizing learning, enhancing accessibility, and identifying systemic inequities. For example, AI tools can convert text to speech, generate real-time captions, or adapt content formats to meet the diverse sensory and cognitive needs of various learners. Additionally, AI can help institutions analyze patterns of exclusion and proactively design learning environments that align with the principles of Universal Design for Learning (UDL).

To use AI tools effectively and ethically, we must first understand what we are working with. As we started this chapter, it was noted that some people perceive AI as a curse. AI is just another aspect of the other curse word, 'change', that challenges the status quo. John Tagg (2012) discusses how loss aversion and the endowment effect sum up the "status quo bias" (p. 10). As humans, we typically do not love change. We crave at least some amount of routine in our lives, and some of us need more of that routine and predictability than others. Artificial intelligence (AI) is a relatively new concept; most scholars point to the mid-1900s, specifically the 1940s or 1950s, depending on how AI is defined, as the birth of AI as we know it today (Gupta & Mangla, 2020).

Despite AI having been in existence for decades, a widespread lack of understanding persists about what AI is and what it is not. Many people conflate AI with Hollywood representations of androids or science fiction storylines about machines taking over the world. In reality, AI encompasses a broad spectrum of technologies, from narrow AI systems that power recommendation engines and voice assistants (think Siri and Alexa) to more complex models used in predictive analytics, autonomous vehicles, and adaptive learning platforms. Without a foundational understanding of these distinctions, it becomes difficult to assess the ethical implications or practical applications of AI in education, accessibility, or any other field. This knowledge gap can fuel fear, resistance, or misuse.

The two types of AI we will focus on are generative AI (e.g., ChatGPT, CoPilot) and traditional or non-generative AI (e.g., spam filters, Sumy). Traditional AI, sometimes called non-generative AI, extractive AI, or analytical AI, does not create new content like generative AI does. These non-generative AI programs recognize patterns and extract information from existing data. They can make predictions, offer suggestions, and summarize text. In contrast, generative AI can create original content by learning patterns in existing data and generating new, unique outputs. Neither of these types of AI is foolproof. We will cover the risks and benefits more later in the chapter.

To move beyond the promise and into practice, we must examine how these technologies are being used in real-world educational contexts. Understanding the types of AI, their capabilities, and their limitations is essential not only for leveraging their benefits but also for safeguarding against unintended consequences. This next section explores how students are currently using AI systems.

Usage and Implications

As educators, administrators, and others observing learning spaces look across the landscape and see a wide variety of learners, they must also recognize that the way those learners use AI may differ just as much as their appearances. Multiple factors—such as age, racial identity, education level, and program of study—influence how and when students utilize AI.

For instance, consider a multilingual nursing student who uses AI to simplify dense medical texts. English may not be their first language, so they rely on AI tools to define unfamiliar terms, summarize readings, and clarify complex instructions. This use of AI serves as a bridge to a deeper understanding and academic confidence.

Now imagine a master's student in public policy and advocacy who has dyslexia. For this learner, AI serves as a tool for accessibility—used to convert readings into audio, summarize lengthy documents, or help structure written assignments. In both cases, AI is not just a convenience; it is a critical support for equitable learning.

Recent data supports these diverse usage patterns. Pew Research (2025) reports that about 26% of U.S. teenagers have used AI tools for schoolwork. A 2024 Digital Education Council (DEC) Global AI Student Survey found that 86% of post-secondary students reported using AI tools to study, with 54% using them weekly and 24% daily. Notably, 33% of students use AI to summarize documents (DEC, 2024). Usage also varies by identity and context: Black and Hispanic teenagers are more likely to utilize AI for schoolwork (Sidoti et al., 2025), and multilingual learners tend to use AI more frequently than their peers who predominantly use English (Dai, 2024). In applied fields such as engineering or healthcare, students report higher rates of generative AI use (Qu et al., 2024).

Despite this widespread adoption, post-secondary institutions are not doing enough to help students use AI effectively. According to the DEC survey, 73% of students believe universities should provide training for faculty on the effective use of AI, and 72% expect their institutions to offer courses on AI literacy (DEC, 2024).

These findings suggest a clear call to action: institutions must move beyond awareness and toward intentional integration of AI into teaching and learning, ensuring that all students, regardless of background or ability, are equipped to use these tools meaningfully and ethically.

ENHANCING ACCESSIBILITY WITH AI

Using proactive approaches, such as Universal Design for Learning (UDL) that incorporates AI, provides students with the scaffolding and choices they need to become expert learners. Reactive approaches, such as providing accommodations for specific needs, can also benefit from AI tools. According to a study by Burgess (2025), disabled students identified several themes that support the integration of AI and UDL in the process of enhancing accessibility. Flexibility and Adaptability are themes that are emphasized, along with having multiple options for accessing content, demonstrating knowledge, and engaging with instructors and peers. AI can enhance these options by adapting content formats (e.g., converting text to audio or generating visual summaries), offering real-time language translation, and supporting personalized learning.

AI-powered tools can also help identify and remove barriers before they impact students, shifting the focus from retrofitting accommodations to designing inclusively from the outset. For example, AI can assist faculty in evaluating course materials for accessibility, suggesting alternative formats, or flagging content that may not align with Universal Design for Learning (UDL) principles. Examples of this include products such as Anthology Ally and YuJa Panorama.

The integration of AI into UDL also supports emotional and psychological well-being by reducing the stigma often associated with requesting accommodations. When inclusive practices are built into the course design and supported by AI systems, students are less likely to feel singled out or burdened by disclosure. As one participant noted, having access to recorded lectures and transcripts available to all students allowed them to engage with material without needing to justify their needs (Burgess, 2025).

Combining Universal Design for Learning (UDL) and Artificial Intelligence (AI) enhances accessibility while also challenging ableist assumptions embedded in traditional educational structures. It models inclusive behavior, supports diverse learning preferences, and empowers students to take ownership of their learning.

Practical Applications

Let's look at a few different scenarios to see how we can put AI into practical use.

Scenario 1

Context: Dr. Smith, a professor of History, has been noticing that one of their students, Alex, seems to struggle with processing the information during lectures. Alex has not disclosed any specific disability, but Dr. Smith wants to ensure that all students have equal access to the course material.

Challenge: Alex often appears overwhelmed by the volume of information presented during lectures and struggles to keep up with note-taking. This affects their ability to participate in class discussions and perform well on assessments.

Solution: Dr. Smith decides to use an AI-powered tool to summarize lecture transcripts. After each lecture, the AI tool generates a concise summary of the key points and main ideas discussed. Dr. Smith then shares these summaries with the entire class, including Alex.

Benefits

1. Improved Comprehension: The AI-generated summaries help Alex quickly grasp the essential information without feeling overwhelmed by the details. This allows Alex to focus on understanding the core concepts rather than getting lost in the minutiae.
2. Enhanced Engagement: With the summarized content, Alex can participate more actively in class discussions and group activities, as they have a clearer understanding of the lecture material.
3. Better Retention: The summaries serve as a valuable study aid for Alex, making it easier to review and retain the information for exams and assignments.
4. Inclusive Learning Environment: By providing summaries to all students, Dr. Smith ensures that everyone benefits from the enhanced accessibility, fostering an inclusive and supportive learning environment.

Outcome

Alex's performance in the course improves significantly. They feel more confident in their ability to keep up with the lectures and contribute to class discussions. Dr. Smith receives positive feedback from other students as well, who appreciate the additional resource.

Scenario 2

Context: Professor Lee teaches a psychology course and has assigned a comprehensive research paper that requires students to integrate various theories, case studies, and empirical data. One of the students, Jamie, has difficulty with short-term memory, which makes it challenging to recall and organize the numerous pieces of information needed for the assignment.
Challenge: Jamie struggles to keep track of the various sources and ideas that need to be included in the research paper. This leads to frustration and difficulty in creating a coherent outline, which is essential for writing a well-structured paper.
Solution: Professor Lee introduces Jamie to an AI-powered tool designed to help with outlining and organizing ideas. Jamie inputs the key points, sources,

and concepts into the AI tool, which then generates a structured outline for the research paper.

Benefit

1. Enhanced Organization: The AI tool helps Jamie organize their thoughts and ideas into a logical structure, making it easier to see how different pieces of information connect.
2. Improved Recall: By using the AI-generated outline, Jamie can quickly reference the key points and sources without having to rely solely on their short-term memory.
3. Reduced Cognitive Load: The AI tool reduces the cognitive load on Jamie by handling the task of organizing information, allowing them to focus on developing their arguments and analysis.
4. Increased Confidence: With a clear and structured outline, Jamie feels more confident in their ability to complete the assignment and produce a high-quality research paper.

Outcome:

Jamie successfully completes the research paper, receiving positive feedback from Professor Lee on the organization and coherence of their work. The use of the AI tool not only helps Jamie manage their short-term memory challenges but also enhances their overall academic performance.

Scenario 3

Context: Jordan is a high school junior in AP Calculus. Jordan has cerebral palsy, which affects fine motor skills, making handwriting, drawing graphs, and writing equations on paper physically challenging. Despite these barriers, Jordan is highly motivated and excels in conceptual understanding.

Challenge: Traditional classroom assessments and note-taking methods rely heavily on handwritten work. Jordan struggles to complete timed written tests and often falls behind in taking notes or showing multi-step problem-solving processes, which are essential in AP math courses. Additionally, the school has a shortage of qualified para-professionals who can serve as scribes for Jordan.

Solution: The school implements an AI-powered math assistant platform tailored for accessibility.

- This includes a speech-to-math interface that allows Jordan to use voice commands to input equations, describe graphs, and solve problems.

- AI handwriting recognition and correction that allows Jordan to use a stylus on a tablet to write. The AI interprets rough or incomplete handwriting and converts it into clean, legible math expressions.
- Integration with the learning management system (LMS) that syncs all of Jordan's work within the AI platform to the LMS, allowing teachers to review and grade Jordan's work.

Benefits

1. Increased Independence: Jordan can complete assignments and assessments without relying on a scribe or extended time accommodations.
2. Real-Time Feedback: The AI platform offers immediate support, reinforcing learning and reducing frustration.
3. Equity in Assessment: Jordan's performance is evaluated based on understanding, not handwriting ability.
4. Confidence Boost: With tools that level the playing field, Jordan participates more actively in class discussions and group work.

Outcome

By the end of the semester, Jordan received a high score on the final exam. The AI tools not only support academic success but also foster greater self-advocacy and confidence. The school expands the use of AI accessibility tools to support other students with diverse learning needs, helping more students and addressing the shortage of available para-professional staff.

Scenario 4

Context: Taylor is a graduate student in a demanding education policy program. Taylor has a traumatic brain injury (TBI), ADHD, and is on the autism spectrum. These intersecting neurodivergent conditions impact executive functioning, particularly around time management, task initiation, and cognitive flexibility. Taylor often delays submitting assignments due to a strong internal drive for perfection, which is compounded by anxiety. The program requires extensive weekly reading, including academic articles, policy briefs, and case law, which Taylor finds cognitively overwhelming, especially in traditional formats.

Challenge: Taylor struggles with managing deadlines due to perfectionism and executive function challenges. Processing large volumes of dense reading material, especially when switching between formats or navigating inaccessible

PDFs and maintaining focus during long study sessions, leading to fatigue and missed comprehension.

Solution: The university's accessibility office collaborates with Taylor to implement a personalized AI support system as a part of Taylor's approved accommodations.

- This includes utilizing an AI-powered reading companion that leverages natural language processing (NLP) to summarize academic texts into concise, digestible bullet points. It also offers multimodal delivery, including audio narrations with adjustable speed, visual highlighting, and simplified summaries. It also allows Taylor to create a concept map that visually outlines key themes and relationships.
- A deadline coach with adaptive nudging that integrates with Taylor's calendar and LMS. It can also break assignments into smaller, more manageable tasks and send gentle, personalized reminders. It uses sentiment analysis to detect stress in Taylor's responses and adjusts tone and frequency accordingly.
- AI writing assistant with confidence mode that helps Taylor draft and revise papers without the pressure of perfection. It offers real-time feedback on clarity, structure, and tone, while encouraging submission of "good enough" drafts. It also includes a confidence meter that tracks progress and celebrates milestones to reduce anxiety.

Benefits

1. Reduced cognitive load through AI-generated summaries and visual aids.
2. Improved time management with proactive, compassionate reminders.
3. Increased self-efficacy by shifting focus from perfection to progress.
4. Greater engagement with course material through accessible, multimodal formats.

Outcome

Taylor completes the semester with all assignments submitted on time for the first time since starting the program. The faculty noted improved clarity and consistency in Taylor's work. Taylor reports feeling more in control, less anxious, and more connected to the learning process. The university begins piloting the AI tools with other neurodivergent graduate students, using Taylor's experience as a model for inclusive innovation.

RISKS AND BENEFITS

As with all things in life, there are risks and benefits that need to be weighed when making decisions. Use of AI is not an exception to this rule, particularly because at the time of this publication, we do not have a lot (if any) parameters in place to minimize many of the risks. There are also numerous benefits to incorporating AI alongside other strategies to create more inclusive learning environments.

Although this is not an exhaustive list of risks, the following are some of the most prevalent and impactful risks noted by researchers such as Gibson (2024). There are digital accessibility gaps. Not all platforms or content have been designed with accessibility in mind. We are seeing increased pressure being put on some platforms due to upcoming deadlines for agencies accountable under Title II of the Americans with Disabilities Act to be compliant with the digital accessibility standard of WCAG 2.1 AA, which will ultimately benefit everyone else at the same time. However, until we improve our ability to ensure digital content is as accessible as possible for as many users as possible, we may be excluding users with disabilities or, at the very least, creating inconsistent experiences.

As previously discussed, AI systems are primarily designed by and for the dominant group, which may reflect or amplify societal biases, leading to unfair treatment or misrepresentation of marginalized groups in educational environments. Natural Language Processing (NLP) programs, for example, that favor a particular language or accent pattern may perpetuate the exclusion of those that differ.

In order for generative AI to keep learning, it needs to increase the amount of data that is collected. That collection of data may contain personal data, which raises concerns about consent, privacy, data security, and potential misuse, especially for those individuals with disabilities. Questions continue to be raised about the ethical implications of using AI. Is there sufficient transparency, accountability, and informed consent with the use of AI? Is there sufficient information available to users prior to use to help them understand how using this type of technology may impact them in the long term? These questions are yet to be answered.

There is also the risk of becoming overly reliant on technology, which can limit our skills in critical thinking and human interaction. A recent study by Essien et al. (2024) highlights the same limitations of AI in relation to critical thinking skills. This may further disadvantage those with limited access to technology or literacy. We have already observed that many individuals are overly confident in the results that AI provides, and some may not be double-checking those results, leading to students facing unintended academic integrity issues due to hallucinated or fabricated data in their assignment submissions.

Despite some significant risks, there are still benefits when AI is used effectively in conjunction with verifications. Many individuals can benefit from enhanced accessibility. Many digital tools can remove physical, sensory, and cognitive barriers, enabling learners to access course content in a format that matches their needs (e.g., screen readers, captions, voice commands). This enhanced accessibility can improve the independence of learners. Students are free to engage with the course materials and complete the required tasks independently, thus fostering confidence and self-reliance.

Along with other aspects that connect to UDL, AI-driven platforms can personalize learning to each individual, including the format, pace, and other preferences. With the ability to customize learning, learners increase their autonomy as they have more control over when, how, and where they engage with the content. Ultimately, when we bridge gaps in educational opportunities by providing equitable access, we can help learners move closer to achieving their goals, regardless of their marginalized status.

CONCLUSION

So here we are – at the end of a chapter that began with a four-letter word (flux), flirted with a six-letter one (change), and tangoed with a ten-letter taboo (disability). If you have made it this far, congratulations! You have survived a whirlwind tour through the tangled jungle of accessibility, AI, and acronyms galore. Furthermore, if your brain feels like it just ran a marathon in a thunderstorm – same.

But here is the thing: education is not just about surviving the storm. It is about learning to dance in the downpour, preferably with tools that will not trip us up. AI, when used thoughtfully (and not just because it is trendy), can be one of those tools. It is not a magic wand, and it definitely will not fix centuries of ableism overnight. However, it can assist us in building literal and metaphorical ramps toward more inclusive, flexible, and human-centered learning environments.

We've seen how Universal Design for Learning (UDL) and AI can team up like the dynamic duo we didn't know we needed. Together, they can reduce barriers, boost autonomy, and maybe – just maybe- make education feel less like a maze and more like a map.

Of course, there are risks. Bias, surveillance, digital divides, and the ever-looming specter of AI hallucinations (no, ChatGPT, Abraham Lincoln did not invent TikTok). But with critical awareness, ethical design, and a healthy dose of skepticism, we can navigate these challenges.

So what's next? That's up to you. Will you be the educator who shrugs off AI as "just another fad"? Or will you be the one who sees its potential to rewrite the rules – and maybe even the syllabus?

Either way, remember: accessibility isn't a feature. It's a foundation. And inclusion isn't a checkbox. It's a commitment. Let's build something better – one byte, one barrier-busting idea, and one brave conversation at a time.

REFERENCES

Burgess, K. (2025). Phenomenological study of disabled student experiences related to inclusive learning environments in public higher education *Dissertations, Theses, and Projects*. 1024.

Cherney, J. (2019). *Ableist rhetoric*. The Pennsylvania State University Press.

Dai, Y. (2024). Why students use or not use generative AI: Student conceptions, concerns, and implications for engineering education. Digital Engineering, 100019.

Digital Education Council. (2024). Global AI Student Survey 2024. Retrieved from https://www.digitaleducationcouncil.com/post/digital-education-council-global-ai-student-survey-2024

Dolmage, J. (2017). *Academic ableism: Disability in higher education*. University of Michigan Press.

Essien, A., Bukoye, O. T., O'Dea, X., & Kremantzis, M. (2024). The influence of AI text generators on critical thinking skills in UK business schools. *Studies in Higher Education (Dorchester-on-Thames), 49*(5), 865–882. https://doi.org/DOI: 10.1080/03075079.2024.2316881

Gibson, R. (2024, September 10). The impact of AI in advancing accessibility for learners with disabilities. *EDUCAUSE Review*. Retrieved from https://er.educause.edu/articles/2024/9/the-impact-of-ai-in-advancing-accessibility-for-learners-with-disabilities[1](https://er.educause.edu/articles/2024/9/the-impact-of-ai-in-advancing-accessibility-for-learners-with-disabilities)

Gupta, N., & Mangla, R. (2020). *Artificial intelligence basics* (1st ed.). Mercury Learning and Information., DOI: 10.1515/9781683925149

Hosking, D. (2008). Critical disability theory: A paper presented at the 4th biennial disability studies conference. www.lancaster.ac.uk

Jun, H. (2009). Ableism. In *Social justice, multicultural counseling & practice: Beyond a conventional approach* (pp. 199–222). SAGE Publications.

Linton, S. (1998). *Claiming Disability: Knowledge and Identity*. New York University Press.

Miller, S. Z. (2019). Disability accommodation requests: Prevalence and preference of review processes at postsecondary institutions in the United States. *Journal of Postsecondary Education and Disability*, *32*(3), 217–226.

National Center for Education Statistics. (2023). Students with disabilities. *Fast Facts*. U.S. Department of Education. https://nces.ed.gov/fastfacts/display.asp?id=60

National Center for Education Statistics. (2024). Degrees conferred by race/ethnicity and sex. *Fast Facts*. U.S. Department of Education. https://nces.ed.gov/fastfacts/display.asp?id=72

Qu, Y., Tan, M. X. Y., & Wang, J. (2024). Disciplinary differences in undergraduate students' engagement with generative artificial intelligence. *Smart Learning Environments*, *11*(1), 51.

Schweik, S. (2009). *The ugly laws: Disability in public*. New York University Press.

Sidanius, J., & Pratto, F. (2004). Social dominance theory: Its agenda and method. *Political Psychology*, *25*, 845–880.

Sidoti, O., Park, E., & Gottfried, J. (2025). Pew Research Center. Retrieved from https://www.pewresearch.org/short-reads/2025/01/15/about-a-quarter-of-us-teens-have-used-chatgpt-for-schoolwork-double-the-share-in-2023/

Tagg, J. (2012). Why Does the Faculty Resist Change? *Change: The Magazine of Higher Learning*, *44*(1), 6–15. DOI: 10.1080/00091383.2012.635987

Weis, R., & Bittner, S. A. (2022). College Students' Access to Academic Accommodations Over Time: Evidence of a Matthew Effect in Higher Education. *Psychological Injury and Law*, *15*, 236–252. DOI: 10.1007/s12207-021-09429-7

Welding, L. (2023, March 29). Students with disabilities in higher education: Facts and statistics. Best Colleges: https://www.bestcolleges.com/research/students-with-disabilities-higher-education

World Health Organization. (2023). Disability and health. *WHO*. https://www.who.int/news-room/fact-sheets/detail/disability-and-healthstatistics/

ADDITIONAL READING

Bowen, J. A., & Watson, C. E. (2024). *Teaching with ai: A practical guide to a new era of human learning*. Johns Hopkins University Press.

Centers for Disease Control and Prevention. (2024). Adult disability status: CDC releases new data. *CDC Newsroom*. https://www.cdc.gov/media/releases/2024/s0716-Adult-disability.html

Dignum, V. (2023). *AI literacy for educators. Zenodo.* https://doi.org/DOI: 10.5281/zenodo.8072950

Gravestein, J. (n.d.). *AI literacy for educators.* Substack. https://jurgengravestein.substack.com/p/ai-literacy-for-educators

U.S. Department of Education, National Center for Education Statistics. (2022). Racial/ethnic enrollment in public schools. *Condition of Education.* https://nces.ed.gov/programs/coe/indicator/cge/racial-ethnic-enrollment

KEY TERMS AND DEFINITIONS

Ableism: the systemic favoring of individuals perceived to have typical physical or mental abilities, resulting in discrimination against those with disabilities or neurodivergent traits.

Charity Model of Disability: portrays people with disabilities as objects of pity who are dependent on the goodwill of others, often assuming they are unable to care for themselves and require help from the broader community.

Generative Artificial Intelligence: a subfield of artificial intelligence focused on creating new content, such as text, images, audio, video, etc., using machine learning that has been trained to recognize patterns and structures from larger datasets rather than analyzing or classifying existing data; (e.g., ChatGPT, CoPilot).

Human Rights Model of Disability: views disability as a natural part of human diversity and emphasizes that all individuals, regardless of actual or perceived impairments, are entitled to the same fundamental rights, freedoms, and dignity.

Medical Model of Disability: frames disability as a problem located within the individual—something broken or deficient that needs to be fixed or cured. It emphasizes impairment as a personal limitation, and when improvement isn't visible, it often implies a lack of effort or will on the part of the individual.

Moral Model of Disability: views disability as a reflection of personal or familial moral failing. It often interprets disability as a form of divine punishment or as a test or opportunity for spiritual growth and character development.

Non-Generative Artificial Intelligence: sometimes referred to as "traditional AI" or "extractive AI", is a subfield of artificial intelligence focused on solving problems using pre-programmed rules, logic, and structured data. It uses only existing data, such as filtering spam or summarizing large amounts of text (e.g., Siri, Alexa, TextSummarizer, Sumy).

Social Model of Disability: recognizes that while individuals may have impairments, disability arises from societal barriers, such as inaccessible environments, systems, or attitudes, that limit inclusion and participation. For example, a person who is blind has a visual impairment, but it becomes a disability when reading materials are only provided in visual formats, excluding alternatives like Braille or audio.

Universal Design: the creation of environments and products that are accessible, understandable, and usable by all people, to the greatest extent possible, without the need for adaptation or specialized design.

Universal Design for Learning: is an educational framework grounded in neuroscience that guides the development of flexible learning environments and teaching practices to accommodate the diverse needs of all learners.

Chapter 9
Pedagogical Perspectives on Artificial Intelligence in Islamic Religious Education:
A Comprehensive Review

Mussa Saidi Abubakari
https://orcid.org/0000-0003-3782-281X
Dig Connectivity Research Laboratory (DCRLab), Uganda & Universiti Brunei Darussalam, Brunei

Gamal Abdul Nasir Zakaria
Universiti Brunei Darussalam, Brunei

Desfa Yusmaliana
https://orcid.org/0000-0001-9979-3933
Universitas Muhammadiyah Bangka Belitung, Indonesia

Ahmad Zaldi
Universitas Islam Internasional Darullughah Wadda'wah, Indonesia

Juraidah Musa
https://orcid.org/0000-0001-5973-0997
Universiti Brunei Darussalam, Brunei

Mulyani Mudis Taruna
https://orcid.org/0000-0002-1140-0208
National Research and Innovation Agency, Indonesia

ABSTRACT

This chapter examines the pedagogical considerations and implications of integrating artificial intelligence (AI) with Islamic Religious Education (IRE). As generative AI reshapes modern education, its role in Islamic-based learning settings warrants significant consideration. The contextualisation of AI in education, with a justification for focusing on IRE, is discussed first. Foundational concepts are defined, which include AI in education (AIEd), and major pedagogical principles common to all Islamic traditions are also discussed, along with their practical

DOI: 10.4018/979-8-3373-3000-6.ch009

applications. Opportunities and challenges are presented. The chapter introduced Islamic pedagogical views and addressed teacher AI readiness, concluding with suggested pedagogical strategies that align with the use of AI and Islamic values. The chapter concludes by calling for collaborative-based initiatives and outlines the next steps in research for curriculum development, professional development, and AI ethics in IRE.

INTRODUCTION

Artificial Intelligence (AI) has emerged as one of the most transformative forces of the 21st century, penetrating virtually every sector, including finance, healthcare, and education (Papakostas, 2025). In the educational arena, AI technologies are revolutionising how teaching and learning occur by enabling personalised learning experiences, instant feedback, intelligent data analytics, and automation of administrative tasks (Tran & Nguyen, 2021). For example, AI-driven systems can adapt instructional content to meet individual student needs, perform complex pattern recognition tasks, such as grading or detecting learning difficulties, and provide virtual tutoring and conversational support via chatbots. This broad adoption of AI in general education – often referred to as AI in Education (AIEd) – is driven by rapid advances in machine learning, natural language processing (NLP), IoT, and data mining, which together allow computers to perform cognitive tasks at scale (Abubakari & Mashoedah, 2021; Abubakari & Suprapto, 2021; Ifenthaler et al., 2024). As a result, educators and policymakers worldwide are exploring AI's implications for improving educational outcomes and efficiency. However, a growing consensus holds that AI should augment, not replace, human educators; maintaining a "human-in-the-loop" approach is considered essential so that the strengths of both AI and teachers are harnessed in tandem. This viewpoint recognises that while AI can handle data-driven personalisation and routine tasks at breathtaking speed, meaningful education also relies on human qualities like empathy, moral judgment, and social interaction (Ifenthaler et al., 2024; Papakostas, 2025).

Within this broader context, attention is turning to the role of AI in religious education – an area traditionally rooted in spiritual formation, ethical guidance, and human mentorship. Unlike many secular subjects, religious education (RE) involves not only cognitive learning but also the transmission of values, identity formation, and often a sense of the sacred. Integrating AI into such a domain raises unique questions and opportunities. In recent years, theological schools and religious educators have begun to experiment with AI tools for tasks like teaching, assessment, and even pastoral support (Papakostas, 2025). Yet, academic scrutiny of AI's impact on religious education has lagged behind its examination in general education.

Researchers have noted that while AI's influence on mainstream education has been extensively studied, its adaptation in religious contexts, where long-standing traditions and communal, face-to-face pedagogies prevail, remains under-explored (Papakostas, 2025). Nevertheless, the pressure to modernise and digitise is increasingly felt even in religious learning, as faith communities seek to engage younger, tech-savvy generations without compromising core values. This convergence of AI and religious education forms a new and complex frontier, sparking both optimism and apprehension among educators and religious leaders.

Islamic Religious Education (IRE) provides a pertinent focus within this frontier, given the global scale of Islamic-based education and the distinct pedagogical principles it entails. Islamic education spans a vast spectrum – from informal study circles and traditional madrasas (Islamic seminaries) to formal school curricula in Muslim-majority countries and weekend religious classes in Muslim-minority societies (Daun & Arjmand, 2021). Across these settings, IRE carries rich concepts such as tarbiyyah (holistic nurturing and upbringing), ta'lim (instruction and transmission of knowledge), and tazkiyah (purification and character development), which together underscore that the goal is not merely intellectual mastery but also moral and spiritual growth (Sabki & Hardaker, 2013; Waghid, 2014). The introduction of AI into IRE thus needs to be examined in light of how it might support or conflict with these aims. There is a strong rationale for focusing on IRE: Muslim communities worldwide are increasingly adopting educational technology, and there is significant interest in leveraging digital tools (including AI) to enhance Qur'ān learning, Islamic studies, and other religious subjects (Salim & Aditya, 2025). At the same time, there are valid concerns that indiscriminate use of AI in religious learning could dilute the authenticity of Islamic teachings or bypass the critical role of the teacher as a murabbi (mentor and spiritual guide) (Thoriquttyas & Rohmawati, 2024). By concentrating on Islamic education, this chapter addresses how AI integration might be tailored to align with Islamic pedagogical values and the expectations of Muslim educators, students, and other stakeholders.

CHAPTER OBJECTIVES, STRUCTURE, AND METHODOLOGY

This article aims to provide a comprehensive scholarly review of pedagogical approaches to integrating AI in Islamic Religious Education. It seeks to (a) conceptualise AI in the educational context and clarify the foundational principles of Islamic pedagogy (Section 2), (b) survey the current applications of AI in IRE and the potential it holds for enhancing various aspects of teaching and learning (Section 3), (c) analyse the pedagogical opportunities created by AI – such as increased engagement, personalisation, and fostering of critical thinking – as well as the challenges and risks – such as loss of context, overreliance on technology, and shifts in teacher roles (Section 4), (d) discuss the ethical and theological considerations that arise from the intersection of AI and Islam, including how innovation is approached in Islamic thought and concerns around bias and privacy (Section 5), (e) evaluate the readiness of IRE teachers and the professional development needed for effective AI integration (Section 6), and (f) propose strategies for integrating AI into IRE in a manner consistent with Islamic values, addressing cognitive, affective, and spiritual dimensions and clarifying the roles of key stakeholders (Section 7). The chapter concludes with a summary and suggestions for future research and practice (Section 8). Through this structured analysis, the chapter aims to contribute to an interdisciplinary dialogue on how AI can be aligned with the educational and spiritual goals of Islamic education in a rapidly evolving digital age.

This chapter adopts a comprehensive narrative review methodology, drawing on peer-reviewed academic literature and open-access scholarly sources to synthesise current knowledge on the integration of Artificial Intelligence (AI) in Islamic Religious Education (IRE). The approach is primarily conceptual and qualitative, aiming to bridge interdisciplinary perspectives from educational technology, Islamic pedagogy, and AI ethics. To ensure scholarly rigour, the literature was selected through systematic searches across multiple reputable academic databases such as SpringerLink, ScienceDirect, Google Scholar, and Taylor & Francis Online, among others. The chapter thematically analysed selected literature and categorised it according to the chapter's conceptual structure. While not an empirical study, this review follows best practices in conceptual research by clearly defining constructs, critically comparing sources, and proposing a framework rooted in Islamic educational theory.

CONCEPTUAL FOUNDATIONS

Artificial Intelligence in Education (AIEd)

Artificial Intelligence in Education (AIEd) refers to the application of AI technologies and algorithms to support and enhance teaching and learning processes in various educational settings. At its core, AI involves creating machines or software that can perform tasks normally requiring human intelligence, such as understanding language, recognising patterns, solving problems, and making decisions (Ifenthaler et al., 2024; Tapalova & Zhiyenbayeva, 2022). In contrast to human cognition, AI systems can process vast amounts of data rapidly and consistently, which opens up new possibilities for data-driven personalisation and efficiency in education (Ifenthaler et al., 2024). AIEd is not a single technology but rather a broad umbrella encompassing a range of tools and approaches that leverage AI techniques in both formal and informal learning environments. Key technologies under the AIEd umbrella include:

- Intelligent Tutoring Systems (ITS) and Adaptive Learning Platforms: AI-driven tutoring programs that adapt to a student's level and pace, providing hints, feedback, and scaffolding in real time. These systems employ techniques like machine learning and cognitive modelling to personalise exercises and explanations, much like a one-on-one tutor would (Huang et al., 2025; Tseng et al., 2024). For instance, an ITS for learning Qur'ān recitation could listen to a student's recitation and highlight errors in pronunciation (tajwīd) or memory lapses, then guide the student to practice the specific verses that need improvement. Further, AI-powered learning management systems adjust the difficulty and sequence of learning materials based on student performance. Through algorithms and predictive analytics, these platforms identify patterns such as which topics a learner is struggling with and then customise the forthcoming lessons to address those gaps (Capuano & Caballé, 2020; Pliakos et al., 2019). In IRE, an adaptive learning app might track a student's progress in memorising hadiths or learning Arabic vocabulary, and then automatically provide more practice on weaker areas, ensuring mastery before moving on.
- Chatbots and Virtual Assistants: Conversational AI agents that can answer students' questions or engage them in dialogue. In an educational context, chatbots can serve as 24/7 teaching assistants. For example, a chatbot might be available to answer questions about Islamic history or jurisprudence by retrieving answers from a knowledge base of verified religious texts. AI chatbots can use natural language processing (NLP) to understand students' queries in either Arabic or other languages and provide instant, context-relevant responses (Munshi et al., 2021; Sholeh et al., 2024). This can be particularly useful in large classes or online learning, where human teachers cannot always respond immediately to every question.
- Predictive Analytics and Early Warning Systems: AI systems that analyse student data (e.g., quiz scores, engagement time, homework completion) to predict outcomes like academic success or risk of dropping out (Aldowah et al., 2019; Musa et al., 2025). Educators can use these insights to intervene early. In Islamic schools, such analytics might help identify students who are disengaging from religious classes so that mentors can provide timely support or counselling, thereby bridging academic data with pastoral care.
- Automated Content Analysis and Curation: AI algorithms can process and categorise large volumes of educational content. For instance, machine learn-

ing models can analyse classical Islamic texts – the Qur'ān, hadith corpora, and fiqh manuals – and tag them by topic, making it easier for teachers and students to retrieve relevant passages. AI can also be used to generate quizzes or summaries of content (Marwa et al., 2025; Semrl et al., 2023). An example is using NLP to generate comprehension questions from a chapter in a Seerah (Prophetic biography) textbook, saving teachers' time in assessment design.

- Natural Language Processing (NLP) for Language Learning: NLP techniques enable speech recognition and automated translation, which are valuable for learning languages of Islamic scholarship (primarily Arabic). AI-driven speech recognition is already being applied to Quranic recitation learning: systems can evaluate a student's recitation against proper pronunciation and rhythm, and provide corrective feedback (Afzal et al., 2023; Alvindo et al., 2024). Likewise, AI translation tools can assist students in understanding Arabic texts by providing initial translations (to be refined by the teacher for accuracy).

In summary, AIEd encompasses a wide collection of technologies – from data mining and neural networks to large language models – all applied with the aim of improving educational delivery and outcomes (Ifenthaler et al., 2024). What distinguishes AIEd is not just the use of advanced software in classrooms, but the intelligence aspect: these systems learn from data about students' behaviours and performance, and then make autonomous decisions (or recommendations) to optimise the learning process. This dynamic, data-informed adaptivity marks a significant shift from one-size-fits-all education towards more tailored learning experiences. For Islamic Religious Education, which often must accommodate students with diverse backgrounds and learning paces (especially in community settings like weekend schools or converts' classes), such personalisation promises to be particularly useful – if implemented thoughtfully. It is important to note, however, that experts caution against viewing AI as a magical solution: AIEd works best when complementing human educators (Ifenthaler et al., 2024; Papakostas, 2025). Even in cutting-edge classrooms, the role of teachers remains critical in guiding AI's use and adding the human dimensions of motivation, moral judgment, and empathy that machines lack.

Pedagogical Principles in Islamic Religious Education (IRE)

Islamic pedagogy is grounded in a holistic vision of education that integrates intellectual, moral, and spiritual development. Classical Islamic scholarship articulates several key concepts to describe education's multifaceted nature, notably taʿlim, tarbiyyah, and tazkiyah, among others. Taʿlīm refers to the act of teaching or instruction – the imparting of knowledge, often of revealed or canonical texts. It is concerned with the intellectual transmission of information, such as teaching the content of the Qur'ān, hadith (Prophetic traditions), creed (aqidah), and law (fiqh). Tarbiyyah, on the other hand, comes from a root meaning to nurture or foster growth (Zuraidah et al., 2024). It denotes upbringing and holistic education, emphasising character formation, ethical training, and personal development in accordance with Islamic values. Tarbiyyah is about guiding students to develop virtues (such as honesty, patience, humility) and to integrate Islamic principles into their daily behaviour. It is closely tied to the concept of adab – proper conduct and manners – which some scholars (e.g. Naquib al-Attas) have highlighted as central to Islamic education (Al-Attas, 2007). Tazkiyah means purification, often used in the context of purifying the soul. In pedagogy, tazkiyah points to the spiritual dimension of education: the cultivation of sincere faith (iman), God-consciousness (taqwa), and inner spirituality. Thus, an Islamic educational process traditionally aims not only to produce knowledgeable individuals but also people of noble character and spirituality. As one study succinctly puts it, Islamic education's goal goes beyond knowledge transfer to forming morals and spirituality that are in accordance with religious teachings (Zuraidah et al., 2024). The concept of tarbiyyah encapsulates this broader mandate by focusing on shaping the student's character through a curriculum infused with Qur'anic and Prophetic teachings.

In classical settings, these pedagogical principles manifested in specific methods. Traditional madrasa education was often teacher-centric and text-centric: students sat with a learned scholar, memorised and recited texts (like Qur'an, hadith compilations, or didactic poems in theology and law), and received oral commentary and moral guidance. The personal relationship between teacher and student (often described as one of mentorship or even spiritual parenthood) was paramount (Paramboor & Ibrahim, 2013). The teacher (ustādh or shaykh) was expected not only to convey factual knowledge but also to serve as a role model (uswah hasanah) in conduct, embodying the teachings of Islam. Memorisation and repetition were widely used techniques – in part because mastery of the sacred texts was a priority, and also because of limited access to written materials in pre-modern times. Alongside rote learning, traditional Islamic pedagogy employed discussion and debate in advanced stages (for example, the dialectical method in jurisprudence known as munazarah or the question-and-answer style in hadith circles) (Abbas, 2017). Importantly, all of this took place in a spiritually infused environment: learning was often framed as an act of worship (`ibādah), begun with the correct intention (niyyah) and invocations for divine aid. Success was measured not just by academic achievement but by the student's growth in piety and good character.

Contemporary Islamic Religious Education, especially in formal school systems, has had to adapt to modern pedagogical frameworks and institutional constraints (Abubakari, Zakaria, et al., 2024; Abubakari, 2025a). In many Muslim-majority countries today, IRE is part of the national curriculum in public schools, taught in classrooms with curricula and assessments similar to secular subjects. This modernisation of IRE means that contemporary Muslim education often blends traditional approaches with methods borrowed from modern education science (Abubakari, Zakaria, & Musa, 2023; Baiza, 2022). For example, a typical Islamic Studies class in a modern school might include group discussions, audio-visual presentations, and project-based learning (methods common in Western pedagogy) alongside traditional practices like memorisation of short sūrahs or prayers. Indeed, contemporary Muslim education bears the influence of both the traditional Muslim approach to knowledge and the modern Western education system (Baiza, 2022). There is also an increasing emphasis on critical thinking and context in IRE curricula today, moving beyond rote learning to ensure students understand and can apply Islamic teachings in contemporary life (Altinyelken, 2021). For instance, rather than just memorising a list of moral virtues, students might engage in activities to critically reflect on how those virtues apply to issues like social media use or environmental responsibility. Despite these updates, the fundamental pedagogical values remain influential. Many educators still see their role in terms of tarbiyyah – caring for and mentoring students in a holistic sense. In practice, this means IRE teachers often take a keen interest in their students' character development and spiritual well-being, not just their exam scores. The ideal IRE lesson interweaves factual learning (e.g., understanding a Qur'anic verse's meaning) with moral exhortation (encouraging students to implement that verse's lessons in daily life) and spiritual reflection (perhaps a short classroom dua (prayer) or moment of reflection to internalise the lesson).

However, challenges exist in contemporary practice. Some critics point out that in certain settings, IRE can become overly textbook-driven and exam-oriented, potentially losing some of the traditional richness of mentorship and spirituality (Amzat, 2022). Others note that the diversity of student backgrounds (especially in the West, where an IRE class may include students from various cultures or levels of prior Islamic knowledge) requires more creative and differentiated teaching approaches than the one-size-fits-all methods of old (Memon et al., 2021; Syah, 2016). As Islamic pedagogy evolves, scholars and practitioners are actively exploring ways to revitalise it by returning to foundational concepts and also by incorporating proven methods from global educational research. An emerging contemporary Islamic pedagogy has been described, which integrates faith and identity with modern skills like critical thinking and global citizenship (Memon, 2021). In sum, the pedagogical principles of IRE straddle a dynamic tension: continuity with tradition (ensuring that the transmission of the sacred knowledge and values remains authentic and effective) and engagement with contemporary methodologies (ensuring that teaching is pedagogically sound and relevant to today's learners).

INTEGRATION OF AI IN ISLAMIC RELIGIOUS EDUCATION

Current Applications and Trends

The integration of AI into Islamic Religious Education is already underway, with a variety of applications emerging across the Islamic world and in Muslim communities globally. One prominent area of AI application is in Qur'an learning and recitation. AI-powered Qur'an apps have gained popularity for helping Muslims memorise and recite the Qur'an with correct pronunciation (tajwīd). For instance, AI-driven applications (an AI companion for Qur'an study) leverage advanced speech recognition to provide real-time feedback on a user's recitation (Bashir et al., 2023; Farooq & Imran, 2021). A learner can recite verses aloud, and the app will highlight mistakes in pronunciation or lapses in memorisation, allowing for immediate correction. These apps often use deep learning models trained on extensive audio recordings of Qur'anic recitation to detect errors in applying tajwīd rules (rules of recitation). Research in this domain includes developing deep neural networks for automatic evaluation of tajwīd rules. Early studies show that such models can successfully identify errors in elongation (madd), nasalisation (ghunnah), and other tajwīd principles, achieving high accuracy in recognising whether a rule was correctly applied (Al-Ayyoub et al., 2018; Balula et al., 2021). The benefit of these AI systems is that students can practice independently and receive guided feedback, which is especially useful in contexts where access to qualified Qur'an teachers is limited. In countries

Beyond recitation, AI is making inroads in facilitating the study of Islamic texts. Hadith databases and search engines have existed in digital form for years, but AI techniques are now enhancing their functionality. NLP allows for more intelligent querying of hadith corpora (Azmi et al., 2019). For example, one can ask a system a question in natural language (e.g., "What did the Prophet say about honesty in business?") and an AI-powered engine can retrieve relevant hadiths by understanding synonyms and context, not just exact keyword matches. An innovative project in this vein is the development of a knowledge graph for Hadith. In 2024, researchers presented a methodology for generating a semantic knowledge graph from hadith literature (Butt et al., 2024). By extracting and interlinking entities (people, places, concepts) and the relationships between them in six canonical hadith collections, the system allows scholars and students to navigate hadith information relationally. For instance, one could trace all narrations involving a particular companion of the Prophet, or explore conceptually related hadiths across different collections. This goes beyond simple text search; it is an AI-driven way to explore Islamic knowledge, potentially unveiling connections that a reader might not easily find manually. The SemanticHadith project, as it is known, illustrates how AI can assist in organising and retrieving religious knowledge more richly, supporting both casual learners and researchers in Islamic studies (Kamran et al., 2023).

AI is also being applied to the domain of fatwas (religious rulings) and jurisprudence. Several Muslim-majority countries have shown interest in AI systems to manage the volume of fatwa requests from the public. These "fatwa engines" rely on large repositories of existing fatwas and an AI technique known as case-based reasoning, where the system attempts to find a precedent fatwa that matches the user's query scenario (Ab Rahim et al., 2025; Munshi et al., 2021). A study by Alshithisri (2024) delved into the impacts of AI on fatwa issuance, noting that such AI systems compile past rulings and attempt to provide guidance accordingly. However, the study found numerous obstacles to relying on AI for fatwas, including the complexities of language and context (Alshithisri, 2024). Subtle differences in question wording or context can lead to significantly different rulings in Islamic law, and AI struggles with this nuanced understanding. Moreover, the same study highlighted strong caution among Muslim jurists: "Muslim scholars unanimously agree that artificial intelligence should not be employed in the production of fatwas" (Alshithisri, 2024: p.2504). This indicates that while AI can assist in disseminating information (e.g., retrieving a prior ruling or providing a summary), the authoritative process of issuing a new fatwa is still seen as the domain of qualified human scholars. Nonetheless, AI is used in related ways, such as categorising incoming questions, translating fatwas into various languages, or offering a ranked list of previous fatwas that might be relevant to a query.

In both Muslim-majority and minority contexts, AI's current applications in IRE are also seen in educational administration and support. In large Islamic universities, AI-driven systems help personalise course recommendations or study plans for students of Shari'ah (Islamic law) and Islamic studies (Syukur et al., 2024). For example, an intelligent system might analyse a student's academic record and suggest elective courses in Qur'anic sciences or Arabic language to strengthen areas of weakness. In countries like Turkey and Malaysia, where public Islamic schools and universities are numerous, AI-based learning management systems are being tested to improve student engagement and track progress. In Muslim-minority settings, a case study from a non-Muslim context is informative: A recent empirical study in Lesotho investigated secondary school teachers' perceptions of integrating AI in religious studies classes. Teachers acknowledged that AI tools (like educational software or search engines) could provide students with wider access to religious knowledge beyond the local curriculum, for example, by retrieving information about Islamic history or practices globally (Kurata et al., 2025). However, they also expressed concern about the accuracy of online information and the need for teachers to guide students in verifying AI-provided content against authentic sources (since misinformation is a risk). This reflects a general trend: educators see AI as a means to augment resources and reach, especially where trained teachers or libraries are scarce, but remain cautious about its content reliability and interpretative limitations.

Another trend in AI for IRE is the development of multilingual translation tools for religious content. AI translation services have dramatically improved, enabling texts like the Qur'an, Hadith, and scholarly articles to be translated between Arabic and English, for instance, with increasing fluency (Noha Abdullah Alowedi & Arif Ahmed Mohammed Hassan Al-Ahdal, 2023; Wasehudin et al., 2024). This has the potential to democratise access to classical knowledge, though accuracy in religious translation is paramount and often requires human review. In summary, current applications of AI in Islamic Religious Education span from interactive learning tools for Qur'an and Hadith to information retrieval systems for religious knowledge and virtual assistants for basic religious queries. Global examples include AI-powered Qur'an recitation apps, semantic hadith search engines aiding scholars worldwide, and pilot AI fatwa response systems (with cautious oversight) (Abdi et al., 2020; Daily Sabah, 2025; Munshi et al., 2021). In Muslim-minority contexts, AI primarily serves to connect learners with resources and distant teachers, mitigating the lack of local expertise. Thus, the AI trend in IRE is clear: AI is gradually being woven into the fabric of Islamic education, though often in supportive roles and under careful human supervision to ensure fidelity to authentic teachings.

Pedagogical Opportunities of AI to Support IRE

Personalised and Adaptive Learning:

The most frequently cited benefit of AI in any educational context is its ability to personalise learning. In IRE, personalisation is particularly valuable because students often have widely varying levels of prior knowledge and skill – for instance, in a single class, some students might already know how to read Arabic while others are beginners. AI systems can tailor instruction to each student's level (Abubakari & Suprapto, 2021; Bhutoria, 2022). Personalised learning plans can ensure that a student who has already memorised certain prayers is not forced to repeat them unnecessarily, while another who is struggling with a concept (e.g., the rules of wudu (ablution)) gets additional practice. Studies in Indonesia have shown that AI-based personalisation can significantly increase students' understanding of Islamic concepts by allowing them to learn at their own pace (Salim & Aditya, 2025). From the teacher's perspective, AI personalisation provides data dashboards indicating each learner's progress. Teachers receive analytics that can help them design more effective interventions – for example, identifying that a group of students who have difficulty with a particular topic (say, distinguishing different schools of Islamic law in fiqh) and thus need a remedial session (Abubakari, Shafik, et al., 2024;

Salim & Aditya, 2025). Ultimately, by accommodating individual differences, AI has the potential to uphold the Islamic pedagogical principle of ta'lim (delivering knowledge) more effectively to each student.

Intelligent Tutoring and Practice:

AI's capability to function as a tireless tutor can greatly supplement classroom learning in IRE. ITS can be available to students outside class hours, providing practice and guidance in a way that was not feasible before (Syahrizal et al., 2023). For example, an AI tutor for learning Hadith terminology could quiz a student on the definitions of terms like sahih, hasan, da'if (hadith grades), and offer explanations whenever the student errs, patiently continuing until mastery is achieved. Similarly, for learning Arabic (a foundational skill in IRE), AI-driven language tutors can engage students in interactive exercises, correct their pronunciation, and even carry out simple conversational practice. These tutors can use multimedia, like showing how to write Arabic letters or playing audio of how a word is pronounced, and then evaluating the student's attempt. The benefit for IRE is that students get instant feedback and can practice without waiting for the next class or the teacher's availability. In primary education settings, such as elementary madrasas, research has found that integrating AI tutoring with an emotional intelligence approach – i.e., making the AI respond supportively and encouragingly – can make learning more interactive and enjoyable, thereby improving young students' engagement in religious lessons (Priyanto et al., 2025). The use of AI tools alongside a focus on emotional and spiritual connection helped strengthen students' internalisation of religious and emotional values, although it was noted that success relied on collaboration between the technology, teachers, and a holistic curriculum (Priyanto et al., 2025). This suggests AI tutors are most effective when they complement, rather than replace, the human touch provided by teachers.

Natural Language Processing for Islamic Texts:

The application of NLP and related AI technologies to Islamic textual sources holds great promise for both students and scholars (Azmi et al., 2019). One potential is language assistance: many students of Islam struggle with classical Arabic. AI translation and transliteration tools can make foundational texts more accessible. For example, an AI tool might allow a student to hover over an Arabic verse and see an accurate translation and explanation in their native language. It could also parse complex sentences from a tafsīr (Qur'anic exegesis) text and summarise the main point in simpler terms. Additionally, AI can help in textual analysis and research. A student working on a project about Islamic ethics could use an AI-powered search to find all occurrences of the term "justice" ('adl) across the Qur'ān and hadith corpus, something that would have been immensely time-consuming manually. Researchers have shown how AI-based religious text analysis systems can digitise and simplify the understanding of complex religious texts (Butt et al., 2024; El Ganadi et al., 2024). By identifying themes, cross-referencing verses with similar messages, and even performing morphological analysis of Arabic words, AI tools can provide learners with deeper and more structured insights into texts that might otherwise require years of traditional study to navigate. This does not diminish the need for scholarly learning, but it can act as "training wheels" for students, giving them a head start and building their confidence in engaging with primary sources.

Enhanced Accessibility for Diverse Learners:

AI technology has a notable capacity to improve inclusive education, which is relevant for IRE as well. Learners with disabilities or special needs can benefit from AI-driven assistive tools (Pagliara et al., 2024). For instance, speech-to-text and text-to-speech technologies can help hearing-impaired or visually-impaired students participate more fully in Islamic classes. An AI-powered system could transcribe a teacher's lecture or a sermon in real time for a student who cannot hear, displaying the text on the student's devices. Conversely, for a student who is blind, an AI system could read out textbooks or translate Qur'anic Arabic verses into audible outputs. There are also AI tools that convert text into sign language through animated avatars, which could be used to teach deaf students how to perform prayers (alāh) by showing the postures via the avatar. Research on AI in inclusive education indicates that such tools "markedly enhance accessibility and active involvement" for students with various impairments (Abdelwahab et al., 2025; Ahmed et al., 2025). In the Islamic education context, this could mean that a child with dyslexia might use an AI reading app to help read the Qur'an (highlighting words as it reads them aloud), or a student with attention-deficit issues might use an AI tutor that breaks lessons into shorter, engaging snippets. By catering to individual needs, AI can help ensure that "no child is left behind" in religious learning, echoing the Islamic ethos of making knowledge available to all and accommodating differences (as the Prophet Muhammad adjusted his teaching style according to his audience's needs).

Engagement and Motivation through Gamification:

Another potential is increasing student engagement through AI-driven platforms. AI can drive sophisticated educational games and simulations that make learning about Islam interactive and fun, especially for younger learners. Imagine an AI-driven game where students virtually "travel" through Muslim historical civilisations, solving quests that require answering questions about Islamic beliefs or identifying moral lessons from stories of the Prophets. The AI in the game can adjust the difficulty based on the learner's responses, ensuring they remain challenged but not frustrated. Recent studies have indeed shown that AI-based gamified learning in Islamic education can boost students' motivation and participation (Attarwiyah et al., 2025; Muslimah & Arliansyah, 2024). The adaptability means that if a student is breezing through, the game introduces harder tasks; if they are struggling, it provides hints or simplifies the challenge. Beyond games, AI can facilitate simulations – for example, an AI-powered virtual reality experience of Hajj that allows students to "perform" the pilgrimage in a classroom, with the AI explaining each step and checking if they remember the required prayers or actions. Such immersive learning can deepen understanding and emotional connection to the material.

Fostering Critical Thinking and Ethical Reasoning

It might seem counterintuitive, but AI can also be used to cultivate critical thinking rather than rote learning. By providing a vast array of information and viewpoints, AI tools can encourage students to analyse and evaluate what they encounter. For instance, a class might use a generative AI (like an Islamic version of ChatGPT fine-tuned on scholarly sources) to pose a complex ethical question ("What is the Islamic perspective on environmental conservation?"). The AI could generate a nuanced answer drawing from Qur'an, hadith, and scholarly opinions. Students would then be tasked with evaluating that answer: Does it align with what they have learned? Is the reasoning sound? This exercise trains them in critical engagement with content. Moreover, AI can present simulated ethical dilemmas or role-playing scenarios. An AI system might simulate a dialogue where the student has to advise a peer on an ethical issue (e.g., dealing with bullying, or making ethical choices in using social media) – the AI takes the role of the peer, asking questions or even challenging the student's answers. Such AI-mediated dialogic simulations have been highlighted as a didactically valuable opportunity in religious and ethics education (Papakostas, 2025). They allow students to practice reasoning and moral decision-making in a safe environment. Some researchers noted that incorporating AI-based learning in Islamic education can contribute to fostering critical thinking among students (Hartati et al., 2024; Raehang et al., 2025), likely because the interactive and personalised nature of AI encourages students to think actively rather than passively receive information. For example, when an AI tutor asks, "Why do you think this verse was revealed?" and offers hints, it nudges the student to engage in deeper interpretation.

AI IMPLEMENTATION CHALLENGES IN IRE

For all the optimism surrounding AI's potential in Islamic education, some equally significant challenges and concerns must be addressed. These challenges span pedagogical, practical, and even theological dimensions. Recognising them is critical to developing a balanced approach to AI integration. Key challenges include:

Decontextualisation of Religious Knowledge

A foremost concern is that AI tools might present Islamic knowledge in a fragmented or decontextualised manner, undermining the holistic understanding that traditional education strives for. Islamic teachings are deeply context-sensitive – verses of the Qur'an have occasions of revelation, hadiths have contexts and conditions, and legal rulings depend on circumstances. An AI, especially a naïve one, might supply an answer or a religious quote without the necessary context, leading students to misconstrue its meaning. For example, a student might ask an AI about a complex legal issue; the AI might retrieve a classical ruling and present it without explaining the societal context in which that ruling was given, or without noting differing opinions. This could confuse the student or give a skewed view of Islam as overly rigid or irrelevant, when in fact, a teacher would have contextualised it properly. Nasution et al. (2025), in their phenomenological study of AI in Islamic high schools, observed that while AI enhanced access to religious knowledge and even stimulated critical reflection, it also led to "spiritual narrative fragmentation" and "theological oversimplification". Essentially, bits of knowledge were floating around without the narrative glue that usually holds them together in a meaningful way (Nasution et al., 2025). For instance, students might learn many facts via AI quizzes but fail to see the bigger spiritual message connecting them. This challenge of decontextualisation can weaken the tarbiyyah aspect – the nurturing of a coherent Islamic worldview – and reduce learning to information snippets. The risk is that students become "Google Muslims," with lots of isolated information but little understanding. Overcoming this challenge requires intentional instructional design: AI systems must be programmed or used in ways that preserve context (through explanatory notes, source references, etc.), and teachers must actively help students piece the fragments into a whole.

Overreliance on AI and Authority

Another significant challenge is the possibility of students (or even teachers) placing undue trust in AI outputs regarding religious matters. If an AI app consistently provides quick answers to religious questions, users might start treating it as an authority. This is problematic because AI lacks true understanding – it cannot grasp divine intent, spiritual subtleties, or moral weight the way a trained and pious scholar can. There is a danger of what we might term "fatwa by algorithm," where people prefer asking an app over consulting a knowledgeable person, leading to superficial or even incorrect guidance. A recent work on AI in Religious Education explicitly flags the risk of theological distortion and epistemic conformity – AI might give answers that are distorted (due to biased training data or simplistic algorithms), and users might conform to them without question (Papakostas, 2025). In an IRE context, if students use AI tools to get answers for assignments or personal religious queries, they might not develop the habit of critical verification against authentic sources. They might also not learn to appreciate the scholarly process – the years of study, the methodology of deriving rulings – because AI makes it appear as if answers are instant and clear-cut. This ties into the Islamic concept of taqlid (blind following) versus tadabbur (deliberation); we don't want AI to become an object of blind following. Moreover, an AI could inadvertently propagate mistakes or one-sided views (depending on its training data). For example, suppose an AI is trained predominantly on one school of law's texts. In that case, it might always give answers according to that school, making students unaware of the diversity of Islamic thought. Overreliance could also reduce students' engagement in discussion and reflection – why discuss when the app "knows" the answer? This challenge calls for strong guidelines and digital literacy education (Abubakari, Zakaria, Musa, et al., 2023; Abubakari & Kalinaki, 2024): students and teachers need to understand AI's limitations. Some theological voices might emphasise that ilm (knowledge) in Islam comes with chains of transmission and human insight (basirah) that a machine cannot replicate; thus, an AI can be a tool, but not a mufti or a spiritual guide.

Undermining the Teacher's Role and Spiritual Relationship

Islamic pedagogy highly values the teacher-student relationship, not just as a conduit of knowledge, but as a bond of respect, character moulding, and often spiritual mentorship (the concept of murabbi who shapes the student's tarbiyah). The introduction of AI could strain this relationship. If students start turning to AI for answers or if AI handles many teaching tasks, the perceived role of the teacher may diminish. Teachers themselves might feel threatened or disoriented by AI's presence, unsure of where they now add value. Nasution et al. (2025) found that teachers in their study were "polarised between adaptation and resistance" to AI's presence, indicating that not all educators are comfortable with these tools. Some might resist using AI out of fear that it encroaches on their traditional authority and the affective aspect of teaching. And indeed, a critical challenge is ensuring that AI does not replace the human touch. An AI can't provide genuine empathy, listen to a student's problems after class, or impart wisdom through real-life examples – all things IRE teachers often do. The relational and formational aspects of religious education (such as mentoring a student in improving their character or inspiring them through one's personal stories) must remain central. As one study concluded, AI may enrich RE when used thoughtfully, but it must not replace the relational and formational aspects central to RE (Papakostas, 2025). A more subtle point is that in Islam, knowledge is traditionally taken heart-to-heart, almost like a transmission of not just data but also light (nur) and blessings (barakah). Relying entirely on impersonal tools could deprive learning of this spiritual dimension. For instance, reciting the Qur'ān to a qualified teacher is considered superior because the teacher links you back through a chain to the Prophet – something an app cannot do so far. Thus, maintaining the authority and spiritual role of teachers is a challenge. It requires re-envisioning the teacher's role: rather than being the sole source of information, the teacher becomes a facilitator, a context-giver, and most importantly, the spiritual and ethical mentor who interprets and guides the use of the information that AI provides. Students must continue to see their teachers as role models and ultimate guides in their learning journey, with AI as a supplementary aid. One protective measure, as seen in Harvard Divinity School's approach, is to explicitly forbid treating AI as a source of religious authority, thereby reinforcing that human scholarship and spiritual discernment are the final arbiters (Papakostas, 2025).

Quality and Authenticity of AI-Provided Content

Another challenge is ensuring that the content delivered or generated by AI is accurate and in line with authentic Islamic teachings. AI systems are only as good as their data and algorithms. If an AI's training data includes non-authentic or biased sources, it might present those as equally valid knowledge. For example, an AI scraping the internet might pick up a misleading interpretation of a hadith from a fringe blog and give it to a student without caution. This could inadvertently introduce incorrect ideas. In a worst-case scenario, an AI could be manipulated (through adversarial attacks or simply through user prompts) to produce blasphemous or inappropriate content, as has been seen with some mainstream AI chatbots when users intentionally or unintentionally trigger certain outputs. In a classroom, if a student asks a sensitive question (say about gender roles or jihad) and the AI gives a tactless or contextless answer, it could do real harm by reinforcing stereotypes or confusing the student. Ensuring quality control is a non-trivial challenge. It means curating the AI's knowledge base, constantly monitoring outputs, and ideally involving scholars in the development process of Islamic AI tools. Without such measures, we risk what could be called "algorithmic Ifta' errors." It's worth noting that even advanced AI ethics research calls for oversight; researchers argue for community-wide frameworks to manage ethics in AI in education (Holmes et al., 2022). In the IRE context, that implies oversight by educational authorities and Islamic scholars to certify or supervise the AI's content. Until that is in place, educators must remain vigilant and probably double-check AI-provided material before it reaches students.

Technological and Infrastructure Challenges

From a practical standpoint, many Muslim educational institutions, especially in less affluent regions, face infrastructure gaps – unreliable internet, lack of devices, and limited technical support. Implementing AI might widen the "digital divide" if not everyone has equal access. Some studies have highlighted that infrastructure limitations in some regions can exacerbate the gap between urban and rural schools in implementing AI in IRE (Abubakari, Shafik, et al., 2024; Achruh et al., 2024). If some schools have AI labs and others barely have electricity, for instance, AI could inadvertently increase inequity in educational quality. Even within a classroom, if AI tools are accessed via personal devices, students who cannot afford smart devices or data plans could be left out. Therefore, logistical challenges of hardware, software, and maintenance are significant. Teachers also need training, and without it, they might misuse or underuse the AI tools, leading to frustration and abandonment of otherwise beneficial technologies. Another technical barrier is language support. Not all AI models currently handle Arabic or other languages from the Muslim world as well as they handle English (Abubakari, 2025b). While progress is rapid (with new Arabic LLMs being developed), there can still be limitations in, for example, understanding complex Arabic grammar in a student's input or generating responses in less common languages. If an AI tutor misinterprets a question posed in broken Arabic or struggles with a regional dialect, it may provide incorrect help, frustrating the learner.

ETHICAL AND THEOLOGICAL CONSIDERATIONS FOR AI INTEGRATION

Integrating AI into Islamic Religious Education not only raises pedagogical questions but also prompts deeper ethical and theological reflection. Islamic tradition has a rich framework for engaging with new phenomena, grounded in principles such as ijtihad (independent reasoning in legal and ethical matters) and maqasid al-shari'ah (the objectives or higher intents of Islamic law) (Elmahjub, 2023). These principles guide Muslims in evaluating innovations like AI: what benefits (maslahah) it brings, what harms (mafsadah) it may entail, and how it aligns with the preservation of key values such as faith, life, intellect, progeny, and property – the five oft-cited maqā id.

From an Islamic theological perspective, technology is generally seen as a tool that humans develop using the intellect (ʻaql) granted by God. The prevailing view among contemporary scholars is that AI, like other technologies, is permissible (halal) in principle unless it is used in a manner that contravenes Islamic teachings. This echoes a jurisprudential maxim: the basic ruling on things is permissibility unless there is evidence to prohibit. In the context of AI, scholars have reasoned that it can be considered an extension of human capabilities, essentially leveraging the intelligence that God has endowed human beings with, to create systems that can process information and make decisions (Mohadi & Tarshany, 2023; Raquib et al., 2022). However, this permissibility is not a blank check; it comes with the condition that AI's use must not violate ethical and religious boundaries. One key ethical consideration is intention (niyyah). In Islam, actions are judged by intentions, as per a famous hadith. The use of AI in education should thus be intentioned towards enhancing learning and serving the cause of Islamic knowledge, rather than, say, showing off technological prowess or commercial exploitation. If educators and institutions adopt AI, the underlying intention should be to fulfil their duty of tarbiyyah and ta'lim better, seeking God's pleasure by improving how students learn about Islam. This intentionality ensures that AI remains a servant to the higher goals of IRE rather than an end in itself.

Maqasid al-shari'ah (Higher Objectives of Islamic Law) provide a holistic lens to examine AI's role (Elmahjub, 2023; Raquib et al., 2022). For example, one of the maqā id is the preservation of al-ʻaql (intellect). AI in education should serve to preserve and enhance human intellect, not make it redundant or harm it. An overuse of AI (especially things like over-automation or reliance on AI for thinking) could make students intellectually lazy or passive, which would be contrary to preserving intellect. On the other hand, AI that provides knowledge and aids learning clearly serves the preservation and enrichment of intellect. Another maq ad is the preservation of al-din (faith or religion). AI's impact on faith can be argued in two ways: positively, it can spread knowledge of Islam widely and efficiently, supporting the preservation of religion by educating more people. Negatively, if misused, it might introduce doubts or errors or diminish the human elements of spirituality. Thus, alignment with maqasid requires maximising the benefit (spreading authentic knowledge, making education accessible) and minimising the harm (preventing errors, ensuring the tech doesn't erode spiritual practice).

Islamic thought also values maslahah (public interest) and ʻadl (justice). These values lead to concerns about bias and fairness in AI (Abubakari, 2025b). If an AI educational tool inadvertently favours one linguistic group (say Arabic speakers) over others in terms of quality of content, it could be seen as unjust or creating disparity. Ensuring inclusive design is an ethical imperative. Additionally, the concept of amanah (trust) applies to data: student data collected by AI systems is an amānah that must be protected—hence, issues of privacy and consent become not just legal, but moral duties. Moreover, the privacy concern in AI (surveillance, data collection) intersects with the Islamic emphasis on dignity and privacy (satr). Islamic ethics would demand that an AI system should not expose a student's weaknesses or personal information without consent and necessity. Schools using AI need clear policies about data, aligning with both legal standards and ethical norms of confidentiality. This is especially sensitive in religious learning, where sometimes personal reflections or questions (for instance, about one's doubts or sins in an Islamic context) might be shared with an AI tutor; such data is deeply personal and arguably should be treated with the same confidentiality as a counsellor or teacher would give.

Another theological consideration is the human-AI interaction in terms of the delegation of roles. Humans are considered *khalifah* (stewards) of God on earth, tasked to use their reason and moral agency to make decisions. If AI systems start making decisions in education (like deciding curricula or disciplining students via automated systems), one might ask: Are we handing over aspects of our *khilafah* to machines? Most would say AI lacks moral agency and cannot bear responsibility; thus, final decisions, especially moral ones, should remain with humans. This stance is reflected in scholars' nearly unanimous opinion that AI cannot issue fatwas autonomously. A fatwa is a moral-legal response requiring accountability before God and the community, something only a human jurist can carry. By extension, any interpretive act that has moral weight should involve human oversight. Theologically, this ensures that *niyyah* and *taqwa* (God-consciousness) – qualities of the heart – are part of the decision process, which an AI as a tool cannot possess.

There are also futuristic ethical questions under discussion: If AI systems become very advanced (e.g., using humanoid robots or very life-like avatars to teach), is there any theological issue in, say, having a robot lead a basic Islamic lecture or remind people of prayer times? While a robot imam for prayers is clearly unacceptable (because the imam must be a sane adult Muslim with intention, etc.), a robot could technically recite the adhan or a dua. Scholars might debate the propriety of that: Does it remove the human element of worship too much? Such scenarios are hypothetical but worth pondering as technology advances.

On the matter of bias, consider algorithmic bias that might conflict with Islamic values. For instance, if a training dataset for an AI tutoring system contains subtle secular biases (like portraying religious practice as a secondary aspect of life), it might influence the AI's interactions or content prioritisation in ways that downplay the importance of religious practice. Ensuring that an Islamic education AI is trained or adjusted with data reflecting Islamic values is important. This is akin to how one would choose textbooks: we ensure they have the right perspective; similarly, the "knowledge base" of an AI should be scrutinised.

From a theological lens, one could argue that using AI in education should be seen as part of the Islamic concept of seeking knowledge (talab al-'ilm), which is a form of worship if done for God's sake. In that sense, AI is just a new means (wasīla) to fulfil an age-old religious duty. Historical analogies are sometimes drawn to past Muslim scholars who used the latest tools of their times – the paper and printing press, or travel on camels, then steamships – to propagate knowledge. AI is a tool of our time. However, those analogies also remind us that every tool had its detractors initially (e.g., printing presses for the Qur'an were controversial centuries ago). Over time, the community engaged in ijtihad and determined how best to use those tools in line with Islamic principles. Similarly, a scholarly discourse is emerging on AI ethics from an Islamic perspective (Elmahjub, 2023). An article on Maqasid al-Shari'ah and AI ethics argues that the ethical challenges of AI, such as privacy and manipulation, correlate with essential values in maqā id theory, and that an Islamic framework can contribute to global AI ethics discussions (Raquib et al., 2022). The conclusion from that discourse is that Muslim thinkers see value in proactively shaping AI development with ethical considerations (like ensuring privacy, avoiding manipulation, and ensuring justice), rather than rejecting AI outright. This proactive engagement is in itself an ethical stance, practising stewardship by guiding technology towards good.

In summary, the ethical and theological considerations surrounding AI in IRE revolve around ensuring that the use of AI aligns with Islamic values and does not undermine them. Key points include maintaining human agency and moral responsibility, securing justice and avoiding bias, protecting privacy, and upholding the sanctity of religious learning. There is an optimistic but cautious outlook: AI is part of the God-given creative capacity of humans and can be used for enormous good, but it must be checked by ethical guidelines rooted in Islamic teachings. It's also worth noting that some theologians stress humility and reliance on God (*tawakkul*) – meaning that while we use these means, we ultimately trust in God to grant beneficial knowledge and understanding. The presence of advanced tools should not lead to a false sense of self-sufficiency. In an Islamic classroom with AI, a teacher might remind students: "We use these tools by the grace of Allah, but we always ask Him for true knowledge and wisdom." This kind of perspective keeps the theological principle that knowledge (`ilm) is a light from God, and tools are just facilitators, not the ultimate source.

TEACHER READINESS AND PROFESSIONAL DEVELOPMENT

Digital Competence of IRE Educators and Learners

The successful integration of AI in Islamic Religious Education hinges not only on the technology itself but on the people using it, especially teachers, who are the linchpins of the educational process. A critical factor is the digital competence of IRE educators (Abubakari, 2024b; Abubakari et al., 2025; Budiyanti et al., 2022). Many Islamic studies teachers, particularly those who trained in traditional methods or graduated years before the current tech wave, may have had little exposure to advanced educational technology during their training. Some might be highly proficient in classical Arabic or Quranic sciences but less comfortable navigating software, online platforms, or data analytics dashboards. Bridging this gap is essential. If teachers lack basic digital literacy, they may find AI tools intimidating or burdensome and thus avoid or underutilise them. In a sense, there is a generation gap challenge: students today (especially at secondary and higher levels) might be quite tech-savvy (often termed "digital natives"), whereas some teachers could be "digital immigrants" trying to adapt (Benini & Murray, 2014; García et al., 2020). This can invert the usual knowledge hierarchy and potentially cause classroom management or credibility issues if not addressed (imagine a student having to help the teacher use the app – it can undermine the teacher's authority subtly).

Students, too, have varying degrees of digital competence (Abubakari, Zakaria, Musa, et al., 2023; Abubakari & Kalinaki, 2024). While many youths are good at using smartphones or playing games, they may not automatically know how to use an AI learning app effectively. There is a need to teach digital study skills: for instance, how to critically evaluate what an AI outputs (not taking everything at face value), or how to manage time when learning with an app (since these can be engaging, some students might over-rely on apps for quick answers rather than doing deep thinking, or conversely, spend too much time on one aspect of learning because the app makes it fun, at the expense of other tasks). Thus, part of readiness is also preparing learners to be smart users of AI – essentially building AI literacy among students. A study in Vietnam on AI in Christian education found that openness to AI varied across generations; notably, the youngest generation (Gen Z) was most prepared to adopt it, whereas older church personnel were more hesitant (Tran & Nguyen, 2021). In an IRE setting, that might analogously mean students will often be more eager and quicker to embrace tech than their teachers or school administrators. The disparity itself is something to manage; ideally, harness student enthusiasm (perhaps by even involving tech-savvy students as "tech helpers" in class) while ensuring teacher authority and pedagogy lead the way.

Professional Development and Training Programs

Professional development tailored for IRE educators is critical to ensure that the integration of AI is effective, ethical, and sustainable. As AI is a relatively new frontier in education, many teachers will not have encountered it in their initial teacher training programs. Thus, in-service training and continuous development opportunities are needed. These should cover not just the "how-to" of the technology but also pedagogical strategies and ethical guidelines for its use. For professional development to be effective, it should be contextualised for IRE. Generic tech-integration training might not touch on issues like correct recitation feedback or hadith content accuracy, whereas an IRE-focused program will. By aligning training with the subject matter, teachers see the relevance. For instance, part of the training could be "Using AI for Qur'an Tajwid: Dos and Don'ts," which is directly useful to many IRE teachers.

Recognising the challenge of digital and AI literacy gaps, many scholars emphasise that teacher readiness is as important as student readiness when implementing AI (Ifenthaler et al., 2024). In contexts like Lesotho's religious studies teachers or others studied, perceptions and comfort levels with AI varied widely (Kurata et al., 2025). For IRE, teacher attitudes might also be influenced by concerns we have discussed – spiritual or ethical reservations. A teacher might be confident digitally but resistant mentally because they fear negative impacts, as found by a recent study- some teachers are resistant, while others adapt (Nasution et al., 2025). Readiness is thus both skill-based and mindset-based. On the skills side, educators need training in basic computer use, familiarisation with specific AI tools (how to interpret an AI recommendation, how to troubleshoot when the system errors, etc.), and an understanding of concepts like algorithmic bias or data privacy so that they can oversee these tools responsibly. On the mindset side, they may need reassurance and theological/ethical framing to feel comfortable that using AI is aligned with their role as Islamic educators.

APPROACHES FOR EFFECTIVE AI INTEGRATION IN IRE

Clear AI Guidelines for Learners and Teachers

It is essential to develop clear guidelines on how AI tools should be used in the learning process. Schools and madrasas can formulate an "AI use policy" that defines the scope of AI assistance – for example, clarifying that AI tutors can be used for practice and research, but final verification of religious answers should be done with a teacher or trusted sources. Such guidelines help set the right expectations among students, teaching them to use AI as a supplementary resource rather than an infallible authority (Abubakari, 2024a). In higher education settings, policies on academic integrity should be updated to address AI (e.g., requiring students to disclose if an AI was used to generate any part of an assignment, similar to citing a source). This encourages honest and ethical use of AI.

Institutions should also integrate AI literacy into their curriculum. Just as digital literacy is now taught, students should be instructed on how to query AI effectively, how to cross-check its answers, and the Islamic ethics of seeking knowledge (so they don't, for instance, use AI to seek forbidden knowledge or misuse it for cheating). By making AI literacy part of learning objectives, schools acknowledge its presence and prepare students to engage with it responsibly. As Chan & Hu (2023) highlighted, understanding users' perceptions and concerns can inform well-crafted guidelines and strategies for effective GenAI implementation. For Islamic institutions in particular, it might be wise to establish a Shariah advisory board for educational technology. This board can continuously review new AI tools or content updates to ensure they meet religious standards, similar to how Islamic banks have Shariah boards. Their endorsement can reassure the community that the tool is sound. They can also issue guidance on complex issues, such as whether using AI-generated voices for Quran recitation in class is permissible. This pre-emptive governance helps avoid confusion and conflict later. Studies advocate for trustworthy principles in global Islamic education when adopting AI, suggesting that alignment with Islamic values must be evaluated at each step (Wiranto & Suwartini, 2023).

Professional Training and Capacity Building

Investing in teacher training is one of the most critical steps for successful AI integration. Educators need hands-on workshops and continuous support to become proficient with AI tools. This training should cover both technical operation (how to use the software, interpret data, and troubleshoot common issues) and pedagogical integration (best practices for blending AI activities with traditional teaching). Teachers could benefit from seeing model lessons where AI is used effectively. Sharing success stories or having tech-savvy teachers mentor others can build confidence. As some researchers concluded, the potential of AI will only be realised if teachers and learners receive adequate training and support (Chan & Hu, 2023; Lestari et al., 2024).

Additionally, capacity building is not just for teachers and learners – school administrators and curriculum developers should also be trained to understand AI's capabilities and constraints so that they can make informed decisions about resource allocation and curriculum design. Perhaps short certification courses in "AI in Education" can be developed in collaboration with universities, targeting

Islamic educators. Governments and educational organisations could subsidise these programs, recognising that upskilling the workforce is a public good. Such initiatives can be realised, possibly through partnerships between tech firms and Islamic educational boards.

Collaboration Among Diverse Stakeholders

Multi-disciplinary collaboration is vital to create AI solutions that are both technologically robust and religiously sound. Technologists (AI developers, data scientists) bring expertise in what is feasible and how to implement it. Religious scholars (ulama) ensure that the content and methods respect Islamic teachings and address the nuanced requirements of religious instruction. Educators ensure that the tools actually meet classroom needs and align with pedagogy. Regular workshops or panels that bring these groups together can spark innovations and address concerns early. For instance, an IRE institution looking to implement AI could host a hackathon including local Islamic studies teachers and AI developers to brainstorm solutions for, say, an intelligent quiz generator for a fiqh class.

One concrete form of collaboration could be developing shared open-source Islamic datasets and models. Different institutions working in silos may each train AI on similar Islamic texts – a collaborative effort could pool resources to create one high-quality, wide-ranging dataset of Quran, Hadith, classical books, and contemporary fatwas (with proper permissions). This would benefit all who then use it to train AI for educational purposes. It also allows scholars to audit and approve the dataset collectively. In essence, an "Ummah-wide" effort where, for example, experts from various International Islamic universities contribute to a central Islamic AI knowledge base could ensure global relevance and acceptance. Collaboration is also needed at the implementation stage. For example, when rolling out an AI tutor in a school, it is crucial to involve Islamic studies teachers, who are familiar with classroom dynamics, and software developers, who can adjust the tool based on teacher feedback. Students and parents can also be part of feedback loops. Institutions could form a small committee at the school, comprising a tech coordinator, a senior Islamic studies teacher, and perhaps a student representative, to monitor the AI program's effectiveness and report any issues. This ensures constant communication between the technical and educational sides. Thus, such collaborative approaches align with recommendations that a collaborative approach involving AI developers, communication experts, and qualified Islamic scholars is necessary for the effective and respectful use of AI in religious outreach and education (Abubakari, Shafik, et al., 2024; Hakim & Anggraini, 2023). When all stakeholders are at the table, the resulting implementation is more likely to be holistic and sustainable.

CONCLUSION AND FUTURE DIRECTIONS

In this chapter, through a comprehensive review, we have examined how Artificial Intelligence can be pedagogically integrated into Islamic Religious Education in a manner that respects and enhances the core values of Islamic pedagogy. We began by contextualising AI in contemporary education and noting its encroachment into religious education, including Islamic contexts, highlighting both enthusiasm and caution in the community. We identified that while AI in Education (AIEd) offers powerful tools – such as personalised learning via intelligent tutors, instant feedback through NLP, and vast information access – its adoption in IRE must be carefully aligned with *ta lim*, *tarbiyyah*, and *tazkiyah*, the triad of transmitting knowledge, nurturing character, and fostering spirituality.

Our exploration of current applications showed that AI is already aiding Qur'ān memorisation, hadith research, and even fatwa advisory, in both Muslim-majority nations and among diaspora communities. These innovations demonstrate clear potential: AI can increase efficiency and engagement (for example, making rote learning more interactive) and provide customisation (an app can adjust to each student's memorisation pace). Furthermore, we saw that AI can support inclusivity, helping students with disabilities access religious content more easily (Ahmed et al., 2025). The pedagogical opportunities identified include enhanced feedback loops, differentiated instruction, and possibilities for fostering critical thinking and ethical reasoning through AI-mediated activities (Papakostas, 2025). For instance, AI can simulate ethical dilemmas or present multiple viewpoints on a theological question, which teachers and students can then discuss, thereby encouraging deeper reflection and understanding.

However, our analysis also underscored significant challenges. AI's strengths in delivering information can become weaknesses if they lead to fragmented, context-less learning or an overreliance on machine answers. A consistent theme was the irreplaceability of the teacher's spiritual and interpersonal role – as mentor, moral exemplar, and interpreter of knowledge. We stressed that AI should augment but never supplant the teacher or the rich teacher-student relationship that is at the heart of Islamic pedagogy. Ethically, we delved into how Islamic principles like justice, privacy, and the higher objectives of Shari'ah (Maqasid) can guide the responsible use of AI (Raquib et al., 2022). It became clear that any technological integration must be evaluated not just on educational efficacy but on its impact on students' moral and spiritual development – a perspective sometimes overlooked in secular EdTech discussions. While this review has covered considerable ground, it also highlights areas ripe for further research. We conclude by suggesting several future research avenues:

- ***Empirical Impact Studies*:** There is a need for empirical research assessing the impact of AI integration on IRE outcomes across cognitive, affective, and spiritual domains. For example, a longitudinal study could compare two groups of students – one experiencing AI-enhanced IRE and a control group with traditional instruction – measuring not only academic performance (e.g., Islamic studies exam scores, memorisation rates) but also changes in attitudes (interest in religious learning, self-efficacy) and indicators of spiritual engagement (frequency of voluntary religious activities, qualitative self-reports of faith). Such studies would provide evidence on what works and what caution is warranted, helping to fine-tune integration strategies.
- ***Curriculum and Content Development*:** Research can focus on developing curriculum models or specific content for AI tools that embody Islamic pedagogical principles. For instance, designing an AI-driven Seerah (Prophetic biography) curriculum that allows students to "chat" with a historical simulation of a Companion of the Prophet, then studying how that affects their understanding and emotional connection to the material. Content research might also involve creating high-quality open-access datasets of Islamic knowledge (Qur'an, hadith, jurisprudence, biographies) annotated by scholars, which can be used to train AI models. This ensures that the knowledge base of future Islamic EdTech AI is authentic and comprehensive.
- ***AI Ethics and Policy in Islamic Education*:** Building on our ethical discussion, more focused research can be done to develop Islamic frameworks for AI ethics in education. This could involve ijtihād by contemporary scholars to issue guidance (*fatawa* or resolutions) on matters like: Is it acceptable to use AI to emulate human reciters for learning Qur'an (given issues of listening to recorded vs. live recitation)? How to handle data privacy from an Islamic legal perspective (does uploading student data to a cloud violate any trust (amānah) principles)? Also, policy research might explore how Muslim-majority education systems are beginning to incorporate AI, doing case studies of countries like Malaysia, Indonesia, or the UAE that are experimenting with AI in religious curricula, extracting best practices and lessons learned.
- ***Teacher Training Efficacy Studies*:** Since teacher readiness is key, research should look at professional development approaches (like the ones we described) to identify which models most effectively empower IRE teachers with tech integration without losing their distinctive pedagogical strengths. Action research by teachers implementing AI in their classes and reflecting on it can yield rich insights. This also extends to student perspective research – how do students, especially in different age groups, perceive the use of AI in their religious learning? Does it make them more interested, or do some

find it less "sacred"? Understanding student reception will guide a more nuanced implementation.

- ***Innovative AI Applications for IRE*:** Future research and development can explore creative new applications: e.g., intelligent tutoring systems for Arabic calligraphy (since calligraphy has spiritual dimensions in Islam, can AI help teach it while conveying its meditative aspect?), or VR simulations of historical events like the Battle of Badr to teach lessons in faith and strategy – measuring learning outcomes from those. Another frontier might be adaptive assessment – using AI to evaluate open-ended student responses about ethical dilemmas in light of Islamic criteria, which is very challenging but could transform assessment in IRE by going beyond multiple-choice knowledge tests to assessing depth of understanding and moral reasoning.

In conclusion, the integration of Artificial Intelligence in Islamic Religious Education stands at a delicate but promising juncture. If guided by thoughtful pedagogy, ethical safeguards, and continuous collaboration between educators and technologists, AI has the potential to significantly enhance IRE, making learning more accessible, engaging, and tailored, while upholding the spiritual and moral fabric that is its foundation. The journey forward will require balance: embracing beneficial innovations (a spirit of *ijtihad*) without losing sight of the wisdom in traditional methods (honouring the legacy of *turath*). As our review has illustrated, with principled frameworks and stakeholder commitment, it is possible to chart a path where technology serves as a tool to help shape not just knowledgeable minds but also virtuous souls, in line with the highest aims of Islamic education.

REFERENCES

Ab Rahim, S. F., Ab Rahman, M. F., Abdullah Thaidi, H. A., Nik Mohd Azimi, N. N. M. A., & Jailani, M. R. (2025). Artificial Intelligence for Fatwa Issuance: Guidelines And Ethical Considerations. *Journal of Fatwa Management and Research*, *30*(1), 76–100. DOI: 10.33102/jfatwa.vol30no1.654

Abbas, T. (2017). Traditional and Modern Muslim Education at the Core and Periphery: Enduring Challenge. In Daun, H., & Arjmand, R. (Eds.), *Handbook of Islamic Education, International Handbooks of Religion and Education* (pp. 1–12). Springer International Publishing., DOI: 10.1007/978-3-319-53620-0_13-1

Abdelwahab, M. M., Al-Karawi, K. A., & Semary, H. E. (2025). A Systematic Review of Assistive Technology for Enhancing the Students with Disabilities. *Journal of Disability Research*, *4*(2). Advance online publication. DOI: 10.57197/JDR-2024-0117

Abdi, A., Hasan, S., Arshi, M., Shamsuddin, S. M., & Idris, N. (2020). A question answering system in hadith using linguistic knowledge. *Computer Speech & Language*, *60*, 101023. DOI: 10.1016/j.csl.2019.101023

Abubakari, M. S. (2024a). Overviewing the Maze of Research Integrity and False Positives Within AI-Enabled Detectors: Grammarly Dilemma in Academic Writing. In Mutawa, A. (Ed.), *Impacts of Generative AI on the Future of Research and Education* (pp. 335–366). IGI Global., DOI: 10.4018/979-8-3693-0884-4.ch013

Abubakari, M. S. (2024b). The digital frontier within Islamic education: Research gaps overview in digital competence. *Journal of Computing Research and Innovation*, *9*(2), 317–331. DOI: 10.24191/jcrinn.v9i2.435

Abubakari, M. S. (2025a). Digital Technologies Adoption in Islamic Education for Fostering Lifelong Learning Culture: Pilot Survey Preliminary Insights. In Anshari, M., Almunawar, M. N., & Ordóñez de Pablos, P. (Eds.), *Multi-Industry Digitalization and Technological Governance in the AI Era* (pp. 103–126). IGI Global., DOI: 10.4018/979-8-3373-1681-9.ch005

Abubakari, M. S. (2025b). Overviewing Biases in Generative AI-Powered Models in the Arabic Language: AI Fairness for Sustainable Future. In Syafrudin, M., Fitriyani, N. L., & Anshari, M. (Eds.), *Achieving Sustainability in Multi-Industry Settings With AI* (pp. 361–390). IGI Global., DOI: 10.4018/979-8-3373-2530-9.ch013

Abubakari, M. S., & Kalinaki, K. (2024). Digital Competence in Islamic Education for Lifelong Learning: Preliminary Analysis Using DigComp 2.1 Framework. In Hawamdeh, M. M. K., & Abdelhafid, F. (Eds.), *Embracing Technological Advancements for Lifelong Learning* (pp. 1–31). IGI Global., DOI: 10.4018/979-8-3693-1410-4.ch001

Abubakari, M. S., & Mashoedah. (2021). The Internet of Things (IoT) as an Emerging Technological Solution for the Covid-19 Pandemic Mitigation: An Overview. *Journal of Physics: Conference Series*, *1737*(1), 012003. DOI: 10.1088/1742-6596/1737/1/012003

Abubakari, M. S., & Suprapto, S. (2021). Educational Data Mining to Predict Students Performance Based on Deep Learning Neural Network. Proceeding International Conference On Health, Social Sciences And Technology, 1(1), 13–16. https://ojs.poltekkespalembang.ac.id/index.php/icohsst/article/view/697

Abubakari, M. S., Shafik, W., & Hidayatullah, A. F. (2024). Evaluating the Potential of Artificial Intelligence in Islamic Religious Education: A SWOT Analysis Overview. In AI-Enhanced Teaching Methods (pp. 216–239). IGI Global. DOI: 10.4018/979-8-3693-2728-9.ch010

Abubakari, M. S., Zakaria, G. A. N., & Musa, J. (2023). Digital Learning Acceptance in Islamic Education: Validity and Reliability Testing of the Modified Technology Acceptance Model. *Canadian Journal of Educational and Social Studies*, *3*(6), 27–42. DOI: 10.53103/cjess.v6i1.185

Abubakari, M. S., Zakaria, G. A. N., & Musa, J. (2024). Perceived compatibility and students' intention to adopt digital technologies in Islamic education institutions. *Cogent Education*, *11*(1), 2430869. DOI: 10.1080/2331186X.2024.2430869

Abubakari, M. S., Zakaria, G. A. N., & Musa, J. (2025). Validating the DigComp framework among university students across different educational systems. *Discover Education*, *4*(1), 200. DOI: 10.1007/s44217-025-00652-x

Abubakari, M. S., Zakaria, G. A. N., Musa, J., & Kalinaki, K. (2023). Assessing Digital Competence in Higher Education: A Gender Analysis of DigComp 2.1 Framework in Uganda. SAGA. *Journal of Technology and Information System*, *1*(4), 114–120. DOI: 10.58905/saga.v1i4.210

Achruh, A., Rapi, M., Rusdi, M., & Idris, R. (2024). Challenges and Opportunities of Artificial Intelligence Adoption in Islamic Education in Indonesian Higher Education Institutions. International Journal of Learning. *Teaching and Educational Research*, *23*(11), 423–443. DOI: 10.26803/ijlter.23.11.22

Afzal, M. R., Ali, A., Mashwani, W. K., Anam, S., Zubair, M., & Qammar, L. (2023). Recitation of The Holy Quran Verses Recognition System Based on Speech Recognition Techniques. UMT Artificial Intelligence Review, 3(2), 01–20. DOI: 10.32350.umt-air.32.01

Ahmed, S., Rahman, M. S., Kaiser, M. S., & Hosen, A. S. M. S. (2025). Advancing Personalized and Inclusive Education for Students with Disability Through Artificial Intelligence: Perspectives, Challenges, and Opportunities. *Digital*, *5*(2), 11. DOI: 10.3390/digital5020011

Al-Attas, S. M. N. (2007). Knowledge and Education in Islam. In Secularism and Spirituality (pp. 166–179). DOI: 10.5281/zenodo.29436

Al-Ayyoub, M., Damer, N. A., & Hmeidi, I. (2018). Using Deep Learning for Automatically Determining Correct Application of Basic Quranic Recitation Rules. International Arab Journal of Information Technology, 15(3A Special Issue), 620–625.

Aldowah, H., Al-Samarraie, H., & Fauzy, W. M. (2019). Educational data mining and learning analytics for 21st century higher education: A review and synthesis. *Telematics and Informatics*, *37*, 13–49. DOI: 10.1016/j.tele.2019.01.007

Alshithisri, D. A. B. A. (2024). A Study of the Legal and Fiqhi Impact of AI on Issuing Fatwas. *Kurdish Studies*, *12*(1), 2504–2511. DOI: 10.58262/ks.v12i1.174

Altinyelken, H. K. (2021). Critical thinking and non-formal Islamic education: Perspectives from young Muslims in the Netherlands. *Contemporary Islam*, *15*(3), 267–285. DOI: 10.1007/s11562-021-00470-6

Alvindo, F., Setiawan, N. A., & Nugroho, H. A. (2024). Al-Quran Recitation or Sound Processing Analysis : A Systematic Literature Review on Methods. *2024 International Conference on Electrical Engineering and Computer Science (ICECOS)*, 54–58. DOI: 10.1109/ICECOS63900.2024.10791189

Amzat, I. H. (2022). *Supporting Modern Teaching in Islamic Schools: Pedagogical Best Practice for Teachers*. Routledge., DOI: 10.4324/9781003193432

Attarwiyah, N. M., Wasi'ah, I. R., & Jennah, S. N. (2025). Bridging Tradition and Technology : Gamification in Modern Islamic Boarding Schools. *Journal of Social Studies and Education*, *02*(02), 97–110.

Azmi, A. M., Al-Qabbany, A. O., & Hussain, A. (2019). Computational and natural language processing based studies of hadith literature: A survey. *Artificial Intelligence Review*, *52*(2), 1369–1414. DOI: 10.1007/s10462-019-09692-w

Baiza, Y. (2022). Are Contemporary Islamic Education and Their Pedagogical Approaches Fit for Purpose? A Critique and Way Forward. In Amzat, I. H. (Ed.), *Supporting Modern Teaching in Islamic Schools* (pp. 17–30). Routledge., DOI: 10.4324/9781003193432-3

Balula, N. O., Rashwan, M., & Abdou, S. (2021). Automatic Speech Recognition (ASR) Systems for Learning Arabic Language and Al-Quran Recitation: A Review. *International Journal of Computer Science and Mobile Computing*, *10*(7), 91–100. DOI: 10.47760/ijcsmc.2021.v10i07.013

Bashir, M. H., Azmi, A. M., Nawaz, H., Zaghouani, W., Diab, M., Al-Fuqaha, A., & Qadir, J. (2023). Arabic natural language processing for Qur'anic research: A systematic review. *Artificial Intelligence Review*, *56*(7), 6801–6854. DOI: 10.1007/s10462-022-10313-2

Benini, S., & Murray, L. (2014). Challenging Prensky's Characterization of Digital Natives and Digital Immigrants in a Real-World Classroom Setting. In Guikema, J. P., & Williams, L. (Eds.), *Digital literacies in foreign and second language education* (Vol. 12, pp. 69–85).

Bhutoria, A. (2022). Personalized education and Artificial Intelligence in the United States, China, and India: A systematic review using a Human-In-The-Loop model. *Computers and Education: Artificial Intelligence*, *3*, 100068. DOI: 10.1016/j.caeai.2022.100068

Budiyanti, S., Ulum, I. M., Jaenudin, A., & Aisyah, S. (2022). PAI Teacher Digital Competency Based on Teaching Level. QALAMUNA: Jurnal Pendidikan, Sosial. *Dan Agama*, *14*(2), 275–286. DOI: 10.37680/qalamuna.v14i2.1937

Butt, N. A., Basharat, A., & Kamran, A. B. (2024). Semantic Enrichment of Hadith Corpus - Knowledge Graph Generation from Islamic Text. Semantic Web Journal. https://www.semantic-web-journal.net/system/files/swj3651.pdf

Capuano, N., & Caballé, S. (2020). Adaptive Learning Technologies. *AI Magazine*, *41*(2), 96–98. DOI: 10.1609/aimag.v41i2.5317

Chan, C. K. Y., & Hu, W. (2023). Students' voices on generative AI: Perceptions, benefits, and challenges in higher education. *International Journal of Educational Technology in Higher Education*, *20*(1), 43. DOI: 10.1186/s41239-023-00411-8

Sabah, D. (2025). Saudi Arabia unveils AI "Fatwa Robot," new pilgrim flow technology. Daily Sabah. https://www.dailysabah.com/life/saudi-arabia-unveils-ai-fatwa-robot-new-pilgrim-flow-technology/news

Daun, H., & Arjmand, R. (2021). Globalisation and Islamic Education. In Zajda, J. (Ed.), *Third International Handbook of Globalisation, Education and Policy Research* (pp. 451–463). Springer International Publishing., DOI: 10.1007/978-3-030-66003-1_25

El Ganadi, A., Aftar, S., Gagliardelli, L., Bergamaschi, S., & Ruozzi, F. (2024). The Impact of Generative AI on Islamic Studies: Case Analysis of "Digital Muhammad ibn Ismail Al-Bukhari." 2024 2nd International Conference on Foundation and Large Language Models (FLLM), 179–187. DOI: 10.1109/FLLM63129.2024.10852480

Elmahjub, E. (2023). Artificial Intelligence (AI) in Islamic Ethics: Towards Pluralist Ethical Benchmarking for AI. *Philosophy & Technology*, *36*(4), 73. DOI: 10.1007/s13347-023-00668-x

Farooq, J., & Imran, M. (2021). Mispronunciation Detection in Articulation Points of Arabic Letters using Machine Learning. 2021 International Conference on Computing, Electronic and Electrical Engineering (ICE Cube), 1–6. DOI: 10.1109/ICECube53880.2021.9628251

García, A. C., Gil-Mediavilla, M., Álvarez, I., & Casares, M. de los Á. (2020). The Influence of Social Networks within Educational and Social Fields: A Comparative Study between Two Generations of Online Students. *Sustainability*, *12*(23), 9941. DOI: 10.3390/su12239941

Hakim, A., & Anggraini, P. (2023). Artificial Intelligence in Teaching Islamic Studies: Challenges and Opportunities. *Molang: Journal Of Islamic Education*, *1*(02), 57–69. DOI: 10.32806/6ynvg541

Hartati, R., & Fujiantie, J., & Ries Dyah Fitriyah. (2024). Generative Artificial Intelligence Integration for the Education of Islamic Communication and Broadcasting. *Jurnal Komunikasi Islam*, *14*(2), 345–365. DOI: 10.15642/jki.2024.14.2.345-365

Holmes, W., Porayska-Pomsta, K., Holstein, K., Sutherland, E., Baker, T., Shum, S. B., Santos, O. C., Rodrigo, M. T., Cukurova, M., Bittencourt, I. I., & Koedinger, K. R. (2022). Ethics of AI in Education: Towards a Community-Wide Framework. *International Journal of Artificial Intelligence in Education*, *32*(3), 504–526. DOI: 10.1007/s40593-021-00239-1

Huang, X., Xu, W., & Liu, R. (2025). Effects of Intelligent Tutoring Systems on Educational Outcomes. *International Journal of Distance Education Technologies*, *23*(1), 1–25. DOI: 10.4018/IJDET.368420

Ifenthaler, D., Majumdar, R., Gorissen, P., Judge, M., Mishra, S., Raffaghelli, J., & Shimada, A. (2024). Artificial Intelligence in Education: Implications for Policymakers, Researchers, and Practitioners. Technology. *Knowledge and Learning*, *29*(4), 1693–1710. DOI: 10.1007/s10758-024-09747-0

Kamran, A. B., Abro, B., & Basharat, A. (2023). SemanticHadith: An ontology-driven knowledge graph for the hadith corpus. *Journal of Web Semantics*, *78*, 100797. DOI: 10.1016/j.websem.2023.100797

Kurata, L., Ayanwale, M. A., Molefi, R. R., & Sanni, T. (2025). Teaching religious studies with artificial intelligence: A qualitative analysis of Lesotho secondary schools teachers' perceptions. *International Journal of Educational Research Open*, *8*, 100417. DOI: 10.1016/j.ijedro.2024.100417

Lestari, J. T., Darmayanti, R., & Arifin, Z. (2024). Integration of Artificial Intelligence in Islamic Education Curriculum. *Journal of Pergunu and Contemporary Islamic Studies*, *1*(1), 55–78. https://jurnal.pcpergunukotapasuruan.org/index.php/jpcis/article/view/12

Marwa, N. K., Anwar, S., & Firmansyah, M. I. (2025). Implementation of Artificial Intelligence in Islamic Education Learning at Elementary School. Edu Cendikia. *Jurnal Ilmiah Kependidikan*, *4*(03), 1676–1686. DOI: 10.47709/educendikia.v4i03.5413

Memon, N. A. (2021). Islamic Pedagogy for Islamic Schools. In *Oxford Research Encyclopedia of Education*. Oxford University Press., DOI: 10.1093/acrefore/9780190264093.013.1515

Memon, N. A., Alhashmi, M., & Abdalla, M. (2021). Curriculum Renewal for Islamic Education (N. A. Memon, M. Alhashmi, & M. Abdalla (eds.); 1st Editio). Routledge. DOI: 10.4324/9780429276811

Mohadi, M., & Tarshany, Y. (2023). Maqasid Al-Shari'ah and the Ethics of Artificial Intelligence. *Journal of Contemporary Maqasid Studies*, *2*(2), 79–102. DOI: 10.52100/jcms.v2i2.107

Munshi, A. A., AlSabban, W. H., Farag, A. T., Rakha, O. E., Al Sallab, A. A., & Alotaibi, M. (2021). Towards an Automated Islamic Fatwa System: Survey, Dataset and Benchmarks. *International Journal of Computer Science and Mobile Computing*, *10*(4), 118–131. DOI: 10.47760/ijcsmc.2021.v10i04.017

Musa, S., Abubakari, M. S., & Abdulwahab, L. O. (2025). Evaluating the Potential of Adapting Artificial Intelligence (AI) in Small and Medium Enterprises for Competitive Advantage. In Anshari, M., Almunawar, M. N., & Ordóñez de Pablos, P. (Eds.), *Multi-Industry Digitalization and Technological Governance in the AI Era* (pp. 233–266). IGI Global., DOI: 10.4018/979-8-3373-1681-9.ch012

Muslimah, M., & Arliansyah, A. (2024). Gamification Method in Increasing Motivation towards Studying the Al-Quran and Islamic Perspectives. *Jurnal Pendidikan Agama Islam*, *4*(1), 181–190.

Nasution, S., Pohan, A. J., & Hayati, N., Khairurrijal, & Nur, K. (2025). Islamic Religious Education in the Post-Human Era : Embracing Artificial Intelligence through Transformative Spirituality. *Jurnal Penelitian Pendidikan Islam*, *13*(1), 26–43. DOI: 10.36667/jppi.v13i1.2170

Alowedi, N. A., & Al-Ahdal, A. A. M. H. (2023). Artificial Intelligence based Arabic-to-English machine versus human translation of poetry: An analytical study of outcomes. *Journal of Namibian Studies : History Politics Culture*, *33*(2), 1523–1538. DOI: 10.59670/jns.v33i.800

Pagliara, S. M., Bonavolontà, G., Pia, M., Falchi, S., Zurru, A. L., Fenu, G., & Mura, A. (2024). The Integration of Artificial Intelligence in Inclusive Education: A Scoping Review. *Information (Basel)*, *15*(12), 774. DOI: 10.3390/info15120774

Papakostas, C. (2025). Artificial Intelligence in Religious Education: Ethical, Pedagogical, and Theological Perspectives. *Religions*, *16*(5), 563. DOI: 10.3390/rel16050563

Paramboor, J., & Ibrahim, B. (2013). Philosophical Aspects of 'Murabbi'- A Contextual Analysis with Special Reference to Globalization Of Education. *Journal of Education and Practice*, *4*(26), 151–156.

Pliakos, K., Joo, S.-H., Park, J. Y., Cornillie, F., Vens, C., & Van den Noortgate, W. (2019). Integrating machine learning into item response theory for addressing the cold start problem in adaptive learning systems. *Computers & Education*, *137*, 91–103. DOI: 10.1016/j.compedu.2019.04.009

Priyanto, D., Annas, A. N., Djollong, A. F., Khaerul, K., & Arafat, Y. (2025). Integration Of Artificial Intelligence In Learning Islamic Religious Education Based On Emotional Intelligence In Primary Schools. *Journal of International Multidisciplinary Research*, *3*(5), 15–22. DOI: 10.62504/jimr1238

Raehang, Assingkily, M. S., & Ahmad, M. (2025). Integrating Artificial Intelligence into Madrasah Learning: A Mixed-Methods Study of Intelligent Media Development and Implementation. *Cendekiawan : Jurnal Pendidikan Dan Studi Keislaman*, *4*(1), 608–618. DOI: 10.61253/cendekiawan.v4i1.322

Raquib, A., Channa, B., Zubair, T., & Qadir, J. (2022). Islamic virtue-based ethics for artificial intelligence. *Discover Artificial Intelligence*, *2*(1), 11. DOI: 10.1007/s44163-022-00028-2

Sabki, A. A., & Hardaker, G. (2013). The madrasah concept of Islamic pedagogy. *Educational Review*, *65*(3), 342–356. DOI: 10.1080/00131911.2012.668873

Salim, M. A., & Aditya, R. B. (2025). Integration of Artificial Intelligence in Islamic Education: Trends, Methods, and Challenges in the Digital Era. *Journal of Modern Islamic Studies and Civilization*, *3*(01), 74–89. DOI: 10.59653/jmisc.v3i01.1368

Semrl, N., Feigl, S., Taumberger, N., Bracic, T., Fluhr, H., Blockeel, C., & Kollmann, M. (2023). AI language models in human reproduction research: Exploring ChatGPT's potential to assist academic writing. *Human Reproduction (Oxford, England)*, *38*(12), 2281–2288. DOI: 10.1093/humrep/dead207

Sholeh, M., Rusydiyah, E. F., & Abu Bakar, M. Y. (2024). Integration of AI Chatbots in Islamic Religious Education: Potential and Challenges from a Doctoral Student Perspective. AL-ISHLAH. *Jurnal Pendidikan*, *16*(2), 2105–2121. DOI: 10.35445/alishlah.v16i2.5409

Syah, M. N. S. (2016). Challenges of Islamic Education in Muslimworld : Historical, Political, and Socio-Cultural Perspective. QIJIS: Qudus International Journal of Islamic Studies, 4(1). http://journal.stainkudus.ac.id/index.php/QIJIS/article/download/1580/1449

Syahrizal, S., Yasmi, F., & Mary, T. (2023). Discourse on Artificial Intelligence Design Using ITS and SDLC Methods in Building Islamic Religious Education Learning Applications. *Journal of Pragmatics and Discourse Research*, *3*(1), 46–28. DOI: 10.51817/jpdr.v3i1.330

Syukur, F., Maghfurin, A., & Marhamah, U., & Phaosan Jehwae. (2024). Integration of Artificial Intelligence in Islamic Higher Education: Comparative Responses between Indonesia and Thailand. *Nazhruna: Jurnal Pendidikan Islam*, *7*(3), 531–553. DOI: 10.31538/nzh.v7i3.13

Tapalova, O., & Zhiyenbayeva, N. (2022). Artificial Intelligence in Education: AIEd for Personalised Learning Pathways. *Electronic Journal of e-Learning*, *20*(5), 639–653. DOI: 10.34190/ejel.20.5.2597

Thoriquttyas, T., & Rohmawati, N. (2024). How Far Artificial Intelligence influenced Mu'allim, Murabbi, and Mudarris? Transhumanism and Diffusion of Innovation Theory's Perspective. Suhuf. *International Journal of Islamic Studies*, *36*(2), 139–154. DOI: 10.23917/suhuf.v36i2.6302

Tran, K., & Nguyen, T. (2021). Preliminary Research on the Social Attitudes toward AI's Involvement in Christian Education in Vietnam: Promoting AI Technology for Religious Education. *Religions*, *12*(3), 208. DOI: 10.3390/rel12030208

Tseng, Y.-J., Yadav, G., Hou, X., Wu, M., Chou, Y.-S., Chen, C. C., Wu, C.-C., Chen, S.-G., Lin, Y.-J., Liao, G., & Koedinger, K. R. (2024). ActiveAI: The Effectiveness of an Interactive Tutoring System in Developing K-12 AI Literacy. Technology Enhanced Learning for Inclusive and Equitable Quality Education: *19th European Conference on Technology Enhanced Learning, EC-TEL 2024*, 452–467. DOI: 10.1007/978-3-031-72315-5_31

Waghid, Y. (2014). Islamic Education and Cosmopolitanism: A Philosophical Interlude. *Studies in Philosophy and Education*, *33*(3), 329–342. DOI: 10.1007/s11217-013-9390-3

Wasehudin, W., Aslihah, A., Sirojudin, R., & Yuttana, Y. (2024). Artificial Intelligence's Impact on the Development of Islamic Religious Education Learning at a Public Junior High School of Cilegon, Indonesia. Hanifiya. *Jurnal Studi Agama-Agama*, *7*(1), 193–198. DOI: 10.15575/hanifiya.v7i2.37787

Wiranto, E. B., & Suwartini, S. (2023). Artificial Intelligence and Trustworthy Principles in Global Islamic Education. *Ushuluddin International Conference (USICON)*, 6, 64–87.

Zuraidah, Y., Rianti, S., & Rahmadani, J. S. (2024). Implementation of the Concept of Tarbiyah in the Islamic Education Curriculum. *JUDIKIS: Jurnal Pendidikan Islam*, *1*(3), 119–128. DOI: 10.70938/judikis.v1i3.47

Chapter 10
Designing an AI Supported Teaching Module With STEM Approach for Science Education

Nagihan Kadıoğlu
https://orcid.org/0000-0003-4911-8985
Hacettepe University, Turkey

İlayda Sayın
Milli Eğitim Bakanlığı, Turkey

Özge Özyalçın Oskay
Hacettepe University, Turkey

ABSTRACT

The integration of Artificial Intelligence (AI) applications into education is possible in all disciplines, and teaching abstract concepts becomes significantly easier by providing an individualized learning environment. In Turkey, considering the developing technology, the 21st century and the goals of the Ministry of National Education (MoNE), the use of technology in education and especially the use of AI applications, which have recently come to the fore, has become a necessity. With STEM, individuals are expected to have 21st century skills by combining mathematics, engineering, science and technology disciplines. Individuals of our age are expected to actively use technology in their lives, have a say in society, make the right decisions, and be productive. For this reason, in this study, an EBA teaching

DOI: 10.4018/979-8-3373-3000-6.ch010

module was developed with an AI-supported and STEM approach. With the design of an AI-supported EBA teaching module, it is aimed to create more effective learning experiences by better understanding individual differences and student needs.

Educational technology is a field of study based on theoretical and practical foundations that designs effective and goal-oriented teaching environments by utilizing information, technology, and educational sciences to support individuals' learning processes (Tüysüz & Çümen, 2016). Artificial intelligence, which is growing in popularity and frequency of use, is one such educational technology. With technological developments, the use of artificial intelligence applications in education has attracted attention. Artificial intelligence in education is an interdisciplinary field that focuses on transforming and developing instructional design, learning processes, and assessment methods by applying artificial intelligence technologies in education (Xu & Ouyang, 2022).

In research on artificial intelligence in education, it is possible to encounter a wide variety of applications in almost every field, including not only knowledge-based but also data- and logic-based artificial intelligence and artificial intelligence applications (İncemen & Öztürk, 2024). Artificial intelligence applications used in education can also be named according to the characteristics of applications such as expert systems, intelligent tutoring systems, or dialogue-based tutoring systems. The adaptability of artificial intelligence applications allows the content of the subject to be customized and personalized according to student needs. Thus, the positive contribution of the personalized learning environment to the comprehension and retention of the subject also contributes to the overall quality of learning.

In particular, the integration of artificial intelligence applications into education across all disciplines, the provision of individualized and personalized learning environments, and the teaching of abstract concepts have become significantly easier. However, it is crucial for students to be knowledgeable about these applications so that they can envision a future in which AI is integrated. In this context, artificial intelligence applications combined with the STEM approach enable students to acquire 21st-century skills such as analytical thinking, problem solving, and developing innovative ideas. The visualization and interaction opportunities offered by artificial intelligence in fields such as science, which involve abstract concepts, help students understand concepts in a more concrete way. Equipping students with a deep understanding of technology to meet the requirements of the future further emphasizes the importance of using these innovative systems in education.

1. THE USE OF ARTIFICIAL INTELLIGENCE IN EDUCATION

Artificial intelligence has entered the world of technology as systems that simulate human intelligence and human reasoning principles through databases and mimic decision-making processes using this reasoning (Williamson & Eynon, 2020). These technologies analyze and interpret large amounts of data using machine learning algorithms and deep learning techniques.

UNESCO (2017) defines artificial intelligence as a way to make education more personalized, flexible, inclusive, and engaging by processing real-time data. Artificial intelligence has a wide range of applications, from healthcare to the financial sector, from the automotive industry to customer service. Artificial intelligence technology, which emerged based on theoretical foundations rooted in the "Boolean Circuit Model of the Brain" developed by McCulloch and Pitts (1943) to mathematically explain how neurons in the brain function, has seen a notable increase in its effective and widespread use in the field of education, particularly over the past decade (Chen et al., 2020). The development of artificial intelligence-based systems has not only changed the human profile expected to be cultivated by education systems, but has also changed the structure and functioning of education (Coşkun & Gülleroğlu, 2021). Artificial intelligence tools facilitate the work of education administrators, teachers, and students by systematizing the preparation of educational materials, instructional design, and assessment processes (Humphry & Fuller, 2023; West et al., 2023; Zheng & He, 2021). Artificial intelligence systems used in education can provide more detailed results than traditional assessment methods because they analyze large amounts of data obtained from students (Coşkun & Gülleroğlu, 2021).

Artificial intelligence applications in different educational fields can be classified as "Intelligent Tutoring Systems" (Bahçeci and Gürol, 2010; Uzun et al., 2021), "Expert Systems" (Atalay and Çelik, 2017; Çoşkun and Gülleroğlu, 2021; Uzun et al., 2021), and "Chatbots" (cited in İncemen & Öztürk, 2024).

Intelligent tutoring systems have separate knowledge structures related to teaching content and strategies, and provide step-by-step guidance with appropriate learning materials and activities based on the student's subject proficiency and success level. These computer-assisted systems aim to facilitate effective learning by continuously updating the process with feedback, hints, and explanations to continuously update the difficulty level, Expert systems can be defined as systems that possess only information related to a specific field, similar to a person who is an expert in that field. These systems are primarily used in distance education (Coşkun & Gülleroğlu, 2021). Chatbots, on the other hand, can be defined as simple programs that respond to simple commands with a single line or as digital assistants that learn and evolve to allow for more customization in information gathering and processing (İncemen & Öztürk, 2024).

Some examples of artificial intelligence-based educational software are as follows:

1. EBA system: A virtual assistant application for distance learning.
2. Gradescope: An online classroom assessment platform that provides objectivity in assessment, reduces teachers' workload, and can be used with free membership (Gradescope, 2023).
3. Querium: A private tutoring learning platform that helps students acquire chemistry, mathematics, and STEM-related skills and personalizes learning (Querium, 2023).
4. Duolingo: A language learning platform.
5. Udemy, Coursera, KhanAcademy: Massive online learning platforms.
6. ChatGPT: An artificial intelligence chatbot developed by OpenAI and released in November 2022 (OpenAI, 2024).

There are many advantages to using artificial intelligence technology in education. When used correctly and effectively, integrating artificial intelligence into education allows learners to study whenever and wherever they want, supports learning at their own pace by providing individualized learning environments, meets learning needs with personalized feedback, analyzing learning data to predict future performance and determine student-specific methods, saving time through digital content, identifying learning gaps and misconceptions in large student groups, and contributing to the concretization of abstract concepts through tools such as virtual laboratories and machine learning (Cavalcanti et al., 2021; Chen et al., 2021; Chiu, 2021; Jang et al., 2022 cited in Çolak Yazıcı & Erkoç, 2023).

For example, it can provide personalized learning experiences for students by offering content and activities tailored to each student's needs (Zawacki-Richter et al., 2019). They can reduce teachers' workload and identify weaknesses by monitoring student performance. These tools can identify trends through data analysis and contribute to the shaping of educational policies. They also play an important role in providing instant feedback to students and optimizing virtual learning environments. Artificial intelligence also contributes to educational activities as a support tool in areas related to school management, such as curriculum planning, personnel planning, exam management, facility management, and security (Holmes et al., 2019). The effective use of artificial intelligence technologies in the classroom is possible with teachers taking on a central role in deciding when and how to apply these tools; in addition, data obtained from artificial intelligence contributes to teachers planning educational resources in the most efficient way (İşler & Kılıç, 2021).

However, it should not be forgotten that artificial intelligence tools are still a very new and constantly evolving technology. There are situations where AI can be useful, but there are also situations where it can pose a threat. Issues such as data protection, emotions, and sustainability are important problems that need to be considered (Vázquez-Cano, 2021). The fact that AI-powered chatbots such as ChatGPT threaten the integrity of the education system by enabling cheating on exams and unethical assistance with homework, exposing the system's vulnerability to external influences; meanwhile, teachers' lack of awareness and use of these current technologies puts students without access to resources at a disadvantage (Adeshola & Adepoju, 2024).

While whether artificial intelligence poses a threat to humanity has been a subject of debate for a long time, the inability of computer science to model only the "what" and "how" questions, but not the "why" question and, consequently, human-specific qualities such as consciousness and will, it can be said that artificial intelligence has not yet reached the cognitive and moral depth necessary to compete with the human mind (Coşkun & Gülleroğlu, 2021).

2. ARTIFICIAL INTELLIGENCE AND ETHICS

Studies on the use of artificial intelligence and ethics have examined the ethical implications of this technology in various fields. This section focuses on ethical issues that arise or may arise in K-12 educational settings.

Adams et al., 2023 examined the current principles shaping artificial intelligence ethics policies for children and K-12 education through content analysis and concluded that transparency; fairness and justice; do no harm; responsibility; privacy; doing good; freedom and autonomy, as well as four new principles specific to K–12 education: pedagogical appropriateness, children's rights, artificial intelligence literacy, and teacher well-being. Akgün and Greenhow (2021) listed the ethical concerns and challenges teachers face in using artificial intelligence at the K–12 level, which vary according to the age and developmental level of students, as fundamental problems such as privacy, surveillance, autonomy, bias, and discrimination. Celik et al. (2022) provide an overview of research on teachers' use of artificial intelligence applications and machine learning in their study, which highlights the challenges reported by teachers regarding AI use: "Limited reliability of algorithms," "Limited technical capacity of AI," "Limited technical infrastructure for AI in schools," "Inability to apply AI systems to multiple environments," "Inefficiency of AI in assessment and measurement," "Teachers' lack of technological knowledge regarding AI use," "Teachers' indifference toward AI," "Slow AI feedback," and "Limited AI adaptive feedback."

Since artificial intelligence technologies profoundly affect individuals' decision-making processes, it is important to introduce students to the basic concepts of artificial intelligence technology in schools, despite possible negative attitudes, and to draw attention to the ethical aspects of artificial intelligence applications according to their usage, type, and characteristics (Burgsteiner et al., 2016). The ethical use of artificial intelligence technologies in education is possible not only through the development of technical infrastructure but also through individuals' ability to understand and use these technologies consciously. Artificial intelligence literacy is a multidimensional skill set shaped by three fundamental axes: acquiring knowledge, understanding how it works, and living with AI. It enables individuals to comprehend how AI technologies work and critically evaluate their impact on social life. It goes beyond educational applications and plays an important role in terms of digital citizenship and ethical awareness (Casal-Otero et al., 2023). Therefore, artificial intelligence literacy reveals people's abilities to understand, use, and interact with artificial intelligence applications (Kong et al., 2023).

3. STEM AND SCIENCE EDUCATION

Rapid advances in science and technology have significantly increased the need for skilled labor in societies. Especially in today's world, where political and economic transformations continue unabated, reforms in education aimed at nurturing individuals who can adapt to these changes have come to the fore. One such reform is the proposal to incorporate innovative thinking and engineering education into primary and secondary education. Along with this approach, STEM programs, which integrate education with engineering applications and are formed from the initial letters of the words "science," "technology," "engineering," and "mathematics," are being widely discussed and implemented around the world.

Although the STEM concept first entered our lives in the early 2000s, the foundations of this approach were laid by the United States' efforts to increase its competitive strength in science and technology in the competition that began between the Soviet Union and the United States with the launch of the Sputnik satellite (Jolly, 2009).

The aim of STEM education is to teach mathematics, engineering, science, and technology disciplines in an integrated manner. Through the combination of these disciplines, the aim is to equip individuals with skills that are considered essential for the 21st century, such as communication skills, entrepreneurial spirit, critical thinking ability, collaboration, leadership qualities, problem solving, creativity, and flexible thinking. These innovative methods integrated into the education system aim to ensure that students acquire not only academic knowledge but also the skills they will need throughout their lives.

STEM aims to prepare young minds for the future by instilling analytical thinking and problem-solving skills at an early age. This helps build a strong foundation of technical knowledge and boosts students' ability to come up with creative ideas and innovate. Also, STEM education helps students gain the scientific and technical skills that are critical for competing in the global economy. In this context, partnerships between educators, governments, and the private sector support efforts to make STEM education more widespread and effective.

In addition, STEM education strives to cultivate scientifically literate individuals in order to remain competitive in the ongoing global race and sustain this competitiveness (National Academy of Engineering- [NAE] and National Research Council-[NRC], 2009). STEM education, especially when implemented at the K-12 level, plays an important role in increasing students' scientific literacy levels and preparing them for future careers (National Academy of Engineering & National Research Council, 2014).

One of the main reasons why it has become important to incorporate STEM into education systems is that students in countries with advanced economies are less likely to choose science, mathematics, technology, and engineering fields (Nugent et al., 2015). However, in some education systems where STEM is incorporated, there is a strong focus on science and mathematics, while the critical role of engineering and technology in preparing students for an increasingly digital world is often overlooked (McDonald, 2016). To implement effective STEM education in classrooms, it is important to focus on all four dimensions and deliver STEM education to students through an interdisciplinary and transdisciplinary approach.

Science courses play a critical role in the success of STEM education in terms of enabling students to apply the knowledge they have learned in their daily lives. Although students generally perceive science courses as difficult, when visual elements and interactive activities are incorporated, science courses can be considered among the courses that are easy to understand and achieve high learning success (Kadirhan & Korkmaz, 2020).

4. THE USE OF ARTIFICIAL INTELLIGENCE IN STEM EDUCATION

Globalization and rapid advances in technology have increased the need for qualified human resources in STEM (Science, Technology, Engineering, and Mathematics) fields. Recognizing these developments, many countries have begun to prioritize application-based learning, critical thinking, and interdisciplinary interaction in STEM education (Sun et al., 2024).

The integration of AI into STEM education offers a powerful interdisciplinary teaching method that allows students to actively use relevant AI applications while also researching interdisciplinary knowledge (Yang et al., 2024).

The use of generative AI-based chatbots such as ChatGPT in STEM education and their potential benefits is a new area of educational research with a wide range of research gaps (Feser, 2024). Thanks to generative artificial intelligence using algorithms and machine learning techniques to produce content such as text, images, video, or music, educators can create interactive and engaging learning experiences tailored to each student's different needs and interests (Al Darayseh & Mersin, 2025). The application of AI is aligned with STEM practices and supports STEM learning as it supports and enhances inquiry, facilitates interdisciplinary knowledge and creativity, and promotes higher order thinking skills such as computation, problem solving, and critical thinking (Kohnke & Zaugg, 2025). Teachers' willingness to integrate AI technology into learning environments can accelerate the adoption of innovative teaching methods, the discovery of new educational models, the provision of richer learning experiences, and the overall improvement of educational quality (Sun et al., 2024).

The Historical Structure of Science Course Curricula in Turkey:

The 2000 Science Course Curriculum was the most comprehensive program of the Republican era. This program was the first to use the term "achievement," and the course name was changed to "Science and Technology" with the addition of technology achievements. The program was designed to enable students to gain deeper knowledge of science topics and apply this knowledge in their daily lives.

The program was updated in 2005 using a constructivist approach. This approach aims to encourage students to take an active role in the learning process and to make what they learn more permanent through experience. The program includes various examples to show students that science and technology are two disciplines that are interconnected.

In 2013, the vision of the program was to ensure that students grew up to be scientifically literate individuals. In this context, many activities and projects were included in the program to develop students' scientific process skills. In doing so, importance was given to the development of skills such as critical thinking, problem solving, research, and teamwork. Additionally, information about the historical development of science, the lives of famous scientists, and their discoveries is provided to increase students' interest in science (MEB, 2013).

In the curriculum updated in 2018, "The competencies that students will need at both the national and international levels in their personal, social, academic, and professional lives have been determined in the Turkish Qualifications Framework (TYÇ). The TYC identifies eight key competencies. These are: 1. Communication in the mother tongue 2. Communication in foreign languages 3. Mathematical competence and basic competence in science/technology 4. Digital competence 5.

Learning to learn 6. Social and civic competence 7. Initiative and entrepreneurship 8. Cultural awareness and expression" (MEB, 2018).

The 2018 program retains the foundations of the 2013 program while offering a more innovative and interdisciplinary structure to adapt to today's dynamic world. In particular, science and engineering applications have been included within the framework of the STEM (Science, Technology, Engineering, Mathematics) approach, with the aim of developing skills such as design-oriented thinking, problem solving, and creative productivity. The updated curriculum aims to contribute to economic life and the development of material culture by combining science and the process of acquiring scientific knowledge with technology production and entrepreneurship. In this context, science, engineering, and entrepreneurship applications have been made an integral part of the course, parallel to each unit (MEB, 2018).

Finally, the latest curriculum revision will be implemented gradually starting with preschool, 1st, 5th, and 9th grades in the 2024-2025 academic year. The 2024 Science Course Curriculum is a teaching program based on the Türkiye Century Education Model, a model that supports the individual's social, moral, physical, and cognitive development and is based on a holistic education approach (Bilir, 2025).

As mentioned above, when examining the structure of artificial intelligence, it is seen to emerge at the intersection of mathematics, engineering, computer science, and natural sciences. In this respect, artificial intelligence, with its interdisciplinary structure, directly aligns with the theoretical foundations of the STEM approach. Therefore, it is important to include the use of artificial intelligence in STEM education in current curricula. At this point, the most suitable platform for disseminating applications that adapt artificial intelligence to science curricula and STEM applications throughout the country is the EBA platform affiliated with the Ministry of National Education.

5. EDUCATION INFORMATION NETWORK (EBA)

The Education Information Network (EBA) is an online social education platform established in 2012 by the General Directorate of Innovation and Education Technologies (YEĞİTEK) under the Ministry of National Education (MEB) with the aim of providing e-content for all grade levels and subjects, and made available to individuals free of charge.

The content on EBA is continuously updated by experts in their fields, supported by organizations with experience in online publishing, and constantly developed with the contributions of teachers and students (Gacanoğlu and Nakiboğlu, 2019). In line with contemporary educational understanding, students can access digital content such as lecture notes and homework assignments via EBA independently of time and place, and can also share this content with their peers and teachers (Çiftçi & Aydın, 2020). The textbooks, lesson topics, animations, simulations, and experiment activities in EBA serve as a digital library (Demir et al., 2018). In addition to sections where students can review lessons, EBA also has sections where they can view notes prepared by their teachers, access presentations, and take tests. The EBA platform has separate infrastructures for students and parents, allowing parents to monitor their children's progress through EBA.

At the end of 2019, the Covid-19 pandemic entered our lives and affected the entire world, prompting many countries to impose various restrictions to combat the pandemic. This situation also affected the education sector and made it necessary to switch to distance learning to ensure that education and teaching activities were not interrupted. When viewed specifically in the context of Türkiye, this extraordinary situation increased the use of EBA and made it an important material used in education.

As a result, EBA is an educational platform that functions as an alternative service, enabling students who are unable to attend formal education due to various difficulties and inequality of opportunity caused by extraordinary circumstances such as pandemics to continue their education outside of school by providing a learning environment tailored to their individual efforts (Taş & Buran, 2024).

6. CHATGPT-SUPPORTED MODULE DESIGN RELATED TO THERMAL INSULATION

The lesson module developed within the scope of this study is related to the topic of "Matter and Heat" in Unit 4 of the 6th grade curriculum in the 2018 Science Teaching Program. The Matter and Heat unit covers the classification of materials in terms of heat transfer, the importance of thermal insulation in buildings, family and national economy and the efficient use of resources, the criteria for selecting thermal insulation materials used in buildings, and the development of alternative thermal insulation materials.

The fact that one of the authors of the study is based in Malatya province has led to the idea that the topic of thermal insulation could be presented in a context that is interesting and meaningful for students, taking into account the climatic characteristics of the region. This will help to facilitate the effective learning of the lesson objectives. The course module developed for the study was designed taking into account the socio-cultural and educational conditions of Malatya province, located in the Eastern Anatolia Region of Türkiye. Malatya has a continental climate with very low humidity, very hot summers, and very cold winters. Frost and snowfall continue throughout the winter season in Malatya province. There is no spring season; instead, there is a sharp transition from winter to scorching heat. Therefore, thermal insulation is a necessity in this city. Based on these climatic conditions, the development of thermal insulation materials with students is a regional need. Due to this need, the topic of thermal insulation was chosen for STEM education, and artificial intelligence support was integrated into this process. Artificial intelligence support has helped students quickly identify thermal insulation materials and develop new material content from existing materials. Additionally, the thermally insulated houses developed by the students were evaluated objectively by ChatGPT. In the study, recycling materials such as Styrofoam foam, wooden sticks, fibre, cotton, leather, straw, peanut and walnut shells, egg cartons, play dough, plastic fork and spoon handles, plastic bottles, and materials such as gouache paint, rock wool, glue, coloured papers, pencils, scissors, utility knife, computer or iPad, thermometer, stopwatch were provided by the teacher for students to design heat insulated houses. Students made their own creative designs by using any of these materials. They were given the opportunity to make use of ChatGPT while preparing their designs.

After completing the design phase, in order to develop students' critical thinking skills and gain different perspectives, each group presented their products in detail and conducted classroom discussions on the advantages and limitations of the materials they chose. During the evaluation process, the scientific validity of the criteria used by students in their material selection, the feasibility of their designs, and their innovative aspects were taken into account.

The layers of the designed insulated houses and the materials used were examined in detail, and the teacher provided the necessary feedback. Students had the opportunity to redesign their designs based on the teacher's feedback. This process is expected to contribute to the improvement of students' designs. After the students finalized their designs, the final evaluation stage was initiated. Since the aim of this stage is for students to possess the ability to transfer theoretical knowledge into practical design processes and reconstruct it with a critical perspective, their application skills, analytical thinking abilities, and problem-solving capacities are evaluated holistically. For the evaluation phase, criteria such as the Student Self-Assessment Form and Cognitive Process Science Rubric can be suggested for teachers to evaluate their students individually. At this stage, ChatGPT's rubric perception and evaluation performance was tested in advance by scoring another dataset that had been previously scored by teachers. After ChatGPT was trained, the main evaluation phase began. The assessment process is completed by scoring the student on a scale of 1 to 100 using an evaluation rubric prepared in advance by the teacher with the support of ChatGPT.

It is very important for students to have knowledge about the use of artificial intelligence in order to conduct research using ChatGPT. Since artificial intelligence has the potential to be one of the important technological skills of the 21st century, it is critical for non-experts to develop their artificial intelligence skills in order to benefit from the advantages and avoid the disadvantages of artificial intelligence (Çelebi et al., 2023). Therefore, before using this course module, the teachers first ensured that the students were familiarised with artificial intelligence. Different artificial intelligence tools were introduced to the students and they were informed about how they could use them. Here, the AI literacy level of the teachers who teach the students is also an issue to be considered (Tan & Tang, 2025). Therefore, it is very important that the teachers who will use this course module have knowledge about the use of artificial intelligence and ethics.

These ChatGPT-supported activities on thermal insulation are uploaded to the EBA platform and shared with students.

Table 1. ChatGPT-Supported Thermal Insulation Course Module

Course Name:	**Science**
Class:	6th Grade
Unit No.-Name:	Unit 4: Matter and Heat
Topic:	Matter and Heat
Recommended Course Hours:	4+4 Hours
Student Outcomes/Goals and Behaviors:	F.6.4.3.1. Classifies materials based on their thermal conductivity. F.6.4.3.2. Determines the criteria for selecting thermal insulation materials used in buildings. F.6.4.3.3. Develops alternative thermal insulation materials. F.6.4.3.4. Discusses the importance of thermal insulation in buildings in terms of family and national economy and the effective use of resources.

continued on following page

Table 1. Continued

Course Name:	Science
Outcomes related to STEM activities	**Science:** Understands the concepts of heat conductors and heat insulators. Understands the concepts of heat flow and direction. Establishes a connection between national and family economics and heat insulation. Researches and presents alternative heat insulation materials. Determines the criteria for selecting heat insulation materials. Provides examples of heat insulation from everyday life. Establishes a relationship between thermal insulation and other disciplines. **Technology:** Gathers information about new thermal insulation technologies and materials. Understands the connection between thermal insulation materials and technology. **Engineering:** Designs a thermally insulated house based on the information they have acquired about thermal insulation. **Mathematics:** Performs mathematical calculations about the heat-insulated house they designed. Uses a ruler and compass. **Social Product Gains** Presents the heat-insulated house products they created to their friends and explains their features. Interacts with their peers during group work, exchanges ideas, and actively participates in the learning process.
Unit Concepts and Symbols:	Heat conductor, heat insulator, heat flow, heat insulation, heat insulation materials, energy efficiency, energy saving
Methods and Techniques to be Applied:	Presentation, question and answer, brainstorming, pair and group discussion, butter-and-bread technique
Scientific Process Skills	Observation, classification, drawing conclusions, making inferences, forming hypotheses, using and interpreting data, designing and conducting experiments, using spatial and temporal relationships
Explanations:	In the butter-and-bread technique, students think individually about a problem or question and then discuss their ideas in groups. They present the conclusions they reach collectively to the class. This technique enables students to engage in active learning.
Materials Used	Styrofoam, wooden sticks, fiber, cotton, leather, EVA foam, straw, peanut and walnut shells, egg cartons, modeling clay, plastic forks and spoon handles, plastic bottles, gouache paint, rock wool, glue, colored paper and pencils, scissors, craft knife, computer or iPad, thermometer, stopwatch (different materials can also be used as insulation materials)

continued on following page

Table 1. Continued

Course Name:	Science
References	Bayraktar, D., & Bayraktar, E. (2016). Mevcut binalarda Isı yalıtımı uygulamalarının değerlendirilmesi. *Mehmet Akif Ersoy Üniversitesi Fen Bilimleri Enstitüsü Dergisi*, *7*(1), 59-66. Bektaş, V., Çerçevik, A. E., & Kandemir, S. Y. (2017). Binalarda ısı yalıtımının önemi ve ısı yalıtım malzemesi kalınlığının yalıtıma etkisi. *Bilecik Şeyh Edebali Üniversitesi Fen Bilimleri Dergisi*, *4*(1), 36-42. FlipHTML5. (2023). 6. Sınıf Fen Bilimleri Isı Yalıtımı Konu Anlatımı. https://fliphtml5.com/swqza/wlkv/basic Levent, S. (2023, Şubat 5). Isı yalıtımı ile yüzde 60'a varan tasarruf mümkün. Hürriyet. https://www.hurriyet.com.tr/yazarlar/sefer-levent/isi-yalitimi-ile-yuzde-60a-varan-tasarruf-mumkun-42655026 Milli Eğitim Bakanlığı. (2018). *6. Sınıf Fen Bilimleri Ders Kitabı*. Ankara: MEB Yayınları.
Measurement and Evaluation	Brainstorming, information gathering, and product development notebooks Student Self-Assessment Form Cognitive Process Science Rubric Product evaluation with ChatGPT
Knowledge-Based Life Problem (KBLP):	BTHP: (Open-ended, multiple solutions, 21st century life, product-process integration). Students are asked to design a residence using traditional, natural, ecological, and recycled insulation materials, specifying the main, inner, and outer layers for each group. The residences will be evaluated, and the best insulated house will be selected by ChatGPT using the teacher rubric at the end of the process. Limitations: (Time, budget, materials to be used, environmentally friendly, functionality, or information used). You should pay attention to some key features that are emphasized. These features include durability, fire resistance, being lightweight and environmentally friendly, providing sound insulation, being water-resistant, preventing moisture and mold, being easy to apply, and having a low construction cost for a living space. The total estimated time for the course and design process is 4+4 class hours.

continued on following page

Table 1. Continued

Course Name:	Science
Course Content: **a. Introduction to the Course**	The teacher enters the classroom with two teacups and begins the lesson. One cup is made of cardboard and the other is made of glass. The lesson begins by asking the students which cup of tea burns their hands. They are asked to conclude that heat spreads better in some objects than in others. They are asked to make predictions about the distance between particles in objects that conduct heat well and those that do not. After the students give their answers, an example from daily life is given involving cooking with a wooden spoon and a metal spoon. They are asked which spoon will heat up more while cooking. Based on all these questions, students who conclude that heat spreads well in some materials and less well in others recall the concepts of heat conductors and heat insulators they learned in 5th grade. Based on these concepts, the topic of heat insulation is introduced. The question-and-answer method is used to reveal students' prior knowledge about heat insulation and its purposes. Students are asked to establish a relationship between the concepts of heat insulation and heat insulators, thus reaching the conclusion that the concept of heat insulation can be designed with heat insulating materials. In addition, based on their prior knowledge from 5th grade about matter and heat, students are reminded that heat is energy that flows from hot to cold. Then, a news article about thermal insulation is read, and a discussion is held with students about the contributions of thermal insulation to the country's and household economies. After the necessary prior learning has been provided, some old buildings in Türkiye are mentioned (such as the Harran Houses in the city of Şanlıurfa, which were built using materials such as egg whites, soil, corn husks, and straw). Students are asked to design a thermally insulated house using alternative, traditional, and ecological materials to be built in the province of Malatya. The following guidelines are read to the students.
	LET'S DEVELOP AN ALTERNATIVE HEAT INSULATION MATERIAL Malatya is a city that is quite cold in winter and quite hot in summer. To make living in this city easier, you decide to design a living space using traditional natural and ecological materials. Your task is to design residential buildings by determining the main, inner, and outer layers using some traditional, natural, ecological, and recycled thermal insulation materials. You need to pay attention to some basic features that are emphasized. These features are longevity, fire resistance, lightness and environmental friendliness, sound insulation, water resistance, moisture and mold prevention, easy application and low cost.

continued on following page

Table 1. Continued

Course Name:	Science
Course Content: **b. Trial:**	The teacher divides the students into groups of 4 students each. At this stage, artificial intelligence (ChatGPT) support is sought to answer the questions of what is thermal insulation, what are the criteria of thermal insulation materials, what are traditional, alternative and ecological thermal insulation materials. Students working as a group acquire the necessary theoretical knowledge in a short time with the support of ChatGPT. Since the source of information and the accuracy of the information provided by artificial intelligence is not clearly known, the accuracy of the information obtained by the students is checked by the teacher. *(The important point at this stage is that students test the accuracy of the information provided by ChatGPT. It is known that chat robots supported by artificial intelligence such as ChatGPT etc. provide false or untrue information. Therefore, it is very important that students are aware of this. At this stage, the role of the teacher comes to the fore. Students verify the information they obtain from ChatGPT under the guidance of the teacher by using the text that will be given to them in the next stage). Thermal insulation is a technical subject with a wide range of applications. Integrating artificial intelligence into STEM activities saves time on research. Students can find answers to the technical details they want to learn in a short time. They record their ideas about the product they will design in the idea development notebook.
Course Content: **c.Supporting:**	Read the following text on thermal insulation. Thermal Insulation In our daily lives, we need to maintain the temperature of some substances. For example, we want our lemonade to stay cold and our tea to stay hot. For this, the heat flow of the substances and environments that we want to maintain their temperature should be slowed down. To slow down the heat flow, substances that do not conduct heat well, i.e. heat insulators, are used. Maintaining the temperature of substances for a certain period of time by using heat insulators such as air, wood, plastic is called thermal insulation. The fact that drinks in a thermos and food stored in plastic foam maintain their temperature for a long time can be given as examples of thermal insulation. In our daily lives, there are situations where thermal insulation is necessary, as well as situations where heat conduction is necessary. For example, in order to cook our meals, our pots and calorifiers must be made of heat conductors in order to keep warm. Thus, heat flow can take place quickly. Heat flows from a hot substance to a cold substance. Since the inside of the house is warmer than the outside in winter, the heat flow is from the inside to the outside. With thermal insulation, the heat flow from inside to outside is slowed down. In this way, houses can be heated using less fuel in winter. In summer, the heat flow is from outside to inside as the outside is warmer than the inside of the house. With thermal insulation, the heat flow from outside to inside is slowed down. In this way, the inside of the houses can be kept cool without using electric vehicles. The areas with the highest heat loss in homes are the roof, windows, doors and walls. Thermal insulation should be applied to these areas to prevent these losses. The material to be used varies according to the area to be insulated. For example; glass wool is used on roofs, wood on floors, plastic foam on walls, double-glazed systems with deaerated air on windows.

continued on following page

Table 1. Continued

Course Name:	Science
	Insulation Materials (See Figure 1)
	When making thermal insulation, materials that do not conduct heat well are used. Heat flow can be slowed down by thermal insulation on the exterior walls of buildings, windows, roofs, installation pipes, ventilation ducts, sections in contact with the ground and sections separating floors. The materials used in thermal insulation are called **insulation materials.** Plastic foam, wood, stone wool, tar, glass wool and silicone wool are some insulation materials used in thermal insulation. These materials are selected in accordance with the area to be insulated, taking into account features such as combustion properties, places of use and lifetime. Students who have acquired all this information are enabled to blend and explain the information they have gained from both ChatGPT and the text by using question and answer and discussion methods on the subject. "Determine the thermal insulation materials and the properties they should have in the houses you will design. Determine which of these materials can be used as internal insulation, which ones as external insulation and which ones as coating materials. According to the properties of thermal insulation materials, design a heat insulated house suitable for the conditions of our province and draw it on the additional paper to be given to you." The design process is initiated with the directive. Students who have knowledge about traditional thermal insulation materials and those who have knowledge about thermal insulation and alternative thermal insulation materials with the support of ChatGPT are given the task of developing a thermal insulation material with certain properties or improving existing materials and asked to test the materials and evaluate their performance. Materials such as Styrofoam foam, wooden sticks, fiber, cotton, leather, eva, straw, peanut and walnut shells, egg cartons, play dough, plastic fork and spoon handles, plastic bottles, gouache paint, rock wool can be used during the design of heat insulated houses.

continued on following page

Table 1. Continued

Course Name:	Science
Course Content d. Elaboration	The designs are discussed and finalized. In each house, containers filled with hot water at 100 degrees are placed and a thermometer is placed. The final temperatures at the end of a certain period of time are recorded. An idea is reached about the success level of thermal insulation of each house. Write down all the mathematical calculations used in the designed system in your product development notebook. How can you improve the system to reduce the disadvantages? Calculate the energy savings for Malatya province based on the energy expenditures of houses with and without thermal insulation.
Course Content: e.Evaluation	Questions are asked about the properties and selection criteria of thermal insulation materials used in buildings. Students give information about the different thermal insulation materials they have developed and each group shares its opinion about the advantages and disadvantages of these materials. The students' tasks of selecting and recreating thermal insulation materials according to certain criteria are evaluated by the teacher on a group basis. Necessary feedback and corrections are made about the inner middle and outer layers of the insulated houses; ceiling, floor and roof materials. Their practical skills and analytical thinking abilities are evaluated. For individual assessment, the Student Self-Assessment Form and the Cognitive Process Science Rubric can be used. The houses, which are finalized with the self-assessments of both the teacher and the students, are scored out of 100 with an evaluation rubric prepared by the teacher in advance with the support of ChatGPT in order to contribute to an objective evaluation. *(At this stage, in order to evaluate the scoring performance of ChatGPT with the evaluation rubric, it is recommended that ChatGPT be asked to score another data set that has already been scored by the teachers. In this way, ChatGPT's perception and evaluation performance of the rubric can be tested beforehand. Additional commands may need to be given to ChatGPT in order for it to evaluate as desired). Since an unbiased evaluation is made in this project competition, the measurement results will be free from errors and the results of the competition will be easily accepted by the students.

In this module design, ChatGPT is used in two ways: as a tool for students to acquire knowledge and as a tool to help teachers evaluate student performance.

Figure 1. Insulation Figures

Yalıtım malzemesi	Maliyet	Kullanım ömrü	Çevre dostu mu?	Yanma özelliği	Kullanım alanları
Plastik köpük 	Düşük	Uzun ömürlü	Zararlı	Kolay yanar.	İç ve dış cep-helerde
Ahşap 	Orta	Kısa ömürlü	Zararsız	Kolay yanar.	İç ve dış döşemelerde
Taş yünü 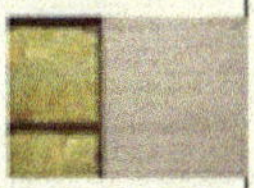	Düşük	Uzun ömürlü	Zararsız	Yanmaz.	Tavan, iç ve dış duvarlarda
Cam yünü 	Düşük	Uzun ömürlü	Zararsız	Zor yanar.	Çatı, iç ve dış duvarlar ve tesisat borularında
Silikon yünü 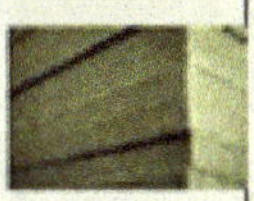	Çok düşük	Uzun ömürlü	Zararsız	Zor yanar.	Dış cephelerde

(FlipHTML5, 2023)

7. CONCLUSION

The 21st century is considered the starting point of the digital age, with the information explosion that came with the unexpected growth in technology (Beers, 2011). Technological tools are constantly updating themselves before we even realize it. It is expected that individuals of our time will be able to adapt to these rapidly advancing technological developments by actively using technology in their lives, having a say in society, making the right decisions, being productive, and possessing the skills required by the age. In this context, it is important for teachers to design educational materials in line with the requirements of the age and to closely follow technological developments. Considering the current state of artificial intelligence, it is thought that developing the skills to use and manage it effectively is more meaningful than competing with it (Coşkun & Gülleroğlu, 2021). Therefore, it is believed that an EBA teaching module developed with artificial intelligence support and a STEM approach will play a critical role in helping both teachers and students adapt to this rapid technological transformation and will transform educational processes to meet the needs of our era.

The design of an AI-supported EBA teaching module can enable the creation of more effective learning experiences by better understanding individual differences and student needs in Türkiye's education system, thereby increasing students' academic achievements and interest in STEM fields and cultivating competent individuals for the future.

REFERENCES

Adams, C., Pente, P., Lemermeyer, G., & Rockwell, G. (2023). Ethical principles for artificial intelligence in K-12 education. *Computers and Education: Artificial Intelligence, 4*, 100131. DOI: 10.1016/j.caeai.2023.100131

Adeshola, I., & Adepoju, A. P. (2024). The opportunities and challenges of ChatGPT in education. *Interactive Learning Environments, 32*(10), 6159–6172.

Al Darayseh, A., & Mersin, N. (2025). Integrating generative AI into STEM education: Insights from science and mathematics teachers. *International Electronic Journal of Mathematics Education, 20*(3), em0832. Advance online publication. DOI: 10.29333/iejme/16232

Atalay, N., & Çelik, H. (2017). Uzman sistemler ve eğitimde uygulamaları. *Eğitimde Kuram ve Uygulama, 13*(2), 123–140.

Bahçeci, D., & Gürol, M. (2010). Akıllı öğretim sistemleri ve eğitimde kullanımı. *Eğitim Teknolojisi Kuram ve Uygulama, 1*(1), 1–14.

Beers, S. (2011). *21st century skills: Preparing students for their future.*

Bilir, U. (2025). Türkiye'de 2018 ve 2024 yılları fen bilimleri dersi öğretim programlarının temel ögeler açısından karşılaştırılması. *Milli Eğitim Dergisi, 54*(246), 793–836. DOI: 10.37669/milliegitim.1532604

Burgsteiner, H., Kandlhofer, M., & Steinbauer, G. (2016, March). Irobot: Teaching the basics of artificial intelligence in high schools. *Proceedings of the Thirtieth AAAI Conference on Artificial Intelligence*. Arizona, AAAI.

Casal-Otero, L., Catala, A., Fernández-Morante, C., Taboada, M., Cebreiro, B., & Barro, S. (2023). AI literacy in K-12: A systematic literature review. *International Journal of STEM Education, 10*(1), 29. DOI: 10.1186/s40594-023-00418-7

Celik, I., Dindar, M., Muukkonen, H., & Järvelä, S. (2022). The promises and challenges of artificial intelligence for teachers: A systematic review of research. *TechTrends, 66*(4), 616–630. DOI: 10.1007/s11528-022-00715-y

Coşkun, F., & Gülleroğlu, H. D. (2021). Yapay zekânın tarih içindeki gelişimi ve eğitimde kullanılması. [JFES]. *Ankara University Journal of Faculty of Educational Sciences, 54*(3), 947–966. DOI: 10.30964/auebfd.916220

Çelebi, C., Demir, U., & Karakuş, F. (2023). Yapay zekâ okuryazarlığı konulu çalışmaların sistematik derleme yöntemiyle incelenmesi. *Necmettin Erbakan Üniversitesi Ereğli Eğitim Fakültesi Dergisi, 5*(2), 535–560. DOI: 10.51119/ereegf.2023.67

Çiftçi, B., & Aydın, A. (2020). Eğitim bilişim ağı (EBA) platformu hakkında fen bilimleri öğretmenlerinin görüşleri. *Türkiye Kimya Derneği Dergisi Kısım C. Kimya Eğitimi*, *5*(2), 111–130. DOI: 10.37995/jotcsc.765647

Çolak Yazıcı, S., & Erkoç, M. (2023). Fen bilimleri grubu öğretmenlerinin uzaktan eğitim sürecinde yapay zekâ kullanma durumlarının analizi. *Dokuz Eylül Üniversitesi Buca Eğitim Fakültesi Dergisi*, (58), 2682–2704.

Demir, D., Özdinç, F., & Ünal, E. (2018). Eğitim bilişim ağı (EBA) portalına katılımın incelenmesi. *Erzincan Üniversitesi Eğitim Fakültesi Dergisi*, *20*(2), 407–422.

Feser, M. S. (2024). Parents' vıews on the use of AI-based chatbots such as ChatGPT in high school (STEM) education. *Journal of Baltic Science Education*, *23*(1), 4–8.

Gacanoğlu, C., & Nakiboğlu, C. (2019). Eğitim bilişim ağı (EBA) platformunun değerlendirilmesi. *Eğitim ve Teknoloji Dergisi*, *9*(2), 55–70.

Gradescope. (2023). Deliver and grade your assessments anywhere. deliver and grade your assessments anywhere. https://www.gradescope.com/

Holmes, W., Bialik, M., & Fadel, C. (2019). *Artificial intelligence in education: Promises and implications for teaching and learning*. Center for Curriculum Redesign.

Humphry, T., & Fuller, A. L. (2023). Potential ChatGPT use in undergraduate chemistry laboratories. *Journal of Chemical Education*, *100*(4), 1434–1436. DOI: 10.1021/acs.jchemed.3c00006

İncemen, S., & Öztürk, G. (2024). Farklı eğitim alanlarında yapay zekâ: Uygulama örnekleri. *International Journal of Computers in Education*, *7*(1), 27–49.

İşler, B., & Kılıç, M. (2021). Eğitimde yapay zekâ kullanımı ve gelişimi. *Yeni Medya Elektronik Dergisi*, *5*(1), 1–11.

Jolly, J. L. (2009). The national defense education act, current STEM initiative, and the gifted. *Gifted Child Today*, *32*(2), 50–53.

Kadirhan, M., & Korkmaz, Ö. (2020). The effects of learning blended with eba content on students' academic achievement and attitudes toward science course. *Trakya Eğitim Dergisi*, *10*(1), 64–75.

Kohnke, S., & Zaugg, T. (2025). Artificial Intelligence: An untapped opportunity for equity and access in STEM education. *Education Sciences*, *15*(1), 68.

Kong, S. C., Cheung, W. M. Y., & Tsang, O. (2023). Evaluating an artificial intelligence literacy programme for empowering and developing concepts, literacy and ethical awareness in senior secondary students. *Education and Information Technologies*, *28*(4), 4703–4724.

McCulloch, W. S. ve Pitts, W. (1943). A logical calculus of the ideas immanent in nervous activity. *The Bulletin of Mathematical Biophysics*, *5*(4), 115–133.

McDonald, C. V. (2016). STEM education: A review of the contribution of the disciplines of science, technology, engineering and mathematics. *Science Education International*, *27*(4), 530–569.

MEB. (2013). *İlköğretim kurumları (ilkokullar ve ortaokullar) fen bilimleri dersi (3, 4, 5, 6, 7 ve 8. sınıflar) öğretim programı*. Milli Eğitim Bakanlığı Talim ve Terbiye Kurulu.

MEB. (2018). *Fen Bilimleri Dersi (İlkokul ve Ortaokul 3, 4, 5, 6, 7 ve 8. Sınıflar) Öğretim Programı*. Milli Eğitim Bakanlığı.

National Academy of Engineering & National Research Council. (2014). *STEM Integration in K-12 Education: Status, Prospects, and an Agenda for Research*. The National Academies Press., DOI: 10.17226/18612

NRC. (National Research Council) (2009*). Learning science in informal environments: People, places, and pursuits.* Washington, DC: National Academies Press.

Nugent, G., Barker, B., Welch, G., Grandgenett, N., Wu, C. R., & Nelson, C. (2015). A model of factors contributingto STEM learning and career orientation. *International Journal of Science Education*, *37*(7), 1067–1088. DOI: 10.1080/09500693.2015.1017863

Open, A. I. (2024). ChatGPT [Large language model]. https://chat.openai.com

Querium (2023). *Master Critical STEM Skills*. Querium. https://www.querium.com/

Sun, F., Tian, P., Sun, D., Fan, Y., & Yang, Y. (2024). Pre-service teachers' inclination to integrate AI into STEM education: Analysis of influencing factors. *British Journal of Educational Technology*, *55*(6), 2574–2596.

Tan, Q., & Tang, X. (2025). Unveiling AI literacy in K-12 education: A systematic literature review of empirical research. *Interactive Learning Environments*, ***•••***, 1–17. DOI: 10.1080/10494820.2025.2482586

Taş, H. ve Buran, O. (2024). Eğitim bilişim ağındaki (eba) ortaokul matematik ders videolarının incelenmesi. *Kesit Akademi Dergisi*, *10*(39), 568–587.

Tüysüz, C., & Çümen, V. (2016). EBA ders web sitesine ilişkin ortaokul öğrencilerinin görüşleri. *Uşak Üniversitesi Sosyal Bilimler Dergisi, 9*(27/3), 278-296.

UNESCO. (2017). *Data revolution to measure equity in education for SDGs #CIES2017.* UNESCO Institute for Statistics.

Uzun, A. M., Yıldırım, S., & Çelik, E. (2021). Eğitimde yapay zekâ uygulamaları: Akıllı öğretim ve uzman sistemler. *Eğitimde Yeni Yönelimler Dergisi*, *5*(3), 45–60.

Vázquez-Cano, E. (2021). Artificial intelligence and education: A pedagogical challenge for the 21st century. *Educational Process: international journal, 10*(3): 7-12.

West, J. K., Franz, J. L., Hein, S. M., Leverentz-Culp, H. R., Mauser, J. F., Ruff, E. F., & Zemke, J. M. (2023). An analysis of AI-generated laboratory reports across the chemistry curriculum and student perceptions of ChatGPT. *Journal of Chemical Education, 100*(11), 4351–4359. DOI: 10.1021/acs.jchemed.3c00581

Williamson, B., & Eynon, R. (2020). Historical threads, missing links, and future directions in AI in education. *Learning, Media and Technology*, *45*(3), 223–235. DOI: 10.1080/17439884.2020.1798995

Xu, W., & Ouyang, F. (2022). The application of AI technologies in STEM education: A systematic review from 2011 to 2021. *International Journal of STEM Education*, *9*(1), 59. DOI: 10.1186/s40594-022-00377-5

Yang, Y., Sun, W., Sun, D., & Salas-Pilco, S. Z. (2024). Navigating the AI-Enhanced STEM education landscape: A decade of insights, trends, and opportunities. *Research in Science & Technological Education*, •••, 1–25. DOI: 10.1080/02635143.2024.2370764

Zawacki-Richter, O., Marín, V. I., Bond, M., & Gouverneur, F. (2019). Systematic review of research on artificial intelligence applications in higher education – Where are the educators? *International Journal of Educational Technology in Higher Education*, *16*(1), 39.

Zheng, H. U., & He, W. (2021, March). Relevant concepts, key technologies and typical application scenarios of AI+ education. [). IOP Publishing.]. *Journal of Physics: Conference Series*, *1861*(1), 012059.

Chapter 11
Fostering Critical Thinking in AI-Assisted English Language Learning Environments

Vivit Rosmayanti
https://orcid.org/0000-0002-3648-9878
Universitas Negeri Makassar, Indonesia

ABSTRACT

Artificial Intelligence (AI) is revolutionizing English Language Teaching (ELT) by enhancing critical thinking skills in learners. Critical thinking is crucial for the competent use of a foreign language, allowing students to analyze, synthesize information, evaluate language use, apply it to real life, and reflect on it. AI can improve thinking skills in ELT by providing personalized environments, real-time feedback, tailored challenges, and interactivity. AI-empowered applications, such as language learning apps and virtual classrooms, can build critical skills and enhance language proficiency simultaneously. Teachers can design learning tasks that encourage reflection, inquiry, and discussion, promoting critical thinking and identifying gaps in understanding complex ideas. AI-based tools can be implemented in ways that minimize infringement on students' education and personal liberties, ensuring the teacher's functions and responsibilities are preserved.

INTRODUCTION

The implementation of AI technology in English teaching opens a myriad of opportunities for both students and teachers. It is essential to note that AI technologies,

DOI: 10.4018/979-8-3373-3000-6.ch011

including Intelligent Tutoring Systems (ITS) and language processing tools, enable every learner to access content tailored to their unique skill set and proficiency levels, thereby facilitating learning and engagement. According to Wei's research, the students employing AI-assisted tools demonstrated notable improvements in their self-regulation, motivation, and overall language learning outcomes, which led to enhanced levels of engagement with the technology (Wei, 2023). Gyawali (2023) argue that ITS also has natural language processing and machine learning capabilities, which enable it to provide learners with individualized feedback, enhancing its effectiveness in teaching languages in all educational paradigms. Such features of ITS not only make it applicable for personalized language teaching, but also make it possible to promote active participation in the learning processes.

No aspect of critical thinking in the context of English language learning and acquisition is equally significant. Critical thinking represents the ability to analyze, evaluate, or synthesize information, which enables learners to comprehend the sophisticated elements and meanings of language comprehensively. As noted by Gligorea et al., (2023), there is a need to support traditional skills such as critical thinking in conjunction with AI learning environments nowadays. Development of critical thinking skills is significant in situations where students are expected to work together and come up with new solutions, which is often the case with constructivist pedagogical approaches. The use of AI technologies has the potential to make a priceless contribution to this process by providing challenges in the form of real-world scenarios that require analysis (Nurjanah et al., 2024). Also, Amin (2023) highlights the contribution of AI in enabling greater interaction with the content of the language as it encourages practical application of critical thinking, for instance, in forming dialogues or solving problems within the language learning context.

There is a very strong need to develop learners' critical thinking skills to create AI-supported foreign language learning environments. Concerning the implementation of AI, there are positive aspects such as learning customization and instantaneous feedback, but there are also negative sides to overdependence on AI technology that need to be addressed. As noted by Çela et al. (2024) concerning the application of AI, tools may be useful, but if they are not implemented with a thought process, there is a risk of diminishing critical cognitive skills. With that said, it is reasonable to suggest that the use of AI technologies in learning pathways needs to be carefully planned to support the development of critical thinking skills instead of stifling them. Çela et al. (2024) Underlined UNESCO's advocacy for technology in education, where there is a need to protect cognitive skills that are essential for learning and thinking.

The interactive and motivating learning environments AI technology offers enable the support of critical thinking in English Language Teaching (ELT). As Kolegova and Levina demonstrate in their study, AI systems can provide a variety of learning resources and opportunities for authentic interactions with language, which enhances learners' analytical and critical engagement with language content. Instructors do not need to guide learners with everything on a step-by-step basis anymore since certain tools, such as chatbots and virtual tutors, are available. Learners can engage with the content meaningfully, making what was previously viewed as language acquisition a vibrant process of negotiation and meaning-making. This improvement can foster the development of overcoming thinking skills, where learners are actively the ones exposed to information and not passively being impeded. Additionally, Idham et al., (2022) argue that the integration of AI into education systems comes with the benefits of advanced data analytics, which allows for comprehensive personalized feedback that can direct learners to Dewey's reflective inquiry cycle on language use.

To sum up, the crossing of AI technology and critical thinking within the context of English language learning is one of the modern developments in pedagogy. AI can not only adapt to students' learning needs and facilitate the development of language skills, but also assist in the acquisition of higher-order thinking skills necessary for communication. On the other hand, creating an environment that fully capitalizes on technological advantages while nurturing critical thinking skills is challenging and requires a well-defined educational approach and continuous study. Educators can develop powerful, critically engaging language learning opportunities by applying AI technologies without sidelining critical considerations, enabling learners to grapple with the challenges of communication in the modern world.

UNDERSTANDING CRITICAL THINKING IN THE CONTEXT OF ENGLISH LANGUAGE LEARNING

As one of the major competencies in English language learning (ELL), critical thinking has, and continues to, reshape the processes involved in acquiring and utilizing a language. Reasoning in familiar or novel contexts by analyzing, evaluating, and synthesizing information requires a set of skills and elements, which include analysis, evaluation, inference, interpretation, problem-solving, and is termed as 'critical thinking'. As Rios et al. (2020) noted, these skills allow learners not only to understand complex language patterns but also to use language in different contexts. The addition of these skills to the ELL curriculum enables learners to take responsibility for their learning, which helps foster a culture of inquiry and reflective thought instead of rote memorization (Nugraini et al., 2022).

The intersection of critical thinking and language proficiency is profound because advanced critical thinking is linked with having an advanced language proficiency. Learners who possess language skills alongside critical thinking skills are competent in analyzing and interpreting texts, considering diverse viewpoints, as well as expressing themselves, which improves their proficiency. For example, participation in group problem-solving activities enables the development of critical thinking skills, which enhances and promotes communicative proficiency in English (Xu et al., 2023). In addition, Nugraini et al. argue that critical thinking is not simply an appendage to the skill set, but a core determinant that affects the ability of the learners to understand and produce language as they need to solve real-world problems through language (Nugraini et al., 2022).

The application of critical thinking occurs in the different uses of language, including the analysis of texts, debates, and discussions. These activities require not only competence with language but also higher-order skills such as meaning interpretation, argument crafting, and rebuttal formulation. In regard to critical thinking and fostering it, Mugisha et al., (2021) state that text analysis helps learners measure diverse viewpoints, integrating multiple narratives into a single coherent anchor that can be complexly construed and insightfully evaluated. Likewise, participating in debates helps learners apply the practice of using appropriate language because they have to defend their positions and argue against opposing arguments (Romadhoni et al., 2022).

Analytical thinking has a lot of importance for language learning, even with questioning, problem-solving, and reflection. Asking questions serves as a generator of critical exploration and goes deeper to examine the inferences and assumptions underlying any language content. As noted Ab.Wahid (2022), there is a need to apply problem posing techniques within the language class so learners are able to ask questions of great importance that aid their learning and exploration of language. Such problem-solving processes enable learners to with practical language use which is a paramount element for fluent and competent language skills. Reflection strategies enable students to shift their thought processes about the learning experiences, making it more visible the structure and function of language (Lionenko & Huzar, 2023).

Combining critical thinking with reflection, for learners of a language, helps evaluate their varying pathways and use and learning of a language. The inclusion of reflection in instruction enhances the evaluative skills of learners and become critical about their actions and decisions within the language skills (Grecu, 2023). For learners, when provided tuition where they can pose and reflect on questions, they are taught to become inquisitive, independent, which in turn fosters the need to learn even when they are outside of class settings in a new world.

In conclusion, we can say that critical thinking is a part of English language learning from a much wider perspective than a mere English learner. It covers many areas to such an extent that learners can evaluate, express, and use language meaningfully and contextually. The interplay of critical thinking and language skills helps not only to master comprehension and expression but also prepares learners to interact with the myriad systems of language in a well-informed and critical manner. When teachers propose strategies that include inquiry and problem solving, they enable learners to develop those critical thinking skills needed for academic work and in the world outside.

AI'S ROLE IN SUPPORTING CRITICAL THINKING

The applications of AI technologies are crucial to the development of critical thinking skills in learners and have greatly improved language learning. With the advancement of AI technologies, chatbots, adaptive learning technologies, and AI educational assessments have all become key components of modern educational frameworks. As an example, chatbots serve as artificial English tutors that learners can simulate conversations with in order to enhance their English language competencies beyond the boundaries of the classroom. With the adoption of AI chatbots in EFL classes, students have had access to a wealth of new learning opportunities, including enhanced oral practice and assessment (Yang et al., 2022). Such participation affords learners instant access to support and motivates them to think critically about what they need to do to respond and move through the conversation. According to Xue-wei (2023) adaptive learning systems, they also personalize education through tailoring instructional materials to the learner's level of achievement on previously given tasks, making the learners continuously face optimal challenges.

AI enhances cognitive engagement by offering personalized challenges and customized feedback. AI systems have the capability to analyze learner data, which allows educators to tailor specific interventions to promote critical thinking. For example, numerous adaptive systems can present complex scenarios or problems to learners that require language skills to be used analytically, thus engaging learners in evaluation and synthesis (Annamalai et al., 2022). AI facilitates the creation of inquiry-based learning environments that fundamentally deepen students' understanding of content, enabling students to challenge, conclude, and explain their assumptions, hallmarks of critical thinking.

Additionally, AI technologies can foster the advancement of critical thinking skills by providing challenges that require learners to defend their responses. For instance, AI chatbots and educational software can ask learners open-ended questions that compel them to defend a particular position or consider opposing views. Such challenges can be especially important during class debates where learners are required to use reasoning, as they interact with different uses of language, contexts, or culture. Annamalai et al. attest that students deepen their understandings of the intricacies of language during chatbot interactions by examining the answers they provide concerning the questions posed (Annamalai et al., 2022). Such activities help enhance language competence, but more importantly, develop the understanding associated with critical thinking.

Different tools and systems demonstrate the efficacy of AI in stimulating critical thinking in language learners. For instance, many AI-assisted language teaching systems can include game-like exercises that require thinking as well as active participation. Doulngo, for instance, applies AI to tailor lessons to individual users' progress, so that learners are always challenged with tasks that require critical thinking. Also, some online debate tools with AI capabilities can foster critique and reflection by having students defend their stances on relevant issues in structured discussions.

The use of AI-generated feedback, such as that offered by ChatGPT, is beneficial for learners as it prompts essays and encourages critical thinking about the content. This type of feedback enables students to receive fast edits through AI, allowing them to modify their writing afterward. The design of AI tools promotes critical approaches to writing as students are encouraged to think about different perspectives and question their writing outputs (Pitychoutis, 2024). AI tools assist students not only in formulating well-structured arguments but also enable and enhance learners' critical engagement with the materials.

Chatbots, especially noted for their capability to offer conversational practice, also reduce the affective filter that comes with language learning. These systems, through their design, promote social presence and participation, which help learners overcome the anxieties of using language, grappling with what-if questions that challenge mental frameworks, and wondering with uncertainty towards critique (Merelo et al., 2022). In this light, AI-based conversational agents profoundly accelerate the journey towards achieving fluency and language mastery alongside cognitive development.

As highlighted, AI frameworks designed to enhance ELL environments critically assess and influence students' capabilities to think independently. Beyond offering personalized learning pathways, adaptive chatbots and other AI technologies raise a learner's mental involvement by providing individualized challenges, prompts for engagement, and actionable insights through feedback. These systems guide learners through the intricacies of the language while fostering the essential skills needed for powerful communication. Continuous investigation of the applications of AI technologies will remain pivotal for empowering learners to unlock critical thinking skills, using AI technologies for language learners, as innovations in language education heighten.

PEDAGOGICAL STRATEGIES FOR INTEGRATING CRITICAL THINKING WITH AI TOOLS

The use of AI technologies in teaching language skills is perhaps one of the most innovative ways they can be used to teach learners the art of critical thinking. Designing activities using AI that foster critical thinking may include debates, problem-solving activities, and the use of open questions. For example, sharing student AI-controlled debating chambers can enhance the students' reasoning and argumentative skills, enabling them to think out loud as they respond to different sides of the debate. Ruiz-Rojas et al. (2024) Observe that the use of generative AI tools promotes students' collaborative working, which enhances their critical thinking and communication skills (Ruiz-Rojas et al., 2024). The AI can be designed in such a way to assist the learners to analyze the situation and synthesize information from different resources and construct sound arguments to defend their stand, which will indeed prepare them for real-world discourse.

The assimilation of AI feedback prompts students to think reflectively and conduct self-assessments through self-monitoring. AI tools offer feedback that permits learners to monitor their performance in real time. Such real-time feedback offers powerful learning incentives as students can identify their strengths and shortcomings. Capinding & Dumayas explained that AI adapts to learners individually at all levels of learning and all levels of their skill development, which proves helpful to students, encouraging learning adjustments. AI Drives Change suggests AI can help learners change their perceptions of self-evaluation by making them reconsider their thought patterns and responses, which makes choosing to believe in intelligence a choice and adopting self-regulation a pathway to success (Mayasari et al., 2024). Also, as Mayasari et al argue, AI is particularly helpful for fostering self-regulation, enabling students to shift their study patterns based on the feedback, thus changes administered creating fertile ground.

The contribution of scaffolding and guidance within an AI-assisted learning environment is paramount. Providing adequate AI scaffolds ensures learners are fully supported while engaging with language tasks, which are enhanced by AI technologies. In this scenario, teachers function at the meso level, where they employ AI as a form of assistance to patient care devices and allow them to attempt more sophisticated tasks over time (Walter, 2024). This technique supports the pedagogical theory from Kong et al, which concentrates on employing self-regulated learning strategies where AI is freely utilized in teaching academic writing. Throughout the AI learning stages, educators have the opportunity to foster collaboration by designing processes that learners can follow for autonomous completion. Therefore, provided that AI technologies are appropriately implemented, they can help scaffold learners' interactions and dialogues, thereby promoting more profound critical thought (Kong, 2024).

Partnering with AI aids in developing educational materials that offer interactive tasks, which heighten the learning experience. Simulations and role play foster participation, active engagement with materials through different perspectives language can be employed within real-life situations. In addition, AI-augmented simulations can provide context for language use for learners to grapple with multifaceted sociocultural interaction. This enables proficient language development while necessitating critical reflection of one's actions within the simulation (Hyde et al., 2024). In addition, while practicing negotiation skills with students, practitioners employing AI tools can preset prompts that expand reasoning to counterarguments and formally supported claims in order to prepare the students further for critical thinking.

The unique opportunities that come along with natural language processing AI tools have made it easier for language learners to interact with content in new, exciting ways. For example, students who are tasked to write on a particular topic or provided a written piece to critique AI-generated texts are stimulated to evaluate arguments, which enhances their reasoning skills. Such activities help students develop analytical skills by evaluating content for relevance and how compelling the arguments made were, thus nurturing an environment of critical scrutiny (Woo et al., 2023). Woo mentioned that with such tools, students can apply critical self-reflection, which helps in improving metacognitive skills.

The merging of critical thinking instruction and AI implementation in tools offers an elaborate approach to facilitating language learning activities. As a through-classroom AI-powered activity design aimed at debates, problem-solving, and open question generation, robust learning environments that constructively channel critical engagement can be rich. AI-driven reflections and self-assessments enhance contemplative thought, while adequate scaffolding and guidance nurture further students' progress in completing the language tasks at hand. Collaboration with AI systems such as ChatGPT in the formatting of interactive activities augments the teaching and learning experience by enabling learners to approach language learning tasks constructively and creatively. With the swift advancement of technologies within the education sector, these strategies underscore the growing importance of AI tools as pedagogical resources aimed at transforming students into thoughtful, competent communicators.

CHALLENGES AND ETHICAL CONSIDERATIONS IN FOSTERING CRITICAL THINKING WITH AI

Encouraging critical thinking in AI-enabled educational contexts involves risks and challenges, both normatively and ethically. One of the greatest challenges is the use of AI tools that contain biases. These biases may affect the way learners are able to undertake critical thinking. AI systems are put through a training regimen using datasets, which might unavoidably comprise certain biases and stereotypes that damage the neutrality and the quality of the information presented. Jha & Singh (2024) further underlines that discriminatory assumptions made on AI applications pose a threat to vital discourse on issues strategic for the learning and development of the learners from a critical thinking perspective. Such biases affect the ability to analyze and evaluate, arguably the most fundamental aspects of critical thinking, and therefore pose troubling challenges for the educational quality embedded in the technologies touted for use in learning environments (Moustaghfir & Brigui, 2024).

The incorporation of AI into educational systems is further complicated by ethical issues about data privacy, autonomy, and the instructional role of teachers in AI-aided settings. As AI systems capture and scrutinize considerable amounts of personal data for machinized tailoring of learning experiences, securing that information and applying it ethically to avert misuse poses the greatest challenge. Hazari (2024) pushes for the grave need of frameworks that AI ethics literacy seeks to resolve with curriculum design, questioning student complexities and responsibilities stemming from such curricula. Additionally, while there is a gradual shift in AI's role as an instructor towards more active participation, it becomes important to ensure that educators still serve as facilitators so that autonomy and critical engagement with the students' learning are preserved. The teachers in these settings have to remain as comprehensible guides who use AI information in a constructive way, which drives the learners toward judgment and not mere acknowledgment (Zakaria, 2025).

Another critical issue is the implications of AI technology on students' creativity and autonomous decision-making. The evolution of AI technology might lead students to rely on it excessively, which may hinder their imagination and independent thinking. Kuyumcu advocates that AI may be beneficial to learning, but teachers must not use technology excessively at the expense of creative thinking and expression. This particular excerpt about creativity in education was noted by different researchers in the area. Also, the prevalence of AI technology, which can create content that is replicative of learners' works, undermines the unique elements of human creativity (Khatri & Karki, 2023). Hence, there is a need to formulate approaches that facilitate the appreciation of human thought and creative reasoning to minimize the use of AI as the primary cognitive processor rather than a supplement to the intellect.

To alleviate issues of overdependence on AI technologies can be dealt with through ensuring proper interfacing between human agencies and AI systems. As previously mentioned by Elsayary, adopting an educational philosophy that encourages fostering partnership as opposed to dependence can help alleviate the dangers presented by over-reliance on technology (ElSayary, 2025). Adopting such a framework requires a constructive engagement where students are educated on using AI as a tool that augments reasoning and creativity rather than doing it for them. This allows for control on the part of learners, where they are able to think critically about the information that is put forth by AI technologies (Pepin et al., 2025).

As was noted, even though AI-powered tools have the capabilities of being used to enhance critical reasoning among learners, challenges and ethical issues surrounding them need particular focus. Issues starting from the biases that are baked into the AI model, ethical ones like data privacy, and the role of a teacher all pose questions that need a balance put towards them while integrating AI tools into comment educational settings. Most importantly, integrating AI technology to different education levels should ensure that they can use such tools to aid crafts rather than be hindrances to innovation and independent guardians of ideas. Teaching these values and ethics allows for the creation of active modern citizens. Making sure the technology does not outstage the teacher preserves the balance that facilitates aimed human and AI collaboration, flexible without losing focus.

PRACTICAL GUIDELINES FOR EDUCATORS

Best practices for incorporating AI tools that foster critical thinking in the classroom

Implementing classroom AI tools that promote higher-order thinking skills requires complex pedagogical approaches that balance technology and educational aims. As with any innovation of this magnitude, the integration must be fairly meticulous and consider the new AI technology's academic merits and demerits. For instance, educators should start by implementing a range of AI-based activities. The use of chatbots in role-play scenarios can aid learners in developing critical discussion and debate skills, as they are required to provide articulation and justify reasoning. This promotes fluency and enhances critical thinking, as students must analyze, create, and evaluate information while conversing with an AI (Hading et al., 2024).

AI can also assist with problem-solving activities featuring open-ended questions, which prompt inquiry-based learning. Behaviors that Liu and Wang note indicate that AI offers solutions and aids learners in working through difficult scenarios with critical thinking (Liu & Wang, 2024). Tasks such as these require students to respond to questions using well-structured, reasoned responses enveloped in non-considerable reasoning, combining the interactivity of AI in a learning context that shifts the paradigm from traditional to active learning. All these activities, when designed with precise guiding goals and content, leverage the technology-pedagogy interface around constructivism and critique the use of AI for learning.

Educators must leverage AI-generated input to promote reflection and self-evaluation. Students can enhance their metacognitive capabilities through AI systems that offer timely and detailed feedback, enabling students to determine both their robust and not-so-strong features (Jin et al., 2023). This fosters an ongoing cycle of learning in which learners evaluate their achievement and progress level and subsequently adapt their learning approaches (Walter, 2024). Educators can build a culture of reflective practice vital for developing learners¿ critical thinking skills by personalizing feedback for students.

Another key approach is building more advanced structural support within AI-assisted settings. The integration of AI tools must be accompanied by adequate guidance from educators to ensure that students effectively navigate the complexities of technology (Çela et al., 2024). Instructive feedback includes advanced critique of AI-supplied solutions, which students are encouraged to question the trustworthiness of the AI's output, leading them to form well-rounded conclusions (Moustaghfir & Brigui, 2024). In this way, that kind of guidance helps learners gain the freedom to manage their learning even as AI becomes part of their learning experience, while emphasizing the need for robust critical thinking.

Moreover, meaningful interactive tasks with AI-generated collaborative work should be performed. AI-assisted role-playing activities and simulations have the potential to enhance rich experiential learning (Shaik et al., 2022). These techniques permit learners to actively engage in realistic scenarios where they can exercise reasoning and critical thinking skills relevant to problem solving. For example, AI can be used to conduct subject-specific case studies that require students to evaluate situations and develop able responses (Berbenyuk et al., 2024).

As well, using AI technology in pedagogy, ethical considerations have to be included in the development of curricula. The ethics discussions regarding AI in teaching, such as algorithmic biases, need to be incorporated into teaching materials for students to think and engage actively about the issue (Hao, 2024). This strategy is essential based on the need to expose students to the consequences of AI technologies and encourage them to develop a logic of responsibility while working with these technologies. Professionally fostered development for educators is necessary to guide the appropriate use of AI tools in the classroom. Training should be designed that help teachers incorporate AI in such a way that promotes critical thinking while preserving educational value (Peng et al., 2023). This also requires crafting plans to mitigate the risks brought by reliance on technology, and having knowledge of what AI can do.

In summary, optimal strategies for fostering critical thinking using AI in the classroom focus on integrating various AI applications, multilingual scaffolding, feedback systems, and conversations on ethics, which all serve to strengthen the students' critical thinking skills. If technology is thoughtfully integrated as per educational goals, it can enhance learning environments, increasing students' critical thinking skills and enabling them to deal with the realities of the modern, digital world.

How teachers can guide students in using AI effectively to support critical thinking

The impact of artificial intelligence (AI) on modern education is extensive. It transforms teachers into learning facilitators. AI is an advanced technology that requires critical thinking for its effective use. Enhancing students' thinking skills begins with effective use of AI, and teachers remain central to students being able to use AI and other technologies cognitively. AI can be incorporated into instruction through collaborative teaching. In addition, teachers are able to stimulate ethical concern, context-based AI course training, and foster a culture of collaboration in the classroom.

First, encouraging a mindset of inquiry in students is of the utmost importance. Joseph F. Johnson suggests that educators stimulate learners to attempt to explore the relevant questions with AI tools. To foster critical thinking, enable learners to engage in dialogue aimed at evaluating AI responses, and to incorporate differing perspectives from other disciplines. A robust primary education equips students with the ability to not take answers from AI at face value, but to problematize its responses logically. This is deeply rooted in a theory cited in Barbara G. Walker, Eric B. Shuster, and Pamela E. Walker's book, "Discovering Modern C Information," which teaches that questioning commonly accepted realities yields a simpler life. Cultivating a culture of inquiry helps in enabling students to assume full control over the searching process.

Another educator's responsibility is to provide tailored training on AI tools. This training should focus on the particular objectives and goals of the students as well as the specific features of the AI tool in use. As stated by Ahn and others, having the ability to navigate through AI tools profoundly increases the ability of students to make use of these technologies meaningfully. Teachers should design training classes that involve active participation where learners use AI tools to address real-life issues, and therefore, the tools are used in a meaningful context. Contextualized training not only builds confidence in the use of AI but also enables students to reinforce critical thinking skills through authentic application of the tools used.

Moreover, teachers must note the social and ethical aspects related to the application of AI technologies. Ramasamy suggests that teaching AI's potential biases and limitations can help students cultivate AI literacy that is more nuanced. Teachers can invite their students to analyze the social ramifications of AI outputs and the impact of AI algorithms on people and societies. It is the responsibility of educators to help learners understand that AI can serve as a great support; however, without critical scrutiny, over-reliance on AI may result in serious misdiagnoses and the disabling of reasoning abilities.

Also, the creation of collaborative environments for learning is critical in mentoring students on the use of AI in relation to fostering critical thinking. Student dialogues and interactions can be stimulated through AI-enabled collaborative activities, which enhance the overall engagement and participation of the learners as they share ideas and challenge each other's conclusions. A collaborative inquiry-based approach utilizing AI provides students with opportunities for constructive disputes aimed at challenging their ideas and igniting further investigation. Educators must develop activities where students are required to work in groups and use AI tools to investigate multifaceted issues from different angles and defend their conclusions with evidence derived from their analyses. Societal problems require engagement with multiple perspectives, which students develop along with crucial communicative skills through this collaboration.

Additionally, educators may incorporate AI-enabled feedback into their pedagogy to assist students in contemplating on deeper levels. When students receive AI-generated feedback tailored to their attributes, they are more likely to consider the reasoning and strategies that led to their conclusions. Educators may guide conversations around the AI-generated feedback and invite students to think about the reasoning behind their answers and other possible explanations. Connecting AI feedback with reflective practices gives educators a means to increase metacognitive awareness and understanding of reasoning elements.

Instructing students to use AI for critical thinking also requires teaching them to model appropriate use of technology. Influencing the way students pose questions to AI, how they evaluate the information provided by AI, and how they approach the results given by AI offers an important teaching opportunity. Through this instruction, students learn to apply information from AI responsibly and understand that critical thinking is a process that occurs in cycles. When educators apply sophisticated critical thinking using AI, students are likely to imitate such practices in their engagement with technology.

At last, teachers need to know the most recent changes in AI technology and their effects on education. In their work, educators need to pursue advanced AI research that is actively being published to refine their focus, which requires teaching them how to use research effectively. Specialized discussion groups and professional development workshops on AI in education help educators understand how to respond to many current issues and evolving trends as well as how to strategize to address the challenges of effective teaching in the age of technology. With this knowledge, educators can tailor their instruction to use the strengths of AI and minimize its weaknesses.

To summarize, students' use of AI to enhance critical AI thinking is facilitated best by teacher guidance. In fostering inquiry, contextual training, modeling ethical considerations, modeling AI concept interactions, collaborating with students to pose questions for debriefing sessions, and staying up to date with evolving technology, AI-powered educators enable students to grapple autonomously and critically with technology's complexities. Under such a model, teachers instill in students the culture of critical thinking and prepare them to thrive in an AI-dominated world.

Encouraging a balanced approach: Combining traditional methods with AI-enhanced critical thinking tasks.

Integrating AI tools along with traditional ones enhances the development of critical thinking skills while engineering a rich learning environment. Innovative approaches to critical thinking facilitated through AI systems are superb, but equally important are traditional practices like direct instruction, peer teaching, and experiential learning, which provide a holistic development of thinking skills. This integration allows learners to harness fundamental knowledge along with sophisticated analytical skills effectively.

An example of using direct instruction models AI tools to create a robust approach to teaching critical thinking tasks, AI-guided, and the content taught through direct instruction. Teachers can employ guiding lectures and discussions to explain essential concepts to the students and apply the same principles to AI-guided exercises. After the initial explanations of grammar or writing, teachers can allow the students to engage with AI writing assistants to formulate and polish their drafts. AI feedback gives students an opportunity to enhance their critical thinking abilities along with their writing skills. Instruction shifts from the teacher to the learner through the interaction of the student and AI, which improves student engagement.

In addition, traditional experiences of collaborative learning with peers can be enhanced with AI-driven tasks that stimulate deeper analytical discourse. In a discussion or project-based class, the teacher could employ an AI tool to gather/ perform analyses and present the results to the learners for further exploration. With this approach, students are offered the opportunity to wrestle with pertinent materials in a data, evidence, and information-driven manner and to foster collective inquiry and discussion. For example, groups can evaluate trends, challenge their assumptions, and develop arguments supporting or repudiating the AI-generated insights based on data-driven research results. While these combinations cultivate critical thinking skills, they also provide opportunities for the development of effective communication skills for the students as they work in diverse groups to solve multifaceted problems collaboratively.

Moreover, the application of AI technologies in simulating realistic activities can enhance hands-on learning experiences. Students can be given stimulating and challenging scenarios through case-based problem simulations or role-playing exercises, together with AI-generated simulations. For instance, in language classes, students can work with AI platforms that simulate real-life situations, such as debates, where they are expected to actively use the language and make strategic assessment decisions. Such simulations motivate the learners to be more adaptable as well as be able to solve problems creatively and reflect on their learning in engaging ways.

Employing AI within the feedback and formative assessment activities is yet another way of integrating traditional methods with technology to stimulate critical thinking. With traditional assessment practices, teachers outline learning objectives and expected outcomes, which can then be accompanied by AI tools to personalize feedback. This advanced feedback helps students understand their learning pathways, accentuating progress together with instruction, as To and Xu noted, emphasizing the need to integrate metacognitive alongside critical analytical skills development. The multi-faceted experience of receiving formative feedback from educators in addition to AI tailored to their needs becomes enriching, in that it addresses varied preferences and requirements within the teaching-learning interface.

To promote a nurturing environment with the help of AI alongside conventional methods, fostering question posing techniques is critical. Strategies that encourage learners to inquire within lesson discussions, mentoring by adults, or AI complement circulate through traditional tutoring mechanisms and strengthen critical thinking. Educators can introduce inquiry by encouraging students to ask reflective questions about their reasoning and the AI's responses before, during, and after AI engagements. This kind of critical examination enhances AI interactivity while independently building curiosity as learners navigate the learning process to deepen their AI-induced active thinking abilities.

As with any other tool, educators need to have a balanced understanding of the advantages and disadvantages of the technology being used. AI tools can help students with critical thinking tasks; however, an over-dependence on such tools will adversely affect creativity and independent thought. This can be avoided by creating a balance where the traditional educational norms are preserved while focusing on the innovative features of AI-enhanced critical thinking skills paired with creativity. Such balance allows technology to be utilized meaningfully and appropriately, thus allowing students to integrate real-world contexts into their learning.

To conclude, the positioning of AI in education encourages a well-rounded approach guided by focusing on diverging from traditional methods to activate AI-enhanced critical thinking tasks to advance deep learning development shifts at all levels. By using whole group instruction, a combination of group and individual work, hands-on learning, and purposeful questions, learners can master the essential

AI-powered skills blended with robust thinking paradigms in a rich learning space. This innovation about education deepens students' understanding of how to think critically while fostering their capacity to responsibly function within an evolving, technologically advanced society.

THE FUTURE OF CRITICAL THINKING IN AI-ASSISTED ENGLISH LANGUAGE LEARNING

AI-assisted English language learning as a branch of education is analyzed from the perspective of critical skills development, and it is evident that the advancing technology and synergistic pedagogical practices motivate learners and teachers alike. It is now universally accepted that new trends and technologies will create critical thinking opportunities through constructive learning and improved learning experience customization. As technology develops, the use of AI in natural language processing, speech recognition, and tutoring will be typical in educational settings. Gyawali (2022) have advanced the claim that intelligent tutoring systems (ITS) can be used by learners to receive tailored assistance for self-evaluation and, therefore, encourage reflective thinking in their learning processes. According Gyawali (2022), these systems, they provide seamless adaptability to learners' progress by offering appropriate challenges and resources to encourage advanced cognitive processes.

In addition, the use of machine learning and data analytics tools enables AI to track trends in students' performance and engagement, enabling easier addressing of learning gaps. Liu and Wang's study documents the positive influences of AI integration in English literature classes on students' critical thinking skills (Liu & Wang, 2024). While AI systems learn from individual and collective data, they suggest specific measures that refine critical thinking about language as well as texts and contexts, alongside prompting students to take on multidisciplinary challenges. This allows educators to move towards a more student-centered and inquiry-based pedagogical framework that helps build the many emerging competencies needed in today's society.

The restructuring of educational systems concerning Artificial Intelligence (AI) requires that instructors embrace new teaching methodologies while still protecting their core autonomy in education. In this sense, a teacher's influence will be more pronounced in properly guiding students to apply AIs to critical thinking exercises rather than rote learning (Li & Xu, 2022). In an AI-infused context, there will be greater emphasis for teachers to select suitable AI applications to be used in a given educational setting and offer instructional guidance as learners confront intricate information systems. Through guided inquiry and analysis of AI outputs, students can develop the skills necessary to make distinctions on the usefulness and relevance of information, thus enhancing their critical thinking capabilities.

The next decade anticipates a peak in the use of AI technology alongside critical thinking into language teaching. Educators will utilize AI technologies within the classroom to construct workplace pathways designed to facilitate inquiry and creative expression, as well as to guide learning tailored to each individual. AI technology may be utilized to improve students' satisfaction with learning by offering current information and tailored teaching (Dewi et al., 2021). This evolving feedback loop will allow teachers to enhance their teaching approaches using ever-present insights from AI technologies.

As AI technology develops, there is a possibility of the emergence of collaborative AI, where students co-create knowledge with AI. This kind of interaction would challenge students to think critically about AI-generated information and improve their perspectives while forming new ideas. Educators will propose conversations about these collaborations, guiding learners to analyze the contribution of AI and its impact on their perspectives concerning language and culture.

The consideration of ethical AI frameworks for language learning will continue to take precedence. Teachers have a responsibility to ensure their students build proper cybernetic ethics as human reasoning and machine learning systems converge. This involves understanding the nuances of bias concerning AI's societal implications, including the content created by AI systems. Moybeka et al. argue that the use of Artificial Intelligence in teaching languages has the potential to affect pupils' motivation and, therefore, requires a more nuanced ethical approach to its pedagogical use (Moybeka et al., 2023).

CONCLUSION

Assimilating AI technologies into English learning instruction has given rise to new ways of fostering learners' critical thinking skills. A salient aspect of AI's role in promoting critical thinking in English language teaching and learning is its usefulness in developing critical thinking as an essential communication and analytical skill. Students' advanced engagement AI tools, such as intelligent tutoring systems, chatbots, and adaptive learning systems, can be tailored to give prompt feedback and present tasks that stimulate intellectually demanding activity.

AI tools and applications are growing at a rapid pace. Technologies like natural language processing and machine learning will likely develop, creating more advanced interactivity and greater efficiency for automatic tailoring tailored to each learner's requirements. Tools powered by AI have greatly improved students' critical thinking skills. This observation validates the critical role of these AI tools in enhancing vital thinking processes for learning languages. The changing nature of teaching with AI incorporates the notion of a facilitator. Teachers now need to encourage students to use AI tools critically, ethically, and constructively, which builds a focus on deeper inquiry beyond surface-level engagements with technology.

In the language instruction domain, the incorporation of critical thinking and the application of technological instruction aids suggest that AI tools will become more integrated into pedagogical practices over the coming decade. Teaching will remain dynamic as educators continue to change their approaches to align with AI systems, incorporating both the technological and humanistic sides of education. Language teaching and learning will further enhance learners' critical reflection and analysis skills due to the integration of AI.

While these advancements are embraced, it is important to note the consideration of educational ethics relating to pedagogical responsibility in teaching English using AI tools. Addressing the barriers of biases with AI algorithms and data privacy issues related to autonomy for learners will promote responsible technology use and advocacy of learners' interests. Moreover, the integration of AI should not undermine the need for traditional education systems, which encourage creativity, critical thought, and interpersonal skills.

Summarizing our discussion, while we are at the beginning of a new phase involving advancement in technology, there is a great possibility for artificial intelligence to transform the development of critical thinking skills in English learning. With the rapid developments in technology, educators are tasked to cultivate spaces that develop language skills and enable learners to become responsible, critical thinkers. The path forward is to nurture innovation carefully alongside ethical considerations in order to ensure that the next generation is prepared for success in a world where interconnectivity and technology pervade daily life activities.

REFERENCES

Ab.Wahid, N. T. (2022). Developing Critical Thinking Skills in Secondary School Students: The Potential for Strategic Management Through Problem-Posing Instructional Strategy. *International Journal of Academic Research in Progressive Education and Development, 11*(3). Advance online publication. DOI: 10.6007/ijarped/v11-i3/15505

Amin, M. Y. M. (2023). AI and chat GPT in language teaching: Enhancing EFL classroom support and transforming assessment techniques. *International Journal of Higher Education Pedagogies, 4*(4), 1–15.

Annamalai, N., Eltahir, M. E., Alsalhi, N. R., Zakarneh, B., & Zyoud, S. H. (2022). Investigation of Malaysian ESL Students' Learning Experience of the Smartphone Applications for English Language Learning. *International Journal of English Language and Literature Studies, 11*(4), 202–211. DOI: 10.55493/5019.v11i4.4678

Berbenyuk, A., Powell, L., & Zary, N. (2024). *Feasibility and Educational Value of Clinical Cases Generated Using Large Language Models*. https://doi.org/DOI: 10.3233/shti240705

Çela, E., Fonkam, M., & Potluri, R. M. (2024). Risks of AI-Assisted Learning on Student Critical Thinking. *International Journal of Risk and Contingency Management, 12*(1), 1–19. DOI: 10.4018/ijrcm.350185

Dewi, H. K., Putri, R. E., Rahim, N. A., Wardani, T. I., & Pandin, M. G. R. (2021). *The Use of Ai (Artificial Intelligence) in English Learning Among University Student: Case Study in English Department, Universitas Airlangga*. https://doi.org/DOI: 10.31235/osf.io/x3qr6

ElSayary, A. (2025). *Transforming Education*. 89–102. https://doi.org/DOI: 10.4018/979-8-3693-7332-3.ch006

Gligorea, I., Cioca, M., Oancea, R., Gorski, A.-T., Gorski, H., & Tudorache, P. (2023). Adaptive learning using artificial intelligence in e-learning: A literature review. *Education Sciences, 13*(12), 1216.

Grecu, V. (2023). Investigating Critical Thinking Among Engineering Students in Romania. *Acta Universitatis Cibiniensis Technical Series, 75*(1), 21–29. DOI: 10.2478/aucts-2023-0003

Gyawali, Y. P. (2022). Artificial Intelligence in English Language Teaching: Navigating the Future With Emerging Perspectives. *Journal of Language and Linguistics in Society, 26*, 21–27. DOI: 10.55529/jlls.26.21.27

Gyawali, Y. P. (2023). Exploring Dimensions of Teacher Education in Nepal: Perspectives, Challenges, and Reform Opportunities. *Journal of General Education and Humanities*, *2*(4), 285–298. DOI: 10.58421/gehu.v2i4.128

Hading, E. F., Rustan, D. R. H. P., & Ruing, F. H. (2024). EFL Students' Perceptions on the Integration of AI in Fostering Critical Thinking Skills. *Glens*, *2*(1), 1–10. DOI: 10.61220/glens.v2i1.466

Hao, H. (2024). Moderating Role of Depression in the Association Between Leisure Activity and Cognitive Function Among the Disabled Older People. *Frontiers in Public Health*, *12*. Advance online publication. DOI: 10.3389/fpubh.2024.1345699

Hazari, S. (2024). Justification and Roadmap for Artificial Intelligence (AI) Literacy Courses in Higher Education. *Journal of Educational Research and Practice*, *14*(1). Advance online publication. DOI: 10.5590/jerap.2024.14.1.07

Hyde, S. J., Busby, A., & Bonner, R. L. (2024). Tools or Fools: Are We Educating Managers or Creating Tool-Dependent Robots? *Organizational Behavior Teaching Review*, *48*(4), 708–734. DOI: 10.1177/10525629241230357

Idham, S. Y., Subramaniam, I., Khan, A., & Mugair, S. K. (2022). The Effect of Role-Playing Techniques on the Speaking Skills of Students at University. *Theory and Practice in Language Studies*, *12*(8), 1622–1629.

Jha, A., & Singh, S. R. (2024). *Integrating Artificial Intelligence in Media Education*. 297–328. https://doi.org/DOI: 10.4018/979-8-3373-1017-6.ch010

Jin, S.-H., Im, K., Yoo, M., Roll, I., & Seo, K. (2023). Supporting Students' Self-Regulated Learning in Online Learning Using Artificial Intelligence Applications. *International Journal of Educational Technology in Higher Education*, *20*(1). Advance online publication. DOI: 10.1186/s41239-023-00406-5

Khatri, B. B., & Karki, P. D. (2023). Artificial Intelligence (AI) in Higher Education: Growing Academic Integrity and Ethical Concerns. *Nepalese Journal of Development and Rural Studies*, *20*(01), 1–7. DOI: 10.3126/njdrs.v20i01.64134

Kong, S.-C. (2024). A Pedagogical Design for Self-Regulated Learning in Academic Writing Using Text-Based Generative Artificial Intelligence Tools: 6-P Pedagogy of Plan, Prompt, Preview, Produce, Peer-Review, Portfolio-Tracking. *Research and Practice in Technology Enhanced Learning*, *19*, 30. DOI: 10.58459/rptel.2024.19030

Li, P., & Xu, Q. (2022). Computational Modeling of Bilingual Language Learning: Current Models and Future Directions. *Language Learning*, *73*(S2), 17–64. DOI: 10.1111/lang.12529

Lionenko, M., & Huzar, O. (2023). Synergy of Reflection and Critical Thinking: A Catalyst for Students' Intellectual Growth. *Journal of Vasyl Stefanyk Precarpathian National University*, *10*(3), 75–82. DOI: 10.15330/jpnu.10.3.75-82

Liu, W., & Wang, Y. (2024). The Effects of Using <scp>AI</Scp> Tools on Critical Thinking in English Literature Classes Among <scp>EFL</Scp> Learners: An Intervention Study. *European Journal of Education*, *59*(4). Advance online publication. DOI: 10.1111/ejed.12804

Mayasari, N., Sastraatmadja, A. H. M., Suparman, T., Mutiara, I. I., & Maqfirah, P. A. (2024). Effectiveness of Using Artificial Intelligence Learning Tools and Customized Curriculum on Improving Students' Critical Thinking Skills in Indonesia. *The Eastasouth Journal of Learning and Educations*, *2*(02), 111–118. DOI: 10.58812/esle.v2i02.302

Merelo, J. J., Castillo, P. Á., Mora, A. M., Barranco, F., Abbas, N., Guillén, A., & Tsivitanidou, O. (2022). *Exploring the Role of Chatbots and Messaging Applications in Higher Education: A Teacher's Perspective*. 205–223. https://doi.org/DOI: 10.1007/978-3-031-05675-8_16

Moustaghfir, S., & Brigui, H. (2024). Navigating Critical Thinking in the Digital Era: An Informative Exploration. *International Journal of Linguistics Literature and Translation*, *7*(1), 137–143. DOI: 10.32996/ijllt.2024.7.1.11x

Moybeka, A. M., Syariatin, N., Tatipang, D. P., Mushthoza, D. A., Dewi, N. P. J. L., & Tineh, S. (2023). Artificial Intelligence and English Classroom: The Implications of AI Toward EFL Students' Motivation. *Edumaspul - Jurnal Pendidikan*, *7*(2), 2444–2454. https://doi.org/DOI: 10.33487/edumaspul.v7i2.6669

Mugisha, M., Uwitonze, A. M., Chesire, F., Senyonga, R., Oxman, M., Nsangi, A., Semakula, D., Kaseje, M., Lewin, S., Sewankambo, N., Nyirazinyoye, L., Oxman, A. D., & Rosenbaum, S. (2021). Teaching Critical Thinking About Health Using Digital Technology in Lower Secondary Schools in Rwanda: A Qualitative Context Analysis. *PLoS One*, *16*(3), e0248773. DOI: 10.1371/journal.pone.0248773

Nugraini, A. R., Iswari, R. S., & Anggraito, Y. U. (2022). Development of Sets-Based Booklets to Improve Critical Thinking Skills and the Effectiveness of Biotechnology Learning in SMA/MA. *Journal of Innovative Science Education*, *11*(3), 261–269. DOI: 10.15294/jise.v10i1.51437

Nurjanah, A., Salsabila, I. N., Azzahra, A., Rahayu, R., & Marlina, N. S. (2024). Artificial Intelligence (AI) Usage in Today's Teaching and Learning Process: A Review. *Syntax Idea*, *6*(3), 1517–1523. DOI: 10.46799/syntax-idea.v6i3.3126

Peng, M., Xie, J., Mao-hua, X., & Liu, Y. (2023). Artificial Intelligence Education in Primary and Secondary Schools From the Perspective of Thinking Quality. *Journal of Contemporary Educational Research*, *7*(4), 41–46. DOI: 10.26689/jcer.v7i4.4875

Pepin, B., Buchholtz, N., & Salinas-Hernández, U. (2025). A Scoping Survey of ChatGPT in Mathematics Education. *Digital Experiences in Mathematics Education*, *11*(1), 9–41. DOI: 10.1007/s40751-025-00172-1

Pitychoutis, K. M. (2024). *Harnessing AI Chatbots for EFL Essay Writing: A Paradigm Shift in Language Pedagogy*. https://doi.org/DOI: 10.31235/osf.io/xrvth

Rios, J. A., Ling, G., Pugh, R., Becker, D., & Bacall, A. (2020). Identifying Critical 21st-Century Skills for Workplace Success: A Content Analysis of Job Advertisements. *Educational Researcher*, *49*(2), 80–89. DOI: 10.3102/0013189x19890600

Romadhoni, M., Andania, R. A., & Yen, A.-C. (2022). Students' Critical Thinking on Argumentative Essay Writing Through Cooperative Learning. *Education and Human Development Journal*, *7*(2), 1–12. DOI: 10.33086/ehdj.v7i2.2941

Ruiz-Rojas, L. I., Salvador-Ullauri, L., & Acosta-Vargas, P. (2024). Collaborative Working and Critical Thinking: Adoption of Generative Artificial Intelligence Tools in Higher Education. *Sustainability*, *16*(13), 5367. DOI: 10.3390/su16135367

Shaik, T., Tao, X., Li, Y., Dann, C., McDonald, J., Redmond, P., & Galligan, L. (2022). A Review of the Trends and Challenges in Adopting Natural Language Processing Methods for Education Feedback Analysis. *IEEE Access : Practical Innovations, Open Solutions*, *10*, 56720–56739. DOI: 10.1109/access.2022.3177752

Walter, Y. (2024). Embracing the Future of Artificial Intelligence in the Classroom: The Relevance of AI Literacy, Prompt Engineering, and Critical Thinking in Modern Education. *International Journal of Educational Technology in Higher Education*, *21*(1). Advance online publication. DOI: 10.1186/s41239-024-00448-3

Wei, L. (2023). Artificial Intelligence in Language Instruction: Impact on English Learning Achievement, L2 Motivation, and Self-Regulated Learning. *Frontiers in Psychology*, *14*. Advance online publication. DOI: 10.3389/fpsyg.2023.1261955

Woo, D. J., Wang, Y., Susanto, H., & Guo, K. (2023). Understanding English as a Foreign Language Students' Idea Generation Strategies for Creative Writing With Natural Language Generation Tools. *Journal of Educational Computing Research*, *61*(7), 1464–1482. DOI: 10.1177/07356331231175999

Xu, E., Wang, W., & Wang, Q. (2023). The Effectiveness of Collaborative Problem Solving in Promoting Students' Critical Thinking: A Meta-Analysis Based on Empirical Literature. *Humanities & Social Sciences Communications, 10*(1). Advance online publication. DOI: 10.1057/s41599-023-01508-1

Xue-wei, Z. (2023). A Chinese Study of Foreign English Teachers Employment in Online Recruitment Advertisements. *Academic Journal of Humanities & Social Sciences*, *6*(24). Advance online publication. DOI: 10.25236/ajhss.2023.062418

Yang, Y.-T. C., Chen, Y.-C., & Hung, H.-T. (2022). Digital storytelling as an interdisciplinary project to improve students' English speaking and creative thinking. *Computer Assisted Language Learning*, *35*(4), 840–862.

Zakaria, N. Y. K. (2025). Exploring the Impact of AI on Critical Thinking Development in ESL: A Systematic Literature Review. *Arab World English Journal, 1*, 330–347. DOI: 10.24093/awej/ai.19

KEY TERMS AND DEFINITIONS

Adaptive Learning Systems: Computer-based platforms that personalize instruction by adjusting tasks and resources according to a learner's progress, ensuring optimal challenges for skill development.

Artificial Intelligence (AI): A branch of computer science that enables machines to perform tasks that typically require human intelligence, such as language processing, problem-solving, and decision-making.

Chatbots: AI-powered conversational agents designed to simulate human dialogue, often used in language learning to provide practice, feedback, and interactive engagement.

Critical Thinking: The cognitive ability to analyze, evaluate, and synthesize information to make informed judgments, solve problems, and reflect on learning processes.

Ethical Considerations: The principles and moral concerns related to the responsible use of AI in education, including issues of bias, data privacy, fairness, and the role of teachers.

Feedback Mechanisms: Processes or systems, often AI-driven, that provide learners with timely evaluations of their performance, helping them adjust strategies and improve outcomes.

Intelligent Tutoring Systems (ITS): AI-based educational tools that deliver personalized instruction, guidance, and feedback to learners, simulating one-on-one tutoring experiences.

Language Proficiency: The ability to effectively use a language across various contexts, including speaking, writing, listening, and reading, often enhanced by critical thinking skills.

Natural Language Processing (NLP): A field of AI that enables machines to understand, interpret, and generate human language, supporting applications such as translation, text analysis, and chatbots.

Self-Regulated Learning: A learning approach where students take active control of their study process by setting goals, monitoring progress, and adapting strategies, often supported by AI tools.

Chapter 12
Generative Artificial Intelligence's Impact on English Language Education:
Implications on Linguistic Imperialism and Critical Pedagogy in Post-Secondary Education

Brenda McDermott
https://orcid.org/0009-0007-5547-3357
University of Calgary, Canada

Roxanne Ross
https://orcid.org/0000-0003-0511-2389
University of Calgary, Canada

ABSTRACT

In this chapter, the authors discuss the impacts of the ongoing privileging of Standard English (SE) on English as an additional language (EAL) post-secondary students and explore the ways in which the introduction of Generative Artificial Intelligences (Gen AI) offer the potential to both expand L2 learners' access to SE and reinforce biases of linguistic imperialism. Drawing on current research on Gen AI integration within L2 pedagogy, the authors propose strategies grounded in critical pedagogy aimed at supporting L2 learners' critical language use in the context of Gen AI tools in ways that challenge SE norms and honour diverse cultural and linguistic identities.

DOI: 10.4018/979-8-3373-3000-6.ch012

INTRODUCTION

The advent of generative artificial intelligence (GenAI) tools has revolutionized various aspects of education, particularly academic writing instruction. These tools, such as ChatGPT, have the potential to transform how students learn and practice writing. This is particularly true for English as L2[1] students studying in Western post-secondary institutions, where preferences for Standard English (SE) can pose barriers to academic success and may be experienced as discriminatory (Page, 2023; Sterzuk, 2015). Concerns about the legitimacy of writing as a practice and educators' responses to circumvent students' use of GenAI highlight how this linguistic privilege is embedded in educational practices. For example, biases in GenAI detection tools that falsely label L2 writers as AI-generated underscore the existing discrimination within L2 writers' experiences (Liang et al., 2023).

In the context of L2 pedagogy, early research exploring applications of GenAI in academic writing instruction suggests that GenAI tools offer unprecedented opportunities for L2 students to enhance academic writing skills (Fathi & Rahimi, 2024) thus aiding them in meeting SE norms of expression more easily. While the potential for GenAI tools to challenge current linguistically imperialist practices exists, their integration into educational settings continues to raise pedagogical concerns related to assessment practices and academic integrity. This has resulted in calls for, and in some cases the adoption of, practices that limit student use of GenAI entirely. Adding further complexity to this discussion are deeper ethical issues related to GenAI systems' predominant reliance on English-language data (Lai et al., 2023), thereby reinforcing SE's dominance.

This chapter explores these questions by examining the impact of GenAI on linguistic imperialism and Standard English (SE) in post-secondary education, and its potential to destabilize SE privilege by aiding L2 learners in attaining SE-associated advantages. At the same time, the authors examine GenAI's capacity to reaffirm this privilege through its limited recognition of World Englishes. The chapter proposes critical pedagogical practices to navigate the integration of GenAI in academic writing instruction in a manner that promotes equity and inclusivity. It concludes with a brief overview of emerging critical pedagogical approaches to supporting L2 students' academic writing success, such as applications of critical digital pedagogy (Baskara, 2024) and critical reflection (Britton & Lorimer Leonard, 2020).

STANDARD ENGLISH AND ACADEMIC WRITING

Language is not a neutral medium of communication; it is deeply embedded in social, cultural, and political power structures. In academic contexts, the privileging of Standard English (SE) reflects and reproduces these hierarchies, reinforcing linguistic imperialism and marginalizing alternative ways of knowing and expressing (Clements & Petray, 2021). This privileging is particularly evident in post-secondary institutions, where English language standards are upheld through the internationalization of higher education, often under the guise of neutrality and meritocracy (Sharma & Hussein, 2021).

The dominance of SE is not accidental but historically rooted in colonial legacies. One way to understand linguistic imperialism is through Kachru's (1990) model of World Englishes. It illustrates how English is stratified globally, with the Inner Circle (e.g., UK, US, Canada, Australia) setting linguistic norms that the Outer and Expanding Circles are expected to emulate. This model reveals how SE becomes the benchmark for legitimacy, positioning native English speakers, particularly historically white speakers, as ideal communicators and marginalizing those from linguistically diverse backgrounds.

This global linguistic hierarchy is perpetuated through educational practices that equate SE with academic excellence. Phillipson (1997) critiques this dynamic as a form of linguistic imperialism, where the teaching and assessment of SE serve to maintain colonial power structures in subtle, non-coercive ways. These practices disadvantage L2 writers and suppress variation within native Englishes with the Inner Circle. For instance, Anya (2020) and Ogunniyi & O'Neil (2022) show how African American English and other non-standard varieties are devalued in academic settings, revealing that linguistic bias affects both L1 and L2 speakers whose expression deviates from the norm. This privileging of SE is further institutionalized through academic language policies. Sterzuk (2015) argues that in Canada, such policies function to homogenize linguistic diversity, reinforcing settler colonial privilege under the rhetoric of multiculturalism. Similarly, Clements and Petray (2021) challenge the myth of a neutral SE in the U.S., showing how it is used to stigmatize individuals based on race, class, and gender. Shin and Sterzuk (2019) note that rigid language policies in writing assessments disproportionately affect L2 and Indigenous students. Mahboob and Szenes (2010) further argue that such evaluations can lead to race-based grading discrimination, where students are penalized for not conforming to dominant linguistic norms. Dobinson et al. (2019) add that standardized rubrics often provide vague or overly technical feedback, making it difficult for linguistically diverse students to improve.

Importantly, the enforcement of SE is often justified through claims of clarity and accessibility. However, as Ishaque and Khan (2018) argue, these claims obscure the fact that SE is not inherently more comprehensible but is instead socially constructed as superior. Heng Hartse and Kubota (2014) highlight how academic editing practices reinforce this construction by treating stylistic differences as errors, particularly in L2 writing, thereby framing deviation from SE as a deficit rather than a difference. Pérez-Llantada (2013) and Trahar et al. (2019) demonstrate that rhetorical differences rooted in cultural norms are often misinterpreted as errors, contributing to lower publication rates for L2 scholars.

Together, these studies reveal a consistent pattern: academic writing practices, from classroom assessments to publication standards, are structured in ways that uphold SE as the norm. This not only marginalizes linguistic diversity but also sustains broader systems of inequality rooted in colonial histories. Addressing these issues requires a critical examination of how language is used in academic spaces—not as a neutral tool, but as a mechanism of power.

FROM LINGUISTIC IMPERIALISM TO ALGORITHMIC POWER: THE ROLE OF GENAI IN ACADEMIC WRITING

The privileging of Standard English (SE) in academic writing is not merely a matter of stylistic preference—it is a mechanism of power that upholds colonial legacies and marginalizes linguistic diversity. As explored above, this power is enacted through institutional policies, editorial practices, and assessment standards that frame SE as the benchmark of academic legitimacy. However, these mechanisms are not confined to human institutions alone. With the rise of GenAI tools these linguistic hierarchies are increasingly encoded into the technologies and their Large Language Models (Smith et al., 2025).

GenAI systems are not neutral tools; they are trained on vast datasets that overwhelmingly reflect dominant linguistic and cultural norms. GenAI tools produce written output, predominantly in English (OpenAI, n.d.; Ramesh, Sitaram & Shoudhoury, 2023). These Natural Language Processing (NLP) models are created through machine learning, which requires a large amount of data. As Levendowski (2018) and Smith et al. (2025) note, the training data for large language models (LLMs) is largely drawn from freely available online content, much of which is written in SE and produced within Western, English-dominant contexts. This bias in training material reflects a similar linguistic hierarchy to those criticized by Phillipson (1997) as supporting linguistic imperialism. NLP models are not only more fluent in SE but also more likely to reproduce its stylistic conventions, rhetorical patterns, and implicit biases. In doing so, GenAI tools reinforce the very linguistic hierarchies that critical pedagogy seeks to dismantle. In fact, GenAI's creation of written output that reflects SE is one of its strengths. GenAI weaknesses the tools may hallucinate when creating content and sources (Peres et al., 2023; Wach et al., 2023) or struggle to form conclusions that follow disciplinary expectations with complex material (Pedersen, 2023). Therefore, these tools may not always create meaningful, complex content, but they can reproduce the linguistic markers of SE.

The increased performance of the GenAI tools and their predominately SE output may highlight why many concerns around the technology have focused on the development and assessment of the writing, particular composition. Several authors have expressed concerns that GenAI may disincentivize composition skills (Chan & Hu, 2023; Huang, 2023; Pedersen, 2023). For example, Mohammadkarimi's (2023) survey of post-secondary educators identifies that many educators believe that GenAI will have a negative impact on skill development, particularly critical thinking and research skills. Some educators responding by increasing restrictions on writing conditions to preserve academic integrity (Laupichler et al., 2022). This includes a growing reliance on in-class, timed writing assessments under heightened supervision (Huang, 2023), which limits students' ability to engage in revision, reflection, or access external supports such as writing centres. While intended to deter misuse of AI tools, these measures disproportionately disadvantage diverse learners, particularly L2 students, who benefit from extended time, feedback, and scaffolding to develop their writing skills. Moreover, such practices risk reinforcing nativist language expectations, privileging students who already write fluently in SE while marginalizing those whose linguistic backgrounds differ. In this context, the use of GenAI not only destabilizes traditional grading norms but also exposes and potentially amplifies existing inequities in language assessment (Cheuk, 2021).

Institutional responses to GenAI have largely centered on concerns about academic integrity, often overlooking the deeper pedagogical and equity implications. Xiao et al. (2023) found that universities in English-speaking countries are more likely to implement GenAI-related policies, yet these policies tend to focus narrowly on disclosure and plagiarism prevention. As Dang and Wang (2024) observed, few institutions explicitly address the unique needs of L2 learners or the linguistic biases embedded in both GenAI tools and their detection systems. Tools such as GPTZero and Turnitin's AI detection system have been shown to disproportionately flag L2 writing as AI-generated due to its more predictable syntax and vocabulary (Liang et al., 2023). These false positives are not simply technical glitches—they reflect and reinforce the same linguistic hierarchies that privilege SE and marginalize diverse Englishes. GenAI detectors are a future institutionalization of linguistic imperialism. As Otterbacher (2023) and Woelfel (2023) argue, these systems equate human authorship with stylistic idiosyncrasies more common among native speakers, thereby upholding a narrow, racialized standard of what constitutes "authentic" writing. In this way, both GenAI tools and their detection counterparts operate within a shared ideological framework that centers SE as the linguistic ideal, further entrenching the marginalization of L2 voices in academic spaces.

PEDAGOGICAL DILEMMAS: LEVELING THE FIELD OR REINFORCING THE NORM FOR L2WRITERS

Despite the concerned regarding GenAI reaffirm SE priveledge, a large body of literature on GenAI and L2 writers stresses the ways in which GenAI provides opportunities for immediate feedback and customized learning (Calma et al., 2022; Koltovskaia, 2020; O'Neill & Russel, 2019; Shin & Kim, 2022). For example, Wang and others (2023) noted that GenAI helps address language barriers through providing translation services. Other scholars discuss how Automated Writing Evaluation and Feedback Tools, such as Grammarly, provide support for L2 language acquisition (Godwin-Jones, 2022). Wang and Dang's (2024) systematic review of pedagogical uses of GenAI in L2 writing instruction concluded that the most frequent pedagogical focus was correcting language errors and that reviewed studies demonstrated these tools were successful in reducing errors in students' written work

The immediacy and increased access to feedback that GenAI offers L2 learners has been highlighted as a primary benefit of pedagogical applications of AI in L2 writing instruction (Fathi & Rahimi, 2024). This increased access to immediate feedback has also been shown to enhance L2 learners' motivation (Huang & Mizumoto, 2025) and confidence and reduce anxiety (Fathi & Rahimi, 2024).

These initial findings related to GenAI pedagogical applications in L2 academic writing have led some scholars to reflect on GenAI's capacity to potentially level the playing field (James & Andrews, 2024). However, alongside positive results in relation to GenAI's impact on students' written linguistic performance, studies have also highlighted a number of challenges related to students' and scholars' concerns regarding overreliance on GenAI (Wang & Dang, 2024) as well as GenAI's limitations in providing feedback with an appropriate level of context (Hwang et al., 2023). For instance, in their study comparing students' experiences with teacher feedback and ChatGPT feedback, Lu et al. (2024) found that ChatGPT more frequently included less specific feedback. Although the study demonstrated students with higher levels of performance preferred this type of feedback, finding it a "source of inspiration" (p. 622), many students appreciated the greater specificity and direction of teacher feedback. Overall their study demonstrated that despite not being informed of the source of the feedback (ChatGPT or teacher provided), teachers' suggestions for revision were implemented more frequently. While Lu et al.'s (2024) study focused on the benefits that all students experienced in their writing performance and critical thinking skills from blending teacher and GenAI feedback, their findings also suggest that using GenAI tools for pedagogical feedback could have varied results depending on students' L2 proficiency.

However, as Kim and Danilina (2025) have pointed out, one of the more pressing concerns regarding GenAI and L2 research and pedagogy's current focus on "skill enhancement. They stress that this narrative reinforces "assumptions about multilingual students' lack of writing skills and knowledge of Anglo-centric writing norms" (p. 3). Medina (2024) has also argued that while GenAI does present the potential to support students' ability to access common linguistic forms of SE, without careful approaches, GenAI "reinforces the colonial project of English education, silences non-dominant voices, and disrupts the opportunities for new ways of making meaning" (p. 75). This raises important questions regarding how GenAI pedagogical research and practice can support L2 learners with critical access to languages of power while at the same time providing opportunities for students and educators to critique GenAI's potential as a reinforcing agent of linguistic imperialism (Britton & Lorimer Leonard, 2020).

CRITICAL PEDAGOGY IN THE AGE OF GENAI: NAVIGATING EQUITY AND CONFORMITY FOR L2 LEARNERS

Developing a GenAI pedagogy that meaningfully supports L2 learners has become a central concern in recent scholarship, particularly as educators grapple with the dual imperatives of providing equitable access and resisting linguistic conformity. From an academic literacies' perspective, Kim and Dalinina (2025) advocate for a "multilayered approach…[that] fosters multilingual writers' critical awareness of competing literacy practices, writing norms, and the power imbalances embedded in both GenAI technologies and academic writing itself" (p. 3). This call aligns with broader movements toward critical digital pedagogy, as articulated by Baskara (2024) who examines the educational implications of ChatGPT through the lens of Paulo Freire's (2005) critical pedagogy. Critical digital pedagogy, like its foundational counterpart, seeks to "foster agency, greater empowerment, and social justice" through dialogic and reflective educational practices in digital spaces (Smith, 2024, p. 68). Morris and Stommel (2018) further define this approach as grounded in community relationships, and the inclusion of diverse voices, emphasizing the "need to reimagine communication across cultural and political boundaries" (para. 22). They advocate for learning environments where both students and teachers are active co-constructors of knowledge, rather than the banking model (Freire, 2005) in which students are passive vessel received information.

Baskara's (2024) application of this framework to GenAI highlights both its potential and its pitfalls. While tools like ChatGPT may "democratize" (p. 58) knowledge and "promote dialogue" (p. 64) through their conversational interfaces, they also risk encouraging passive consumption and reinforcing dominant linguistic norms. Critical digital pedagogy offers a promising foundation for educators seeking to integrate GenAI in ways that are dialogic, inclusive, and responsive to the lived experiences of L2 learners. Rather than positioning GenAI as a neutral tool, this approach invites educators to critically engage with its design, outputs, and implications—ensuring that pedagogical strategies do not simply facilitate access to SE but also empower students to question and reshape the linguistic hierarchies that structure academic writing.

PROMISING PRACTICES: INTEGRATING GENAI INTO CRITICAL PEDAGOGY OF WRITING INSTRUCTION

Promising practices are beginning to emerge at the intersection of critical pedagogy and GenAI integration, offering educators concrete strategies to support L2 learners without reinforcing linguistic conformity. These approaches aim to balance the potential of GenAI to provide linguistic access with the need to preserve students' diverse linguistic identities and foster critical engagement. The section below presents current research on pedagogical applications of GenAI from the perspective of critical digital pedagogy. Although calls for critical approaches to GenAI pedagogy are increasing, both praxis-oriented scholarship and empirical research remain limited. Qian's (2025) recent systematic review of GenAI pedagogical applications highlights a growing emphasis on using these tools to support critical thinking, dialogic learning, and student-teacher interaction. Drawing from this emerging body of literature, the following examples illustrate instructional strategies that reflect the principles of critical digital pedagogy and demonstrate how GenAI can be used not only to support writing development but also to challenge linguistic hierarchies and empower multilingual learners.

Integrating Prompt Generation

Building on these emerging pedagogical frameworks, one area gaining particular attention is the role of prompt generation in shaping how learners engage with GenAI tools. As GenAI systems rely heavily on user input to generate meaningful and contextually relevant responses, the ability to craft effective prompts becomes a critical literacy in itself (Lee & Palmer, 2025). While research on how best to support learners in developing prompt literacy is currently limited, these skills are essential to democratizing access and enhancing learner agency and an important consideration for enacting a critical digital pedagogy lens when introducing GenAI into educational environments.

Developing prompt literacy not only enhances the quality of GenAI output but also empowers learners to use these tools with greater intentionality and agency. A key component to equitable access and discerning use of GenAI tools is, therefore, the cultivation of skills in designing prompts that align with specific learning goals and reflect an understanding of both content and context. Bender (2024) provides an illustrative example of the "procedural knowledge" (p. 163) involved in applying a GenAI tool to the task of analyzing a poem. Students share an initial and refined prompt followed by a successful result. In their illustration, they demonstrate that the success of ChatGPT's output relies on a learner's knowledge of the task itself, for example, in providing ChatGPT with prominent theme from the poem and requesting an illustrative quotation to be the focus of the tool's analysis This example illustrates the importance of procedural knowledge in GenAI interactions by demonstrating how the refinement of prompts can significantly influence the quality of AI-generated responses. Building on this foundation, Cain (2024) offers a more structured framework for effective GenAI prompting, emphasizing three key components—*content knowledge*, *critical thinking*, and *iterative design*—that are particularly useful when considering how to support learners in developing prompt literacy. Cain's framework encourages considering how learners can enact their existing knowledge of a subject along with their goals for engaging with GenAI, to design more effective prompts as well as to develop critical strategies for "scrutinizing the AI's responses—ranging from bias detection to relevance assessment" (p. 50). Learning tasks can focus students on engaging in iterative prompting, a process of designing an initial prompt, evaluating the output it generates and applying this information to refine further prompts to achieve a learner's writing goal.

This approach emphasizes the use of multiple, sequential prompts—structured as a dialogue or chain-of-thought—to help learners refine their interactions with GenAI tools. It supports the development of procedural knowledge, encouraging students to build on prior prompts and responses to improve clarity, depth, and relevance. Critically, this method also exposes the limitations of GenAI systems, which often struggle to generate meaningful responses without highly structured, SE-aligned input. As Ranalli (2021) notes, these tools are designed with SE writers in mind, meaning their usability and effectiveness are significantly reduced for learners whose linguistic traditions deviate from those norms. Through iterative prompting, students can begin to recognize how GenAI's performance is shaped by its training data—and how that may exclude or misrepresent their own language practices.

This emphasis on intentional and iterative prompt design is particularly relevant in the context of L2 instruction, where learners benefit from structured opportunities to engage critically with language. One illustrative case study that applies these principles is Hwang et al.'s (2025) exploration of prompt generation as a tool to support vocabulary development and conceptual understanding among L2 students. Students in the study interacted with GenAI to develop and refine a generated image of a word to support dual coding. Students first were supported with content knowledge in that they were provided with information on historical derivations and cultural contexts for the word. In addition, they were asked to draw their own image based on their understanding of the word. This was followed by engagement in iterative prompting of the GenAI tool to create an image that they felt represented their understanding of the word best. Lastly, students were asked to reflect on their interactions with the tool. They concluded that through this process, learners demonstrated a high level of engagement in language learning as well as an appreciation for GenAI tools in supporting their learning. One important addition to this activity that we might suggest would be to equip students to assess generated images for biases through an initial exercise that provides students with examples of images that demonstrate bias as identified by scholars such as Nyaaba et al. (2024). Conducting their own analysis of the images they later generate as part of the activity could be included within the reflective task.

When considering the use of the prompt generation in an L2 context, it is important to consider the key features of the existing the research. This approach centers on student reflection as a tool for learning. Learners analyze how changes in word choice, tone, and structure affect the quality and relevance of GenAI-generated responses. This fosters more intentional and critical language use, helping students understand the rhetorical impact of their linguistic decisions (Pérez-Llantada, 2013). More importantly, it creates space for students to observe how GenAI may misunderstand or misrepresent non-Standard English (non-SE) expressions, such as dialects, idioms, or culturally specific phrasing. Zaini (2018) warns that automated writing feedback (AWF) can lead students to internalize biased feedback, encouraging them to suppress their sociolinguistic traits in favor of conforming to dominant norms. Reflective assessment helps students resist this pressure by critically examining the assumptions embedded in GenAI feedback and recognizing the value of their own linguistic identities.

Adopting a Process-Oriented Focus

Informed by decades of scholarship in composition studies, the process-oriented approach to writing emphasizes writing as a recursive, developmental act—one that values invention, drafting, revision, and reflection over the mere production of polished texts (Bender, 2024). This pedagogical stance is increasingly relevant in the age of GenAI, where the temptation to use tools as content creators risks undermining the learning process itself. Recent literature in GenAI and education reflects this concern. Qian's (2025) systematic review identifies learning support as one of the three primary pedagogical uses of GenAI, alongside automated feedback and critical thinking development. However, scholars caution that students may misuse GenAI to bypass learning, "exploit[ing] GenAI for academic credit without engaging in learning process" (Chang et al., 2023). These concerns echo long-standing debates in composition about authorship, originality, and the role of tools in writing.

To address these challenges, a process-based integration of GenAI—particularly for L2 learners—offers a promising path forward. Rather than treating GenAI as a shortcut to a final product, this approach positions it as a scaffold for learning, supporting students through the stages of writing while fostering critical digital literacy and writer agency.

Several articles discuss ways to incorporate GenAI into the traditional writing process. Lin (2024) discusses a collaborative framework in which the GenAI tool supports co-writing. Woo et al. (2025) describes a computer in the loop, where the GenAI tools support text-editing to L2 students during the composition process. A detailed example of a process-based approach to composition which integrates GenAI is provided by Kong et al. (2024) in the form of a six-part framework. Kong et al. (2024) offer a compelling pedagogical model grounded in self-regulated learning (SRL) and aligned with the values of composition studies. Their six-part framework—plan, prompt, preview, produce, peer-review, and portfolio-tracking—mirrors the recursive nature of writing and supports students in managing both their cognitive and emotional engagement with writing tasks.

- Plan: Students begin by identifying a writing goal or topic, echoing the pre-writing and invention stages in composition.
- Prompt: Learners use GenAI to explore ideas, generate content, or gather information—treating the tool as a brainstorming partner rather than a ghostwriter.
- Preview: Students critically assess the AI's output for accuracy, bias, and relevance, engaging in the kind of rhetorical analysis central to composition pedagogy.
- Produce: Learners synthesize GenAI outputs with their own research and perspectives, emphasizing writer agency and voice.
- Peer-Review: Collaborative feedback reinforces writing as a social process and supports revision.
- Portfolio-Tracking: Students reflect on their development over time, comparing their own writing with GenAI-generated texts and evaluating their growth.

Kong et al.'s (2024) framework and its encouragement to consider GenAI in the context of theories of learning, such as SRL, can guide the creation of meaningful, process-oriented learning activities that emphasize student agency and reflection where GenAI tools support their learning and performance. The authors emphasize that although their proposed model focuses on an academic writing task, they aimed for their design to be applicable for using GenAI in students' lives more broadly.

When viewed through the lens of critical pedagogy, as advocated by Williams and Condon (2016), this model also challenges the idealization of native or L1 writers by foregrounding writing as a communicative act embedded in cultural and social contexts. When integrated into Kong's stages—particularly during the plan, prompt, and preview phases—this perspective invites students to consider how GenAI interprets and responds to different language varieties, and to question why certain forms (typically SE) are privileged in AI-generated outputs.

- The plan phase: Students might begin by identifying a writing goal that draws on their cultural background or multilingual identity. For example, students may write a personal narrative that incorporates idioms or expressions from their home language. This planning stage invites students to reflect on how their linguistic choices communicate meaning and identity, and to anticipate how GenAI might respond to non-Standard English inputs.
- In the prompt phase: Students can experiment by crafting two different prompts for the same task—one using Standard English and another using a culturally specific dialect or phrasing. For instance, a student might ask GenAI to describe the meaning of a proverb in both SE and in a regional variation of English. This allows students to observe how GenAI interprets and responds to different linguistic registers, and to begin questioning the assumptions embedded in the tool's training data.
- During the preview phase: Students critically assess the AI-generated outputs, comparing how the tool handled the SE prompt versus the non-SE version. They might notice that the SE version yields a more coherent or confident response, while the non-SE version is misunderstood or flagged as unclear.

Combining author-focused dialogue with Kong's process model transforms GenAI from a passive writing aid into a site of inquiry, where students actively negotiate meaning, identity, and power in their writing. Through this process, students are not only developing writing skills but also cultivating critical digital literacy and asserting their agency as multilingual writers navigating AI-mediated environments.

Dialogue and Co-Creation

As GenAI continues to reshape educational practices and everyday communication, it presents a powerful opportunity for educators and students to engage in dialogue and co-construct knowledge about its broader implications. Paulo Freire's (2005) problem-posing model of education challenges the traditional banking models. It promotes a collaborative, dialogic learning environment in which both students and instructors actively participate in shaping understanding. Within the context of the GenAI, two forms of dialogic learning have been highlighted, student-instructor conversation and student-GenAI interactions.

In a recent educational blog titled *Conversation as care: Why talking to students about AI is our most essential task right now*, Jarenski (2024) shares a personal anecdote about entering into meaningful dialogue with students about the role of GenAI in education. They pose the question, "How do you feel about writing more with AI, when you think about it in relation specifically to your heart and your authenticity?" (para. 4)—a prompt that invites students to reflect not only on the tool itself but on their identities as writers. Jarenski argues that engaging students in open, reflective conversations about GenAI is an essential act of pedagogical care, especially given the technology's far-reaching implications, the uneven distribution of technical knowledge among students, and its potential to exacerbate classroom inequities. These conversations are not one-sided; rather, they model a dialogical learning relationship in which both instructor and students explore the ethical, emotional, and intellectual dimensions of GenAI together.

Practical guidance for fostering this kind of dialogue is increasingly available through post-secondary teaching and learning centres. For example, Ohio State University's (n.d.) *AI teaching strategies: Having conversations with students* offers instructors tools for initiating transparent, reflective discussions, including conversation starters and strategies for modeling critical engagement. The guide also emphasizes the importance of flexibility and responsiveness, recognizing that students may have varying levels of comfort and access when it comes to interacting with GenAI tools. Moreover, it raises important ethical considerations, such as the implications of asking students to submit their academic writing to GenAI platforms that may use this content for training purposes. These concerns intersect with broader issues of intellectual property and "epistemic inequality" raised by Jiang et al. (2024 p. 926), as students risk becoming an "exploited workforce" (p. 926) in machine learning systems. Together, these insights underscore the need for co-created, critically reflective classroom spaces where students and instructors can navigate the complexities of GenAI through ongoing, reciprocal dialogue.

Exploring GenAI's potential to function as dialogic partners in educational settings can further foster awareness of language as a social situated construction. Tang et al. (2024) examine this potential through the lens of Bakhtin's concept of heteroglossia, which emphasizes the inherently dialogic nature of language—where every utterance exists in relation to others within a "chain of discourse" (Artemeva, 2004, p. 9). Applying this framework to GenAI interactions allows educators to reposition GenAI not as a definitive source of knowledge, but as a participant in a broader, socially situated dialogue. Tang et al. argue that this perspective "redistributes epistemic authority from the technology itself to the wider community of knowers underscoring the importance of human expertise in validating and contextualizing knowledge" (p. 495). Their pedagogical model involves a four-step process: students pose a question, reflect critically on the AI's response, engage in further prompting to deepen the dialogue, and finally summarize their understanding in their own words. This process illustrates Bakhtin's "chain of utterances," where meaning emerges not from isolated statements but from the evolving relationship between questions and responses (Tang et al., 2024, p. 498).While this work involves a small sample in the context of high school students rather than post-secondary institutions, Tang et al.'s (2024) application of dialogic interaction through the lens of Bahktin's heteroglossia offers a promising conceptual positioning of the role GenAI as a conversation partner rather than a holder of knowledge and includes a prominent pedagogical step that engages students in critical thinking. Within this framework, GenAI is not treated as a neutral or authoritative tool, but as a participant in a shared inquiry—one that invites critical examination of language, power, authorship, and the sociocultural dynamics embedded in digital technologies.

While GenAI is often positioned as a dialogic partner in education, this conceptual framing must be grounded in a critical understanding of the system's epistemic limitations. As Habgood-Coote (2024) argues, GenAI systems—like search engines—are not neutral conveyors of knowledge but are embedded within broader socio-technical systems that reflect and reproduce structures of "white ignorance." These systems are trained on large-scale web crawls that disproportionately represent dominant cultural and linguistic norms, often marginalizing or misrepresenting non-dominant perspectives. Similarly, Luo et al. (2024) demonstrate that GenAI tools like ChatGPT exhibit significant language and cultural bias, frequently defaulting to Anglo-American viewpoints regardless of the user's linguistic or cultural context. This results in a form of epistemic narrowing, where the AI appears to engage in dialogue but actually mirrors back a limited, culturally filtered worldview. Thus, while GenAI may simulate conversation, its dialogic capacity is constrained by the biases and blind spots of its training data, making it essential for educators and learners to approach these tools with critical awareness and not as authoritative or contextually sensitive interlocutors.

Situated in lived experiences and real-world applications

Integrating GenAI in L2 settings in ways that support critical digital literacy needs to begin with a consideration of the individual identities of students and the experiences they bring to the learning environment (Kim & Danilina, 2025). This is critical to support students' development of academic writing in the context of GenAI tools as well as engage students in culturally responsive classrooms that honour their multilingual and multicultural identities and lived experience (Song, 2025). Nyaaba et al. (2024) demonstrate current risks of cultural imperialism through several illustrations of western bias embedded within GenAI. Their discussion, supported by examples, ranges from predominate depictions of whiteness to biases towards western ways of knowing in GenAI responses as well as overt instances of harmful stereotypes. Their discussion focuses on developing broader "human-centric and liberatory" (para. 1) approaches in GenAI tool development to mitigate harmful perpetuations of bias. In relation to pedagogical practice, however, they emphasize the potential alienating impact of existing biases on non-western students as they engage with GenAI tools and recommend a focus on prompting skills that include cultural references to improve culturally responsive outputs.

An example of GenAI learning activity design that aims to provide "ample opportunities to invest and engage in students' multiliteracies development that goes beyond the traditional forms of academic literacies" is presented by Song (2025, p. 88). Song details an action research initiative, describing three activities ranging from creating a cooking show which enabled students to engage in cultural knowledge around a recipe of their choice to developing a roleplay connected to real-world scenarios, such as preparing for an interview or renting an apartment. Alongside these activities, Song designed tailored GenAI activities to scaffold learners' research processes or assist them by providing culturally and socially situated knowledge where relevant. Learners also engaged in "cross-checking the meanings and contexts of the new knowledge and cultural connotations with the familiar context of learners' first languages and cultures" (p. 97), for example comparing western resume formats with resume formats prevalent in China. Song's approach exemplifies an innovative pedagogical method for embracing multiliteracies into L2 teaching supported by GenAI, in ways that honour students' identities, create space for critical reflection and encourage a "diversity as power/empowerment" (p. 87) frame, and mitigate risks of cultural and linguistic imperialism embedded within GenAI tools.

A critical pedagogical approach to GenAI in educational settings should also incorporate reflection and offer learners opportunities to reflect on conditions of power for the purposes of promoting equity (Baskara, 2024). As discussed above, GenAI tools have the potential to exacerbate linguistic imperialism, thus, applications of critical digital pedagogy must consider ways in which learners can actively explore biases embedded within the content it generates. Kim and Danilini (2025) suggest for instance, that educators could engage learners in "critiqu[ing] a GenAI generated text, considering cultural biases and the hegemony of English to challenge the limitations inherent in GenAI technologies" (p.3). This approach reflects Britton and Lorimer Leonard (2020) focus on critical language awareness, which involves attending to and questioning the ways in which some languages and language norms hold dominance. Although their approach is not presented within the context of

GenAI, they similarly recommend providing opportunities for students to engage in critical reflection in ways that challenge their existing assumptions.

TOWARD CRITICAL ENGAGEMENT: REFLECTING ON POWER, LANGUAGE, AND AI

In the context of GenAI and critical educational approaches, Darvin (2025) offered a number of suggestions for engaging learners in critical digital literacy activities. Many of these activities are embedded in the promising practices discussed, including

1. Asking a platform to revise a text they have written and analyzing the extent to which the revision changes the voice, stance and style they originally employed;
2. Using different platforms to achieve the same writing task, comparing interactions with the tools, and reflecting on the extent to which the designs and responses of these platforms shaped such interactions;
3. Uploading the same text to different platforms and comparing the writing feedback and recommended rhetorical strategies they provide;
4. Prompting a platform to generate images for a narrative they have written, and examining the patterns in which identities are represented in such images; and
5. Engaging in translanguaging while asking the GenAI platform for feedback on their writing, and comparing the extent to which the tools recognize their L1s and provide sufficient responses. (Darvin, 2025, p. 5).

LIMITATIONS

Integrating GenAI into L2 instruction presents promising opportunities, but it also comes with significant limitations that educators must critically consider. One major concern is material inequity among students, as highlighted by Darvin (2025). Access to GenAI tools often depends on the availability and quality of technology—students with only smartphones may face usability challenges compared to those with laptops or desktops. Furthermore, many GenAI platforms offer tiered services, where premium features—such as advanced writing support, translation accuracy, or extended usage—are locked behind paywalls. This creates a digital divide, privileging students who can afford these services and disadvantaging those who cannot. Such disparities risk reinforcing existing educational inequities, making it essential for educators to adopt inclusive strategies that ensure equitable access and meaningful engagement with GenAI tools for all learners.

The integration of GenAI into L2 instruction raises significant privacy concerns that educators must carefully consider. As highlighted in both Xiang (2024) and Liu et al. (2024), GenAI models are often trained on vast, uncurated datasets that may include sensitive personal information, such as biometric data, private communications, or identifiable user content, often without informed consent. These models can inadvertently memorize and regurgitate such data, posing risks of unintended disclosure. In educational settings, where students may input personal narratives, voice recordings, or culturally specific content into AI tools, the potential for privacy breaches becomes particularly acute. Moreover, the lack of transparency around how student data is stored, used, or potentially retrained into future models exacerbates these risks. Without robust privacy safeguards, including differential privacy techniques and clear data governance policies, the use of GenAI in L2 classrooms could compromise student confidentiality and trust, especially among vulnerable or marginalized learners.

CONCLUSION

This chapter aimed to highlight long standing issues of linguistic imperialism alongside more recent scholarship critiquing GenAI's role in reinforcing the privileging of SE in the context of L2 academic writing pedagogy. Alongside this discussion, in acknowledgement of the potential that GenAI tools present for improving L2 students' access to language learning, rather than advocating for limiting GenAI pedagogical integration, this chapter offered an exploration of current scholarship of L2 GenAI pedagogy through the lens of critical pedagogy and critical digital pedagogy. Throughout our discussion, we both report on and extend pedagogical examples of process-oriented and dialogic learning activities designed to support L2 learners in developing agency and critical approaches to both utilize GenAI tools effectively while challenging their cultural and linguistic biases. In shaping this chapter, it is clear that while there is a growing body of research exploring pedagogical applications of GenAI, more studies examining the application of critical pedagogical approaches is urgently needed to foster ethical and inclusive approaches to GenAI pedagogy for L2 post-secondary students.

REFERENCES

Anya, U. (2020). African Americans in world language study: The forged path and future directions. *Annual Review of Applied Linguistics*, *40*, 97–112. DOI: 10.1017/S0267190520000070

Artemeva, N. (2004). Key concepts in rhetorical genre studies: An overview. *Discourse and Writing/Rédactologie, 20*(1), 3–38. DOI: 10.31468/cjsdwr.524

Baskara, F. (2024). ChatGPT and critical digital pedagogy: Examining the potential and challenges for educational practice. *Proceeding of The International Conference of Innovation, Science, Technology, Education, Children, and Health, 4*(1), 57–73. DOI: 10.62951/icistech.v4i1.80

Bender, S. M. (2024). Awareness of Artificial Intelligence as an essential digital literacy: ChatGPT and Gen-AI in the classroom. *Changing English, 31*(2), 161–174. DOI: 10.1080/1358684X.2024.2309995

Britton, E. R., & Lorimer Leonard, R. (2020). The social justice potential of critical reflection and critical language awareness pedagogies for L2 writers. *Journal of Second Language Writing*, *50*, 100776. DOI: 10.1016/j.jslw.2020.100776

Cain, W. (2024). Prompting change: Exploring prompt engineering in large language model AI and its potential to transform education. *TechTrends*, *68*(1), 47–57. DOI: 10.1007/s11528-023-00896-0

Calma, A., Cotronei-Baird, V., & Chia, A. (2022). Grammarly: An instructional intervention for writing enhancement in management education. *International Journal of Management Education*, *20*(3), 100704. DOI: 10.1016/j.ijme.2022.100704

Chan, C. K. Y., & Hu, W. (2023). Students' voices on generative AI: Perceptions, benefits, and challenges in higher education. *International Journal of Educational Technology in Higher Education*, *20*(1), 43. DOI: 10.1186/s41239-023-00411-8

Chang, D. H., Lin, M. P.-C., Hajian, S., & Wang, Q. Q. (2023). Educational design principles of using AI chatbot that supports self-regulated learning in education: Goal setting, feedback, and personalization. *Sustainability*, *15*(17), 12921. DOI: 10.3390/su151712921

Cheuk, T. (2021). Can AI be racist? Color-evasiveness in the application of machine learning to science assessments. *Science Education*, *105*(5), 825–836. DOI: 10.1002/sce.21671

Clements, G., & Petray, M. (2021). Languaging matters. In *Linguistic discrimination in US higher education: Power, prejudice, impacts, and remedies* (pp. 189–202). Routledge.

Dang, A., & Wang, H. (2024). Ethical use of generative AI for writing practices: Addressing linguistically diverse students in U.S. universities' AI statements. *Journal of Second Language Writing*, *66*, 101157. DOI: 10.1016/j.jslw.2024.101157

Darvin, R. (2025). The need for critical digital literacies in generative AI-mediated L2 writing. *Journal of Second Language Writing*, *67*, 101186. DOI: 10.1016/j.jslw.2025.101186

Dobinson, T., Mercieca, P., & Kent, S. (2019). World englishes in academic writing: Exploring Markers' responses. In Dobinson, T., & Dunworth, K. (Eds.), *Literacy unbound: Multiliterate, multilingual, multimodal* (pp. 11–30). Springer., DOI: 10.1007/978-3-030-01255-7_2

Fathi, J., & Rahimi, M. (2024). Utilising artificial intelligence-enhanced writing mediation to develop academic writing skills in EFL learners: S qualitative study. *Computer Assisted Language Learning*, •••, 1–40. DOI: 10.1080/09588221.2024.2374772

Godwin-Jones, R. (2022). Partnering with AI: Intelligent writing assistance and instructed language learning. *Language Learning & Technology*, *26*(2), 5–24.

Habgood-Coote, J. (2024). Search engines, white ignorance, and the social epistemology of technology. *Philosophy (London, England)*, *99*(3), 479–510. DOI: 10.1017/S003181912400007X

Heng Hartse, J., & Kubota, R. (2014). Pluralizing English? Variation in high-stakes academic texts and challenges of copyediting. *Journal of Second Language Writing*, *24*, 71–82. DOI: 10.1016/j.jslw.2014.04.001

Huang, J., & Mizumoto, A. (2025). The effects of generative AI usage in EFL classrooms on the L2 motivational self system. *Education and Information Technologies*, *30*(5), 6435–6454. DOI: 10.1007/s10639-024-13071-6

Huang, K. (2023, January 19). Alarmed by A.I. chatbots, universities start revamping how they teach. *New York Times*. https://www.nytimes.com/2023/01/16/technology/chatgpt-artificial-intelligence-universities.html

Hwang, M., Lee, K. H., & Lee, H. K. (2025). A word to the wise: Crafting impactful prompts for ChatGPT. *System*, *133*, 103756. DOI: 10.1016/j.system.2025.103756

Hwang, W.-Y., Nurtantyana, R., Purba, S. W. D., Hariyanti, U., Indrihapsari, Y., & Surjono, H. D. (2023). AI and recognition technologies to facilitate english as foreign language writing for supporting personalization and contextualization in authentic contexts. *Journal of Educational Computing Research, 61*(5), 1008–1035. DOI: 10.1177/07356331221137253

Ishaque, M., & Khan, R. (2018). Empowering English speakers through diversification and promotion of World Englishes. *Advances in Language and Literary Studies, 9*(6), 93. DOI: 10.7575/aiac.alls.v.9n.6p.93

James, T., & Andrews, G. (2024). Levelling the playing field through GenAI: Harnessing artificial intelligence to bridge educational gaps for equity and disadvantaged students. *Widening Participation and Lifelong Learning: the Journal of the Institute for Access Studies and the European Access Network, 26*(3), 250–260. DOI: 10.5456/WPLL.26.3.250

Jarenski, S. (2024). *Conversation as care: Why talking to students about AI is our most essential task right now*. University of Michigan. https://dearbornhub.net/conversation-as-care-why-talking-to-students-about-ai-is-our-most-essential-task-right-now/

Jiang, J., Vetter, M. A., & Lucia, B. (2024). Toward a 'more-than-digital' AI literacy: Reimagining agency and authorship in the postdigital era with ChatGPT. *Postdigital Science and Education, 6*(3), 922–939. DOI: 10.1007/s42438-024-00477-1

Kachru, B. (1990). World Englishes and applied linguistics. *World Englishes, 9*(1), 3–20. DOI: 10.1111/j.1467-971X.1990.tb00683.x

Kim, J., & Danilina, E. (2025). Towards inclusive and equitable assessment practices in the age of GenAI: Revisiting academic literacies for multilingual students in academic writing. *Innovations in Education and Teaching International, 1–5*. Advance online publication. DOI: 10.1080/14703297.2025.2456223

Koltovskaia, S. (2020). Student engagement with automated written corrective feedback (AWCF) provided by Grammarly: A multiple case study. *Assessing Writing, 44*, 100450. DOI: 10.1016/j.asw.2020.100450

Kong, S.-C., Lee, J. C.-K., & Tsang, O. (2024). A pedagogical design for self-regulated learning in academic writing using text-based generative artificial intelligence tools: 6-P pedagogy of plan, prompt, preview, produce, peer-review, portfolio-tracking. *Research and Practice in Technology Enhanced Learning, 19*, 030. https://doi.org/ DOI: 10.58459/rptel.2024.19030

Lai, C. Y., Cheung, K. Y., & Chan, C. S. (2023). Exploring the role of intrinsic motivation in ChatGPT adoption to support active learning: An extension of the technology acceptance model. *Computers and Education: Artificial Intelligence*, *5*, 100178. DOI: 10.1016/j.caeai.2023.100178

Laupichler, M. C., Aster, A., Schirch, J., & Raupach, T. (2022). Artificial intelligence literacy in higher and adult education: A scoping literature review. *Computers and Education: Artificial Intelligence*, *3*, 100101. DOI: 10.1016/j.caeai.2022.100101

Lee, D., & Palmer, E. (2025). Prompt engineering in higher education: A systematic review to help inform curricula. *International Journal of Educational Technology in Higher Education*, *22*(1), 7. DOI: 10.1186/s41239-025-00503-7

Levendowski, A. (2018). How copyright law can fix artificial intellience's implicit bias problem. *Washington Law Review (Seattle, Wash.)*, *93*, 579–630.

Liang, W., Yuksekgonul, M., Mao, Y., Wu, E., & Zou, J. (2023). GPT detectors are biased against non-native English writers. *Patterns (New York, N.Y.)*, *4*(7), 100779. DOI: 10.1016/j.patter.2023.100779 PMID: 37521038

Lin, Z. (2024). Techniques for supercharging academic writing with generative AI. *Nature Biomedical Engineering*, *9*(4), 426–431. DOI: 10.1038/s41551-024-01185-8 PMID: 38499642

Liu, Y., Huang, J., Li, Y., Wang, D., & Xiao, B. (2024). Generative AI model privacy: A survey. *Artificial Intelligence Review*, *58*(1), 33. DOI: 10.1007/s10462-024-11024-6

Lu, Q., Yao, Y., Xiao, L., Yuan, M., Wang, J., & Zhu, X. (2024). Can ChatGPT effectively complement teacher assessment of undergraduate students' academic writing? *Assessment & Evaluation in Higher Education*, *49*(5), 616–633. DOI: 10.1080/02602938.2024.2301722

Luo, Q., Puett, M., & Smith, M. (2024). *A "perspectival" mirror of the elephant: Investigating language bias on Google, ChatGPT, YouTube, and Wikipedia.* arXiv preprin*t.* arXiv: 2303.16281

Mahboob, A., & Szenes, E. (2010). Linguicism and racism in assessment practices in higher education. *Linguistics and the Human Sciences*, *3*(3), 325–354. DOI: 10.1558/lhs.v3i3.325

Medina, D. (2024). *Generative AI in Writing Education.* Routledge., DOI: 10.4324/9781003493563-5

Mohammadkarimi, E. (2023). Teachers' reflections on academic dishonesty in EFL students' writings in the era of artificial intelligence. *Journal of Applied Learning & Teaching*, *6*(2). Advance online publication. DOI: 10.37074/jalt.2023.6.2.10

Morris, S., & Stommel, J. (2018). *An urgency of teachers*. Pressbooks. https://pressbooks.pub/criticaldigitalpedagogy/

Nyaaba, M., Wright, A., & Choi, G. (2024). *Generative AI and digital neocolonialism in global education: Towards an equitable framework*. arXiv preprint. arXiv: 2406.02966

O'Neill, R., & Russel, A. (2019). Stop! Grammar time: University students' perception of automated feedback program Grammarly. *Australasian Journal of Educational Technology*, *35*(1), 42–56.

Ogunniyi, V., & O'Neil, K. (2022). "We can do this in our classes, but what about students in other classes and out in the world?": How educators imagine code-meshers and their audiences. *Journal of College Reading and Learning*, *52*(4), 321–351. DOI: 10.1080/10790195.2022.2116127

Ohio State University. (n.d.). *AI teaching strategies: Having conversations with students*. https://teaching.resources.osu.edu/teaching-topics/ai-teaching-strategies-having

Otterbacher, J. (2023). Why technical solutions for detecting AI-generated content in research and education are insufficient. *Patterns (New York, N.Y.)*, *4*(7). Advance online publication. DOI: 10.1016/j.patter.2023.100796 PMID: 37521044

Page, C. (2023). Academic language development and linguistic discrimination. *Comparative and International Education*, *52*(2). Advance online publication. DOI: 10.5206/cie-eci.v52i2.15000

Pedersen, I. (2023). The rise of generative AI and enculturating AI writing in postsecondary education. *Frontiers in Artificial Intelligence*, *6*. Advance online publication. DOI: 10.3389/frai.2023.1259407 PMID: 37635912

Peres, R., Schreier, M., Schweidel, D., & Sorescu, A. (2023). On ChatGPT and beyond: How generative artificial intelligence may affect research, teaching, and practice. *International Journal of Research in Marketing*, *40*(2), 269–275. DOI: 10.1016/j.ijresmar.2023.03.001

Pérez-Llantada, C. (2013). 'Glocal' rhetorical practices in academic writing. *European Journal of English Studies*, *17*(3), 251–268. DOI: 10.1080/13825577.2013.867180

Phillipson, R. (1997). Realities and myths of linguistic imperialism. *Journal of Multilingual and Multicultural Development*, *18*(3), 238–248.

Qian, Y. (2025). Pedagogical applications of generative AI in higher education: A systematic review of the field. *TechTrends*. Advance online publication. DOI: 10.1007/s11528-025-01100-1

Ranalli, J. (2021). L2 student engagement with automated feedback on writing: Potential for learning and issues of trust. *Journal of Second Language Writing*, *52*, 100816. DOI: 10.1016/j.jslw.2021.100816

Sharma, B. K., & Hussein, I. (2021). Discourses of professional identities and linguistic capital formation of international STEM faculty. *Journal of English for Academic Purposes*, *52*, 100997. DOI: 10.1016/j.jeap.2021.100997

Shin, H., & Sterzuk, A. (2019). Discourses, practices, and realities of multilingualism in higher education. *TESL Canada Journal*, *1*, 147–159. DOI: 10.18806/tesl.v36i1.1307

Shin, Y., & Kim, G. (2022). The effect of automated written feedback through Grammarly. *Multimedia-Assisted Language Learning*, *25*(2), 84–102.

Smith, E. (2024). Building critical digital literacies for social media through educational development. *Journal of Contemporary Issues in Education*, *19*(2), 64–89. DOI: 10.20355/jcie29599

Smith, G., Fleisig, E., Bossi, M., Rustagi, I., & Yin, X. (2025). *Standard language ideology in AI-Generated Language*. arXiv preprint. arXiv: 2406.08726

Song, H. (2025). When ELT meets AI: Reshaping EDI-centric EAP teaching. *Multicultural Education Review*, *17*(1), 84–100. DOI: 10.1080/2005615X.2025.2467807

Sterzuk, A. (2015). 'The standard remains the same': Language standardisation, race and othering in higher education. *Journal of Multilingual and Multicultural Development*, *36*(1), 53–66. DOI: 10.1080/01434632.2014.892501

Tang, K. S., Cooper, G., Rappa, N., Cooper, M., Sims, C., & Nonis, K. (2024). A dialogic approach to transform teaching, learning & assessment with generative AI in secondary education: A proof of concept. *Pedagogies*, *19*(3), 493–503. DOI: 10.1080/1554480X.2024.2379774

Trahar, S., Juntrasook, A., Burford, J., von Kotze, A., & Wildemeersch, D. (2019). Hovering on the periphery? 'Decolonising' writing for academic journals. *Compare: A Journal of Comparative Education*, *49*(1), 149–167. DOI: 10.1080/03057925.2018.1545817

Wach, K., Duong, C. D., Ejdys, J., Kazlauskaitė, R., Korzynski, P., Mazurek, G., Paliszkiewicz, J., & Ziemba, E. (2023). The dark side of generative artificial intelligence: A critical analysis of controversies and risks of ChatGPT. *Entrepreneurial Business and Economics Review*, *11*(2), 7–30. DOI: 10.15678/EBER.2023.110201

Wang, H., & Dang, A. N. (2024). *Enhancing L2 writing with Generative AI: A systematic review of pedagogical integration and outcomes*. DOI: 10.13140/RG.2.2.19572.16005

Wang, T., Lund, B. D., Marengo, A., Pagano, A., Mannuru, N. R., Teel, Z. A., & Pange, J. (2023). Exploring the potential impact of Artificial Intelligence (AI) on international students in higher education: Generative AI, chatbots, analytics, and international student success. *Applied Sciences (Switzerland)*, *13*(11). DOI: 10.3390/app13116716

Williams, J., & Condon, F. (2016). Translingualism in composition studies and second language writing: An uneasy alliance. *TESL Canada Journal*, *33*(2), 1. DOI: 10.18806/tesl.v33i2.1234

Woelfel, K. (2023). *Late applications: Disproportionate effects of Generative AI-Detectors on English learners*. Center for Democracy and Technology. https://cdt.org/insights/brief-late-applications-disproportionate-effects-of-generative-ai-detectors-on-english-learners/

Woo, D., Yu, Y., & Guo, K. (2025). *Exploring EFL secondary students' AI-generated text editing while composition writing*. arXiv preprint. arXiv: 2505.17041

Xiang, A. (2024). Fairness & privacy in an age of Generative AI. *Science and Technology Law Review*, *25*(2). DOI: 10.52214/stlr.v25i2.12765

Xiao, P., Chen, Y., & Bao, W. (2023). *Waiting, banning, and embracing: An empirical analysis of adapting policies for Generative AI in higher education*. arXiv preprint. arXiv: 2305.18617

Zaini, A. (2018). Word processors as monarchs: Computer-generated feedback can exercise power over and influence EAL learners' identity representations. *Computers & Education*, *120*, 112–126. DOI: 10.1016/j.compedu.2018.01.014

ENDNOTE

1. The authors wanted to acknowledge the limitation of the term English Language Learners as it implies a deficit model of the language that the article

criticizes. As a result, the author has chosen to refer to L2 students; however, L2 is also a flawed concept. The authors also recognize the limitation of the L2 as it fails to reflect the multilingual backgrounds of these writers, of which English is one of many spoken and written languages.

Chapter 13
The New Age Pedagogy: Addressing the Learning Dimensions and Ethical Challenges of the Use of AI in Higher Education

Adorn Verma
GNA University, India

Pramendra Singh
https://orcid.org/0000-0002-9142-265X
Marwadi University, India

ABSTRACT

In the world of digitalization, Artificial Intelligence (AI) is bringing a deep revolution in higher education. This study examines the emergence of New Age Pedagogy, a learner-centered AI enhanced model that prepares different pupils' cognitive, emotional, social and metacognitive needs. AI-based tools, from intelligent tutoring systems to personalized and instant analytical feedback, increase learner participation, performance, and self-regulation, helping cultivate different learning methods and contributing to effective educational impact. The issue of using the AI calls pressing ethical questions such as data privacy misconception, algorithmic bias, academic dishonesty, and transparency and trust erosion. Such risks emphasize the necessity of strong ethics of governance, reflective curriculum design and humanity-AI partnership. The chapter argues for incorporating ethics in educational frameworks and advocates for participatory and interdisciplinary approaches to policy making focused on the ecological interrelations of AI, systems within an educational space.

DOI: 10.4018/979-8-3373-3000-6.ch013

1. INTRODUCTION

The quick technological advancement during the last decade brought major shifts to how humans interact with their environment, especially in educational systems. Artificial intelligence (AI) is the most transformable technical achievement that fundamentally alters the processes of creating and acquiring knowledge and delivering information today. The educational environment of higher education implements AI as an integrated teaching component beyond its role in administrative tasks and content distribution (Baillifard et al., 2023). Different AI technological implementations, including smart tutoring software, predictive analytic frameworks, and adaptive learning systems, modify how teachers interact with students and how both parties engage with educational content. The migration requires educators to readjust their educational frameworks while thinking about ethical implications and the foundation of their educational theories (Maity and Deroy, 2024).

Modern pedagogical practices will be understood through the term "New Age Pedagogy." This progressive method combines teaching techniques with emerging technology adoption, specifically AI, to build an integrated platform that improves the whole learning process (Katsamakas et al., 2024). Experienced educators must handle their responsibilities carefully when deploying such technologies since these environments possess intellectual formative elements as well as complex social and ethical considerations (Halkiopoulos and Gkintoni, 2024). The purpose of New Age Pedagogy is to unite technology modifications with education's multidimensional learning processes. Hence, education continues to be human-connected and socially comprehensive in the time of digital disruption (McDonald et al., 2024).

This study is primarily developed through a review of the existing literature on AI in higher education, with particular focus on pedagogical and ethical challenges. The author writes from the positionality of an Assistant Professor who mentors doctoral students and conducts research on the use of AI in higher education. While the discussion is not based on empirical classroom data, this professional background informs the interpretation of the literature and frames the critical perspective adopted throughout the research.

The primary purpose of this research exists in two critical elements which guide its development. The study examines the points where AI engages different learning domains, including cognitive processes, emotional dynamics, social elements, and self-regulation capabilities, to foster better educational results within higher education systems (Sajja et al., 2024). The research examines the ethical problems when AI is integrated into educational teaching methods and learning practices (Popenici and Kerr, 2017). The introduction of AI into modern learning systems brings four main challenges to educational institutions, which consist of problems with data security and biased algorithms, together with academic honour and AI system transparency

(Halkiopoulos and Gkintoni, 2024). The educational values of fairness, trust, autonomy, and accountability face challenges stemming from specific issues.

Learning processes involving memory, attention, reasoning, and problem-solving experience major disruptions via AI systems, which produce adaptive feedback elements while adapting both learning paths and assessment automation features (Maity and Deroy, 2024). The educational tools that improve comprehension possess the capacity to dissolve complex intellectual development into numerical data, which fails to capture emotional learning processes. Terms like sentiment analysis and affective computing, stemming from AI enable emotional data collection and emotional response capabilities among learners (Halkiopoulos and Gkintoni, 2024). The implementation of these promising technologies introduces serious worry about both electronic monitoring of emotions and the natural connection between instructors and their students (McDonald et al., 2024).

The redefinition of learning's social elements involves transforming how people interact while maintaining communication and sensitivity towards different cultures. Access inequality to AI tools can create unintentional social gaps while the technology supports worldwide collaboration and student-learner interactions through virtual platforms. AI systems have potential as tools to develop the metacognitive dimension of learning because they provide learners with reflective prompts and self-regulated learning aid systems (Halkiopoulos and Gkintoni, 2024). Excess use of AI presents the danger that human independence for critical thought and self-efficacy development will become compromised. Educational technology tools create both ethical problems alongside multiple teaching challenges and obstacles. Student data collection and subsequent analysis for AI model production create substantial privacy and surveillance concerns. Implementing digital profiling and data management by institutions requires decisions about consent procedures, data rights, and future effects of digital data (Chan, 2023). The systematic maintenance of educational outcomes becomes worse or stronger because of biased data and flawed design within AI algorithms. The growth of AI content generation and automated assessment systems makes academic honesty evaluation more challenging for educators who must reconsider their evaluation practices and intellectual work requirements. Understanding how AI systems operate is necessary for students and faculty members because they must grasp AI decisions that influence educational outcomes (McDonald et al., 2024).

Implementing AI into higher education requires a framework combining technological ability with education goals and moral accountability. This report supports an explicit reformation of educational teaching methods to guide the utilisation of AI while promoting the core educational principles and societal objectives. To integrate AI responsibly, the educational system needs human-machine alliances, ethical teaching plan development, and complete protection for every stakeholder's rights. The method should be adaptable as it understands both AI's continuous change and different uses of its technology across multiple settings. The report presents an AI Ecological Education Policy Framework, which studies the joint operation of technological platforms and educational systems with ethical considerations. The framework bases its approach on sustainability, inclusivity, and interdependency to guarantee both innovation and future-forward education that maintains equity when integrating AI (Chan, 2023). This ecological perspective of education as an interconnected system develops policies that support long-term health outcomes for educational institutions, students, and teaching staff. The report's final sections point ahead regarding educational systems requiring complex understanding and partnership design with diverse groups for AI advancement and multi-disciplinary studies of education alongside computer science, ethics, sociology, and psychology. Strategies must lead the way when using AI in education because they allow navigation through educational uncertainties while building teaching methods that match technology sophistication (Katsamakas et al., 2024).

This research project undertakes an in-depth and analytical evaluation of how AI influences higher education teaching practices. The study balances theory with practical knowledge because educating students with AI tools is unavoidable yet critical to the fulfilment of human progress, social equality, and democratic principles. Our current position between educational renewal and innovative technology demands a creative perspective on modern teaching and learning practices in the twenty-first century. The redesign of education systems requires technical possibilities, clear moral principles, deep teaching expertise, and a united desire to achieve the full success of all students.

To guide the reader through the following discussion, this study is structured around four key questions:

1. How does AI reshape the cognitive, emotional, social, and metacognitive dimensions of learning in higher education?
2. What ethical challenges arise from AI-enabled pedagogical practices, such as privacy, bias, academic integrity, and transparency?
3. How can New Age Pedagogy integrate AI while preserving human-centric educational values?
4. What institutional and policy frameworks are necessary to ensure responsible and inclusive AI adoption in higher education?

2. UNDERSTANDING NEW AGE PEDAGOGY

The digital age speeds up transformations within higher education, leading educational institutions to challenge traditional teaching models through restructuring and innovation. The evolving sense of how present-day learners learn differently from students of the past enables this educational reform. The rise of adaptive interconnected education patterns established New Age Pedagogy as an educational approach that uses emerging technological ecosystems represented by AI and various others. The teaching methods of New Age Pedagogy replace traditional lecture-based instruction with student-focused dynamic educational practices (Strielkowski et al., 2025). The approach emphasises being flexible rather than rigid, offering customized learning instead of standardized programs, and involves students in collaborative education delivery. The approach shows constant change because it adapts to modern digital systems developments and cultural value transformations while responding to worldwide proficiency demands. The distinctive feature of this teaching model goes beyond adopting new tools because it rebuilds the foundation that shapes the classroom interactions between teachers and learners (Morrow et al., 2023). Within New Age Pedagogy, the educator takes on multiple functions, including facilitator, mentor, and learning architect, instead of being considered the primary knowledge source. The pedagogical model enables learners to be energetic meaning creators through their active involvement with various information sources found in interactive multimodal learning platforms (Widiatna, 2020).

The educational evolution takes place through an extensive transformation in understanding how knowledge operates. Modern society requires teaching students to master digital literacy alongside cultural, emotional, and ethical literacy. Schoolchildren must now learn to handle advanced information networks, demonstrate analytical skills for content, and connect with various fields of learning (Buckley and Kukhareva, 2021). Because of these needs, pedagogical strategies must be designed with adaptable frameworks that enable different learning patterns yet still uphold academic standards. The essential quality of New Age Pedagogy consists of integrating knowledge with real-world circumstances. Academic developers now create learning experiences that mirror real-world issues to help students convert theoretical knowledge into practical solutions for society, innovation development, and ethical problems. Student interest increases, thereby developing a vital lifelong learning disposition, which is central in times of perpetual change. The educational transformation depends fundamentally on technology, although it remains an essential component without other alternatives (Commission - for Education, 2017). New Age Pedagogy advocates for the defined and careful use of digital tools, including AI, augmented reality, and learning analytics systems as educational methodologies. This purpose bypasses mechanical conversion of traditional approaches through the development of fresh approaches, which escalate inventive power while fostering inquiry functions and collaborative learning activities. The new educational approach of New Age Pedagogy establishes an intelligent educational system which breaks away from traditional inflexible instructional frameworks and adapts to meaningful learning contexts at present and in the future (Pandey et al., 2023). The approach understands that contemporary education escapes conventional physical classrooms and fixed teaching plans. Knowledge development occurs across networks, platforms, and communities because co-learning is continuous, and adaptability plays a central role (Rohi et al., 2025).

3. AI AND LEARNING DIMENSIONS IN HIGHER EDUCATION

The application of AI in education is supported by digital technology, but does not oppose the tradition of education. AI affects education through system management functions and how students receive knowledge as well as process and think about it. AI technologies analyse current feedback touchpoints to create individualized educational material, which students receive in real-time. This section explores the impact of AI across four core dimensions of learning in higher education: cognitive, emotional, social, and metacognitive.

3.1 Cognitive Dimension

Brain learning relies heavily on intellectual operations to perform reasoning, analysis, and memory functions. Performance analysis in new AI systems helps educators schedule dynamic educational timing for students and personalize their practice schedules. During testing, students can benefit from personalized learning paths generated through the combination of concept mapping software and AI tutors who perform continuous assessment activities (Baillifard et al., 2023). The adaptive learning operations conducted by Educational AI platform systems have replaced traditional educational methods within digital learning environments. AI technology helps discover learning gaps that remain unobserved in typical large classroom settings. Technology delivers early intervention and stress reduction to students through its capability to intervene immediately after they face difficulties independently. The intervention system enables teachers to detect learning difficulties before they escalate into confused states for students. The ability of AI to use text-based and visual elements combined with interactive design improves student retention of taught content. New educational systems built on AI platforms develop methods to enhance cognitive student performance (Halkiopoulos and Gkintoni, 2024).

In practice, educators often face challenges in balancing AI-driven personalization with the need to cultivate independent critical thinking among students. While adaptive systems can accelerate learning progress, they may also encourage over-reliance on automated feedback, reducing opportunities for students to struggle productively and develop resilience. This tension reflects a key pedagogical challenge in integrating AI tools into cognitive learning processes.

3.2 Emotional Dimension

The study has proven that emotions are critical in student learning because they influence motivation levels and attention and help increase student resilience. Current programs that analyse student emotions work with facial expression analysis, digital communication detection, and voice tone recognition systems. Educational technology tools help teachers adjust their classroom setup to meet the emotional requirements of their students. An AI system measures student emotion by recording their interactions and automatically adjusting tasks according to student needs during cognitive breaks, and it delivers motivational messages. The system tracks student emotional development within hybrid and online formats to establish areas for educational interactions that connect emotionally, even when human teachers might not detect these changes. Virtual assistants combined with affective computing functions now assist in real-time responses through chatbots to help students feel less distant in remote education platforms. The emotional capabilities of AI systems create important concerns about monitoring individuals without their consent. Secure systems must handle emotional data storage because personal data with sensitive characteristics occurs naturally. Students require assurance that no one will misread or abuse their emotional displays (Keshishi and Hack, 2023). Emotionally intelligent AI systems will be effective when their processes remain transparent, thereby working alongside educators instead of working alone. Through AI educational tools, teachers receive assistance in their interactions with students who achieve better outcomes without negatively impacting their classroom confidence.

3.3 Social Dimension

Educational groups enable students to acquire social learning knowledge as they work together in their group activities. The social dimension of education undergoes complex changes due to AI through new approaches to learner connections, communication, and knowledge co-creation methods. Computer-human interaction systems utilizing AI functions as control and moderation systems to eliminate improper content, thus generating inclusive educational discussions on platforms (Salloum et al., 2025). The implementation of recommendation algorithms to suggest collaborations between students effectively increases the quality of social learning interactions in education. AI tools help teachers identify objectionable content and provide equal student participation possibilities. Social learning processing requires processing unnoticeable social indications, including body language and humour, which AI systems have not yet mastered to an effective level. Systematic improvements should be added to AI technology to enhance interaction with humans instead of seeking to replace existing relationships. AI faces challenges interpreting natural social learning aspects involving emotional signals and body language that human interpreters efficiently process. Students show a tendency to rely more on automated feedback systems instead of engaging with meaningful instructor and peer discussions. AI systems should strengthen human dialogue instead of occupying every human connection option. Each function within the system allows students to guide each other through group projects that build a comprehensive set of capabilities. Institutions should guarantee digital equity for their students when implementing socially enabling AI technologies (Keshishi and Hack, 2023).

From a student perspective, AI-enabled collaborative platforms foster global peer-to-peer learning opportunities. However, day-to-day classroom practices reveal obstacles such as unequal access to devices, reduced opportunities for face-to-face discussion, and potential disengagement when social interactions are mediated predominantly by AI systems. Educators must adapt their teaching strategies to maintain genuine human connections while leveraging the efficiency of AI tools in facilitating social learning.

3.4 Metacognitive Dimension

Students who want to become self-directed learners need metacognitive abilities to understand and actively direct their learning activities. This system provides students with immediate feedback about their learning gaps in real-time. The dashboard visuals allow students to monitor their academic progress through visual representations of how they manage their time, distribute their results, and allocate study time. Students can evaluate their educational approaches by taking advantage of built-in operational tools located in learning management systems through reflective assessment quizzes. Improvements in educational achievement emerge through individual student recommendations produced by analysing their program behaviours (Steinert et al., 2023). An AI tutor can detect persistent excellence in visual tasks from students and then generate diagram-based revision recommendations. AI reveals previously hidden educational aspects by converting them into explicit educational resources for teachers and students to use. AI systems understand student-and-content interactions to create feedback that reveals the reason behind mistakes and their detection. The use of AI in engagement systems helps students improve their problem-solving abilities. AI systems need proper adjustment to facilitate metacognitive development in learners. Students lose their independence for self-directed learning whenever systems provide excessive directive guidance. The most beneficial outcomes emerge from AI tools when they permit students to perform independent exploration and experimentation while they investigate their work through reflection instead of delivering pre-established solutions. Through AI systems, students learn to think independently by using them to create learning goals during academic struggles (Salloum et al., 2025).

By addressing these four dimensions, AI demonstrates its potential to streamline educational processes and enrich the overall learning experience, complementing traditional methods while introducing new pathways for student growth and institutional effectiveness. These cognitive, emotional, social, and metacognitive enhancements are reflected in the real-world applications observed in higher education institutions. At the IITs, AI-enabled adaptive tutoring systems deliver personalized content (cognitive), track student engagement, and provide feedback (emotional and metacognitive), improving overall learning outcomes. Similarly, predictive analytics at the South African university identifies at-risk students early, allowing timely interventions that support both emotional well-being and social integration within the academic community. In Brazil, AI-driven plagiarism detection tools uphold academic integrity, reinforcing metacognitive awareness of ethical scholarship while fostering a collaborative and fair learning environment. Table 1 summarises the application of AI in higher education, highlighting its impact across cognitive, emotional, social, and metacognitive learning dimensions. It also outlines the associated benefits and challenges observed in institutional implementations.

Table 1. AI in higher education, including learning dimensions, benefits, and challenges.

Dimension	Role of AI tools	Benefits	Challenges
Cognitive	Adaptive learning, predictive analytics	Personalized learning, early intervention	Reduced critical thinking, over-reliance on automation
Emotional	Sentiment analysis, chatbots	Motivation, resilience, emotional support	Privacy risks, emotional surveillance
Social	Virtual collaboration, AI moderation	Inclusive interaction, global connectivity	Reduced human contact, digital divides
Metacognitive	Dashboards, reflective AI tutors	Goal-setting, self-regulation, reflective practice	Over-guidance, diminished independence

4. ETHICAL CHALLENGES IN AI-ENABLED HIGHER EDUCATION

The more the use of AI is integrated within academic systems, it creates a range of ethical issues, which higher education institutions find themselves working against. AI is more efficient, personalized, and explorative, and from these come severe queries about responsibility, fairness, and autonomy. Institutional ethical stewardship is of utmost importance not just because it ensures institutional credibility but also because it prevents learners and educators from the unintended consequences. A part of this chapter discusses central ethical dilemmas associated with the application of AI in the sphere of higher education: data privacy, classroom bias, academic integrity and transparency.

4.1 Data Privacy and Security

AI systems used in education need masses of data to be effective. These systems find sensitive private information such as attendance logs and submission of assignments, as well as behaviour and biometric data. The gathering and processing of such information entails inherent risk, especially in such cases where privacy safeguards are weak or not definite. Illegal access or breaches may endanger student identity, their learning history or even their psychological profiles. It is an urgent matter of the lack of clarity regarding the issue of consent. Students cannot always be certain about how their information is being collected, used, and shared. The legal wording in user agreements is unclear (Campbell et al., 2025). Therefore, people can find it hard to consent when they are informed. Further, third-party tools embedded in learning platforms may have different data practices, making the risk compounded. The other possible vulnerability is in data storage and retention. Imprisons institutions if it lacks robust measures of cybersecurity or it does not routinely weed out information that is no longer required. Cyberattacks aimed at educational databases have already shown the world the life consequences of insecure systems. Educational institutions must adopt an open data governance policy focusing on student rights and anonymisation methods, and develop clear opt-out options. The use of ethical AI begins with human respect for digital areas and the understanding that personal data should be used for educational purposes, not surveillance or monetary profit (Ghimire and Edwards, 2024).

4.2 Bias and Fairness

AI algorithms are not neutral; they adopt the biases found in their training data and the thinking assumptions embedded in their design. In educational settings, this can lead to differential treatment of students, most particularly from marginalized or underrepresented groups. For example, predictive models used to determine student performance may, by accident, discriminate in favor of one demographic group and against another, not because of actual performance, but by inference of past patterns. This manifests in admissions systems, automated grading programs, and academic advising systems. Unchecked, such discrepancies instead propagate systemic inequalities instead of correcting them. In addition, opaque decision-making processes make it impossible for students or educators to challenge or understand why this or that outcome occurs, i.e. why a student is marked as at risk, or assigned a lower mark by an algorithm (Campbell et al., 2025). Fairness in AI is not a people problem but an engineering one. It includes the regular audit of the datasets, including model training, and the involvement of different stakeholders in development. Institutions must also understand that bias is not a pure computational problem, it is a social one. What is asked in the questions, what is gathered in the data, and what gets automated are all reflective of underlying values. To maintain fairness, universities ought to use accountability frameworks to oversee the effect AI has on various student groups. Equally important is creating spaces for feedback and a grievance mechanism. AI has to be aligned towards the education goal of equity, not efficiency.

4.3 Academic Integrity

Panels of academic dishonesty are being made more complicated by integrating AI in educational premises. How tools equipped with AI can write essays, solve equations, or perform research simulations blur the boundary between learning and outsourcing. As generative technologies continue to progress, differentiating between original student work and products from generative technologies becomes ever more challenging. To some, AI tools are learning tools, which increase manoeuvring; to others, they are the enablers of academic dishonesty. The issue of disagreeing morally is the intention and the context of use. For instance, with AI it is possible to check grammar or brainstorm ideas which may be acceptable, while what one cannot do is to submit work written using AI as merely one's own, which creates concerns over authenticity and authorship (Madaio et al., 2022). Instructors are presented with new difficulties in terms of evaluating how students perceive a concept. Traditional forms of testing will be insufficient if students are mainly dependent on external algorithms for solving problems. Similarly, Plagiarism tools cannot always pick up AI-generated content to leave room for gaps in enforcement. Higher education institutions must change their integrity policies to accommodate these changing realities. This would involve part revision of codes of conduct, educating students on the responsible use of ethical AI, and creating assessments that call for critical thinking, creativity, and reflection, which machines find hard to replace. Integral, just as it promotes a culture where integrity is valued intrinsically. Punitive measures will not solve the causes of dishonesty. Institutions must weigh innovation and accountability such that academic performance continues to be an important measure of humanity in terms of work and intellectual development (Chinta et al., 2024).

4.4 Transparency and Explainability

One major ethical issue of AI enhanced education is the obscurity of the logic of algorithms and how they make decisions. Many AI systems work as "black boxes", providing results without explaining their logic. This kind of opaqueness is detrimental, especially when the outcome is out of proportion to the impact on students' academic paths. Students and educators should be able to know how AI tools come up with conclusions, whether making predictions of academic risk, suggesting learning materials or even grading assignments. If a decision seems, to the users, arbitrary or inexplicable, users may lose confidence in the fairness and reliability of the system. In addition, the inability to challenge or appeal against algorithmic decisions undermines educational agency (Gillani et al., 2023). Explainability is especially important in an assessment situation. For example, if an AI scores a student's work lower than it's supposed to, the learner should be able to access a rationale for the decision. Transparency is a learning environment, while opacity hides error and destroys accountability. Creating explainable AI denotes adopting user-friendly interfaces to battle human entrapsment, data visualization, and override. Educational institutions should also require algorithmic disclosure from technology vendors, such as model limitations, training data sources, and update procedures. Transparency is not simply a strictly technical problem, it is an ethical imperative. It ensures that AI would be an educational partner, avoiding being an invisible authority (O'Brien and O'Keeffe, 2022). In cases when learners and teachers participate as informed actors in the AI-driven processes, the educational environment becomes more just, empowering, and trusting..

5. TRANSFORMING PEDAGOGICAL MODELS: INTEGRATING AI RESPONSIBLY

The need for AI in higher education is not a matter of altering tools, but of revising the whole set of educational frameworks from the ground up. Pedagogical integration entails harmonistics of AI technologies with the values of teaching and learning, such that they facilitate human performance, rather than replacing it.

During institutional reimaginings of pedagogical models, the care they bring must also be balanced with innovation, so that technological solutions are augmented and bring forward academic objectives. This section describes practical strategies for the integration of responsible AI, which are collaboration, ethics, governance, policy, and sustainability.

5.1 Human-AI Collaboration

Treat the technology as a collaborator and not a replacement of it, this has been one of the most successful strategies for the artificial integration. Instructors can allow AI to perform repetitive and data-intensive tasks (e.g. grading quizzes, tracking participation), thereby saving them time to do more important, meaningful engagement with their students. In this hybrid model, AI supports the educators by offering leads or scaffolding while the key remains human-based in its mentorship, contextual judgement and ethical guidance. In a classroom learning environment, AI can facilitate learning by modulating the content delivery or suggesting individualized resources. However, such essential features are used with intent. Educators must constitute an active presence, interpret the AI feedback, and ensure this feedback facilitates pedagogical aspirations. This symbiotic relationship uses everyone's strengths: the computational power of AI to work with numbers, of course and the human comfort-above-all approach of the educator to use their emotional intelligence and critical thinking. Besides, students ought to be taught to work meaningfully with AI. This involves judging AI-generated suggestions critically, asking questions about outputs, and knowing the limitations (Holstein and Aleven, 2022). Instead of building dependency, responsible use makes learners consider AI as a tool to support discovery and a source for making decisions. Augmentation, and not automation, characterizes a human-AI partnership. By presenting AI as a supporter rather than a replacement, the institutions are able to preserve the integrity of a learning experience while enjoying the efficiencies and personalization that are AI's privilege (Mollick and Mollick, 2023).

5.2 Ethical Curriculum Integration

Higher education must incorporate ethical understanding into the curriculum directly and thus to ready students for a world of intelligent systems. Rather than as a niche subject within the confines of all AI ethics, institutions should encourage interdisciplinary approaches that link the use of technology to people's lives. Such integration founds many forms. For example, modules on responsible design may become part of engineering programmes, and algorithmic decision-making in business courses. In the humanities, students may explore how AI influences the narratives, access to information and cultural norms. Such views prepare moments of illicit ethical challenges for the latter in making the right decisions. Furthermore, as ethical curriculum design includes encouraging reflective practices, students should be made to question critically: Who benefits from this technology? Bias can thus be hidden in the system? How are decisions justified? These questions form digital citizenship and a sense of accountability in the spaces of technology. Project-based learning can be an energetic means of this integration. Students develop practical exposure on dealing with complex ethical trade-offs by engaging in true-to-life case studies (displays of AI, for example, in medicine, surveillance, hiring). It deepens their understanding of technology and educates them on transparency, justice, and equality values. Incorporating ethics at all times during the learning process creates a situation where students aren't only receiving technology; they're moulding it. Ethical curriculum integration prepares learners for moral literacy, which is essential for coherent participation in an AI-dominated world (Holstein and Aleven, 2022).

5.3 Policy and Governance Frameworks

For AI in education, there needs to be a responsible strategy informed by whole institutional policies and a sound governance configuration. AI adoption can become fragmented, inconsistent or even disastrous without proper frameworks. Effective governance ensures that deploying AI tools works with the institution's mission, values, and regulations. Roles and responsibilities are two of the main elements of governance. Who controls approval on AI tools? Who regulates their effect on students? How are risks evaluated? Such clarification prevents misuse and ensures a timely reaction to arising issues. In addition, oversight bodies (AI ethics committees or digital innovation boards) can continuously review the tools in use. Policies should also address vendor selection, data management and algorithmic accountability (Ghimire and Edwards, 2024). For instance, imposing technology providers to be transparent with model working, using their data, and updating management allows institutions to make informed decisions. Transparency clauses and data protection requirements should be inviolable. The other very important area in policies is user education. Institutions need to train the faculty and students on ways to interact with the AI systems safely. Policies must also encourage digital literacy so that all stakeholders should come into grips with their roles and responsibilities in an AI-mediated environment. It's not just about control, but stewardship (Ghimire and Edwards, 2024). It protects innovation from undermining the educational community. No frills policy frameworks establish a culture of accountability, trust and common purpose in the age of intelligent systems.

5.4 AI Ecological Education Policy Framework

An ecological view of AI education looks at the larger systems in which learning takes place; it's technological, social, environmental, and cultural. AI ecological education policy framework, as displayed in Fig. 3. An AI ecological education policy architecture prompts institutions to go beyond individual instruments and consider those interrelated networks that determine responsible technology consumption. The integration of AI in higher education is not confined to the Global North. In India, initiatives such as the National Education Policy (NEP 2020) emphasize AI-enabled personalized learning pathways. In Brazil, AI applications are being tested to support large public universities in scaling student advising systems. Similarly, in South Africa, AI-based platforms are being employed to improve access and inclusivity in distance learning. These diverse efforts highlight that AI adoption is shaped by socio-economic realities and policy frameworks, underscoring the importance of context-specific strategies within the proposed AI Ecological Education Policy Framework.

This approach values the fact that AI operates in ecosystems consisting of data infrastructures, institutional hierarchies, public policies, and the student community. The ecological policy framework, therefore, encourages general thinking, pressing decision makers to evaluate the impacts of choices on one sphere (e.g., data sourcing) and another (e.g., equity or sustainability). For instance, institutions may future-proof their policies with green AI policies focused on energy efficiency, leading to less environmental footprint of machine learning systems (Chan, 2023). Also, they could impose integral design standards to guarantee that AI systems do not forget different needs and identities. Such policies are not merely technical – they are moral obligations to fairness, sustainability and access. An ecological framework also supports adaptability. Apparently, it does not impose rules as it encourages principles that change with technological development. These might be values such as openness, interoperability, and community participation. In so doing, institutions remain agile, responsive, and true to their ethical compass. Finally, this policy framework promotes collaboration between departments and fills the gap between disciplines such as IT, pedagogy, ethics and administration. It creates a place where policy is not something to be considered later but rather an essential ingredient in educational change (Ghimire and Edwards, 2024). When institutions base their approach to AI practices on an ecological mindset, these practices can become sustainable, context-sensitive, and relevant to the long-term academic goals.

5.5 Toward a Sustainable AI Future in Higher Education

A sustainable future with AI in education needs vision, inclusivity, and ever-growing reflection. Here, sustainability goes beyond being environmentally friendly; it also means long-term relevance, equity, and ethical integrity of AI use in academic life. A sustainable future for AI treasures the long-lasting over the new. Institutions should focus on tools that can gain long-term benefits and be maintained responsibly, supporting the core of the education requirement rather than incorporating all the latest technology trends. This requires evidence-based decision making, strong pilot programs and regular impact diagnoses. Sustainability of AI planning also needs to be based on equity. While digital divides continue, institutions must ensure that access to AI enhanced learning tools shall not become the right of the privileged few. This involves allocating resources to underfunded departments, supporting students with poor connectivity, and designing inclusive interfaces that are accessible regardless of ability or learning mode. Another essential thing is cultivating a culture of collective responsibility (Ogundare and Araya, 2023). Faculty, students, technologists and administrators must collaborate to determine the future of AI in education. The provision of open doorways to feedback, fostering participatory design, and facilitating multi-disciplinary research are important strategies for keeping the use of AI effective/ethical. Finally, sustainability means preparing generations to manage and ask themselves about their societal role. Education must also enable the students to use AI and understand its other implications so that it can be shaped to their needs. Through this, higher education institutions can set the precedent for the future design of a world where technology augments the human learning experience instead of depleting it. Table 2 outlines key pedagogical and policy recommendations for the responsible integration of AI in higher education, highlighting strategies for collaboration, ethics, governance, and sustainability.

Table 2. Pedagogical and policy recommendations for responsible AI integration.

Strategy	Practical action	Expected outcome
Human-AI collaboration	Use AI for administrative tasks, keep educators central	Preserves human connection and trust
Ethical curriculum	Integrate AI ethics across disciplines	Students develop critical digital citizenship
Policy & governance	Establish AI ethics committees, transparency rules	Institutional accountability and fairness
Inclusive frameworks	Provide equitable access to AI tools, context-aware adoption	Reduces digital divides
Sustainability planning	Long-term ecological approach to AI integration	Ensures adaptive and inclusive practices

6. FUTURE DIRECTIONS

AI uses in higher education have become an integral aspect of the landscape, and one must plan beyond short-term implementation and on longer-term strategies, though. The world today is how it is because of simplification and a concomitant information explosion, and what AI can achieve for education will depend on how well institutions manage complexity, welcome diversity, and foster cross-disciplinary collaboration. Such future directions focus more than just on technological growth, but on human-centred innovation that can be congruent with education values and societal ambitions.

6.1 Embracing Complexity

The education landscape is inherently complex, and AI does not make it simpler; it makes it more complicated. Institutions are ready for a future mandate, a change in the way they will either solve or prevent problems, from linear problem-solving approaches to systems thinking that will see the institutions understand and deal with interdependencies, feedback loops and contextual variations. That is to say, embrace vagueness and design educative systems that are flexible, adaptive and resilient. For instance, while the role played by AI is out of the classroom, interventional mechanisms within institutional regimes, social order, and cultural stories get played out. Too simple a focus on performance metrics or automation can fail to understand the ways learning occurs in complex terms. The monostrative value of embracing complexity challenges assumptions, respects various forms of intelligence and admits that some results are unpredictable and unquantifiable. Also, educational leaders should create a setting for experimentation, where experimentation should be welcomed and failure should be seen as a learning opportunity. Downloadable versions of agile models of curriculum development, ethical foresight exercises, and scenario planning can equip institutions with the agility to counter the quick pace of change. By increasing complexity, such a thinking style will move away from the reductionist models and towards the more holistic, student-centred model of higher education. This orientation allows creating more inclusive, context-aware, future-proof pedagogical models that accommodate the wealth of human learning and encounter diversity.

6.2 Participatory Design Approaches

Ministers are especially interested in the implications of new educational technology, and students, teachers, and other support staff must have a say in how that technology is used to shape the learning experience. Participatory design focuses on user agency and co-creation and helps ensure that those technologies correspond to educators' actual needs and values. Engaging users early in the design process allows developers to surface hidden problems, understand the culture and determine the potential ethical issues. For example, students can explain the ways in which some AI tools support inequities or neglect individual learning styles. Educators can demonstrate the disruptions caused by automation to critical thinking or diminished pedagogic flexibility. Whereas consultation invites collaboration, participatory perspectives encourage actual co-operation. Design sprints, focus tests, and pilots can be used as venues for an iterative test and revision process. This makes innovation more democratic and legitimizes and caters for AI solutions. Institutions that use participatory frameworks show that they are investing in transparency and inclusiveness. They acknowledge that technology should work for the users, not the other way around. Further, co-designed AI tools are more likely to succeed in practice because they are grounded in the everyday and shaped by diverse voices. In the end, good participatory design creates trust, makes things more accessible, and helps make the use of AI in education ethical. It re-establishes the dynamics of support from top-down imposition to collaborative transformation.

6.3 Interdisciplinary Research

Being a technological issue is not the case of AI in education; it is a multidimensional phenomenon, which touches upon pedagogy, psychology, ethics, sociology, and, well, more. For us to properly appreciate and wisely pursue this integration, interdisciplinary research must become the leading focus in academic research for the future. An excellent understanding of what AI can do comes when experts from different fields come together. Educators will have a say on learning theory, ethicists on the moral implications, psychologists on the cognitive outcomes, but technologists will then develop the algorithms. When such disciplines work together, they produce more robust, balanced, context-specific innovations. Interdisciplinary groups can examine critical questions such as: What influence does the AI have on the teacher-student relationship? How do the students react to emotions from AI feedback? What can AI systems be culturally diverse? Such is not questioning that any one discipline can answer by itself. Further, interdisciplinary research stimulates the development of methodological innovation. By using both qualitative and quantitative approaches, it is possible to carry out more meaningful assessments with regard to AI interventions. Case studies, ethnographies and longitudinal analysis complement technical evaluation to provide a complete picture of what works, for whom, and under what conditions. Sponsoring agencies and academic journals should facilitate such an integrated approach through cross-divisional grants and publications. Institutions can, in turn, create transdisciplinary research centres of AI in education in which innovation is guided by complexity and reflection about ethics. The future of AI in higher education will not be solely determined by discovery on the technological frontier, rather both accomplishments out of combining disciplinary silos and creating collaborative knowledge production will also have an integral role to play, as it will correspond to the entire range of the human experience.

7. CONCLUSION

AI integration offers a tremendous opportunity and mammoth ethical obligations at the threshold of the transformation of higher education. This report has discussed the way AI remakes learning on the cognitive, emotional, social, and metacognitive dimensions, enlivening education by personalisation, feedback, and engagement. Coincidentally, it also introduces the theme that is ethically quite critical, for example, with regard to data privacy, bias, academic integrity, and transparency. Evolution to new age pedagogy requires more than adopting trends of the times; it requires a redefinition of purpose and the design and governance of educational environments. AI must be embedded in society in such a way as to augment, rather than override human agency. In doing so responsibly, institutions must develop human-AI collaboration and merge ethics in worlds, curricula, and policy frameworks that will guarantee equity and accountability. Moving forward, future trajectories should focus on complexity, participatory design and inter-disciplinary research, respectively. By doing so, educational innovation is grounded in human values and needs in society. Learners, educators, and policymakers need to be empowered so that they can be partners in co-creating technological futures that are inclusive, fair, and sustainable in the long term. Ultimately, the mindful use of AI in higher education is not a destination; it is a journey that should continually be reconsidered, and for which its constant adaptation should be demanded, while it is a shared stewardship. Consistent with pedagogical intentions and ethical commitments, higher education institutions could use technology to respond to the digital age and actively create a more just, alive, and learner-centred future.

REFERENCES

Baillifard, A., Gabella, M., Lavenex, P.B., Martarelli, C.S., 2023. Implementing Learning Principles with a Personal AI Tutor: A Case Study 1–17.

Buckley, C., & Kukhareva, M. (2021). Making Inspiration Mainstream: Innovative Pedagogies for the Real World. In *Applied Pedagogies for Higher Education* (pp. 269–297). Springer International Publishing., DOI: 10.1007/978-3-030-46951-1_12

Campbell, M., Barthwal, A., Joshi, S., Shouli, A., & Shrestha, A. K. 2025. Investigation of the Privacy Concerns in AI Systems for Young Digital Citizens: A Comparative Stakeholder Analysis, in: *2025 IEEE 15th Annual Computing and Communication Workshop and Conference (CCWC)*. IEEE, pp. 00030–00037. https://doi.org/DOI: 10.1109/CCWC62904.2025.10903925

Chan, C. K. Y. (2023). A comprehensive AI policy education framework for university teaching and learning. *International Journal of Educational Technology in Higher Education, 20*, 38. DOI: 10.1186/s41239-023-00408-3

Chinta, S.V., Wang, Z., Yin, Z., Hoang, N., Gonzalez, M., Quy, T. Le, Zhang, W., 2024. FairAIED: Navigating Fairness, Bias, and Ethics in Educational AI Applications 1–47.

Commission - for Education, E.D., 2017. "Transforming higher education: how we teach in the digital age" Key messages from the joint PLA in. Eur. Commision 7.

Ghimire, A., & Edwards, J. 2024. From Guidelines to Governance: A Study of AI Policies in Education, in: Communications in Computer and Information Science. pp. 299–307. https://doi.org/DOI: 10.1007/978-3-031-64312-5_36

Gillani, N., Eynon, R., Chiabaut, C., & Finkel, K. (2023). Unpacking the "Black Box" of AI in Education. *Journal of Educational Technology & Society, 26*. Advance online publication. DOI: 10.30191/ETS.202301_26(1).0008

Halkiopoulos, C., & Gkintoni, E. (2024). Leveraging AI in E-Learning: Personalized Learning and Adaptive Assessment through Cognitive Neuropsychology—A Systematic Analysis. *Electronics (Basel), 13*, 3762. DOI: 10.3390/electronics13183762

Holstein, K., & Aleven, V. (2022). Designing for human–AI complementarity in K-12 education. *AI Magazine, 43*, 239–248. DOI: 10.1002/aaai.12058

Katsamakas, E., Pavlov, O. V., & Saklad, R. (2024). Artificial Intelligence and the Transformation of Higher Education Institutions: A Systems Approach. *Sustainability, 16*, 6118. DOI: 10.3390/su16146118

Keshishi, N., & Hack, D. S. (2023). Emotional Intelligence in the Digital Age: Harnessing AI for Students' Inner Development. *J. Perspect. Appl. Acad. Pract., 11*. Advance online publication. DOI: 10.56433/jpaap.v11i3.579

Madaio, M., Blodgett, S. L., Mayfield, E., & Dixon-Román, E. (2022). Beyond "fairness. In *The Ethics of Artificial Intelligence in Education* (pp. 203–239). Routledge., DOI: 10.4324/9780429329067-11

Maity, S., Deroy, A., 2024. Generative AI and Its Impact on Personalized Intelligent Tutoring Systems 1–5.

McDonald, N., Johri, A., Ali, A., Hingle, A., 2024. Generative Artificial Intelligence in Higher Education: Evidence from an Analysis of Institutional Policies and Guidelines 1–24.

Mollick, E. R., & Mollick, L. 2023. Assigning AI: Seven Approaches for Students, with Prompts. SSRN Electron. J. https://doi.org/DOI: 10.2139/ssrn.4475995

Morrow, E., Zidaru, T., Ross, F., Mason, C., Patel, K. D., Ream, M., & Stockley, R. (2023). Artificial intelligence technologies and compassion in healthcare: A systematic scoping review. *Frontiers in Psychology, 13*. Advance online publication. DOI: 10.3389/fpsyg.2022.971044 PMID: 36733854

O'Brien, K. A., & O'Keeffe, M. (2022). Reimagining the role of technology in sport officiating: How artificial intelligence (AI) supports the design and delivery of ecologically dynamic development processes. *Managing Sport and Leisure*, •••, 1–13. DOI: 10.1080/23750472.2022.2126996

Ogundare, O., Araya, G.Q., 2023. Comparative Analysis of CHATGPT and the evolution of language models 1–10.

Pandey, A., Mittal, M., Ahmad, K., & Sharma, V. (2023). New Age Teaching Pedagogy. In *Redefining Virtual Teaching Learning Pedagogy* (pp. 59–73). Wiley., DOI: 10.1002/9781119867647.ch4

Popenici, S. A. D., & Kerr, S. (2017). Exploring the impact of artificial intelligence on teaching and learning in higher education. *Research and Practice in Technology Enhanced Learning, 12*, 22. DOI: 10.1186/s41039-017-0062-8 PMID: 30595727

Rohi, M. P., Boymau, L. T., Birri Bolen Nimanuho, M. S., & Mbuik, S. M. (2025). Generative AI and education: Digital pedagogies, teaching innovation and learning design. *Asia Pacific Journal of Education, 00*, 1–4. DOI: 10.1080/02188791.2025.2473282

Sajja, R., Sermet, Y., Cikmaz, M., Cwiertny, D., & Demir, I. (2024). Artificial Intelligence-Enabled Intelligent Assistant for Personalized and Adaptive Learning in Higher Education. *Information (Basel)*, *15*, 596. DOI: 10.3390/info15100596

Salloum, S. A., Alomari, K. M., Alfaisal, A. M., Aljanada, R. A., & Basiouni, A. (2025). Emotion recognition for enhanced learning: Using AI to detect students' emotions and adjust teaching methods. *Smart Learn. Environ.*, *12*, 21. DOI: 10.1186/s40561-025-00374-5

Steinert, S., Avila, K.E., Ruzika, S., Kuhn, J., Küchemann, S., 2023. Harnessing Large Language Models to Enhance Self-Regulated Learning via Formative Feedback 1–9. https://doi.org/DOI: 10.1186/s40561-024-00354-1

Strielkowski, W., Grebennikova, V., Lisovskiy, A., Rakhimova, G., & Vasileva, T. (2025). AI -driven adaptive learning for sustainable educational transformation. *Sustainable Development (Bradford)*, *33*, 1921–1947. DOI: 10.1002/sd.3221

Widiatna, A. D. (2020). Transformasi Pendidikan Calon Katekis Dan Guru Agama Katolik Di Era Digital. *JPAK J. Pendidik. Agama Katolik*, *20*, 66–82. DOI: 10.34150/jpak.v20i2.280

Chapter 14
Transforming Higher Education:
The Central Role of AI in Personalized Learning for University Students

Anselmus Sudirman
https://orcid.org/0000-0001-5520-9838
Universitas Sarjanawiyata Tamansiswa, Yogyakarta, Indonesia

ABSTRACT

This chapter examines the potential of Artificial Intelligence (AI) to transform higher education, with a focus on personalized learning. The ability of AI to tailor educational experiences significantly improves student engagement, motivation, and academic achievement. The integration of AI introduces ethical challenges, such as data privacy concerns, algorithmic bias, and the need for human oversight in educational practices. Furthermore, although AI can automate specific educational processes, the role of lecturers is crucial in delivering pedagogical interpretation and emotional support. The implementation of balanced strategies integrates AI with conventional teaching methods, recognizing the significance of human insight in fostering critical thinking and maintaining academic integrity. Higher education institutions can responsibly leverage AI's capabilities to develop inclusive, personalized, and equitable learning environments by fostering collaboration among lecturers, policymakers, and technology providers.

DOI: 10.4018/979-8-3373-3000-6.ch014

INTRODUCTION

Artificial Intelligence (AI) is emerging as a fundamental element in transforming higher education by providing personalized learning opportunities and enhancing student engagement. As educational institutions adopt AI, they encounter an imperative to guarantee fair access to its revolutionary capabilities. This necessity is especially evident in different countries, where varied, multicultural, and multilingual environments demand personalized AI models developed from representative datasets. National initiatives must focus on the equitable allocation of AI tools to prevent exacerbating the educational disparity between privileged and underprivileged regions (Haetami, 2025).

The incorporation of AI in higher education offers significant benefits and unique obstacles, particularly in varied and evolving areas such as Indonesia. The potential of AI in personalized learning is in its capacity to address specific student requirements, tailoring educational resources to diverse tempos and methodologies. Nonetheless, actualizing this promise necessitates the deliberate application of AI that honors and embodies cultural, linguistic, and socio-economic variety. Localized AI models are not simply a technology modification but an essential advancement in transforming educational experiences to be more inclusive, reflecting the intricacies of the educational environment.

By creating AI systems trained on datasets that reflect the country's diverse characteristics, educational institutions can guarantee that these technologies significantly enhance all learning environments. National measures are vital in mitigating gaps, as the equitable deployment of AI tools is needed to avert the deepening of educational inequality. In the absence of a proactive strategy, there is a danger that AI may exacerbate existing disparities instead of alleviating them, so further hindering underprivileged people's access to quality education. Prioritizing equity in AI implementation promotes educational inclusivity and advances societal objectives of fairness and equal opportunity, guaranteeing that the transformative potential of artificial intelligence is utilized to benefit all learners, regardless of their background or geographical location.

AI presents significant prospects to transform personalized learning extensively, enhancing the responsiveness and student-centricity of education. Notwithstanding these benefits, the extensive integration of AI in education poses intricate problems, including the reinforcement of existing inequities and the inability to achieve complete personalization due to disparate infrastructure and access (Ruano-Borbalan, 2025). Nonetheless, AI's contribution to improving creative pedagogical approaches, foreign language acquisition, and research-oriented fields is significant and indicates its capacity to dissolve distinctions between formal and informal educational frameworks.

As they go towards this AI-driven revolution, educational institutions must reconcile technological innovation with ethical accountability. Data privacy, computational biases, and the potential for employment displacement are critical issues that must not be disregarded. To enable AI to realize its potential as an equalizing force, institutions must implement comprehensive policies that integrate their many objectives, necessitating substantial infrastructure investments and adequate teacher training (Farooq et al., 2024). Collaborative initiatives with industry partners will be essential for the integration of AI tools and the preparation of students for an AI-driven employment landscape.

The ethical dilemmas arising from the swift expansion of AI, such as academic dishonesty and misuse, necessitate novel solutions. Upholding academic integrity in AI-enhanced educational settings necessitates transparency and ethical utilization of AI techniques, including detection plugins like Turnitin. Encouraging critical thinking and reformulating assessment methods to include new and regulated formats can reduce misuse (Mulaudzi & Hamilton, 2025). Institutions must establish ethical norms and guarantee that AI is utilized as a mechanism for equity rather than division.

The practical ramifications of AI's incorporation into educational systems are extensive. AI-driven platforms can augment accessibility to personalized learning experiences, markedly improving educational outcomes, particularly for students with disabilities or from marginalized areas (Silva et al., 2024). Nonetheless, maintaining human engagement is essential to avert the erosion of pedagogical interpretation and emotional assistance. AI ought to enhance, not supplant, human understanding, underscoring the imperative of empowering lecturers, with AI serving as an exoskeleton to boost instruction (Mariyono & Hd, 2025).

The distinctive educational framework of Indonesia highlights the necessity of collaboratively creating AI tools with local lecturers to guarantee representative training datasets and ethical AI applications. Regulatory measures are essential to rectify inadequate frameworks in data privacy and student information security. Formulating national policies that direct the ethical and inclusive application of AI in education would facilitate AI's role as an instrument for inclusive transformation (Merino-Campos, 2025).

The promise of AI in enhancing personalized learning outcomes and educational analytics offers considerable opportunities and problems. AI-driven adaptive algorithms can customize educational techniques to meet personalized learning requirements, improving engagement and academic success while providing lecturers with essential insights into student progress. A balanced approach in which AI enhances traditional teaching is essential to avoid over-reliance and achieve optimal educational outcomes (Bhatia et al., 2024).

The revolutionary potential of AI in higher education depends on addressing ethical issues, fostering human-machine collaboration, improving policy frameworks, and facilitating lifelong learning. As universities aggressively utilize AI for educational advancement, they can markedly enhance student satisfaction, retention, and academic performance, equipping learners to excel in a dynamic global workforce. By connecting AI capabilities with educational objectives, lecturers can preserve a human-centered approach, ensuring that AI functions not as a substitute for human understanding but as an intelligent collaborator in educational advancement (Ruano-Borbalan, 2025).

THE TRANSFORMATION OF HIGHER EDUCATION THROUGH AI-DRIVEN PERSONALIZED LEARNING

Artificial Intelligence (AI) is transforming the educational landscape, with the potential to revolutionize personalized learning in higher education. Utilizing adaptive technologies and real-time analytics, AI can tailor educational experiences to meet individual learning needs and preferences (Farooq et al., 2024). The impact of AI on education is significant, as it enables a more personalized, inclusive, and engaging learning environment while addressing longstanding educational challenges (Mariyono & Hd, 2025).

Personalized learning, as an educational strategy, aims to offer personalized instructional methods, content delivery, and pacing modifications to accommodate the varied learning styles and abilities of students (Kaswan et al., 2024). Artificial intelligence technologies, including machine learning algorithms and natural language processing, play a crucial role in the development of intelligent tutoring systems, adaptive learning platforms, and recommendation engines that offer personalized academic support and enhance understanding (Revathy J. et al., 2025).

The potential of AI to revolutionize higher education is demonstrated through its ability to personalize educational experiences on a large scale, a challenge that has historically been difficult for lecturers employing traditional methods. The implementation of AI in educational environments facilitates real-time analysis of student performance, thereby guiding the creation of personalized learning pathways and adaptive curriculum frameworks (Revathy J. et al., 2025). This method enhances student engagement and academic achievement while providing lecturers with critical insights into student progress, facilitating timely interventions and support (Silva et al., 2024).

While the integration of AI in higher education holds significant promise, it also presents various challenges. Ethical considerations, including data privacy, algorithmic fairness, and the risk of excessive dependence on AI technologies, present substantial concerns (Galindo et al., 2024). The responsible and equitable use of AI requires strong regulatory frameworks that tackle data confidentiality, algorithmic biases, and ethical guidelines to protect educational stakeholders (Ruano-Borbalan, 2025).

Maximizing AI's transformative potential in education requires balancing technological innovation with traditional pedagogical practices. This perspective considers AI as a "exoskeleton" that enhances human teaching instead of replacing it, highlighting the significance of human insights and emotional intelligence in educational settings (Mariyono & Hd, 2025). Lecturers are essential in interpreting AI outputs and customizing interventions to meet the distinct needs of their students, ensuring that technology enhances rather than replaces human expertise (Bhatia et al., 2024).

Furthermore, the fair distribution of AI tools and digital infrastructure is essential to avoid worsening educational inequalities, especially in areas with restricted access to technology (Haetami, 2025). Efforts to create localized AI models that embody the multicultural and multilingual diversity of educational environments, particularly in Indonesia, are crucial for promoting inclusive and representative educational changes (Silva et al., 2024).

As higher education institutions seek to leverage AI's capabilities, the training of lecturers and the development of skills are essential. Equipping lecturers with the necessary competencies to integrate AI into teaching practices fosters a workforce capable of navigating and influencing the future of education (Farooq et al., 2024). Additionally, promoting ethics education for both students and lecturers will enhance critical thinking and the responsible use of AI tools in academic environments (Mulaudzi & Hamilton, 2025).

AI serves as a significant catalyst for educational transformation, possessing the potential to greatly influence personalized learning in higher education. Prioritizing ethical AI use, ensuring equitable access, and fostering human-machine collaboration allows educational institutions to create a learning environment in which AI enhances educational objectives while upholding a human-centered approach (Rane, 2025). The future of higher education depends on our capacity to manage the complexities of AI integration, promoting technological progress while preserving the fundamental values of higher education.

AI-driven personalized learning has significant potential to transform higher education into a more adaptive, equitable, and student-centered environment. The journey toward fully realizing AI's potential in education presents challenges concerning ethics, accessibility, and the relationship between technology and human insight. However, proactive strategies aimed at addressing these issues can facilitate successful integration. Institutions should adopt AI as a supportive element in human teaching, creating an educational setting where technological tools enhance the pedagogical process instead of complicating or overshadowing it. Investing in teacher training, ethical frameworks, and representative AI models enables higher education to maximize the potential of AI, ensuring that all students receive personalized learning experiences that improve engagement, motivation, and overall academic success. As we explore the transformative capabilities of AI, educational policies and practices must evolve concurrently to foster innovation while safeguarding the fundamental values of human-centered learning. Therefore, the future of higher education depends on our capacity to integrate AI responsibly, ensuring a balance between technological advancement and principles of integrity and inclusion.

EXPLORING THE ETHICAL IMPLICATIONS OF AI IN THE TRANSFORMATION OF HIGHER EDUCATION

The integration of artificial intelligence in higher education presents various ethical challenges that necessitate careful consideration to effectively leverage its potential. The swift integration of AI-driven personalized learning demonstrates its ability to customize educational experiences according to individual requirements, thereby improving student engagement and success (Silva et al., 2024). Nonetheless, in addition to these advantages, concerns regarding data privacy, algorithmic bias, and ethical standards necessitate thorough strategies to guarantee the responsible application of AI in educational settings (Mulaudzi & Hamilton, 2025).

Data privacy represents a significant issue in the application of AI within higher education. AI systems designed to personalize educational experiences frequently depend on comprehensive data collection, which includes sensitive information about students. It is essential to implement strong safeguards to protect this data, especially in areas where regulatory frameworks are still lacking. Implementing transparent data governance protocols and ethical standards for AI deployment is crucial for safeguarding student privacy and building trust in AI technologies (Haetami, 2025). Collaborations between educational institutions and technology providers can establish clear roles and responsibilities, thereby ensuring data security and ethical compliance (Mariyono & Hd, 2025).

Algorithmic bias represents a considerable challenge in the integration of AI into higher education. AI models developed using non-representative datasets are likely to reinforce existing inequalities, as algorithms may unintentionally favor specific demographics over others (Ruano-Borbalan, 2025). To address this issue, it is essential to develop AI models that are trained on diverse datasets, reflecting the multicultural and multilingual educational contexts, such as those found in Indonesia (Silva et al., 2024). Ensuring the representativeness of training data allows AI to promote educational equity instead of worsening existing disparities (Haetami, 2025).

The ethical application of AI in education necessitates the maintenance of human oversight in AI-assisted learning. AI has the capacity to automate diagnostics and personalize content; however, the roles of pedagogical interpretation and emotional support are essential elements that only lecturers can fulfill (Revathy J. et al., 2025). Lecturers must engage in the interpretation of AI outputs and customize interventions to meet the distinct needs of students, ensuring that technology enhances human insights rather than supplants them (Bhatia et al., 2024). This approach centered on human factors enhances educational outcomes while maintaining the integrity of the teaching profession (Farooq et al., 2024).

Furthermore, it is essential to establish ethical guidelines to mitigate academic dishonesty and the misuse of AI technologies (Mulaudzi & Hamilton, 2025). Higher education institutions must promote transparency in AI-assisted academic work by urging students to disclose their use of AI and by redesigning assessments to include innovative formats that uphold academic integrity (Asy'ari & Sharov, 2024). Ethical education programs are essential for fostering critical thinking skills in students, enabling them to engage responsibly with AI tools (Vivitsou, 2023).

Investment by institutions in teacher training is essential for the effective integration of AI technologies in education, while addressing ethical concerns (Farooq et al., 2024). Equipping lecturers with the skills to navigate AI-driven platforms enables them to utilize technology effectively while preserving a human-centered learning environment (Revathy J. et al., 2025). Moreover, providing ethical training for both students and lecturers can enable responsible AI usage, thereby promoting an inclusive and transparent educational environment (Xu et al., 2025).

The transformative potential of AI in higher education is significant; however, its success depends on the development of ethical frameworks that ensure a balance between innovation and accountability (Rane, 2025). Prioritizing equity, diversity, and human oversight in AI-driven educational practices enables institutions to leverage AI's capabilities to improve personalized learning while protecting essential educational values (Galindo et al., 2024). Future initiatives must prioritize the co-design of AI tools in collaboration with local lecturers and the formulation of policies that govern the ethical use of AI, ensuring that its advantages are accessible to all learners, irrespective of their geographic or socio-economic circumstances (Haetami, 2025).

In essence, addressing the ethical aspects of AI is essential for harnessing its transformative capabilities in higher education. Addressing data privacy, algorithmic bias, and ethical standards enables educational institutions to cultivate an environment in which AI acts as a catalyst for positive educational change, promoting personalized, inclusive, and equitable learning experiences for all (Silva et al., 2024). A balanced approach that integrates ethical considerations with technological innovation will be essential for harnessing AI's full potential in transforming the future of education.

The effective transformation of higher education via AI-driven personalized learning necessitates a comprehensive understanding of the ethical considerations associated with these technologies. Proactively addressing issues of data privacy, algorithmic bias, and the essential role of human oversight enables institutions to create a learning environment where technological advancements enhance educational integrity and equity rather than detract from them. Collaboration among educational stakeholders—policymakers, lecturers, and technologists—is crucial in creating frameworks that prioritize ethical AI use and guarantee that its benefits are available to all students, irrespective of their socio-economic or geographic conditions. Looking ahead, it is essential to balance innovation with ethical responsibility to harness AI's transformative potential. This approach will enhance the educational experience and equip students to succeed in a diverse and rapidly changing world.

THE CENTRAL ROLE OF AI IN ENHANCING PERSONALIZED LEARNING IN HIGHER EDUCATION

Artificial Intelligence (AI) has radically altered the higher education landscape, especially in individualized learning. As global education systems strive to address varied learning styles, AI offers a promising resource for customizing educational experiences to meet individual requirements. Various aspects of AI's pivotal role can improve personalized learning and its significant influence on academic results in higher education. Through a comprehensive analysis of contemporary research and perspectives from many educational settings, we aim to highlight the transformative potential of AI in fostering a more engaging, efficient, and inclusive learning environment for students.

AI-driven personalized learning represents a fundamental transformation from conventional "one-size-fits-all" educational strategies to ways personalized to individual students' distinct requirements, preferences, and capabilities. Pratama et al. (2023) demonstrate that most students recognize the importance of AI in education, showing substantial consensus on its ability to function as virtual instructors and intelligent assistants. The incorporation of AI technology, including machine learning algorithms and data analytics, allows for adaptive content delivery and real-time feedback, enhancing comprehension and engagement among learners (Kaswan et al., 2024). This transition highlights AI's capacity to revolutionize education by developing personalized learning trajectories that enhance student engagement and performance.

AI's Transformative Potential in Higher Education

The revolutionary promise of AI in higher education is apparent in its capacity to improve student engagement, maximize learning outcomes, and reduce educational disparities (Ayeni et al., 2024). AI-driven tools, such intelligent tutoring systems and recommendation engines, utilize extensive educational data to provide insights that facilitate tailored training (Khan, 2025). Naseer et al. (2024) noted a significant 25% enhancement in academic performance and engagement among students employing AI-driven platforms, highlighting the efficacy of individualized learning interventions. These improvements indicate that AI can substantially enhance academic achievement by offering resources personalized to students' specific strengths and shortcomings.

Notwithstanding its advantages, the integration of AI in personalized learning poses significant obstacles that require resolution to guarantee ethical and equitable application. Lecturers and institutions encounter challenges including privacy issues, ethical dilemmas, and potential biases included in AI algorithms (Kaswan et al., 2024). Vorobyeva et al. (2025) underscore the need for professional development for lecturers to proficiently incorporate AI tools into teaching, stressing the necessity for holistic methodologies that tackle technological, pedagogical, and ethical concerns. These difficulties require collaboration among lecturers, technologists, and politicians to create rules that promote inclusive and equitable AI integration in education.

Effective AI applications in educational environments offer significant insights into their revolutionary impact. The Jizzakh Presidential School utilized AI-driven technologies to enhance student engagement and conceptual comprehension in mathematics, establishing a benchmark for lecturers worldwide (Akramovna, 2024). In institutions around Pakistan, AI-driven learning platforms exhibited notable enhancements in student performance and happiness, highlighting the tangible advantages of tailored, AI-enhanced education (Naseer et al., 2024). These instances illustrate AI's ability to cultivate dynamic and efficient learning environments, providing lecturers with strategies to utilize AI within their institutions.

As artificial intelligence increasingly integrates with education, it is imperative to address concerns around privacy, bias, and data security (Bhutoria, 2022). Chang and Lu (2019) propose a technology-driven personalized learning approach that prioritizes student autonomy and feedback, fostering an environment that encourages responsible AI utilization. Furthermore, equitable access to AI technology must be guaranteed to avert the intensification of current educational inequalities. These arguments highlight the necessity for ethically robust and inclusive strategies for AI incorporation in education.

The future of AI in personalized learning is filled with possible advancements that are set to transform educational experiences. Advancements in AI-driven predictive models, as illustrated by Lokare & Jadhav (2024), provide lecturers with instruments to customize instructional approaches depending on students' learning preferences and cognitive requirements. Research by Ellikkal & Rajamohan (2025) indicates that integrating self-determination theory ideas into AI-driven education can improve student motivation and academic achievement. These directives underscore the continuous advancement of AI technology and its function in developing more tailored, efficient, and captivating educational experiences for learners.

AI plays a pivotal role in advancing individualized learning in higher education, facilitating a more inclusive and dynamic educational environment. By catering to unique student requirements, enhancing learning trajectories, and augmenting engagement, AI fosters opportunities for academic achievement that surpass traditional pedagogical approaches. As institutions incorporate AI into their educational frameworks, they must deliberately address ethical considerations, equal access, and practical implementation challenges. The ongoing cooperation among educational stakeholders will be crucial in achieving AI's full potential. As technology and education increasingly converge, AI's revolutionary influence heralds an era of individualized learning, ultimately enabling learners to excel in varied and intricate situations. This chapter's ideas establish a foundation for lecturers and institutions aiming to utilize AI, directing them towards a future of tailored and efficient learning experiences.

The incorporation of Artificial Intelligence (AI) in higher education has proven revolutionary, providing unparalleled chances for individualized learning. As educational institutions endeavor to address the varied requirements of students, AI becomes an essential instrument for personalizing learning experiences, enhancing engagement, and maximizing outcomes. This chapter will examine the substantial advantages AI offers for individualized learning, while recognizing the associated obstacles. This chapter aims to direct lecturers, policymakers, and technologists towards the successful and responsible implementation of AI in higher education by thorough study and empirical data.

Promoting Personalized and Adaptive Learning

AI technology has transformed education by enabling customization and adaptive learning, personalizing educational content to meet each student's distinct requirements. Kaswan et al. (2024) emphasize AI's capacity to employ machine learning algorithms for personalized learning, resulting in a personalized and immersive experience that improves student engagement and understanding. Adaptive learning systems enable students to advance at their own speed, therefore catering to varied learning styles and capabilities. AI-driven platforms adopted by universities, as examined by Naseer et al. (2024), exhibit measurable enhancements in academic performance and engagement, highlighting the transformative effect of individualized educational trajectories.

Improving Student Involvement, Motivation and Educational Analytics

One of the most significant advantages of AI in personalized learning is its ability to improve student engagement and motivation. Pratama et al. (2023) underscore the significance of AI in fostering stimulating educational settings via virtual instructors and adaptive evaluations. AI technologies promote enhanced understanding and stimulate student engagement in their educational journey by providing tailored feedback and immediate assistance. The study by Xu et al. (2025) highlights that AI-driven individualized feedback serves as a significant motivator, enhancing students' goal attainment and self-efficacy. This personalized assistance fosters a greater sense of connection to educational endeavors, resulting in enduring motivation and academic achievement.

Artificial intelligence markedly enhances educational analytics, offering instructors essential insights into student performance and learning dynamics. Shoaib et al. (2024) emphasize that AI-driven systems can forecast student success and risk factors, facilitating proactive interventions that enhance student retention and achievement. These analytics enable lecturers to refine instructional tactics and enhance learning results by addressing individual needs and problems. The augmented data capabilities provided by AI promote a culture of informed decision-making in educational institutions, resulting in more efficient and focused support for students.

The incorporation of AI in individualized education, albeit advantageous, necessitates meticulous attention to ethical and privacy issues. Haetami (2025) emphasizes the necessity of establishing comprehensive legal frameworks and ethical norms to safeguard student data and guarantee algorithmic equity. Transparent data governance protocols are crucial for cultivating trust and encouraging appropriate AI utilization in educational settings. Kousa and Niemi (2023) promote explicability and accountability in artificial intelligence systems, guaranteeing that their functions are comprehensible and reliable. By confronting these difficulties, institutions may establish a secure and equitable educational environment that optimizes AI's capabilities.

Challenges for Integrating AI into Personalized Learning

The effective incorporation of AI in higher education offers both obstacles and prospects. Vorobyeva et al. (2025) emphasize the necessity for holistic techniques that concurrently tackle technological, educational, and ethical concerns. Cooperative initiatives among lecturers, technologists, and policymakers are essential for the effective and inclusive application of AI. Caucheteux et al. (2024) underscore the significance of incorporating many viewpoints, particularly those of students, in the development and implementation of AI systems. By employing a comprehensive strategy that includes all stakeholders, institutions may reduce risks and harness AI's transformative potential for individualized learning.

Incorporating AI into personalized learning presents numerous obstacles that must be resolved to achieve its maximum potential. The primary worry is data privacy and security, as AI systems depend on the collection and analysis of extensive student information (Haetami, 2025). Educational institutions must implement stringent data governance policies to safeguard sensitive information and ensure ethical usage. Ruano-Borbalan (2025) emphasizes the risk of algorithmic bias, which may result in disparities in educational achievements if AI systems are not well calibrated to prevent the reinforcement of existing prejudices. Lecturers must diligently monitor AI outputs to guarantee that individualized learning experiences are equitable and inclusive.

A significant obstacle of AI integration into personalized learning is the necessity for considerable investment in technology infrastructure. Institutions must dedicate resources to develop and sustain sophisticated AI-driven systems, necessitating substantial financial investment (Ruano-Borbalan, 2025). This investment transcends hardware and software, incorporating teacher training and support systems to guarantee that lecturers can proficiently utilize AI tools in their instructional methodologies. Haetami (2025) emphasizes the necessity of governmental policies that prioritize the equal allocation of AI resources to ensure that students in underprivileged areas are not marginalized. Moreover, cultivating partnerships with technology suppliers is essential to remain abreast of swift developments in AI.

Academic integrity and ethical considerations pose additional hurdles in the incorporation of AI. The capacity of AI to automate jobs and analyze data generates apprehensions regarding academic dishonesty, especially in evaluation methods (Muludzi & Hamilton, 2025). Lecturers must adopt creative tactics, like AI detection tools and restructured examinations, to maintain academic integrity while enabling students to ethically utilize AI resources. Moreover, there exists a risk of excessive dependence on AI, potentially undermining human judgment and pedagogical skill if AI systems are regarded as substitutes rather than supplements to human lecturerss (Farooq et al., 2024). Formulating ethical criteria for AI implementation in education guarantees that technology enhances rather than supplants conventional teaching techniques.

Ultimately, the incorporation of AI necessitates traversing intricate regulatory frameworks, which may impede its extensive implementation. National rules regulating AI implementation and advancement in education are inadequately designed, resulting in deficiencies in supervision and accountability (Haetami, 2025). Silva et al. (2024) propose that harmonizing innovation with regulation is crucial for promoting technological progress while safeguarding the rights and privacy of both students and lecturers. Cooperative initiatives among educational institutions, governmental bodies, and technology vendors are essential to formulate explicit ethical criteria and legal protections for AI in personalized learning. Addressing these difficulties is essential for sustainably leveraging AI's transformational potential.

Opportunities For The Integration Of Artificial Intelligence Into Personalized Learning

Notwithstanding the limitations, the incorporation of AI into personalized learning offers various options that can substantially improve educational experiences. Artificial intelligence facilitates the personalization of educational trajectories, adapting teaching strategies and materials to meet the specific requirements of each student (Merino-Campos, 2025). By utilizing adaptive algorithms and machine learning models, educational institutions may provide tailored learning experiences that accommodate various learning styles and preferences, hence enhancing engagement and academic achievement. The capacity to deliver immediate feedback and assistance allows students to traverse their educational paths more efficiently, utilizing AI-driven systems that perpetually adapt to enhance learning results.

Another opportunity exists in AI's ability to optimize administrative operations, allowing lecturers to concentrate on instruction and student assistance. Automated grading systems and intelligent tutoring platforms alleviate instructors' workloads by managing mundane activities, enabling them to focus on personalized education and the development of critical thinking abilities (Silva et al., 2024). This automation supports Ruano-Borbalan's (2025) claim that AI serves as a "exoskeleton" for lecturers, enhancing their capabilities rather than supplanting them. As AI systems assume administrative responsibilities, lecturers can allocate increased time and resources to investigating creative pedagogical approaches and fostering deeper engagement with students.

The incorporation of AI into personalized learning enhances educational analytics, supplying institutions with critical insights about student progress and learning practices. Utilizing AI-driven analytics, lecturers can discern patterns and trends that guide interventions, guaranteeing prompt help for students needing extra assistance

(Silva et al., 2024). The extensive data produced by AI systems enhances instructional tactics, hence enhancing teaching efficacy and student results. This ability to convert data into actionable insights enables schools to identify educational deficiencies and customize their curricula to accommodate changing student requirements.

Moreover, AI can promote inclusivity and accessibility in education by customizing learning materials and resources to accommodate the requirements of students with impairments or those from underprivileged areas (Mariyono & Hd, 2025). AI-driven personalized learning platforms can be tailored to meet diverse accessibility needs, guaranteeing equal access to quality education for all students. The creation and application of AI solutions that emphasize inclusivity can help close the digital divide, fostering a fairer educational environment. By utilizing AI's ability for personalization, educational institutions can provide tailored learning experiences that address individuals' individual circumstances and obstacles.

Although the integration of AI into personalized learning poses considerable hurdles, it provides transformative prospects that can improve educational results and experiences. By addressing ethical considerations, investing in infrastructure, and promoting collaboration, educational institutions can leverage AI's promise to personalize learning experiences, automate administrative tasks, enhance analytics, and promote inclusion. With deliberate and purposeful integration, AI can function as a potent instrument in transforming individualized learning, enabling students to thrive in a changing educational environment. This chapter offers insights to assist lecturers and policymakers in the responsible and effective utilization of AI for educational innovation as it transforms teaching techniques and learning approaches.

AI possesses significant potential to improve personalized learning in higher education by providing personalized educational experiences that address individual requirements and preferences. AI can foster an inclusive and dynamic learning environment that enhances academic success through adaptive learning, student engagement, educational analytics, and ethical considerations. Realizing AI's full potential necessitates deliberate integration and ongoing collaboration across educational stakeholders. By synchronizing AI capabilities with educational objectives, schools can equip students for a swiftly changing global workforce while tackling ethical and practical concerns. This chapter offers guidance for lecturers and policymakers on the responsible and successful utilization of AI as it transforms the educational landscape.

THE APPLICATION OF ARTIFICIAL INTELLIGENCE IN PERSONALIZED LEARNING WITHIN HIGHER EDUCATION: CASE STUDIES AND EXAMPLES

The incorporation of artificial intelligence (AI) in education signifies a significant change, facilitating a more personalized and adaptive learning experience for students across all levels. This transformation is reshaping traditional educational paradigms and improving the effectiveness of instructional methodologies across various disciplines (Kaswan et al., 2024). Notable applications of AI in education include Intelligent Tutoring Systems (ITS) and adaptive learning platforms, which have significantly enhanced personalized instruction and skill development (Bhatia et al., 2024).

Intelligent Tutoring Systems (ITS) Facilitating Personalized Learning Experiences

Intelligent Tutoring Systems (ITS) utilize Artificial Intelligence (AI) technology to enhance educational experiences by providing personalized learning pathways customized to the specific needs of each learner. Farooq et al. (2024) emphasize that ITS employs sophisticated machine learning algorithms and natural language processing to evaluate student performance, preferences, and areas needing enhancement in real time. These systems tailor instruction by examining learning behaviors, thereby enhancing the delivery of instructional content and engaging students effectively. By modifying teaching tactics according to real-time data, ITS guarantees that students obtain the requisite help to address knowledge deficiencies, thereby improving their academic achievement. This tailored method enables students to assume responsibility for their educational experience, promoting an atmosphere favorable to continuous involvement and success.

The application of machine learning and natural language processing in Intelligent Tutoring Systems enables advanced evaluation and modification of educational materials to align with individual learning profiles. According to Kaswan et al. (2024), machine learning algorithms in Intelligent Tutoring Systems evaluate complex patterns in student interactions, allowing the system to discern strengths, weaknesses, and learning style preferences. Natural language processing enhances this procedure by analyzing student replies to customize instructional content and feedback. This dynamic adaptability guarantees that ITS delivers educational experiences tailored to each student's distinct needs, hence improving understanding and engagement. Consequently, ITS revolutionizes conventional educational methods, providing a more sophisticated and individualized teaching strategy that markedly enhances student learning outcomes.

The immediate feedback and customized resources offered by ITS greatly improve student understanding and involvement in diverse educational settings. As stated by Asy'ari & Sharov (2024), the promptness of feedback in ITS allows students to swiftly recognize and correct misconceptions, hence enhancing comprehension and retention of content. Personalized resources, including personalized exercises and specific learning modules, offer students concentrated chances to practice and enhance abilities in identified areas of need. This focused assistance not only targets certain skill deficiencies but also fosters an engaging and participative learning atmosphere. By providing resources specifically tailored to individual needs, ITS fosters a learning environment that encourages students to engage deeply with content, ultimately optimizing their academic potential.

Intelligent Tutoring Systems have exhibited adaptability and efficacy across multiple disciplines, resulting in improved learning outcomes in areas such as mathematics, sciences, language acquisition, and vocational education. Revathy J. et al. (2025) observe the varied utilization of ITS in customizing educational experiences to meet subject-specific needs, hence enhancing student competence and proficiency. In language acquisition, ITS has significantly enhanced learning via interactive exercises, tailored vocabulary recommendations, and real-time conversational practices (Lyu & Salam, 2025). These systems adjust to enhance the learner experience, leading to better language proficiency and communicative ability. In science education, ITS offers students the chance to participate in interactive problem-solving sessions, enhancing critical thinking and deepening comprehension of essential topics (Caucheteux et al., 2024). The capacity of ITS to adjust to diverse educational situations highlights its significance as a transformative instrument in creating more effective and tailored learning environments.

ITS greatly enhances critical thinking skills and conceptual understanding among students by fostering interactive and solution-oriented educational experiences. Caucheteux et al. (2024) demonstrate that ITS in science education enhances problem-solving sessions, requiring students to apply theoretical knowledge in practical contexts, so effectively bridging the divide between theory and practice. By prompting students to explore various ideas and engage in reflective thought, ITS cultivates an environment that enhances creativity and analytical abilities. These interactive workshops enhance students' capacity to synthesize material and foster confidence in applying acquired concepts in practical scenarios. By emphasizing critical engagement and problem-solving, ITS significantly contributes to fostering a comprehensive learning experience that enables students to address intricate educational issues.

A key feature of ITS is its capacity to manage extensive data to inform and modify teaching tactics, ensuring that learning is precisely aligned with students' changing requirements. Merino-Campos (2025) emphasizes that the data-driven methodology of ITS provides lecturers with insights into student performance, facilitating proactive modifications and personalized interventions. These findings are essential for designing instructional pathways that adapt to student progress, thus enhancing learning experiences. Furthermore, the predictive analytics features of ITS provide insight into possible learning obstacles, enabling lecturers to proactively resolve issues and refine teaching strategies. By aligning real-time data with educational tactics, ITS markedly improves the accuracy and efficacy of personalized learning initiatives.

The ethical ramifications of integrating Intelligent Tutoring Systems into education require meticulous evaluation to guarantee the proper application of AI technology in safeguarding academic integrity and data privacy. Mulaudzi and Hamilton (2025) underscore the imperative for institutions to implement transparent data governance frameworks and ethical norms to alleviate concerns linked to AI. ITS must comply with privacy rules to safeguard sensitive student information while assuring the security of acquired data. Furthermore, lecturers must possess the competencies required to appropriately analyze AI outputs, ensuring human oversight to enhance automated insights. By tackling these ethical and privacy issues, ITS can function as a mechanism for equitable educational progress, allowing institutions to harness AI's promise while protecting students' rights.

The future of Intelligent Tutoring Systems depends on their capacity to adapt and change according to new educational demands, consistently refining and improving personalized learning experiences. Haetami (2025) asserts that the partnership between lecturers and technology developers is essential for aligning Intelligent Tutoring Systems (ITS) with pedagogical objectives. As Intelligent Transportation Systems grow, they must incorporate inclusive design principles to accommodate various student groups and address educational disparities. By emphasizing collaborative development and ethical execution, ITS can achieve its maximum potential as a revolutionary educational instrument, cultivating an atmosphere where individualized learning transcends traditional limits. By doing so, ITS will maintain its leadership in educational innovation, enabling students through personalized and significant learning experiences.

Intelligent Tutoring Systems signify a substantial progression in educational personalization, providing personalized learning experiences that address the unique requirements of individual students across diverse fields. ITS employs AI technology to deliver flexible, data-informed, and interactive learning pathways that improve understanding, engagement, and analytical reasoning. The potential of Intelligent Tutoring Systems as facilitators of individualized learning is substantial; nevertheless, achieving this potential necessitates the resolution of ethical issues and the promotion of inclusive and collaborative development. As institutions increasingly incorporate ITS into educational settings, these systems are set to revolutionize pedagogical practices, facilitating transformative learning experiences that equip students for success in a complex and dynamic world.

Advancements Impacting University Students' Understanding and Skill Acquisition

Advancements in AI have notably impacted students' understanding and skill acquisition in higher education (Strielkowski et al., 2025). AI-driven systems have been incorporated into curricula at universities globally to evaluate and enhance student learning outcomes (Shoaib et al., 2024). These systems employ data analytics to pinpoint areas of student difficulty or success, allowing lecturers to provide more focused teaching interventions and support.

Recent studies indicate that AI applications enhance students' self-efficacy, motivation, and digital literacy within university environments (Xu et al., 2025). AI enhances students' goal-setting and achievement through personalized feedback and adaptive learning pathways, thereby fostering greater academic engagement and success (Merino-Campos, 2025). The incorporation of AI in higher education curricula provides students with essential digital skills and competencies necessary for the contemporary workforce, thereby aligning educational goals with industry requirements (Ruano-Borbalan, 2025).

Advancements in artificial intelligence have significantly influenced students' comprehension and skill development in higher education. AI-driven technologies have been integrated into university curricula worldwide to assess and improve student learning results (Strielkowski et al., 2025). These systems utilize data analytics to identify areas of student struggle or achievement, enabling lecturers to deliver more targeted instructional interventions and assistance. AI technology can assess patterns in student performance and detect comprehension gaps, facilitating personalized teaching approaches that enhance learning efficiency (Shoaib et al., 2024). Additionally, AI systems produce detailed reports on student progress that assist instructors in customizing their teaching approaches to meet individual learning requirements, hence improving academic performance and skill development.

Recent research demonstrates that AI apps improve students' self-efficacy, motivation, and digital literacy in university settings (Xu et al., 2025). AI technologies offer individualized feedback that enhances students' confidence by affirming their learning advancements and identifying areas for development. This personalized engagement promotes accountability and ownership of one's educational path, enhancing self-directed learning and motivation (Merino-Campos, 2025). Moreover, AI tools compel students to enhance their digital skills by interacting with technology-driven learning platforms, equipping them for the progressively digital workforce. Integrating these tools into university courses enables institutions to cultivate important digital skills necessary for addressing modern industry requirements.

Artificial intelligence improves students' goal-setting and accomplishment by providing tailored feedback and adaptive learning pathways, therefore promoting enhanced academic engagement and performance. Adaptive learning technologies enable students to advance at their own speed, providing personalized content that aligns with their capabilities and learning preferences (Shoaib et al., 2024). This method optimizes learning efficiency while enhancing student satisfaction by addressing individual educational needs and preferences. Increased engagement is apparent when students pursue specific objectives within tailored learning frameworks, building confidence through ongoing feedback and reinforcement. Consequently, students are more adept at addressing intricate academic problems, resulting in effective skill acquisition and a profound comprehension of course content.

The integration of AI into higher education curricula equips students with vital digital skills and capabilities required for the modern workforce, thus matching educational objectives with industrial demands (Ruano-Borbalan, 2025). AI-driven educational settings prioritize digital literacy by promoting student engagement with sophisticated technological tools and platforms. This exposure enhances their comprehension of digital interfaces and equips them for positions necessitating technical expertise. Moreover, AI technologies replicate real-world settings, enabling students to practice and enhance their skills in problem-solving, critical thinking, and innovation. As a result, university graduates enter the labor market with a competitive advantage, equipped with the digital proficiency and agility desired by contemporary enterprises.

Furthermore, AI promotes collaborative learning experiences that augment skill acquisition and comprehension among university students. AI-driven systems frequently have functionalities that facilitate virtual collaboration, enabling students to collaborate on projects and assignments regardless of geographical constraints (Strielkowski et al., 2025). These platforms foster collaboration and enhance communication skills, as students work together to address challenges and exchange knowledge. This virtual connection reflects the interconnected nature of the global workforce, equipping students to participate in collaborative initiatives in professional contexts. AI-facilitated collaboration enables students to acquire useful insights from their peers, thereby enhancing their learning experience and promoting the exchange of varied ideas and solutions.

Although AI offers distinct benefits in education, concerns concerning ethical considerations and data protection must be resolved to enhance its effect on student learning. The dependence on data-driven AI systems requires diligence in safeguarding student information and guaranteeing the ethical application of AI technology (Ruano-Borbalan, 2025). Universities must establish stringent data governance rules and ethical standards to protect student privacy and cultivate trust in AI applications. Furthermore, sustaining human supervision in AI-assisted education is crucial to harmonize technical interventions with compassionate and individualized academic assistance. Confronting these problems will enhance the effectiveness of AI in improving university students' comprehension and skill development, facilitating a responsible incorporation of AI technology in academia.

Improvements in artificial intelligence have significantly impacted students' comprehension and skill development in higher education. AI-driven systems are essential for recognizing educational problems and achievements, facilitating more personalized and effective teaching methodologies. The utilization of AI enhances students' self-efficacy and motivation while providing them with essential digital literacy skills necessary for future employment in technology-driven sectors. AI technologies facilitate goal-setting and academic achievement through the provision of individualized learning experiences. Furthermore, AI cultivates collaborative learning environments that equip students for teamwork and communication in professional contexts. Although AI offers significant educational advantages, it is essential to address data privacy and ethical issues to optimize its beneficial effects. As institutions increasingly utilize AI in educational environments, meticulous attention to these issues will guarantee that AI-enhanced learning progresses responsibly, improving both student results and institutional objectives.

Adaptive Learning Platforms and the Personalized Learning Pathways

Adaptive learning platforms exemplify a significant application of AI in personalized education, facilitating the personalized learning pathways and content delivery across diverse curricula (Silva et al., 2024). These platforms employ advanced algorithms to assess students' learning patterns and preferences, thereby dynamically modifying the instructional content and pace to meet individual needs (Mariyono & Hd, 2025). These systems enhance the educational experience by storing and processing historical learning data, thereby optimizing student engagement and achievement (Rane, 2025).

Adaptive learning platforms have been extensively utilized in K-12 and higher education environments to improve student-centered learning (Vivitsou, 2023). In K-12 classrooms, these systems enable teachers to differentiate instruction, allowing them to address the diverse needs of students, including those with disabilities or from underserved backgrounds (Revathy J. et al., 2025). In higher education, adaptive platforms have been effectively incorporated into hybrid and online learning environments, aiding students in navigating their personal learning trajectories and academic objectives (Bhatia et al., 2024).

Adaptive learning platforms represent notable progress in the utilization of AI in personalized education, serving as catalysts for personalized learning pathways and content across various curricula. These systems utilize sophisticated algorithms to evaluate students' learning habits and preferences, adjusting instructional content and pace to accommodate individual requirements (Silva et al., 2024). These technologies improve educational experiences by archiving and analyzing historical learning data, therefore maximizing student engagement and success (Rane, 2025). Ultimately, adaptable platforms serve as a revolutionary instrument in educational environments, facilitating more personalized and effective learning experiences for students.

These advanced platforms have transformed the educational landscape by utilizing AI algorithms to examine extensive data on student interactions and performance. Mariyono & Hd (2025) underscore the significance of adaptive learning systems in evaluating real-time data to modify instructional strategies and resources based on the specific requirements of each student. Utilizing this information, the platform can customize learning pathways and guarantee that each student receives content according to their learning style. Moreover, the platforms enable ongoing optimization through the incorporation of feedback loops, facilitating iterative enhancements in content distribution. Adaptive learning platforms facilitate personalized educational experiences that promote student performance through a dynamic approach.

The capacity of adaptive learning platforms to improve student engagement and performance is crucial to their increasing implementation in educational environments. Rane (2025) emphasizes that these systems analyze past learning data to guide instructional tactics, facilitating deeper student engagement with the topic. Adaptive platforms enhance educational engagement by delivering content that aligns with students' interests and learning styles, resulting in better academic performance. Furthermore, the personalized learning experiences mitigate frustration and disengagement by maintaining students' challenges at suitable levels, thereby enhancing motivation and achievement. Ultimately, adaptive learning platforms foster a friendly and dynamic educational atmosphere that promotes student achievement.

Adaptive learning platforms have been widely employed in K-12 settings to enhance student-centered learning. Vivitsou (2023) demonstrates how these methods facilitate differentiated learning, addressing the varied requirements of students, including those from marginalized backgrounds and individuals with disabilities. By customizing educational experiences, lecturers may create a more inclusive and supportive learning environment in which every student can flourish. Furthermore, adaptive platforms aid lecturers in recognizing and rectifying learning deficiencies, facilitating focused interventions to promote comprehensive growth. Consequently, these platforms are essential in converting the conventional educational model into a more personalized and dynamic learning experience for young students.

Adaptive learning tools have been successfully integrated into hybrid and online higher education settings, assisting students in managing their learning paths and academic goals. Bhatia et al. (2024) underscore the significance of these platforms in delivering tailored assistance and resources that correspond with students' objectives, thus enriching their academic experience. Adaptive systems provide students with enhanced flexibility in balancing their education with other obligations through self-paced learning. Moreover, the platforms facilitate the cultivation of lifelong learning competencies by promoting student autonomy in their educational pursuits. Adaptive learning platforms offer a framework in higher education that facilitates tailored learning routes, enabling students to realize their academic potential.

Although adaptive learning platforms provide significant advantages, their use in educational environments presents problems. Institutions must confront ethical issues related to data privacy and guarantee algorithmic equity to avert biases (Merino-Campos, 2025). Furthermore, the integration of these platforms necessitates substantial investment in technology infrastructure and lecturers' training (Bhatia et al., 2024). These issues require joint efforts among lecturers, technologists, and policymakers to facilitate successful integration. Notwithstanding these challenges, the capacity of adaptive learning systems to improve educational results renders them a worthwhile investment for schools dedicated to providing personalized education.

Adaptive learning platforms represent a significant advancement in AI's contribution to personalized education, providing a robust framework for tailoring curricular content and learning trajectories to meet the specific needs of individual students. These platforms, spanning K-12 to higher education, augment engagement and achievement through the utilization of AI algorithms that assess real-time data and tailor learning experiences. Despite the limitations in their implementation, the transformative potential of adaptive learning systems highlights their significance in promoting dynamic and personalized educational experiences. As schools use adaptive platforms, the emphasis is on maintaining a balanced and ethical approach that safeguards students' rights while promoting optimal learning results. Adaptive learning systems serve as foundational elements in the quest for personalized education, enabling students to excel in ever-intricate and varied educational settings.

Examples of Effective Applications in Higher Education

Various case studies demonstrate the successful implementation of AI in higher education. AI tools, including intelligent tutoring systems and adaptive learning platforms, have played a crucial role in offering personalized support to students with learning disabilities, such as autism spectrum disorder (Diviya et al., 2025). Assistive technologies such as speech-to-text and predictive models enhance inclusivity and accessibility, enabling lecturers to provide timely interventions for at-risk students (Ruano-Borbalan, 2025).

In higher education, AI applications encompass not only classroom settings but also administrative processes, where AI-driven systems enhance resource allocation, scheduling, and student support (Shoaib et al., 2024). Campus Management Systems (CMS) that incorporate AI student success predictors automate grading processes, forecast student risks, and enhance retention rates by analyzing patterns in student data and enabling proactive interventions (Farooq et al., 2024). This integration enhances decision-making and optimizes efficiency and resource management within educational institutions (Lytras et al., 2024).

Additionally, AI-driven Massive Open Online Courses (MOOCs) provide a large-scale method for personalized learning, attracting learners from various backgrounds and locations (Alexandre et al., 2024). These courses employ AI to deliver tailored learning resources and assessments, promoting learner autonomy and engagement, regardless of physical proximity to educational institutions (Kousa & Niemi, 2023).

The incorporation of AI applications may transform the educational landscape by facilitating personalized learning experiences tailored to the unique needs and aspirations of individual students. Intelligent Tutoring Systems, adaptive learning platforms, and other AI-driven tools are pivotal in transforming higher education and K-12 environments, enhancing student outcomes, engagement, and skill development (Kaswan et al., 2024). To fully harness the transformative potential of AI, educational institutions must address ethical considerations, ensure data privacy, and provide equitable access to AI technologies, thereby creating an inclusive and resilient educational ecosystem for learners globally (Haetami, 2025). Embracing AI in a balanced, ethical, and human-centered manner can enhance the future of education, yielding significant benefits for students, lecturers, and society at large.

The increasing influence of artificial intelligence in education indicates that this technological revolution has the potential to redefine paradigms in higher education and provide students with personalized, adaptive learning experiences. Realizing this potential requires a multifaceted approach that incorporates ethical considerations into all aspects of AI deployment. Clear protocols, diverse datasets, and a focus on human-centric teaching enable educational institutions to effectively navigate the complexities associated with AI integration. The effectiveness of AI in reshaping education hinges not solely on technological progress but also on our shared dedication to safeguarding individual rights and fostering social equity. Ongoing dialogue and collaboration among lecturers, technologists, policymakers, and the academic community can position AI as a significant ally in advancing inclusive and transformative education. In shaping the future of higher education, prioritizing ethics is essential to ensure that technology serves as a tool for empowerment and enhances access to quality education for all learners.

IMPLICATIONS

The incorporation of Artificial Intelligence (AI) in higher education has significant implications for theories, pedagogies, and practices, providing transformative opportunities alongside notable challenges. As educational institutions increasingly adopt AI-driven tools, it is essential to examine and understand the implications to fully harness AI's potential in reshaping the educational landscape.

Theoretical Implications

The integration of AI requires a reassessment of educational theories, especially those concerning learning and motivation. The Technology Acceptance Model (Mulaudzi & Hamilton, 2025) provides a framework for understanding the attitudes of lecturers and students towards AI technologies. With the increasing prominence of AI in educational contexts, theories of cognitive and motivational development must evolve to consider how AI-driven personalized learning environments affect student engagement and intrinsic motivation (Xu et al., 2025). Theories of constructivism, traditionally focused on the learner's active construction of knowledge, may evolve to include the role of AI in offering adaptive scaffolding and personalized learning experiences tailored to individual needs. The self-determination theory, which highlights autonomy, competence, and relatedness, is being applied in AI environments that can enhance these elements through personalized learning paths and adaptive feedback (Farooq et al., 2024).

Pedagogical Implications

The role of AI in pedagogy is significant, providing innovative methods for teaching and learning. The concepts of personalized learning are transformed by AI's capacity to deliver real-time analytics and feedback, thereby significantly improving instructional methods (Silva et al., 2024). Pedagogical models should evolve to utilize AI's ability to personalize learning experiences, enhancing student engagement and academic performance through personalized content and pacing (Kaswan et al., 2024). The flipped classroom model may be improved through the integration of AI-powered tools that provide personalized pre-class learning materials and post-class assessments, thereby optimizing classroom interactions for higher-order thinking and collaborative problem-solving. Lecturers should integrate AI as complementary tools, allowing them to concentrate on fostering critical thinking and creativity instead of being burdened by administrative tasks (Mariyono & Hd, 2025).

The role of AI as a pedagogical tool indicates a necessity for greater focus on ethics and critical thinking skills within educational curricula (Mulaudzi & Hamilton, 2025). With the growing interaction between students and AI, curricula need to incorporate training on ethical AI usage and data privacy concerns to equip students for responsible technological engagement (Vivitsou, 2023). Additionally, AI's capacity to support differentiated instruction enables lecturers to more effectively address diverse student needs, especially in special education settings where conventional approaches may be inadequate (Diviya et al., 2025).

Practical Implications

AI significantly alters the operations of educational institutions, impacting student management systems and administrative processes. The emergence of AI-driven Campus Management Systems (CMSs) that automate grading, predict student risks, and forecast retention outcomes signifies a transition towards greater efficiency and improved academic decision-making (Shoaib et al., 2024). The implementation of AI in these systems necessitates stringent standards of privacy and accountability to safeguard student data and maintain ethical practices (Haetami, 2025).

Furthermore, AI compels lecturers to reevaluate their methodologies following the technology's potential. Professional development and training are essential, ensuring lecturers have the requisite skills to effectively integrate AI into their teaching (Farooq et al., 2024). As artificial intelligence assumes an increasing number of routine tasks, lecturers are liberated to concentrate on interactions that truly necessitate human empathy and insight, essential components in educational settings (Revathy J. et al., 2025).

As AI is set to influence assessment practices, lecturers should evaluate the potential of adaptive learning platforms and AI-driven assessments to enhance fairness and comprehensiveness in evaluation methods (Merino-Campos, 2025). The potential for bias in AI underscores the need for transparent and equitable algorithmic processes, which necessitates that lecturers engage in continuous evaluation and calibration efforts (Mulaudzi & Hamilton, 2025).

AI significantly impacts educational practices by fostering AI literacy in students, preparing them to effectively navigate and utilize these technologies in their personal and professional lives (Caucheteux et al., 2024). Institutions should integrate AI literacy into their curricula to guarantee that students possess a thorough understanding of AI's capabilities and constraints (Strielkowski et al., 2025).

The implications of AI integration into higher education for theories, pedagogies, and practices are extensive and intricate. Educational institutions must modify their theoretical frameworks, pedagogies, and operational practices to harness AI's potential for transformative change, while ensuring the maintenance of ethical standards and a focus on human-centered learning. With meticulous implementation, AI can significantly enhance educational experiences and equip students to succeed in a digital landscape.

CONCLUSION

The integration of artificial intelligence (AI) into personalized learning experiences marks the onset of a new era in higher education, offering transformative opportunities that remain largely untapped. Artificial intelligence can transform education by personalizing learning experiences, increasing student engagement, and promoting academic achievement. Nevertheless, navigating this transformation necessitates careful consideration of the ethical and practical aspects associated with these technological advancements.

Establishing robust ethical frameworks is essential to ensure that AI integration in education upholds fundamental values. Concerns regarding data privacy are significant, as AI systems require the collection of substantial student data to provide tailored learning experiences. Protecting sensitive information is a priority for educational institutions, requiring transparent data governance protocols that ensure student privacy while facilitating technological innovation. Furthermore, it is essential to address algorithmic biases to prevent the continuation of existing inequalities. AI systems must be trained on diverse and representative datasets that accurately reflect the multicultural and multilingual realities of educational environments, thus fostering inclusivity and equitable access to learning opportunities.

Furthermore, although AI demonstrates significant potential in automating diagnostics and personalizing content, the role of lecturers is essential for upholding the quality and integrity of education. Human oversight guarantees that pedagogical interpretation and emotional support remain integral to AI-assisted learning processes. Lecturers, utilizing insights derived from AI outputs, can customize interventions to meet the distinct needs and aspirations of their students, fostering a collaborative relationship between technology and human understanding. This method enhances personalized instruction while promoting critical thinking and creativity, which are essential in a progressively automated environment.

Investment by institutions in teacher training and development is crucial for effectively managing the complexities associated with AI integration. Lecturers must effectively utilize AI technologies to improve learning experiences, ensuring adherence to ethical standards and a continued emphasis on the human-centered nature of education. Training initiatives that equip lecturers with essential skills can foster the responsible and innovative application of AI tools, promoting an educational ecosystem that prioritizes transparency and accountability.

Moreover, cultivating a culture of responsible AI usage and academic integrity among students begins with implementing ethical education programs that emphasize critical engagement with technology. Students ought to be encouraged to investigate the capabilities and limitations of AI, fostering informed opinions that direct their utilization of these powerful tools. Redesigning assessment strategies to include innovative formats and promoting transparency in AI-assisted academic work enables higher education institutions to effectively reduce the risks associated with academic dishonesty and misuse.

The future of AI in higher education depends on a balanced approach that integrates technological innovation with ethical responsibility. Collaboration among educational stakeholders—policymakers, lecturers, and technologists—is essential for creating inclusive policies that guarantee the equitable distribution of AI benefits among diverse learner populations. Institutions that prioritize ethical, human-centered practices can leverage AI's transformative potential to foster an adaptive and equitable learning environment, thereby enhancing students' educational experiences and equipping them to succeed in a dynamic global landscape. In short, although AI offers significant potential for personalized learning and educational transformation, its effective integration requires adherence to ethical standards, human oversight, and equitable access. By adopting these principles, higher education can adeptly address the complexities of AI, realizing its full potential to transform the future of learning for everyone.

REFERENCES

Akramovna, X. D. (2024). The Role of Artificial Intelligence in Personalized Learning. *International Conference on Language Education: Modern Experiences and Future Prospects*, 144–147. https://doi.org/https://doi.org/10.5281/zenodo.14201229

Alexandre, F., Comte, M.-H., Lagarrigue, A., & Viéville, T. (2024). *Learning Artificial Intelligence Through Open Educational Resources*., DOI: 10.1007/978-3-031-55272-4_3

Asy'ari, M., & Sharov, S. (2024). Transforming Education with ChatGPT: Advancing Personalized Learning, Accessibility, and Ethical AI Integration. *International Journal of Essential Competencies in Education*, *3*(2), 119–157. https://doi.org/https://doi.org/10.36312/ijece.v3i2.242

Ayeni, O. O., Al Hamad, N. M., Chisom, O. N., Osawaru, B., & Adewusi, O. E. (2024). AI in education: A review of personalized learning and educational technology. *GSC Advanced Research and Reviews*, *18*(2), 261–271. DOI: 10.30574/gscarr.2024.18.2.0062

Bhatia, A., Bhatia, P., & Sood, D. (2024). Leveraging AI to Transform Online Higher Education: Focusing on Personalized Learning, Assessment, and Student Engagement. *International Journal of Management and Humanities*, *11*(1), 1–6. https://papers.ssrn.com/sol3/papers.cfm?abstract_id=4959186

Bhutoria, A. (2022). Personalized education and Artificial Intelligence in the United States, China, and India: A systematic review using a Human-In-The-Loop model. *Computers and Education: Artificial Intelligence*, *3*, 100068. DOI: 10.1016/j.caeai.2022.100068

Caucheteux, C., Hodgkins, L.-B., Batifol, V., Fouché, L., & Romero, M. (2024). *Students' Perspective on the Use of Artificial Intelligence in Education* (pp. 101–113). https://doi.org/DOI: 10.1007/978-3-031-55272-4_8

Chang, J., & Lu, X. (2019). The Study on Students' Participation in Personalized Learning Under the Background of Artificial Intelligence. *2019 10th International Conference on Information Technology in Medicine and Education (ITME)*, 555–558. https://doi.org/DOI: 10.1109/ITME.2019.00131

Diviya, M., Subramanian, M., Prabu, M., & Murugan, T. (2025). Revolutionizing Special Education: The Impact of AI and Data Science on Personalized Learning. In *Driving Quality Education Through AI and Data Science* (pp. 73–90). IGI Global. https://doi.org/DOI: 10.4018/979-8-3693-8292-9.ch004

Ellikkal, A., & Rajamohan, S. (2025). AI-enabled personalized learning: Empowering management students for improving engagement and academic performance. *Vilakshan - XIMB. Journal of Management*, *22*(1), 28–44. DOI: 10.1108/XJM-02-2024-0023

Farooq, U., Malik, S. A., & Syed, A. S. (2024). Revolutionizing Higher Education: The Transformative Impact of Artificial Intelligence on Teaching, Learning, and Career Preparation. *ShodhKosh: Journal of Visual and Performing Arts*, *5*(3). Advance online publication. DOI: 10.29121/shodhkosh.v5.i3.2024.3239

Haetami, H. (2025). AI-Driven Educational Transformation in Indonesia: From Learning Personalization to Institutional Management. *Al-Ishlah: Jurnal Pendidikan*, *17*(2), 1819–1832. DOI: 10.35445/alishlah.v17i2.7448

Kaswan, K. S., Dhatterwal, J. S., & Ojha, R. P. (2024). AI in personalized learning. In *Advances in Technological Innovations in Higher Education* (pp. 103–117). CRC Press., DOI: 10.1201/9781003376699-9

Khan, S. M. (2025). AI-based personalized learning in medical education. In *Fundamentals of AI for Medical Education, Research and Practice* (pp. 145–166). Elsevier. https://doi.org/DOI: 10.1016/B978-0-443-33584-6.00007-4

Kousa, P., & Niemi, H. (2023). Artificial Intelligence Ethics from the Perspective of Educational Technology Companies and Schools. In *AI in Learning: Designing the Future* (pp. 283–296). Springer International Publishing. https://doi.org/DOI: 10.1007/978-3-031-09687-7_17

Lokare, V. T., & Jadhav, P. M. (2024). An AI-based learning style prediction model for personalized and effective learning. *Thinking Skills and Creativity*, *51*, 101421. DOI: 10.1016/j.tsc.2023.101421

Lytras, M. D., Serban, A. C., Alkhaldi, A., Aldosemani, T., & Malik, S. (2024). Transformative Learning for Future Higher Education: The Artificial Intelligence-enabled Learning Revolution 2035. In *Digital Transformation in Higher Education, Part B* (pp. 231–241). Emerald Publishing Limited. https://doi.org/DOI: 10.1108/978-1-83608-424-220241009

Lyu, W., & Salam, Z. A. (2025). AI-powered personalized learning: Enhancing self-efficacy, motivation, and digital literacy in adult education through expectancy-value theory. *Learning and Motivation*, *90*, 102129. DOI: 10.1016/j.lmot.2025.102129

Mariyono, D., & Hd, A. N. A. (2025). AI's role in transforming learning environments: A review of collaborative approaches and innovations. *Quality Education for All*, *2*(1), 265–288. DOI: 10.1108/QEA-08-2024-0071

Merino-Campos, C. (2025). The Impact of Artificial Intelligence on Personalized Learning in Higher Education: A Systematic Review. *Trends in Higher Education*, *4*(2), 17. DOI: 10.3390/higheredu4020017

Mulaudzi, L. V., & Hamilton, J. (2025). Lecturer's Perspective on the Role of AI in Personalized Learning: Benefits, Challenges, and Ethical Considerations in Higher Education. *Journal of Academic Ethics*. Advance online publication. DOI: 10.1007/s10805-025-09615-1

Naseer, F., Khan, M. N., Tahir, M., Addas, A., & Aejaz, S. M. H. (2024). Integrating deep learning techniques for personalized learning pathways in higher education. *Heliyon*, *10*(11), e32628. DOI: 10.1016/j.heliyon.2024.e32628 PMID: 38961899

Pratama, M. P., Sampelolo, R., & Lura, H. (2023). Revolutionizing Education: Harnessing the Power of Artificial Intelligence for Personalized Learning. *KLASIKAL : JOURNAL OF EDUCATION, LANGUAGE TEACHING AND SCIENCE*, *5*(2), 350–357. DOI: 10.52208/klasikal.v5i2.877

Rane, N. L. (2025). Education 4.0 and 5.0: integrating Artificial Intelligence (AI) for personalized and adaptive learning. *Journal of Artificial Intelligence and Robotics*. https://doi.org/DOI: 10.61577/jaiar.2024.100006

Revathy, J. S., Sachdeva M., R., M. S., A., & T. G., M. D. (2025). Transforming Personalized Learning With Artificial Intelligence. In *Driving Quality Education Through AI and Data Science* (pp. 311–332). IGI Global. https://doi.org/DOI: 10.4018/979-8-3693-8292-9.ch014

Ruano-Borbalan, J.-C. (2025). The transformative impact of artificial intelligence on higher education: A critical reflection on current trends and future directions. *International Journal of Chinese Education*, *14*(1). Advance online publication. DOI: 10.1177/2212585X251319364

Shoaib, M., Sayed, N., Singh, J., Shafi, J., Khan, S., & Ali, F. (2024). AI student success predictor: Enhancing personalized learning in campus management systems. *Computers in Human Behavior*, *158*, 108301. DOI: 10.1016/j.chb.2024.108301

Silva, G., Godwin, G., & Jayanagara, O. (2024). The Impact of AI on Personalized Learning and Educational Analytics. [ITEE]. *International Transactions on Education Technology*, *3*(1), 36–46. DOI: 10.33050/itee.v3i1.669

Strielkowski, W., Grebennikova, V., Lisovskiy, A., Rakhimova, G., & Vasileva, T. (2025). AI-driven adaptive learning for sustainable educational transformation. *Sustainable Development*, *33*(2), 1921–1947. DOI: 10.1002/sd.3221

Vivitsou, M. (2023). Perspectives and Metaphors of Learning: A Commentary on James Lester's Narrative-Centered AI-Based Environments. In *AI in Learning: Designing the Future* (pp. 125–136). Springer International Publishing. https://doi .org/DOI: 10.1007/978-3-031-09687-7_8

Vorobyeva, K. I., Belous, S., Savchenko, N. V., Smirnova, L. M., Nikitina, S. A., & Zhdanov, S. P. (2025). Personalized learning through AI: Pedagogical approaches and critical insights. *Contemporary Educational Technology*, *17*(2), ep574. DOI: 10.30935/cedtech/16108

Xu, Q., Liu, Y., & Li, X. (2025). Unlocking student potential: How AI-driven personalized feedback shapes goal achievement, self-efficacy, and learning engagement through a self-determination lens. *Learning and Motivation*, *91*, 102138. DOI: 10.1016/j.lmot.2025.102138

Zavalevskyi, Y., Kyrilenko, S., Kijan, O., Bessarab, N., & Mosyakova, I. (2024). The role of AI in individualizing learning and creating personalized programs. *Revista Amazonia Investiga*, *13*(73), 200–208. DOI: 10.34069/AI/2024.73.01.16

Chapter 15
The Future of AI in Indian Higher Education

Sneh Lata
https://orcid.org/0009-0007-8195-6491
G.C. Rithoj, Gurugram University, Gurugram, India

ABSTRACT

This chapter explores the transformative potential of Artificial Intelligence (AI) in Indian higher education by analyzing current trends, benefits, challenges, and future prospects. It highlights how AI is reshaping pedagogy, enhancing personalized learning, streamlining administrative processes, and preparing students for future job markets. Drawing on secondary data and literature, the study identifies key barriers such as infrastructural gaps, faculty readiness, cost, ethical concerns, and linguistic limitations. The chapter concludes with forward-looking policy recommendations to promote inclusive, scalable, and ethical AI adoption across diverse educational contexts in India.

1. INTRODUCTION

Artificial Intelligence (AI) is rapidly reshaping the contours of global education, catalyzing an unprecedented transformation in teaching methodologies, administrative operations, and academic research. In the context of India—a nation with a vast and diverse educational landscape—AI adoption is emerging as a critical enabler for addressing long-standing systemic challenges such as low gross enrollment ratios (GER), disparities in access, outdated pedagogy, and administrative inefficiencies. While the global AI in education market is expected to reach USD 20 billion by 2027

DOI: 10.4018/979-8-3373-3000-6.ch015

(MarketsandMarkets, 2022), India's AI market alone is projected to touch USD 7.8 billion by 2025, with education cited as a primary growth sector (NASSCOM, 2021).

The convergence of digital transformation and educational reform has been accelerated by policy developments such as the National Education Policy (NEP) 2020, which explicitly promotes the integration of emerging technologies—including AI—into the curriculum and institutional frameworks. AI holds particular promise in personalizing learning pathways, supporting at-risk students, automating routine tasks, and enabling data-driven decision-making at all levels of higher education administration. Institutions such as the Indian Institutes of Technology (IITs) and Indian Institutes of Management (IIMs) have taken the lead in incorporating AI-centric modules, courses, and research initiatives. Meanwhile, the proliferation of EdTech platforms such as Byju's, upGrad, and Vedantu has further underscored the potential of AI to democratize access to high-quality learning experiences. Despite these advancements, the application of AI in Indian higher education is still nascent and unevenly distributed. Disparities in digital infrastructure, lack of faculty training, and ethical concerns about data privacy and algorithmic bias continue to hinder holistic integration. According to a 2022 AICTE report, less than 50% of rural Indian universities have access to high-speed internet, creating a digital chasm that limits the scalability of AI innovations (AICTE, 2022). Moreover, a 2021 FICCI survey revealed that only 35% of Indian faculty had undergone any form of AI training, illustrating the urgent need for robust capacity-building initiatives.

Ethical and legal concerns also loom large. The use of AI-based assessments and predictive analytics raises questions about transparency, accountability, and student data protection. There is a growing recognition that while AI can enhance educational equity, it also risks amplifying existing inequalities if not thoughtfully implemented. According to NITI Aayog's National AI Strategy (2018), the ethical deployment of AI in education must be guided by principles of fairness, inclusivity, and explainability.

Against this backdrop, this chapter seeks to provide a comprehensive, data-driven analysis of AI's transformative potential in Indian higher education. It synthesizes secondary data from scholarly journals, policy documents, industry whitepapers, and government reports to evaluate the state of AI adoption, identify key benefits and limitations, and project future trajectories. Through this examination, the chapter also aims to provide actionable recommendations for policymakers, educators, and administrators seeking to harness AI responsibly and effectively.

1.1. Review Of Related Literature

The global discourse on AI in education has increasingly emphasized its potential to enhance personalization, accessibility, and administrative efficiency. Scholars such as Luckin et al. (2016) argue that AI technologies, particularly intelligent tutoring systems and adaptive learning platforms, can fundamentally reconfigure traditional pedagogical models by providing real-time, personalized feedback and automating repetitive tasks. Their analysis outlines how AI enables a shift from one-size-fits-all instruction to student-centered learning, thereby improving engagement and retention rates.

In the Indian context, Banerjee and Mishra (2022) conducted a pivotal study on adaptive learning systems deployed by EdTech firms like Byju's. Their findings suggest a 30% increase in student engagement and measurable improvements in performance in online courses where AI-driven customization was employed. These outcomes align with earlier global research by Holmes et al. (2019), who found similar engagement benefits among learners using adaptive learning technologies in Western education systems. AI's administrative applications also warrant attention. Gupta et al. (2021) investigated AI-powered virtual assistants in Indian private universities, demonstrating that automated student support services significantly reduced response times and improved overall student satisfaction. The study noted that such tools are especially valuable during high-traffic periods like admissions and examinations. Similarly, AI is revolutionizing assessment and evaluation practices. Ernst & Young (2022) report that automated grading and AI-enabled proctoring tools are increasingly being used in Indian higher education institutions to address faculty shortages and reduce the workload. These technologies offer consistent evaluation and minimize human error, although their reliability and fairness have occasionally been questioned. Echoing this, Selwyn (2019) critiques the opaque nature of some AI algorithms and calls for greater transparency in how student data is used and analyzed.

On the research front, institutions such as IIT Madras and IISc Bangalore have integrated AI tools like IBM Watson into research workflows, especially in fields like engineering and public health. A study by Rajan and Rao (2021) found that AI-augmented research methodologies led to a 20% acceleration in problem-solving outcomes, primarily by enabling more efficient data analysis and hypothesis testing. Government policy has played a catalytic role in shaping AI adoption. NEP 2020's push for digital integration and skill development, combined with NITI Aayog's AI strategy, has created a supportive regulatory framework. Programs like "AI for All," co-launched by CBSE and Intel in 2021, have laid the groundwork for AI literacy among students and faculty alike. However, despite these advances, several scholars have highlighted the significant challenges that persist. The digital divide remains a central issue. According to the AICTE (2022) report, internet access in many rural institutions is either unreliable or entirely absent, creating barriers to AI deployment. Kumar and Singh (2020) emphasize that such infrastructural deficits disproportionately impact marginalized communities and rural learners, thereby exacerbating educational inequality.

Ethical concerns are equally critical. A 2022 NITI Aayog report on AI ethics in education calls for robust data governance policies, emphasizing that student data must be anonymized, securely stored, and used only with informed consent. Scholars such as Williamson and Eynon (2020) further argue that AI's reliance on historical data could perpetuate existing biases, particularly in predictive analytics used for admissions or academic counseling. Faculty readiness is another barrier. The FICCI (2021) report found that while there is widespread enthusiasm for AI among educators, a majority lack hands-on training and practical exposure to AI tools. This gap impairs the effective implementation of AI in classroom settings. Studies by Sharma and Kapoor (2021) suggest that faculty development programs need to be more inclusive, ongoing, and context-specific to address these gaps effectively. Another underexplored dimension in the literature is the cultural and pedagogical compatibility of AI tools in Indian institutions. Indian classrooms are often characterized by high student-to-teacher ratios, multilingual environments, and exam-oriented pedagogies. Scholars such as Jha (2020) argue that for AI to be truly transformative, it must be adapted to these socio-cultural contexts rather than merely imported from Western models.

While a growing body of literature documents the benefits and challenges of AI in education, few studies offer a holistic, India-specific analysis that integrates pedagogical, ethical, and infrastructural dimensions. Most research either focuses narrowly on technology adoption or remains policy-centric, without bridging the gap between theory and on-ground realities. Furthermore, there is a lack of longitudinal studies assessing the long-term impact of AI on student outcomes, equity, and institutional transformation in India.

This chapter fills this critical gap by offering a comprehensive, data-driven analysis of the future of AI in Indian higher education, synthesizing diverse perspectives to provide actionable insights.

1.2 Conceptual Framework

The integration of Artificial Intelligence (AI) into higher education, particularly in a diverse and populous country like India, necessitates a multi-dimensional conceptual framework. This framework must consider not only technological capabilities but also educational philosophies, institutional readiness, ethical responsibilities, and legal infrastructures. The future of AI in Indian higher education must be situated within a holistic understanding of how AI reshapes the objectives, methods, governance, and equity dimensions of academic ecosystems.

At the heart of this conceptual framework is the notion of *transformative pedagogy*—the idea that AI does not merely enhance existing educational processes but has the capacity to fundamentally alter them. Pedagogy, traditionally centered around human interactions, is evolving into a hybrid model where AI systems serve as co-educators, facilitators, and assessors. The conceptual foundation rests on constructivist and connectivist learning theories. Constructivism posits that learners construct knowledge through active engagement and contextual understanding, which AI facilitates by offering adaptive learning pathways and personalized feedback. Connectivism, a theory advanced by Siemens and Downes, emphasizes the role of digital networks in shaping learning. AI, through its data-driven insights and networked capabilities, embodies connectivist ideals by connecting students to resources, peers, and mentors in real time.

The technological scaffolding of this framework involves AI tools such as intelligent tutoring systems, adaptive learning algorithms, Natural Language Processing (NLP) engines, automated assessment tools, and learning analytics dashboards. These tools are conceptualized not as replacements for teachers but as enhancers of the teaching-learning process. For example, AI-powered platforms like Coursera, Khan Academy, and Byju's use real-time performance analytics to tailor content delivery, aligning it with students' individual learning curves. Within this framework, learning becomes non-linear, student-centered, and responsive to real-time feedback—a significant shift from traditional models of fixed curricula and summative assessment.

However, AI's transformative potential is not solely contingent on its functionality; it is deeply embedded in the socio-economic and institutional contexts in which it is deployed. The Indian higher education system is characterized by heterogeneity—ranging from globally competitive IITs to resource-constrained rural colleges. Therefore, the conceptual framework incorporates *contextual adaptability* as a key pillar. AI tools must be sensitive to linguistic diversity, infrastructural disparities, and varying levels of digital literacy. This implies a design imperative: AI systems for Indian higher education should be multilingual, mobile-friendly, and capable of functioning in low-bandwidth environments.

Institutional readiness forms another axis of the framework. Readiness is not limited to infrastructure but includes faculty training, administrative willingness, leadership vision, and policy alignment. Drawing from Fullan's model of educational change, any systemic shift must involve the alignment of *capacity building*, *policy mandates*, and *incentive systems*. The AI implementation roadmap must be co-created by faculty, students, administrators, and policymakers, ensuring shared ownership and trust. Faculty resistance, a recurring challenge in tech-based reforms, can be mitigated through continuous professional development, exposure to global best practices, and opportunities for experimentation.

Ethical considerations are foundational to this framework. The deployment of AI in educational settings involves massive data collection—on student behavior, performance, preferences, and even emotions. This raises profound questions about *data privacy, algorithmic bias, surveillance, and autonomy*. The ethical lens draws from principles of *data minimization*, *informed consent*, *transparency*, and *fairness*. For instance, predictive analytics tools that identify "at-risk" students must be evaluated not only for their accuracy but also for their potential to reinforce stereotypes or penalize certain demographic groups. Ethical AI in education also involves the human-in-the-loop principle, wherein final decisions affecting students must always involve human oversight.

The legal dimension of the framework interacts closely with the ethical one. Currently, India lacks a comprehensive legal framework governing AI in education. The proposed *Digital Personal Data Protection Act* and the guidelines of the *National Education Policy 2020* offer broad principles but lack enforceable directives specific to AI usage. The conceptual framework anticipates the development of legal instruments that define institutional obligations, data fiduciary responsibilities, and mechanisms for redressal. In this context, the role of regulatory bodies like the University Grants Commission (UGC), AICTE, and National Assessment and Accreditation Council (NAAC) becomes critical. These institutions must evolve to assess and accredit not just academic quality but digital and AI readiness.

A crucial dimension of this framework is *equity and inclusion*. AI systems, if poorly designed, can exacerbate existing inequalities. Students from rural, tribal, or economically marginalized backgrounds are at risk of exclusion due to lack of access to devices, connectivity, or AI-compatible content in their languages. This conceptualization draws on Sen's capability approach, which emphasizes expanding individuals' real freedoms and opportunities. AI in higher education must thus be evaluated not just on efficiency metrics but on its contribution to democratizing access, enhancing learner agency, and reducing structural barriers. Projects like AI-4Bharat, which develop open-source NLP models in Indian languages, are essential components in building inclusive AI ecosystems.

The policy landscape shapes and is shaped by AI integration. The NEP 2020 provides a strategic impetus for digital transformation, encouraging the use of AI in assessment, content creation, and personalized learning. However, implementation has been uneven. Hence, the conceptual framework includes *policy coherence* as a guiding principle. AI integration must align with other national programs like *Digital India*, *SWAYAM*, *National Digital Education Architecture (NDEAR)*, and *National Academic Bank of Credits (ABC)*. These initiatives must not operate in silos but reinforce each other through inter-ministerial coordination, shared databases, and unified standards for data interoperability. An emerging facet of the framework is the *AI-powered research ecosystem*. Beyond teaching and administration, AI is transforming how knowledge is produced, validated, and disseminated. Indian institutions are increasingly using AI tools for data analytics, meta-research, literature review automation, and simulation modeling. This shift necessitates new forms of research literacy where students and faculty are trained in digital epistemologies, algorithmic thinking, and AI ethics. The framework proposes the integration of AI research methods into postgraduate curricula across disciplines—not only in engineering or computer science but in social sciences, humanities, and management.

Another pillar in this framework is *student agency and well-being*. While AI promises personalization, it can also lead to hyper-surveillance and reduced student autonomy if not carefully managed. The framework draws on self-determination theory, which emphasizes autonomy, competence, and relatedness as essential for motivation. AI systems should be designed to empower students to set their own goals, monitor their progress, and make informed choices rather than merely nudging them toward algorithmic decisions. Institutions must ensure that student data is not commodified and that AI usage respects students' right to opt out, access their data, or challenge algorithmic decisions.

Capacity-building forms the operational backbone of this framework. Institutions must invest in skilling their human capital—students, faculty, and administrators—to effectively interact with AI systems. This involves developing AI literacy curricula, organizing workshops, creating AI research clusters, and fostering collaborations with EdTech startups and international universities. A robust feedback mechanism must also be institutionalized to evaluate AI tools in real time and recalibrate their deployment based on student outcomes and user satisfaction.

The sustainability of AI in higher education is a long-term consideration within the framework. Sustainability here is not only environmental (e.g., energy-intensive AI computation) but also financial and pedagogical. Institutions must conduct cost-benefit analyses before adopting AI systems and explore open-source alternatives where feasible. A sustainable AI strategy also means avoiding over-reliance on proprietary tools that lead to vendor lock-in or data dependency. Pedagogically, AI tools should supplement—not replace—human interaction, especially in emotionally or morally complex teaching contexts.

Interdisciplinarity is a meta-principle that cuts across the entire framework. AI in higher education must not be ghettoized into engineering departments or IT cells. Instead, the framework encourages co-creation involving diverse academic voices—philosophers, linguists, sociologists, economists, and ethicists. Courses like "AI and Society," "Philosophy of Algorithms," or "AI and Ethics in Law" can help students understand AI not just as a technical artifact but as a socio-technical system shaped by values, power, and politics. Lastly, the conceptual framework is dynamic and iterative. AI technology evolves rapidly, and so must institutional responses. The framework is designed to be regularly updated based on emerging research, technological innovation, and stakeholder feedback. Institutions should adopt a "learning organization" approach where experimentation is encouraged, failures are documented, and best practices are scaled.

Figure 1. Conceptual Framework

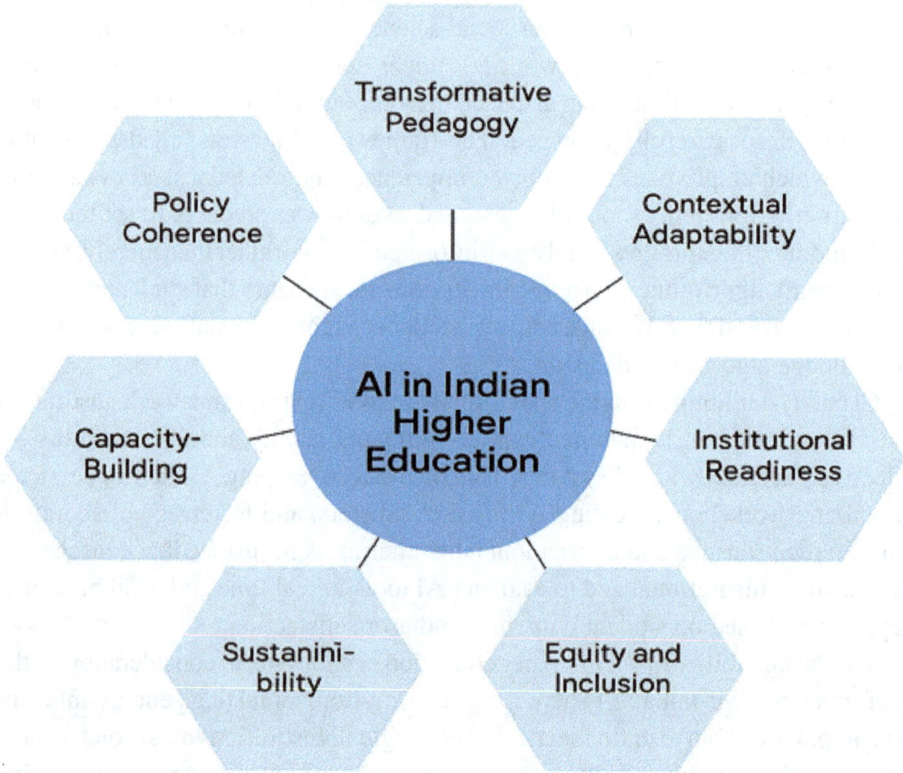

In sum, the conceptual framework for AI in Indian higher education is built on the following interconnected pillars: transformative pedagogy, contextual adaptability, institutional readiness, ethical and legal governance, equity and inclusion, policy coherence, research innovation, student agency, capacity-building, sustainability, and interdisciplinarity. These elements collectively provide a blueprint for responsible, inclusive, and effective AI integration. By addressing not just the "what" and "how" but also the "why" of AI adoption, the framework aims to guide educators, policymakers, researchers, and technologists in shaping a future-ready higher education system rooted in Indian realities and global best practices.

2. RESEARCH METHODOLOGY

This chapter is based entirely on secondary data and adopts a qualitative-descriptive research methodology. The research draws upon an extensive review of literature from academic journals, whitepapers, government reports, and publications from industry associations such as NASSCOM, FICCI, and AICTE. Key documents include the National Education Policy (2020), NITI Aayog's National AI Strategy (2018), and reports from EdTech companies and international consultancies like Ernst & Young.

The methodology involved thematic coding and content analysis of the selected sources to identify key patterns, emerging trends, and policy implications concerning AI integration in Indian higher education. Credible academic databases such as JSTOR, Scopus, and Google Scholar were used to gather peer-reviewed studies, while official government websites provided policy data and statistics. Emphasis was placed on triangulating information from multiple sources to ensure reliability and comprehensiveness. The focus remained on extracting insights relevant to pedagogical transformation, administrative efficiency, ethical considerations, and infrastructural challenges. Since the study is exploratory in nature, it does not involve any hypothesis testing but instead aims to provide an integrated understanding of the opportunities and barriers to AI adoption. The findings serve as a foundation for future empirical research and strategic interventions in the field.

3. AI AND HIGHER EDUCATION IN INDIA

Artificial Intelligence (AI) has emerged as a transformative force across global industries, with education being one of its most promising frontiers. In the Indian context, higher education faces a set of unique challenges—massification, quality disparities, skill mismatches, and underfunded infrastructure. These challenges, however, have also made India an ideal testbed for innovation-driven solutions such as AI. Over the past decade, AI has gradually entered the discourse around higher education reform, spurred by national policies, international collaborations, and private sector initiatives.

India has over 1,100 universities and more than 43,000 colleges, catering to around 40 million students (AISHE, 2021-22). However, Gross Enrollment Ratio (GER) remains at 28.4%, with stark disparities between urban and rural, and male and female learners. The NEP 2020 targets increasing GER to 50% by 2035, and AI is seen as a key enabler for reaching this milestone. The integration of AI can help address faculty shortages, promote personalized learning, and bring administrative transparency.

In recent years, the Indian government has taken steps to promote AI across educational institutions. The National AI Strategy (NITI Aayog, 2018) identified education as one of the five focus areas for AI adoption. Additionally, programs such as "Responsible AI for Youth" (launched in 2020) and the collaboration between CBSE and Intel on "AI for All" have laid the groundwork for AI literacy and integration at the school and higher education levels. The Ministry of Education's 2022 initiative on AI-based skill development in partnership with Microsoft and IBM marked another milestone in policy-driven AI adoption. AICTE's approval of AI-focused courses in engineering colleges, and the launch of AI centers in premier institutions such as IIT Hyderabad, IIIT-Delhi, and IISc Bangalore, have contributed to building a solid academic ecosystem around AI. However, despite these advances, India's progress in integrating AI into mainstream higher education remains uneven. A majority of state and private universities lack the infrastructure and human capital to deploy AI-based systems effectively. Faculty awareness and training continue to be significant bottlenecks.

The following table summarizes some key indicators reflecting the current state of AI and higher education in India:

Table 1. Key Statistics on AI and Higher Education in India

Indicator	Data	Source
Total number of universities	1,113	AISHE Report 2021-22
Colleges in India	43,796	AISHE Report 2021-22
Gross Enrollment Ratio (GER) in Higher Education	28.4%	AISHE Report 2021-22
Target GER by 2035 (NEP)	50%	NEP 2020
AI-related job growth rate (2019–2023)	30.8% CAGR	NASSCOM Report, 2022
Percentage of Indian HEIs offering AI courses	~12%	AICTE, 2022
Institutions with dedicated AI research labs	110+	MHRD & AICTE, 2022
Percentage of faculty trained in AI pedagogy	35%	FICCI Survey, 2021

Despite growing government and corporate interest, a significant rural-urban digital divide persists. A 2022 AICTE report reveals that over 60% of rural colleges lack access to high-speed internet and digital classrooms, limiting their capacity to implement AI-based systems. Additionally, private EdTech companies, while innovative, mostly cater to urban learners, leaving behind a vast underrepresented student population.

Thus, the current landscape of AI in Indian higher education is one of promise mixed with challenges. Bridging the infrastructural, pedagogical, and policy gaps is crucial to realize the full potential of AI in democratizing and modernizing higher education in India.

4. THE ROLE OF AI IN TRANSFORMING INDIAN HIGHER EDUCATION

Artificial Intelligence is not merely a technological upgrade—it represents a paradigm shift in the way education is conceived, delivered, and assessed. In the context of Indian higher education, where diversity in language, resources, and learner backgrounds is enormous, AI offers tailored solutions that can bridge systemic gaps and elevate learning experiences.

Personalized Learning:

One of the most transformative applications of AI in higher education is its capacity to personalize the learning process. Unlike traditional classroom models, AI-powered systems analyze students' learning patterns, strengths, and weaknesses to provide customized content. Tools like Coursera's adaptive assessments, or Indian EdTech startups like Embibe and Byju's, have demonstrated AI's ability to offer personalized feedback and practice recommendations. A 2022 study by KPMG India found that students using AI-based learning tools showed a 23% increase in retention and comprehension scores.

Intelligent Tutoring Systems and Virtual Labs:

AI-driven tutoring systems provide real-time assistance to students outside classroom hours. Platforms like Carnegie Learning and India's own Toppr use natural language processing (NLP) and machine learning to simulate human-like interactions. These systems can solve mathematical problems, explain concepts, and even suggest learning schedules. AI-based virtual labs, such as those promoted under the MHRD's Virtual Lab initiative, allow students in remote areas to conduct experiments online thus democratizing access to quality education.

Smart Content Generation and Translation:

AI is now being used to create smart content, such as digital textbooks, automated note summaries, and even voice-based content in regional languages. Tools powered by GPT and similar large language models (LLMs) are enabling institutions to transcribe and translate academic content into multiple Indian languages, aligning with NEP 2020's emphasis on mother tongue instruction. According to a 2021 report by the Ministry of Education, AI-enabled translation systems have already been deployed in 200+ universities to facilitate multilingual learning.

Predictive Analytics and Student Support:

Predictive analytics is helping institutions monitor student progress and proactively offer support. For example, Bennett University uses AI algorithms to identify students at risk of dropping out based on attendance, grades, and behavioral indicators. Early warning systems like these improve retention and reduce drop-out rates, especially among first-generation learners. A McKinsey study (2021) noted that predictive analytics led to a 15–18% reduction in attrition rates across several Indian institutions.

Automating Administrative Tasks:

AI streamlines administrative functions such as admissions, scheduling, and grading. Chatbots are being used for student inquiries, document submission, and academic counseling. Institutions like Amity University and SRM Institute have adopted AI-powered chat systems that handle over 10,000 student queries per month. Automated grading systems, especially in multiple-choice formats and language processing-based evaluation of essays, are significantly reducing faculty workload and ensuring consistency.

Enhancing Research Capabilities:

AI has opened new frontiers in academic research. From data mining and meta-analysis to citation management and plagiarism detection, AI tools are expediting scholarly productivity. The Indian Council of Social Science Research (ICSSR) reported in 2022 that researchers using AI for data analysis and simulation saved 30–40% of their research time. Furthermore, interdisciplinary fields such as computational social sciences and bioinformatics are gaining momentum due to AI's integrative capabilities.

Virtual Reality (VR) and Augmented Reality (AR) Integration:

While not AI per se, the fusion of AI with AR/VR technologies is enhancing immersive learning experiences. AI-driven VR tools are being used in medical colleges for surgical simulations and in architecture schools for 3D modeling. Institutions like Manipal Academy of Higher Education have adopted AI-AR technologies to simulate real-world environments, offering experiential learning that would otherwise be logistically unfeasible.

Ethical Governance and Fairness:

While AI offers immense benefits, its deployment in higher education must be ethically governed. Algorithms must be transparent, data usage should respect privacy laws, and decision-making processes must avoid bias. The 2021 NITI Aayog draft paper on "Responsible AI" calls for the creation of institutional AI ethics committees. Universities like Ashoka and IIIT-B have already set up such bodies to oversee the responsible use of AI in curriculum and administration.

Skill Development and AI Curriculum Integration:

To prepare students for an AI-driven future, Indian universities are incorporating AI courses into their core and elective curricula. As per AICTE data (2022), over 600 institutions now offer undergraduate and postgraduate programs in AI and machine learning. Moreover, new-age interdisciplinary degrees combining AI with business, law, or humanities—are gaining popularity. The World Economic Forum (2023) highlighted that AI and data science are among the top five most in-demand skills in India.

Challenges and the Way Forward:

Despite these transformative effects, there are considerable barriers to AI's universal adoption in Indian higher education:

- **Digital Infrastructure Deficit**: Particularly in Tier-2 and Tier-3 cities and rural areas.
- **Faculty Training**: Most faculty lack the technical skills to implement or supervise AI systems.
- **Cost of Implementation**: AI tools and platforms are expensive, limiting access to private institutions or elite government colleges.

- **Language and Cultural Barriers**: AI systems need better localization to cater to India's linguistic diversity.

Moving forward, policy support must be sustained and scaled. Public-private partnerships, faculty development programs, and multilingual AI platforms are critical to democratizing access and ensuring that AI doesn't deepen existing inequalities.

5. CHALLENGES IN AI ADOPTION IN INDIAN HIGHER EDUCATION

While the integration of Artificial Intelligence (AI) into Indian higher education holds enormous transformative potential, the path toward widespread adoption is fraught with challenges. These hurdles range from infrastructural and financial constraints to faculty training, ethical concerns, and language localization issues. Despite policy encouragement and selective success stories in elite institutions, the systemic incorporation of AI across the entire spectrum of Indian higher education remains limited.

5.1 Digital Infrastructure Divide

One of the most critical barriers is the uneven distribution of digital infrastructure across urban and rural areas. According to the All India Survey on Higher Education (AISHE) 2021–22, over 60% of colleges are located in rural or semi-urban areas. A large proportion of these institutions still struggle with unreliable internet access, outdated computer labs, and minimal exposure to EdTech.

Table 2. Internet Access and ICT Facilities in HEIs

Indicator	Percentage of HEIs	Source
HEIs with reliable internet (urban)	89%	AISHE, 2021–22
HEIs with reliable internet (rural)	38%	AISHE, 2021–22
HEIs with smart classrooms	31%	FICCI-EY Report, 2022
HEIs with AI-enabled platforms	12%	AICTE Report, 2022

These disparities mean that AI applications remain concentrated in metros and Tier-1 cities, further widening the rural-urban education gap.

5.2 Faculty Awareness and Training

Another challenge is the lack of AI literacy among faculty members. A 2021 survey conducted by NASSCOM and AICTE revealed that only 35% of faculty members across Indian universities had any form of exposure to AI tools or teaching methodologies. Most teacher training programs are not equipped to train instructors on integrating AI into curriculum design, pedagogy, or student assessments.

Table 3. Faculty Preparedness in AI Education

Parameter	Value	Source
Faculty with formal AI training	18%	NASSCOM-AICTE Survey, 2021
Institutions offering AI training for faculty	24%	AICTE, 2022
Teachers who feel confident using AI tools	27%	FICCI Higher Education Summit, 2022

This lack of preparedness limits the effective deployment of AI tools, particularly in institutions that do not have dedicated departments for data science or computer engineering.

5.3 High Cost of Implementation

AI systems, particularly those offering advanced functionalities like predictive analytics, adaptive learning, and AI chatbots, require substantial investment. For many state universities and private colleges operating on tight budgets, the cost of implementing and maintaining AI infrastructure is prohibitive. According to a 2022 FICCI-EY report, the average cost of implementing an institution-wide AI-based Learning Management System (LMS) can range from 20 lakh to 1 crore depending on the size and complexity. This financial hurdle is particularly steep for non-autonomous institutions dependent on state funding.

5.4 Fragmented Policy Implementation

Although policies like NEP 2020, the National Digital Education Architecture (NDEAR), and NITI Aayog's AI strategy have mentioned AI as a transformative tool, on-the-ground implementation is fragmented. Bureaucratic red tape, inadequate monitoring mechanisms, and lack of cross-institutional coordination often delay or dilute AI-focused programs. Furthermore, there is a lack of clarity on data privacy and ethical frameworks in education technology. Without a national-level AI ethics charter for educational institutions, concerns about bias, surveillance, and algorithmic accountability persist.

5.5 Language and Cultural Barriers

India's linguistic diversity presents a unique challenge for AI systems, which often function optimally in English or globally dominant languages. Despite efforts to develop NLP tools in Indian languages, AI interfaces still struggle with accurate translation, contextual comprehension, and dialect-specific nuances.

Table 4. Language Readiness in AI Tools

Language Compatibility	Percentage of AI Tools Supporting	Source
English	100%	AI4Bharat, 2022
Hindi	45%	AI4Bharat, 2022
Tamil, Telugu, Bengali	~25%	Ministry of Education, 2020
Tribal/Regional Dialects	<5%	UNESCO India Report, 2021

This language gap restricts equitable access and undermines efforts toward inclusive education.

5.6 Ethical, Legal, and Privacy Concerns

The ethical dimensions of AI in education are still under-researched in India. Questions related to data collection, informed consent, algorithmic bias, and surveillance are gaining attention globally but are yet to be addressed systematically in the Indian education landscape.

As per a report by the Internet Freedom Foundation (2023), less than 10% of Indian educational institutions using EdTech platforms have a publicly available data policy or AI ethics charter. This regulatory vacuum can lead to misuse of student data and opaque decision-making processes.

5.7 Lack of Research and Localization

While top-tier institutions like IITs and IIITs are advancing AI research, the vast majority of HEIs lack funding, collaboration networks, or interdisciplinary platforms to explore localized AI applications. Research papers on AI in Indian education are often theoretical and lack empirical grounding.

6. KEY RECOMMENDATIONS

The transformative potential of Artificial Intelligence (AI) in Indian higher education is immense, but its success hinges on coordinated and inclusive strategies. Based on a comprehensive analysis of current trends, institutional realities, and policy frameworks, this chapter offers several key recommendations aimed at policymakers, academic institutions, faculty, EdTech developers, and civil society actors. These recommendations are not only intended to guide the immediate next steps but also provide a roadmap for long-term, sustainable, and ethical AI integration in India's higher education landscape.

To begin with, the foundation of AI integration must rest on *inclusive digital infrastructure*. AI cannot thrive without reliable internet connectivity, robust data systems, and access to devices. Despite various national programs such as Digital India and BharatNet, a large proportion of higher education institutions, particularly in rural and tribal regions, lack the basic infrastructure required to deploy AI solutions. Therefore, the government must prioritize last-mile digital infrastructure connectivity. It is recommended that schemes like Rashtriya Uchchatar Shiksha Abhiyan (RUSA) and Samagra Shiksha Abhiyan be extended and restructured to include AI-readiness components—funding not only broadband and smart classrooms but also backend systems, digital libraries, and device provisioning for students. In parallel, public-private partnerships (PPPs) should be encouraged to build shared infrastructure, particularly for resource-poor state universities and colleges.

Equally crucial is *faculty capacity-building*. Without trained educators, even the most advanced AI tools risk remaining underutilized. It is recommended that a national-level Faculty AI Readiness Program be launched by the Ministry of Education in collaboration with the All India Council for Technical Education (AICTE), University Grants Commission (UGC), and leading industry partners like Microsoft, Google, and IBM. This program should offer structured AI certification courses for teachers, including modules on AI literacy, ethical use, AI in pedagogy, and AI-driven assessment. These should be modular, online-offline hybrid, and credit-based to ensure flexible participation. Beyond training, faculty must be incentivized to integrate AI in their classrooms through academic credits, promotions, and research grants tied to AI implementation.

Another pressing need is the *development of multilingual and culturally relevant AI systems*. India's educational diversity, with 22 officially recognized languages and hundreds of regional dialects, demands AI solutions that go beyond English-language interfaces. AI developers and policymakers must work collaboratively to promote open-source NLP models in Indian languages. The National Language Translation Mission and platforms like AI4Bharat can play a central role. Additionally, AI-based learning content should reflect regional contexts, cultural narratives, and locally relevant examples to ensure contextual learning. Institutions should also promote research into culturally embedded AI design, involving linguists, anthropologists, and sociologists alongside technologists.

One of the structural recommendations is to *establish Institutional AI Ethics Committees (IAECs)* across all higher education institutions that deploy AI tools. These bodies should be modeled after Institutional Review Boards (IRBs) and be mandated to oversee the ethical deployment of AI—reviewing data usage policies, auditing algorithms for bias, ensuring consent and privacy safeguards, and establishing redressal mechanisms for students. Nationally, a *Central AI Ethics Board for Education* should be constituted under the Ministry of Education, comprising ethicists, legal experts, AI developers, and educators. This board would define guidelines, standards, and periodic review processes that all institutions must follow. AI deployment in education must adhere to principles of transparency, fairness, explainability, and accountability.

In tandem with ethical oversight, *legal frameworks for AI governance in education* must be strengthened. As India moves toward implementing the Digital Personal Data Protection Act (DPDP Act), special provisions related to educational data must be carved out. These should include mandatory parental or guardian consent for AI-based learning tools in undergrad settings, secure data storage practices, opt-out rights, and algorithmic transparency. The UGC and AICTE should also update their accreditation parameters to include "AI data compliance" as a criterion. Institutions found misusing student data or deploying opaque AI systems should face penalties or risk losing accreditation.

Curricular reform is another key area where AI can be both a tool and a subject of study. Indian higher education curricula must evolve to prepare students for an AI-driven world. Firstly, AI literacy should be embedded into undergraduate education across disciplines—not just in STEM but also in social sciences, law, management, and humanities. This includes basic AI concepts, ethical reasoning, data handling, and critical engagement with algorithms. Secondly, interdisciplinary programs must be promoted, such as AI and Law, AI and Public Policy, AI and Education, and AI and Gender Studies. Universities should be encouraged to set up AI Centers of Excellence and offer micro-credentials and stackable courses through SWAYAM, NPTEL, and private EdTech platforms.

In addition to curricular changes, institutions must focus on *AI-integrated pedagogical innovation*. Teachers should be encouraged and supported to experiment with AI-based tools like intelligent tutoring systems, adaptive assessments, plagiarism checkers, chatbot assistants, and learning analytics dashboards. For this, institutions should create sandboxes or controlled environments where teachers and students can test and evaluate new tools without fear of failure. Annual grants and innovation fellowships can be introduced to reward educators and departments that effectively integrate AI in teaching and learning. Cross-institutional sharing of best practices must be facilitated through knowledge exchange forums, conferences, and innovation clusters.

On the research front, it is recommended that *AI-based educational research be institutionalized* through dedicated funding, publication incentives, and cross-disciplinary teams. Research should not be limited to technical dimensions but must include impact evaluations, ethical analyses, and longitudinal studies on AI's effect on learning outcomes, student behavior, dropout rates, and teacher performance. National research councils such as ICSSR and SERB must initiate AI-Education research calls. Institutions should also collaborate with EdTech firms to co-design tools based on empirical insights and localized evidence.

Given the growing concern around AI's potential to exacerbate inequality, deliberate steps must be taken to *ensure inclusion and equity*. AI-based solutions should prioritize marginalized learners—first-generation college-goers, students with disabilities, rural and tribal students, and those studying in non-English medium institutions. UGC and NAAC should revise their equity indicators to include AI-readiness and AI-access criteria. Government schemes providing free tablets and data vouchers should be linked to AI-based platforms already in use at institutions. Moreover, assistive AI technologies—like screen readers, voice-based navigation, and AI-powered sign language translation—must be integrated for differently-abled learners.

An important recommendation is to *create collaborative platforms for stakeholders* in the AI-education ecosystem. AI integration requires synergy between various actors—educators, students, EdTech startups, government agencies, civil society organizations, and researchers. A national platform such as the *AI in Education Alliance* should be established to foster dialogue, co-create solutions, and resolve conflicts. This platform could be modeled on IndiaStack and host APIs, datasets, whitepapers, guidelines, and use-case repositories. It would facilitate pilot programs, crowdsourced innovations, and scale-up strategies for successful models.

Another strategic recommendation is to *reform accreditation and ranking systems* to reward AI adoption that is ethical, inclusive, and outcome-driven. Agencies like NAAC and NIRF should develop AI-readiness indices that measure institutional capacity, innovation in teaching, equity outcomes, faculty training, and student experience. Institutions that demonstrate high-quality, low-cost, and inclusive AI integration should be awarded extra credits, higher rankings, or additional funding support. This would incentivize not just adoption but thoughtful and contextualized adoption.

From a financial standpoint, *funding for AI implementation in higher education needs to be diversified and decentralized.* Government budgets should allocate special AI innovation grants to under-resourced colleges. In parallel, CSR funds from technology companies should be directed—through a structured AI-in-Education CSR Policy—toward building infrastructure, supporting AI fellowships, and funding student AI research projects. Crowdfunding models, alumni networks, and philanthropic foundations must also be tapped into, especially to support women, SC/ST, and differently-abled students in accessing AI-based learning environments.

The institutional culture must also shift towards *experimental learning ecosystems*, where risk-taking, failure, and iteration are normalized. Institutions must develop feedback loops to continuously monitor, adapt, and improve AI systems. Student voices must be integral to this process—through student councils, grievance redressal platforms, and participatory tech audits. Periodic surveys, focus groups, and user reviews should be institutionalized to understand how AI tools are affecting academic freedom, mental health, and learner motivation.

Finally, *internationalization and global collaboration* are key for India's AI in education journey. Indian universities should actively participate in global consortia on AI ethics, EdTech standards, and open-source AI development. Faculty and student exchange programs should be built around AI themes. Participation in platforms like UNESCO's AI in Education Working Group or OECD's Future of Education and Skills 2030 will help Indian institutions remain abreast of global trends, innovations, and ethical benchmarks.

CONCLUSION

The integration of Artificial Intelligence (AI) into Indian higher education marks a significant inflection point in the evolution of academic systems, practices, and aspirations. This chapter has provided a comprehensive and interdisciplinary exploration of how AI is reshaping pedagogical paradigms, administrative processes, curriculum design, and student support services across India's vast and diverse higher education landscape. From elite research institutions to resource-constrained state universities, AI is beginning to influence how knowledge is delivered, acquired, and assessed. Despite its transformative potential, AI adoption in Indian academia remains uneven and beset with critical challenges—ranging from infrastructure deficits and faculty unpreparedness to regulatory ambiguities, ethical dilemmas, and linguistic exclusions. While leading institutions have embraced AI tools for research and teaching innovation, a large segment of colleges still struggle with basic digital readiness. The fear of surveillance, algorithmic bias, and data misuse also looms large in the absence of comprehensive ethical and legal safeguards. To navigate this complex terrain, this chapter proposed a robust conceptual framework rooted in transformative pedagogy, institutional readiness, inclusion, policy coherence, and ethical governance. It also advanced detailed recommendations emphasizing faculty development, infrastructure equity, multilingual AI design, ethical oversight, and collaborative platforms to ensure that AI adoption is responsible, inclusive, and sustainable. AI should not be treated merely as a technological intervention but as a socio-cultural force that can reimagine education. With the right blend of vision, capacity, and regulation, AI can democratize access to quality higher education, enhance learning outcomes, and align academic institutions with the needs of an AI-driven future workforce. However, this transformation must be guided by human-centric values—equity, transparency, accountability, and cultural sensitivity.

Ultimately, the future of AI in Indian higher education lies in balancing innovation with introspection, automation with autonomy, and personalization with public good. By adopting this balanced approach, India can become not only a consumer but also a global leader in ethical and inclusive AI-enabled education.

REFERENCES

AI4Bharat. (2022). Language Tools for Bharat. https://ai4bharat.org/

Aayog, N. I. T. I. (2018). *National Strategy for Artificial Intelligence #AIforAll.* Government of India.

All India Council for Technical Education. (2022). Annual Report 2021-22. AICTE.

All India Survey on Higher Education. (2022). AISHE Report 2021-22. Ministry of Education, Government of India.

FICCI-EY. (2022). Higher Education in India [Federation of Indian Chambers of Commerce and Industry.]. *Vision (Basel)*, •••, 2040.

Holmes, W., Bialik, M., & Fadel, C. (2019). *Artificial Intelligence in Education: Promises and Implications for Teaching and Learning*. Center for Curriculum Redesign.

India, K. P. M. G. (2022). *Emerging Trends in AI-Driven Learning Ecosystems.* KPMG Publications.

Internet Freedom Foundation. (2023). *Data Privacy in Indian EdTech: An Overview.* IFF Publications.

Jha, P. (2020). EdTech and India's Digital Future: The Role of Artificial Intelligence. *Economic and Political Weekly*, *55*(30), 25–30.

Kumar, S., & Singh, M. (2020). AI in Indian Universities: Policy and Practice. *Indian Journal of Education Policy*, *7*(3), 34–50.

Luckin, R., Holmes, W., Griffiths, M., & Forcier, L. B. (2016). *Intelligence unleashed: An argument for AI in education*. Pearson Education.

Ministry of Education. (2020). National [Government of India.]. *Educational Policy*, •••, 2020.

NASSCOM & AICTE. (2021). *AI Readiness among Indian Faculty and Institutions.* NASSCOM Reports.

Selwyn, N. (2019). *Should Robots Replace Teachers? AI and the Future of Education*. Polity Press.

UNESCO. (2021). *AI and Education: Guidance for Policymakers.* UNESCO Publishing.

UNESCO. (2022). *Ethics of Artificial Intelligence in Education: Promoting inclusive and quality education*. UNESCO.

Williamson, B., & Eynon, R. (2020). Historical threads, missing links, and future directions in AI in education. *Learning, Media and Technology*, *45*(3), 223–235.

World Economic Forum. (2023). Future of Jobs Report 2023. WEF.

Zawacki-Richter, O., Marín, V. I., Bond, M., & Gouverneur, F. (2019). Systematic review of research on artificial intelligence applications in higher education–where are the educators? *International Journal of Educational Technology in Higher Education*, *16*(1), 1–27. DOI: 10.1186/s41239-019-0171-0

Chapter 16
The Ethics of Using Artificial Intelligence in Language Research

Bora Demir
https://orcid.org/0000-0001-8187-3206
Çanakkale Onsekiz Mart University, Turkey

Selami Aydin
https://orcid.org/0000-0003-1614-874X
Faculty of Education Sciences, İstanbul Medeniyet University, Turkey

ABSTRACT

Artificial intelligence (AI) has become increasingly integrated into language research by providing opportunities, while researchers' perceptions of ethical issues AI usage in research seem untouched in the research context. This study aims to explore language researchers' perceptions of the ethical implications of AI in research practices. In this qualitative research, data were collected through written responses from 20 language researchers and analyzed thematically. The study concluded that while AI offers efficiency and innovation, researchers are concerned with ethical risks, institutional policies, and clearer guidelines to ensure responsible AI use in language research. To maintain the integrity and sustainability of AI in language research, some practical recommendations for language researchers are also noted regarding language researchers, university administrators, policymakers, and academic publishers.

DOI: 10.4018/979-8-3373-3000-6.ch016

INTRODUCTION

Research on foreign language teaching is critical in understanding the complexities of human communication, cultural understanding, social interaction, and educational advancement. It investigates how language functions as a fundamental tool for conveying ideas, emotions, and cultural values, facilitating mutual understanding and cooperation among individuals and communities (Canagarajah, 2012). In addition, in an increasingly interconnected world, communicating across linguistic boundaries is critical for international collaboration, economic development, and social integration (Byram, 2020). Thus, foreign language teaching equips learners with linguistic skills and promotes intercultural competence, enabling individuals to navigate diverse cultural contexts (Deardorff, 2020). It also enhances comprehension of cognitive processes and contributes to various applied fields such as education, psychology, sociology, and technology (Qiao & Zhao, 2023). From a pedagogical perspective, developments in the mentioned field have practical implications for curriculum design, teacher training, and the development of language learning technologies (Kern, 2006).

Ethics plays a crucial role in foreign language teaching research, as it ensures the protection of participants' rights, the integrity of data, and the responsible dissemination of findings since research often involves human subjects, including students, teachers, and language learners, who may be vulnerable to exploitation or harm (Dörnyei, 2020). From this perspective, following ethical principles safeguards against potential harms such as breaches of confidentiality, misrepresentation, and cultural insensitivity (Zimmer, 2018). Ethical frameworks, such as informed consent, confidentiality, and respect for cultural differences, are essential to maintaining trust and integrity in foreign language teaching research (Hultgren et al., 2016). Ethical considerations also promote the fair treatment of research subjects and the respectful handling of linguistic data, which is crucial when working with vulnerable populations or sensitive information (De Costa, 2016a). Moreover, by upholding ethical standards, researchers maintain public trust and contribute to the credibility and validity of their scholarly work (Miteu, 2024). In this regard, it can be stated that ethical considerations protect individuals involved in research and enhance the overall quality and applicability of findings, ensuring that studies contribute meaningfully to theoretical advancements and practical implementations in language education.

AI in language research presents a complex landscape, offering notable opportunities for efficiency and collaboration, posing significant ethical risks related to integrity and data use, and generating unresolved tensions as researchers view it simultaneously as both a valuable tool and a potential threat. First, regarding opportunities, AI tools and environments bring certain benefits to language research and ethics. For instance, AI has the ability to understand the input and process information by reasoning and rationalization (Gilson et al., 2023). Researchers can use AI tools to write and edit documents, formulate general and specific research questions, and find discussion points (Dowling & Lucey, 2023). AI tools can also be used as collaborators by responding to human feedback (Aydın & Zeinolabedini, 2024; Sayici & Aydın, 2025). In this way, they can write, rewrite, proofread, and edit the papers (Lin, 2023). These advantages also bring important legal and ethical considerations that must be addressed within established regulatory frameworks. Within this scope, the legal and ethical use of AI in language research requires alignment with established frameworks such as the General Data Protection Regulation (GDPR) and Institutional Review Board (IRB) guidelines. The former, the GDPR, emphasizes transparency, purpose limitation, and explicit informed consent, raising particular concerns about whether consent remains adequate when data are processed by algorithms that may generate unforeseen inferences. The latter, IRB, ensures that research protocols protect participant rights, confidentiality, and data use. Together, GDPR and IRB frameworks highlight that informed consent in AI-assisted language research goes beyond formality, ensuring specificity, accountability, and trust in the research process. Nevertheless, these benefits cannot be considered without ethical considerations and academic integrity. Second, AI usage in language research may have certain risks. For instance, using AI may be a source of problems regarding copyright, fabrication, manipulation, plagiarism, and authorship (Grimaldi & Ehrler, 2023; Lin, 2023). Some other problems can be encountered regarding data privacy, misinterpretations, and oversimplification (Yao et al., 2024). Similarly, overreliance on AI tools during the research process needs to be questioned regarding data ownership and consent when data are collected without explicit knowledge or agreement (Holmes et al., 2019). Moreover, language researchers encounter some potential problems, such as difficulties in obtaining informed consent in multilingual learning settings (Schembri & Jahić Jašić, 2022) and cultural bias in research design and implementation in research settings (Pelzang & Hutchinson, 2018). It is also evident that overreliance on AI in the research process may result in attrition in research and academic writing skills and inequalities in opportunities to access technology (Berg, 2023). To this end, it can be pointed out that language researchers need a high level of awareness and knowledge when the abovementioned complexities are considered.

THEORETICAL FRAMEWORK

Language research

According to Nunan (1992, p. 3), research is "a systematic process of inquiry consisting of three elements or components: a question, problem, or hypothesis, data, analysis, and interpretation of data." From this perspective, it can be inferred that research includes certain steps, such as a problem statement, narrowing a general question to a research question or hypothesis, reviewing the previous research, designing a research method, choosing data collection tools and analysis techniques, and reporting the results within the scope of the ethical issues (Seliger & Shohamy, 1989). More specifically, research is designed to be systematic, empirical, and objective for examining phenomena, acquiring new knowledge, and validating theories within the scope of basic, applied, and practical types. To conclude, the term research can be defined as the process that includes formulating research questions, reviewing the relevant literature, designing appropriate research types and designs, choosing data collecting tools, analyzing the data, and preparing a well-designed report (Denkci Akkaş et al., 2022; Elmas & Aydin, 2017).

Ethics

Research ethics refers to the standards and principles guiding responsible and ethical research issues (Comstock, 2012) and ensures the protection of participants, data integrity, and the credibility of the whole process (Petrova et al., 2016). Research ethics includes several aspects: honesty and integrity, objectivity, confidentiality and anonymity, non-maleficence, responsible publication, fairness and non-discrimination, and compliance with legal guidelines (Weinbaum et al., 2019). From this perspective, it can be noted that research ethics is a set of principles that ensure the integrity, transparency, and fairness of research while protecting the rights and well-being of participants (Haneef & Agrawal, 2024). Moreover, it involves obtaining informed consent, maintaining confidentiality, avoiding harm, and ensuring honesty in data collection, analysis, and reporting (Petrova et al., 2016). As a final point, adhering to ethical guidelines fosters trust in research, promotes credibility, and upholds legal and institutional standards (Weinbaum et al., 2019).

Artificial intelligence

AI is a combination of linguistics and computer science, performs multitasks including learning, adapting, and understanding knowledge (Aydın, 2024), and it can reactivate the current knowledge using a creative language (Korteling et al.,

2021; Sarker, 2022). Considering its effectiveness in education and research, three characteristics can be listed. First, *intelligence* is the ability to understand and process information within rationalization and reasoning (Gilson et al., 2023). Second, *versatility* is the ability to adapt to different functions, such as generating texts and writing and editing documents (Dowling & Lucey, 2023). Third, *collaboration* is the act of sharing and producing knowledge, including conversational capacity as a collaborator by listening, reading, and responding depending on human feedback (Aydın, 2024; Lin, 2023). These characteristics highlight the transformative and innovative role of AI in education and research and show its potential to enhance knowledge processing, adaptability, and human-machine collaboration in research. In addition to these characteristics, AI ethics in language research can be linked to broader frameworks such as algorithmic bias and AI transparency. Algorithmic bias demonstrates how AI systems may reproduce systemic inequalities and marginalize underrepresented perspectives (Noble & Dubljević, 2022), a risk particularly relevant in language research where Western-centric sources often dominate datasets. Similarly, Mitchell (2025) emphasizes the importance of transparency, noting that researchers should be able to understand and explain how AI systems generate their outputs in order to ensure accountability.

These theoretical principles intersect with emerging empirical concerns, creating a bridge between abstract ethical frameworks and the realities of current research practices. While ethics has long been central to applied linguistics and language education, explicit attention to AI within this domain has only recently begun to emerge. One reason is that research on AI ethics has traditionally been situated within fields such as computer science, philosophy, or educational technology, leaving language research relatively untouched. Another is the rapid pace of AI advancements, which has outstripped the ability of disciplinary frameworks to adapt. As a result, while ethical issues such as confidentiality, transparency, and fairness have been widely discussed in general research contexts, their implications for AI-supported language research remain underexplored, as clarified below.

Previous research

Current research shows that ethics plays a pivotal role in language research. For instance, in a qualitative study, De Costa (2016) aimed to highlight the personal and professional challenges researchers encounter when navigating ethical issues in applied linguistics. The study identified recurring themes such as informed consent, power dynamics, and the ethical implications of cross-cultural research and concluded that ethical decision-making was often context-dependent and required researchers to balance methodological rigor with moral responsibility. In a similar study, Sterling and Gass (2017) examined how researchers in applied linguistics perceived ethical issues. In this survey-based study, they concluded that more experienced researchers tended to view certain scenarios as less problematic than their less experienced counterparts. The study also highlighted the reliance on institutional review board requirements and gaps in ethical training.

While no study directly focuses on ethical considerations regarding AI in the context of language research, several studies underline the transformative role of AI in language research. For example, Alaqlobi et al. (2024) focused on addressing the problem of understanding how AI technologies were being utilized in applied linguistics and the potential ethical considerations arising from their integration. While the study aimed to review research on AI in areas such as language learning, translation, and discourse analysis, it also concluded that there was a need for ethical guidelines to address issues related to data privacy, bias, and the responsible use of AI in linguistic studies. In another review study, Zainuddin et al. (Zainuddin et al., 2024) examined the responsibility of AI and ethical use in language education from the broadest perspective. Regarding ethics, they emphasized the problem of balancing AI's innovative potential with ethical concerns such as data privacy, bias, and the need for transparency in AI-driven educational tools. Aljabr and Al-Ahdal (2024) also evaluated the role of AI as an educational tool from ethical and pedagogical perspectives. This mixed-methods study found a high level of positive perceptions among teachers regarding the ethical use of AI in teaching and its pedagogical implications in the learning process. In addition, Huang et al. (2023) investigated the integration of AI in language education, aiming to identify prevailing trends, research challenges, and practical applications. Employing a systematic review methodology, they found the transformative potential of AI in areas such as personalized learning, assessment, and feedback while emphasizing the need for ethical guidelines to address data privacy, bias, and the responsible use of AI in educational settings. Last, Groenewald et al.(2024) explored the applications of AI in linguistics research, specifically focusing on language acquisition and analysis. The study concluded that AI had a transformative potential in linguistic research, particularly in enhancing language learning and analyzing linguistic data. They also addressed concerns such as data privacy, bias, and the ethical challenges posed by the integration of AI in language research.

Overview Of The Current Study

Several reasons guided the current study. From the broadest perspective, research is of critical importance in understanding the complexities of human communication, cultural understanding, social interaction, and educational advancement. Moreover, ethics plays a crucial role in foreign language teaching research since it ensures the protection of participants' rights, the integrity of data, and the responsible dissemination of findings. It is also evident that AI tools and environments may bring certain benefits to language research, while AI usage in language research may have certain drawbacks and ethical problems. Within this scope, there is a need to focus on ethical considerations regarding how language researchers perceive and use AI tools and environments in research activities. On the other hand, while current literature focuses on the pivotal role of ethics in applied linguistics (De Costa, 2016b; Sterling & Gass, 2017), no study directly focuses on how researchers perceive the ethics of AI usage in their research activities. In other words, while current research examines the transformative and innovative role of AI in language research, ethical issues in the research context remain untouched. For instance, while several studies imply a need for ethical guidelines for using AI in linguistic studies, ethical issues concerning AI are investigated in the context of language learning and teaching. To this end, given the rapid integration of AI into language teaching and research, there is an urgent need for studies that focus on the responsible and ethical use of AI in academic settings, specifically on how researchers perceive ethical considerations within the scope of AI. In this way, it will be possible to examine existing challenges, propose ethical guidelines, and offer practical recommendations for researchers and future research. With these concerns in mind, the current study aims to explore how language researchers perceive the ethics of using AI in language research.

RESEARCH CONTEXT

The study that explores the ethical perceptions of AI usage in language research used a synthetic approach, which focuses on the integration of various language components, and heuristic purpose, which involves exploratory and discovery, at a conceptual level, since it aimed to construct a comprehensive understanding of the phenomenon without a preconceived assumption and research question. At the operational level, the study used a qualitative research design to identify the patterns and themes without manipulation or experimentation. Thus, the study preferred using open-ended responses to allow the participants to express their opinions in detail. The data collected were analyzed using the thematic analysis to ensure a systematic, structured, and flexible framework (Seliger & Shohamy, 1989).

Participants

The participants in the study were 20 language researchers from various universities. The age range of the participants was 26 to 54, with a mean score of 39.5. The group consisted of 11 female and nine male researchers, reflecting a balanced distribution. Regarding their educational background, 15 participants had a Ph.D.

degree, while five had a master's degree. Their research experience in years ranged from 3 to 32, with a mean score of 14.3. There were several reasons behind the selection of participants. First, it was necessary to include both novice and senior researchers to understand their ethical perceptions of AI in language research at different career stages. Second, the gender distribution was intentional for balanced representation. Third and last, there was a need to combine the perspectives of novice researchers with experience in using AI and those with extensive experience in language research. As a final note, the sample size in the study was considered sufficient, as recurring patterns confirmed data saturation (Guest et al., 2006)

Tools

The study used a background questionnaire and responses to structured questions. The background questionnaire interrogated the participants' age, gender, educational background, and research experience in years. For several reasons, written responses to structured questions were used to explore their perceptions of ethical considerations in AI usage in language research. First, they allow participants to express detailed and reflective views by reducing ambiguity and enabling systematic responses. Second, they provide flexibility, adaptability, consistency, and comparability (Seliger & Shohamy, 1989).

Procedure

After informing the participants about the purpose and significance of the study, they were assured that their participation was voluntary, that their privacy would be protected, and that the collected data would be used exclusively for scientific purposes. They were also informed that the study did not have any social or psychological risks. Then, participants were provided with a background questionnaire to gather demographic information and asked to submit responses to structured questions, as given below:

- What strategies do you use to uphold ethical integrity when employing AI tools?
- How do you evaluate whether AI-generated content aligns with ethical research standards?
- Are current ethical guidelines adequate for addressing AI's role in language research? Why/why not?
- How do you maintain transparency when documenting AI's contribution to your work?

The questions aimed to explore their general perceptions of AI in language research, its ethical implications, potential risks, decision-making processes related to ethical integrity, the role of institutional policies, and future directions for ethical AI integration in language research.

Analysis

After designing the structured questionnaire in accordance with the purpose of the study, participants were selected through purposeful sampling based on their experience in language research and AI utilization. Before full data collection, a pilot study was conducted with two researchers to clarify and refine the questions. After finalizing the questionnaire, participants were given time to respond to their own pace via their emails. The collected data were then analyzed using thematic analysis to identify recurring themes and patterns in ethical perceptions of AI in language research. Three independent coders analyzed the data separately to ensure saturation, validity, and trustworthiness, categorizing responses into themes and comparing their findings. The rationale behind using three coders was to obtain data triangulation by cross-checking the codes and themes. This approach aimed to provide a comprehensive and unbiased interpretation of the data while maintaining the integrity of the participants' perspectives in a realistic research setting (Denzin, 2017; Patton, 1990).

RESULTS

The findings obtained from the study are presented under five main themes. The first theme, general *perceptions,* included participants' overall views on the role of AI in language research and its impact on ethical standards. The second theme, *ethical risks*, presented findings regarding the risks and challenges experienced by language researchers. The third theme examined ethical *decision-making* before the data on *institutional policies* were presented. Finally, *future directions* within the participants' perceptions were noted.

General perceptions

Participants express mixed opinions on the impact of AI in language research. First, most of them believed that AI had significantly accelerated research practices. They stated that AI-supported applications were increasingly used in learning research regarding idea generation, data organization and analysis, table and figure generation, language enhancement in academic writing, and feedback. However, they also believed that serious concerns about ethical issues and reliability, particularly regarding data confidentiality and the trustworthiness of AI-generated content. Moreover, some argued that AI currently undermines ethical integrity because many researchers rely on AI tools to bypass essential research processes, such as critical literature review, data analysis, and synthesis. This overreliance on AI, as they suggested, weakens researchers' engagement with their work and raises questions about academic responsibility and intellectual honesty, as one participant commented:

"In my opinion, in the short term, it undermines the ethical standards because many people make AI do fulfill their own responsibilities skipping several vital phases of research such as review of literature, reading-analyzing and synthesizing-, truly understanding, analyzing and presenting data. On the other hand, when people realize and question these ethical issues (when they fully recognize there are ethical problems or these are violating the ethics), AI can be beneficial in resetting the ethical principles and standards which comply with the requirement of the digital era. AI is an inevitable and a vital element."

Some also noted that AI might eventually contribute to redefining ethical standards as ethical concerns become more widely recognized and addressed. Regarding the role of AI in language research, they suggested that AI could facilitate discussions on research integrity by clarifying which aspects of the research could remain human-led and which aspects AI could ethically assist. In addition, for researchers, AI could be used to detect ethical violations and have a potential role in defining ethical boundaries, as stated below:

"It can open debates about the areas and extent of the real qualifications and responsibilities of researchers so we can decide which parts should be carried out by the researchers and for which parts and how AI can be used. AI technologies can also help to detect ethical violations also in the research where AI is not used."

Participants' perspectives reveal notable differences across career stages, reflecting how professional experience shaped both opportunities and concerns. For instance, while mid-career researchers tended to frame AI as a collaborator that could extend intellectual work, early-career researchers often emphasized efficiency and skill development, pointing out how AI supported their everyday practices. Moreover, senior academics expressed stronger caution and ethical reservations, often linking them to professional responsibility. As one researcher remarked:

"The risk of confidentiality breaches in large models makes me reluctant to trust AI in sensitive research contexts." Another added: "If younger colleagues over-rely on AI, they may lose touch with critical methodological skills that define good scholarship."

Ethical risks

According to the participants, several significant ethical risks are associated with AI-driven language research. One of the most serious concerns was the potential for fabricated studies. Additionally, some participants worried that researchers might be over-reliant on AI. For them, another major issue was the risk of inaccurate or unreliable AI-generated information, which could distort future research and mislead scholars, as two participants noted:

"There are several serious risks in AI-driven language research. First, some fake studies can be produced and published by some researchers using AI without authorities or readers notice them in the short run. Second, some researchers may make AI do their own job. Third, some incorrect or unreliable information offered by AI may be involved in publications and may distort and mislead the further research or practices in the field."

Regarding data confidentiality and informed consent, participants pointed out that AI platforms often lack transparency in their data policies. Moreover, they stated that many researchers felt uncertain whether AI tools had clear privacy, security, and ethical data processing guidelines; thus, they suggested that AI developers could establish clear transparency policies to address these concerns, as one researcher commented:

"They need to have a policy about confidentiality or informed consent, but we have no idea whether they do or not. They do not offer any explanations. First, they need to have a policy about confidentiality or informed content (we have no idea whether they do or not). They need to have more elaborated interfaces or menus/subsections. However, nothing is clear yet. They do not offer any explanations so I cannot suggest anything about whether or how they can assure confidentiality."

Moreover, some participants expressed concerns about AI-generated citations and references, as AI fabricated sources or provided unverifiable references. Additionally, the lack of proper attribution for AI-generated content raised issues related to plagiarism and authorship, as one participant explained:

"I know it offers fake or incorrect citations or references. Also, it generates a lot of information without any references. Therefore, there may emerge direct or indirect plagiarism when using AI. On the other hand, claiming authorship when getting or using content generated by AI will cause ethical violations as well. As for the dilemma, while not being able to decide if it is ethical or how ethical to use AI in language research on one hand, I cannot be sure whether I can trust AI tools."

Participants also believed that AI could manipulate research outcomes and introduce bias. Many noted that AI-generated content often oversimplified complex research topics, leading to superficial or generalized findings. In addition, since AI systems were typically trained on Western-centric datasets, there was a risk of bias in the information they produced.

Ethical governance

Participants shared conflicting perspectives on their strategies to uphold ethical integrity when employing AI tools in language research. For instance, while some researchers stated that they did not use AI for research purposes, others mentioned that they limited AI usage to idea generation or visualization rather than relying on it for core research tasks, as one participant noted:

"To keep ethical when benefitting from AI in research, I would just use it to get some ideas or to generate some visuals for my paper, and I would report that I used it for such purposes while preparing my paper."

Participants also expressed uncertainty about the capacity of AI to produce reliable scientific materials. Thus, they emphasized cross-checking AI-generated results with original data to prevent misleading interpretations, as one participant explained:

"If it is used for the analysis of the already collected data, for example, I would compare the findings with the real raw data to prevent any misleading results. I would also try to make sure it ensures the confidentiality of the participants."

Regarding the adequacy of current ethical guidelines for AI in language research, participants generally agreed that while existing frameworks provided a necessary foundation, they were insufficient in addressing full ethical implications, as one participant stated:

"They are good in terms of the provision of a framework. However, they are not enough because, in my opinion, nobody exactly knows the real potential or, on the other hand, real limitations, risks, or drawbacks of AI in terms of all the elements or aspects of ethical issues."

In terms of maintaining transparency when documenting the contributions of AI to research, participants emphasized the importance of explicitly reporting the extent of AI usage in their studies. However, many also maintained that AI could not replace the researcher's core responsibilities.

Participants believe that various institutional policies guide their ethical use of AI in research, primarily emphasizing national and academic regulations. For instance, many referred to the ethics guide the Higher Council of Education prepared, which outlines principles, risks, and best practices for using AI in research. Moreover, guidelines set by academic publishers and journals served as reference points for ensuring ethical compliance, as one participant noted:

"First of all, the ethics guide for using AI in research prepared by the Higher Council of Education introduces the main principles to follow, the factors to

consider, and the main risks to avoid. Therefore, it is one of the main sources of guidelines in using AI in my research."

Regarding whether universities could follow stricter ethical frameworks for AI in language studies, participants largely agreed that institutions could be more active in regulating AI usage. For instance, some researchers noted that many scholars were not aware of the capacity of AI; thus, they emphasized that universities could first develop a clear understanding of the role of AI in research, as one participant explained:

"Many researchers either exaggerate or undermine the potential or functions of AI, and many tend to use it ignoring its ethical risks or neglecting reliability or confidentiality issues." ... "Institutions first need to fully understand AI and its role in research and then prepare clear and comprehensive guidelines."

Participants also identified several barriers regarding ethical standards when using AI tools. One major concern was the pressure to publish quickly, while another challenge was the overestimation of the capabilities of AI, with some researchers assuming AI-generated content was inherently reliable.

FUTURE DIRECTIONS

Participants identified several ethical challenges and proposed strategies to ensure responsible and sustainable use of AI in language research. One of the most frequently mentioned recommendations was the need for more effective AI detection tools to distinguish between human-generated and AI-assisted academic work. Some participants suggested that theses, articles, and book chapters could undergo AI detection processes as a standard requirement. Some participants pointed out the importance of stronger consequences for ethical violations, suggesting that sanctions could be stricter for those misusing AI in research. Many participants also stressed the importance of educating researchers and students about responsible AI usage. They proposed that AI ethics training could be mandatory, and researchers could be required to obtain certification in ethical AI use before utilizing such tools, as one participant explained:

"There is pressing need to more reliable AI detector tools. Theses, articles, book chapters must be undergone AI detection process. Sanctions must be stricter. I'm not saying dismissal from work. But researchers violating the rules (ethical rules) must be fined. Responsible AI use must be taught to every stake holder. And having this certificate must be an obligation. Universities ethical committees must work more effectively."

Participants generally agreed that AI could be used as a supporting tool rather than a primary research generator when asked about practical advice. They suggested that AI could assist in idea generation, problem-solving, and learning the basics of a specific topic. One participant described this balance. Some participants also predicted that new AI tools would be developed specifically to counteract the adverse effects of other AI tools. However, they acknowledged that such solutions would likely be costly and could create disparities between institutions with different levels of funding, as one participant noted:

"I believe in a short period of time, we will have some AI tools to mitigate the negative effects of other AI tools on research. But of course, this won't be free of charge. People or institutions will have to spend fortunes to have such tools."

Participants also expressed skepticism about whether publishers and funding bodies would enforce strict ethical regulations on AI use. Some argued that publishers had a financial interest in allowing AI-generated content, as it contributed to the rapid publication and increased revenue from article processing charges. Last, participants mostly agreed that AI could not replace the researcher's role in analyzing and discussing findings, as one participant strongly emphasized:

"We should eliminate AI tools from the process of article writing. Discussing findings, relating those findings to real life, education, or other fields is the researcher's job. If AI does this, then there is no need for researchers."

CONCLUSIONS AND DISCUSSION

Four conclusions can be drawn based on the findings presented above. The first conclusion is that AI is increasingly used in language research for idea generation, data organization, and academic writing support, while concerns exist about data confidentiality, reliability, and academic integrity. In other words, researchers seem to be still confused regarding the ethical impact of AI tools, as some suggest that there is a need to redefine ethical standards, while AI is a source of fear regarding academic responsibility. The second conclusion is that researchers identify several key ethical risks, including academic integrity violations, plagiarism, misinformation, potential AI-generated fabrications, and the lack of transparency regarding data confidentiality and informed consent. They also point to improper attribution of AI-generated content in referencing and citation practices, as well as the bias introduced by Western-centric datasets and the oversimplification of complex research topics. Thus, researchers adopt varying strategies such as avoiding AI altogether, while others use it selectively for tasks such as visualization and brainstorming. However, there is no consensus on whether AI-generated content aligns with ethical research standards, leading many to verify AI outputs manually. Current ethical guidelines are regarded as a useful but insufficient framework, making transparency in reporting AI use and self-regulation crucial for safeguarding academic integrity.

The third conclusion is that institutional policies on AI in language research are still evolving; national regulations and academic publisher guidelines are the primary ethical reference points. Thus, researchers believe that universities should have a more active role in regulating AI use in research by ensuring that ethical concerns are balanced with the potential benefits of AI. Some other barriers to ethical AI use include the pressure to publish, overestimating the capacity of AI, and an overall lack of awareness of AI-related ethical risks. The fourth and last conclusion is that researchers demand more effective AI detection tools to ensure research integrity. They suggest that AI detection should become a standard practice for publications within this scope. They also believe that stricter ethical regulations and consequences for AI misuse are needed to eliminate unethical practices in language research and that universities should implement AI ethics training and certification. However, they think that these solutions may be expensive and create disparities between well-funded and underfunded institutions. Considering these conclusions, it can be inferred that a notable contradiction exists in that participants regard AI as both a threat and a solution in language research. On the one hand, they emphasize risks such as plagiarism, fabricated content, unreliable outputs, and the erosion of academic responsibility. On the other hand, they recognize the potential of AI to accelerate research, support idea generation, and even assist in detecting ethical violations. This ambivalence may be partly explained by the contexts of their research, with some studies more focus on practical applications and others more alert to ethical risks, as well as by career stage, with early-career researchers often more open to experimentation and senior academics more cautious about responsibility.

These conclusions can also be interpreted in light of existing legal frameworks such as the GDPR and the European Union Artificial Intelligence Act (EU AI Act), which add further weight to researchers' ethical concerns. Issues of data confidentiality and informed consent directly connect to the GDPR for transparent and secure data processing, while worries about bias and accountability align with categorization of AI by the EU AI Act as high-risk systems requiring documentation, risk management, and human oversight. In this sense, participants' calls for transparency, effective detection tools, and stronger institutional policies not only reflect ethical responsibility but also resonate with evolving legal obligations, highlighting that safeguarding research integrity involves both moral and regulatory compliance.

Pedagogical implications

Several pedagogical implications can also be noted within the scope of the conclusions obtained from the study. From a broad perspective, the results of the current study align with the theoretical emphasis on ethics as a cornerstone of research integrity (Deardorff, 2020; Hultgren et al., 2016), particularly in safeguarding participants' rights and ensuring cultural sensitivity. On the other hand, the study presents novel ethical challenges that extend beyond traditional frameworks, such as data ownership, algorithmic bias, and the risk of overreliance on technology, since the theoretical framework underscores the importance of informed consent and confidentiality (Petrova et al., 2016), multilingual data, ethics training within the scope of AU usage. The results also resonate with prior research on ethical perceptions in applied linguistics regarding ethical judgments (Sterling & Gass, 2017) and context-dependent ethical decision-making (De Costa, 2016a). On the other hand, the conclusions in the current study diverge in terms of AI reliance on Western-centric datasets from the findings in previous research, while earlier studies are associated with human-centric research design (Pelzang & Hutchinson, 2018). Regarding cultural inclusivity and bias mitigation, the findings align with the results emphasizing intercultural competence in language education (Byram, 2020). To this end, the current study provides a bridge between traditional research ethics and the ethical complexities introduced by AI. For instance, while existing theories emphasize universal principles like honesty and non-maleficence (Weinbaum et al., 2019), the findings reveal that AI necessitates redefining these principles to address unique challenges such as algorithmic transparency and intellectual property rights within the scope of fairness and non-discrimination (Haneef & Agrawal, 2024). Moreover, the study contributes to the related literature in terms of ethical guidelines tailored to AI in language research (Alaqlobi et al., 2024; Tlili et al., 2023). More specifically, while prior studies focused on the transformative potential of AL (Groenewald et al., 2024), the current study explains specific risks, such as academic integrity violations and skill attrition, whereas the findings overlap the previous research in terms of transparency and institutional accountability (Zainuddin et al., 2024). On the other hand, it should be emphasized that the current study contextualizes the concerns mentioned in the previous research, including multilingual consent processes and culturally sensitive data interpretation. In conclusion, the present study is significant since it highlights the alignment and divergence of AI-related ethical concerns in language research with traditional research ethics and emphasizes the transformative potential of AI usage by identifying specific risks such as academic integrity violations, algorithmic bias, and overreliance on AI-generated content. Additionally, the findings suggest the necessity of developing ethical guidelines tailored specifically to AI in language research, addressing transparency, institutional accountability, and multilingual consent processes to ensure culturally sensitive data interpretation.

Practical recommendations

Some practical recommendations for language researchers can be noted regarding language researchers, university administrators, policymakers, and academic publishers. First, researchers should be aware that AI can be used for idea generation, data organization, and academic writing support, while they should overreliance on AI-generated content. In other words, researchers should critically evaluate AI outputs and ensure that they do not compromise research integrity. Second, they should maintain transparency by explicitly reporting the extent and purpose of AI usage in their studies. In addition, proper citation should be mandatory to prevent issues related to plagiarism and authorship by following ethical guidelines within the scope of academic honesty and responsibility. To achieve these, researchers should verify AI-generated information against credible sources to prevent misinformation and fabricated data. Second, universities should be more active in setting and enforcing ethical policies on AI use in language research. Policies should balance the benefits of AI and ethical risks by ensuring that researchers have clear, up-to-date guidelines on AI integration into research activities. University administrations should also implement training and certification programs to ensure that researchers are well-informed about responsible AI use, as offered by the Digital Research Ethics Collaboratory. Third, academic publishers should develop guidelines for authors and integrate AI detection tools to safeguard research integrity and adopt existing AI-detection technologies to ensure the integrity of submitted manuscripts. Fourth, policymakers should develop standardized ethical frameworks regarding AI usage in academic research, ensure transparency in AI-generated research content, and invest in developing AI detection tools. Fifth, AI developers should provide clear documentation on how their models function, integrate built-in mechanisms that detect ethical violations, implement features that help users comply with research ethics guidelines, adopt data privacy measures, and ensure equitable representation of different languages, cultures, and academic perspectives. Moreover, they should collaborate with universities and regulatory institutions and provide interactive ethics training modules to help researchers understand responsible AI usage in academic settings, specifically in language research. As a final recommendation, the above-mentioned stakeholders should align their practices with established legal frameworks such as the GDPR and the IRB guidelines, particularly by revising informed consent procedures to clarify how AI tools may process participant data.

Limitations and recommendations for further research

The study is not without limitations. First, the study was confined to a qualitative research design administered with 20 novice and experienced participants. Second, only one data collection tool, which might limit a deeper understanding of research ethics in language research, was used in the study. Third, the study focused on self-reported perceptions rather than actual and realistic practice. Lastly, the participants in the study were mostly Ph.D. holders in the field.

Some recommendations for further research can be noted. First, language researchers should examine how language researchers perceive AI ethics, focus on AI policies and ethical guidelines, and the role of AI in plagiarism and ethical risks, and explore the credibility of AI-generated research content, particularly in literature reviews, data analysis, and academic writing in longitudinal, multilingual, and cross-cultural language studies. To achieve these aims, further research should be designed to be qualitative for a better and deeper understanding of research ethics in the context of language research. Moreover, scale development and descriptive studies are necessary for describing the perceptions and real experiences in AI ethics in language research. Experimental studies should also be performed to test the effectiveness of training concerning AI ethics. Finally, researchers should conduct correlational studies to explore the relationships between AI ethics and certain demographic, cognitive, emotional, psychological, and social variables.

AUTHOR CONTRIBUTIONS

All authors contributed equally to the conception, design, data collection, analysis, and writing of this study.

FUNDING

This research received no external funding.

ETHICAL APPROVAL

Ethical approval was obtained from the Institutional Review Board of a state university.

INFORMED CONSENT STATEMENT

Informed consent was obtained from all participants involved in the study.

DATA AVAILABILITY STATEMENT

The data supporting the findings of this study are available from the corresponding author upon reasonable request.

CONFLICTS OF INTEREST

The authors declare no conflicts of interest.

REFERENCES

Alaqlobi, O., Alduais, A., Qasem, F., & Alasmari, M. (2024). Artificial intelligence in applied (linguistics): A content analysis and future prospects. *Cogent Arts & Humanities, 11*(1). Advance online publication. DOI: 10.1080/23311983.2024.2382422

Aljabr, F., & Al-Ahdal, A. (2024). Ethical and pedagogical implications of AI in language education: An empirical study at Ha'il University. *Acta Psychologica, 251*, 104605. DOI: 10.1016/j.actpsy.2024.104605

Aydın, S. (2024). Using ChatGPT in foreign language research: An overview. *Innovational Research in ELT*, *5*(1), 20–26. DOI: 10.29329/irelt.2024.1045.2

Aydın, S., & Zeinolabedini, M. (2024). Integrating artificial intelligence into foreign language learning: Learners' perspectives. *11th EJER Congress*.

Berg, C. (2023). *The case for generative AI in scholarly practice*. SSRN Electronic Journal. https://doi.org/DOI: 10.2139/ssrn.4407587

Byram, M. (2020). *Teaching and assessing intercultural communicative competence*. Multilingual Matters., DOI: 10.21832/BYRAM0244

Canagarajah, S. (2012). *Translingual practice*. Routledge., DOI: 10.4324/9780203073889

Comstock, G. (2012). *Research ethics: A philosophical guide to the responsible conduct of research*. Cambridge University Press.

De Costa, P. (2016a). *Ethics in applied linguistics research: Language researcher narratives*. Routledge.

De Costa, P. (2016b). Situating aff ect, ethics, and policy in LTI research. In *Reflections on Language Teacher Identity Research* (pp. 166–171). Routledge.

Deardorff, D. (2020). *Manual for developing intercultural competencies*. UNESCO.

Denkci Akkaş, F., Tekin, I., & Aydın, S. (2022). Does developing research skills increase academic motivation among foreign language learners? *The Literacy Trek*, *8*(2), 142–164. DOI: 10.47216/literacytrek.1124192

Denzin, N. (2017). *Sociological methods: A sourcebook*. Routledge.

Dörnyei, Z. (2020). *Innovations and challenges in language learning motivation*. Routledge., DOI: 10.4324/9780429485893

Dowling, M., & Lucey, B. (2023). ChatGPT for (Finance) research: The Bananarama Conjecture. *Finance Research Letters*, *53*, 1–6. DOI: 10.1016/j.frl.2023.103662

Elmas, E., & Aydin, S. (2017). Pre-service foreign language teachers' perceptions of research skills: A qualitative study. *The Qualitative Report*, *22*(12), 3088–3101. DOI: 10.46743/2160-3715/2017.3194

Gilson, A., Safranek, C., Huang, T., Socrates, V., Chi, L., Taylor, R., & Chartash, D. (2023). How does ChatGPT perform on the United States Medical Licensing Examination? The implications of Large Language Models for medical education and knowledge assessment. *JMIR Medical Education*. Advance online publication. DOI: 10.2196/45312

Grimaldi, G., & Ehrler, B. (2023). AI et al.: Machines are about to change scientific publishing forever. *ACS Energy Letters, 8*(1), 878–880. https://doi.org/DOI: 10.1021/acsenergylett.2c02828

Groenewald, E., Rani, S., Singla, P., Howard, E., & Groenewald, C. (2024). Artificial intelligence in linguistics research: Applications in language acquisition and analysis. *Naturalista Campano*, *28*(1), 1253–1262. DOI: 0.1016/j.actpsy.2024.104605

Guest, G., Bunce, A., & Johnson, L. (2006). How many interviews are enough? *Field Methods*, *18*(1), 59–82. DOI: 10.1177/1525822X05279903

Haneef, I., & Agrawal, M. (2024). Ethical issues in educational research. *Asian Research Journal of Arts & Social Sciences*, *22*(5), 29–38. DOI: 10.9734/arjass/2024/v22i5535

Holmes, W., Bialik, M., & Fadel, C. (2019). *Artificial intelligence in education: Promise and implications for teaching and learning*. Centre for Curriculum Redesign.

Huang, X., Zou, D., Cheng, G., Chen, X., & Xie, H. (2023). Using artificial intelligence in TESOL: Some ethical and pedagogical considerations. *Journal of Educational Technology & Society*, *26*(1), 112–131. https://onlinelibrary.wiley.com/doi/10.1002/tesq.3320

Hultgren, A. K., Erling, E. J., & Chowdhury, Q. (2016). Ethics in language and identity research. In Preece, S. (Ed.), *The Routledge handbook of language and identity* (pp. 15–30). Routledge., DOI: 10.1080/00437956.2017.1347315

Kern, R. (2006). Perspectives on technology in learning and teaching languages. *TESOL Quarterly*, *40*(1), 183–120. DOI: 10.2307/40264516

Korteling, J., van de Boer-Visschedijk, G., Blankendaal, R., Boonekamp, R., & Eikelboom, A. (2021). Human- versus artificial intelligence. *Frontiers in Artificial Intelligence*, *4*. Advance online publication. DOI: 10.3389/frai.2021.622364

Lin, Z. (2023). Why and how to embrace AI such as ChatGPT in your academic life. *PsyArXiv*, 1–5. https://doi.org/DOI: 10.31234/osf.io/sdx3j

Mitchell, T. (2025). Trust and transparency in artificial intelligence. *Philosophy & Technology*, *38*(3), 1–30. DOI: 10.1007/s13347-025-00916-2

Miteu, G. (2024). Ethics in scientific research: A lens into its importance, history, and future. *Annals of Medicine and Surgery (London)*, *86*(5), 2395–2398. DOI: 10.1097/MS9.0000000000001959

Noble, S., & Dubljević, V. (2022). Ethics of AI in organizations. In *Human-Centered Artificial Intelligence* (pp. 221–239). Elsevier., DOI: 10.1016/B978-0-323-85648-5.00019-0

Nunan, D. (1992). *Research methods in language learning*. Cambridge University Press.

Patton, M. (1990). *Qualitative evaluation and research methods*. Sage Publications Ltd.

Pelzang, R., & Hutchinson, A. (2018). Establishing cultural integrity in qualitative research. *International Journal of Qualitative Methods*, *17*(1). Advance online publication. DOI: 10.1177/1609406917749702

Petrova, E., Dewing, J., & Camilleri, M. (2016). Confidentiality in participatory research. *Nursing Ethics*, *23*(4), 442–454. DOI: 10.1177/0969733014564909

Qiao, H., & Zhao, A. (2023). Artificial intelligence-based language learning: Illuminating the impact on speaking skills and self-regulation in Chinese EFL context. *Frontiers in Psychology*, *14*. Advance online publication. DOI: 10.3389/fpsyg.2023.1255594

Sarker, I. (2022). AI-based modeling: Techniques, applications and research issues towards automation, intelligent and smart systems. *SN Computer Science*, *3*(2), 1–20. DOI: 10.1007/s42979-022-01043-x

Sayici, S., & Aydın, S. (2025). Using artificial intelligence in foreign language teaching: Teachers' perspectives. *Proceedings of The World Conference on Education and Teaching*, *4*(1), 1–10. https://doi.org/DOI: 10.33422/etconf.v4i1.1016

Schembri, N., & Jahić Jašić, A. (2022). Ethical issues in multilingual research situations: A focus on interview-based research. *Research Ethics*, *18*(3), 210–225. DOI: 10.1177/17470161221085857

Seliger, H. W., & Shohamy, E. (1989). *Second language research methods*. Oxford University Press.

Sterling, S., & Gass, S. (2017). Exploring the boundaries of research ethics: Perceptions of ethics and ethical behaviors in applied linguistics research. *System*, *70*, 50–62. DOI: 10.1016/j.system.2017.08.010

Tlili, A., Shehata, B., Adarkwah, M., Bozkurt, A., Hickey, D., Huang, R., & Agyemang, B. (2023). What if the devil is my guardian angel: ChatGPT as a case study of using chatbots in education. *Smart Learning Environments*, *10*(1), 1–24. DOI: 10.1186/s40561-023-00237-x

Weinbaum, C., Landree, E., Blumenthal, M., Piquado, T., & & Gutierrez, C. (2019). *Ethics in scientific research*. RAND Corporation.

Yao, Y., Duan, J., Xu, K., Cai, Y., Sun, Z., & Zhang, Y. (2024). A survey on large language model (LLM) security and privacy: The Good, The Bad, and The Ugly. *High-Confidence Computing*, *4*(2), 100211. DOI: 10.1016/j.hcc.2024.100211

Zainuddin, N., Suhaimi, N., Jaffar, M., Norwawi, N., Sahrir, M., Wan Daud, W., & Abdul Ghani, M. (2024). Responsible and ethical use of artificial intelligence in language education: A systematic review. *Forum for Linguistic Studies*, *6*(5), 316–325. DOI: 10.30564/fls.v6i5.7092

Zimmer, M. (2018). Addressing conceptual gaps in big data research ethics: An application of contextual integrity. *Social Media + Society*, *4*(2). Advance online publication. DOI: 10.1177/2056305118768300

Chapter 17
Integrating AI in Teacher Training:
Preparing Future Educators for Technology-Enhanced Classrooms

Andi Asrifan
https://orcid.org/0000-0002-9934-6129
Universitas Negeri Makassar, Indonesia

Rismawati Sudirman
https://orcid.org/0000-0001-8046-6764
Universitas Muhammadiyah Palopo, Indonesia

Andi Nur Maharani Islami
https://orcid.org/0009-0004-1651-592X
Universitas Negeri Makassar, Indonesia

Muhammad Yusri Bachtiar
Universitas Negeri Makassar, Indonesia

Fausiah Fausiah
STIM LPI Makassar, Indonesia

Mariani Loise
Politeknik Maritim AMI Makassar, Indonesia

ABSTRACT

The incorporation of Artificial Intelligence (AI) in education necessitates a fundamental reevaluation of teacher competencies, training methodologies, and educational equality. This study examines the necessity for the evolution of teacher education to equip educators for AI-enhanced learning settings via curriculum redesign, pedagogical innovation, ethical contemplation, and systemic support. It underscores the significance of AI literacy, digital fluency, equal access, and adaptive assessment methodologies. The report promotes inclusive and sustainable AI training ecosystems based on foresight and human-centered principles by examining worldwide policy trends and best practices. The examination of mentorship, educator views,

DOI: 10.4018/979-8-3373-3000-6.ch017

and institutional preparedness provides a comprehensive framework. Empowering educators to take charge in AI-enhanced classrooms is crucial for fostering equitable and ethical digital futures in education.

INTRODUCTION

The swift incorporation of artificial intelligence into educational frameworks has radically transformed the perceptions of teaching, learning, and professional identity in modern education. As AI tools progressively impact curriculum design, assessment methodologies, and instructional decision-making, teacher education encounters mounting demand to adapt in pedagogically sound, ethically responsible, and socially fair manners. Equipping educators for this changing environment necessitates not only technical skills but also a profound engagement with matters of equity, agency, and professional identity. This chapter examines the reconfiguration of teacher education to tackle these difficulties by harmonizing global policy frameworks, pedagogical methodologies, and ethical standards within AI-enhanced educational settings.

1.1 Rethinking Teacher Competencies in the Age of AI

The rapid incorporation of Artificial Intelligence (AI) into educational settings has fundamentally altered the capabilities necessary for instructors in the 21st century. Conventional teaching skillsets, although still valuable, are inadequate for managing the complexities of AI-driven, technology-enhanced classrooms (Bauer et al., 2025). As digital agents increasingly undertake roles such as personalized feedback, adaptive assessment, and content generation, educators must enhance their AI literacy, data-informed decision-making capabilities, and ethical judgment concerning algorithmic processes.

Modern teacher training must surpass traditional models and adopt a transformative competency framework rooted in Technological Pedagogical Content Knowledge (TPACK), augmented to incorporate AI-specific expertise (Mikeladze et al., 2024). Educators must understand both the operation of AI-powered technologies and their impact on learner agency, the perpetuation of prejudice, and power relations inside the classroom. In this setting, teacher education institutions must transition to a comprehensive competency development model that incorporates critical thinking, computational literacy, and ethical considerations regarding data utilization.

Furthermore, the competencies of prospective instructors should extend beyond just individual technical proficiency. The advancement of collaborative intelligence—cooperating with AI systems to co-create learning experiences—is increasingly regarded as fundamental to contemporary pedagogical functions (Filo et al., 2024). Educators must acquire the ability to critically assess AI-generated outputs, organize content that aligns with educational objectives, and offer socio-emotional support that AI cannot reproduce.

This redefinition necessitates a focus on diversity and contextual awareness. In areas with persistent infrastructural deficiencies, the integration of AI in teacher training must be customized to address digital disparities and promote equitable access to technology-enhanced educational resources. Competencies for future-ready educators must arise from a contextually informed and morally sound framework, harmonizing technological advancement with pedagogical rigor and human-centered principles. Ultimately, reevaluating teacher abilities in the era of AI transcends a mere technical enhancement; it constitutes a redefinition of the essence of being an educator within an increasingly automated yet deeply human educational environment (Mikeladze et al., 2024). Institutions must proactively develop teacher education programs that equip educators to lead the AI transition in education rather than merely follow it.

1.2 Global Trends and Policy Drivers for AI in Education

The incorporation of Artificial Intelligence (AI) in education has transitioned from a theoretical concept to a strategic necessity influenced by global trends and regulatory changes. Governments, international organizations, and educational institutions are formulating frameworks to harness AI's promise while addressing ethical, legal, and pedagogical concerns (Bond et al., 2024; Hong, 2024). These policy measures embody a worldwide agreement: education systems prepared for the future must be technologically enhanced, data-driven, and equitable.

UNESCO's Recommendation on the Ethics of Artificial Intelligence has functioned as a seminal text at the policy level, advocating for the establishment of human-centered AI ecosystems in education across nations (Hong, 2024). It underscores inclusive access, algorithmic transparency, and the enhancement of educators' capabilities. The OECD's AI Principles advocate for the development of trustworthy AI, emphasizing the necessity of teacher training to guarantee significant human oversight in AI-facilitated learning (Ifenthaler et al., 2024).

In Asia, nations such as South Korea and Singapore have developed AI masterplans that incorporate digital literacy and AI ethics into teacher education curricula. South Korea's AI Education Competency Framework requires organized AI training for both pre-service and in-service educators, whereas Singapore's EdTech Plan promotes AI-assisted tailored learning paths facilitated by trained teachers. The European Commission's Digital Education Action Plan (Goosen, 2025; Han, 2025).

These global trends are further bolstered by public-private partnerships and multilateral initiatives, such as the AI and Education Working Group within the Global Partnership on Artificial Intelligence (GPAI), which promotes cross-sector collaboration to develop scalable teacher training models (Ahmad, 2025). Concurrently, EdTech businesses are progressively integrating their solutions with these legislative frameworks, providing AI technologies that necessitate proficient facilitation by adequately educated educators.

Notwithstanding these advancements, inequities persist. Policy drivers frequently prioritize innovation while neglecting implementation deficiencies in low- and middle-income nations. The World Bank cautions that deficient infrastructure and inadequate teacher preparation could intensify existing educational disparities if AI implementation occurs without systemic backing (Jain & Raghuram, 2023). Global AI education policies are swiftly advancing, presenting both a framework and an obligation: to develop teacher education that is proactive, equitable, and morally founded. As AI transforms education, educators must be prepared to navigate—not simply adjust to—this evolving world.

1.3 The Digital Divide and Equity Concerns in AI Training Access

The incorporation of Artificial Intelligence (AI) in education presents transformative potential, however it concurrently intensifies enduring systemic disparities, especially over access to teacher training. The digital divide—evidenced by inequalities in infrastructure, connectivity, digital literacy, and institutional preparedness—constitutes a significant obstacle to equitable AI integration in teacher education (Tunjera & Chigona, 2023). In the absence of deliberate design and policy intervention, AI-driven solutions may exacerbate existing educational marginalization instead of alleviating it.

Worldwide, pre-service and in-service educators in marginalized groups frequently encounter restricted access to dependable internet, modern gear, and AI-enhanced teaching resources. The differences are both technological and socio-cultural, shaped by language difficulties, gender norms, rural-urban disparities, and varying perspectives of AI's role in education (Roshanaei et al., 2023).

Resource limitations in teacher training institutions frequently impede the implementation of complete AI educational methods. Numerous teacher preparation programs are deficient in teachers with experience in AI or data-driven pedagogy, leading to disjointed or cursory exposure to emerging technologies (Roshan et al., 2024). Moreover, commercial AI tools often exhibit Western-centric content and algorithmic reasoning, hence constraining their contextual applicability in many educational settings, especially in the Global South.

Addressing equity issues in AI training access requires a multifaceted approach: strategic investments in digital infrastructure, incorporation of underrepresented perspectives in AI tool development, and creation of culturally attuned training models. Initiatives like UNESCO's AI for Inclusive Education and UNICEF's Re-imagine Education campaign underscore localized capacity-building, promoting AI ecosystems that emphasize equity, transparency, and accessibility (Nuankaew et al., 2025). Closing the digital divide in AI-enhanced teacher education is not solely a technological task; it is a moral obligation. Equity must be integrated at every stage of policy, design, and implementation to guarantee that all educators, irrespective of location or background, are equipped to interact effectively with AI in the classroom.

DESIGNING AI-INFUSED PEDAGOGY AND CURRICULUM

Creating pedagogy and curricula that effectively incorporate artificial intelligence necessitates a transition from a technology-focused approach to a learning-centered intentionality. Curriculum design should prioritize explicit learning outcomes, pedagogical coherence, and ethical considerations, rather than viewing AI as a mere supplement or instructional expedient. This section underscores that AI-enhanced pedagogy must synchronize teaching tactics, assessment methodologies, and learner support with overarching educational objectives, such as critical thinking, equity, and the development of professional identity. By concentrating on intentional curriculum development, educators may guarantee that AI augments learning processes while maintaining human discernment, pedagogical autonomy, and contextual significance across varied educational environments.

2.1 Curriculum Models for AI Literacy and Digital Fluency

As Artificial Intelligence (AI) becomes a fundamental element of educational institutions, teacher training programs must be restructured to incorporate AI literacy and digital fluency as essential competencies (Rachbauer et al., 2025). Conventional curricula frequently prioritize content knowledge and general teaching methodologies; however, in the era of intelligent systems, educators must also cultivate the ability to comprehend, critically evaluate, and pedagogically incorporate AI technologies.

In this context, AI literacy encompasses more than just technical knowledge. It encompasses the capacity to understand essential AI concepts—such as machine learning, algorithmic logic, and natural language processing—alongside a knowledge of the ethical, social, and pedagogical ramifications of these technologies in educational environments (Black et al., 2024). Digital fluency entails the proficient and flexible utilization of digital resources to enhance teaching, learning, and professional cooperation. This dual emphasis necessitates curriculum models that are adaptable, interdisciplinary, and attuned to advancing educational technology.

Numerous new frameworks have arisen to direct curriculum development in this field. The AI + Education Competency Framework established by ISTE. These approaches emphasize the necessity of contextualizing AI instruction to local circumstances, ensuring that educators are not only consumers but reflective practitioners and co-designers of AI-enhanced pedagogies (Daher, 2025; Ren & Wu, 2025).

Effective curriculum models promote experiential and inquiry-based learning methodologies. Incorporating project-based learning (PBL), scenario simulations, and design thinking laboratories enables pre-service educators to investigate AI applications in genuine scenarios. This pragmatic approach cultivates both technical skills and the cognitive flexibility required to adjust to new tools and educational settings. Curricular change must be both iterative and participative (Knoblauch & Joost, 2025; Tokay et al., 2024). Involving teacher educators, policy-makers, and technologists in joint curriculum development guarantees coherence between educational objectives and technical capabilities. An effectively organized, AI-integrated curriculum empowers prospective educators to lead with assurance, integrity, and innovation in technology-enhanced learning environments.

2.2 Pedagogical Approaches for AI-Enhanced Instruction

The incorporation of Artificial Intelligence (AI) into educational practices necessitates both technology accessibility and a transformation in pedagogy. Educators must implement and modify pedagogical strategies that utilize AI's advantages while preserving human-centered learning (Bauer et al., 2025; Ifenthaler et al., 2024). Effective pedagogical tactics for AI-enhanced training are founded on constructivist, customized, and data-driven learning paradigms.

A notable method is blended learning, wherein AI tools facilitate differentiated training, adaptive feedback, and real-time performance monitoring. Intelligent Tutoring Systems (ITS) provide tailored pacing and scaffolding informed by learner analytics, so augmenting both autonomy and achievement (Kestin et al., 2025). When utilized with educational intent, such tools can transform the teacher's position from material provider to facilitator and mentor, thereby allocating more time for social-emotional engagement and advanced cognitive tasks.

A notable approach is flipped learning, wherein AI systems—such as generative content makers and recommender engines—prepare students prior to in-class sessions, hence optimizing classroom time for inquiry-based and collaborative endeavors (Kwan et al., 2025; Tata et al., 2025). This model promotes active learning and enhances digital fluency, particularly when combined with reflective and metacognitive tactics. Moreover, learning analytics dashboards enable instructors to track student progress, recognize misconceptions, and intervene proactively, hence improving the responsiveness and inclusivity of education.

Project-based learning (PBL) is enhanced by AI applications, especially when students tackle real-world issues with AI-supported technologies such as chatbots, simulations, or data visualization platforms. Educators can create multidisciplinary projects that enable students to investigate ethical questions, sustainability concerns, or global challenges related to AI, fostering critical thinking and civic duty (Mouta et al., 2023; Urmeneta et al., 2024). In this concept, AI functions as a co-inquirer instead of a passive instrument, fostering creative participation.

Pedagogical techniques must be grounded in ethical awareness and critical digital pedagogy. Educators must to be instructed not only in the use of AI tools but also in critically examining its assumptions, biases, and societal ramifications. Pedagogical models must prioritize inclusivity, accessibility, and cultural responsiveness to avert the marginalization of underrepresented learners (Hoggan & Kloubert, 2020; Roshanaei et al., 2023). AI-enhanced instruction necessitates a reconfiguration of pedagogy. By harmonizing instructional methodologies with the strengths of AI while maintaining educational principles, teacher training can develop educators who exemplify intentionality, ethics, and creativity.

2.3 Assessment Strategies for AI-Integrated Competencies

The advent of Artificial Intelligence (AI) in educational settings requires a fundamental reevaluation of assessment methodologies in teacher training. Educators are required to develop AI-integrated competencies, encompassing technical expertise, pedagogical innovation, and ethical judgment; consequently, assessment models must adapt to represent these multifaceted skill sets (Mosher et al., 2024). Traditional evaluation approaches, including written examinations and standardized tests, inadequately reflect the dynamic, practical, and reflective characteristics of AI-related pedagogical practices.

Effective evaluation in AI-enhanced teacher training must highlight performance-based and formative assessment methodologies. E-portfolios provide a comprehensive perspective on the development of pre-service teachers by recording lesson ideas utilizing AI tools, thoughts on algorithmic bias, and documentation of student participation in AI-enhanced classrooms (Estaiteyeh & McQuirter, 2024; Saimon et al., 2024). These portfolios correspond with constructivist methodologies and enable teacher educators to evaluate both technological implementation and pedagogical rationale.

Simulation-based evaluations are an additional new approach. Trainees can utilize AI-enhanced virtual environments to engage with digital avatars, adaptive learning systems, or classroom analytics dashboards, showcasing educational decision-making in real-time (Karakaya et al., 2025; Mosher et al., 2024). These simulations facilitate the cultivation of practical skills in secure, regulated environments and provide detailed feedback for enhancement.

Moreover, self- and peer-assessment are essential in fostering introspective and collaborative skills. In assessing AI integration, it is crucial for teacher candidates to exhibit procedural expertise while also expressing their ethical reasoning, cultural responsiveness, and critical thoughts on the role of technology in educational settings. This method promotes metacognitive awareness and collective accountability for learning (Hoggan & Kloubert, 2020).

The utilization of AI techniques in assessment requires critical examination. Although AI can deliver prompt feedback and monitor student advancement over time, it also poses the potential of entrenching prejudice and simplifying intricate human skills into measurable measures. Consequently, teacher training programs must instruct educators to critically analyze AI-generated evaluation data and augment it with human judgment (Du et al., 2024; Onesi-Ozigagun et al., 2024). Evaluation methodologies for AI-integrated competencies should transcend technical checklists to adopt comprehensive, genuine, and ethically-based frameworks. By synchronizing assessment techniques with the intricacies of AI-augmented pedagogy, teacher education may guarantee the development of reflective, proficient, and future-oriented educators.

EMPOWERING EDUCATORS THROUGH CONTINUOUS AI PROFESSIONAL DEVELOPMENT

Facilitating ongoing professional development for educators is crucial for the sustained and ethical incorporation of artificial intelligence in education. As AI tools and applications advance swiftly, educators necessitate continuous opportunities to enhance AI literacy, pedagogical proficiency, and critical awareness. Professional development must evolve beyond singular technical training to organized, reflective learning trajectories that foster experimentation, collaboration, and ethical decision-making. This section emphasizes the significance of enduring professional learning ecosystems that empower educators to integrate AI-enhanced methodologies into varied classroom environments, while preserving professional autonomy, instructional integrity, and a dedication to educational justice.

3.1 In-Service Training Models for AI Pedagogy

The swift progression of Artificial Intelligence (AI) technology in education necessitates both pre-service training and ongoing professional development for in-service educators. Due to the rapidly changing landscape of AI tools and their ethical, educational, and operational ramifications, professional development frameworks must be restructured to guarantee that educators stay proficient, certain, and critically reflective in AI-enhanced teaching settings (Al-Zahrani & Alasmari, 2024; Pietsch & Mah, 2024).

Effective in-service training for AI pedagogy must adopt modular, flexible, and context-sensitive frameworks. The combined microcredentialing concept integrates asynchronous online training on AI principles with live, practice-focused seminars (Karakaya et al., 2025). This approach facilitates personalized learning trajectories, permitting educators to develop competencies progressively while supporting their varied schedules and degrees of experience.

A viable option is the practice-based mentorship paradigm, wherein seasoned educators proficient in AI integration act as instructional coaches for their colleagues. These coaching relationships establish communities of practice that encourage collaborative experimentation, collective lesson design, and critical evaluation of the impact of AI in the classroom (Isma'il et al., 2024). This technique diminishes opposition and promotes grassroots ownership of technology-enhanced pedagogy by utilizing peer expertise.

Action research cycles serve as an effective mechanism for the advancement of AI pedagogy. In this methodology, educators recognize particular classroom difficulties, apply AI-assisted treatments, and assess results through continuous reflection (Isma'il et al., 2024; Kelley & Wenzel, 2025). This model enhances educational comprehension and places educators as co-creators of contextually pertinent AI techniques. Action research cultivates vital digital agency when combined with institutional support and access to ethical AI frameworks.

Notwithstanding these advancements, obstacles remain—especially in resource-constrained environments. Numerous educators indicate insufficient institutional infrastructure, restricted access to high-quality training resources, and ambiguity concerning the consequences of AI for equity and privacy. Consequently, institutional support—comprising national policy alignment, funding mechanisms, and engagement with EdTech developers—is crucial for the expansion of effective in-service training programs (Fundi et al., 2024). Comprehensive in-service training models are essential for teacher preparedness in the age of AI. Training should extend beyond technological skills to foster pedagogical innovation, ethical awareness, and adaptable professionalism, empowering educators to drive revolutionary change in AI-enhanced learning settings.

3.2 Teacher Beliefs and Attitudes Towards AI Integration

Educator perceptions and attitudes are essential factors in the adoption and effective deployment of Artificial Intelligence (AI) in educational environments. Although legislation, infrastructure, and training programs are crucial, the psychological preparedness and perceptions of educators frequently influence the efficacy of AI integration in educational settings (Cubio, 2025; Granström & Oppi, 2025). Comprehending these assumptions is essential for formulating professional development techniques that are both effective and enduring.

Empirical research indicate that educators display a range of attitudes concerning AI, from optimism and interest to anxiety and resistance. Favorable dispositions are frequently linked to previous experience with AI tools, perceived utility, and self-assurance in navigating technological transitions. Educators who acknowledge AI's capacity to customize learning, facilitate varied education, and alleviate administrative tasks are more likely to investigate its uses in the classroom (Morić et al., 2024; Ofosu-Ampong, 2024). Nonetheless, in the absence of sufficient assistance, even well-meaning educators may find it challenging to implement their favorable attitudes in reality.

In contrast, negative or ambivalent opinions are often associated with perceived dangers, including employment displacement, ethical ambiguity, and data privacy issues. Numerous educators convey concern over excessive dependence on algorithmic systems or the erosion of pedagogical autonomy in AI-augmented settings (Jose & Jose, 2024; Pikhart & Al-Obaydi, 2025). Moreover, restricted digital self-efficacy and insufficient institutional trust in EdTech providers further impede acceptance. Cultural and cultural elements additionally affect teacher attitudes. In low-resource or rural environments, where infrastructure and training are irregular, educators may perceive AI as an exclusive or unattainable advancement. Conversely, in more technologically advanced settings, educators may demonstrate increased autonomy and experimentation using AI-assisted technologies.

To positively alter views, professional development must encompass emotive, cognitive, and social components. Reflective discourse, peer modeling, and scenario-based talks regarding ethical concerns help elucidate AI and promote critical involvement. Moreover, conceptualizing AI as a pedagogical ally rather than a substitute can assist in redefining teacher identity in the context of technology (Mikeladze et al., 2024). Educators' ideas regarding AI are not fixed obstacles but rather dynamic factors influenced by experience, context, and dialogue. Fostering knowledgeable, confident, and morally conscious attitudes is crucial for developing AI-ready educators capable of leading innovation with purpose and integrity.

3.3 Mentorship and Peer-Learning Models for AI Proficiency

The integration of Artificial Intelligence (AI) technologies in contemporary classrooms necessitates that teachers develop expertise through persistent, relational, and community-oriented learning methods, rather than solely relying on formal training. Effective techniques include mentorship and peer-learning frameworks that assist educators in managing the challenges of AI adoption through shared experiences, mutual support, and collaborative reflection (Ma et al., 2025; Nagaraj et al., 2023).

Mentorship models utilize the knowledge of seasoned educators—either formally educated in AI or early adopters of EdTech tools—who assist their colleagues through structured learning. These mentors deliver practical demos, collaboratively design lessons utilizing AI tools, and furnish immediate input on implementation difficulties (Abuhassna, 2024). These relationships cultivate trust and create secure environments for experimentation, which is particularly crucial when addressing ethical issues or engaging with unfamiliar technologies.

In addition to mentorship, peer-learning communities are frequently structured as Professional Learning Communities (PLCs) or communities of practice. These frameworks promote collaborative exploration of AI pedagogy, allowing educators to jointly develop lesson plans, exchange thoughts on classroom experiences, and evaluate the pedagogical efficacy of AI applications. The iterative aspect of peer learning cultivates critical thinking and adaptive problem-solving, which are vital for addressing the evolving landscape of AI technologies (Elstad & Eriksen, 2024; Mishra, 2024). Innovative concepts like digital peer networks and social learning platforms are especially effective in transcending geographical and institutional barriers. Educators can connect with international colleagues, share techniques, and obtain curated AI teaching resources through webinars, forums, and collaborative digital workspaces. These platforms facilitate the democratization of information dissemination and ensure fair access to innovative methods.

Nonetheless, the successful execution of mentorship and peer-learning programs necessitates institutional backing. This encompasses time allocations in instructional schedules, acknowledgment of mentorship responsibilities, and investment in coordinating systems. In the absence of structural support, such models are prone to becoming informal and unsustainable (Grassley & Lambe, 2015; Platz & Hyman, 2013). Mentorship and peer-learning frameworks are essential for enhancing teacher confidence, resilience, and proficiency in AI teaching. By basing AI training on collaborative human connections, these methods guarantee that technology integration is rooted in common values, professional development, and pedagogical integrity.

ETHICAL AND POLICY CHALLENGES IN AI-DRIVEN EDUCATION

The incorporation of artificial intelligence in education presents intricate ethical and policy dilemmas that surpass just technological aspects. Concerns regarding data privacy, algorithmic bias, accountability, and transparency increasingly influence the design, use, and governance of AI systems in educational institutions. Confronting these difficulties necessitates cohesive policy frameworks that integrate technology innovation with educational principles and social accountability. This section analyzes how ethical principles and regulatory frameworks might guide the responsible application of AI in education, ensuring that technological progress promotes equity, safeguards learner autonomy, and bolsters trust among educators, students, and the broader community.

4.1 Data Privacy and Surveillance in AI Tools for Educators

The implementation of Artificial Intelligence (AI) tools in education prompts significant concerns over data privacy and monitoring, especially as these technologies progressively influence teaching, evaluation, and classroom management. AI-driven systems provide robust solutions, including real-time analytics, automated feedback, and adaptive learning environments, yet they frequently function by gathering, processing, and analyzing extensive amounts of personal data from students and educators (Durak & Onan, 2025).

The ramifications for educators are complex. Artificial intelligence systems integrated inside Learning Management Systems (LMS), classroom surveillance software, and predictive analytics platforms routinely collect data on educator conduct, teaching strategies, and interpersonal dynamics (Calderwood, 2025; Kumar et al., 2019). These systems—frequently used without sufficient consent or comprehension—can result in unintentional surveillance cultures, in which educators perceive themselves as being observed, assessed, or restricted by obscure algorithms. The decline of professional autonomy and trust can compromise instructional freedom and teacher well-being.

Moreover, data privacy frameworks are frequently inadequately established or applied inconsistently in educational environments. Numerous educational institutions lack comprehensive policies governing data storage, access permissions, and usage reasons. Commercial EdTech providers may adhere to terms of service that emphasize data monetization at the expense of ethical stewardship, so exacerbating issues of governance and accountability (Hakimi et al., 2021; Hasan, 2023).

Algorithmic bias and data misuse pose significant hazards to marginalized communities, as AI systems educated on biased datasets may perpetuate systemic disparities. Educators operating in such environments may be assessed using inadequate metrics, resulting in reputational damage or professional detriment (Jose et al., 2025).

To alleviate these dangers, teacher training must incorporate digital rights literacy, enabling educators to critically evaluate the tools they utilize, champion transparent data practices, and engage in legislative discussions. Educational institutions must form ethical review boards, implement privacy-by-design principles, and assure adherence to national and international data protection requirements, including GDPR and FERPA. Protecting data privacy in AI-driven education transcends technological concerns; it encompasses ethical considerations, equity, and educational justice (Eden et al., 2024; Shukla & Taneja, 2024). Educators must be prepared to traverse this landscape with alertness, articulation, and a profound comprehension of their rights and obligations in the digital era.

4.2 Algorithmic Bias and Fairness in Teaching Tools

The expansion of AI-based educational technologies has heightened debates over algorithmic bias and the necessity of equity. Although AI offers efficiency, customisation, and scalability, it functions through computational models trained on historical data that may perpetuate current societal biases. Consequently, algorithmic systems employed in education—spanning automated grading instruments to learning analytics dashboards—pose a risk of perpetuating or exacerbating injustices in classrooms unless they are deliberately created and rigorously assessed (Baker & Hawn, 2021).

Algorithmic bias can emerge in various forms. Predictive algorithms evaluating student performance may harm learners from marginalized backgrounds if the training datasets lack diversity or contextual sensitivity. Automated language tools can display cultural or linguistic biases, and adaptive learning platforms may misinterpret learner requirements due to the uniform logic ingrained in their algorithms (Boateng & Boateng, 2025; Li, 2024). In these instances, AI may inadvertently perpetuate preconceptions and generate unequal outcomes for marginalized student groups, rather than promoting equity.

The notion of fairness in artificial intelligence is intricate and multifarious. Definitions vary from statistical parity (equitable treatment of demographic groups) to individual fairness (treating analogous learners identically). Nonetheless, fairness must also consider contextual equity, acknowledging that certain kids necessitate tailored support due to systemic obstacles (Castelnovo et al., 2022). Educators and policymakers must transcend mere technical fairness measurements and engage with ethically informed and pedagogically pertinent interpretations of justice.

Educators are essential in recognizing and mitigating algorithmic prejudice. Teacher training programs must prepare educators to interrogate the impartiality of AI systems, identify nuanced biases in outputs, and promote inclusive design. Transparency in AI tool functionality, elucidation of algorithmic conclusions, and collaborative co-design with educators and learners are critical measures for achieving fairness (Barnes & Hutson, 2024; Fitas, 2025). Guaranteeing equity in AI-driven educational tools is not merely a technical modification; it is a pedagogical and ethical need. As AI integrates into educational environments, educators must be empowered as pivotal actors capable of identifying prejudice, ensuring accountability, and collaboratively developing just and equitable educational technologies.

4.3 Policy Frameworks for Responsible AI in Education

As Artificial Intelligence (AI) becomes increasingly integrated into educational systems, the formulation of comprehensive policy frameworks is crucial to guarantee responsible, ethical, and equitable implementation. These frameworks function as regulatory mechanisms that oversee AI development, deployment, and governance in educational settings, harmonizing innovation with the safeguarding of human rights, privacy, and pedagogical integrity (Bond et al., 2024; Zhu et al., 2025).

UNESCO's Recommendation on the Ethics of Artificial Intelligence serves as a fundamental policy statement at the worldwide level, promoting human-centered, inclusive, and transparent AI ecosystems. It emphasizes the necessity for governments to create legal and institutional frameworks to oversee the application of AI in education, encompassing teacher training and accountability systems (Chan, 2023; Hong, 2024). The OECD AI Principles also underscore the necessity of trustworthiness, explainability, and democratic engagement as essential conditions for the use of AI in public sectors, such as educational institutions.

National policy frameworks differ in breadth and development. Countries such as Finland and Singapore have spearheaded AI education programs that incorporate digital ethics, AI literacy, and professional development into national curricula for educators. Finland's National AI Strategy mandates AI ethics modules for teacher educators, whereas Singapore's EdTech Masterplan incorporates ongoing capacity-building initiatives in accordance with data governance principles (Mekheimer, 2025; Park et al., 2023).

Notwithstanding these advancements, disparities remain in numerous contexts, particularly in the Global South, where disjointed legislation, insufficient enforcement, and restricted stakeholder engagement impede the appropriate application of AI. Policies frequently omit to involve educators substantively in AI governance, resulting in top-down strategies that overlook local educational contexts and equality issues (Lainjo & Tsmouche, 2023).

To tackle these difficulties, policy frameworks must incorporate multi-stakeholder engagement, contextual awareness, and educational pertinence. Educators, learners, guardians, technologists, and members of civic society should together formulate AI education policies that embody collective values and address community requirements. Furthermore, rules must be flexible, including regular evaluation processes to address technological advancements and new ethical issues (Bagstad et al., 2025; Devi, 2023). The implementation of responsible AI in education necessitates policy coherence. An effective, inclusive, and progressive policy framework is essential for empowering educators, protecting learners, and guaranteeing that AI augments—rather than undermines—the objective of education as a public benefit.

SHAPING THE FUTURE OF TEACHER EDUCATION IN AN AI WORLD

Transforming teacher education for an AI-driven future necessitates a reevaluation of how educators are equipped to manage uncertainty, technology advancements, and shifting professional responsibilities. Future-oriented teacher education should prioritize the development of adaptive competence, ethical judgment, and lifetime learning abilities, rather than concentrating exclusively on contemporary technologies or trends. This section examines how teacher education programs might proactively address rising demands, appropriately incorporate AI, and maintain the human aspects of teaching, beyond immediate implementation issues. By integrating innovation with educational principles, teacher education can significantly contribute to ensuring that AI promotes, rather than undermines, professional identity, equity, and pedagogical intent.

5.1 Emerging AI Tools and Their Educational Applications

The advancement of Artificial Intelligence (AI) has produced a new array of intelligent instruments ready to revolutionize educational methodologies. These developing AI tools increase educational delivery and broaden the pedagogical possibilities—promoting personalization, automation, and deeper engagement. In teacher training programs, comprehending the capabilities, limitations, and educational ramifications of these tools is essential for equipping educators for 21st-century classrooms (Black et al., 2024; Mosher et al., 2024).

The AI-driven intelligent tutoring system (ITS) is among the most impactful tools. Systems like Carnegie Learning and Squirrel AI dynamically adjust educational content in real time according to student reactions and learning characteristics. They provide many paths, prompt feedback, and scaffolding that facilitates mastery learning (Hariyanto et al., 2025). For educators, ITS can offer analytics that guide training and pinpoint learning deficiencies.

A fast expanding category is generative AI, including OpenAI's ChatGPT, Google Gemini, and Anthropic's Claude. Large language models (LLMs) can aid educators in lesson preparation, topic development, rubric formulation, and reflective pedagogy (Gabriel, 2024). Despite their potency, their application prompts apprehensions about accuracy, prejudice, and excessive dependence, necessitating critical literacy in prompt engineering and AI ethics.

Learning analytics platforms are increasingly gaining popularity. Platforms such as Classcraft and Brightspace employ machine learning to assess student behavior, attendance, involvement, and emotional trends. This facilitates predictive modeling and early interventions, helping instructors to implement proactive techniques. Nonetheless, these platforms require a comprehensive understanding of data interpretation and a robust dedication to student privacy (Coughlan et al., 2021; Montoro et al., 2019). Furthermore, AI-driven immersive solutions, such as virtual reality (VR) integrated with AI tutors and augmented reality (AR) simulations, provide experiential learning settings for teacher trainees. These instruments enable educators to implement classroom management, differentiated education, and culturally sensitive pedagogy within secure, simulated environments.

The instructional potential of these instruments is contingent upon their deliberate integration, informed by pedagogical objectives, ethical considerations, and ongoing professional growth. Educators must possess not only the knowledge of utilizing AI but also an understanding of its appropriate applications and timing for its utilization. Nascent AI technologies have transformative possibilities in education (Black et al., 2024; Huynh et al., 2025). Teacher preparation must prepare future educators to critically interact with these technologies, optimizing their advantages while properly addressing their difficulties.

5.2 Scenario Planning and Foresight in Teacher Education

In a period characterized by swift technology advancement and educational upheaval, scenario planning and foresight are increasingly acknowledged as vital instruments for equipping future educators for an AI-augmented environment. Instead of perceiving the future as a definitive conclusion, foresight practices push teacher education institutions to accept ambiguity, foresee several possibilities, and develop adaptive capacity in educators (Akanzire et al., 2025; Nyaaba & Zhai, 2024).

Scenario planning is the development of various credible future narratives that take into account evolving trends, technological advancements, and socio-political factors. In the realm of AI in education, scenarios may encompass entirely automated learning settings, hybrid human-AI co-teaching models, or even opposition against algorithmic education. These scenarios assist teacher trainees in examining how various futures may influence pedagogy, equality, data governance, and professional identity (Mouta et al., 2023).

Integrating foresight into teacher preparation fosters a future-oriented attitude that is strategic, reflective, and ethically informed. Educators proficient in foresight possess the ability to assess AI tools for both their current effectiveness and its future ramifications on student autonomy, privacy, and the educational social contract (Meletiou-Mavrotheris et al., 2025). They are more adept at scrutinizing the assumptions inherent in AI systems and at collaboratively designing learning environments that are prepared for the future and consistent with human values. Foresight can be included into teacher education through design thinking workshops, future scenario development, and policy simulation exercises. These methods foster both innovative and critical thinking, enabling teacher candidates to simulate their roles as innovators, policy shapers, and ethical stewards within education systems influenced by advanced technologies. Crucially, foresight in teacher education must be comprehensive and collaborative.

Marginalized voices, sometimes disregarded in discussions defining the future, must be deliberately incorporated to guarantee equal perspectives on AI's function in education. Additionally, institutional leadership must cultivate cultures that prioritize long-term perspectives and engage in ongoing horizon scanning to adjust curricula as needed. Scenario planning and foresight convert teacher education from a reactive approach to a proactive framework for shaping educational futures (Bol & Staring, 2018). As AI transforms education, providing educators with foresight tools enables them to not only endure upheaval but to navigate it with vision, empathy, and intention.

5.3 Sustainable and Inclusive AI Training Ecosystems

Establishing sustainable and inclusive AI training ecosystems is essential for empowering educators to excel in digitally transformed classrooms. These ecosystems extend beyond singular workshops or isolated interventions; they constitute a holistic framework of policies, partnerships, pedagogies, and support systems that adapt to the requirements of educators and the ethical imperatives of AI-driven education (Amiri et al., 2025).

An enduring AI training ecosystem is defined by its capacity to consistently adjust to technology advancements while preserving educational integrity. This necessitates the integration of AI competencies into pre-service teacher curricula, ensuring that AI literacy and ethical reasoning are fundamental elements of professional identity development (Rütti-Joy et al., 2023). Furthermore, in-service training should be bolstered by established professional development frameworks that are consistently revised, informed by research, and attuned to contextual realities.

Simultaneously, inclusion must serve as a fundamental value. Numerous educators, especially in underprivileged and rural areas, have obstacles in obtaining AI training due to deficiencies in digital infrastructure, language constraints, or the absence of culturally pertinent resources. Consequently, inclusive ecosystems must emphasize equitable access, create multilingual and contextually relevant material, and use gender-sensitive strategies in both content and delivery (Moulaei et al., 2023).

Collaborative partnerships are essential for sustaining these ecosystems. Governments, universities, teacher associations, EdTech businesses, and civil society organizations must collaboratively develop frameworks for AI training that harmonize innovation with ethical accountability (Yan & Liu, 2024). Collaboration between public and private sectors can provide technological expertise and financial resources, while educational stakeholders offer pedagogical knowledge and practical insights.

Moreover, sustainability relies on feedback and governance mechanisms that provide ongoing assessment and adjustment. AI training programs must have systems for collecting instructor feedback, evaluating effects on instructional practices, and guaranteeing conformity with overarching educational objectives and data protection regulations. A sustainable and inclusive AI training ecosystems represent not just technical frameworks but also social, cultural, and ethical obligations (Bagstad et al., 2025; Khan et al., 2025). By investing in egalitarian, dynamic, and values-driven ecosystems, we enable educators to not only adapt to AI-enhanced education but also to actively influence its direction for the advantage of all learners.

CONCLUSION

The emergence of Artificial Intelligence (AI) in education signifies a fundamental transformation that redefines the duties, responsibilities, and capabilities of educators in the 21st century. As digital agents undertake more educational and administrative responsibilities, educators must possess not only technical expertise but also ethical judgment, cultural awareness, and critical engagement with AI tools. This shift necessitates that teacher education transcends conventional subject delivery by integrating AI literacy and digital fluency as essential components of both pre-service and in-service training.

The crux of this transition lies in the establishment of sustainable and inclusive ecosystems, which include curricula, professional development, mentorship, and policy frameworks, that are responsive to varied circumstances and technological progress. Scenario planning and foresight methodologies ought to be integrated into teacher education to cultivate future-oriented attitudes and resilience. Simultaneously, concerns regarding algorithmic bias, data privacy, and infrastructure inequity must be confronted to prevent the intensification of educational disparities.

The research highlights that mentorship, peer-learning networks, and collaborative curriculum development improve teacher preparedness and assurance in utilizing AI tools. Furthermore, equity-centered strategies are crucial for closing the digital divide and promoting substantive involvement among educators of diverse backgrounds. Responsible AI integration necessitates participatory policy-making that involves educators as co-designers of digital futures. Equipping educators for AI-enhanced education is a complex task necessitating ethical, pedagogical, and structural coherence. Teachers should be empowered as active agents of change, capable of influencing educational technologies to promote human dignity, equity, and the public good, rather than becoming passive beneficiaries of innovation. An approach to AI in education that prioritizes human needs would guarantee that technology acts as a facilitator of inclusive, transformative, and lifelong learning for everyone.

REFERENCES

Abuhassna, H. (2024). The Information Age for Education via Artificial Intelligence and Machine Learning: A Bibliometric and Systematic Literature Analysis. *International Journal of Information and Education Technology (IJIET)*, *14*(5), 700. DOI: 10.18178/ijiet.2024.14.5.2095

Ahmad, F. B. (2025). AI-Powered Chatbots for Mobile Teacher Training: Enhancing Interactive Learning Experiences. [iJIM]. *International Journal of Interactive Mobile Technologies*, *19*(17), 41. DOI: 10.3991/ijim.v19i17.54387

Akanzire, B. N., Nyaaba, M., & Nabang, M. (2025). Generative AI in teacher education: Teacher educators' perception and preparedness. *Journal of Digital Educational Technology*, *5*(1). Advance online publication. DOI: 10.30935/jdet/15887

Al-Zahrani, A. M., & Alasmari, T. (2024). Exploring the impact of artificial intelligence on higher education: The dynamics of ethical, social, and educational implications. *Humanities & Social Sciences Communications*, *11*(1). Advance online publication. DOI: 10.1057/s41599-024-03432-4

Amiri, S. M. H., Islam, M. M., & Akter, N. (2025). Educating the future: AI's role in shaping next-generation pedagogies. *International Journal of Science and Research Archive*, *15*(1), 621. DOI: 10.30574/ijsra.2025.15.1.1036

Bagstad, K. J., Balbi, S., Adamo, G., Athanasiadis, I. N., Affinito, F., Willcock, S., Magrach, A., Hayashi, K., Harmáčková, Z. V., Niamir, A., Smets, B., Buchhorn, M., Drakou, E. G., Alfieri, A., Edens, B., Morales-Salinas, L., Vári, Á., Sanz, M. J., & Villa, F. (2025). Interoperability for ecosystem service assessments: Why, how, who, and for whom? *Ecosystem Services*, *72*, 101705. DOI: 10.1016/j.ecoser.2025.101705

Baker, R. S., & Hawn, A. (2021). Algorithmic Bias in Education. *International Journal of Artificial Intelligence in Education*, *32*(4), 1052. DOI: 10.1007/s40593-021-00285-9

Barnes, E., & Hutson, J. (2024). Navigating the ethical terrain of AI in higher education: Strategies for mitigating bias and promoting fairness. *Forum for Education Studies.*, *2*(2), 1229. DOI: 10.59400/fes.v2i2.1229

Bauer, E., Greiff, S., Graesser, A. C., Scheiter, K., & Sailer, M. (2025). Looking Beyond the Hype: Understanding the Effects of AI on Learning. *Educational Psychology Review*, *37*(2). Advance online publication. DOI: 10.1007/s10648-025-10020-8

Black, N. B., George, S., Eguchi, A., Dempsey, J. C., Langran, E., Fraga, L., Brunvand, S., & Howard, N. R. (2024). A Framework for Approaching AI Education in Educator Preparation Programs. *Proceedings of the AAAI Conference on Artificial Intelligence, 38*(21), 23069. DOI: 10.1609/aaai.v38i21.30351

Boateng, O., & Boateng, B. (2025). Algorithmic bias in educational systems: Examining the impact of AI-driven decision making in modern education. *World Journal of Advanced Research and Reviews, 25*(1), 2012. DOI: 10.30574/wjarr.2025.25.1.0253

Bol, E., & Staring, M. (2018). Becoming a Future-Proof Teacher: Futures Education Integrated in a Teacher in Training Program. *World Futures Review, 10*(4), 323. DOI: 10.1177/1946756718784002

Bond, M., Khosravi, H., de Laat, M., Bergdahl, N., Negrea, V., Oxley, E., Pham, P., Chong, S. W., & Siemens, G. (2024). A meta systematic review of artificial intelligence in higher education: A call for increased ethics, collaboration, and rigour. *International Journal of Educational Technology in Higher Education, 21*(1). Advance online publication. DOI: 10.1186/s41239-023-00436-z

Calderwood, S. J. (2025). *Surveillance Digitisation, Performativity, and Teacher-Student Relationships in a Blended Learning Setting*. Postdigital Science and Education., DOI: 10.1007/s42438-024-00537-6

Castelnovo, A., Crupi, R., Greco, G., Regoli, D., Penco, I. G., & Cosentini, A. (2022). A clarification of the nuances in the fairness metrics landscape. *Scientific Reports, 12*(1), 4209. DOI: 10.1038/s41598-022-07939-1

Chan, C. K. Y. (2023). A comprehensive AI policy education framework for university teaching and learning. *International Journal of Educational Technology in Higher Education, 20*(1). Advance online publication. DOI: 10.1186/s41239-023-00408-3

Coughlan, T., Lister, K., & Lucassen, M. (2021). Representing the Unseen with "Our Journey": A Platform to Capture Affective Experiences and Support Emotional Awareness in University-Level Study. *Journal of Formative Design in Learning, 5*(1), 39. DOI: 10.1007/s41686-021-00055-9

Cubio, M. J. V. (2025). The Influence of Privacy, Bias, and Surveillance Concerns on Teachers' Willingness to Use Artificial Intelligence in Education. *International Journal of Research and Innovation in Social Science, 3192*. Advance online publication. DOI: 10.47772/ijriss.2025.903sedu0240

Daher, R. F. (2025). Integrating AI literacy into teacher education: A critical perspective paper. *Discover Artificial Intelligence, 5*(1). Advance online publication. DOI: 10.1007/s44163-025-00475-7

Devi, A. (2023). Ethical Considerations in Using Artificial Intelligence to Improve Teaching and Learning. *Tuijin Jishu/Journal of Propulsion Technology, 44*(4), 1031. https://doi.org/DOI: 10.52783/tjjpt.v44.i4.966

Du, K., Geiger, J., Killen, T., Porta, A. E., & O'Brien, T. (2024). The Paradigm Shift in Education in Big Data Era: Exploring the Intersection of Historical Assessment Frameworks and AI-Powered Assessment Methods in Education. *Journal of Education and Training Studies*, *12*(2), 22. DOI: 10.11114/jets.v12i2.6582

Durak, H. Y., & Onan, A. (2025). A systematic review of AI-based feedback in educational settings [Review of *A systematic review of AI-based feedback in educational settings*]. *Journal of Computational Social Science, 8*(4). Springer Nature. https://doi.org/DOI: 10.1007/s42001-025-00428-1

Eden, C. A., Chisom, O. N., & Adeniyi, I. S. (2024). Integrating AI in education: Opportunities, challenges, and ethical considerations. *Magna Scientia Advanced Research and Reviews*, *10*(2), 6. DOI: 10.30574/msarr.2024.10.2.0039

Elstad, E., & Eriksen, H. M. (2024). High School Teachers' Adoption of Generative AI. [NJCIE]. *Nordic Journal of Comparative and International Education*, *8*(1). Advance online publication. DOI: 10.7577/njcie.5736

Estaiteyeh, M., & McQuirter, R. (2024). Generative or Degenerative?! Implications of AI Tools in Pre-Service Teacher Education and Reflections on Instructors' Professional Development. *Brock Education Journal*, *33*(3). Advance online publication. DOI: 10.26522/brocked.v33i3.1176

Filo, Y., Rabin, E., & Mor, Y. (2024). An Artificial Intelligence Competency Framework for Teachers and Students: Co-created with Teachers. *European Journal of Open Distance and E-Learning*, *26*, 93. DOI: 10.2478/eurodl-2024-0012

Fitas, R. (2025). Inclusive education with AI: Supporting special needs and tackling language barriers. *AI and Ethics*. Advance online publication. DOI: 10.1007/s43681-025-00824-3

Fundi, M., Sanusi, I. T., Oyelere, S. S., & Ayere, M. (2024). Advancing AI education: Assessing Kenyan in-service teachers' preparedness for integrating artificial intelligence in competence-based curriculum. *Computers in Human Behavior Reports*, *14*, 100412. DOI: 10.1016/j.chbr.2024.100412

Gabriel, S. (2024). Generative AI and Educational (In)Equity. *Proceedings of the International Conference on AI Research.*, *4*(1), 133. https://doi.org/DOI: 10.34190/icair.4.1.3153

Goosen, Prof. W. (2025). Designing AI Literacy Curricula for Higher Education: A Comparative Framework. *International Journal of Research and Innovation in Social Science*, *9*(26), 8439. DOI: 10.47772/ijriss.2025.903sedu0637

Granström, M., & Oppi, P. (2025). Assessing teachers' readiness and perceived usefulness of AI in education: An Estonian perspective. *Frontiers in Education, 10*. Advance online publication. DOI: 10.3389/feduc.2025.1622240

Grassley, J. S., & Lambe, A. (2015). Easing the Transition From Clinician to Nurse Educator: An Integrative Literature Review [Review of *Easing the Transition From Clinician to Nurse Educator: An Integrative Literature Review*]. *Journal of Nursing Education, 54*(7), 361. Slack Incorporated (United States). https://doi.org/DOI: 10.3928/01484834-20150617-01

Hakimi, L., Eynon, R., & Murphy, V. A. (2021). The Ethics of Using Digital Trace Data in Education: A Thematic Review of the Research Landscape [Review of *The Ethics of Using Digital Trace Data in Education: A Thematic Review of the Research Landscape*]. *Review of Educational Research, 91*(5), 671. SAGE Publishing. https://doi.org/DOI: 10.3102/00346543211020116

Han, X. (2025). Improving pre-service teachers' AI competencies: A quasi experimental study. *Frontiers in Psychology, 16*. Advance online publication. DOI: 10.3389/fpsyg.2025.1642465

Hariyanto, H., Kristianingsih, F. X. D., & Maharani, R. (2025). Artificial intelligence in adaptive education: A systematic review of techniques for personalized learning. *Discover Education*, *4*(1). Advance online publication. DOI: 10.1007/s44217-025-00908-6

Hasan, R. (2023). Understanding EdTech's Privacy and Security Issues: Understanding the Perception and Awareness of Education Technologies' Privacy and Security Issues. *Proceedings on Privacy Enhancing Technologies. Privacy Enhancing Technologies Symposium*, *2023*(4), 269. DOI: 10.56553/popets-2023-0110

Hoggan, C., & Kloubert, T. (2020). Transformative Learning in Theory and Practice. *Adult Education Quarterly*, *70*(3), 295. DOI: 10.1177/0741713620918510

Hong, C. (2024). The Ethical Challenges of Educational Artificial Intelligence and Coping Measures: A Discussion in the Context of the 2024 World Digital Education Conference. *Science Insights Education Frontiers, 20*(2), 3263. https://doi.org/DOI: 10.15354/sief.24.re339

Huynh, T.-N., Le, T.-T., Dang, B., An, B. T., Vu, C.-T., & Nguyen, A. (2025). Mindset matters: Fostering teachers' responsible AI use through professional development. *Journal of New Approaches in Educational Research, 14*(1). Advance online publication. DOI: 10.1007/s44322-025-00043-y

Ifenthaler, D., Majumdar, R., Gorissen, P., Judge, M., Mishra, S., Raffaghelli, J. E., & Shimada, A. (2024). Artificial Intelligence in Education: Implications for Policymakers, Researchers, and Practitioners. *Technology Knowledge and Learning, 29*(4), 1693. DOI: 10.1007/s10758-024-09747-0

Isma'il, A., Aliu, A., Ibrahim, M., & Sulaiman, A. B. (2024). Preparing Teachers of the Future in the Era of Artificial Intelligence. *Journal of Artificial Intelligence Machine Learning and Neural Network, 44*, 31. DOI: 10.55529/jaimlnn.44.31.41

Jain, K., & Raghuram, J. N. V. (2023). Unlocking potential: The impact of AI on education technology. *Multidisciplinary Reviews, 7*(3), 2024049. DOI: 10.31893/multirev.2024049

Jose, B., Verghis, A. M., Varghese, S., Mumthas, S., & Cherian, J. (2025). From tools to co-learners: Entangled humanism and the co-evolution of intelligence in AI education. *Frontiers in Education, 10*. Advance online publication. DOI: 10.3389/feduc.2025.1632990

Jose, J., & Jose, B. J. (2024). Educators' Academic Insights on Artificial Intelligence: Challenges and Opportunities. *Electronic Journal of e-Learning, 0*. Advance online publication. DOI: 10.34190/ejel.21.5.3272

Karakaya, K., Alpat, M. F., Uçar, H., Karakaya, Ö., & Bozkurt, A. (2025). Preparing teachers for the algorithmic educational landscape: A critical mapping of generative AI integration in language teacher education. *Technology in Language Teaching & Learning, 7*(2), 102841. DOI: 10.29140/tltl.v7n2.102841

Kelley, M., & Wenzel, T. (2025). Advancing Artificial Intelligence Literacy in Teacher Education Through Professional Partnership Inquiry. *Education Sciences, 15*(6), 659. DOI: 10.3390/educsci15060659

Kestin, G., Miller, K., Klales, A., Milbourne, T., & Ponti, G. (2025). AI tutoring outperforms in-class active learning: An RCT introducing a novel research-based design in an authentic educational setting. *Scientific Reports, 15*(1), 17458. DOI: 10.1038/s41598-025-97652-6

Khan, S., Mazhar, T., Shahzad, T., Khan, M. A., Rehman, A. U., Saeed, M. M., & Hamam, H. (2025). Harnessing AI for sustainable higher education: Ethical considerations, operational efficiency, and future directions. *Discover Sustainability*, *6*(1). Advance online publication. DOI: 10.1007/s43621-025-00809-6

Knoblauch, C., & Joost, R. (2025). The Potential of Artificial Intelligence in Education. [iJAC]. *International Journal of Advanced Corporate Learning*, *18*(1), 28. DOI: 10.3991/ijac.v18i1.51197

Kumar, P., Vitak, J., Chetty, M., & Clegg, T. (2019). The Platformization of the Classroom: Teachers as Surveillant Consumers. *Surveillance & Society*, *17*, 145. DOI: 10.24908/ss.v17i1/2.12926

Kwan, P., Kadel, R. W., Memon, T. D., & Hashmi, S. S. (2025). Reimagining Flipped Learning via Bloom's Taxonomy and Student–Teacher–GenAI Interactions. *Education Sciences*, *15*(4), 465. DOI: 10.3390/educsci15040465

Lainjo, B., & Tsmouche, H. (2023). Impact of Artificial Intelligence On Higher Learning Institutions. *International Journal of Education Teaching and Social Sciences*, *3*(2), 96. DOI: 10.47747/ijets.v3i2.1028

Li, C. (2024). Adam Edmett, Neenaz Ichaporia, Helen Crompton, and Ross Crichton: Artificial Intelligence and English Language Teaching: Preparing for the Future. *Journal of China Computer-Assisted Language Learning*. Advance online publication. DOI: 10.1515/jccall-2023-0032

Ma, Y., Yufang, S., Ming-da, L., Zhang, Y., Chai, W., Huang, A., & Zhao, X. (2025). Preparing Students for an AI-Driven World: Generative AI and Curriculum Reform in Higher Education. *Frontiers of Digital Education.*, *2*(4). Advance online publication. DOI: 10.1007/s44366-025-0067-6

Mekheimer, M. A. (2025). Effective technology integration in higher education: A mixed-methods study of professional development. *Education and Information Technologies*. Advance online publication. DOI: 10.1007/s10639-025-13750-y

Meletiou-Mavrotheris, M., Bakogianni, D., Danidou, Y., Paparistodemou, E., & Kofteros, A. (2025). Investigating Student Teacher Engagement with Data-Driven AI and Ethical Reasoning in a Graduate-Level Education Course. *Education Sciences*, *15*(9), 1179. DOI: 10.3390/educsci15091179

Mikeladze, T., Meijer, P. C., & Verhoeff, R. P. (2024). A comprehensive exploration of artificial intelligence competence frameworks for educators: A critical review [Review of *A comprehensive exploration of artificial intelligence competence frameworks for educators: A critical review*]. *European Journal of Education, 59*(3). Wiley. https://doi.org/DOI: 10.1111/ejed.12663

Mikeladze, T., Meijer, P. C., & Verhoeff, R. P. (2024). A comprehensive exploration of artificial intelligence competence frameworks for educators: A critical review [Review of *A comprehensive exploration of artificial intelligence competence frameworks for educators: A critical review*]. *European Journal of Education, 59*(3). Wiley. https://doi.org/DOI: 10.1111/ejed.12663

Mishra, Mr. S. (2024). Revolutionizing Education: The Impact of AI-Enhanced Teaching Strategies. *International Journal for Research in Applied Science and Engineering Technology*, *12*(9), 9. DOI: 10.22214/ijraset.2024.64127

Montoro, M. Á., Colón, A. M. O., Moreno, J. R., & Steffens, K. (2019). Emerging technologies. Analysis and current perspectives. *Digital Education Review*, *186*. Advance online publication. DOI: 10.1344/der.2019.35.186-201

Morić, Z., Mršić, L., Filjak, M., & Đambić, G. (2024). Integrating a Virtual Assistant by Using the RAG Method and VERTEX AI Framework at Algebra University. *Applied Sciences (Basel, Switzerland)*, *14*(22), 10748. DOI: 10.3390/app142210748

Mosher, M., Dieker, L., & Hines, R. (2024). The Past, Present, and Future Use of Artificial Intelligence in Teacher Education. *Journal of Special Education Preparation*, *4*(2), 6. DOI: 10.33043/8aa9855b

Moulaei, K., Moulaei, R., & Bahaadinbeigy, K. (2023). Barriers and facilitators of using health information technologies by women: a scoping review [Review of *Barriers and facilitators of using health information technologies by women: a scoping review*]. *BMC Medical Informatics and Decision Making, 23*(1). BioMed Central. https://doi.org/DOI: 10.1186/s12911-023-02280-7

Mouta, A., Sánchez, E. M. T., & Llorente, A. M. P. (2023). Design of a future scenarios toolkit for an ethical implementation of artificial intelligence in education. *Education and Information Technologies*, *29*(9), 10473. DOI: 10.1007/s10639-023-12229-y

Nagaraj, B., & Kalaivani, A., R, S. B., Akila, S., Sachdev, H. K., & Kumar, N. K. S. (2023). The Emerging Role of Artificial Intelligence in STEM Higher Education: A Critical Review. *International Research Journal of Multidisciplinary Technovation*, *1*. Advance online publication. DOI: 10.54392/irjmt2351

Nuankaew, P., Nasa-Ngium, P., & Nuankaew, W. S. (2025). Artificial intelligence and educational data mining technologies for the 4th SDG quality education: A systematic review [Review of *Artificial intelligence and educational data mining technologies for the 4th SDG quality education: A systematic review*]. *International Journal of Innovative Research and Scientific Studies*, *8*(3), 4217. DOI: 10.53894/ijirss.v8i3.7468

Nyaaba, M., & Zhaı, X. (2024). Generative AI Professional Development Needs for Teacher Educators. *Journal of AI*, *8*(1), 1. DOI: 10.61969/jai.1385915

Ofosu-Ampong, K. (2024). Beyond the hype: Exploring faculty perceptions and acceptability of AI in teaching practices. *Discover Education*, *3*(1). Advance online publication. DOI: 10.1007/s44217-024-00128-4

Onesi-Ozigagun, O., Ololade, Y. J., Eyo-Udo, N. L., & Ogundipe, D. O. (2024). Revolutionizing education through AI: A comprehensive review of enhancing learning experiences [review of revolutionizing education through AI: A *comprehensive review of enhancing learning experiences*]. *International Journal of Applied Research in Social Sciences, 6*(4), 589. Fair East Publishers. https://doi.org/DOI: 10.51594/ijarss.v6i4.1011

Park, J., Teo, T. W., Teo, A., Chang, J., Huang, J., & Koo, S. (2023). Integrating artificial intelligence into science lessons: Teachers' experiences and views. *International Journal of STEM Education, 10*(1). Advance online publication. DOI: 10.1186/s40594-023-00454-3

Pietsch, M., & Mah, D.-K. (2024). Leading the AI transformation in schools: It starts with a digital mindset. *Educational Technology Research and Development.* Advance online publication. DOI: 10.1007/s11423-024-10439-w

Pikhart, M., & Al-Obaydi, L. H. (2025). Reporting the potential risk of using AI in higher Education: Subjective perspectives of educators. *Computers in Human Behavior Reports, 18*, 100693. DOI: 10.1016/j.chbr.2025.100693

Platz, J., & Hyman, N. (2013). Mentorship [Review of *Mentorship*]. *Clinics in Colon and Rectal Surgery, 26*(4), 218. Thieme Medical Publishers (Germany). https://doi.org/DOI: 10.1055/s-0033-1356720

Rachbauer, T., Graup, J., & Rutter, E. (2025). Digital literacy and artificial intelligence literacy in teacher training. *Forum for Education Studies.*, *3*(1), 1842. DOI: 10.59400/fes1842

Ren, X., & Wu, M. L. (2025). Examining Teaching Competencies and Challenges While Integrating Artificial Intelligence in Higher Education. *TechTrends*, *69*(3), 519. DOI: 10.1007/s11528-025-01055-3

Roshan, S., Iqbal, S., & Qing, Z. (2024). Teacher Training and Professional Development for Implementing AI-Based Educational Tools. *Journal of Asian Development Studies*, *13*(2), 1972. DOI: 10.62345/jads.2024.13.2.154

Roshanaei, M., Olivares, H., & Lopez, R. R. (2023). Harnessing AI to Foster Equity in Education: Opportunities, Challenges, and Emerging Strategies. *Journal of Intelligent Learning Systems and Applications*, *15*(4), 123. DOI: 10.4236/jilsa.2023.154009

Rütti-Joy, O., Winder, G., & Biedermann, H. (2023). Building AI Literacy for Sustainable Teacher Education. *Zeitschrift Für Hochschulentwicklung*, *18*(4), 175. DOI: 10.21240/zfhe/18-04/10

Saimon, M., Mtenzi, F., Lavicza, Z., Fenyvesi, K., Arnold, M., & Diego-Mantecón, J. M. (2024). Applying the 6E learning by design model to support student teachers to integrate artificial intelligence applications in their classroom. *Education and Information Technologies*. Advance online publication. DOI: 10.1007/s10639-024-12795-9

Shukla, R. P., & Taneja, S. (2024). Ethical Considerations and Data Privacy in Artificial Intelligence. In *Advances in educational technologies and instructional design book series* (p. 86). IGI Global., DOI: 10.4018/979-8-3693-2440-0.ch005

Tata, T. S., Heri, H. S., & Kurniawan, K. (2025). Navigating the Generative AI Revolution in Education: A Systematic Review of Applications, Ethical Considerations, and Future Directions [Review of *Navigating the Generative AI Revolution in Education: A Systematic Review of Applications, Ethical Considerations, and Future Directions*] [JANAPATI]. *Jurnal Nasional Pendidikan Teknik Informatika*, *14*(2). Advance online publication. DOI: 10.23887/janapati.v14i2.90367

Tokay, I., Ağar, S., & Elmas, M. (2024). The Significance of Artificial Intelligence in University Education System and Course Syllabuses. *Creative Education*, *15*(5), 739. DOI: 10.4236/ce.2024.155045

Tunjera, N., & Chigona, A. (2023). Investigating Effective Ways to Use Artificial Intelligence in Teacher Education. *European Conference on E-Learning*, *22*(1), 331. https://doi.org/DOI: 10.34190/ecel.22.1.1625

Urmeneta, A., Roméro, M., Petre, V., veanu, G., Lepage, A., Collin, S., Alexandre, F., Comte, M.-H., Lagarrigue, A., Viéville, T., Durampart, M., Bonfils, P., Galy, I., Camponovo, J., Tressols, F., Boulord, C., Borgne, Y. L., Corieri, P., Caucheteux, C., . . . Girard, M.-A. (2024). Creative Applications of Artificial Intelligence in Education. In *Palgrave studies in creativity and culture*. https://doi.org/DOI: 10.1007/978-3-031-55272-4

Yan, Y., & Liu, H. (2024). Ethical framework for AI education based on large language models. *Education and Information Technologies*. Advance online publication. DOI: 10.1007/s10639-024-13241-6

Zhu, H., Sun, Y., & Yang, J. (2025). Towards responsible artificial intelligence in education: A systematic review on identifying and mitigating ethical risks. *Humanities & Social Sciences Communications*, *12*(1). Advance online publication. DOI: 10.1057/s41599-025-05252-6

ADDITIONAL READING

Asri, A. (2024). Utilization of artificial intelligence in improving student outcomes in higher education. *Paradoks: Journal of Educational Research*, *8*(2), 56–69. DOI: 10.29333/paradoks.2024.990

Daher, R. (2025). Integrating AI literacy into teacher education: A critical perspective. *Journal of AI in Education*, *5*, 217. DOI: 10.1007/s44163-025-00475-7

Garzón, J. (2025). Systematic review of artificial intelligence in education: Emerging trends and challenges. *Interaction*, *9*(8), 84. DOI: 10.3390/hi9080084

Gayed, J. M. (2025). Educators' perspective on artificial intelligence: Equity, preparedness, and development. *Cogent Education*, *12*(1), 2024–2045. DOI: 10.1080/2331186X.2024.2447169

Jud, M. (2025). AI insights into initial teacher education: Predictive models for preservice dropout risk. *Journal of Education and Technology*, *53*(4), 311–329. DOI: 10.1080/02619768.2025.2535624

Mohamad, A. F. B. N., Sharibudeen, N., & Selvam, K.. (2025). Artificial intelligence in education: A tool for equity or a barrier to inclusion. *Environment and Social Psychology*, *10*(10), 4016. DOI: 10.59429/esp.v10i10.4016

Tan, X., Cheng, G., & Ling, M. H. (2024). Artificial intelligence in teaching and teacher professional development: A systematic review. *Computers and Education: Artificial Intelligence, 100355*. Advance online publication. DOI: 10.1016/j.caeai.2024.100355

Tripathi, T. (2025). Teaching and learning with AI: Teachers' beliefs, practices, and challenges. *Frontiers in Education, 10*, 165121. DOI: 10.3389/feduc.2025.1651217

KEY TERMS AND DEFINITIONS

AI Literacy: The capacity of educators to understand, evaluate, and pedagogically apply artificial intelligence concepts, tools, and implications in educational contexts.

Algorithmic Bias: Systematic distortions in AI system outputs that result from biased data, design choices, or assumptions, leading to unfair or unequal educational outcomes.

Artificial Intelligence In Education: The use of computational systems capable of learning, reasoning, and adaptation to support teaching, learning, assessment, and educational decision-making.

Collaborative Intelligence: A pedagogical approach in which educators and learners work alongside AI systems as co-creators of learning rather than passive users of technology.

Digital Divide: Inequities in access to digital infrastructure, skills, and resources that shape unequal participation in AI-enhanced education and teacher training.

Ethical AI: The development and use of artificial intelligence guided by principles of transparency, fairness, accountability, privacy protection, and human-centered values.

Teacher Competencies: The integrated set of knowledge, skills, attitudes, and ethical capacities required for educators to teach effectively in AI-enhanced learning environments.

Teacher Professional Development: Ongoing learning processes that support in-service educators in acquiring AI literacy, pedagogical innovation skills, and ethical awareness.

Technology-Enhanced Pedagogy: Instructional practices that intentionally integrate digital and AI-based tools to improve learning while preserving pedagogical purpose and human judgment.

Chapter 18

Transformative Alliances: A Collaborative Model for AI Integration in Teacher Training

Alicia Drelick
https://orcid.org/0000-0002-4485-5858
Rowan University, USA

Cecile H. Sam
https://orcid.org/0000-0002-3949-9940
Rowan University, USA

Jill Perry
https://orcid.org/0000-0002-2551-5161
Rowan University, USA

Kathryn M. Luet
Rowan University, USA

Beth Wassell
Rowan University, USA

Andrea Hawkman
Rowan University, USA

ABSTRACT

This chapter presents a collaborative model for integrating generative AI into teacher preparation through a multidisciplinary faculty alliance. Formed at a large public university, the group comprises faculty from various content areas, special education, and leadership who share a commitment to the ethical and practical use of AI. Together, they revised course content, modeled transparent AI practices, and developed flexible, tiered classroom policies. The alliance fosters shared learning, professional development, and the creation of co-created materials. Emphasizing co-creation, digital literacy, and inclusive pedagogy, this model supports preservice teachers in critically and ethically engaging with AI. The chapter provides a replicable framework for educator preparation programs as they navigate AI's evolving role in teaching and learning.

DOI: 10.4018/979-8-3373-3000-6.ch018

INTRODUCTION

Since the arrival of generative AI (GenAI) that is easily accessible to students, higher education has been left to determine an appropriate response to this transformative technology. Early studies suggest that the higher education community has mixed feelings about GenAI. On one hand, early adopters tout GenAI's potential advantages in advancing research, outsourcing administrative tasks, and improving teaching and learning outcomes for students (Cornish & Larter, 2024; Mah, & Groß, 2024). On the other hand, resistors have cited concerns about its usage, including academic integrity issues, environmental concerns, and the devaluing of human work and creativity (Mah & Groß, 2024).

Higher education institutions often respond to emerging issues, like those caused by GenAI, by forming interdisciplinary committees or task forces. These groups aim to break down boundaries and synthesize ideas into clear policies and value statements (Hannon et al., 2018). While the results can be meaningful, the work is not without challenges. Collaboration across disciplines is hindered by the isolating, competitive dynamics of the tenure and promotion process, particularly at research-intensive institutions. Institutional structures and a lack of incentive to collaborate also serve as barriers to collaboration (Tolman et al., 2021). In schools of education, additional silos, organized by areas of expertise, can restrict information sharing, communication, and joint professional growth (Stolz, 2021). At the same time, as faculty begin to find their footing in meeting increasing expectations in teaching, research, and service, they need support from colleagues (Trust et al., 2017). To break through these barriers, faculty members must invest in relationships, build trust, articulate shared goals, and establish clear lines of communication (Roper, 2021; Tolman et al., 2021).

In interdisciplinary collaborations, faculty need to move beyond specialized content expertise and engage in holistic, cross-disciplinary thinking (Roper, 2021). Roper (2021) argues that a fear of losing one's disciplinary identity hinders effective interdisciplinary collaboration. While interdisciplinary work requires faculty to integrate and reframe their disciplinary perspectives, multidisciplinary alliances offer an alternative approach. In this model, faculty contribute as experts in their own fields, making distinctions and drawing conclusions that apply primarily within their disciplinary frameworks (Hannon et al, 2018). Multidisciplinary alliances across education faculty, such as those that bring together experts in science, technology, engineering and mathematics (STEM) education, the humanities, special education, and school administration, can be beneficial when participants address shared challenges, such as the integration of emerging technologies, while remaining grounded in their own disciplines and responsive to their students.

This chapter highlights how a multidisciplinary GenAI alliance in a College of Education at a large, public mid-Atlantic institution organized its work around shared, practice-driven questions. Rather than seeking a single model, our alliance used common, broad questions to focus our work, coordinate efforts, exchange ideas, build common language, and grow our collective knowledge.

1. What might a faculty learning alliance around GenAI look like? In what ways might others create their own alliances?
2. What issues are surfacing in classroom use (e.g., integrity, privacy, overreliance, accuracy) and how might we respond?
3. What modifications to course policies, activities, and discussions have we made to incorporate GenAI? How, when, and why might our approach vary?
4. How can we share emerging practices and policies within the college and beyond?

In this chapter, after a brief review of relevant literature, we discuss how the group formed, the structure of our collective and individual work, and our efforts to expand knowledge and pedagogical practices around GenAI. We also share specific examples of emerging pedagogical practices and AI-related policies. Our goal as an alliance was to cultivate a dynamic, evolving landscape of innovative practices and policy.

BACKGROUND

To meaningfully support faculty integration of GenAI, our alliance first examined previous work on GenAI in higher education and the evolving demands of teacher preparation in the digital age. This section focuses on key themes in the literature: faculty perceptions of GenAI; institutional responses to this emerging technology; and shifts to teacher education. The emergent understandings that we gained from our initial review informed the alliance's collaboration on GenAI implementation, frameworks, and practices.

Faculty Perspectives on GenAI in Higher Education

The introduction of GenAI has shifted the learning landscape, causing tensions in faculty perspectives on its adoption and use on college campuses (Cornish & Larter, 2023; Niemi, 2024). Scholars have identified valid fears and reservations regarding the use of AI. For example, some researchers have explored concerns about the effects of AI use on student academic integrity and cheating (Cornish & Larter, 2024; Mah, & Groß, 2024). In addition to this ethical conundrum, data privacy also presents a challenge (Zhai, 2024; Al-Mughairi & Bhaskar, 2024). Others fear students will develop an overreliance on AI tools, leading to a diminishing return on student critical-thinking skills, the very skill faculty seek to foster in higher education (Cornish & Larter, 2023; Zhai, 2024; Al-Mughairi & Bhaskar, 2024). Cornish and Larter (2023) cite factual inaccuracies, hallucinations in the form of factual citations, and superficial responses as major limitations to using AI as a brainstorming or research tool. Al-Mughairi and Bhaskar (2024) also note that a lack of institutional support for infrastructure, training, or policy can serve as a barrier for some who may be curious about using AI.

Despite these concerns, other faculty largely view AI as a tool that provides new pedagogical opportunities (Mah & Groß, 2024). Al-Mughairi and Bhaskar (2024) note the faculty find value in the ability for GenAI to personalize lessons, save time and make lessons more innovative. Students find GenAI to be an effective brainstorming tool, particularly when they dive deep into responses (Cornish & Larter, 2023). Mah and Groß (2024) assert that faculty members' views and practices on the adoption of GenAI in their teaching is underexplored; as such, effective applications and emerging views are still being reported.

Institutional Responses and Policy Frameworks

In response to the increasing integration of GenAI into more tasks, institutions of higher education have been developing policies to guide student use (Lou, 2024; Wang et al., 2024). In reviewing the GenAI policies of 140 universities, McDonald and colleagues (2025) found that approximately 60% encouraged the use of GenAI, with stipulations that varied significantly across the sample. Wang et al. (2024) note that many universities allow instructors to decide their own policy. Sample syllabus templates and statements are often provided to model different levels of acceptable GenAI use (McDonald et al., 2025; Wang et al., 2024).

Wang and colleagues (2024) are critical of GenAI policies that overemphasize the misuse of GenAI for writing. Luo (2024) suggests that universities and faculty begin to rethink what constitutes “original work” (p. 656). A more collaborative and inclusive approach to developing policies that connect faculty and students can yield policies that better reflect today's content-creation landscape (Luo, 2024). Easton (2024) calls this the post-plagiarism era, where individuals co-create their work with GenAI.

Preparing Future Educators for the GenAI Era

Today’s educators must navigate not only curriculum and pedagogy, but also an increasingly complex digital landscape. In response, teacher preparation programs are called to adapt. Teacher educators must prepare educators for the future classroom, not the past (Easton, 2024). Easton (2024) remembers another crossroads:

> *Remember when people asked us back in the early 1990s if they could turn off the internet?" Back then, with puzzled looks on our faces, we replied, "No, you can't just turn off the internet." Here we are, 30 years later, with some colleagues saying we should ban artificial intelligence (AI) or somehow pretend it does not exist. (p. 12)*

Not only do we need to acknowledge the presence of GenAI in teacher preparation, but we also need to ensure that preservice teachers have sufficient understanding to adopt and integrate it into their teaching and learning (Zhai, 2024). Zhai (2024) believes we must shift from having teachers act as facilitators to adopting mindsets that enable them to collaborate and innovate with GenAI, leveraging their understanding to co-create new ideas with their students. Zhai (2023) also advocates for empowering preservice teachers with GenAI tools that can reduce their workload such as designing assessments, lesson plans, and materials. Understanding the evolving demands of digital-age teaching sets the stage for considering how AI literacy fits within educator preparation.

Embracing GenAI as an education disruptor introduces a whole new skill set in teacher readiness (Niemi, 2021). Shifting teachers from content-deliverers to coaches who can center humans within the GenAI loop is critical (Niemi, 2021; USDOE; 2023). Easton (2024) stresses the importance of building digital literacies into programs that promote ethical awareness and critical engagement with GenAI tools. Policies that prohibit or discourage the use of GenAI can be detrimental in preservice teachers' ability to develop their own perspectives on ethical GenAI use (Easton, 2024). This emerging scholarship about such needed shifts in teacher preparation, institutional responses, and faculty perceptions of GenAI use informed the group that we ultimately established -- the Multidisciplinary GenAI Alliance.

Forming Our Multidisciplinary Alliance

At our institution and within the College of Education, we could see the research-described tensions around GenAI in practice. In 2023, the University started an AI Teaching Ambassadors initiative, bringing faculty representatives from all colleges together to learn about GenAI and examine its promise and pitfalls. Within this group, faculty engagement around GenAI varied for a range of reasons, including college leadership's encouragement or discouragement; ethical concerns; and comfort with emergent technology. Each Ambassador was tasked with producing one college-level deliverable; these deliverables ranged from how-to guides for crafting effective prompts to restrictive policy language.

Meanwhile, the university convened various GenAI-focused cross-institutional groups (e.g., AI Executive Research Committee and AI Student Ethics Committee). The existing Academic Integrity Committee took up the work of addressing the rising concerns around academic integrity and student GenAI use. Of these efforts, ethics committees proved the most active and effective, balancing institution-wide guidance with disciplinary differences. Even so, we observed persistent disconnects among faculty on what constitutes appropriate GenAI use. As the technology advanced, university messaging and policies remained unclear. Faculty were left to make sense of GenAI for themselves and within our own disciplines, and this is where the Alliance had its genesis.

Our Alliance began with a simple question between colleagues: "What are you doing about AI in your class?" After several informal conversations, the pair decided to invite others to join their discussion, creating a more formal working group around AI. Membership grew organically, with some faculty members being invited to join based on their expressed interest in working with AI and others asking to participate when they learned about the group's existence. Everyone was welcome.

In its current form, the Alliance includes faculty at multiple ranks from content-area teacher education (e.g., humanities education, world languages education, STEM education), elementary and special education, administrative and educational leadership, and higher-education faculty development. In addition to deep content knowledge, members bring expertise in equity, culturally relevant pedagogy, accessibility, and educational policy. The members share a commitment to preparing future educators to use GenAI effectively and informally in practice. In 2023 and 2024, the Alliance met bi-weekly with an agenda set by the group. Over these two academic years, the Alliance developed a shared understanding of how educational stakeholders engage with GenAI tools, exploring both challenges and potential. Its work included IRB-approved studies conducted by subgroups, as well as informal evidence gathered through shared documents and end-of-semester reflections.

Grounding Our Work: Theoretical and Ethical Foundations for GenAI Integration

As we began, we grounded our approach in guidance from the U.S. Department of Education (2023), which suggested the following tenets for GenAI use in education more broadly:

- Emphasize Humans in the Loop
- Align AI Models to a Shared Vision

- Design Using Modern Learning Principles
- Prioritize Strengthening Trust
- Inform and Involve Educators
- Focus R&D on Addressing Context and Enhancing Trust and Safety
- Develop Education-specific Guidelines and Guardrails

We also drew on the International Society for Technology in Education (ISTE) Standards for students, educators, and leaders (2024) to frame ethical, practical uses of GenAI for teaching, learning, and educator productivity. Additionally, as our College is dedicated to inclusive practices, we grounded our work in Universal Design for Learning (UDL) (CAST, 2023) to ensure learning experiences were accessible, purposeful, and engaging. Culturally relevant pedagogy (Ladson-Billings, 1995; 2021) further guided both our own engagement with GenAI and our focus on preparing preservice teachers to use these tools ethically to support racially, ethnically, linguistically, and socioeconomically diverse learners.

Beyond conceptual approaches, we prioritized two competencies: helping preservice teachers formulate purposeful prompts, and teaching them to critically evaluate AI outputs. To develop competencies in our classes, we used two heuristics as guides. For prompting, we drew on the *CLEAR* framework (Concise, Logical, Explicit, Adaptive, Restrictive), which supports the development of prompt-engineering skills and can foster critical thinking and digital literacy (Lo, 2023; Seung et al., 2025). Using *CLEAR* can help students maximize the quality of what GenAI produces and optimize its use. For output critique, we used the EDIT framework to have students "evaluate the content for language, facts & structure; Determine accuracy and corroborate sources; Identify biases and misinformation; Transform the content to reflect any necessary adjustments" (Fitzpatrick et al., 2023, p. 100). This framework helps students navigate and define co-creating with GenAI (Easton, 2024). In our work, these frameworks served not as strict rules to be followed, but rather as tools to advance practice and research-aligned goals.

Our review of faculty perspectives, institutional responses, and educator-preparation responsibilities suggested a clear need for coordinated action. While GenAI policies and practices were still emerging, our Alliance agreed on a shared goal: build capacity for responsible, inclusive, and practical integration of GenAI across programs. Rather than waiting for top-down mandates, we prioritized collaboration, experimentation, and reflection. In the next section, we outline strategies and solutions we developed, highlighting how we redesigned instruction, learning experiences, and policies through cross-disciplinary collaboration.

SOLUTIONS AND RECOMMENDATIONS

Our ongoing work as an Alliance reflects five priorities: (1) updating course curricula and assignments; (2) engaging in collective professional development; and (3) refining course-level policies on AI use; (4) conducting empirical research; and (5) enhancing our practices by embedding emerging technologies. We have also collaborated with college, university, and K-12 partners to share insights and strategies for incorporating GenAI into teacher preparation and teacher learning programs. By integrating GenAI into our educational practices and supporting future educators in using these tools effectively, the Alliance advances our vision of transformative education. Together, we aim to equip preservice teachers to use AI tools effectively and ethically and competently, fostering equitable and inclusive teaching practices (Jin, 2024). In the sections that follow, we outline some of the outcomes of our work.

Reimagining Teacher Practice with GenAI

When reflecting on how to integrate GenAI, we first discussed what activities and assignments were no longer working in our classes. This discussion was guided by a series of questions, including:

- How do we want students to engage with learning materials?
- What do we want students to take away from our classes?
- Does it make sense to have students summarize an academic article on a discussion board anymore? Is that a relevant task in today's world?
- Is assigning a research paper or literature review (e.g., about learning theories) an effective way to assess students' comprehension of the topic?

The presence of GenAI challenged us to revisit our course content and refocus assignments on personal experience and direct alignment with fieldwork, making the assignments even more practical.

Furthermore, this moment of reflection provided an opportunity to redesign tasks to align with Universal Design for Learning guidelines (CAST, 2024) in an effort to increase student engagement and overall accessibility. Finally, we looked for opportunities to embed GenAI into our courses to prepare preservice teachers to navigate their future P-12 classrooms.

In embracing the use of GenAI, it was essential to be transparent with students about our expectations and our own use of GenAI when applicable. Disclosing and citing GenAI provides a moment of transparent pedagogy and opens discussion. We also worked to delineate tasks reserved for human expertise from those that can be enhanced through a GenAI thought partner with students. For example, tasks requiring a reflection are just that, a personal reflection, and should not be a GenAI-approved task. However, for tasks like lesson planning and creating supplemental materials, we needed to provide structure, support, and time to explore GenAI and its capabilities.

Equipping Preservice Teachers for AI Integration

Developing Lesson Plans

In our respective programs, which focus on different grade levels and subject-area concentrations, we all introduced the use of GenAI. We outlined practical and ethical engagement within the appropriate context for each group. We then challenged our preservice teachers to create lesson plans using GenAI with a specific focus on culturally relevant, equitable, and inclusive teaching practices. Overall, students reported using GenAI as a "thought partner." They also recognized the shifting roles of educators in today's world. Presevice teachers noted that GenAI was a good starting point, but there were often some inaccuracies and a lack of depth of understanding. In co-developing lesson plans with GenAI, our students found they were responsible for checking output for accuracy, adapting it to align with their own pedagogical and equity goals, and infusing knowledge of their own students into activities.

From a faculty perspective, we saw the benefits of GenAI in supporting preservice teachers with tasks in lesson planning that typically pose a challenge such as generating essential questions. Additionally, GenAI provided ideas for modifications, accommodations, and Universal Design supports to address the needs of diverse learners. Nevertheless, prompting for these elements must be done in a way that respects student privacy, providing an opportunity for discussion on the ethical use of GenAI.

Finding and Creating Teaching Materials

Another effective use of GenAI with preservice teachers has been to create or locate teaching materials. When planning lessons, preservice teachers can create prompts to find materials that offer more diverse representation in their curriculum. This provides a range of content that might be outside of a preservice teacher's personal experiences or knowledge, which they might consider for lessons. These materials should be reviewed through a culturally responsive and inclusive lens to ensure they are appropriate for the classroom.

Preservice teachers can also use GenAI to create lesson materials, including basic materials such as quizzes, outlines, and slide decks. Within their specialty, we explored how to leverage GenAI to ethically streamline tasks, such as generating data collection for progress monitoring individual goals, creating problem sets, developing rubrics, and themed vocabulary lists for world language classes. With support and exploration, students can stretch their skill set to create custom images or videos to complement their lessons.

GenAI for Differentiation, Equity, and Inclusion

A promising application of GenAI in our education preparation work has been for supporting differentiated instruction. Leveraging the principles of UDL (CAST, 2023), we encouraged preservice educators to co-develop materials and learning experiences that provide multiple means of engagement, representation, and expression, making them more accessible from the outset. Further, individualized supports can be generated with additional prompting. In addition to differentiation, we framed GenAI as a tool to support culturally relevant pedagogy (Ladson-Billings, 1995; 2021). This can be particularly helpful for finding resources outside of a preservice teacher's lived experience.

Using GenAI for these tasks required significant scaffolding from instructors. In many cases, we noticed that GenAI did not provide equity-driven outputs. Thus, educator judgment, critical consciousness, and the intentional application of pedagogical approaches are required. These experiences often served as an "ah-ha" moment, emphasizing the need for human expertise and personal connections with students. GenAI can be a tool to build differentiated and culturally responsive lessons and materials, but they are only as good as the prompts provided and still require educator evaluation.

Developing Transparent, Tiered AI Use Policies

How does one navigate this post-plagiarism era, an era in which faculty can shape their own policies around the use of GenAI? These policies have lasting implications, not only for preservice teachers but also for the students they will one day serve. How can faculty evolve their teaching practices to help future educators become effective GenAI collaborators and co-creators? There are many ways to approach this challenge, but we found that navigating it through a multidisciplinary alliance strengthened our own leadership and our capacity to support preservice teachers.

In some cases, the decision to adopt a GenAI policy is left to an instructor. While some guidance may be provided by a university, department, or program, it may be all or nothing, such as "No GenAI." Students and instructors may bear the responsibility of navigating the implementation of such vague policies. For example, the statements below were provided by our university as suggestions to be used on faculty syllabi.

Table 1. University-Proposed Syllabus Statements

No GenAI	Some GenAI
In this course any use of generative artificial intelligence will be considered a violation of academic integrity and will be treated accordingly. According to the University policy, students committing any act of academic dishonesty may fail the assignment, fail the course, or face other sanctions. All violations of academic integrity must be reported. To avoid plagiarism, students should provide appropriate documentation whenever quoting, paraphrasing, summarizing, or otherwise using the language or ideas of others.	Although generative AI can be used as a tool to support learning (e.g., in obtaining feedback or generating ideas), work submitted by a student should be that of the student and not the work of an AI system. If you include material generated by an AI program, it should be cited like any other reference material. Ultimately, the student bears responsibility for any inaccuracies or misinformation. If you have questions about how AI may be used to complete assignments within the scope of this academic integrity policy, please reach out to your instructor.

As we navigate the post-plagiarism world (Eaton, 2024) and, as Lou (2024) suggests, we redefine "originality" of work, we must first acknowledge that policies outlawing GenAI may be harmful to teacher preparation programs. We must move towards co-created policies with preservice teachers that have emerged from our collaborative discussions. In upcoming semesters, we plan to adopt policies reflective of multiple levels of GenAI use. We plan to define each level with students and engage in discussions about which level would be appropriate for various assignments and assessments in our courses.

Student input will be considered for implications for output for GenAI use and not. For example, students like to use GenAI to "polish up" their assignments. So, if GenAI is not expected to be used, grammar and spelling are not part of the grading requirement. Additionally, if GenAI is encouraged, then instructors might ask to see how students are using it, and an explanation of AI use can be built into the assignment as part of the submission process. This system provides clearer guidelines at the assignment level and allows students to use GenAI responsibly and ethically, with support in their coursework.

Figure 1. Basic 3-tier GenAI policy for assignments.

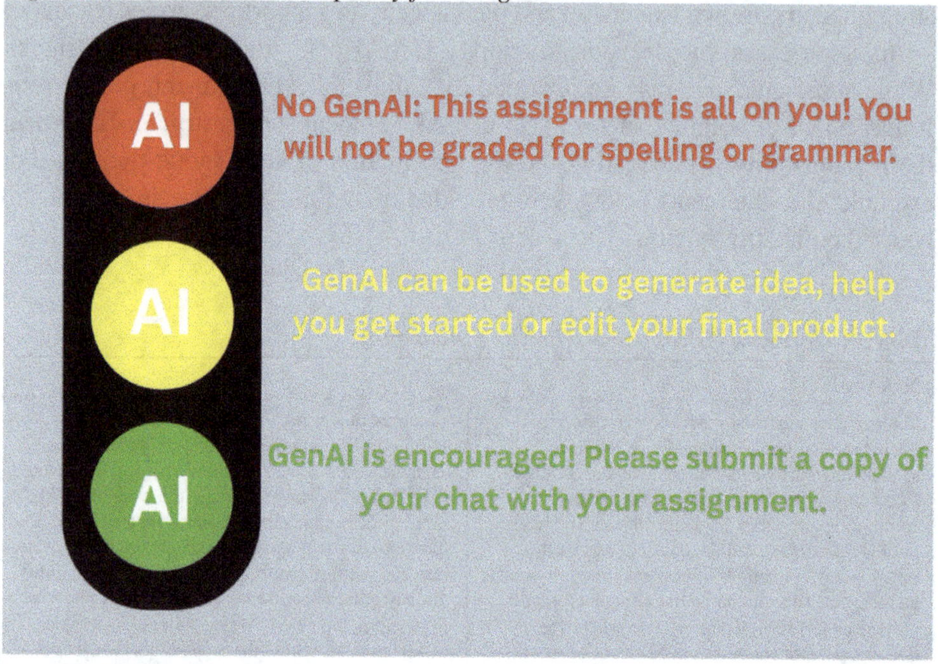

Source: Image created in Canva.

Sharing, Scaling, and Sustaining the Work

Our multidisciplinary alliance has met both formally and informally over the course of two academic years. We have engaged in research together, presented at national conferences, and facilitated professional development for K-12 teachers. Our ongoing conversations and engagements have challenged each other to stay abreast of the constant changes and newly emerging tools. In turn, we take our knowledge back to our respective programs. Some of us co-teach and are able to model the use of GenAI tools and teaching practices directly with colleagues. Others share new ideas in team meetings or simply share resources with course instructors. We have also hosted a lunch and learn event to share tools and resources for embedding AI into teacher education. Our collaboration and multidisciplinary approach has extended our reach and voice, breaking through traditional silos that isolate us.

Developing Your Own Alliance

Starting a multidisciplinary alliance around GenAI begins with curiosity and conversation. Finding colleagues who are interested in GenAI and its implications in teacher preparation is a good starting point. It is important to remember that the goal of a multidisciplinary alliance is not to seek out like-minded individuals or those from the same background. Rather, varying perspectives are what make an alliance like this meaningful and the results applicable to various programs.

After securing some colleagues who want to engage on GenAI, begin identifying pressing issues for your college, such as the ethical use of GenAI or how to embrace GenAI in a way that keeps pace with evolving pedagogy. After identifying a problem, work together to explore various solutions. Remember: the goal is not to propose a single solution, but to examine a range of practices that can be deployed. To keep pace with new technologies in teaching and learning, faculty cannot do it alone; collaboration is essential.

FUTURE RESEARCH DIRECTIONS

Faculty perspectives and practices of utilizing GenAI in higher education is an emerging research topic (Mah & Groß, 2024). Faculty in teacher preparation programs grapple with the implications of GenAI on K12 classroom teachers and what that means in their college courses. More research is needed, specifically on the faculty perspective of GenAI in teacher preparation. Examining patterns across programs and disciplines can be useful as well as examining faculty adoption based on their stages in their careers or discipline. These results can have implications on professional development and preservice teacher program design.

Furthermore, examining the skills needed for digital literacy in education is warranted. With this knowledge, we must evaluate what knowledge and skills to prioritize in teacher preparation programs. Further work is warranted to investigate how preservice teachers understand the evolving roles of teachers in GenAI-enriched classrooms. This can help faculty develop programs and learning experiences that better foster preservice teachers' identity and agency as critical, co-creators with Gen-AI.

Finally, there is an opportunity to explore a faculty- and student-co-created GenAI policy for ethical use. Unpacking policies and their rationale with both parties might allow us to move past our current understanding of "originality" of work, as Lou (2024) called for. Researchers can also examine how this process shapes the classroom culture, autonomy, academic integrity and overall GenAI use.

CONCLUSION

It is easy for faculty to settle comfortably into siloed departments and programs within higher education. But when an educational disruption like GenAI enters everyday conversation and practice, collaboration is not just helpful; it is essential. By forming a multidisciplinary alliance, faculty can bring together diverse expertise to engage complex problems with collective solutions. One of the benefits of this collaboration is that experts from various disciplines and backgrounds bring their ideas, which provide a variety of options for addressing complex, emerging issues. These diverse perspectives offer innovative approaches that no one person could design alone. Through conversations and the exchange of ideas and resources, faculty can take what is best for their students and their practice. In doing so, faculty can prepare future educators to not only use GenAI tools but to think critically, act ethically, teach inclusively, and co-create in a rapidly changing landscape. GenAI is constantly evolving. Don't go it alone. Form an alliance. Prepare the future together.

REFERENCES

Al-Mughairi, H., & Bhaskar, P. (2024). Exploring the factors affecting the adoption of AI techniques in higher education: Insights from teachers' perspectives on ChatGPT. *Journal of Research in Innovative Teaching & Learning*. https://doi.org/ DOI: 10.1108/JRIT-09-2023-0129

CAST. (2024). Universal design for learning guidelines version 3.0 [graphic organizer]. Lynnfield, MA: Author. https://udlguidelines.cast.org

Cornish, D., & Larter, Z. (2023). "I Don't Have to Write an Essay Ever Again!": University Student Reflections on ChatGPT in the Classroom. *Journal of Educational Technology Systems*, *52*(3), 325–334. DOI: 10.1177/00472395231219267

Eaton, S. E. (2024). Pre-service teacher education in a postplagiarism world: Incorporating GenAI into teacher training. *Brock Education Journal, 33*(3), 11–16. https://journals.library.brocku.ca/brocked

Fitzpatrick, D., Fox, A., & Weinstein, B. (2023). *The AI Classroom: The Ultimate Guide to Artificial Intelligence in Education*. The Hitchhiker's Guide for Educators Series.

Hannon, J., Hocking, C., Legge, K., & Lugg, A. (2018). Sustaining interdisciplinary education: Developing boundary crossing governance. *Higher Education Research & Development*, *37*(7), 1424–1438. DOI: 10.1080/07294360.2018.1484706

Jin, Y. (2024). Letter from the new editor of CITE-General: Editorial transition. *Contemporary Issues in Technology & Teacher Education*, *24*(1), 36–42.

Ladson-Billings, G. (1995). Toward a theory of culturally relevant pedagogy. *American Educational Research Journal*, *32*(3), 465–491. DOI: 10.3102/00028312032003465

Ladson-Billings, G. (2021). Three Decades of Culturally Relevant, Responsive, & Sustaining Pedagogy: What Lies Ahead? *The Educational Forum*, *85*(4), 351–354. DOI: 10.1080/00131725.2021.1957632

Lo, L. S. (2023). The CLEAR path: A framework for enhancing information literacy through prompt engineering. *Journal of Academic Librarianship*, *49*(4), 102720.

Luo (Jess), J. (2024). A critical review of GenAI policies in higher education assessment: A call to reconsider the "originality" of students' work. Assessment &amp. *Evaluation in Higher Education*, *49*(5), 651–664. DOI: 10.1080/02602938.2024.2309963

Mah, D.-K., & Groß, N. (2024). Artificial intelligence in higher education: Exploring faculty use, self-efficacy, distinct profiles, and professional development needs. *International Journal of Educational Technology in Higher Education*, *21*, 58. DOI: 10.1186/s41239-024-00490-1

McDonald, N., Johri, A., Ali, A., & Hingle, A. (2025). Generative artificial intelligence in higher education: Evidence from an analysis of institutional policies and guidelines. *Computers in Human Behavior: Artificial Humans*, *3*(1), 100121. DOI: 10.1016/j.chbah.2025.100121

Niemi, H. (2021). AI in learning: Preparing grounds for future learning. *Journal of Pacific Rim Psychology*, *15*, 1–12. DOI: 10.1177/18344909211038105

Roper, L. (2021). Encouraging interdisciplinary collaboration: A study of enablers and inhibitors across silos in higher education. *Interdisciplinary Journal of Partnership Studies*, *8*(1), 6. Advance online publication. DOI: 10.24926/ijps.v8i1.3687

Seung, Y., & Park, J.CIDDL Team. (2025). *Generative AI prompt engineering for educators*. The Center for Innovation, Design, and Digital Learning.

Stolz, S. (2021). Time for critical reimagining and breaking of silos in teacher education. *Teacher Education Quarterly*, *48*(1), 97–102.

Tolman, E. R., Ferguson, D. G., Hubble, G., Kaloi, M., Niu, M., & Jensen, J. L. (2021). Barriers to teaching evolution in higher education. *Evolution (New York)*, *14*, 12. DOI: 10.1186/s12052-021-00151-1

Trust, T., Carpenter, J. P., & Krutka, D. G. (2017). Moving beyond silos: Professional learning networks and professional learning. *LEARNing Landscapes*, *11*(1), 109–124. DOI: 10.36510/learnland.v11i1.913

U.S. Department of Education, Office of Educational Technology. (2023). *Artificial intelligence and future of teaching and learning: Insights and recommendations*. Washington, DC.

Wang, H., Dang, A., Wu, Z., & Mac, S. (2024). Generative AI in higher education: Seeing ChatGPT through universities' policies, resources, and guidelines. *Computers and Education: Artificial Intelligence*, *7*, 100326. DOI: 10.1016/j.caeai.2024.100326

Zhai, X. (2023). ChatGPT for next generation science learning. *XRDS: Crossroads*, *29*, 42–46. DOI: 10.1145/3589649

Zhai, X. (2024). Transforming teachers' roles and agencies in the era of generative AI: Perceptions, acceptance, knowledge, and practices. *Journal of Science Education and Technology*, *29*(3), 42–64. DOI: 10.1007/s10956-024-10174-0

ADDITIONAL READING

Acut, D. P., Gamusa, E. V., Pernaa, J., Yuenyong, C., Pantaleon, A. T., Espina, R. C., Sim, M. J., & Garcia, M. B. (2025). AI Shaming Among Teacher Education Students: A Reflection on Acceptance and Identity in the Age of Generative Tools. In Garcia, M., Rosak-Szyrocka, J., & Bozkurt, A. (Eds.), *Pitfalls of AI Integration in Education: Skill Obsolescence, Misuse, and Bias* (pp. 97–122). IGI Global Scientific Publishing., DOI: 10.4018/979-8-3373-0122-8.ch005

Bowen, J. A., & Watson, C. E. (2024). *Teaching with AI : A Practical Guide to a New Era of Human Learning*. Johns Hopkins University Press.

Eaton, S. E. (2024). Pre-service teacher education in a postplagiarism world: Incorporating GenAI into teacher training. *Brock Education Journal, 33*(3), 11–16. https://journals.library.brocku.ca/brocked

KEY TERMS AND DEFINITIONS

Co-Creation: collaborative process in which humans and AI tools generate content, ideas, or products together. In the classroom, this may involve students or teachers using GenAI to draft, refine, or reimagine lesson materials or assessments, with human oversight and adaptation.

Multidisciplinary Alliance: collaborative group composed of faculty or practitioners from different academic disciplines or professional areas who work together to address complex challenges. In teacher preparation, this model supports innovative responses to emerging issues like AI integration while maintaining disciplinary depth and shared pedagogical values.

Post-Plagiarism Era: a conceptual shift in education where the focus moves beyond traditional definitions of plagiarism to address co-creation with AI tools. In this era, originality is reframed to include ethical use, transparency, and the development of human-AI partnerships in academic work (Easton, 2024).

About the Contributors

Kristen Carlson currently serves as the program coordinator for the doctorate in Educational Leadership at Minnesota State University Moorhead. She also serves as the Director of Teacher Education leading efforts to prepare educators for contemporary classrooms, ensuring alignment with state and national licensure standards while advancing innovative teaching practices. Dr. Carlson has an extensive background teaching graduate courses in instructional design, technology integration, and educational leadership. Her work emphasizes creating equitable, student-centered learning environments and integrating technology to enhance teaching and learning. A scholar-practitioner, Dr. Carlson has led projects on online learning best practices, curriculum redesigns, and mentored faculty and doctoral learners in adopting research-driven instructional strategies. Dr. Carlson's commitment to educational equity, innovation, and lifelong learning informs her leadership and scholarship. With a strong focus on bridging theory and practice, she continues to shape the field of teacher preparation and technology integration through collaborative research, mentorship, and professional development initiatives.

***

Mussa S Abubakari, PhD, is an enthusiastic educational technology researcher and associate researcher with the Dig Connectivity Research Laboratory (DCRLab) in Kampala, Uganda, since 2024. He's an instructor in the Department of Physics and Mathematics at Kondoa Islamic Secondary School, Tanzania. He has a PhD in Educational Technology from Sultan Hassanal Bolkiah Institute of Education, Universiti Brunei Darussalam, and graduated in 2025. Dr. Mussa obtained a Master of Education degree in Electronics and Informatics Engineering at Yogyakarta State University, Indonesia, in July 2021. He obtained his BSc. in Telecommunications Engineering at the University of Dodoma in June 2016. His academic and research interests include educational technology, technology-enhanced learning, technology acceptance, open and distance learning, generative AI, and digital competence, among others. He has over 15 journal articles published in internationally reputable journals, several book chapters, and papers presented at international conferences.

Aisha Naz Ansari is working as a Research Specialist at Aga Khan University, Institute for Educational Development, Pakistan. She is a member of Evidence Synthesis Infrastructure Collaboration managed by Cochrane. She has experience of working on Educational Technology, including Artificial Intelligence in higher education. She is an AFHEA by UK considering excellence in teaching. She has published more than 15 research articles, systematic reviews, and research blogs in international and national journals and prestigious forums. She has completed a systematic review on the use of ChatGPT in higher education as the principal investigator. She has also been involved in facilitating workshops and short courses on the use of AI use for teachers and graduate students. Her research areas include systematic reviews, educational technology, educational psychology, teacher education, public-private partnerships, education policy, and classroom teaching and learning. Email: aisha.naz22@alumni.aku.edu

Andi Asrifan is an accomplished educator and academic leader with a Doctorate in Education, specializing in English Language Education from Universitas Negeri Makassar. With a strong academic foundation, he holds a Master's degree in the same field and a Bachelor's degree in Secondary Education. His dissertation focused on developing bilingual educational materials, reflecting his commitment to enhancing language education. Dr. Asrifan has extensive experience in various educational roles, including serving as the Head of the International Affairs Office at Politeknik Negeri Nunukan and as the Head of the Institute for Student Development and Alumni at Universitas Muhammadiyah Sidenreng Rappang. He is also an active member of several professional organizations, including the Linguistics Society of Indonesia and TEFLIN. In addition to his administrative roles, Dr. Asrifan is a passionate advocate for educational innovation and has participated in numerous international conferences and webinars, sharing his insights on language teaching and curriculum development. His dedication to professional development is evident through his participation in various training programs.

Selami Aydın, a professor in the Department of English Language Teaching at Istanbul Medeniyet University, focuses on the psychological and technological dimensions of language education. His research examines affect, emotion, and technology in developing basic language skills. He teaches ELT courses in undergraduate and graduate programs, focusing on technology, psychology, research skills, and statistics.

Kristin L. Burgess, Ed.D. Kristin L. Burgess serves as the Director of the Center for Accessibility Resources and Community Faculty in the College of Community Studies and Public Affairs at Metropolitan State University in Saint Paul, Minnesota. She also holds the role of interim ADA Coordinator. With a career rooted in justice and equity, Kristin brings a justice model lens to both her professional and personal endeavors, advocating for inclusive practices across higher education and public service. Kristin holds a Doctor of Education in Leadership from Minnesota State University, Moorhead, where her research contributed to the growing body of literature on the experiences of disabled students in higher education, with a focus on inclusive learning environments and the impacts of ableism. She earned her Master of Public Policy from the Humphrey School of Public Affairs, concentrating on disability policy, and a Graduate Certificate in Disability Policy and Services from the University of Minnesota's College of Education and Human Development. Her academic journey began with a Bachelor of Human Services in Disability Studies from Metropolitan State University. She is also a Certified Americans with Disabilities Act Coordinator. Her professional background includes service in several Minnesota state agencies, including the Department of Transportation (MnDOT), the Minnesota Housing Finance Agency, the Department of Employment and Economic Development, the State Senate Research Office, the Minnesota Council on Disability, and the Olmstead Implementation Office. Across these roles, she has championed accessibility, equity, and systemic change. Outside of academia and policy, Kristin is deeply engaged in her local community. She lives in south central Minnesota with her husband and their four cats. A licensed amateur radio operator, she volunteers at community events such as food distributions, town festivals, and endurance races. She also serves as a head election judge, a role she has held for over two decades. Kristin is an avid handcyclist and adaptive kayaker, recently completing a 1,000-kilometer summer challenge with her daughter.

Sheryl Burgstahler founded and directed Accessible Technology Services—which includes the DO-IT (Disabilities, Opportunities, Internetworking, and Technology) Center and the IT Accessibility Technology (ITAT) Team—1992-2023 at the University of Washington (UW). These dynamic groups promote (1) the development of self-determination skills, use of mainstream and assistive technology, and other interventions to support the success of students with disabilities in postsecondary education and careers and (2) the universal design (UD) of learning opportunities, physical spaces, websites, documents, multimedia, and services to ensure that they are accessible to, usable by, and inclusive of individuals with disabilities they are accessible to, usable by, and inclusive of individuals with disabilities. ITAT focuses its efforts at the University of Washington; the DO-IT Center reaches national and international audiences with the support of federal, state, corporate, foundation, and private funds. SherylBurgstahler@outlook.com Dr. Burgstahler is also an affiliate professor in the UW College of Education and Disability Studies program at the UW and in the Disability Studies and Services programs at City University of New York, where she teaches online. Much of Dr. Burgstahler's teaching and research focus on the successful transition of students with disabilities to postsecondary studies and careers and on the application of UD to technology, teaching and learning activities, physical spaces, and student services; the incorporation of UD topics in mainstream curriculum; and the adoption of a UD Framework to inform all diversity equity, and inclusion (DEI) and other practices in higher education within an Inclusive Campus Model. Dr. Burgstahler has delivered hundreds of presentations and has more than 100 publications that include the books Creating Inclusive Learning Opportunities in Higher Education: A Universal Design Toolkit (2020) and Universal Design in Higher Education: From Principles to Practice (2015), both published by Harvard Education Press. In her retirement, Dr. Burgstahler teaches disability studies courses online, publishes articles, delivers presentations, and engages in part-time work.

Bora Demir holds a PhD in English Language Teacher Education and was promoted to Associate Professor in 2023. He is currently a faculty member at the School of Foreign Languages, Çanakkale Onsekiz Mart University. He has published extensively in national and international journals and edited volumes on various aspects of language teaching and language teacher education. Since 2019, he has been the founder and Editor-in-Chief of the academic journal Innovational Research in ELT. His main research interests include technology-assisted language teaching, cognitive dimensions of language learning, and the psychological aspects of language learning and teaching, with a particular focus on teacher education contexts.

Fausiah, S.E., M.Si has been a lecturer since 2002 with a strong academic background in Financial Management. She earned both her Bachelor's and Master's degrees in Financial Management from the Graduate School of Universitas Hasanuddin (Unhas), where she developed her expertise in corporate finance, investment, and managerial decision-making. With over two decades of teaching experience, she has been actively contributing to higher education as a faculty member at STIM LPI Makassar, where she teaches courses and supervises students in finance and management. Beyond her academic responsibilities, Fausiah is also engaged in various organizational activities, reflecting her commitment to both professional and community development. Her long-standing dedication to teaching and leadership in academic and organizational contexts underscores her role as a respected educator and mentor in the field of financial management.

Pooja Jaiswal received the B.Sc. degree in science from J.K. Institute of Applied Physics & Technology, University of Allahabad (U.P.) in 2007. She received the B.Tech & M.Tech degrees in Electronics and Communication from J.K. Institute of Applied Physics & Technology, University of Allahabad (U.P.) in 2010 & 2012. Her research interests include quantum computing and image processing with deep learning and their applications. Presently she is pursuing a PhD from the J.K. Institute of Applied Physics & Technology, University of Allahabad, India.

Iva Katzarska-Miller is a Professor of Psychology at Transylvania University in Lexington, Kentucky. She teaches classes related to cultural psychology and social justice. Her research interests focus on global citizenship, intergroup relations, and AI pedagogy.

Mariani Loise, SH., MH is a dedicated lecturer with more than twenty years of experience in academia. She began her academic journey with a degree in Psychology from Universitas Medan Area, followed by a Bachelor of Law from Universitas Hasanuddin. She later pursued her Master's degree in Law at Universitas Hasanuddin, further strengthening her expertise in the field. This diverse educational background has provided her with a strong interdisciplinary foundation, allowing her to approach complex academic issues with both psychological and legal perspectives. Currently, she serves as a lecturer at Politeknik Maritim AMI (POLIMARIM) Makassar, where she contributes to teaching, mentoring, and academic development. Beyond her teaching role, she is often invited as a speaker in various academic and non-academic forums, sharing her insights on law, education, and professional development. Her extensive knowledge and experience make her an authoritative voice in the topics explored in this book.

Andi Nur Maharani Islami, S.Pd., M.Pd., is a lecturer at the Department of Early Childhood Teacher Education, Faculty of Education, Universitas Negeri Makassar, Indonesia. She obtained her Bachelor's degree in Early Childhood Teacher Education from Universitas Negeri Makassar and later earned a Master's degree in Early Childhood Education from Universitas Negeri Yogyakarta. Her scholarly interests cover digital literacy, pedagogy in the digital era, character education, children's cognitive and social development, as well as the design and implementation of innovative learning media for young learners. Throughout her academic career, she has actively engaged in teaching, research, and community service while contributing to the development of more adaptive and future-oriented early childhood education practices. Her research has particularly emphasized the integration of digital tools into learning processes to enhance literacy, creativity, and social interaction among children, reflecting her commitment to bridging traditional pedagogical approaches with emerging educational technologies. In addition to her university roles, she has been invited as a speaker and trainer at various seminars, workshops, and professional development programs organized by educational institutions and professional associations, addressing themes closely aligned with her expertise. She continues to contribute to advancing the quality of early childhood education in Indonesia and beyond.

Shivani Mishra is a research scholar in English literature and a faculty member in the Department of Applied Sciences and Humanities, with over fifteen years of teaching experience. Her research interests include contemporary Indian fiction, cultural materialism, neoliberalism, and the intersection of literature and social change. She has published several papers in reputed journals, with a focus on the works of Aravind Adiga, exploring themes of class, materialism, and capitalism. Passionate about interdisciplinary studies, she integrates literary criticism with cultural and social theories to offer fresh academic perspectives.

Juraidah Musa is an Assistant Professor in Educational Technology at Sultan Hassanal Bolkiah Institute of Education, UBD. Her research focuses on digital technologies in education, with a special interest in digital game-based learning, and innovative teaching approaches to enhance learning experiences in the 21st-century classrooms.

Tushar NA received a B.Tech degree in electronics and communication from U.P.T.U., Lucknow (U.P.), in 2007. I received the M.B.A. degree in R.T.M. from Jiwaji University, Gwalior (M.P.), in 2009. I am a "gold medalist" in M.E. in Communication Control and Networking from M.P.C.T. Gwalior, M.P. My research interests include antenna and microwave communication, QCA design, and deep learning and their applications. Presently I am pursuing a Ph.D. and acting as an assistant professor at the United College of Engineering & Research, Prayagraj, India.

Julie Perino is the Co-Director of the Bingham Center for Teaching Excellence at Transylvania University in Lexington, KY. She teaches classes on digital rhetoric, writing, and research writing. Her research interests include digital rhetoric, writing transfer research, and inclusive pedagogies.

|Jill Perry - Contributing Author|Jill Perry is a mathematics educator and scholar whose work explores students' mathematical reasoning, communication, and identity. As Director of Rowan's Faculty Center, she supports faculty across disciplines in inclusive pedagogy, educational development, and SoTL. Her work bridges research, practice, and leadership in service of equity and student success.

Nandita Pradhan is the head of the ECE and CRT department. She did B.E. in Electronics and Telecommunication Engineering in 1985, M.E. in Communication Systems from the Govt. Engineering College, Jabalpur in 1991 and Ph.D. in Electronics and Communication Engineering from AKTU, Lucknow. She began her professional journey as a Lecturer in the Department of ECE at Government Engineering College, Jabalpur in 1985 and served in that position until 1997. Currently she worked as a Head of the Department of ECE in United Group of Institutions, Prayagraj, India.

Rismawati is a distinguished academic and consultant with a robust focus on sustainability reporting. She currently holds the position of lecturer and Head of the Quality Assurance Institute at Universitas Muhammadiyah Palopo, where she has been pivotal in ensuring the quality of university processes and outputs since February 2020. Additionally, she serves as an Assurer for Sustainability Reporting at the National Center for Sustainability Reporting in Jakarta, specializing in the evaluation of sustainability reports for mining companies across Indonesia. Her academic qualifications are extensive, comprising a Bachelor's degree in Economics and Accounting, a Master's degree in Accounting Science, and a Doctorate in Accounting from Universitas Brawijaya, Malang. Rismawati is also a certified specialist in sustainability reporting, risk management, and tax planning, holding several prestigious certifications including Certified Sustainability Reporting Specialist (CSRS), Certified Risk Management Practitioner (CRMP), Certified Management Accountant (CMA) and Certified Enterprise Risk Analysis (CERA). In her professional capacity, she has provided consultancy services in financial management and tax compliance for companies such as PT. Reski Barito Timur and PT. Helay Raya. Furthermore, she has authored multiple publications on Social Accounting, Sustainability Accounting, Management Accounting and CSR, contributing significantly to the academic community. Her interests in reading, writing, and travel reflect her commitment to lifelong learning and professional growth in her field.

Vivit Rosmayanti, S.Pd.I., M.Pd was born in Botta on June 26, 1987. She has over 10 years of experience teaching at the University. She obtained a bachelor's degree in English Education from Alauddin State Islamic University. She completed her master's and doctoral degrees in English Education from Makassar State University. She is currently a lecturer in the Post Graduate Program, Department of English Education at Makassar State University, South Sulawesi, Indonesia. She is also actively writing research articles to be published in nationally and internationally accredited journals. She has written in some chapter books, monographs, and reference books. She is interested in teaching methods for teaching English. Her research interests include language teaching methodology, ICT instruction, and ESP teaching. She can be contacted at email: rosmayantivivit@gmail.com

Cecile H. Sam is an Associate Professor at Rowan University. Her current research focus is on the ethical dimensions of faculty work and leadership in educational contexts, with a developing interest the ways technology shapes our experience and understanding of education.

Wasswa Shafik (Member, IEEE) received a Bachelor of Science degree in information technology from Ndejje University, Uganda, a Master of Engineering degree in Information Technology (Computer and Communication Networks) from Yazd University, Iran, and a PhD in Computer Science with the School of Digital Science, Universiti Brunei Darussalam, Brunei Darussalam. He is also the Founder and Research Director of the Dig Connectivity Research Laboratory (DCRLab) after serving as a Research Associate at the Network Interconnectivity Research Laboratory at Yazd University. Prior to this, he worked as a Community Data Analyst at Population Services International (PSI-Uganda), a Community Data Officer at the Programme for Accessible Health Communication (PACE-Uganda), a Research Assistant at the Socio-Economic Data Centre (SEDC-Uganda), Uganda, an Assistant Data Officer at TechnoServe, Kampala, Uganda, and Asmaah Charity Organization as Cheif Executive Officer. He has hundreds of publications with renowned publishers. His research interests include Artificial Intelligence, Neural Networks, Computer Vision, Smart Agriculture, Digital Health, and Green Computing.

Pramendra Singh is an Assistant Professor at Faculty of Management Studies, Marwadi University, India. He has more than eight years of teaching and research experience. He has done three post graduate degrees, two in Tourism & Travel Management and one in History. He did his doctorate (PhD) from Jiwaji University, India in 2018. He has in his credit more than thirty research papers and book chapters published by internationally reputed publishers. He has been a part of various academic activities as resource person and speaker. He also published five books on tourism interlinking it with sustainability and technology. His research interest areas are travel & tourism management, marketing, entrepreneurship, higher education and sustainability.

Mulyani Mudis Taruna, born in Brebes on January 31, 1967. Education: Bachelor's degree from the Faculty of Tarbiyah, IAIN Walisongo Semarang (1991), and Master's degree from Yogyakarta State University, Research and Evaluation of Education Program (2001). He has participated in the Religious Researcher Capacity Building Program (PKPA) in Jakarta, Advanced Functional Researcher Training and Development at the LIPI Training Center in Cibinong in 2013, and Academic

Writing Training at Gadjah Mada University. Previously, he was an associate researcher at the Semarang Religious Research and Development Center and is currently an associate researcher at the Center for Religious and Belief Research at the National Research and Innovation Agency (BRIN). Some of his published works include: Cultivating Character in The Digital Age: Umar Ibn Ahmad Bārājā's Moral Education Framework for Society 5.0 (Analisa, 2024). Digital learning models: experience of online learning during the pandemic (IJERE, 2025), Islamic boarding school policy in response to the transmission of transnational religious ideologies in Klaten, Indonesia (Cogent Education, 2025), Digital learning models: experience of online learning during the pandemic (Ijere, 2025), Critical communication of disaster preparedness areas for informational strategies in disaster management in Indonesia (Progress in Disaster Science, 2024), Exploring the influence of regional economic pillars on library service equity in Indonesia (Malaysian Journal of Library and Information Science, 2024), Cultivating Character in The Digital Age: Umar Ibn Ahmad Bārājā's Moral Education Framework for Society 5.0 (Analisa, 2024), Challenges in Islamic education curriculum development: A comparative study of Indonesia, Pakistan, and India (International Journal of Learning, Teaching and Educational Research, 2024), Challenges and Opportunities in Early Childhood Religious and Moral Education: A Perspective from the Evaluation of Logical Models (Nazhruna: Jurnal Pendidikan Islam, 2024), Community Perception of Madrasah Education Services in Central Java (Journal of Education, Jakarta Research and Development Center for Religion; 2022), and Intellectual Interaction Open Inclusive Understanding Of Islamic Religious Groups In Banyumas District (Journal Seybold Report; 2022), Pesantren Education Model in the Hindu Community (Litbangdiklat Press, 2022), Vocational Education in Madrasah Aliyah in Central Java (Proceedings; Asia Pacific International Conference on Industrial Engineering and Operations Management, 2022), Online Learning Discrimination in Private Schools (Smart Journal of the Semarang Religious Research and Development Center; 2021), Nationalism and Nationality Expression in Salafiyah, Salafi, and Khalafi Islamic Boarding Schools in Indonesia (Journal Linguistica Antverpiensia; 2021), Formal Diniyah Education; Center for the Cadre Development of Tolerant Ulama (Rizqiputra, 2018).

Pankaj Vaishnav is a seasoned academic and researcher with extensive experience in English Language Teaching (ELT). Having taught at both undergraduate and postgraduate levels, Dr. Pankaj has worked with a diverse international student body, spanning 17 countries. A published author, Dr. Pankaj's work, 'Current Trends and Future Prospects in English Language Teaching', has garnered international recognition. HIs research spans a wide array of topics, including innovations in ELT, task-based learning, and cultural identity in language learning, particularly in

Oman. Dr. Pankaj continues to explore cutting-edge research at the intersection of linguistics, technology, and cultural studies, with ongoing projects in ESP and STEM education.

Adorn Verma is a tourism educator and researcher with expertise in sustainable tourism, tourist psychology, and the application of AI in higher education. She holds a Ph.D. in Tourism Management from IGNTU, M.P. and has taught at institutions including Central Tribal University of Andhra Pradesh, Vishwakarma University and NITHM. Dr. Verma has published widely in peer-reviewed journals and serves as a reviewer and editorial board member for international research publications. Her work combines academic rigor with practical insight, focusing on ethical, technological, and socio-cultural dimensions of tourism and education. Currently, She is an Assistant Professor at GNA university where she teaches Aviation Management, Basics of Airlines & Ticketing, and Tourism Marketing.

JJ Wallace is an Associate Professor of Health and Exercise Science and the Digital Liberal Arts Fellow at Transylvania University in Lexington, KY. Her research focuses on integrating technology into pedagogical practices within the liberal arts. Her work leverages engaged learning strategies to incorporate emerging technologies, such as virtual reality (VR) and artificial intelligence (AI), into the classroom, thereby enhancing educational outcomes.

Ajit Kumar Yadav was born on 1 July 1984. He holds a Master's degree in Electrical Engineering from Motilal Nehru National Institute of Technology (MNNIT), Prayagraj, and a Bachelor's degree in Electrical Engineering from the Institute of Engineering and Technology (IET), MJP Rohilkhand University, Bareilly. He is currently serving as an Assistant Professor in the Department of Electrical Engineering at United College of Engineering and Research, Prayagraj. Over the course of his career, he has gained fourteen years of teaching experience, along with two years of industry experience, which together shape his balanced and practical approach to engineering education.

Desfa Yusmaliana is a researcher and a PhD candidate at the SHBIE Faculty, Universiti Brunei Darussalam. Her research focuses on innovation in Islamic education, specifically through the development of a learning model that integrates environmental education and creative imagination. With a strong background in pedagogy, she aims to bridge the gap between religious teachings and contemporary challenges such as environmental issues and corruption. Through her research, Desfa hopes to produce a practical framework that can assist educators in shaping students' character to be one of integrity, environmentally conscious, and grounded in spiritual values.

Gamal Abdul Nasir Zakaria is an Associate Professor in Islamic Education & Arabic Language Education at Sultan Hassanal Bolkiah Institute of Education, Universiti Brunei Darussalam. His research interests include Islamic Education Teaching and Learning, Arabic Language, Pedagogy and Education, Professional Development, ICT and Islamic Education.

Ahmad Zaldi, PhD (Candidate), is a dedicated Islamic education researcher and doctoral candidate at the Sultan Hassanal Bolkiah Institute of Education (SHBIE), Universiti Brunei Darussalam, where he has been pursuing his PhD by research in Islamic Education since 2023. He is a seasoned educator with more than two decades of teaching experience in Indonesia, having served as a lecturer in Islamic Religious Education at the Bandung State Polytechnic (Politeknik Negeri Bandung) for 13 years and as a religious studies teacher at the Laboratory Junior High School of Universitas Pendidikan Indonesia (UPI) for 14 years. Mr. Zaldi holds a Master's degree in General Education from Universitas Pendidikan Indonesia (2009) and a Bachelor's degree in Arabic Language Education (2007) from the same university. His academic and research interests include Islamic education, character development, educational moderation, pesantren-based education, integration of knowledge and practice, classical Islamic curriculum, and the use of technology in Islamic learning environments. Ahmad Zaldi has authored and co-authored multiple journal articles in the field of Islamic education published in reputable academic journals. His works focus on topics such as Islamic moderation in schools, educational leadership, digital integration in religious teaching, and sociocultural perspectives on religious literacy. He has also contributed to national and international seminars and continues to expand his scholarly contributions as part of his PhD journey.

Index

Symbols

A

B

C

D

E

F

G

H

I

K

U

www.ingramcontent.com/pod-product-compliance
Lightning Source LLC
LaVergne TN
LVHW061529290926
849162LV00004B/719